PRAISE FOR OTHER *FEARLESS CRITIC* RESTAURANT GUIDES
(FORMERLY OFF THE MAP PRESS)

"**Deft, unblushing prose**...good friends to the honest diner, they call it as they see it."
—T. Susan Chang,
Food & Travel Correspondent,
Boston Globe

"A **clever and engaging** culinary tour."
—Tim Zagat, Co-Founder,
Zagat Survey

"**Exceptionally experienced restaurantgoers**...knowledgeable and enthusiastic about eating well."
—*Yale Daily News*

"**Immensely useful, written with panache**, as respectful of 'Roadfood' as of 'fine-dining'...one of the **most compelling** restaurant guides we've seen."
—Jane and Michael Stern,
Authors, *Roadfood*

"**Not just a useful book—a pleasure to read.** The only people who won't find it a pleasure are the owners of some of the really bad restaurants it warns us about."
—David Ball, Professor Emeritus
of French and Comparative
Literature, Smith College

"**Scathing** and **scintillating**."
—*New Haven Register*

ABOUT THE AUTHORS

ROBIN GOLDSTEIN has authored three books of restaurant reviews and written for more than 30 travel guides, including *Fodor's Italy*, *Fodor's Argentina*, *Fodor's Chile*, and *Fodor's Hong Kong*. He has also served as chief food critic for the *New Haven Advocate* and as *Metro New York*'s "Fearless Critic" columnist. Robin has an A.B. from Harvard University, a J.D. from Yale Law School, and a certificate in cooking from the French Culinary Institute in New York. He currently lives in South Austin, where he can often be spotted exiting La Mexicana Bakery at 3am with a bag full of barbacoa.

REBECCA MARKOVITS is a member of an increasingly rare species: the Native Austinite. She left town briefly for her undergraduate studies at Yale, where she learned to love the pizza pie; and for an M.Phil. in English Literature at Oxford, where she soaked in rain and curries. When Rebecca gleefully returned to Austin, she put all of her education to good use by sitting around and eating. She has four siblings, all of whom are chazers.

MONIKA POWE NELSON is an Austin native and daughter of Pacific Northwest transplants. She spent some of her palate-forming years in the Hawaiian Islands, as well as some long summers in France, making her crave brisket, lefse, fresh fish, and stinky cheeses in equal proportions. Monika is a graduate of both the University of Texas at Austin and the California Culinary Academy in San Francisco. She spent 14 years as a professional chef both in Austin and California. Monika currently resides in the Hill Country with her husband and two sons, who refuse to eat anything that isn't yellow.

THE
FEARLESS
CRITIC

AUSTIN
RESTAURANT
GUIDE

WWW.FEARLESSCRITIC.COM

FIRST EDITION, 2006-2007

Printed in the United States of America

ISBN 0-9740143-3-8

THE
FEARLESS
CRITIC

AUSTIN
RESTAURANT
GUIDE

CONTENTS

ABOUT THE CONTRIBUTING WRITERS

Clifford Antone was the illustrious founder of Antone's, renowned for its husbandry of such luminaries as Stevie Ray Vaughan. His untimely death in the summer of 2006 was a profound loss to the city.

Jane Cohen, the Umbrian culinary ambassador to Austin, is the Edward Clark Centennial Professor at the University of Texas School of Law and also the University's foremost expert on duck prosciutto.

Sarah E. Fisher, with her interdisciplinary degree in art history, anthropology, and religious studies, is a proud member of the best-educated food-service industry in the United States.

J.J. Hermes is Editor-in-Chief of *The Daily Texan*, the University of Texas at Austin's undergraduate daily. At the scouting combine, he reportedly typed a 4.58-second paragraph with philosophical implications.

John Kelso is a humor columnist for the *Austin American-Statesman*, so we won't try to one-up him by writing anything even remotely funny in this space.

Bob Schneider is a beloved Austin singer-songwriter whose recording *I'm Good Now* was named as one of the top 10 albums of 2004 by *Rolling Stone*'s Lynne Margolis. Also, he loves his breakfast tacos.

Mark Strama was elected to the Texas House of Representatives in 2004, but we can attest to the fact that he still pays for his queso.

ACKNOWLEDGMENTS

From Rebecca Markovits: I'd like to gratefully acknowledge the help of a number of people on whom I relied, as is my way, innocently and without question. First and foremost, of course, my parents, Inga and Dick Markovits, who not only raised me on some of the best cooking this side of the pond, but also gave, unhesitatingly, as is their way, their standard emotional and financial support. Without them I would be, without a doubt, more lucratively employed.

All four of my siblings are excellent cooks, adding much to my culinary know-how (Jule in particular put up with drafts and whinings), but a special thank you goes out to Daniel, who got me into this mess in the first place, and whom I still owe dinner for the pleasure.

Thanks, also, to Robin Goldstein, for his tireless advice, discussion, and editing, and to Monika Powe Nelson, for showing me how an enterprise this gluttonous could be executed in style.

A great many people were invaluable as eating companions at 160 restaurants, giving sage criticisms and spicy witticisms, which I unabashedly stole for any number of my reviews. I'd like in particular to thank two of them, Simine Vazire and Marty Toohey, for putting up with more than their share of middling dinners.

Most of all, of course, I owe a tremendous thank you to my favorite fella, Asher, for his unflagging company at meal after meal after meal, his late-night editing, his countless useful comments, and his ability to make even the eighth mediocre Mexican meal of the week a jolly night out. The couple that eats together, well, grows together. My portion of this book is for him. –RM

From Monika Powe Nelson: To my husband Daniel, for nudging me in this direction and continuing to nudge when nudging was necessary. To my parents, Scot and Carolyn, and the wonderful Anti-Leah, for all their love, interest, last minute babysitting, and support. Without y'all I couldn't have done this. Thank you. To my most constant and lively dinner companions: Lauren, Suzanna, Camille, and Papa Ed. Your enthusiasm and charm made every meal we shared more than something to write about.

To the dozens of other friends and family who answered "Yes!" when I needed a lunch date at 10:30 in the morning, I thank you for your forbearance and grace. And to Jack and Reid, my favorite food detectives, I promise never to make y'all eat out again. –MPN

From Robin Goldstein and Fearless Critic Media: My deepest thanks go first to Rebecca Markovits and Monika Powe Nelson, for their fearlessly brilliant food criticism, for their incisive editing, for their gracious adaptations to our stylistic quirks, and for putting up with the hurry-up-and-wait publishing routine (next edition, we promise Swiss precision). I am eternally grateful, too, for the monumental work of our enthusiastic and meticulous Associate Editors, Ashley Carker, Shay Fan, Kathryn Fondren, Alexis Herschkowitsch, and Romina Olson. Your labor of love shines through this book.

The unwavering support and boundless generosity of Susan Stubbs, Barry Goldstein, Lu and Hal Stubbs, and Rosie Goldstein has been as incredible as ever—I barely noticed that you were all a half a country away (or that this book was twice as long as the last). And I would like to express my most heartfelt appreciation for the contributions of David Menschel—for his business partnership, for his artistic patronage, for his insightful editing, and for his spiritual leadership and wisdom.

In Austin, I would like to express my deep appreciation to Nancy and Tom Hudson, whose gracious, completely unexpected hospitality allowed this entire project to get off its feet. Thanks also to Sarah Fisher, Asher Price, Antonella Olson, Chiara Bercu, and Nicole Jones—among the many people who helped Fearless Critic Media in Austin.

Help can show up in the most unlikely places: I had the good fortune to meet Vikki Gates Cuddy in an airplane cabin, and Jane Cohen and Larry Sager in the Italian countryside. I also had the good fortune to find people willing to put up with me and my notebook through many a meal: Nicole Angotti, Emma Graves Fitzsimmons, Lisa Simmons, and erstwhile impaustinites Benjamin Rosenblum, Daniel Frommer, and Jake Katz. The person most willing to put up with me has been Ashley, and for her sweetness I am endlessly grateful.

Heartfelt shoutouts to the Fearless Critic Media Cabinet: Clare Murumba, Duncan Levin, Samantha Lazarus, Giuliano Stiglitz, Steve Maslow, Justin Nowell, Benjamin Lima, Nate Baum-Snow, Daniel Horwitz, Andrea Armeni, Christine Kim, Michelle Gonzalez, Matt Lombardi, Julian Faulkner, and Roy Ip. I would also like to dedicate my work on this book to the sincere hope that León Cayetano Armeni Guerrero, ya nacido campeón, will someday come up and fix (or at least conquer) our country. And may this be the first of many publications to sing León's praises. —RG

PREFACE

It was on a buffalo hunt in 1838 that Mirabeau B. Lamar, then Vice President of the Republic of Texas, was first captivated by the beauty and natural resources of this particular bend of the Colorado River—a land known as Waterloo. "Here," said Lamar, "should reside the seat of the future empire."

Maybe what Lamar had really liked most about the city that would become Austin was his buffalo steak. For even as oil rushes, shipping industries, airports, and professional sports franchises have lured activity to other parts of Texas over the past century and a half, this city's gastronomical dominion over the rest of the state remains secure. But then, perhaps the greatest of empires—Napoleon's, for instance—are really, at their core, just culinary movements.

Sam Houston was cursing Lamar's idea by 1842, when, fearful of Mexican advances, he tried to move the capital of Texas northward. The new Austinites, already defiant, refused to turn over the Texas national archives to Houston, resulting in the brief and bloodless Archives War. Even then, Austin was a place at the center of the Lone Star that never seemed particularly aligned with any of its points.

That cultural and culinary independence remain every bit as strong today. You look at Houston, and it really clings more to the Southern comfort-food traditions that lord over the Gulf of Mexico and the American Southeast. Dallas, meanwhile, seems firmly implanted as the southern stronghold of Midwestern strip-steakland, while San Antonio remains an inescapably Tex-Mex town even as its restaurants start to yup out.

It's not that Austin's expansive restaurant scene doesn't dabble in each one of those noble Texan traditions—it's that we almost fetishize them. We have the yoke-choked, cowboy-hatted steakhouses that echo with boozy insider stock tips, and we have the sombrero-shaded Tex-Mex haciendas where the faucets flow with queso—yet these places sometimes seem to render the rest of Texas in the artificially exotic way that an outsider would, like a faux-Japanese hibachi house or a faux-Italian villa.

But our homages to Texas tradition remain in harmonious denial of the city's political battles. Professors of comparative literature sit at populist picnic tables amidst piles of post oak and drool over slow smokers with briskets-to-be; buff college athletes gingerly mix wasabi into their sushi-combination soy-sauce tubs; organic-gardening activists unashamedly plop down at chain restaurants and dip their chips into oozing bowls of yellow cheese. At Austin's dinner table, there is no culture war.

Still, our city's kitchens find themselves most at home when they traverse another culinary plane entirely. Austin's chefs are a different breed, transfixed by some concept either far further East or far further West, something less themed, something more animistic. Do not call Austin "Weird." Call it...enchanted. Like the town itself, Austin's food doesn't speak—it *sings*. It hums to the tunes of shamans in shantytowns along the Rio Grande. It whistles along with chile farmers on the Indian reservations of the American Southwest. It solemnly chants, all dressed in white, alongside the Krishna vegans. It hits the precise notes of a string quartet echoing through a foofy French ballroom. It sings an empathetic lullaby of *Fast Food Nation* lyrics to the free-range farmer. And it drunkenly croons to the tortured tunes of unfathomably skinny punk acousticians that play for nothing more than a free bottle of Lone Star and a cool boy or girl to go home with, if only for a night.

If there is an uncomfortable tension running through the cuisine of Austin, it is not that between South and Southwest but rather that between rural wisdom and urban ambition. Next to the great big rack of ribs on the old smoker sits a pot of chipotle aïoli with the potential to overwhelm the subtle smokiness of the meat. You love the queso that's dripping across the axis venison burgers, but you wish the sandwiches weren't done up as "panini" that squeeze all their precious juices out onto on the press. Sometimes you just don't want smoked duck sprinkled on your nachos, alfalfa sprouts in your whole-wheat taco, soy sauce in your empanada, or kaffir lime leaves bedding your elk steak. Yet it is this same willingness to risk failure for the sake of experimentation that can sometimes make Austin's food so great.

Still, when we dine at Uchi, the #1-rated restaurant in this First Edition, although we appreciate many of the restaurant's fusion flights of fancy, we must admit that we find ourselves more often ordering their simple pieces of nigiri sushi—the silky tuna, the buttery salmon, the springy Japanese black bass. The fish is shipped over ice in jumbo jets that take off each day from Tokyo's Narita airport, concealing no greater, or lesser, ambition than the small miracle of arriving in Austin. Such simple but astonishing tricks are now coming together to form the backbone of a new wave of American cuisine, a truly modern movement that deeply values the provenance of ingredients. You can see that school of thought taking hold not only in some of Austin's newer restaurants, but also in its world-class upscale food stores, where pride of place is no longer limited to Elgin sausage. At Central Market and Whole Foods, people are even starting to buy Texas wine these days.

But let us not forget that Austin food is college food, too. Take time to notice the youthful beauty of the very simplest of culinary transactions that occur within the extended arms of this town's great campuses: The cup of coffee that costs whatever the dude behind the counter (or is it a she?) feels like charging you. The ratty but well-loved Thai joint whose noodles taste indescribably better after 2am. The Mexican martinis supposedly so strong that they'll only sell you two of them. The scoop of ice cream that's smashed and bashed and twirled into submission by a tattooed philosopher-king.

Even in the places where Austin is at its most inescapably American—amidst strip malls and "lifestyle center" shopping plazas, beneath whirring tangles of highway interchange and red-and-white bullseye logos—you'll find surprises like Vietnamese supermarkets that draw in University professors, and pawn-shop-taquerías with steaming metal vats whose lids conceal the city's best barbacoa. And even many of the locally-based fast-food chains seem cosmopolitan, their gaze focused on a faraway place. It is as though the city's culinary heartbeat is attached to a solar-powered pacemaker whose rhythm is controlled by short-wave frequencies from the skies above.

A lot of the time it works, and some of the time it doesn't. But there are two tenets of Austin dining that you really cannot argue with. The first is that the prices are consistently reasonable, with precious few exceptions, and this goes a long time toward excusing the flaws, when they do occur. Just as you're about to complain about a slightly overcooked piece of steak, or a slightly bland serving of chips and salsa, stop and remember how much less taste those same few dollars would get you in Boston, Chicago, or San Francisco. There may be no city in the United States that rivals Austin's ratio of quality to price.

The second tenet is that even the most spectacular culinary experiences in Austin are presented to customers without even a glimmer of pretense, almost no matter where you dine. That pattern of sauces that spreads across your plate of Gulf red snapper, like an impressionist oil painting of guajillo beurre blanc, coriander crème fraîche, and smoked poblano salsa, is described modestly and simply on the menu; and it's actually just there to complement the tastes of the fresh, crusted fish and the sticky corn pudding, not to look like the Mexican flag or to be photographed for a glossy magazine.

For Austin is not a city whose cuisine has ever been conceived as performance art. Rather, the food here makes an unapologetic beeline for the pleasure centers of the brain. Even at many of Austin's top tables, your server might well describe your wine as "awesome," and perhaps even indulge in a glass of it with you if you offer. And when you're done with dinner, he or she will certainly ask if you want to take your leftovers home in a doggie bag. There will be not a murmur of disapproval from anyone in the restaurant when you do, because this is a place in which even the elitists understand that good food is not just there to be admired—it is there to be eaten. –RG

THE FEARLESS CRITIC SYSTEM

Welcome to the Fearless Critic restaurant guide to Austin, Texas. As you may have gathered, the Fearless Critic is not just a single person. Our three authors have reviewed and rated 390 places to eat in the Austin area, with the constant help of a hungry, intrepid, and tireless network of Associate Editors, Contributing Editors, and Contributing Writers.

The hallmarks of the Fearless Critic philosophy are candor, rigor, and independence. We do not accept advertising from restaurants. As food critics, we always visit restaurants incognito, and when we taste, we ignore lofty reputations, other reviews, and newspaper "awards." We visit most restaurants several times, and most of our reviews are informed by years of repeat visits (as well as the collective knowledge and experience of our informal, top-secret panel of local restaurantgoers). As writers, we are brutally honest, but we also try to be entertaining whenever possible.

In order to qualify for inclusion, an establishment must, at a minimum, serve food. Of course, we haven't included every single restaurant in Austin; except in special cases, we've omitted national chains, corner pizza joints, and generic fast-food-style purveyors with little to distinguish them. We're sure that we have also unwittingly omitted some true out-of-the-way gems, and for that we apologize in advance (and encourage you to let us know about them by emailing us at feedback@fearlesscritic.com, so that they might be included in the next edition). But we hope that these pages will also turn you on to a lot of little places with which you might not be familiar, and we hope we've done a generally fair job covering the majority of eateries worth knowing about within the city of Austin. We have also included several notable restaurants in other towns in the Hill Country and elsewhere.

As you'll see once you start reading, the Fearless Critic's style is relentlessly opinionated—something you might not be used to when you read a restaurant review. We're happy to wax poetic if we love a place, but as big fans of the First Amendment, we're also not the least bit afraid to be completely frank if a place is overpriced, rude, or just plain bad. We see the purpose of a restaurant guide as not merely to tell the reader where to go, but also to tell the reader where *not* to go. Your hard-earned dollars matter a lot to us, and we hope that the $14.95 you've spent on this book will save you untold amounts of money in the future by preventing you from wasting hundreds of dollars on potentially bad meals. Therein, we believe, lies much of the usefulness of food criticism.

So, welcome to a new kind of restaurant review, and a new kind of restaurant guide. We hope you'll be a convert.

THE RATING SCALE

There are two numerical ratings assigned to each restaurant: a food rating and an experience rating. Each rating is out of 10 points.

Food (1-10): This rating is strictly a measure of whether the food on offer is appetizing or objectionable, insipid or delicious. Don't be surprised to find a greasy spoon outscoring a historic, upscale, sit-down establishment, for one simple reason: the food just tastes better. Close your eyes, open your mind (and your mouth), and give everything a chance. Purveyors of sweets and specialty markets are ineligible for this rating, as they don't attempt to serve meals.

Experience (1-10): Many guides rate the "service" and "décor" at a restaurant, but rather than counting the number of pieces of silverware on the table or the number of minutes and seconds before the food arrives, we ask ourselves a simple question: does being here make us happy? The most emphatic "yes" inspires the highest rating. We don't give out points for tablecloths or tuxedos. We reward warm lighting, comfortable accommodations, a finely realized theme, and a strong sense of place. If it's a place steeped in history, or just an eminently classic Austin joint (think Spider House, Magnolia, or Hill's), we give bonus points for that, because it's certainly part of the experience. The dim glow of candles, dark wood, and old Texas paraphernalia at your local dive might just garner more accolades than the proliferation of accoutrements at a stuffy "continental" restaurant.

Also figured into the experience rating is the question of whether you'll love or loathe the prospect of interacting with the people who stand between you and your meal. We don't expect the burger-flipper at a greasy spoon to start spouting off elaborate wine adjectives, but if a restaurant's staff is unusually helpful and caring, or extraordinarily enthusiastic and knowledgeable about what's coming out of the kitchen, then the experience rating will reflect that. On the flip side, if the staff is consistently indifferent or condescending—or seems to have gone on strike—then points will be deducted from the experience rating of the restaurant, which happens as often at high-priced places as it does at corner take-out joints. Consider this a nonviolent revolution in the food-review world. Viva.

The math: Keep in mind that we use the whole 10-point scale, and that there's no grade inflation here. Let yourself get used to our system, and don't be scared off by something in the 5 to 6 range. Any score over 8 is truly high praise. Only 22 establishments score 9 or above for food, and only 53 finish at 9 or above for experience. For food, the mean is 6.48, the median is 6.7, and the standard deviation is 1.7. For experience, the mean is 6.89, the median is 7, and the standard deviation is 1.8. Establishments with food scores above 9 are extraordinary; those above 8 are highly recommended; and those above 7 are recommended.

THE OTHER STUFF ON THE PAGE

Average dinner price: This dollar value is a guide to how much, on average, you should expect to spend per person on a full dinner at the restaurant, including one alcoholic beverage, tax, and a 20% tip (for table-service establishments; we encourage you to tip at coffeeshops and take-out joints too, but we don't figure it into the meal price). This is an imperfect science, but we go by what the average person tends to order at each place. At simple take-out places, this might be just a sandwich or the like; at more elaborate sit-down restaurants, we usually figure in the cost of shared appetizers (one for every two people) and desserts (one for every two people). For alcoholic drinks, too, we are guided by what people generally tend to order. At Fadó, it's a beer. At Baby A's, it's a margarita. At Jeffrey's, it's a midrange glass of wine. Keep in mind that at the higher-end restaurants, you will generally spend considerably less than the quoted price if you go for lunch, or if you order iced tea instead of wine. Only restaurants that serve meals are eligible for price estimates; this excludes dessert-and-coffee places, specialty grocery stores, and so on.

Cuisine category: Every establishment in *The Fearless Critic* is associated with one or more cuisine categories. Our "Lists" section (p. 9) includes a cross-referenced guide to all restaurants by cuisine. A few categories require a bit of explanation. **Light American** refers to places that focus on sandwiches, salads, and soups. **New American,** sometimes referred to as "construction cuisine," is a style of cooking pioneered on the West Coast that fuses elements from many world regions, often including Asia. The **Southern** category includes soul food, Cajun, and Louisiana Creole. And the **Latin American** category includes Central American, South American, and Caribbean food, along with so-called "Nuevo Latino" cuisine, but not Mexican food.

Establishment type: We have divided Austin's eating establishments into several categories. The largest category is **casual restaurant,** which means a place with waiter service at tables but a generally laid-back atmosphere without much fuss. An **upmarket restaurant** is a place with more elegant ambitions, marketed as a restaurant for a special occasion or an impressive date. The **counter service** category includes cafeterias, self-service places, and also establishments where you place an order at a counter but it is then brought out to your table. **Take-out** means that virtually nobody eats in, even if there are a couple of tables for that ostensible purpose. We define a **pub** as a place that's fundamentally a bar at heart but also serves food, though the kitchen often closes before the bar. **Café** means a place whose primary business is the provision of coffee or tea, but they must also serve food to be included in the book. We've included a few notable **specialty groceries** in Austin as well; while they are not traditional food-service establishments, all of them serve certain varieties of prepared foods that can be eaten straightaway.

Location: We have divided Austin into distinct neighborhoods to help sort out the restaurants geographically. You can find the delineation of these neighborhoods beginning on p. 22, in the "By Location" portion of the "Lists" section of the book. The map on the facing page illustrates the division of neighborhoods in downtown Austin.

Address: We have included addresses and neighborhood designations for up to three locations. For chains with more than three locations, consult their web sites. For specific directions, we advise that you consult the well-designed Google Maps website (maps.google.com)—though, at press time, its maps improperly label IH-35—or MapQuest (www.mapquest.com).

Special features: These appear in italics, following the address on the page. **Breakfast** and **brunch** generally mean that a restaurant has a special menu, or separate portion of the menu, geared toward those meals, not just that the place is open in the morning. By **date-friendly,** we mean establishments that we find particularly romantic in some way—and that doesn't necessarily mean tuxedoed waiters or high prices. We look for warm lighting, good vibes, and a sense of easy fun. **Delivery** can be limited to a certain geographical range or minimum order. **Kid-friendly** doesn't just mean a couple of high chairs in the corner; it means a place where the little ones will actually be happy, whether for culinary reasons or for the availability of special activities or play areas. Austin is the **live music** capital of the world, and we've flagged places that honor that tradition in any way; this includes establishments that have live music only on certain days or nights, so call ahead if it's atmospherically important to you. **Outdoor dining** can mean anything from a couple of sidewalk tables to a sprawling biergarten. **Wireless Internet** has to be free to qualify—this is Austin, after all. In this vegetarian-friendly city, we are particularly careful when choosing which establishments to flag as **vegetarian-friendly.** The designation is not limited to vegetarian-only places, but we look for menus where vegetarians will not just be accommodated—they'll actually have an ample selection. Vegetarians should also check out our "Vegetarian Dining Guide," a set of cross-referenced lists of vegetarian-friendly places to eat; that section begins on page 54.

Other practical information: We also list a telephone number, a website (if available); and whether, in our estimation, reservations are essential or advisable for dinner. As for the bar, "full" indicates that the establishment is licensed to serve hard liquor and, thus, mixed drinks and cocktails in addition to wine and beer. "Wine and beer" is another type of license; such places might serve just wine, or just beer, or both. There's also a handful of "BYO" restaurants, where you can bring your own wine or beer. We're fans of this concept—it can be a great opportunity to drink that nice bottle that's been sitting around the house, waiting for a good occasion.

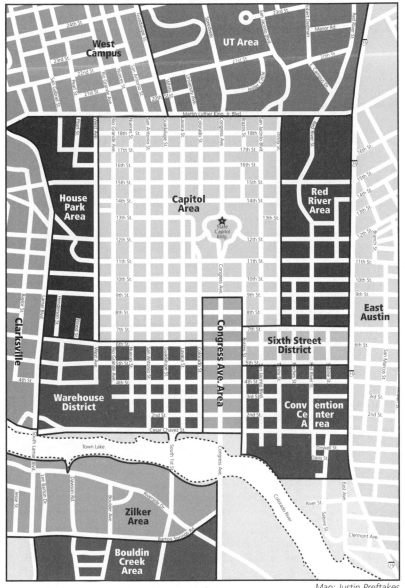

Map: Justin Preftakes

Central Austin Neighborhoods

RELENTLESSLY OPINIONATED

The Fearless Critic is relentlessly opinionated. It is a new kind of restaurant guide. One of our Contributing Editors calls it "in-your-face" restaurant reviewing. One newspaper called it "scathing." And some people have suggested that this style of reviewing is rude to the restaurants. But we consider it rude when an unsuspecting patron, with friends or date in tow, forks over a lot of cash for a bad meal on the strength of a sugar-coated review.

We think that too many restaurant critics have not deigned to embrace the art of simple criticism, thus giving readers the ultimate raw deal. For how is one to choose between two places if both are portrayed in dizzying, worshipful prose? And how frustrating is it to find out that at least one of them was a waste of your time and money? If you're celebrating a special occasion, as one often does by dining out, the sting of disappointment after a bad meal is that much more acute.

We are here to help minimize your pain and maximize your pleasure. In short, our duty is to our readers, not to the restaurants. We do not accept advertising from restaurants, and we never identify ourselves when we dine. We also consult our Contributing Editors, drawing upon their bodies of experience to broaden our personal perspective on each restaurant, and assuring that our experiences were representative. Our goal is to save you the cost, disappointment, and possible discomfort of a bland, overpriced meal—and to point you preemptively in the direction of something better. Helping you choose, every time you eat out, is what makes this endeavor worthwhile for us. And so, within these pages, we tell you exactly what we'd tell a good friend if she called us up and asked what we *really* thought of a place.

This unapologetic approach may take a moment to get used to. But in the end, we believe opinionated commentary to be the highest possible compliment to the local dining scene. That is to say, the food here is definitely worth talking about. Austin has arrived as a culinary town, and it deserves a serious restaurant guide.

We don't expect you to agree with everything we say—sometimes, we don't even agree with each other—but we do hope you can appreciate our conviction that, in food writing, opinion is better expressed openly than buried between the lines. We believe that, over the course of a book full of 390 reviews, we will earn your trust. And whether you concur or dissent, we would love to hear from you; we'd like nothing better than to inspire more relentlessly opinionated diners in Austin. Visit us at **www.fearlesscritic.com** to post your own opinions, or your thoughts on ours.

QUIRKS

Cooking times: as you might notice within these pages, we prefer our meat (and certain kinds of fish) rare. Specifically, our reviews sometimes comment on whether or not establishments are willing to serve a dish as rare as we request it. Although we understand that there are many people who like their meat more cooked than we do, our complaint isn't with restaurants that serve meat medium or medium-well by default; it's with restaurants that refuse to serve meat rare *even upon emphatic request*. Still, people who like their meat cooked medium or more should take our comments with a grain of salt—and skip the following paragraph.

Seasoning: speaking of grains of salt, we complain from time to time about undersalted dishes. Our position is that there is no such thing as salting "to taste" in the professional kitchen. As a matter of chemistry, a certain amount of salt is necessary to bring out the complexity of most savory flavors: meats, fishes, soups, sauces, and so on. If you don't believe us, try this experiment, suggested by Italian food guru Marcella Hazan: pour two half-glasses of red wine, dump some salt into one of them, swirl them both around, and smell both glasses. The salt really brings out the bouquet (you won't want to drink it, though...).

Undersalting is one of the most common ways that an otherwise well-executed dish can fall completely flat. This problem can sometimes be corrected with the salt shaker, but sometimes it's too late, as when the food is deep-fried. Regardless, we think a dish should come to the table properly seasoned and ready to eat, not left in the final stages of preparation. If you want your meal with less salt than normal, you can ask for it that way, and the restaurant should be willing to honor the request. Otherwise, forcing the customer to finish that process is as absurd as plopping a salad down in front of a customer with a whole carrot and a peeler.

"Mains": you won't find the word "entrée" in *The Fearless Critic*. The word is inherently ambiguous, and particularly confusing to foreigners, as the French word "entrée" means "starter" or "appetizer." We're not sure how "entrée" came to mean a main course in the United States, but herein we say "main course," or "main," if that's what we mean.

Fearless grammar: We diverge from certain style conventions in a small handful of ways. For instance, we don't italicize foreign words in this book, as we believe that convention to be cumbersome and distracting. We also do not capitalize dish names unless they're invented by the restaurant, in which case we enclose them in quotation marks.

FEEDBACK

The heart and soul of this endeavor is our firm belief that the world of restaurant reviewing can only be improved by opening outspoken channels of communication between restaurants and their customers. We hope that the honest articulation of our opinions and dining experiences will encourage you to do the same—if you have a bad meal, or a great one, *tell the restaurant.* Tell them what was right and what was wrong. It can only help. And tell us; we've set up an interactive space at **www.fearlesscritic.com**, where readers can express agreement or dissent of any sort. The commentary found on the site is (within limits) unedited and unadulterated. It doesn't require registration, and you can even post anonymously. Please, read some reviews, go try some restaurants, and then log on and let us know what you think. Our critics might respond to posts from time to time. We look forward to hearing from you.

THE FINE PRINT

This entire book is a work of opinion, and should be understood as such. Any and all judgments rendered upon restaurants within these pages, regardless of tense, are intended as statements of pure opinion. Facts have been thoroughly checked with the restaurants in person and via telephone; we have gone to the utmost lengths to ensure that every fact is correct, and that every ingredient in every dish is properly referenced. Any factual errors that nonetheless remain are purely unintentional. That said, menus and plates (not to mention hours of operation) change so frequently at restaurants that any printed book, however new, cannot help but be a bit behind the times. Check in at **www.fearlesscritic.com** for the latest updates, restaurant news, discussion boards, and more.

ABOUT FEARLESS CRITIC MEDIA

Fearless Critic Media is a lean, fiercely independent publishing house founded in 2003 and dedicated to providing useful information in an engaging format. Fearless Critic publishes relentlessly opinionated, irreverent, and comprehensive guides to dining in smaller and midsize American cities and college towns. Look for other Fearless Critic restaurant guides, including *The Menu: New Haven* and *The Menu: Northampton, Amherst, and the Five-College Area*, which can be bought online at amazon.com and barnesandnoble.com as well as at bookstores in the New Haven, Connecticut, and Western Massachusetts areas. For all of the latest information, please visit our publishing website at **www.fearlesscritic.com**.

LISTS

TOP 50 FOOD

<u>LISTED IN ORDER OF FOOD RATING OUT OF 10</u>

Rank			Location	Cuisine	Type	Price
1	Uchi	9.7	South Lamar	Japanese	Upmarket	$69
2	Café at the 4 Seasons	9.6	Convention Center	New American	Upmarket	$73
3	The Driskill Grill	9.4	Congress Ave. Area	New American	Upmarket	$105
4	Café Josie	9.3	Clarksville	Southwestern	Upmarket	$48
5	Wink	9.3	House Park Area	New American	Upmarket	$86
6	Vespaio	9.3	South Congress Area	Italian	Upmarket	$62
7	Castle Hill Café	9.3	Clarksville	Southwestern	Upmarket	$46
8	Café 909	9.3	Marble Falls	New American	Upmarket	$60
9	Zoot	9.2	Tarrytown	New American	Upmarket	$64
10	Fino	9.2	UT Area	Spanish	Upmarket	$50
11	Vespaio Enoteca	9.2	South Congress	Italian	Casual	$32
12	El Chile	9.2	French Place	Mexican	Casual	$31
13	The Salt Lick	9.1	Driftwood	Barbecue	Casual	$17
14	South Congress Café	9.1	South Congress	Southwestern	Upmarket	$42
15	Mikado Ryotei	9.1	Far North	Japanese	Upmarket	$47
16	Kreuz Market	9.1	Lockhart	Barbecue	Counter	$12
17	Aquarelle	9.0	Warehouse District	French	Upmarket	$91
18	Smitty's Market	9.0	Lockhart	Barbecue	Counter	$12
19	Starlite	9.0	Warehouse District	New American	Upmarket	$65
20	Salt Lick 360	9.0	Westlake	Barbecue	Casual	$30
21	Capitol Brasserie	9.0	Warehouse District	French	Upmarket	$48
22	Louie Mueller's	9.0	Taylor	Barbecue	Counter	$10
23	Mirabelle	8.9	Northwest Hills	Southwestern	Upmarket	$46
24	Fonda San Miguel	8.9	North Central	Mexican	Upmarket	$59
25	Musashino	8.9	Northwest Hills	Japanese	Upmarket	$58
26	Manuel's	8.9	Congress Ave. Area	Mexican	Upmarket	$39
27	Hudson's on the Bend	8.8	Lake Travis	Southwestern	Upmarket	$83
28	Taverna	8.8	Warehouse District	Italian	Upmarket	$48
29	Din Ho Chinese BBQ	8.8	Far North	Chinese	Casual	$24
30	Beluga	8.8	Round Rock	Japanese	Upmarket	$40
31	Asti	8.7	Hyde Park	Italian	Upmarket	$37
32	Green Pastures	8.7	Bouldin Creek	American	Upmarket	$67
33	T&S Chinese Seafood	8.7	Far North	Chinese	Casual	$22
34	Rudy's	8.7	Westlake	Barbecue	Counter	$15
35	1886 Café & Bakery	8.6	Congress Ave. Area	American	Upmarket	$31
36	Hill Country Din. Rm.	8.6	Westlake	Southwestern	Upmarket	$68
37	El Borrego de Oro	8.6	St. Edward's Area	Mexican	Casual	$21
38	Ruth's Chris	8.6	Congress Ave. Area	Steakhouse	Upmarket	$74
39	Jeffrey's	8.6	Clarksville	New American	Upmarket	$84
40	Mandola's	8.5	Hyde Park	Italian	Counter	$19
41	Siena	8.5	Westlake	Italian	Upmarket	$55
42	La Traviata	8.5	Congress Ave. Area	Italian	Upmarket	$51
43	Curra's Grill	8.5	St. Edward's Area	Mexican	Casual	$27
44	House Park BBQ	8.5	House Park Area	Barbecue	Counter	$7
45	Sunflower	8.5	Far North	Vietnamese	Casual	$22
46	Shoreline Grill	8.4	Convention Center	New American	Upmarket	$64
47	Málaga	8.4	Warehouse District	Spanish	Upmarket	$47
48	Doña Emilia's	8.4	Convention Center	Latin American	Upmarket	$46
49	Casino El Camino	8.4	Sixth Street District	Burgers	Pub	$12
50	Clay Pit	8.4	Capitol Area	Indian	Upmarket	$33

TOP 50 EXPERIENCE

<u>LISTED IN ORDER OF EXPERIENCE RATING OUT OF 10</u>

Rank			Location	Cuisine	Type	Price
1	Fonda San Miguel	10	North Central	Mexican	Upmarket	$59
2	The Driskill Grill	9.9	Congress Ave. Area	New American	Upmarket	$105
3	Chez Nous	9.9	Sixth Street District	French	Upmarket	$51
4	Café at the 4 Seasons	9.8	Convention Center	New American	Upmarket	$73
5	The Salt Lick	9.8	Driftwood	Barbecue	Casual	$17
6	Zoot	9.7	Tarrytown	New American	Upmarket	$64
7	Mozart's	9.7	Tarrytown	Sweets	Café	
8	Café Josie	9.6	Clarksville	Southwestern	Upmarket	$48
9	Alamo Drafthouse	9.6	Warehouse District	American	Theater	$22
10	Spider House	9.6	UT Area	Light American	Café	$7
11	Vivo Cocina Texicana	9.5	French Place	Mexican	Casual	$28
12	Castle Hill Café	9.5	Clarksville	Southwestern	Upmarket	$46
13	The Broken Spoke	9.5	South Lamar	American	Pub	$24
14	Eastside Café	9.5	French Place	American	Upmarket	$45
15	Moonshine	9.5	Convention Center	American	Upmarket	$36
16	Uchi	9.4	South Lamar	Japanese	Upmarket	$69
17	Chez Zee	9.4	Northwest Hills	American	Casual	$35
18	Amy's Ice Cream	9.4	Clarksville	Sweets	Counter	
19	Green Muse Café	9.4	St. Edward's Area	Light American	Café	$9
20	Jo's Hot Coffee	9.4	South Congress	Light American	Café	$8
21	Freddie's	9.4	Bouldin Creek	American	Casual	$21
22	Capitol Brasserie	9.3	Warehouse District	French	Upmarket	$48
23	Texicalli Grill	9.3	St. Edward's Area	American	Casual	$17
24	Fino	9.3	UT	Spanish	Upmarket	$50
25	South Congress Café	9.3	South Congress	Southwestern	Upmarket	$42
26	Iron Works BBQ	9.3	Convention Center	Barbecue	Counter	$14
27	Magnolia Café	9.3	Tarrytown	American	Casual	$18
28	Siena	9.2	Westlake	Italian	Upmarket	$55
29	Hoover's Cooking	9.2	French Place	Southern	Casual	$25
30	Polvos	9.2	Bouldin Creek	Mexican	Casual	$24
31	Clay Pit	9.2	Capitol Area	Indian	Upmarket	$33
32	Mars	9.2	West Campus	New American	Upmarket	$45
33	Doc's	9.2	South Congress	American	Pub	$22
34	Dirty Martin's	9.2	West Campus	American	Casual	$12
35	Draught House	9.2	Seton Medical Area	American	Pub	$19
36	Ronnie's Real Foods	9.2	Westlake	American	Casual	$24
37	Hudson's on the Bend	9.1	Lake Travis	Southwestern	Upmarket	$83
38	Sam's BBQ	9.1	East Austin	Barbecue	Counter	$11
39	Green Pastures	9.1	Bouldin Creek	American	Upmarket	$67
40	Shady Grove	9.1	Zilker	American	Casual	$23
41	El Chile	9.1	French Place	Mexican	Casual	$31
42	Home Slice Pizza	9.1	South Congress	Pizza	Casual	$18
43	Hyde Park Bar & Grill	9.1	Hyde Park	American	Casual	$28
44	Kreuz Market	9.1	Lockhart	Barbecue	Counter	$12
45	Ruta Maya	9.0	St. Edward's Area	Light American	Café	$6
46	Kerbey Lane Café	9.0	Seton Medical Area	American	Casual	$19
47	Las Manitas	9.0	Congress Ave. Area	Mexican	Casual	$16
48	Casa de Luz	9.0	Zilker	Light American	Counter	$13
49	Ararat	9.0	North Central	Middle Eastern	Casual	$22
50	Hill's Café	9.0	Far South	American	Casual	$27

LISTED IN ORDER OF FOOD RATING OUT OF 10

American

		Location	Type	Price
8.7	Green Pastures	Bouldin Creek	Upmarket	$67
8.6	1886 Café & Bakery	Congress Ave. Area	Upmarket	$31
8.2	Eastside Café	French Place	Upmarket	$45
8.0	Emerald Restaurant	Bee Cave	Upmarket	$80
8.0	Hyde Park Bar & Grill	Hyde Park	Casual	$28
7.7	Dirty Martin's	West Campus	Casual	$12
7.7	Texicalli Grill	St. Edward's Area	Casual	$17
7.6	Hill's Café	Far South	Casual	$27
7.6	Fadó	Warehouse District	Pub	$26
7.3	Eddie V's	Sixth Street District	Upmarket	$63
7.1	Thistle Café on 6th	Warehouse District	Upmarket	$34
7.0	The Jackalope	Sixth Street District	Pub	$12
6.9	The Frisco Shop	Burnet	Counter	$16
6.8	Tom's Tabooley	UT Area	Counter	$8
6.8	Texas Chili Parlor	Capitol Area	Casual	$17
6.7	Pacific Star	Far Northwest	Casual	$24
6.6	Mother's	Hyde Park	Casual	$20
6.6	The Tavern	House Park Area	Pub	$26
6.6	Beck's	South Congress	Pub	$34
6.5	Paradise Café	Sixth Street District	Casual	$25
6.5	Austin Java Co.	Clarksville	Café	$12
6.5	Red River Café	UT Area	Casual	$14
6.4	Moonshine	Convention Center	Upmarket	$36
6.4	Dog Almighty	Burnet	Counter	$5
6.3	Ventana	Burnet	Upmarket	$42
6.3	The Soup Peddler	Bouldin Creek	Take-out	$10
6.2	Kerbey Lane Café	Seton Medical Area	Casual	$19
6.1	Austin Diner	Burnet	Casual	$12
6.1	Shady Grove	Zilker	Casual	$23
6.1	Galaxy Café	Far South	Counter	$15
6.0	Waterloo Ice House	Clarksville	Pub	$22
6.0	Ronnie's Real Foods	Westlake	Casual	$24
6.0	The Paggi House	South Lamar	Pub	$36
6.0	Shoal Creek Saloon	House Park Area	Pub	$23
5.9	Dog & Duck Pub	Capitol Area	Pub	$20
5.9	Hangtown Grill	Westlake	Counter	$14
5.9	Chooby Doo	Far South	Counter	$7
5.9	Magnolia Café	Tarrytown	Casual	$18
5.8	Thistle Café 360	Westlake	Counter	$22
5.8	Russo's Texitally	Marble Falls	Casual	$31
5.8	Arturo's	Capitol Area	Counter	$12
5.8	Chez Zee	Northwest Hills	Casual	$35
5.7	Nau's Enfield Drug	Clarksville	Counter	$5
5.6	Trudy's	UT Area	Casual	$26
5.6	Truluck's	Warehouse District	Upmarket	$66
5.6	The Omelettry	Burnet	Casual	$10
5.6	Crown & Anchor Pub	UT Area	Pub	$13
5.4	Rockin' Tomato	South Lamar	Counter	$17
5.3	Lucy's	Tarrytown	Casual	$33
5.2	Starseeds	French Place	Casual	$18
5.2	The Posse East	UT Area	Pub	$14
5.2	Ringers	Warehouse District	Pub	$24
5.1	Hula Hut	Tarrytown	Casual	$31
5.0	Flip's Satellite Café	Dripping Springs	Casual	$17
5.0	Nutty Brown Café	Dripping Springs	Casual	$29

	American *continued*	Location	Type	Price
4.7	The Broken Spoke	South Lamar	Pub	$24
4.6	EZ's	Seton Medical Area	Counter	$20
4.6	Players	West Campus	Pub	$15
4.5	Draught House	Seton Medical Area	Pub	$19
4.5	Opal Divine's	Warehouse District	Pub	$21
4.5	Hickory Street	Congress Ave. Area	Casual	$23
4.4	Bluebonnet Café	Marble Falls	Casual	$13
4.3	Longhorn Po-Boys	UT Area	Counter	$7
4.2	The Fox & Hound	Capitol Area	Pub	$20
4.2	Alamo Drafthouse	Warehouse District	Theater	$22
4.2	Doc's	South Congress	Pub	$22
4.0	Texadelphia	West Campus	Counter	$13
3.9	Freddie's	Bouldin Creek	Casual	$21
3.3	Mother Egan's	Warehouse District	Pub	$24
3.2	Bee Cave Bistro	Bee Cave	Casual	$37
3.0	Veranda	North Central	Casual	$31
2.9	Maudie's	Tarrytown	Pub	$22

Argentine

8.2	Buenos Aires Café	St. Edward's Area	Counter	$17

Australian

6.8	Boomerang's Pies	UT Area	Counter	$10

Barbecue

9.1	The Salt Lick	Driftwood	Casual	$17
9.1	Kreuz Market	Lockhart	Counter	$12
9.0	Smitty's Market	Lockhart	Counter	$12
9.0	Salt Lick 360	Westlake	Casual	$30
9.0	Louie Mueller's	Taylor	Counter	$10
8.7	Rudy's	Westlake	Counter	$15
8.5	House Park BBQ	House Park Area	Counter	$7
8.3	Cooper's	Llano	Counter	$14
8.2	Sam's BBQ	East Austin	Counter	$11
8.1	Ruby's BBQ	UT Area	Counter	$17
7.8	Black's BBQ	Lockhart	Counter	$11
7.7	Artz Rib House	South Lamar	Casual	$22
7.6	Hill's Café	Far South	Casual	$27
7.4	Stubb's BBQ	Red River Area	Counter	$18
7.3	Green Mesquite	Zilker	Casual	$21
7.1	Lewis' BBQ	East Austin	Counter	$8
6.7	Bee Caves BBQ	Westlake	Counter	$7
6.7	PoKeJo's	Clarksville	Counter	$15
6.5	Iron Works BBQ	Convention Center	Counter	$14
6.5	Jim Bob's BBQ	Bee Cave	Counter	$12
6.4	Richard Jones	St. Edward's Area	Counter	$11
6.2	Bert's BBQ	West Campus	Counter	$8
6.0	Ben's Longbranch	East Austin	Casual	$17
5.9	County Line	Westlake	Casual	$29
5.8	Chisholm Trail	Lockhart	Counter	$11
4.8	Scholtz Garten	Capitol Area	Casual	$20
4.4	The Pit BBQ	Burnet	Counter	$8

Brazilian

6.4	Sampaio's	Burnet	Upmarket	$42
6.0	São Paulo's	UT Area	Casual	$32

Burgers

8.4	Casino El Camino	Sixth Street District	Pub	$12
7.7	Dirty Martin's	West Campus	Casual	$12
7.0	The Jackalope	Sixth Street District	Pub	$12
6.9	BurgerTex	North Central	Counter	$15

	Burgers *continued*	Location	Type	Price
6.8	P. Terry's	South Lamar	Take-out	$6
6.7	Hut's Hamburgers	Warehouse District	Casual	$13
6.5	Red River Café	UT Area	Casual	$14
6.3	Dan's Hamburgers	Far South	Counter	$7
6.2	Fran's	South Congress	Counter	$8
6.0	Top-Notch Burgers	Burnet	Counter	$8
5.7	Nau's Enfield Drug	Clarksville	Counter	$5
5.2	Hill-Bert's Burgers	UT Area	Casual	$10
4.6	Sandy's	Zilker	Take-out	$5
3.9	Freddie's	Bouldin Creek	Casual	$21

Chinese

8.8	Din Ho Chinese BBQ	Far North	Casual	$24
8.7	T&S Chinese Seafood	Far North	Casual	$22
8.3	Pao's Mandarin House	Lake Travis	Casual	$20
8.1	Marco Polo	Southeast	Casual	$24
8.0	Tien Hong	Burnet	Casual	$23
7.5	Sea Dragon	Far North	Casual	$24
7.2	Chinatown	Northwest Hills	Upmarket	$30
6.9	Suzi's China Grill	Westlake	Casual	$31
6.7	Sun Hing	West Campus	Casual	$20
6.6	Peony	Northwest Hills	Casual	$28
6.2	Hunan Lion	South Lamar	Casual	$23
6.0	Lotus Hunan	Westlake	Casual	$22
5.8	Hao Hao	Far South	Casual	$16
5.5	Suzi's China Kitchen	South Lamar	Casual	$23
5.3	Snow Pea	North Central	Casual	$24
5.0	Noodle-ism	Congress Ave. Area	Counter	$19
3.1	CoCo's Café	West Campus	Counter	$8
2.6	Wanfu Too	Zilker	Casual	$21
2.3	Wanfu	Southeast	Casual	$21
2.2	The Magic Wok	West Campus	Counter	$7

French

9.0	Capitol Brasserie	Warehouse District	Upmarket	$48
9.0	Aquarelle	Warehouse District	Upmarket	$91
8.2	Chez Nous	Sixth Street District	Upmarket	$51
8.0	Emerald	Bee Cave	Upmarket	$80

German

4.9	Walburg Mercantile	Walburg	Casual	$29
4.8	Scholtz Garten	Capitol Area	Casual	$20

Greek

7.5	Phoenicia Bakery	South Lamar	Take-out	$6
7.1	Milto's	UT Area	Counter	$11
7.0	Pyramids	North Central	Casual	$15

Hawaiian

6.7	Roy's Austin	Convention Center	Upmarket	$66

Hungarian

8.3	European Bistro	Pflugerville	Upmarket	$37

Ice cream *ranked by ice cream rating only*

9.2	Amy's Ice Cream	Clarksville	Counter	
9.0	Tèo	Seton Medical Area	Counter	
7.9	La Dolce Vita	Hyde Park	Café	
6.1	Paciugo Gelateria	Warehouse District	Counter	

Indian

8.4	Clay Pit	Capitol Area	Upmarket	$33
8.4	Swad	Far North	Counter	$14

	Indian *continued*	Location	Type	Price
7.2	Madras Pavilion	Far North	Casual	$15
7.5	Taj Palace	North Central	Casual	$22
5.0	Cosmic Café	Clarksville	Casual	$16
6.7	Star of India	North Central	Casual	$22
6.2	Sarovar	Burnet	Casual	$25
5.4	Indian Palace	Northwest Hills	Casual	$21
6.9	Bombay Grill	Westlake	Casual	$23
6.8	Shalimar	Far North	Casual	$11
7.3	Bombay Bistro	Arboretum	Upmarket	$30

Indonesian

7.6	Satay	North Central	Casual	$24
3.5	Java Noodles	Southeast	Casual	$19

Irish

8.0	Emerald Restaurant	Bee Cave	Upmarket	$80
7.6	Fadó	Warehouse District	Pub	$26

Italian

9.3	Vespaio	South Congress	Upmarket	$62
9.2	Vespaio Enoteca	South Congress	Casual	$32
8.8	Taverna	Warehouse District	Upmarket	$48
8.7	Asti	Hyde Park	Upmarket	$37
8.5	Mandola's	Hyde Park	Counter	$19
8.5	La Traviata	Congress Ave. Area	Upmarket	$51
8.5	Siena	Westlake	Upmarket	$55
7.8	Cipollina	Clarksville	Counter	$18
7.7	Tuscany	Far North	Counter	$17
7.7	Andiamo	Far North	Upmarket	$50
7.6	Reale's	Far Northwest	Casual	$27
6.9	Brick Oven on 35th	Seton Medical Area	Casual	$26
6.8	Brick Oven	Red River Area	Casual	$22
6.7	Bellagio	Far Northwest	Upmarket	$52
6.1	Frank & Angie's	Warehouse District	Casual	$23
5.6	Tony's Vineyard	West Campus	Upmarket	$37
4.9	Carmelo's	Sixth Street District	Upmarket	$56
3.5	Vinny's	Zilker	Casual	$29
3.2	Romeo's	Zilker	Casual	$28
1.8	Tree House	St. Edward's Area	Upmarket	$36

Japanese

9.7	Uchi	South Lamar	Upmarket	$69
9.1	Mikado Ryotei	Far North	Upmarket	$47
8.9	Musashino	Northwest Hills	Upmarket	$58
8.8	Beluga	Round Rock	Upmarket	$40
8.4	Sushi Sake	Arboretum	Upmarket	$45
7.8	Kyoto	Congress Ave. Area	Upmarket	$37
7.6	Arirang Sushi	Sixth Street District	Casual	$23
7.4	Kenichi	Warehouse District	Upmarket	$82
7.2	Ichiban	Burnet	Casual	$23
7.2	Chinatown	Northwest Hills	Upmarket	$30
6.9	Suzi's China Grill	Westlake	Casual	$31
6.8	Sushi Niichi Express	UT Area	Casual	$17
6.7	Korea Garden	North Central	Casual	$33
6.6	Peony	Northwest Hills	Casual	$28
6.4	Korea House	North Central	Casual	$31
6.3	Maiko Sushi Lounge	Warehouse District	Upmarket	$77
6.1	Silhouette	Congress Ave. Area	Upmarket	$41
6.1	Finn & Porter	Convention Center	Upmarket	$63
5.9	Umi Sushi	Southeast	Upmarket	$56
5.4	Wiki Wiki Teriyaki	Congress Ave. Area	Counter	$10
5.3	Snow Pea	North Central	Casual	$24
4.6	Seoul Restaurant	Far South	Casual	$30

Japanese *continued*	Location	Type	Price
4.4 Koreana	Far North	Upmarket	$31
3.8 Zen	UT Area	Counter	$9

Jewish Deli

6.7 Katz's	Warehouse District	Casual	$23
4.9 Manny Hattan's	Arboretum	Casual	$27

Korean

7.2 Ichiban	Burnet	Casual	$23
6.9 BurgerTex	North Central	Counter	$15
6.7 Korea Garden	North Central	Casual	$33
6.4 Korea House	North Central	Casual	$31
6.1 Koriente	Sixth Street District	Casual	$9
5.3 Snow Pea	North Central	Casual	$24
4.6 Seoul Restaurant	Far South	Casual	$30
4.4 Koreana	Far North	Upmarket	$31

Latin American *includes South American, Central American, Caribbean*

8.4 Doña Emilia's	Convention Center	Upmarket	$46
6.8 Cuba Libre	Warehouse District	Casual	$33
6.8 Habana Calle 6	Sixth Street District	Upmarket	$34
6.4 Mi Colombia	East Austin	Casual	$16
6.3 Costa del Sol	Far North	Casual	$23
6.2 Cocina de Marybel	East Austin	Casual	$15
6.0 El Zunzal	East Austin	Casual	$19
5.2 Elsi's	Burnet	Casual	$19

Light American *sandwiches, salads, soups, and other lunch-type fare*

8.0 Azul	East Austin	Counter	$11
7.9 Café Mundi	East Austin	Café	$11
7.9 Tâm Deli & Café	Far North	Counter	$10
7.9 Portabla	Clarksville	Counter	$9
7.8 Delaware Sub Shop	UT Area	Counter	$8
7.7 Dandelion Café	East Austin	Café	$8
7.7 FoodHeads	UT Area	Counter	$8
7.4 TX French Bread	UT Area	Counter	$8
7.3 Sweetish Hill	Clarksville	Café	$9
7.2 Triumph Café	Northwest Hills	Café	$11
7.1 Garden District	St. Edward's Area	Café	$9
7.1 Upper Crust	Burnet	Café	$6
6.9 The Kitchen Door	Tarrytown	Counter	$9
6.8 Jo's Hot Coffee	South Congress	Café	$8
6.7 Veggie Heaven	West Campus	Casual	$13
6.7 Katz's	Warehouse District	Casual	$23
6.6 Casa de Luz	Zilker	Counter	$13
6.3 Thundercloud Subs	Capitol Area	Counter	$7
6.1 Ba Le	Far North	Counter	$8
6.0 Avenue B Grocery	Hyde Park	Counter	$9
6.0 Green Muse Café	St. Edward's Area	Café	$9
5.9 Nu Age Café	Tarrytown	Casual	$22
5.7 Schlotzsky's	South Lamar	Counter	$8
5.7 NeWorlDeli	Hyde Park	Counter	$13
5.5 The Spider House	UT Area	Café	$7
5.1 Flipnotics	Zilker	Café	$12
5.0 Quack's on 43rd	Hyde Park	Café	$6
4.9 Manny Hattan's	Arboretum	Casual	$27
4.1 Ruta Maya	St. Edward's Area	Café	$6
3.8 Bouldin Creek Café	Bouldin Creek	Café	$8
3.7 Mr. Natural	South Lamar	Counter	$12

Macedonian

7.0 Kebab Palace	Far North	Casual	$11

Malaysian	Location	Type	Price
8.1 Marco Polo	Southeast	Casual	$24

Mexican			
9.2 El Chile	French Place	Casual	$31
8.9 Fonda San Miguel	North Central	Upmarket	$59
8.9 Manuel's	Congress Ave. Area	Upmarket	$39
8.6 El Borrego de Oro	St. Edward's Area	Casual	$21
8.5 Curra's Grill	St. Edward's Area	Casual	$27
8.3 Polvos	Bouldin Creek	Casual	$24
8.3 Azul Tequila	South Lamar	Casual	$30
8.2 Changos Taquería	UT Area	Counter	$11
8.1 El Mesón Taquería	Southeast	Counter	$14
8.1 Oaxacan Tamaleo	North Central	Counter	$7
8.0 Maria's Taco Xpress	South Lamar	Counter	$8
7.8 El Taquito	East Austin	Take-out	$5
7.7 Chuy's	Zilker	Casual	$27
7.6 Las Manitas	Congress Ave. Area	Casual	$16
7.6 A La Carrera	Far Northwest	Casual	$21
7.6 Z' Tejas	Clarksville	Casual	$36
7.5 Little Mexico	Bouldin Creek	Casual	$25
7.5 Mexico Lindo	South Lamar	Casual	$25
7.4 Garibaldi's	Far South	Casual	$21
7.3 Habanero Café	St. Edward's Area	Casual	$9
7.3 Cantina Laredo	Warehouse District	Upmarket	$37
7.2 Serrano's Café	Red River Area	Casual	$28
7.1 El Arroyo	Clarksville	Casual	$28
7.1 Julio's	Hyde Park	Casual	$19
7.0 Las Palomas	Westlake	Casual	$29
7.0 Taquería Arandas	St. Edward's Area	Casual	$8
6.9 El Regio	Southeast	Counter	$10
6.8 Vivo Cocina Texicana	French Place	Casual	$28
6.7 Nuevo León	East Austin	Casual	$24
6.6 Angie's Mexican	East Austin	Casual	$20
6.5 Paradise Café	Sixth Street District	Casual	$25
6.4 Taco Shack	Seton Medical Area	Counter	$5
6.4 Evita's Botanitas	Far South	Casual	$23
6.4 Freebirds	Hyde Park	Counter	$9
6.2 Iron Cactus	Sixth Street District	Pub	$35
6.2 Santa Rita	Seton Medical Area	Casual	$29
6.1 La Mexicana Bakery	Bouldin Creek	Counter	$6
6.0 Juan in a Million	East Austin	Casual	$17
5.8 Taco Cabana	West Campus	Counter	$9
5.6 The Oasis	Northwest Hills	Casual	$32
5.6 Trudy's	UT Area	Casual	$26
5.6 El Azteca	East Austin	Casual	$23
5.4 Güero's	South Congress	Casual	$26
5.2 Chapala	East Austin	Casual	$5
5.1 Hula Hut	Tarrytown	Casual	$31
5.1 Las Palmas	East Austin	Casual	$26
5.0 El Sol y La Luna	South Congress	Casual	$19
4.9 El Mercado	Capitol Area	Casual	$27
4.9 Flores	North Central	Casual	$23
4.9 Matt's El Rancho	South Lamar	Casual	$29
4.8 Jorge's	North Central	Casual	$24
4.4 Jaime's	Red River Area	Casual	$24
4.4 Nueva Onda	St. Edward's Area	Counter	$17
4.2 Doc's	South Congress	Pub	$22
3.8 Marisco Grill	Sixth Street District	Casual	$33
3.7 Tres Amigos	Westlake	Casual	$33
3.6 La Reyna	Bouldin Creek	Casual	$19
3.4 Cisco's	East Austin	Casual	$11
3.1 Dario's	East Austin	Casual	$21
2.9 Maudie's	Tarrytown	Pub	$22

Mexican continued	Location	Type	Price
2.8 Las Cazuelas	East Austin	Casual	$22
2.7 La Feria	South Lamar	Casual	$22
2.6 Baby Acapulco	Zilker	Casual	$23
2.4 El Patio	UT Area	Casual	$15
2.2 El Gallo	St. Edward's Area	Casual	$25
2.0 Jovita's	Bouldin Creek	Casual	$15
1.6 Rosie's	St. Edward's Area	Casual	$22
1.4 Enchiladas y Mas	North Central	Casual	$18

Middle Eastern

	Location	Type	Price
7.6 Jerusalem Gourmet	Southeast	Counter	$9
7.5 Phoenicia Bakery	South Lamar	Take-out	$6
7.3 Byblos	Far North	Counter	$7
7.2 Alborz	North Central	Casual	$28
7.0 Pyramids	North Central	Casual	$15
6.9 Kismet Café	West Campus	Counter	$9
6.8 Tom's Tabooley	UT Area	Counter	$8
6.5 Marakesh	Capitol Area	Casual	$18
5.9 Chooby Doo	Far South	Counter	$7
5.8 Ararat	North Central	Casual	$22
4.3 Longhorn Po-Boys	UT Area	Counter	$7
3.1 Dariush	Capitol Area	Casual	$27

New American

	Location	Type	Price
9.6 Café at the 4 Seasons	Convention Center	Upmarket	$73
9.4 The Driskill Grill	Congress Ave. Area	Upmarket	$105
9.3 Wink	House Park Area	Upmarket	$86
9.3 Café 909	Marble Falls	Upmarket	$60
9.2 Zoot	Tarrytown	Upmarket	$64
9.0 Starlite	Warehouse District	Upmarket	$65
8.6 Jeffrey's	Clarksville	Upmarket	$84
8.4 Shoreline Grill	Convention Center	Upmarket	$64
8.3 Vin Bistro	Seton Medical Area	Upmarket	$64
8.1 Bistro 88	Westlake	Upmarket	$49
7.7 Louie's 106	Sixth Street District	Upmarket	$50
7.5 34th Street Café	UT Area	Upmarket	$44
6.9 219 West	Warehouse District	Upmarket	$32
6.8 Zax Pints & Plates	Zilker	Upmarket	$40
6.7 Roy's Austin	Convention Center	Upmarket	$66
6.5 Mars	West Campus	Upmarket	$45
6.4 Saba Blue Water	Warehouse District	Upmarket	$47
6.1 Finn & Porter	Convention Center	Upmarket	$63
6.0 Judges' Hill	West Campus	Upmarket	$65

Pan-Asian

	Location	Type	Price
8.1 Bistro 88	Westlake	Upmarket	$49
7.6 Satay	North Central	Casual	$24
6.5 Mars	West Campus	Upmarket	$45
5.9 Nu Age Café	Tarrytown	Casual	$22
5.9 Chooby Doo	Far South	Counter	$7
5.1 Hula Hut	Tarrytown	Casual	$31
2.8 Mongolian BBQ	Convention Center	Casual	$17
2.6 Wanfu Too	Zilker	Casual	$21
2.3 Wanfu	Southeast	Casual	$21
1.2 Buffet Palace	North Central	Casual	$14

Pizza ranked by pizza rating, not overall food rating

9.2 Mandola's	Hyde Park	Counter	$19
9.1 Tuscany	Far North	Counter	$17
8.9 Asti	Hyde Park	Upmarket	$37
8.8 Vespaio Enoteca	South Congress	Casual	$32
8.8 Vespaio	South Congress	Casual	$62

Pizza *continued*	Location	Type	Price
8.6 Reale's	Far Northwest	Casual	$27
8.5 Taverna	Warehouse District	Upmarket	$48
7.9 Rounders Pizzeria	Clarksville	Counter	$15
7.8 Cipollina	Clarksville	Counter	$18
7.1 Milto's	UT Area	Counter	$11
7.0 Home Slice Pizza	South Congress	Casual	$18
6.9 Brick Oven on 35th	Seton Medical Area	Casual	$26
6.8 Brick Oven	Red River Area	Casual	$22
6.7 Austin's Pizza	Capitol Area	Counter	$9
6.6 Mangia	UT Area	Casual	$15
6.1 Frank & Angie's	Warehouse District	Casual	$23
5.9 Hangtown Grill	Westlake	Counter	$14
5.4 Rockin' Tomato	South Lamar	Counter	$17
4.9 Mr. Gatti's	West Campus	Casual	$8
4.7 Conan's Pizza	West Campus	Counter	$9
4.6 EZ's	Seton Medical Area	Counter	$20
4.4 Austin Pizza Garden	Oak Hill	Casual	$17

Romanian
7.1 Drakula	Far North	Casual	$23

Russian
6.0 Sasha's	Northwest Hills	Casual	$17

Seafood
8.8 Din Ho Chinese BBQ	Far North	Casual	$24
8.7 T&S Chinese Seafood	Far North	Casual	$22
8.1 Marco Polo	Southeast	Casual	$24
7.3 Eddie V's	Sixth Street District	Upmarket	$63
7.1 Quality Seafood	North Central	Counter	$12
6.7 Pacific Star	Far Northwest	Casual	$24
6.1 Finn & Porter	Convention Center	Upmarket	$63
5.7 Catfish Parlour	Far Northwest	Casual	$23
5.6 Truluck's	Warehouse District	Upmarket	$66
5.3 Lucy's	Tarrytown	Casual	$33
3.8 Marisco Grill	Sixth Street District	Casual	$33

Southern *including soul food, Cajun, and Creole*
8.3 Hoover's Cooking	French Place	Casual	$25
7.9 Nubian Queen Lola's	East Austin	Casual	$10
7.9 Sambet's	Northwest Hills	Counter	$12
7.4 Gumbo's	Capitol Area	Upmarket	$51
7.3 Green Mesquite	Zilker	Casual	$21
7.1 Gene's	East Austin	Casual	$13
6.9 Ms. B's	Northwest Hills	Casual	$27
6.4 Old Pecan St. Café	Sixth Street District	Casual	$29
6.0 Old Alligator Grill	South Lamar	Casual	$30
6.0 Evangeline Café	Far South	Casual	$23
5.7 Catfish Parlour	Far Northwest	Casual	$23
5.5 Threadgill's	North Central	Casual	$24

Southwestern
9.3 Café Josie	Clarksville	Upmarket	$48
9.3 Castle Hill Café	Clarksville	Upmarket	$46
9.1 South Congress Café	South Congress	Upmarket	$42
8.9 Mirabelle	Northwest Hills	Upmarket	$46
8.8 Hudson's on the Bend	Lake Travis	Upmarket	$83
8.6 Hill Country Din. Rm.	Westlake	Upmarket	$68
8.0 Roaring Fork	Congress Ave. Area	Upmarket	$52
7.8 Ranch 616	Capitol Area	Upmarket	$43
7.6 Z' Tejas	Clarksville	Casual	$36
7.5 Mesa Ranch	Northwest Hills	Upmarket	$44
6.5 Y Bar & Grill	Oak Hill	Upmarket	$45

Specialty Groceries

Central Market	Seton Medical Area, Far South
Farm to Market Grocery	South Congress
Fresh Plus	Hyde Park
Grapevine Market	North Central
La Michoacana	East Austin, Far South
Sun Harvest	South Lamar, North Central
Wheatsville Co-Op Deli	UT Area
Whole Foods	Clarksville, Arboretum

Spanish

9.2	Fino	UT Area	Upmarket	$50
8.4	Málaga	Warehouse District	Upmarket	$47
7.7	Louie's 106	Sixth Street District	Upmarket	$50

Steakhouses

8.6	Ruth's Chris	Congress Ave. Area	Upmarket	$74
8.1	Austin Land & Cattle	House Park Area	Upmarket	$60
4.8	Hoffbrau	Warehouse District	Casual	$24
3.3	Dan McKlusky's	Sixth Street District	Upmarket	$63

Thai

7.7	Bangkok Cuisine	Far North	Casual	$24
7.6	Thai Tara	Warehouse District	Casual	$23
7.1	Sawadee	Far South	Casual	$24
6.8	Madam Mam's	West Campus	Casual	$16
6.8	Thai Noodles, Etc.	West Campus	Casual	$14
6.3	Thai Passion	Congress Ave. Area	Casual	$27
5.6	Thai Kitchen	UT Area	Casual	$15

Vietnamese

8.5	Sunflower	Far North	Casual	$22
7.9	Tâm Deli & Café	Far North	Counter	$10
7.9	Le Soleil	Far North	Casual	$26
7.7	Mekong River	Sixth Street District	Casual	$18
7.5	Sea Dragon	Far North	Casual	$24
7.2	Triumph Café	Northwest Hills	Café	$11
6.8	888	Southeast	Casual	$24
6.1	Ba Le	Far North	Counter	$8
5.7	Phô Thai Son	West Campus	Casual	$9
4.1	Hai Ky	Southeast	Casual	$13

LISTED IN ORDER OF FOOD RATING OUT OF 10

Arboretum

		Cuisine	Type	Price
8.9	Manuel's	Mexican	Upmarket	$39
8.4	Sushi Sake	Japanese	Upmarket	$45
7.6	Z' Tejas	Mexican	Casual	$36
7.3	Eddie V's	Seafood	Upmarket	$63
7.3	Bombay Bistro	Indian	Upmarket	$30
7.2	Serrano's Café	Mexican	Casual	$28
6.8	Brick Oven	Italian	Casual	$22
5.6	Truluck's	Seafood	Upmarket	$66
5.4	Wiki Wiki Teriyaki	Japanese	Counter	$10
4.9	Manny Hattan's	Light American	Casual	$27
	Whole Foods	Grocery		

Bee Cave

8.0	Emerald Restaurant	Irish	Upmarket	$80
7.1	El Arroyo	Mexican	Casual	$28
6.5	Jim Bob's BBQ	Barbecue	Counter	$12
3.2	Bee Cave Bistro	American	Casual	$37
1.6	Rosie's Tamale House	Mexican	Casual	$22

Bouldin Creek Area *north of W. Hwy. 290, south of Barton Springs Rd., east of S. Lamar Blvd., west of S. Congress Ave.*

8.7	Green Pastures	American	Upmarket	$67
8.3	Polvos	Mexican	Casual	$24
7.5	Little Mexico	Mexican	Casual	$25
6.3	The Soup Peddler	American	Take-out	$10
6.1	La Mexicana Bakery	Mexican	Counter	$6
3.9	Freddie's	American	Casual	$21
3.8	Bouldin Creek Café	Light American	Café	$8
3.6	La Reyna	Mexican	Casual	$19
2.0	Jovita's	Mexican	Casual	$15

Burnet *on Burnet Rd.*

8.5	Curra's Grill	Mexican	Casual	$27
8.0	Tien Hong	Chinese	Casual	$23
7.5	Phoenicia Bakery	Middle Eastern	Take-out	$6
7.2	Ichiban	Japanese	Casual	$23
7.1	Upper Crust	Light American	Café	$6
7.0	Taquería Arandas	Mexican	Casual	$8
6.9	The Frisco Shop	Steakhouse	Counter	$16
6.4	Sampaio's	Brazilian	Upmarket	$42
6.4	Dog Almighty	American	Counter	$5
6.3	Ventana	American	Upmarket	$42
6.2	Sarovar	Indian	Casual	$25
6.1	Austin Diner	American	Casual	$12
6.0	Top-Notch Burgers	Burgers	Counter	$8
5.6	The Omelettry	American	Casual	$10
5.6	Trudy's	Mexican	Casual	$26
5.2	Elsi's	Latin American	Casual	$19
4.9	El Mercado	Mexican	Casual	$27
4.4	The Pit BBQ	Barbecue	Counter	$8
3.8	Marisco Grill	Mexican	Casual	$33

Capitol Area
north of W. 6th St. west of and including Colorado St., north of 9th St. between Colorado St. and Brazos St., north of E. 7th St. east of and including Brazos St., south of MLK Blvd., east of West Ave., west of and including Trinity St.

8.4	Clay Pit	Indian	Upmarket	$33
7.8	Ranch 616	Southwestern	Upmarket	$43
7.4	Gumbo's	Southern	Upmarket	$51
6.8	Texas Chili Parlor	American	Casual	$17
6.7	Austin's Pizza	Pizza	Counter	$9
6.5	Marakesh	Middle Eastern	Casual	$18
6.3	Thundercloud Subs	Light American	Counter	$7
5.9	Dog & Duck Pub	American	Pub	$20
5.8	Arturo's	American	Counter	$12
4.9	El Mercado	Mexican	Casual	$27
4.8	Scholtz Garten	German	Casual	$20
4.2	The Fox & Hound	American	Pub	$20
4.0	Texadelphia	American	Counter	$13
3.1	Dariush	Middle Eastern	Casual	$27

Cedar Park

7.9	Sambet's	Southern	Counter	$12
2.7	La Feria	Mexican	Casual	$22

Clarksville
north and east of the river, south of MLK Blvd., west of and including Lamar Blvd.

9.3	Café Josie	Southwestern	Upmarket	$48
9.3	Castle Hill Café	Southwestern	Upmarket	$46
8.6	Jeffrey's	New American	Upmarket	$84
7.9	Rounders Pizzeria	Pizza	Counter	$15
7.9	Portabla	Light American	Counter	$9
7.8	CIpollina	Italian	Counter	$18
7.6	Z' Tejas	Mexican	Casual	$36
7.3	Sweetish Hill	Light American	Café	$9
7.1	El Arroyo	Mexican	Casual	$28
6.7	PoKeJo's	Barbecue	Counter	$15
6.5	Austin Java Co.	American	Café	$12
6.0	Waterloo Ice House	American	Pub	$22
5.7	Nau's Enfield Drug	American	Counter	$5
5.0	Cosmic Café	Indian	Casual	$16
	Amy's Ice Cream	Sweets	Counter	
	Whole Foods		Grocery	

Congress Avenue Area
north of the river, south of 9th St., east of Colorado St., west of San Jacinto St.

9.4	The Driskill Grill	New American	Upmarket	$105
8.9	Manuel's	Mexican	Upmarket	$39
8.6	Ruth's Chris	Steakhouse	Upmarket	$74
8.6	1886 Café & Bakery	Light American	Upmarket	$31
8.5	La Traviata	Italian	Upmarket	$51
8.0	Roaring Fork	Southwestern	Upmarket	$52
7.8	Kyoto	Japanese	Upmarket	$37
7.6	Las Manitas	Mexican	Casual	$16
6.3	Thai Passion	Thai	Casual	$27
6.1	Silhouette	Japanese	Upmarket	$41
5.4	Wiki Wiki Teriyaki	Japanese	Counter	$10
5.0	Noodle-ism	Chinese	Counter	$19
4.5	Hickory Street	American	Casual	$23
4.0	Texadelphia	American	Counter	$13

Convention Center Area
north of the river, south of E. 5th St., east of and including Brazos St., west of IH-35

9.6	Café at the 4 Seasons	New American	Upmarket	$73
8.4	Shoreline Grill	New American	Upmarket	$64
8.4	Doña Emilia's	Latin American	Upmarket	$46
6.7	Roy's Austin	New American	Upmarket	$66

Convention Center Area *continued*		*Type*	*Price*
6.5 Iron Works BBQ	Barbecue	Counter	$14
6.4 Moonshine	American	Upmarket	$36
6.1 Finn & Porter	Seafood	Upmarket	$63
2.8 Mongolian BBQ	Pan-Asian	Casual	$17

Driftwood

9.1 The Salt Lick	Barbecue	Casual	$17

Dripping Springs

5.0 Flip's Satellite Café	American	Casual	$17
5.0 Nutty Brown Café	American	Casual	$29
1.6 Rosie's Tamale House	Mexican	Casual	$22

East Austin *south of MLK Blvd., east of IH-35*

8.2 Sam's BBQ	Barbecue	Counter	$11
8.0 Azul	Light American	Counter	$11
7.9 Café Mundi	Light American	Café	$11
7.9 Nubian Queen Lola's	Southern	Casual	$10
7.8 El Taquito	Mexican	Take-out	$5
7.7 Dandelion Café	Light American	Café	$8
7.1 Gene's	Southern	Casual	$13
7.1 Lewis' BBQ	Barbecue	Counter	$8
6.7 Nuevo León	Mexican	Casual	$24
6.6 Angie's Mexican	Mexican	Casual	$20
6.4 Mi Colombia	Latin American	Casual	$16
6.3 Dan's Hamburgers	Burgers	Counter	$7
6.2 Cocina de Marybel	Latin American	Casual	$15
6.0 Juan in a Million	Mexican	Casual	$17
6.0 Ben's Longbranch	Barbecue	Casual	$17
6.0 El Zunzal	Latin American	Casual	$19
5.6 El Azteca	Mexican	Casual	$23
5.2 Chapala	Mexican	Casual	$5
5.1 Las Palmas	Mexican	Casual	$26
3.7 Mr. Natural	Light American	Counter	$12
3.4 Cisco's	Mexican	Casual	$11
3.1 Dario's	Mexican	Casual	$21
2.8 Las Cazuelas	Mexican	Casual	$22
La Michoacana		Grocery	

Far North *north of Research Blvd. west of I-35, north of French Place and Airport Blvd. east of IH-35*

9.1 Mikado Ryotei	Japanese	Upmarket	$47
8.8 Din Ho Chinese BBQ	Chinese	Casual	$24
8.7 T&S Chinese Seafood	Chinese	Casual	$22
8.5 Sunflower	Vietnamese	Casual	$22
8.4 Swad	Indian	Counter	$14
7.9 Le Soleil	Vietnamese	Casual	$26
7.9 Tâm Deli & Café	Vietnamese	Counter	$10
7.7 Bangkok Cuisine	Thai	Casual	$24
7.7 Chuy's	Mexican	Casual	$27
7.7 Tuscany	Italian	Counter	$17
7.7 Andiamo	Italian	Upmarket	$50
7.5 Sea Dragon	Vietnamese	Casual	$24
7.3 Byblos	Middle Eastern	Counter	$7
7.2 Madras Pavilion	Indian	Casual	$15
7.1 Drakula	Romanian	Casual	$23
7.0 Taquería Arandas	Mexican	Casual	$8
7.0 Kebab Palace	Macedonian	Casual	$11
6.9 El Regio	Mexican	Counter	$10
6.8 888	Vietnamese	Casual	$24
6.8 Shalimar	Indian	Casual	$11
6.3 Costa del Sol	Latin American	Casual	$23
6.1 Ba Le	Vietnamese	Counter	$8

Far North continued	Cuisine	Type	Price
5.7 Phô Thai Son	Vietnamese	Casual	$9
4.4 Koreana	Korean	Upmarket	$31
3.7 Tres Amigos	Mexican	Casual	$33
Tèo	Sweets	Counter	

Far Northwest *north and east of and including N. Hwy. 183, west of MoPac*

	Cuisine	Type	Price
8.7 Rudy's	Barbecue	Counter	$15
8.3 Hoover's Cooking	Southern	Casual	$25
7.7 Chuy's	Mexican	Casual	$27
7.6 Reale's	Italian	Casual	$27
7.6 A La Carrera	Mexican	Casual	$21
7.5 Sea Dragon	Vietnamese	Casual	$24
7.1 El Arroyo	Mexican	Casual	$28
6.7 Bellagio	Italian	Upmarket	$52
6.7 Pacific Star	Seafood	Casual	$24
6.5 Austin Java Co.	American	Café	$12
5.7 Catfish Parlour	Southern	Casual	$23
5.4 Rockin' Tomato	Pizza	Counter	$17
4.9 El Mercado	Mexican	Casual	$27
3.7 Tres Amigos	Mexican	Casual	$33
2.6 Baby Acapulco	Mexican	Casual	$23

Far South *south of and including W. Hwy. 290, east of MoPac, west of IH-35*

	Cuisine	Type	Price
7.6 Hill's Café	American	Casual	$27
7.4 Garibaldi's	Mexican	Casual	$21
7.1 Sawadee	Thai	Casual	$24
6.8 Brick Oven	Italian	Casual	$22
6.4 Evita's Botanitas	Mexican	Casual	$23
6.3 Dan's Hamburgers	Burgers	Counter	$7
6.1 Galaxy Café	American	Counter	$15
6.0 Evangeline Café	Southern	Casual	$23
5.9 Chooby Doo	American	Counter	$7
5.8 Hao Hao	Chinese	Casual	$16
5.7 Catfish Parlour	Southern	Casual	$23
5.6 Thai Kitchen	Thai	Casual	$15
4.7 Conan's Pizza	Pizza	Counter	$9
4.6 Seoul Restaurant	Korean	Casual	$30
3.7 Tres Amigos	Mexican	Casual	$33
1.2 Buffet Palace	Pan-Asian	Casual	$14
Central Market		Grocery	
La Michoacana		Grocery	

French Place *north of and including MLK Blvd., south of E. 38½ St., east of and including IH-35, west of and including Airport Blvd.*

	Cuisine	Type	Price
9.2 El Chile	Mexican	Casual	$31
8.3 Hoover's Cooking	Southern	Casual	$25
8.2 Eastside Café	American	Upmarket	$45
6.8 Vivo Cocina Texicana	Mexican	Casual	$28
5.2 Starseeds	American	Casual	$18

House Park Area *north of W. 6th St., south of MLK Blvd., east of Lamar Blvd., west of and including West Ave.*

	Cuisine	Type	Price
9.3 Wink	New American	Upmarket	$86
8.5 House Park BBQ	Barbecue	Counter	$7
8.1 Austin Land & Cattle	Steakhouse	Upmarket	$60
6.6 The Tavern	American	Pub	$26
6.0 Shoal Creek Saloon	American	Pub	$23

Hyde Park *north of and including 38th St., south of and including 51st St., east of and including N. Lamar Blvd., west of IH-35*

8.7	Asti	Italian	Upmarket	$37
8.5	Mandola's	Italian	Counter	$19
8.0	Hyde Park Bar & Grill	American	Casual	$28
7.1	Julio's	Mexican	Casual	$19
6.7	PoKeJo's	Barbecue	Counter	$15
6.6	Mother's	American	Casual	$20
6.4	Freebirds	Mexican	Counter	$9
6.0	Avenue B Grocery	Light American	Counter	$9
5.7	NeWorlDeli	Light American	Counter	$13
5.0	Quack's on 43rd	Light American	Café	$6
	La Dolce Vita	Sweets	Café	
	Fresh Plus		Grocery	

Lake Travis Area *including Lakeway*

8.8	Hudson's on the Bend	Southwestern	Upmarket	$83
8.7	Rudy's	Barbecue	Counter	$15
8.3	Pao's Mandarin House	Chinese	Casual	$20
4.9	Flores	Mexican	Casual	$23
2.7	La Feria	Mexican	Casual	$22

Llano

8.3	Cooper's	Barbecue	Counter	$14

Lockhart

9.1	Kreuz Market	Barbecue	Counter	$12
9.0	Smitty's Market	Barbecue	Counter	$12
7.8	Black's BBQ	Barbecue	Counter	$11
5.8	Chisholm Trail	Barbecue	Counter	$11

Marble Falls

9.3	Café 909	New American	Upmarket	$60
5.8	Russo's Texitally	American	Casual	$31
4.4	Bluebonnet Café	American	Casual	$13

North Central *north of 51st St. east of N. Lamar Blvd., north of W. 45th St. west of N. Lamar Blvd., south of Research Blvd., east of MoPac, west of Airport Blvd.*

8.9	Fonda San Miguel	Mexican	Upmarket	$59
8.5	Curra's Grill	Mexican	Casual	$27
8.1	Oaxacan Tamaleo	Mexican	Counter	$7
7.6	Satay	Indonesian	Casual	$24
7.5	Taj Palace	Indian	Casual	$22
7.2	Alborz	Middle Eastern	Casual	$28
7.1	Quality Seafood	Seafood	Counter	$12
7.0	Pyramids	Middle Eastern	Casual	$15
6.9	BurgerTex	Burgers	Counter	$15
6.9	El Regio	Mexican	Counter	$10
6.9	Suzi's China Grill	Chinese	Casual	$31
6.7	Korea Garden	Korean	Casual	$33
6.7	Star of India	Indian	Casual	$22
6.4	Korea House	Korean	Casual	$31
6.3	Dan's Hamburgers	Burgers	Counter	$7
5.8	Ararat	Middle Eastern	Casual	$22
5.7	Catfish Parlour	Southern	Casual	$23
5.7	Schlotzsky's	Light American	Counter	$8
5.5	Threadgill's	Southern	Casual	$24
5.3	Snow Pea	Chinese	Casual	$24
4.9	Flores	Mexican	Casual	$23
4.8	Jorge's	Mexican	Casual	$24
4.7	Conan's Pizza	Pizza	Counter	$9
4.2	Alamo Drafthouse	American	Theater	$22
3.8	Zen	Japanese	Counter	$9
3.0	Veranda	American	Casual	$31

North Central *continued*		*Type*	*Price*
2.6 Baby Acapulco	Mexican	Casual	$23
1.4 Enchiladas y Mas	Mexican	Casual	$18
1.2 Buffet Palace	Pan-Asian	Casual	$14
Grapevine Market		Grocery	
Sun Harvest		Grocery	

Northwest Hills *north of W. 35th St. and the river, south of N. Hwy. 183, east of the Lake Travis Area, west of and including MoPac*

8.9 Mirabelle	Southwestern	Upmarket	$46
8.9 Musashino	Japanese	Upmarket	$58
7.9 Sambet's	Southern	Counter	$12
7.8 Delaware Sub Shop	Light American	Counter	$8
7.5 Mesa Ranch	Southwestern	Upmarket	$44
7.2 Triumph Café	Vietnamese	Café	$11
7.2 Chinatown	Chinese	Upmarket	$30
6.9 Ms. B's	Southern	Casual	$27
6.9 The Kitchen Door	Light American	Counter	$9
6.6 Mangia	Pizza	Casual	$15
6.6 Peony	Chinese	Casual	$28
6.2 Bert's BBQ	Barbecue	Counter	$8
6.0 Sasha's	Russian	Casual	$17
5.9 County Line	Barbecue	Casual	$29
5.8 Chez Zee	American	Casual	$35
5.6 The Oasis	Mexican	Casual	$32
5.4 Indian Palace	Indian	Casual	$21
5.4 Rockin' Tomato	Pizza	Counter	$17

Oak Hill

7.3 Green Mesquite	Barbecue	Casual	$21
7.2 Serrano's Café	Mexican	Casual	$28
6.5 Y Bar & Grill	Southwestern	Upmarket	$45
6.2 Bert's BBQ	Barbecue	Counter	$8
4.9 Flores	Mexican	Casual	$23
4.9 Mr. Gatti's	Pizza	Casual	$8
4.4 Austin Pizza Garden	Pizza	Casual	$17

Pflugerville

8.3 European Bistro	Hungarian	Upmarket	$37
6.9 BurgerTex	Burgers	Counter	$15

Red River Area *north of 7th St., south of MLK, east of Trinity St., west of IH-35*

7.4 Stubb's BBQ	Barbecue	Counter	$18
7.2 Serrano's Café	Mexican	Casual	$28
6.8 Brick Oven	Italian	Casual	$22
4.4 Jaime's	Mexican	Casual	$24

Round Rock

8.8 Beluga	Japanese	Upmarket	$40
7.4 Gumbo's	Southern	Upmarket	$51
5.8 Hao Hao	Chinese	Casual	$16

Seton Medical Area *north of and including W. 38th St., south of and including W. 45th St., east of MoPac, west of N. Lamar Blvd.*

8.3 Vin Bistro	New American	Upmarket	$64
6.9 Brick Oven on 35th	Italian	Casual	$26
6.4 Taco Shack	Mexican	Counter	$5
6.2 Santa Rita	Mexican	Casual	$29
6.2 Kerbey Lane Café	American	Casual	$19
6.0 Waterloo Ice House	American	Pub	$22
4.6 EZ's	American	Counter	$20
4.5 The Draught House	American	Pub	$19
Tèo	Sweets	Counter	
Central Market		Grocery	

Sixth Street District
north of and including E. 5th St., south of and including E. 7th St., east of and including Brazos St., west of IH-35

				Price
8.4	Casino El Camino	Burgers	Pub	$12
8.2	Chez Nous	French	Upmarket	$51
7.7	Louie's 106	New American	Upmarket	$50
7.7	Mekong River	Vietnamese	Casual	$18
7.6	Arirang Sushi	Japanese	Casual	$23
7.3	Eddie V's	Seafood	Upmarket	$63
7.0	The Jackalope	American	Pub	$12
6.8	Habana Calle 6	Latin American	Upmarket	$34
6.5	Paradise Café	American	Casual	$25
6.4	Old Pecan St. Café	Southern	Casual	$29
6.2	Iron Cactus	Mexican	Pub	$35
6.1	Koriente	Korean	Casual	$9
4.9	Carmelo's	Italian	Upmarket	$56
3.8	Marisco Grill	Mexican	Casual	$33
3.3	Dan McKlusky's	Steakhouse	Upmarket	$63

South Congress
along S. Congress Ave. north of Oltorf St.

9.3	Vespaio	Italian	Upmarket	$62
9.2	Vespaio Enoteca	Italian	Casual	$32
9.1	South Congress Café	Southwestern	Upmarket	$42
7.4	TX French Bread	Light American	Counter	$8
7.0	Home Slice Pizza	Pizza	Casual	$18
6.8	Jo's Hot Coffee	Light American	Café	$8
6.6	Beck's	American	Pub	$34
6.4	Freebirds	Mexican	Counter	$9
6.2	Fran's	Burgers	Counter	$8
5.9	Magnolia Café	American	Casual	$18
5.4	Güero's	Mexican	Casual	$26
5.0	El Sol y La Luna	Mexican	Casual	$19
4.5	Opal Divine's	American	Pub	$21
4.2	Doc's	American	Pub	$22
3.8	Zen	Japanese	Counter	$9
	Amy's Ice Cream	Sweets	Counter	
	Farm to Market		Grocery	

South Lamar Area
along S. Lamar Blvd. north of W. Hwy. 290

9.7	Uchi	Japanese	Upmarket	$69
8.3	Azul Tequila	Mexican	Casual	$30
8.2	Changos Taquería	Mexican	Counter	$11
8.0	Maria's Taco Xpress	Mexican	Counter	$8
7.7	Artz Rib House	Barbecue	Casual	$22
7.5	Mexico Lindo	Mexican	Casual	$25
7.5	Phoenicia Bakery	Middle Eastern	Take-out	$6
6.8	P. Terry's	Burgers	Take-out	$6
6.7	Austin's Pizza	Pizza	Counter	$9
6.2	Hunan Lion	Chinese	Casual	$23
6.2	Kerbey Lane Café	American	Casual	$19
6.0	The Paggi House	American	Pub	$36
6.0	Old Alligator Grill	Southern	Casual	$30
5.8	Taco Cabana	Mexican	Counter	$9
5.7	Schlotzsky's	Light American	Counter	$8
5.6	Trudy's	Mexican	Casual	$26
5.5	Suzi's China Kitchen	Chinese	Casual	$23
5.4	Rockin' Tomato	Pizza	Counter	$17
4.9	Matt's El Rancho	Mexican	Casual	$29
4.9	Mr. Gatti's	Pizza	Casual	$8
4.7	The Broken Spoke	American	Pub	$24
4.2	Alamo Drafthouse	American	Theater	$22
3.7	Mr. Natural	Light American	Counter	$12
2.9	Maudie's	Mexican	Pub	$22
2.7	La Feria	Mexican	Casual	$22
	Sun Harvest		Grocery	

Southeast *south of the river, east of and including IH-35*

				Price
8.1	El Mesón Taquería	Mexican	Counter	$14
8.1	Marco Polo	Chinese	Casual	$24
7.6	Jerusalem Gourmet	Middle Eastern	Counter	$9
6.9	El Regio	Mexican	Counter	$10
6.8	888	Vietnamese	Casual	$24
5.9	Umi Sushi	Japanese	Upmarket	$56
5.8	Taco Cabana	Mexican	Counter	$9
5.7	Phô Thai Son	Vietnamese	Casual	$9
4.1	Hai Ky	Vietnamese	Casual	$13
3.5	Java Noodles	Indonesian	Casual	$19
2.3	Wanfu	Chinese	Casual	$21
1.2	Buffet Palace	Pan-Asian	Casual	$14

St. Edward's Area *north of W. Hwy. 290, south of and including Oltorf St., east of and including S. 1st St., west of IH-35*

8.6	El Borrego de Oro	Mexican	Casual	$21
8.5	Curra's Grill	Mexican	Casual	$27
8.2	Buenos Aires Café	Argentine	Counter	$17
7.7	Texicalli Grill	American	Casual	$17
7.3	Habanero Café	Mexican	Casual	$9
7.1	Garden District	Light American	Café	$9
7.0	Taquería Arandas	Mexican	Casual	$8
6.4	Richard Jones	Barbecue	Counter	$11
6.0	Green Muse Café	Light American	Café	$9
4.4	Nueva Onda	Mexican	Counter	$17
4.1	Ruta Maya	Light American	Café	$6
2.2	El Gallo	Mexican	Casual	$25
1.8	Tree House	Italian	Upmarket	$36
1.6	Rosie's Tamale House	Mexican	Casual	$22

Tarrytown *north and east of of the river, south of and including W. 35th St., west of and including MoPac*

9.2	Zoot	New American	Upmarket	$64
6.9	The Kitchen Door	Light American	Counter	$9
6.6	Mangia	Pizza	Casual	$15
6.3	Thundercloud Subs	Light American	Counter	$7
5.9	Magnolia Café	American	Casual	$18
5.9	Nu Age Café	Light American	Casual	$22
5.3	Lucy's	Seafood	Casual	$33
5.1	Hula Hut	American	Casual	$31
2.9	Maudie's	Mexican	Pub	$22
	Mozart's	Sweets	Café	

Taylor

9.0	Louie Mueller's	Barbecue	Counter	$10

UT Area *north of MLK, south of 38th St., east of Guadalupe St. south of W. 29th St., east of and including N. Lamar Blvd. north of W. 29th St., west of MoPac*

9.2	Fino	Spanish	Upmarket	$50
8.2	Changos Taquería	Mexican	Counter	$11
8.1	Ruby's BBQ	Barbecue	Counter	$17
7.8	Delaware Sub Shop	Light American	Counter	$8
7.7	FoodHeads	Light American	Counter	$8
7.5	34th Street Café	New American	Upmarket	$44
7.4	TX French Bread	Light American	Counter	$8
7.1	Milto's	Greek	Counter	$11
6.8	Sushi Niichi Express	Japanese	Casual	$17
6.8	Boomerang's Pies	Australian	Counter	$10
6.8	Tom's Tabooley	Middle Eastern	Counter	$8
6.6	Mangia	Pizza	Casual	$15
6.5	Red River Café	American	Casual	$14
6.3	Thundercloud Subs	Light American	Counter	$7
6.0	São Paulo's	Brazilian	Casual	$32

UT Area *continued*	Cuisine	Type	Price
5.6 Thai Kitchen	Thai	Casual	$15
5.6 Trudy's	Mexican	Casual	$26
5.6 Crown & Anchor Pub	American	Pub	$13
5.5 The Spider House	Light American	Café	$7
5.2 The Posse East	American	Pub	$14
5.2 Hill-Bert's Burgers	Burgers	Casual	$10
4.3 Longhorn Po-Boys	American	Counter	$7
3.8 Zen	Japanese	Counter	$9
2.4 El Patio	Mexican	Casual	$15
Wheatsville Co-op		Grocery	

Walburg

4.9 Walburg Mercantile	German	Casual	$29

Warehouse District *north of the river, south of and including W. 6th St., east of N. Lamar Blvd., west of and including Colorado St.*

9.0 Aquarelle	French	Upmarket	$91
9.0 Capitol Brasserie	French	Upmarket	$48
9.0 Starlite	New American	Upmarket	$65
8.8 Taverna	Italian	Upmarket	$48
8.4 Málaga	Spanish	Upmarket	$47
7.6 Fadó	Irish	Pub	$26
7.6 Thai Tara	Thai	Casual	$23
7.4 Kenichi	Japanese	Upmarket	$82
7.3 Cantina Laredo	Mexican	Upmarket	$37
7.1 Thistle Café on 6th	American	Upmarket	$34
6.9 219 West	New American	Upmarket	$32
6.8 Cuba Libre	Latin American	Casual	$33
6.8 Jo's Hot Coffee	Light American	Café	$8
6.7 Katz's	Light American	Casual	$23
6.7 Hut's Hamburgers	Burgers	Casual	$13
6.4 Saba Blue Water	New American	Upmarket	$47
6.3 Maiko Sushi Lounge	Japanese	Upmarket	$77
6.1 Frank & Angie's	Pizza	Casual	$23
5.6 Truluck's	Seafood	Upmarket	$66
5.2 Ringers	American	Pub	$24
4.8 Hoffbrau	Steakhouse	Casual	$24
4.5 Opal Divine's	American	Pub	$21
4.2 Alamo Drafthouse	American	Theater	$22
3.3 Mother Egan's	American	Pub	$24
Paciugo Gelateria	Sweets	Counter	
Sticky Toffee	Sweets	Take-out	

West Campus *north of and including MLK Blvd., south of W. 29th St., east of and including N. Lamar Blvd., west of and including Guadalupe St.*

7.7 Dirty Martin's	American	Casual	$12
6.9 Kismet Café	Middle Eastern	Counter	$9
6.8 Thai Noodles, Etc.	Thai	Casual	$14
6.8 Madam Mam's	Thai	Casual	$16
6.7 Austin's Pizza	Pizza	Counter	$9
6.7 Sun Hing	Chinese	Casual	$20
6.7 Veggie Heaven	Light American	Casual	$13
6.5 Mars	New American	Upmarket	$45
6.4 Taco Shack	Mexican	Counter	$5
6.2 Bert's BBQ	Barbecue	Counter	$8
6.2 Kerbey Lane Café	American	Casual	$19
6.0 Judges' Hill	New American	Upmarket	$65
5.8 Hao Hao	Chinese	Casual	$16
4.5 Taco Cabana	Mexican	Counter	$9
5.7 Phô Thai Son	Vietnamese	Casual	$9
5.7 Schlotzsky's	Light American	Counter	$8
5.6 Tony's Vineyard	Italian	Upmarket	$37
4.9 Mr. Gatti's	Pizza	Casual	$8

West Campus *continued*		*Type*	*Price*
4.7 Conan's Pizza	Pizza	Counter	$9
4.6 Players	American	Pub	$15
4.0 Texadelphia	American	Counter	$13
3.1 CoCo's Café	Chinese	Counter	$8
2.2 The Magic Wok	Chinese	Counter	$7
Amy's Ice Cream	Sweets	Counter	
Ken's Donuts	Sweets	Take-out	

Westlake

9.0 Salt Lick 360	Barbecue	Casual	$30
8.7 Rudy's	Barbecue	Counter	$15
8.6 Hill Country Din. Rm.	Southwestern	Upmarket	$68
8.5 Siena	Italian	Upmarket	$55
8.1 Bistro 88	New American	Upmarket	$49
7.8 Delaware Sub Shop	Light American	Counter	$8
7.0 Las Palomas	Mexican	Casual	$29
6.9 Suzi's China Grill	Chinese	Casual	$31
6.9 Bombay Grill	Indian	Casual	$23
6.7 PoKeJo's	Barbecue	Counter	$15
6.7 Bee Caves BBQ	Barbecue	Counter	$7
6.4 Freebirds	Mexican	Counter	$9
6.0 Waterloo Ice House	American	Pub	$22
6.0 Lotus Hunan	Chinese	Casual	$22
6.0 Ronnie's Real Foods	American	Casual	$24
5.9 Hangtown Grill	American	Counter	$14
5.9 County Line	Barbecue	Casual	$29
5.8 Thistle Café 360	American	Counter	$22
5.6 Thai Kitchen	Thai	Casual	$15
4.6 EZ's	American	Counter	$20
3.7 Tres Amigos	Mexican	Casual	$33
2.9 Maudie's	Mexican	Pub	$22

Zilker *north of and including Barton Springs Rd., south of the river, east of MoPac, west of S. Congress Ave.*

7.7 Chuy's	Mexican	Casual	$27
7.3 Green Mesquite	Barbecue	Casual	$21
6.8 Zax Pints & Plates	New American	Upmarket	$40
6.6 Casa de Luz	Light American	Counter	$13
6.5 Austin Java Co.	American	Café	$12
6.1 Shady Grove	American	Casual	$23
5.5 Threadgill's	Southern	Casual	$24
5.1 Flipnotics	Light American	Café	$12
4.6 Sandy's	Burgers	Take-out	$5
3.5 Vinny's	Italian	Casual	$29
3.2 Romeo's	Italian	Casual	$28
2.6 Wanfu Too	Chinese	Casual	$21
2.6 Baby Acapulco	Mexican	Casual	$23

LISTED IN ORDER OF FOOD RATING OUT OF 10

Breakfast	Cuisine	Location	Type	Price
9.6 Café at the 4 Seasons	New American	Convention Center	Upmarket	$73
9.0 Capitol Brasserie	French	Warehouse District	Upmarket	$48
8.6 Hill Country Din. Rm.	Southwestern	Westlake	Upmarket	$68
8.6 El Borrego de Oro	Mexican	St. Edward's Area	Casual	$21
8.6 1886 Café & Bakery	Light American	Congress Ave. Area	Upmarket	$31
8.5 Curra's Grill	Mexican	St. Edward's Area	Casual	$27
8.5 Mandola's	Italian	Hyde Park	Counter	$19
8.3 Polvos	Mexican	Bouldin Creek	Casual	$24
8.2 Changos Taquería	Mexican	UT Area	Counter	$11
8.2 Buenos Aires Café	Argentine	St. Edward's Area	Counter	$17
8.1 Oaxacan Tamaleo	Mexican	North Central	Counter	$7
8.1 El Mesón Taquería	Mexican	Southeast	Counter	$14
8.0 Maria's Taco Xpress	Mexican	South Lamar	Counter	$8
8.0 Azul	Light American	East Austin	Counter	$11
7.9 Café Mundi	Light American	East Austin	Café	$11
7.9 Nubian Queen Lola's	Southern	East Austin	Casual	$10
7.9 Portabla	Light American	Clarksville	Counter	$9
7.8 Cipollina	Italian	Clarksville	Counter	$18
7.7 Dandelion Café	Light American	East Austin	Café	$8
7.7 FoodHeads	Light American	UT Area	Counter	$8
7.7 Tuscany	Italian	Far North	Counter	$17
7.6 Las Manitas	Mexican	Congress Ave. Area	Casual	$16
7.6 A La Carrera	Mexican	Far Northwest	Casual	$21
7.5 Little Mexico	Mexican	Bouldin Creek	Casual	$25
7.5 Mexico Lindo	Mexican	South Lamar	Casual	$25
7.4 Garibaldi's	Mexican	Far South	Casual	$21
7.4 TX French Bread	Light American	UT Area	Counter	$8
7.3 Sweetish Hill	Light American	Clarksville	Café	$9
7.3 Habanero Café	Mexican	St. Edward's Area	Casual	$9
7.2 Triumph Café	Vietnamese	Northwest Hills	Café	$11
7.1 Julio's	Mexican	Hyde Park	Casual	$19
7.1 Upper Crust	Light American	Burnet	Café	$6
7.1 Garden District	Light American	St. Edward's Area	Café	$9
7.1 Quality Seafood	Seafood	North Central	Counter	$12
7.0 Taquería Arandas	Mexican	St. Edward's Area	Casual	$8
7.0 Kebab Palace	Macedonian	Far North	Casual	$11
6.9 The Frisco Shop	Steakhouse	Burnet	Counter	$16
6.9 The Kitchen Door	Light American	Tarrytown	Counter	$9
6.8 Tom's Tabooley	Middle Eastern	UT Area	Counter	$8
6.8 Jo's Hot Coffee	Light American	South Congress	Café	$8
6.7 Katz's	Light American	Warehouse District	Casual	$23
6.7 PoKeJo's	Barbecue	Clarksville	Counter	$15
6.6 The Tavern	American	House Park Area	Pub	$26
6.6 Casa de Luz	Light American	Zilker	Counter	$13
6.6 Angie's Mexican	Mexican	East Austin	Casual	$20
6.5 Jim Bob's BBQ	Barbecue	Bee Cave	Counter	$12
6.5 Austin Java Co.	American	Clarksville	Café	$12
6.5 Red River Café	American	UT Area	Casual	$14
6.4 Evita's Botanitas	Mexican	Far South	Casual	$23
6.4 Richard Jones	Barbecue	St. Edward's Area	Counter	$11
6.4 Taco Shack	Mexican	Seton Medical Area	Counter	$5
6.3 Dan's Hamburgers	Burgers	Far South	Counter	$7
6.3 Costa del Sol	Latin American	Far North	Casual	$23
6.2 Cocina de Marybel	Latin American	East Austin	Casual	$15
6.2 Kerbey Lane Café	American	Seton Medical Area	Casual	$19
6.1 Ba Le	Vietnamese	Far North	Counter	$8
6.1 La Mexicana Bakery	Mexican	Bouldin Creek	Counter	$6
6.1 Galaxy Café	American	Far South	Counter	$15

			Location	Type	Price
6.1	Austin Diner	American	Burnet	Casual	$12
6.0	Avenue B Grocery	Light American	Hyde Park	Counter	$9
6.0	Waterloo Ice House	American	Clarksville	Pub	$22
6.0	Juan in a Million	Mexican	East Austin	Casual	$17
6.0	Judges' Hill	New American	West Campus	Upmarket	$65
6.0	Green Muse Café	Light American	St. Edward's Area	Café	$9
5.9	Magnolia Café	American	Tarrytown	Casual	$18
5.8	Arturo's	American	Capitol Area	Counter	$12
5.8	Taco Cabana	Mexican	West Campus	Counter	$9
5.7	NeWorlDeli	Light American	Hyde Park	Counter	$13
5.7	Nau's Enfield Drug	American	Clarksville	Counter	$5
5.7	Schlotzsky's	Light American	South Lamar	Counter	$8
5.6	The Omelettry	American	Burnet	Casual	$10
5.6	Trudy's	Mexican	UT Area	Casual	$26
5.5	The Spider House	Light American	UT Area	Café	$7
5.2	Starseeds	American	French Place	Casual	$18
5.2	Elsi's	Latin American	Burnet	Casual	$19
5.2	Chapala	Mexican	East Austin	Casual	$5
5.2	The Posse East	American	UT Area	Pub	$14
5.1	Flipnotics	Light American	Zilker	Café	$12
5.1	Las Palmas	Mexican	East Austin	Casual	$26
5.0	Quack's on 43rd	Light American	Hyde Park	Café	$6
5.0	Flip's Satellite Café	American	Dripping Springs	Casual	$17
5.0	El Sol y La Luna	Mexican	South Congress	Casual	$19
4.9	Manny Hattan's	Light American	Arboretum	Casual	$27
4.5	Hickory Street	American	Congress Ave. Area	Casual	$23
4.4	Nueva Onda	Mexican	St. Edward's Area	Counter	$17
4.4	Bluebonnet Café	American	Marble Falls	Casual	$13
4.3	Longhorn Po-Boys	American	UT Area	Counter	$7
4.1	Ruta Maya	Light American	St. Edward's Area	Café	$6
3.8	Bouldin Creek Café	Light American	Bouldin Creek	Café	$8
3.8	Marisco Grill	Mexican	Sixth Street District	Casual	$33
3.7	Mr. Natural	Light American	South Lamar	Counter	$12
3.6	La Reyna	Mexican	Bouldin Creek	Casual	$19
3.4	Cisco's	Mexican	East Austin	Casual	$11
3.1	Dario's	Mexican	East Austin	Casual	$21
2.9	Maudie's	Mexican	Tarrytown	Pub	$22
2.8	Las Cazuelas	Mexican	East Austin	Casual	$22
2.2	El Gallo	Mexican	St. Edward's Area	Casual	$25
1.4	Enchiladas y Mas	Mexican	North Central	Casual	$18
	Ken's Donuts	Sweets	West Campus	Take-out	
	Tèo	Sweets	Seton Medical Area	Counter	
	Central Market		Seton Medical Area	Grocery	
	La Michoacana		East Austin	Grocery	
	Sun Harvest		South Lamar	Grocery	
	Wheatsville Co-op		UT Area	Grocery	
	Whole Foods		Clarksville	Grocery	

Brunch *listed in order of **food** rating; must have special brunch menu to qualify*

9.6	Café at the 4 Seasons	New American	Convention Center	Upmarket	$73
9.2	El Chile	Mexican	French Place	Casual	$31
9.1	South Congress Café	Southwestern	South Congress	Upmarket	$42
9.0	Capitol Brasserie	French	Warehouse District	Upmarket	$48
8.9	Manuel's	Mexican	Congress Ave. Area	Upmarket	$39
8.9	Fonda San Miguel	Mexican	North Central	Upmarket	$59
8.8	Taverna	Italian	Warehouse District	Upmarket	$48
8.7	Green Pastures	American	Bouldin Creek	Upmarket	$67
8.7	T&S Chinese Seafood	Chinese	Far North	Casual	$22
8.6	1886 Café & Bakery	Light American	Congress Ave. Area	Upmarket	$31
8.6	Hill Country Din. Rm.	Southwestern	Westlake	Upmarket	$68
8.5	Curra's Grill	Mexican	St. Edward's Area	Casual	$27
8.4	Doña Emilia's	Latin American	Convention Center	Upmarket	$46
8.3	Hoover's Cooking	Southern	French Place	Casual	$25

	Brunch *continued*	*Cuisine*	*Location*	*Type*	*Price*
8.3	Polvos	Mexican	Bouldin Creek	Casual	$24
8.2	Eastside Café	American	French Place	Upmarket	$45
8.1	Marco Polo	Chinese	Southeast	Casual	$24
8.0	Hyde Park Bar & Grill	American	Hyde Park	Casual	$28
8.0	Tien Hong	Chinese	Burnet	Casual	$23
7.6	Satay	Indonesian	North Central	Casual	$24
7.6	Z' Tejas	Mexican	Clarksville	Casual	$36
7.6	Fadó	Irish	Warehouse District	Pub	$26
7.6	Las Manitas	Mexican	Congress Ave. Area	Casual	$16
7.5	Mesa Ranch	Southwestern	Northwest Hills	Upmarket	$44
7.4	Garibaldi's	Mexican	Far South	Casual	$21
7.4	Stubb's BBQ	Barbecue	Red River Area	Counter	$18
7.1	El Arroyo	Mexican	Clarksville	Casual	$28
6.9	219 West	New American	Warehouse District	Upmarket	$32
6.8	Zax Pints & Plates	New American	Zilker	Upmarket	$40
6.7	Katz's	Light American	Warehouse District	Casual	$23
6.6	Beck's	American	South Congress	Pub	$34
6.6	Mother's	American	Hyde Park	Casual	$20
6.5	Y Bar & Grill	Southwestern	Oak Hill	Upmarket	$45
6.5	Red River Café	American	UT Area	Casual	$14
6.5	Austin Java Co.	American	Clarksville	Café	$12
6.4	Moonshine	American	Convention Center	Upmarket	$36
6.4	Old Pecan St. Café	Southern	Sixth Street District	Casual	$29
6.4	Mi Colombia	Latin American	East Austin	Casual	$16
6.2	Iron Cactus	Mexican	Sixth Street District	Pub	$35
6.2	Kerbey Lane Café	American	Seton Medical Area	Casual	$19
6.2	Santa Rita	Mexican	Seton Medical Area	Casual	$29
6.0	The Paggi House	American	South Lamar	Pub	$36
6.0	Juan in a Million	Mexican	East Austin	Casual	$17
6.0	Judges' Hill	New American	West Campus	Upmarket	$65
6.0	Waterloo Ice House	American	Clarksville	Pub	$22
5.9	Magnolia Café	American	Tarrytown	Casual	$18
5.9	Nu Age Café	Light American	Tarrytown	Casual	$22
5.8	Arturo's	American	Capitol Area	Counter	$12
5.8	Chez Zee	American	Northwest Hills	Casual	$35
5.8	Thistle Café 360	American	Westlake	Counter	$22
5.6	The Omelettry	American	Burnet	Casual	$10
5.6	Tony's Vineyard	Italian	West Campus	Upmarket	$37
5.6	Trudy's	Mexican	UT Area	Casual	$26
5.5	Threadgill's	Southern	North Central	Casual	$24
5.4	Güero's	Mexican	South Congress	Casual	$26
5.2	Starseeds	American	French Place	Casual	$18
5.2	Elsi's	Latin American	Burnet	Casual	$19
5.0	Flip's Satellite Café	American	Dripping Springs	Casual	$17
5.0	Nutty Brown Café	American	Dripping Springs	Casual	$29
5.0	El Sol y La Luna	Mexican	South Congress	Casual	$19
4.9	Manny Hattan's	Light American	Arboretum	Casual	$27
4.9	El Mercado	Mexican	Capitol Area	Casual	$27
4.9	Flores	Mexican	North Central	Casual	$23
4.5	Opal Divine's	American	Warehouse District	Pub	$21
4.5	Hickory Street	American	Congress Ave. Area	Casual	$23
4.4	Nueva Onda	Mexican	St. Edward's Area	Counter	$17
3.5	Vinny's	Italian	Zilker	Casual	$29
3.4	Cisco's	Mexican	East Austin	Casual	$11
3.3	Mother Egan's	American	Warehouse District	Pub	$24
3.2	Romeo's	Italian	Zilker	Casual	$28
3.2	Bee Cave Bistro	American	Bee Cave	Casual	$37
3.0	Veranda	American	North Central	Casual	$31
2.7	La Feria	Mexican	South Lamar	Casual	$22

Delivery *listed in order of **food** rating; some places have minimum orders*

9.0	Salt Lick 360	Barbecue	Westlake	Casual	$30
8.4	Doña Emilia's	Latin American	Convention Center	Upmarket	$46
8.3	Pao's	Chinese	Lake Travis	Casual	$20
8.1	Ruby's BBQ	Barbecue	UT Area	Counter	$17
8.1	Marco Polo	Chinese	Southeast	Casual	$24
8.0	Hyde Park Bar & Grill	American	Hyde Park	Casual	$28
7.9	Rounders Pizzeria	Pizza	Clarksville	Counter	$15
7.7	Mekong River	Vietnamese	Sixth Street District	Casual	$18
7.7	FoodHeads	Light American	UT Area	Counter	$8
7.6	Satay	Indonesian	North Central	Casual	$24
7.5	Taj Palace	Indian	North Central	Casual	$22
7.5	34th Street Café	New American	UI Area	Upmarket	$44
7.2	Serrano's Café	Mexican	Red River Area	Casual	$28
7.1	Thistle Café on 6th	American	Warehouse District	Upmarket	$34
7.1	Drakula	Romanian	Far North	Casual	$23
7.1	Milto's	Greek	UT Area	Counter	$11
6.9	Bombay Grill	Indian	Westlake	Casual	$23
6.9	The Kitchen Door	Light American	Tarrytown	Counter	$9
6.8	Habana Calle 6	Latin American	Sixth Street District	Upmarket	$34
6.7	Austin's Pizza	Pizza	Capitol Area	Counter	$9
6.7	Star of India	Indian	North Central	Casual	$22
6.7	Nuevo León	Mexican	East Austin	Casual	$24
6.7	Sun Hing	Chinese	West Campus	Casual	$20
6.6	Peony	Chinese	Northwest Hills	Casual	$28
6.2	Hunan Lion	Chinese	South Lamar	Casual	$23
6.2	Sarovar	Indian	Burnet	Casual	$25
6.0	Lotus Hunan	Chinese	Westlake	Casual	$22
5.8	Hao Hao	Chinese	Far South	Casual	$16
5.7	NeWorlDeli	Light American	Hyde Park	Counter	$13
5.7	Phô Thai Son	Vietnamese	West Campus	Casual	$9
5.4	Rockin' Tomato	Pizza	South Lamar	Counter	$17
5.4	Wiki Wiki Teriyaki	Japanese	Congress Ave. Area	Counter	$10
5.3	Snow Pea	Chinese	North Central	Casual	$24
5.2	Hill-Bert's Burgers	Burgers	UT Area	Casual	$10
4.9	Manny Hattan's	Light American	Arboretum	Casual	$27
4.3	Longhorn Po-Boys	American	UT Area	Counter	$7
2.8	Las Cazuelas	Mexican	East Austin	Casual	$22
2.6	Wanfu Too	Chinese	Zilker	Casual	$21
2.6	Baby Acapulco	Mexican	Zilker	Casual	$23
2.2	The Magic Wok	Chinese	West Campus	Counter	$7

BYO *bring your own beer or wine; listed in order of **food** rating*

9.1	The Salt Lick	Barbecue	Driftwood	Casual	$17
8.5	House Park BBQ	Barbecue	House Park Area	Counter	$7
8.2	Sam's BBQ	Barbecue	East Austin	Counter	$11
8.2	Buenos Aires Café	Argentine	St. Edward's Area	Counter	$17
7.9	Sambet's	Southern	Northwest Hills	Counter	$12
7.9	Portabla	Light American	Clarksville	Counter	$9
7.2	Madras Pavilion	Indian	Far North	Casual	$15
7.0	Kebab Palace	Macedonian	Far North	Casual	$11
7.0	Pyramids	Middle Eastern	North Central	Casual	$15
6.8	888	Vietnamese	Southeast	Casual	$24
6.7	Veggie Heaven	Light American	West Campus	Casual	$13
6.4	Mi Colombia	Latin American	East Austin	Casual	$16
6.4	Taco Shack	Mexican	Seton Medical Area	Counter	$5
6.4	Dog Almighty	American	Burnet	Counter	$5
6.2	Cocina de Marybel	Latin American	East Austin	Casual	$15
6.0	Ronnie's Real Foods	American	Westlake	Casual	$24
5.9	Nu Age Café	Light American	Tarrytown	Casual	$22
5.8	Ararat	Middle Eastern	North Central	Casual	$22
5.0	Cosmic Café	Indian	Clarksville	Casual	$16
3.4	Cisco's	Mexican	East Austin	Casual	$11

Good date places

			Location	Type	Price
10	Fonda San Miguel	Mexican	North Central	Upmarket	$59
9.9	Chez Nous	French	Sixth Street District	Upmarket	$51
9.9	The Driskill Grill	New American	Congress Ave. Area	Upmarket	$105
9.8	Café at the 4 Seasons	New American	Convention Center	Upmarket	$73
9.8	The Salt Lick	Barbecue	Driftwood	Casual	$17
9.7	Zoot	New American	Tarrytown	Upmarket	$64
9.7	Mozart's	Sweets	Tarrytown	Café	
9.6	Café Josie	Southwestern	Clarksville	Upmarket	$48
9.6	The Spider House	Light American	UT Area	Café	$7
9.6	Alamo Drafthouse	American	Warehouse District	Theater	$22
9.5	Vivo Cocina Texicana	Mexican	French Place	Casual	$28
9.5	Castle Hill Café	Southwestern	Clarksville	Upmarket	$46
9.5	Eastside Café	American	French Place	Upmarket	$45
9.5	Moonshine	American	Convention Center	Upmarket	$36
9.4	Amy's Ice Cream	Sweets	Clarksville	Counter	
9.4	Uchi	Japanese	South Lamar	Upmarket	$69
9.4	Jo's Hot Coffee	Light American	South Congress	Café	$8
9.4	Freddie's	American	Bouldin Creek	Casual	$21
9.4	Green Muse Café	Light American	St. Edward's Area	Café	$9
9.3	South Congress Café	Southwestern	South Congress	Upmarket	$42
9.3	Fino	Spanish	UT Area	Upmarket	$50
9.3	Capitol Brasserie	French	Warehouse District	Upmarket	$48
9.3	Magnolia Café	American	Tarrytown	Casual	$18
9.2	Clay Pit	Indian	Capitol Area	Upmarket	$33
9.2	Mars	New American	West Campus	Upmarket	$45
9.2	Doc's	American	South Congress	Pub	$22
9.2	Siena	Italian	Westlake	Upmarket	$55
9.2	Ronnie's Real Foods	American	Westlake	Casual	$24
9.1	Green Pastures	American	Bouldin Creek	Upmarket	$67
9.1	Home Slice Pizza	Pizza	South Congress	Casual	$18
9.1	El Chile	Mexican	French Place	Casual	$31
9.1	Hudson's on the Bend	Southwestern	Lake Travis	Upmarket	$83
9.0	Lucy's	Seafood	Tarrytown	Casual	$33
9.0	Ararat	Middle Eastern	North Central	Casual	$22
9.0	Ruta Maya	Light American	St. Edward's Area	Café	$6
8.9	Wink	New American	House Park Area	Upmarket	$86
8.9	Ranch 616	Southwestern	Capitol Area	Upmarket	$43
8.9	1886 Café & Bakery	Light American	Congress Ave. Area	Upmarket	$31
8.9	Tèo	Sweets	Seton Medical Area	Counter	
8.9	Musashino	Japanese	Northwest Hills	Upmarket	$58
8.9	Azul	Light American	East Austin	Counter	$11
8.9	Taverna	Italian	Warehouse District	Upmarket	$48
8.8	Emerald	Irish	Bee Cave	Upmarket	$80
8.8	The Oasis	Mexican	Northwest Hills	Casual	$32
8.8	Málaga	Spanish	Warehouse District	Upmarket	$47
8.7	Mirabelle	Southwestern	Northwest Hills	Upmarket	$46
8.7	Vin Bistro	New American	Seton Medical Area	Upmarket	$64
8.6	Vespaio	Italian	South Congress	Upmarket	$62
8.6	Café Mundi	Light American	East Austin	Café	$11
8.6	Aquarelle	French	Warehouse District	Upmarket	$91
8.5	Vespaio Enoteca	Italian	South Congress	Casual	$32
8.5	European Bistro	Hungarian	Pflugerville	Upmarket	$37
8.5	Starlite	New American	Warehouse District	Upmarket	$65
8.4	Bistro 88	New American	Westlake	Upmarket	$49
8.4	Flipnotics	Light American	Zilker	Café	$12
8.4	Rounders Pizzeria	Pizza	Clarksville	Counter	$15
8.4	Güero's	Mexican	South Congress	Casual	$26
8.4	Z' Tejas	Mexican	Clarksville	Casual	$36
8.3	Beck's	American	South Congress	Pub	$34
8.2	Louie's 106	New American	Sixth Street District	Upmarket	$50
8.1	Roaring Fork	Southwestern	Congress Ave. Area	Upmarket	$52
8.1	La Dolce Vita	Sweets	Hyde Park	Café	
8.0	Brick Oven on 35th	Italian	Seton Medical Area	Casual	$26

Good date places *continued*

			Location	Type	Price
8.0	Café 909	New American	Marble Falls	Upmarket	$60
7.7	Gumbo's	Southern	Capitol Area	Upmarket	$51
7.5	Kenichi	Japanese	Warehouse District	Upmarket	$82
7.4	Austin Land & Cattle	Steakhouse	House Park Area	Upmarket	$60
7.4	Cipollina	Italian	Clarksville	Counter	$18
7.3	Iron Cactus	Mexican	Sixth Street District	Pub	$35
7.2	Ruth's Chris	Steakhouse	Congress Ave. Area	Upmarket	$74
7.2	Korea Garden	Korean	North Central	Casual	$33
7.1	Cooper's	Barbecue	Llano	Counter	$14
7.1	La Traviata	Italian	Congress Ave. Area	Upmarket	$51
6.8	Carmelo's	Italian	Sixth Street District	Upmarket	$56
6.7	Habana Calle 6	Latin American	Sixth Street District	Upmarket	$34
6.7	Serrano's Café	Mexican	Red River Area	Casual	$28
6.3	The Jackalope	American	Sixth Street District	Pub	$12
5.3	34th Street Café	New American	UT Area	Upmarket	$44
5.0	The Paggi House	American	South Lamar	Pub	$36

Kid-friendly *listed in order of **food** rating*

9.1	The Salt Lick	Barbecue	Driftwood	Casual	$17
9.1	Kreuz Market	Barbecue	Lockhart	Counter	$12
9.0	Smitty's Market	Barbecue	Lockhart	Counter	$12
9.0	Louie Mueller's	Barbecue	Taylor	Counter	$10
8.8	Din Ho Chinese BBQ	Chinese	Far North	Casual	$24
8.7	Rudy's	Barbecue	Westlake	Counter	$15
8.5	Curra's Grill	Mexican	St. Edward's Area	Casual	$27
8.3	Cooper's	Barbecue	Llano	Counter	$14
8.3	Hoover's Cooking	Southern	French Place	Casual	$25
8.2	Changos Taquería	Mexican	UT Area	Counter	$11
7.8	Black's BBQ	Barbecue	Lockhart	Counter	$11
7.7	Dirty Martin's	American	West Campus	Casual	$12
7.7	Dandelion Café	Light American	East Austin	Café	$8
7.7	Artz Rib House	Barbecue	South Lamar	Casual	$22
7.6	Hill's Café	American	Far South	Casual	$27
7.6	A La Carrera	Mexican	Far Northwest	Casual	$21
7.6	Reale's	Italian	Far Northwest	Casual	$27
7.3	Green Mesquite	Barbecue	Zilker	Casual	$21
7.2	Triumph Café	Vietnamese	Northwest Hills	Café	$11
7.1	Upper Crust	Light American	Burnet	Café	$6
7.1	El Arroyo	Mexican	Clarksville	Casual	$28
7.0	Pyramids	Middle Eastern	North Central	Casual	$15
7.0	Las Palomas	Mexican	Westlake	Casual	$29
7.0	Taquería Arandas	Mexican	St. Edward's Area	Casual	$8
6.9	BurgerTex	Burgers	North Central	Counter	$15
6.9	The Frisco Shop	Steakhouse	Burnet	Counter	$16
6.8	P. Terry's	Burgers	South Lamar	Take-out	$6
6.8	Boomerang's Pies	Australian	UT Area	Counter	$10
6.7	PoKeJo's	Barbecue	Clarksville	Counter	$15
6.7	Hut's Hamburgers	Burgers	Warehouse District	Casual	$13
6.7	Bee Caves BBQ	Barbecue	Westlake	Counter	$7
6.7	Pacific Star	Seafood	Far Northwest	Casual	$24
6.7	Katz's	Light American	Warehouse District	Casual	$23
6.6	Mangia	Pizza	UT Area	Casual	$15
6.5	Jim Bob's BBQ	Barbecue	Bee Cave	Counter	$12
6.4	Moonshine	American	Convention Center	Upmarket	$36
6.4	Freebirds	Mexican	Hyde Park	Counter	$9
6.4	Richard Jones	Barbecue	St. Edward's Area	Counter	$11
6.4	Mi Colombia	Latin American	East Austin	Casual	$16
6.4	Dog Almighty	American	Burnet	Counter	$5
6.3	Dan's Hamburgers	Burgers	Far South	Counter	$7
6.3	Thundercloud Subs	Light American	Capitol Area	Counter	$7
6.2	Fran's	Burgers	South Congress	Counter	$8
6.2	Kerbey Lane Café	American	Seton Medical Area	Casual	$19

6.2	Bert's BBQ	Barbecue	West Campus	Counter	$8
6.1	Shady Grove	American	Zilker	Casual	$23
6.1	Galaxy Café	American	Far South	Counter	$15
6.1	Austin Diner	American	Burnet	Casual	$12
6.1	Frank & Angie's	Pizza	Warehouse District	Casual	$23
6.0	Old Alligator Grill	Southern	South Lamar	Casual	$30
6.0	Top-Notch Burgers	Burgers	Burnet	Counter	$8
6.0	Waterloo Ice House	American	Clarksville	Pub	$22
5.9	Nu Age Café	Light American	Tarrytown	Casual	$22
5.9	Hangtown Grill	American	Westlake	Counter	$14
5.9	County Line	Barbecue	Westlake	Casual	$29
5.9	Magnolia Café	American	Tarrytown	Casual	$18
5.8	Russo's Texitally	American	Marble Falls	Casual	$31
5.8	Thistle Café 360	American	Westlake	Counter	$22
5.8	Taco Cabana	Mexican	West Campus	Counter	$9
5.7	Schlotzsky's	Light American	South Lamar	Counter	$8
5.7	Nau's Enfield Drug	American	Clarksville	Counter	$5
5.7	Catfish Parlour	Southern	Far Northwest	Casual	$23
5.6	The Oasis	Mexican	Northwest Hills	Casual	$32
5.5	Threadgill's	Southern	North Central	Casual	$24
5.1	Hula Hut	American	Tarrytown	Casual	$31
5.0	Nutty Brown Café	American	Dripping Springs	Casual	$29
4.9	El Mercado	Mexican	Capitol Area	Casual	$27
4.9	Mr. Gatti's	Pizza	West Campus	Casual	$8
4.9	Flores	Mexican	North Central	Casual	$23
4.9	Matt's El Rancho	Mexican	South Lamar	Casual	$29
4.8	Scholtz Garten	German	Capitol Area	Casual	$20
4.7	Conan's Pizza	Pizza	West Campus	Counter	$9
4.6	Sandy's	Burgers	Zilker	Take-out	$5
4.6	EZ's	American	Seton Medical Area	Counter	$20
4.5	Hickory Street	American	Congress Ave. Area	Casual	$23
4.4	Austin Pizza Garden	Pizza	Oak Hill	Casual	$17
4.4	Bluebonnet Café	American	Marble Falls	Casual	$13
4.0	Texadelphia	American	West Campus	Counter	$13
3.5	Vinny's	Italian	Zilker	Casual	$29
3.2	Romeo's	Italian	Zilker	Casual	$28
3.1	CoCo's Café	Chinese	West Campus	Counter	$8
2.2	El Gallo	Mexican	St. Edward's Area	Casual	$25
1.2	Buffet Palace	Pan-Asian	North Central	Casual	$14
	Amy's Ice Cream	Sweets	Clarksville	Counter	
	Ken's Donuts	Sweets	West Campus	Take-out	
	Paciugo Gelateria	Sweets	Warehouse District	Counter	
	Sticky Toffee	Sweets	Warehouse District	Take-out	
	Tèo	Sweets	Seton Medical Area	Counter	
	Central Market		Seton Medical Area	Grocery	
	Sun Harvest		South Lamar	Grocery	
	Whole Foods		Clarksville	Grocery	

Live Music *listed in order of* **experience** *rating*

9.8	The Salt Lick	Barbecue	Driftwood	Casual	$17
9.7	Mozart's	Sweets	Tarrytown	Café	
9.6	The Spider House	Light American	UT Area	Café	$7
9.5	The Broken Spoke	American	South Lamar	Pub	$24
9.5	Vivo Cocina Texicana	Mexican	French Place	Casual	$28
9.4	Freddie's	American	Bouldin Creek	Casual	$21
9.4	Chez Zee	American	Northwest Hills	Casual	$35
9.4	Amy's Ice Cream	Sweets	Clarksville	Counter	
9.4	Green Muse Café	Light American	St. Edward's Area	Café	$9
9.4	Jo's Hot Coffee	Light American	South Congress	Café	$8
9.3	Texicalli Grill	American	St. Edward's Area	Casual	$17
9.1	Shady Grove	American	Zilker	Casual	$23
9.0	Hill's Café	American	Far South	Casual	$27
9.0	Maria's Taco Xpress	Mexican	South Lamar	Counter	$8
9.0	Ruta Maya	Light American	St. Edward's Area	Café	$6

			Location	Type	Price
9.0	Lucy's	Seafood	Tarrytown	Casual	$33
9.0	Ararat	Middle Eastern	North Central	Casual	$22
8.9	Ranch 616	Southwestern	Capitol Area	Upmarket	$43
8.8	The Oasis	Mexican	Northwest Hills	Casual	$32
8.8	Bouldin Creek Café	Light American	Bouldin Creek	Café	$8
8.8	Stubb's BBQ	Barbecue	Red River Area	Counter	$18
8.7	Vin Bistro	New American	Seton Medical Area	Upmarket	$64
8.7	Green Mesquite	Barbecue	Zilker	Casual	$21
8.7	Threadgill's	Southern	North Central	Casual	$24
8.6	Café Mundi	Light American	East Austin	Café	$11
8.6	Fadó	Irish	Warehouse District	Pub	$26
8.5	European Bistro	Hungarian	Pflugerville	Upmarket	$37
8.4	Flipnotics	Light American	Zilker	Café	$12
8.4	Hickory Street	American	Congress Ave. Area	Casual	$23
8.4	Güero's	Mexican	South Congress	Casual	$26
8.3	Beck's	American	South Congress	Pub	$34
8.3	FoodHeads	Light American	UT Area	Counter	$8
8.3	The Posse East	American	UT Area	Pub	$14
8.2	Opal Divine's	American	Warehouse District	Pub	$21
8.2	Artz Rib House	Barbecue	South Lamar	Casual	$22
8.0	Walburg Mercantile	German	Walburg	Casual	$29
8.0	Triumph Café	Vietnamese	Northwest Hills	Café	$11
8.0	Sambet's	Southern	Northwest Hills	Counter	$12
8.0	Austin Java Co.	American	Clarksville	Café	$12
7.9	Gene's	Southern	East Austin	Casual	$13
7.9	Galaxy Café	American	Far South	Counter	$15
7.9	Arturo's	American	Capitol Area	Counter	$12
7.9	Cuba Libre	Latin American	Warehouse District	Casual	$33
7.8	Waterloo Ice House	American	Clarksville	Pub	$22
7.6	Nutty Brown Café	American	Dripping Springs	Casual	$29
7.6	Chuy's	Mexican	Zilker	Casual	$27
7.5	Scholtz Garten	German	Capitol Area	Casual	$20
7.5	Curra's Grill	Mexican	St. Edward's Area	Casual	$27
7.5	Julio's	Mexican	Hyde Park	Casual	$19
7.5	El Sol y La Luna	Mexican	South Congress	Casual	$19
7.5	Ken's Donuts	Sweets	West Campus	Take-out	
7.4	Nuevo León	Mexican	East Austin	Casual	$24
7.4	Mother's	American	Hyde Park	Casual	$20
7.4	Jovita's	Mexican	Bouldin Creek	Casual	$15
7.4	Cipollina	Italian	Clarksville	Counter	$18
7.4	The Fox & Hound	American	Capitol Area	Pub	$20
7.4	Las Palomas	Mexican	Westlake	Casual	$29
7.2	Shoal Creek Saloon	American	House Park Area	Pub	$23
7.2	Y Bar & Grill	Southwestern	Oak Hill	Upmarket	$45
7.1	Mother Egan's	American	Warehouse District	Pub	$24
7.0	219 West	New American	Warehouse District	Upmarket	$32
7.0	Manuel's	Mexican	Congress Ave. Area	Upmarket	$39
7.0	Salt Lick 360	Barbecue	Westlake	Casual	$30
7.0	Doña Emilia's	Latin American	Convention Center	Upmarket	$46
6.9	Roy's Austin	New American	Convention Center	Upmarket	$66
6.9	Eddie V's	Seafood	Sixth Street District	Upmarket	$63
6.9	Zax Pints & Plates	New American	Zilker	Upmarket	$40
6.6	Romeo's	Italian	Zilker	Casual	$28
6.6	Mikado Ryotei	Japanese	Far North	Upmarket	$47
6.5	Frank & Angie's	Pizza	Warehouse District	Casual	$23
6.5	Austin Diner	American	Burnet	Casual	$12
6.4	Cosmic Café	Indian	Clarksville	Casual	$16
6.3	Freebirds	Mexican	Hyde Park	Counter	$9
6.3	Tony's Vineyard	Italian	West Campus	Upmarket	$37
6.2	Flores	Mexican	North Central	Casual	$23
6.2	Old Alligator Grill	Southern	South Lamar	Casual	$30
6.2	Hill Country Din. Rm.	Southwestern	Westlake	Upmarket	$68
6.1	Thistle Café on 6th	American	Warehouse District	Upmarket	$34

Live music *continued*

			Location	Type	Price
6.0	São Paulo's	Brazilian	UT Area	Casual	$32
5.9	Evangeline Café	Southern	Far South	Casual	$23
5.9	Baby Acapulco	Mexican	Zilker	Casual	$23
5.8	Marco Polo	Chinese	Southeast	Casual	$24
5.7	Zen	Japanese	UT Area	Counter	$9
5.7	Dog Almighty	American	Burnet	Counter	$5
5.3	Tree House	Italian	St. Edward's Area	Upmarket	$36
5.2	Elsi's	Latin American	Burnet	Casual	$19
5.2	Flip's Satellite Café	American	Dripping Springs	Casual	$17
5.1	Longhorn Po-Boys	American	UT Area	Counter	$7
5.0	Fran's	Burgers	South Congress	Counter	$8
4.1	Azul Tequila	Mexican	South Lamar	Casual	$30
3.9	Oaxacan Tamaleo	Mexican	North Central	Counter	$7
3.8	La Mexicana Bakery	Mexican	Bouldin Creek	Counter	$6
3.4	Tuscany	Italian	Far North	Counter	$17
3.3	Dario's	Mexican	East Austin	Casual	$21
2.0	La Feria	Mexican	South Lamar	Casual	$22
1.6	Dan McKlusky's	Steakhouse	Sixth Street District	Upmarket	$63
1.0	Maiko Sushi Lounge	Japanese	Warehouse District	Upmarket	$77
	Central Market		Seton Medical Area	Grocery	
	Wheatsville Co-op		UT Area	Grocery	
	Whole Foods		Clarksville	Grocery	

Outdoor dining *anything from sidewalk tables to a full garden; listed in order of **food** rating*

9.7	Uchi	Japanese	South Lamar	Upmarket	$69
9.6	Café at the 4 Seasons	New American	Convention Center	Upmarket	$73
9.2	El Chile	Mexican	French Place	Casual	$31
9.2	Vespaio Enoteca	Italian	South Congress	Casual	$32
9.2	Fino	Spanish	UT Area	Upmarket	$50
9.1	The Salt Lick	Barbecue	Driftwood	Casual	$17
9.0	Capitol Brasserie	French	Warehouse District	Upmarket	$48
9.0	Salt Lick 360	Barbecue	Westlake	Casual	$30
8.9	Manuel's	Mexican	Congress Ave. Area	Upmarket	$39
8.8	Taverna	Italian	Warehouse District	Upmarket	$48
8.8	Hudson's on the Bend	Southwestern	Lake Travis	Upmarket	$83
8.7	Rudy's	Barbecue	Westlake	Counter	$15
8.7	Green Pastures	American	Bouldin Creek	Upmarket	$67
8.6	Hill Country Din. Rm.	Southwestern	Westlake	Upmarket	$68
8.5	House Park BBQ	Barbecue	House Park Area	Counter	$7
8.5	Mandola's	Italian	Hyde Park	Counter	$19
8.5	Curra's Grill	Mexican	St. Edward's Area	Casual	$27
8.5	Siena	Italian	Westlake	Upmarket	$55
8.4	Shoreline Grill	New American	Convention Center	Upmarket	$64
8.4	Swad	Indian	Far North	Counter	$14
8.4	Doña Emilia's	Latin American	Convention Center	Upmarket	$46
8.3	Vin Bistro	New American	Seton Medical Area	Upmarket	$64
8.3	Cooper's	Barbecue	Llano	Counter	$14
8.3	Azul Tequila	Mexican	South Lamar	Casual	$30
8.3	Polvos	Mexican	Bouldin Creek	Casual	$24
8.2	Changos Taquería	Mexican	UT Area	Counter	$11
8.2	Buenos Aires Café	Argentine	St. Edward's Area	Counter	$17
8.2	Eastside Café	American	French Place	Upmarket	$45
8.2	Sam's BBQ	Barbecue	East Austin	Counter	$11
8.1	Oaxacan Tamaleo	Mexican	North Central	Counter	$7
8.1	Marco Polo	Chinese	Southeast	Casual	$24
8.1	Ruby's BBQ	Barbecue	UT Area	Counter	$17
8.0	Azul	Light American	East Austin	Counter	$11
8.0	Maria's Taco Xpress	Mexican	South Lamar	Counter	$8
7.9	Portabla	Light American	Clarksville	Counter	$9
7.9	Rounders Pizzeria	Pizza	Clarksville	Counter	$15
7.9	Sambet's	Southern	Northwest Hills	Counter	$12

	Outdoor dining *continued*		*Location*	*Type*	*Price*
7.9	Café Mundi	Light American	East Austin	Café	$11
7.8	Black's BBQ	Barbecue	Lockhart	Counter	$11
7.8	Cipollina	Italian	Clarksville	Counter	$18
7.7	Tuscany	Italian	Far North	Counter	$17
7.7	FoodHeads	Light American	UT Area	Counter	$8
7.7	Artz Rib House	Barbecue	South Lamar	Casual	$22
7.7	Texicalli Grill	American	St. Edward's Area	Casual	$17
7.7	Chuy's	Mexican	Zilker	Casual	$27
7.7	Dirty Martin's	American	West Campus	Casual	$12
7.6	Hill's Café	American	Far South	Casual	$27
7.6	Thai Tara	Thai	Warehouse District	Casual	$23
7.6	Fadó	Irish	Warehouse District	Pub	$26
7.6	Satay	Indonesian	North Central	Casual	$24
7.6	Las Manitas	Mexican	Congress Ave. Area	Casual	$16
7.6	Z' Tejas	Mexican	Clarksville	Casual	$36
7.5	Mexico Lindo	Mexican	South Lamar	Casual	$25
7.4	TX French Bread	Light American	UT Area	Counter	$8
7.3	Cantina Laredo	Mexican	Warehouse District	Upmarket	$37
7.3	Sweetish Hill	Light American	Clarksville	Café	$9
7.3	Green Mesquite	Barbecue	Zilker	Casual	$21
7.2	Serrano's Café	Mexican	Red River Area	Casual	$28
7.2	Triumph Café	Vietnamese	Northwest Hills	Café	$11
7.1	Milto's	Greek	UT Area	Counter	$11
7.1	Garden District	Light American	St. Edward's Area	Café	$9
7.1	Thistle Café on 6th	American	Warehouse District	Upmarket	$34
7.1	Upper Crust	Light American	Burnet	Café	$6
7.1	Lewis' BBQ	Barbecue	East Austin	Counter	$8
7.1	Julio's	Mexican	Hyde Park	Casual	$19
7.1	El Arroyo	Mexican	Clarksville	Casual	$28
7.1	Gene's	Southern	East Austin	Casual	$13
7.0	Pyramids	Middle Eastern	North Central	Casual	$15
7.0	Las Palomas	Mexican	Westlake	Casual	$29
6.9	Kismet Café	Middle Eastern	West Campus	Counter	$9
6.9	The Kitchen Door	Light American	Tarrytown	Counter	$9
6.9	Ms. B's	Southern	Northwest Hills	Casual	$27
6.9	219 West	New American	Warehouse District	Upmarket	$32
6.8	Vivo Cocina Texicana	Mexican	French Place	Casual	$28
6.8	Jo's Hot Coffee	Light American	South Congress	Café	$8
6.8	Zax Pints & Plates	New American	Zilker	Upmarket	$40
6.8	P. Terry's	Burgers	South Lamar	Take-out	$6
6.8	Habana Calle 6	Latin American	Sixth Street District	Upmarket	$34
6.8	Tom's Tabooley	Middle Eastern	UT Area	Counter	$8
6.8	Brick Oven	Italian	Red River Area	Casual	$22
6.8	Thai Noodles, Etc.	Thai	West Campus	Casual	$14
6.8	Cuba Libre	Latin American	Warehouse District	Casual	$33
6.7	Nuevo León	Mexican	East Austin	Casual	$24
6.7	Bellagio	Italian	Far Northwest	Upmarket	$52
6.7	Pacific Star	Seafood	Far Northwest	Casual	$24
6.7	Bee Caves BBQ	Barbecue	Westlake	Counter	$7
6.7	PoKeJo's	Barbecue	Clarksville	Counter	$15
6.7	Roy's Austin	New American	Convention Center	Upmarket	$66
6.6	Beck's	American	South Congress	Pub	$34
6.6	Angie's Mexican	Mexican	East Austin	Casual	$20
6.6	Mangia	Pizza	UT Area	Casual	$15
6.6	The Tavern	American	House Park Area	Pub	$26
6.6	Casa de Luz	Light American	Zilker	Counter	$13
6.6	Mother's	American	Hyde Park	Casual	$20
6.5	Iron Works BBQ	Barbecue	Convention Center	Counter	$14
6.5	Marakesh	Middle Eastern	Capitol Area	Casual	$18
6.5	Y Bar & Grill	Southwestern	Oak Hill	Upmarket	$45
6.5	Austin Java Co.	American	Clarksville	Café	$12
6.5	Red River Café	American	UT Area	Casual	$14
6.5	Jim Bob's BBQ	Barbecue	Bee Cave	Counter	$12

			Location	Type	Price
6.4	Moonshine	American	Convention Center	Upmarket	$36
6.4	Freebirds	Mexican	Hyde Park	Counter	$9
6.4	Sampaio's	Brazilian	Burnet	Upmarket	$42
6.4	Dog Almighty	American	Burnet	Counter	$5
6.4	Taco Shack	Mexican	Seton Medical Area	Counter	$5
6.3	Thundercloud Subs	Light American	Capitol Area	Counter	$7
6.2	Kerbey Lane Café	American	Seton Medical Area	Casual	$19
6.2	Iron Cactus	Mexican	Sixth Street District	Pub	$35
6.2	Santa Rita	Mexican	Seton Medical Area	Casual	$29
6.2	Fran's	Burgers	South Congress	Counter	$8
6.1	Shady Grove	American	Zilker	Casual	$23
6.1	Finn & Porter	Seafood	Convention Center	Upmarket	$63
6.1	Koriente	Korean	Sixth Street District	Casual	$9
6.1	Galaxy Café	American	Far South	Counter	$15
6.1	Frank & Angie's	Pizza	Warehouse District	Casual	$23
6.0	Old Alligator Grill	Southern	South Lamar	Casual	$30
6.0	Ben's Longbranch	Barbecue	East Austin	Casual	$17
6.0	Waterloo Ice House	American	Clarksville	Pub	$22
6.0	Evangeline Café	Southern	Far South	Casual	$23
6.0	São Paulo's	Brazilian	UT Area	Casual	$32
6.0	Green Muse Café	Light American	St. Edward's Area	Café	$9
6.0	Avenue B Grocery	Light American	Hyde Park	Counter	$9
6.0	The Paggi House	American	South Lamar	Pub	$36
6.0	Shoal Creek Saloon	American	House Park Area	Pub	$23
5.9	Hangtown Grill	American	Westlake	Counter	$14
5.9	Chooby Doo	American	Far South	Counter	$7
5.9	County Line	Barbecue	Westlake	Casual	$29
5.9	Dog & Duck Pub	American	Capitol Area	Pub	$20
5.8	Arturo's	American	Capitol Area	Counter	$12
5.8	Thistle Café 360	American	Westlake	Counter	$22
5.8	Russo's Texitally	American	Marble Falls	Casual	$31
5.8	Chez Zee	American	Northwest Hills	Casual	$35
5.8	Taco Cabana	Mexican	West Campus	Counter	$9
5.7	Schlotzsky's	Light American	South Lamar	Counter	$8
5.6	El Azteca	Mexican	East Austin	Casual	$23
5.6	Trudy's	Mexican	UT Area	Casual	$26
5.6	Tony's Vineyard	Italian	West Campus	Upmarket	$37
5.6	The Oasis	Mexican	Northwest Hills	Casual	$32
5.6	Crown & Anchor Pub	American	UT Area	Pub	$13
5.5	The Spider House	Light American	UT Area	Café	$7
5.5	Threadgill's	Southern	North Central	Casual	$24
5.4	Güero's	Mexican	South Congress	Casual	$26
5.3	Lucy's	Seafood	Tarrytown	Casual	$33
5.2	The Posse East	American	UT Area	Pub	$14
5.2	Hill-Bert's Burgers	Burgers	UT Area	Casual	$10
5.1	Las Palmas	Mexican	East Austin	Casual	$26
5.1	Hula Hut	American	Tarrytown	Casual	$31
5.1	Flipnotics	Light American	Zilker	Café	$12
5.0	Flip's Satellite Café	American	Dripping Springs	Casual	$17
5.0	El Sol y La Luna	Mexican	South Congress	Casual	$19
5.0	Nutty Brown Café	American	Dripping Springs	Casual	$29
5.0	Quack's on 43rd	Light American	Hyde Park	Café	$6
5.0	Cosmic Café	Indian	Clarksville	Casual	$16
4.9	Matt's El Rancho	Mexican	South Lamar	Casual	$29
4.9	Carmelo's	Italian	Sixth Street District	Upmarket	$56
4.9	Flores	Mexican	North Central	Casual	$23
4.9	Walburg Mercantile	German	Walburg	Casual	$29
4.8	Scholtz Garten	German	Capitol Area	Casual	$20
4.8	Hoffbrau	Steakhouse	Warehouse District	Casual	$24
4.8	Jorge's	Mexican	North Central	Casual	$24
4.6	Players	American	West Campus	Pub	$15
4.6	EZ's	American	Seton Medical Area	Counter	$20
4.6	Sandy's	Burgers	Zilker	Take-out	$5

Outdoor dining *continued*

			Location	Type	Price
4.5	Opal Divine's	American	Warehouse District	Pub	$21
4.5	Hickory Street	American	Congress Ave. Area	Casual	$23
4.5	The Draught House	American	Seton Medical Area	Pub	$19
4.4	Nueva Onda	Mexican	St. Edward's Area	Counter	$17
4.4	Jaime's	Mexican	Red River Area	Casual	$24
4.3	Longhorn Po-Boys	American	UT Area	Counter	$7
4.2	The Fox & Hound	American	Capitol Area	Pub	$20
4.2	Doc's	American	South Congress	Pub	$22
4.1	Ruta Maya	Light American	St. Edward's Area	Café	$6
4.0	Texadelphia	American	West Campus	Counter	$13
3.9	Freddie's	American	Bouldin Creek	Casual	$21
3.8	Zen	Japanese	UT Area	Counter	$9
3.8	Bouldin Creek Café	Light American	Bouldin Creek	Café	$8
3.8	Marisco Grill	Mexican	Sixth Street District	Casual	$33
3.7	Mr. Natural	Light American	South Lamar	Counter	$12
3.6	La Reyna	Mexican	Bouldin Creek	Casual	$19
3.3	Mother Egan's	American	Warehouse District	Pub	$24
3.2	Bee Cave Bistro	American	Bee Cave	Casual	$37
3.2	Romeo's	Italian	Zilker	Casual	$28
3.0	Veranda	American	North Central	Casual	$31
2.9	Maudie's	Mexican	Tarrytown	Pub	$22
2.7	La Feria	Mexican	South Lamar	Casual	$22
2.6	Baby Acapulco	Mexican	Zilker	Casual	$23
1.8	Tree House	Italian	St. Edward's Area	Upmarket	$36
1.6	Rosie's	Mexican	St. Edward's Area	Casual	$22
	Amy's Ice Cream	Sweets	Clarksville	Counter	
	Mozart's	Sweets	Tarrytown	Café	
	Tèo	Sweets	Seton Medical Area	Counter	
	La Dolce Vita	Sweets	Hyde Park	Café	
	Paciugo Gelateria	Sweets	Warehouse District	Counter	
	Central Market		Seton Medical Area	Grocery	
	Wheatsville Co-op		UT Area	Grocery	
	Whole Foods		Clarksville	Grocery	

Wireless Internet *listed in order of* **experience** *rating*

9.7	Mozart's	Sweets	Tarrytown	Café	
9.6	The Spider House	Light American	UT Area	Café	$7
9.5	Moonshine	American	Convention Center	Upmarket	$36
9.5	Vivo Cocina Texicana	Mexican	French Place	Casual	$28
9.4	Jo's Hot Coffee	Light American	South Congress	Café	$8
9.4	Amy's Ice Cream	Sweets	Clarksville	Counter	
9.4	Freddie's	American	Bouldin Creek	Casual	$21
9.4	Green Muse Café	Light American	St. Edward's Area	Café	$9
9.3	Texicalli Grill	American	St. Edward's Area	Casual	$17
9.3	Capitol Brasserie	French	Warehouse District	Upmarket	$48
9.2	Polvos	Mexican	Bouldin Creek	Casual	$24
9.2	Siena	Italian	Westlake	Upmarket	$55
9.2	Doc's	American	South Congress	Pub	$22
9.1	Home Slice Pizza	Pizza	South Congress	Casual	$18
9.1	El Chile	Mexican	French Place	Casual	$31
9.0	Ruta Maya	Light American	St. Edward's Area	Café	$6
9.0	Hill's Café	American	Far South	Casual	$27
8.9	Tèo	Sweets	Seton Medical Area	Counter	
8.9	Ranch 616	Southwestern	Capitol Area	Upmarket	$43
8.9	1886 Café & Bakery	Light American	Congress Ave. Area	Upmarket	$31
8.8	Shoreline Grill	New American	Convention Center	Upmarket	$64
8.8	Bouldin Creek Café	Light American	Bouldin Creek	Café	$8
8.7	El Arroyo	Mexican	Clarksville	Casual	$28
8.7	Vin Bistro	New American	Seton Medical Area	Upmarket	$64
8.7	Green Mesquite	Barbecue	Zilker	Casual	$21
8.6	Katz's	Light American	Warehouse District	Casual	$23
8.6	Café Mundi	Light American	East Austin	Café	$11

	Wireless Internet *continued*		*Location*	*Type*	*Price*
8.6	Fadó	Irish	Warehouse District	Pub	$26
8.5	Louie Mueller's	Barbecue	Taylor	Counter	$10
8.5	Starlite	New American	Warehouse District	Upmarket	$65
8.5	Garden District	Light American	St. Edward's Area	Café	$9
8.5	European Bistro	Hungarian	Pflugerville	Upmarket	$37
8.4	Flipnotics	Light American	Zilker	Café	$12
8.4	Güero's	Mexican	South Congress	Casual	$26
8.4	Hickory Street	American	Congress Ave. Area	Casual	$23
8.4	Rounders Pizzeria	Pizza	Clarksville	Counter	$15
8.3	The Posse East	American	UT Area	Pub	$14
8.3	Beck's	American	South Congress	Pub	$34
8.3	FoodHeads	Light American	UT Area	Counter	$8
8.3	Peony	Chinese	Northwest Hills	Casual	$28
8.2	Satay	Indonesian	North Central	Casual	$24
8.2	Opal Divine's	American	Warehouse District	Pub	$21
8.1	Milto's	Greek	UT Area	Counter	$11
8.1	Roaring Fork	Southwestern	Congress Ave. Area	Upmarket	$52
8.1	The Tavern	American	House Park Area	Pub	$26
8.1	Quack's on 43rd	Light American	Hyde Park	Café	$6
8.1	La Dolce Vita	Sweets	Hyde Park	Café	
8.0	Triumph Café	Vietnamese	Northwest Hills	Café	$11
8.0	Alborz	Middle Eastern	North Central	Casual	$28
8.0	TX French Bread	Light American	UT Area	Counter	$8
8.0	Austin Java Co.	American	Clarksville	Café	$12
7.9	Arturo's	American	Capitol Area	Counter	$12
7.9	Galaxy Café	American	Far South	Counter	$15
7.9	Cuba Libre	Latin American	Warehouse District	Casual	$33
7.8	Waterloo Ice House	American	Clarksville	Pub	$22
7.8	Maudie's	Mexican	Tarrytown	Pub	$22
7.6	Dandelion Café	Light American	East Austin	Café	$8
7.6	Nueva Onda	Mexican	St. Edward's Area	Counter	$17
7.5	Ken's Donuts	Sweets	West Campus	Take-out	
7.5	Scholtz Garten	German	Capitol Area	Casual	$20
7.5	El Sol y La Luna	Mexican	South Congress	Casual	$19
7.5	Curra's Grill	Mexican	St. Edward's Area	Casual	$27
7.4	Dog & Duck Pub	American	Capitol Area	Pub	$20
7.4	The Fox & Hound	American	Capitol Area	Pub	$20
7.4	Thai Tara	Thai	Warehouse District	Casual	$23
7.4	Cipollina	Italian	Clarksville	Counter	$18
7.2	Shoal Creek Saloon	American	House Park Area	Pub	$23
7.2	Koriente	Korean	Sixth Street District	Casual	$9
7.2	Y Bar & Grill	Southwestern	Oak Hill	Upmarket	$45
7.1	Bert's BBQ	Barbecue	West Campus	Counter	$8
7.0	219 West	New American	Warehouse District	Upmarket	$32
7.0	Brick Oven	Italian	Red River Area	Casual	$22
7.0	Doña Emilia's	Latin American	Convention Center	Upmarket	$46
7.0	Manuel's	Mexican	Congress Ave. Area	Upmarket	$39
6.9	Zax Pints & Plates	New American	Zilker	Upmarket	$40
6.8	Crown & Anchor Pub	American	UT Area	Pub	$13
6.7	Boomerang's Pies	Australian	UT Area	Counter	$10
6.7	Habana Calle 6	Latin American	Sixth Street District	Upmarket	$34
6.7	Serrano's Café	Mexican	Red River Area	Casual	$28
6.6	Romeo's	Italian	Zilker	Casual	$28
6.6	Paradise Café	American	Sixth Street District	Casual	$25
6.6	Portabla	Light American	Clarksville	Counter	$9
6.5	Quality Seafood	Seafood	North Central	Counter	$12
6.5	Sarovar	Indian	Burnet	Casual	$25
6.3	Noodle-ism	Chinese	Congress Ave. Area	Counter	$19
6.3	Bangkok Cuisine	Thai	Far North	Casual	$24
6.3	Freebirds	Mexican	Hyde Park	Counter	$9
6.1	Saba Blue Water	New American	Warehouse District	Upmarket	$47
6.1	Thistle Café on 6th	American	Warehouse District	Upmarket	$34
6.1	Manny Hattan's	Light American	Arboretum	Casual	$27

Wireless Internet *continued*		*Location*	*Type*	*Price*
5.9 Nu Age Café	Light American	Tarrytown	Casual	$22
5.8 Changos Taquería	Mexican	UT Area	Counter	$11
5.7 Wiki Wiki Teriyaki	Japanese	Congress Ave. Area	Counter	$10
5.7 Zen	Japanese	UT Area	Counter	$9
5.6 El Mesón Taquería	Mexican	Southeast	Counter	$14
5.2 Tom's Tabooley	Middle Eastern	UT Area	Counter	$8
5.1 Schlotzsky's	Light American	South Lamar	Counter	$8
5.1 Longhorn Po-Boys	American	UT Area	Counter	$7
4.9 Texadelphia	American	West Campus	Counter	$13
4.8 P. Terry's	Burgers	South Lamar	Take-out	$6
4.5 Swad	Indian	Far North	Counter	$14
4.5 Red River Café	American	UT Area	Casual	$14
4.0 Hao Hao	Chinese	Far South	Casual	$16
3.7 Taco Shack	Mexican	Seton Medical Area	Counter	$5
3.4 Tuscany	Italian	Far North	Counter	$17
1.6 Dan McKlusky's	Steakhouse	Sixth Street District	Upmarket	$63
1.0 Maiko Sushi Lounge	Japanese	Warehouse District	Upmarket	$77
Central Market		Seton Medical Area	Grocery	
Whole Foods		Clarksville	Grocery	

LATE-NIGHT DINING GUIDE

Each of the following lists of late-night options is comprehensive, covering all establishments that will still be open at a given hour on a given night, including take-out options. "Weekday" means Sunday to Thursday or Monday to Thursday; "weekend" means Friday and Saturday. **All lists are ordered by food rating.**

Weekday food after 10pm		*Location*	*Type*	*Price*
9.3 Vespaio	Italian	South Congress	Upmarket	$62
9.3 Wink	New American	House Park Area	Upmarket	$86
9.0 Starlite	New American	Warehouse District	Upmarket	$65
9.0 Capitol Brasserie	French	Warehouse District	Upmarket	$48
8.8 Taverna	Italian	Warehouse District	Upmarket	$48
8.8 Din Ho Chinese BBQ	Chinese	Far North	Casual	$24
8.7 T&S Chinese Seafood	Chinese	Far North	Casual	$22
8.6 Ruth's Chris	Steakhouse	Congress Ave. Area	Upmarket	$74
8.4 Casino El Camino	Burgers	Sixth Street District	Pub	$12
8.2 Sam's BBQ	Barbecue	East Austin	Counter	$11
8.2 Chez Nous	French	Sixth Street District	Upmarket	$51
8.1 Ruby's BBQ	Barbecue	UT Area	Counter	$17
8.0 Emerald	Irish	Bee Cave	Upmarket	$80
8.0 Hyde Park Bar & Grill	American	Hyde Park	Casual	$28
7.8 Kyoto	Japanese	Congress Ave. Area	Upmarket	$37
7.8 El Taquito	Mexican	East Austin	Take-out	$5
7.7 Dirty Martin's	American	West Campus	Casual	$12
7.3 Eddie V's	Seafood	Sixth Street District	Upmarket	$63
7.1 Milto's	Greek	UT Area	Counter	$11
7.0 The Jackalope	American	Sixth Street District	Pub	$12
7.0 Home Slice Pizza	Pizza	South Congress	Casual	$18
7.0 Taquería Arandas	Mexican	St. Edward's Area	Casual	$8
6.9 219 West	New American	Warehouse District	Upmarket	$32
6.8 888	Vietnamese	Southeast	Casual	$24
6.8 Shalimar	Indian	Far North	Casual	$11
6.8 Habana Calle 6	Latin American	Sixth Street District	Upmarket	$34
6.8 P. Terry's	Burgers	South Lamar	Take-out	$6
6.8 Texas Chili Parlor	American	Capitol Area	Casual	$17
6.8 Vivo Cocina Texicana	Mexican	French Place	Casual	$28
6.7 Bellagio	Italian	Far Northwest	Upmarket	$52
6.7 Katz's	Light American	Warehouse District	Casual	$23

	Weekday food after 10pm *continued*		Location	Type	Price
6.7	Austin's Pizza	Pizza	Capitol Area	Counter	$9
6.6	Beck's	American	South Congress	Pub	$34
6.5	Austin Java Co.	American	Clarksville	Café	$12
6.5	Paradise Café	American	Sixth Street District	Casual	$25
6.4	Saba Blue Water	New American	Warehouse District	Upmarket	$47
6.4	Freebirds	Mexican	Hyde Park	Counter	$9
6.3	Maiko Sushi Lounge	Japanese	Warehouse District	Upmarket	$77
6.3	Thai Passion	Thai	Congress Ave. Area	Casual	$27
6.2	Kerbey Lane Café	American	Seton Medical Area	Casual	$19
6.2	Iron Cactus	Mexican	Sixth Street District	Pub	$35
6.1	La Mexicana Bakery	Mexican	Bouldin Creek	Counter	$6
6.1	Shady Grove	American	Zilker	Casual	$23
6.1	Finn & Porter	Seafood	Convention Center	Upmarket	$63
6.1	Silhouette	Japanese	Congress Ave. Area	Upmarket	$41
6.0	Green Muse Café	Light American	St. Edward's Area	Café	$9
5.9	Dog & Duck Pub	American	Capitol Area	Pub	$20
5.9	Magnolia Café	American	Tarrytown	Casual	$18
5.8	Ararat	Middle Eastern	North Central	Casual	$22
5.8	Taco Cabana	Mexican	West Campus	Counter	$9
5.7	Phô Thai Son	Vietnamese	West Campus	Casual	$9
5.6	Tony's Vineyard	Italian	West Campus	Upmarket	$37
5.6	Thai Kitchen	Thai	UT Area	Casual	$15
5.6	Trudy's	Mexican	UT Area	Casual	$26
5.6	Crown & Anchor Pub	American	UT Area	Pub	$13
5.5	The Spider House	Light American	UT Area	Café	$7
5.4	Rockin' Tomato	Pizza	South Lamar	Counter	$17
5.4	Güero's	Mexican	South Congress	Casual	$26
5.2	The Posse East	American	UT Area	Pub	$14
5.2	Ringers	American	Warehouse District	Pub	$24
5.2	Chapala	Mexican	East Austin	Casual	$5
5.2	Starseeds	American	French Place	Casual	$18
5.1	Flipnotics	Light American	Zilker	Café	$12
5.0	Quack's on 43rd	Light American	Hyde Park	Café	$6
4.9	Carmelo's	Italian	Sixth Street District	Upmarket	$56
4.9	Mr. Gatti's	Pizza	West Campus	Casual	$8
4.9	Flores	Mexican	North Central	Casual	$23
4.7	The Broken Spoke	American	South Lamar	Pub	$24
4.7	Conan's Pizza	Pizza	West Campus	Counter	$9
4.6	Players	American	West Campus	Pub	$15
4.6	EZ's	American	Seton Medical Area	Counter	$20
4.6	Sandy's	Burgers	Zilker	Take-out	$5
4.5	Opal Divine's	American	Warehouse District	Pub	$21
4.2	Alamo Drafthouse	American	Warehouse District	Theater	$22
4.2	The Fox & Hound	American	Capitol Area	Pub	$20
4.1	Ruta Maya	Light American	St. Edward's Area	Café	$6
3.9	Freddie's	American	Bouldin Creek	Casual	$21
3.8	Bouldin Creek Café	Light American	Bouldin Creek	Café	$8
3.8	Zen	Japanese	UT Area	Counter	$9
3.3	Mother Egan's	American	Warehouse District	Pub	$24
3.1	CoCo's Café	Chinese	West Campus	Counter	$8
3.0	Veranda	American	North Central	Casual	$31
2.8	Las Cazuelas	Mexican	East Austin	Casual	$22
2.6	Baby Acapulco	Mexican	Zilker	Casual	$23
2.6	Wanfu Too	Chinese	Zilker	Casual	$21
2.3	Wanfu	Chinese	Southeast	Casual	$21
2.2	The Magic Wok	Chinese	West Campus	Counter	$7
	Amy's Ice Cream	Sweets	Clarksville	Counter	
	Ken's Donuts	Sweets	West Campus	Take-out	
	La Dolce Vita	Sweets	Hyde Park	Café	

Weekday food after 11pm

9.0	Capitol Brasserie	French	Warehouse District	Upmarket	$48
8.8	Din Ho Chinese BBQ	Chinese	Far North	Casual	$24

			Location	Type	Price
	Weekday food after 11pm *continued*				
8.7	T&S Chinese Seafood	Chinese	Far North	Casual	$22
8.4	Casino El Camino	Burgers	Sixth Street District	Pub	$12
8.2	Sam's BBQ	Barbecue	East Austin	Counter	$11
8.1	Ruby's BBQ	Barbecue	UT Area	Counter	$17
8.0	Hyde Park Bar & Grill	American	Hyde Park	Casual	$28
7.9	Nubian Queen Lola's	Southern	East Austin	Casual	$10
7.8	El Taquito	Mexican	East Austin	Take-out	$5
7.0	The Jackalope	American	Sixth Street District	Pub	$12
7.0	Taquería Arandas	Mexican	St. Edward's Area	Casual	$8
6.9	219 West	New American	Warehouse District	Upmarket	$32
6.8	Texas Chili Parlor	American	Capitol Area	Casual	$17
6.8	888	Vietnamese	Southeast	Casual	$24
6.7	Katz's	Light American	Warehouse District	Casual	$23
6.5	Paradise Café	American	Sixth Street District	Casual	$25
6.3	Thai Passion	Thai	Congress Ave. Area	Casual	$27
6.2	Kerbey Lane Café	American	Seton Medical Area	Casual	$19
6.1	La Mexicana Bakery	Mexican	Bouldin Creek	Counter	$6
6.1	Silhouette	Japanese	Congress Ave. Area	Upmarket	$41
6.0	Green Muse Café	Light American	St. Edward's Area	Café	$9
5.9	Magnolia Café	American	Tarrytown	Casual	$18
5.8	Taco Cabana	Mexican	West Campus	Counter	$9
5.7	Phô Thai Son	Vietnamese	West Campus	Casual	$9
5.6	Trudy's	Mexican	UT Area	Casual	$26
5.6	Crown & Anchor Pub	American	UT Area	Pub	$13
5.6	Tony's Vineyard	Italian	West Campus	Upmarket	$37
5.6	Thai Kitchen	Thai	UT Area	Casual	$15
5.5	The Spider House	Light American	UT Area	Café	$7
5.4	Rockin' Tomato	Pizza	South Lamar	Counter	$17
5.2	Starseeds	American	French Place	Casual	$18
5.2	Ringers	American	Warehouse District	Pub	$24
5.0	Quack's on 43rd	Light American	Hyde Park	Café	$6
4.9	Mr. Gatti's	Pizza	West Campus	Casual	$8
4.6	Players	American	West Campus	Pub	$15
4.5	Opal Divine's	American	Warehouse District	Pub	$21
4.2	The Fox & Hound	American	Capitol Area	Pub	$20
4.1	Ruta Maya	Light American	St. Edward's Area	Café	$6
3.8	Bouldin Creek Café	Light American	Bouldin Creek	Café	$8
3.0	Veranda	American	North Central	Casual	$31
2.8	Las Cazuelas	Mexican	East Austin	Casual	$22
2.6	Baby Acapulco	Mexican	Zilker	Casual	$23
2.6	Wanfu Too	Chinese	Zilker	Casual	$21
2.3	Wanfu	Chinese	Southeast	Casual	$21
2.2	The Magic Wok	Chinese	West Campus	Counter	$7
	Amy's Ice Cream	Sweets	Clarksville	Counter	
	Ken's Donuts	Sweets	West Campus	Take-out	
	La Dolce Vita	Sweets	Hyde Park	Café	

Weekday food after midnight

9.0	Capitol Brasserie	French	Warehouse District	Upmarket	$48
8.8	Din Ho Chinese BBQ	Chinese	Far North	Casual	$24
8.7	T&S Chinese Seafood	Chinese	Far North	Casual	$22
8.4	Casino El Camino	Burgers	Sixth Street District	Pub	$12
8.2	Sam's BBQ	Barbecue	East Austin	Counter	$11
7.8	El Taquito	Mexican	East Austin	Take-out	$5
7.0	The Jackalope	American	Sixth Street District	Pub	$12
6.7	Katz's	Light American	Warehouse District	Casual	$23
6.3	Thai Passion	Thai	Congress Ave. Area	Casual	$27
6.2	Kerbey Lane Café	American	Seton Medical Area	Casual	$19
6.1	La Mexicana Bakery	Mexican	Bouldin Creek	Counter	$6
5.9	Magnolia Café	American	Tarrytown	Casual	$18
5.8	Taco Cabana	Mexican	West Campus	Counter	$9
5.5	The Spider House	Light American	UT Area	Café	$7
5.2	Starseeds	American	French Place	Casual	$18

				Type	*Price*
4.6	Players	American	West Campus	Pub	$15
4.5	Opal Divine's	American	Warehouse District	Pub	$21
4.2	The Fox & Hound	American	Capitol Area	Pub	$20
4.1	Ruta Maya	Light American	St. Edward's Area	Café	$6
3.0	Veranda	American	North Central	Casual	$31
2.6	Wanfu Too	Chinese	Zilker	Casual	$21
2.3	Wanfu	Chinese	Southeast	Casual	$21
2.2	The Magic Wok	Chinese	West Campus	Counter	$7
	Ken's Donuts	Sweets	West Campus	Take-out	

Weekday food after 1am

8.4	Casino El Camino	Burgers	Sixth Street District	Pub	$12
8.2	Sam's BBQ	Barbecue	East Austin	Counter	$11
7.8	El Taquito	Mexican	East Austin	Take-out	$5
6.7	Katz's	Light American	Warehouse District	Casual	$23
6.3	Thai Passion	Thai	Congress Ave. Area	Casual	$27
6.2	Kerbey Lane Café	American	Seton Medical Area	Casual	$19
6.1	La Mexicana Bakery	Mexican	Bouldin Creek	Counter	$6
5.9	Magnolia Café	American	Tarrytown	Casual	$18
5.8	Taco Cabana	Mexican	West Campus	Counter	$9
5.5	The Spider House	Light American	UT Area	Café	$7
5.2	Starseeds	American	French Place	Casual	$18
4.6	Players	American	West Campus	Pub	$15
4.2	The Fox & Hound	American	Capitol Area	Pub	$20
3.0	Veranda	American	North Central	Casual	$31
2.6	Wanfu Too	Chinese	Zilker	Casual	$21
2.3	Wanfu	Chinese	Southeast	Casual	$21
2.2	The Magic Wok	Chinese	West Campus	Counter	$7
	Ken's Donuts	Sweets	West Campus	Take-out	

Weekday food after 2am

7.8	El Taquito	Mexican	East Austin	Take-out	$5
6.7	Katz's	Light American	Warehouse District	Casual	$23
6.3	Thai Passion	Thai	Congress Ave. Area	Casual	$27
6.2	Kerbey Lane Café	American	Seton Medical Area	Casual	$19
6.1	La Mexicana Bakery	Mexican	Bouldin Creek	Counter	$6
5.9	Magnolia Café	American	Tarrytown	Casual	$18
5.8	Taco Cabana	Mexican	West Campus	Counter	$9
5.2	Starseeds	American	French Place	Casual	$18
4.6	Players	American	West Campus	Pub	$15
2.3	Wanfu	Chinese	Southeast	Casual	$21
	Ken's Donuts	Sweets	West Campus	Take-out	

Weekend food after 10pm

9.7	Uchi	Japanese	South Lamar	Upmarket	$69
9.6	Café at the 4 Seasons	New American	Convention Center	Upmarket	$73
9.3	Wink	New American	House Park Area	Upmarket	$86
9.3	Vespaio	Italian	South Congress	Upmarket	$62
9.2	Fino	Spanish	UT Area	Upmarket	$50
9.1	Mikado Ryotei	Japanese	Far North	Upmarket	$47
9.0	Starlite	New American	Warehouse District	Upmarket	$65
9.0	Capitol Brasserie	French	Warehouse District	Upmarket	$48
8.9	Mirabelle	Southwestern	Northwest Hills	Upmarket	$46
8.9	Fonda San Miguel	Mexican	North Central	Upmarket	$59
8.9	Manuel's	Mexican	Congress Ave. Area	Upmarket	$39
8.9	Musashino	Japanese	Northwest Hills	Upmarket	$58
8.8	Taverna	Italian	Warehouse District	Upmarket	$48
8.8	Din Ho Chinese BBQ	Chinese	Far North	Casual	$24
8.7	Rudy's	Barbecue	Westlake	Counter	$15
8.7	Asti	Italian	Hyde Park	Upmarket	$37
8.7	T&S Chinese Seafood	Chinese	Far North	Casual	$22
8.6	Ruth's Chris	Steakhouse	Congress Ave. Area	Upmarket	$74
8.6	1886 Café & Bakery	Light American	Congress Ave. Area	Upmarket	$31

	Weekend food after 10pm *continued*		Location	Type	Price
8.5	La Traviata	Italian	Congress Ave. Area	Upmarket	$51
8.4	Sushi Sake	Japanese	Arboretum	Upmarket	$45
8.4	Casino El Camino	Burgers	Sixth Street District	Pub	$12
8.4	Málaga	Spanish	Warehouse District	Upmarket	$47
8.4	Doña Emilia's	Latin American	Convention Center	Upmarket	$46
8.4	Clay Pit	Indian	Capitol Area	Upmarket	$33
8.3	Azul Tequila	Mexican	South Lamar	Casual	$30
8.3	Polvos	Mexican	Bouldin Creek	Casual	$24
8.3	Vin Bistro	New American	Seton Medical Area	Upmarket	$64
8.2	Chez Nous	French	Sixth Street District	Upmarket	$51
8.2	Sam's BBQ	Barbecue	East Austin	Counter	$11
8.1	Ruby's BBQ	Barbecue	UT Area	Counter	$17
8.1	Marco Polo	Chinese	Southeast	Casual	$24
8.1	Austin Land & Cattle	Steakhouse	House Park Area	Upmarket	$60
8.0	Emerald	Irish	Bee Cave	Upmarket	$80
8.0	Hyde Park Bar & Grill	American	Hyde Park	Casual	$28
8.0	Roaring Fork	Southwestern	Congress Ave. Area	Upmarket	$52
7.9	Rounders Pizzeria	Pizza	Clarksville	Counter	$15
7.9	Café Mundi	Light American	East Austin	Café	$11
7.9	Nubian Queen Lola's	Southern	East Austin	Casual	$10
7.8	Ranch 616	Southwestern	Capitol Area	Upmarket	$43
7.8	El Taquito	Mexican	East Austin	Take-out	$5
7.8	Kyoto	Japanese	Congress Ave. Area	Upmarket	$37
7.7	Chuy's	Mexican	Zilker	Casual	$27
7.7	Louie's 106	New American	Sixth Street District	Upmarket	$50
7.7	Mekong River	Vietnamese	Sixth Street District	Casual	$18
7.7	Dirty Martin's	American	West Campus	Casual	$12
7.6	Fadó	Irish	Warehouse District	Pub	$26
7.6	Satay	Indonesian	North Central	Casual	$24
7.6	Thai Tara	Thai	Warehouse District	Casual	$23
7.6	Z' Tejas	Mexican	Clarksville	Casual	$36
7.6	Arirang Sushi	Japanese	Sixth Street District	Casual	$23
7.6	Hill's Café	American	Far South	Casual	$27
7.5	Sea Dragon	Vietnamese	Far North	Casual	$24
7.5	Taj Palace	Indian	North Central	Casual	$22
7.4	Gumbo's	Southern	Capitol Area	Upmarket	$51
7.4	Stubb's BBQ	Barbecue	Red River Area	Counter	$18
7.4	Kenichi	Japanese	Warehouse District	Upmarket	$82
7.3	Bombay Bistro	Indian	Arboretum	Upmarket	$30
7.3	Cantina Laredo	Mexican	Warehouse District	Upmarket	$37
7.3	Eddie V's	Seafood	Sixth Street District	Upmarket	$63
7.2	Ichiban	Japanese	Burnet	Casual	$23
7.2	Chinatown	Chinese	Northwest Hills	Upmarket	$30
7.2	Serrano's Café	Mexican	Red River Area	Casual	$28
7.1	Milto's	Greek	UT Area	Counter	$11
7.1	El Arroyo	Mexican	Clarksville	Casual	$28
7.0	Pyramids	Middle Eastern	North Central	Casual	$15
7.0	The Jackalope	American	Sixth Street District	Pub	$12
7.0	Taquería Arandas	Mexican	St. Edward's Area	Casual	$8
7.0	Home Slice Pizza	Pizza	South Congress	Casual	$18
6.9	Suzi's China Grill	Chinese	Westlake	Casual	$31
6.9	El Regio	Mexican	Southeast	Counter	$10
6.9	219 West	New American	Warehouse District	Upmarket	$32
6.8	Shalimar	Indian	Far North	Casual	$11
6.8	Zax Pints & Plates	New American	Zilker	Upmarket	$40
6.8	Habana Calle 6	Latin American	Sixth Street District	Upmarket	$34
6.8	Vivo Cocina Texicana	Mexican	French Place	Casual	$28
6.8	P. Terry's	Burgers	South Lamar	Take-out	$6
6.8	Texas Chili Parlor	American	Capitol Area	Casual	$17
6.8	Cuba Libre	Latin American	Warehouse District	Casual	$33
6.8	888	Vietnamese	Southeast	Casual	$24
6.7	Austin's Pizza	Pizza	Capitol Area	Counter	$9
6.7	Sun Hing	Chinese	West Campus	Casual	$20

		Location	Type	Price
6.7 Pacific Star	Seafood	Far Northwest	Casual	$24
6.7 Bellagio	Italian	Far Northwest	Upmarket	$52
6.7 Star of India	Indian	North Central	Casual	$22
6.7 Katz's	Light American	Warehouse District	Casual	$23
6.6 The Tavern	American	House Park Area	Pub	$26
6.6 Mangia	Pizza	UT Area	Casual	$15
6.6 Peony	Chinese	Northwest Hills	Casual	$28
6.6 Beck's	American	South Congress	Pub	$34
6.5 Austin Java Co.	American	Clarksville	Café	$12
6.5 Mars	New American	West Campus	Upmarket	$45
6.5 Paradise Café	American	Sixth Street District	Casual	$25
6.5 Y Bar & Grill	Southwestern	Oak Hill	Upmarket	$45
6.4 Freebirds	Mexican	Hyde Park	Counter	$9
6.4 Sampaio's	Brazilian	Burnet	Upmarket	$42
6.4 Moonshine	American	Convention Center	Upmarket	$36
6.4 Korea House	Korean	North Central	Casual	$31
6.4 Saba Blue Water	New American	Warehouse District	Upmarket	$47
6.4 Mi Colombia	Latin American	East Austin	Casual	$16
6.4 Old Pecan St. Café	Southern	Sixth Street District	Casual	$29
6.3 Thundercloud Subs	Light American	Capitol Area	Counter	$7
6.3 Thai Passion	Thai	Congress Ave. Area	Casual	$27
6.3 Dan's Hamburgers	Burgers	Far South	Counter	$7
6.3 Maiko Sushi Lounge	Japanese	Warehouse District	Upmarket	$77
6.2 Hunan Lion	Chinese	South Lamar	Casual	$23
6.2 Sarovar	Indian	Burnet	Casual	$25
6.2 Kerbey Lane Café	American	Seton Medical Area	Casual	$19
6.2 Fran's	Burgers	South Congress	Counter	$8
6.2 Santa Rita	Mexican	Seton Medical Area	Casual	$29
6.2 Iron Cactus	Mexican	Sixth Street District	Pub	$35
6.1 Finn & Porter	Seafood	Convention Center	Upmarket	$63
6.1 La Mexicana Bakery	Mexican	Bouldin Creek	Counter	$6
6.1 Shady Grove	American	Zilker	Casual	$23
6.1 Silhouette	Japanese	Congress Ave. Area	Upmarket	$41
6.0 Old Alligator Grill	Southern	South Lamar	Casual	$30
6.0 Shoal Creek Saloon	American	House Park Area	Pub	$23
6.0 São Paulo's	Brazilian	UT Area	Casual	$32
6.0 El Zunzal	Latin American	East Austin	Casual	$19
6.0 Green Muse Café	Light American	St. Edward's Area	Café	$9
5.9 Dog & Duck Pub	American	Capitol Area	Pub	$20
5.9 Magnolia Café	American	Tarrytown	Casual	$18
5.9 Umi Sushi	Japanese	Southeast	Upmarket	$56
5.8 Ararat	Middle Eastern	North Central	Casual	$22
5.8 Chez Zee	American	Northwest Hills	Casual	$35
5.8 Taco Cabana	Mexican	West Campus	Counter	$9
5.7 Phô Thai Son	Vietnamese	West Campus	Casual	$9
5.6 Thai Kitchen	Thai	UT Area	Casual	$15
5.6 Truluck's	Seafood	Warehouse District	Upmarket	$66
5.6 Crown & Anchor Pub	American	UT Area	Pub	$13
5.6 Tony's Vineyard	Italian	West Campus	Upmarket	$37
5.6 Trudy's	Mexican	UT Area	Casual	$26
5.5 The Spider House	Light American	UT Area	Café	$7
5.5 Suzi's China Kitchen	Chinese	South Lamar	Casual	$23
5.4 Güero's	Mexican	South Congress	Casual	$26
5.4 Rockin' Tomato	Pizza	South Lamar	Counter	$17
5.3 Lucy's	Seafood	Tarrytown	Casual	$33
5.2 Starseeds	American	French Place	Casual	$18
5.2 The Posse East	American	UT Area	Pub	$14
5.2 Chapala	Mexican	East Austin	Casual	$5
5.2 Ringers	American	Warehouse District	Pub	$24
5.1 Flipnotics	Light American	Zilker	Café	$12
5.1 Las Palmas	Mexican	East Austin	Casual	$26
5.1 Hula Hut	American	Tarrytown	Casual	$31
5.0 Noodle-ism	Chinese	Congress Ave. Area	Counter	$19

	Weekend food after 10pm *continued*		Location	Type	Price
5.0	Cosmic Café	Indian	Clarksville	Casual	$16
5.0	Nutty Brown Café	American	Dripping Springs	Casual	$29
5.0	Quack's on 43rd	Light American	Hyde Park	Café	$6
4.9	El Mercado	Mexican	Capitol Area	Casual	$27
4.9	Flores	Mexican	North Central	Casual	$23
4.9	Matt's El Rancho	Mexican	South Lamar	Casual	$29
4.9	Mr. Gatti's	Pizza	West Campus	Casual	$8
4.9	Carmelo's	Italian	Sixth Street District	Upmarket	$56
4.9	Manny Hattan's	Light American	Arboretum	Casual	$27
4.8	Jorge's	Mexican	North Central	Casual	$24
4.7	The Broken Spoke	American	South Lamar	Pub	$24
4.7	Conan's Pizza	Pizza	West Campus	Counter	$9
4.6	Players	American	West Campus	Pub	$15
4.6	Sandy's	Burgers	Zilker	Take-out	$5
4.6	EZ's	American	Seton Medical Area	Counter	$20
4.5	Opal Divine's	American	Warehouse District	Pub	$21
4.4	Jaime's	Mexican	Red River Area	Casual	$24
4.4	Austin Pizza Garden	Pizza	Oak Hill	Casual	$17
4.2	Doc's	American	South Congress	Pub	$22
4.2	The Fox & Hound	American	Capitol Area	Pub	$20
4.2	Alamo Drafthouse	American	Warehouse District	Theater	$22
4.1	Ruta Maya	Light American	St. Edward's Area	Café	$6
3.9	Freddie's	American	Bouldin Creek	Casual	$21
3.8	Bouldin Creek Café	Light American	Bouldin Creek	Café	$8
3.8	Marisco Grill	Mexican	Sixth Street District	Casual	$33
3.8	Zen	Japanese	UT Area	Counter	$9
3.7	Tres Amigos	Mexican	Westlake	Casual	$33
3.6	La Reyna	Mexican	Bouldin Creek	Casual	$19
3.5	Vinny's	Italian	Zilker	Casual	$29
3.3	Mother Egan's	American	Warehouse District	Pub	$24
3.2	Romeo's	Italian	Zilker	Casual	$28
3.1	CoCo's Café	Chinese	West Campus	Counter	$8
3.0	Veranda	American	North Central	Casual	$31
2.8	Las Cazuelas	Mexican	East Austin	Casual	$22
2.8	Mongolian BBQ	Pan-Asian	Convention Center	Casual	$17
2.6	Wanfu Too	Chinese	Zilker	Casual	$21
2.6	Baby Acapulco	Mexican	Zilker	Casual	$23
2.3	Wanfu	Chinese	Southeast	Casual	$21
2.2	The Magic Wok	Chinese	West Campus	Counter	$7
2.2	El Gallo	Mexican	St. Edward's Area	Casual	$25
1.8	Tree House	Italian	St. Edward's Area	Upmarket	$36
	Amy's Ice Cream	Sweets	Clarksville	Counter	
	Ken's Donuts	Sweets	West Campus	Take-out	
	La Dolce Vita	Sweets	Hyde Park	Café	
	Tèo	Sweets	Seton Medical Area	Counter	

Weekend food after 11pm

9.0	Capitol Brasserie	French	Warehouse District	Upmarket	$48
8.9	Manuel's	Mexican	Congress Ave. Area	Upmarket	$39
8.8	Taverna	Italian	Warehouse District	Upmarket	$48
8.8	Din Ho Chinese BBQ	Chinese	Far North	Casual	$24
8.7	T&S Chinese Seafood	Chinese	Far North	Casual	$22
8.6	1886 Café & Bakery	Light American	Congress Ave. Area	Upmarket	$31
8.4	Casino El Camino	Burgers	Sixth Street District	Pub	$12
8.4	Málaga	Spanish	Warehouse District	Upmarket	$47
8.3	Azul Tequila	Mexican	South Lamar	Casual	$30
8.2	Sam's BBQ	Barbecue	East Austin	Counter	$11
8.1	Marco Polo	Chinese	Southeast	Casual	$24
8.1	Ruby's BBQ	Barbecue	UT Area	Counter	$17
8.0	Hyde Park Bar & Grill	American	Hyde Park	Casual	$28
7.9	Nubian Queen Lola's	Southern	East Austin	Casual	$10
7.8	El Taquito	Mexican	East Austin	Take-out	$5
7.6	Arirang Sushi	Japanese	Sixth Street District	Casual	$23

	Weekend food after 11pm *continued*		Location	Type	Price
7.1	El Arroyo	Mexican	Clarksville	Casual	$28
7.0	Home Slice Pizza	Pizza	South Congress	Casual	$18
7.0	Taquería Arandas	Mexican	St. Edward's Area	Casual	$8
7.0	The Jackalope	American	Sixth Street District	Pub	$12
6.9	219 West	New American	Warehouse District	Upmarket	$32
6.8	Texas Chili Parlor	American	Capitol Area	Casual	$17
6.8	Shalimar	Indian	Far North	Casual	$11
6.8	Habana Calle 6	Latin American	Sixth Street District	Upmarket	$34
6.8	888	Vietnamese	Southeast	Casual	$24
6.8	P. Terry's	Burgers	South Lamar	Take-out	$6
6.8	Vivo Cocina Texicana	Mexican	French Place	Casual	$28
6.7	Katz's	Light American	Warehouse District	Casual	$23
6.7	Austin's Pizza	Pizza	Capitol Area	Counter	$9
6.6	The Tavern	American	House Park Area	Pub	$26
6.5	Paradise Café	American	Sixth Street District	Casual	$25
6.5	Austin Java Co.	American	Clarksville	Café	$12
6.4	Saba Blue Water	New American	Warehouse District	Upmarket	$47
6.4	Old Pecan St. Café	Southern	Sixth Street District	Casual	$29
6.3	Maiko Sushi Lounge	Japanese	Warehouse District	Upmarket	$77
6.3	Thai Passion	Thai	Congress Ave. Area	Casual	$27
6.2	Kerbey Lane Café	American	Seton Medical Area	Casual	$19
6.2	Iron Cactus	Mexican	Sixth Street District	Pub	$35
6.1	La Mexicana Bakery	Mexican	Bouldin Creek	Counter	$6
6.1	Silhouette	Japanese	Congress Ave. Area	Upmarket	$41
6.0	Green Muse Café	Light American	St. Edward's Area	Café	$9
5.9	Dog & Duck Pub	American	Capitol Area	Pub	$20
5.9	Magnolia Café	American	Tarrytown	Casual	$18
5.8	Chez Zee	American	Northwest Hills	Casual	$35
5.8	Taco Cabana	Mexican	West Campus	Counter	$9
5.7	Phô Thai Son	Vietnamese	West Campus	Casual	$9
5.6	Tony's Vineyard	Italian	West Campus	Upmarket	$37
5.6	Thai Kitchen	Thai	UT Area	Casual	$15
5.6	Crown & Anchor Pub	American	UT Area	Pub	$13
5.6	Trudy's	Mexican	UT Area	Casual	$26
5.5	The Spider House	Light American	UT Area	Café	$7
5.4	Rockin' Tomato	Pizza	South Lamar	Counter	$17
5.2	Ringers	American	Warehouse District	Pub	$24
5.2	Starseeds	American	French Place	Casual	$18
5.1	Flipnotics	Light American	Zilker	Café	$12
5.0	Quack's on 43rd	Light American	Hyde Park	Café	$6
5.0	Noodle-ism	Chinese	Congress Ave. Area	Counter	$19
5.0	Nutty Brown Café	American	Dripping Springs	Casual	$29
4.9	Mr. Gatti's	Pizza	West Campus	Casual	$8
4.9	Manny Hattan's	Light American	Arboretum	Casual	$27
4.7	The Broken Spoke	American	South Lamar	Pub	$24
4.7	Conan's Pizza	Pizza	West Campus	Counter	$9
4.6	Players	American	West Campus	Pub	$15
4.5	Opal Divine's	American	Warehouse District	Pub	$21
4.2	The Fox & Hound	American	Capitol Area	Pub	$20
4.1	Ruta Maya	Light American	St. Edward's Area	Café	$6
3.8	Bouldin Creek Café	Light American	Bouldin Creek	Café	$8
3.8	Marisco Grill	Mexican	Sixth Street District	Casual	$33
3.3	Mother Egan's	American	Warehouse District	Pub	$24
3.0	Veranda	American	North Central	Casual	$31
2.8	Las Cazuelas	Mexican	East Austin	Casual	$22
2.6	Baby Acapulco	Mexican	Zilker	Casual	$23
2.6	Wanfu Too	Chinese	Zilker	Casual	$21
2.3	Wanfu	Chinese	Southeast	Casual	$21
2.2	The Magic Wok	Chinese	West Campus	Counter	$7
	Amy's Ice Cream	Sweets	Clarksville	Counter	
	Ken's Donuts	Sweets	West Campus	Take-out	
	La Dolce Vita	Sweets	Hyde Park	Café	
	Tèo	Sweets	Seton Medical Area	Counter	

Weekend food after midnight

			Location	Type	Price
9.0	Capitol Brasserie	French	Warehouse District	Upmarket	$48
8.8	Din Ho Chinese BBQ	Chinese	Far North	Casual	$24
8.7	T&S Chinese Seafood	Chinese	Far North	Casual	$22
8.4	Casino El Camino	Burgers	Sixth Street District	Pub	$12
8.2	Sam's BBQ	Barbecue	East Austin	Counter	$11
7.8	El Taquito	Mexican	East Austin	Take-out	$5
7.6	Arirang Sushi	Japanese	Sixth Street District	Casual	$23
7.0	Home Slice Pizza	Pizza	South Congress	Casual	$18
7.0	The Jackalope	American	Sixth Street District	Pub	$12
7.0	Taquería Arandas	Mexican	St. Edward's Area	Casual	$8
6.9	219 West	New American	Warehouse District	Upmarket	$32
6.8	P. Terry's	Burgers	South Lamar	Take-out	$6
6.7	Katz's	Light American	Warehouse District	Casual	$23
6.6	The Tavern	American	House Park Area	Pub	$26
6.3	Thai Passion	Thai	Congress Ave. Area	Casual	$27
6.2	Kerbey Lane Café	American	Seton Medical Area	Casual	$19
6.1	La Mexicana Bakery	Mexican	Bouldin Creek	Counter	$6
6.1	Silhouette	Japanese	Congress Ave. Area	Upmarket	$41
5.9	Magnolia Café	American	Tarrytown	Casual	$18
5.8	Chez Zee	American	Northwest Hills	Casual	$35
5.8	Taco Cabana	Mexican	West Campus	Counter	$9
5.6	Trudy's	Mexican	UT Area	Casual	$26
5.5	The Spider House	Light American	UT Area	Café	$7
5.2	Starseeds	American	French Place	Casual	$18
5.0	Noodle-ism	Chinese	Congress Ave. Area	Counter	$19
4.9	Manny Hattan's	Light American	Arboretum	Casual	$27
4.6	Players	American	West Campus	Pub	$15
4.5	Opal Divine's	American	Warehouse District	Pub	$21
4.2	The Fox & Hound	American	Capitol Area	Pub	$20
4.1	Ruta Maya	Light American	St. Edward's Area	Café	$6
3.0	Veranda	American	North Central	Casual	$31
2.8	Las Cazuelas	Mexican	East Austin	Casual	$22
2.6	Wanfu Too	Chinese	Zilker	Casual	$21
2.3	Wanfu	Chinese	Southeast	Casual	$21
2.2	The Magic Wok	Chinese	West Campus	Counter	$7
	Amy's Ice Cream	Sweets	Clarksville	Counter	
	Ken's Donuts	Sweets	West Campus	Take-out	

Weekend food after 1am

9.0	Capitol Brasserie	French	Warehouse District	Upmarket	$48
8.4	Casino El Camino	Burgers	Sixth Street District	Pub	$12
8.2	Sam's BBQ	Barbecue	East Austin	Counter	$11
7.8	El Taquito	Mexican	East Austin	Take-out	$5
7.6	Arirang Sushi	Japanese	Sixth Street District	Casual	$23
7.0	Home Slice Pizza	Pizza	South Congress	Casual	$18
6.9	219 West	New American	Warehouse District	Upmarket	$32
6.7	Korea Garden	Korean	North Central	Casual	$33
6.7	Katz's	Light American	Warehouse District	Casual	$23
6.3	Thai Passion	Thai	Congress Ave. Area	Casual	$27
6.2	Kerbey Lane Café	American	Seton Medical Area	Casual	$19
6.1	La Mexicana Bakery	Mexican	Bouldin Creek	Counter	$6
6.1	Silhouette	Japanese	Congress Ave. Area	Upmarket	$41
5.9	Magnolia Café	American	Tarrytown	Casual	$18
5.8	Taco Cabana	Mexican	West Campus	Counter	$9
5.6	Trudy's	Mexican	UT Area	Casual	$26
5.5	The Spider House	Light American	UT Area	Café	$7
5.2	Starseeds	American	French Place	Casual	$18
5.0	Noodle-ism	Chinese	Congress Ave. Area	Counter	$19
4.6	Players	American	West Campus	Pub	$15
4.2	The Fox & Hound	American	Capitol Area	Pub	$20
3.0	Veranda	American	North Central	Casual	$31
2.8	Las Cazuelas	Mexican	East Austin	Casual	$22
2.6	Wanfu Too	Chinese	Zilker	Casual	$21

	Weekend food after 1am *continued*		Location	Type	Price
2.3	Wanfu	Chinese	Southeast	Casual	$21
2.2	The Magic Wok	Chinese	West Campus	Counter	$7
	Ken's Donuts	Sweets	West Campus	Take-out	

Weekend food after 2am

9.0	Capitol Brasserie	French	Warehouse District	Upmarket	$48
7.8	El Taquito	Mexican	East Austin	Take-out	$5
7.0	Home Slice Pizza	Pizza	South Congress	Casual	$18
6.7	Katz's	Light American	Warehouse District	Casual	$23
6.3	Thai Passion	Thai	Congress Ave. Area	Casual	$27
6.2	Kerbey Lane Café	American	Seton Medical Area	Casual	$19
6.1	La Mexicana Bakery	Mexican	Bouldin Creek	Counter	$6
5.9	Magnolia Café	American	Tarrytown	Casual	$18
5.8	Taco Cabana	Mexican	West Campus	Counter	$9
5.2	Starseeds	American	French Place	Casual	$18
5.0	Noodle-ism	Chinese	Congress Ave. Area	Counter	$19
4.6	Players	American	West Campus	Pub	$15
2.8	Las Cazuelas	Mexican	East Austin	Casual	$22
2.3	Wanfu	Chinese	Southeast	Casual	$21
1.2	Buffet Palace	Pan-Asian	North Central	Casual	$14
	Ken's Donuts	Sweets	West Campus	Take-out	

VEGETARIAN DINING GUIDE

The following lists include only restaurants that we have dubbed "vegetarian-friendly," which means a particularly wide and varied selection of vegetarian options on the menu. ***Except as otherwise noted, all lists are ordered by food rating.***

All vegetarian-friendly establishments

				Type	Price
9.3	Vespaio	Italian	South Congress	Upmarket	$62
9.3	Café Josie	Southwestern	Clarksville	Upmarket	$48
9.2	Vespaio Enoteca	Italian	South Congress	Casual	$32
9.2	El Chile	Mexican	French Place	Casual	$31
9.2	Zoot	New American	Tarrytown	Upmarket	$64
9.0	Aquarelle	French	Warehouse District	Upmarket	$91
8.9	Mirabelle	Southwestern	Northwest Hills	Upmarket	$46
8.8	Taverna	Italian	Warehouse District	Upmarket	$48
8.6	1886 Café & Bakery	Light American	Congress Ave. Area	Upmarket	$31
8.5	Sunflower	Vietnamese	Far North	Casual	$22
8.5	Mandola's	Italian	Hyde Park	Counter	$19
8.4	Clay Pit	Indian	Capitol Area	Upmarket	$33
8.3	Pao's Mandarin House	Chinese	Lake Travis	Casual	$20
8.2	Changos Taquería	Mexican	UT Area	Counter	$11
8.2	Eastside Café	American	French Place	Upmarket	$45
8.1	Bistro 88	New American	Westlake	Upmarket	$49
8.0	Hyde Park Bar & Grill	American	Hyde Park	Casual	$28
8.0	Azul	Light American	East Austin	Counter	$11
7.9	Café Mundi	Light American	East Austin	Café	$11
7.9	Le Soleil	Vietnamese	Far North	Casual	$26
7.9	Portabla	Light American	Clarksville	Counter	$9
7.8	Cipollina	Italian	Clarksville	Counter	$18
7.7	FoodHeads	Light American	UT Area	Counter	$8
7.7	Mekong River	Vietnamese	Sixth Street District	Casual	$18
7.7	Tuscany	Italian	Far North	Counter	$17
7.7	Bangkok Cuisine	Thai	Far North	Casual	$24
7.7	Dandelion Café	Light American	East Austin	Café	$8
7.6	A La Carrera	Mexican	Far Northwest	Casual	$21
7.6	Jerusalem Gourmet	Middle Eastern	Southeast	Counter	$9
7.6	Satay	Indonesian	North Central	Casual	$24

				Type	Price
	All vegetarian-friendly establishments *continued*			*Type*	*Price*
7.5	Sea Dragon	Vietnamese	Far North	Casual	$24
7.5	Phoenicia Bakery	Middle Eastern	South Lamar	Take-out	$6
7.5	Taj Palace	Indian	North Central	Casual	$22
7.4	Stubb's BBQ	Barbecue	Red River Area	Counter	$18
7.3	Bombay Bistro	Indian	Arboretum	Upmarket	$30
7.3	Byblos	Middle Eastern	Far North	Counter	$7
7.2	Chinatown	Chinese	Northwest Hills	Upmarket	$30
7.2	Madras Pavilion	Indian	Far North	Casual	$15
7.2	Alborz	Middle Eastern	North Central	Casual	$28
7.1	Upper Crust	Light American	Burnet	Café	$6
7.0	Pyramids	Middle Eastern	North Central	Casual	$15
6.9	Bombay Grill	Indian	Westlake	Casual	$23
6.9	Suzi's China Grill	Chinese	Westlake	Casual	$31
6.9	Brick Oven on 35th	Italian	Seton Medical Area	Casual	$26
6.8	Brick Oven	Italian	Red River Area	Casual	$22
6.8	Madam Mam's	Thai	West Campus	Casual	$16
6.8	P. Terry's	Burgers	South Lamar	Take-out	$6
6.8	Tom's Tabooley	Middle Eastern	UT Area	Counter	$8
6.8	Jo's Hot Coffee	Light American	South Congress	Café	$8
6.8	Thai Noodles, Etc.	Thai	West Campus	Casual	$14
6.8	Vivo Cocina Texicana	Mexican	French Place	Casual	$28
6.7	Austin's Pizza	Pizza	Capitol Area	Counter	$9
6.7	Veggie Heaven	Light American	West Campus	Casual	$13
6.7	Star of India	Indian	North Central	Casual	$22
6.7	Hut's Hamburgers	Burgers	Warehouse District	Casual	$13
6.6	Mother's	American	Hyde Park	Casual	$20
6.6	Mangia	Pizza	UT Area	Casual	$15
6.6	Casa de Luz	Light American	Zilker	Counter	$13
6.6	Peony	Chinese	Northwest Hills	Casual	$28
6.5	Mars	New American	West Campus	Upmarket	$45
6.5	Marakesh	Middle Eastern	Capitol Area	Casual	$18
6.4	Freebirds	Mexican	Hyde Park	Counter	$9
6.3	The Soup Peddler	American	Bouldin Creek	Take-out	$10
6.3	Thundercloud Subs	Light American	Capitol Area	Counter	$7
6.3	Thai Passion	Thai	Congress Ave. Area	Casual	$27
6.2	Hunan Lion	Chinese	South Lamar	Casual	$23
6.2	Kerbey Lane Café	American	Seton Medical Area	Casual	$19
6.2	Sarovar	Indian	Burnet	Casual	$25
6.1	Frank & Angie's	Pizza	Warehouse District	Casual	$23
6.0	Green Muse Café	Light American	St. Edward's Area	Café	$9
6.0	Sasha's	Russian	Northwest Hills	Casual	$17
5.9	Magnolia Café	American	Tarrytown	Casual	$18
5.9	Nu Age Café	Light American	Tarrytown	Casual	$22
5.9	Chooby Doo	American	Far South	Counter	$7
5.8	Ararat	Middle Eastern	North Central	Casual	$22
5.8	Chez Zee	American	Northwest Hills	Casual	$35
5.7	NeWorlDeli	Light American	Hyde Park	Counter	$13
5.6	The Omelettry	American	Burnet	Casual	$10
5.4	Indian Palace	Indian	Northwest Hills	Casual	$21
5.2	Starseeds	American	French Place	Casual	$18
5.0	Quack's on 43rd	Light American	Hyde Park	Café	$6
5.0	Cosmic Café	Indian	Clarksville	Casual	$16
5.0	El Sol y La Luna	Mexican	South Congress	Casual	$19
5.0	Flip's Satellite Café	American	Dripping Springs	Casual	$17
4.6	EZ's	American	Seton Medical Area	Counter	$20
4.4	Austin Pizza Garden	Pizza	Oak Hill	Casual	$17
4.1	Hai Ky	Vietnamese	Southeast	Casual	$13
3.8	Bouldin Creek Café	Light American	Bouldin Creek	Café	$8
3.8	Zen	Japanese	UT Area	Counter	$9
3.7	Mr. Natural	Light American	South Lamar	Counter	$12
	Amy's Ice Cream	Sweets	Clarksville	Counter	
	Mozart's	Sweets	Tarrytown	Café	
	Paciugo Gelateria	Sweets	Warehouse District	Counter	

All vegetarian-friendly establishments *continued*

			Type	Price
Sticky Toffee	Sweets	Warehouse District	Take-out	
Tèo	Sweets	Seton Medical Area	Counter	
Central Market		Seton Medical Area	Grocery	
Grapevine Market		North Central	Grocery	
Wheatsville Co-op		UT Area	Grocery	
Whole Foods		Clarksville	Grocery	

Vegetarian-friendly establishments with top experience
*listed in order of **experience** rating*

9.7	Zoot	New American	Tarrytown	Upmarket	$64
9.7	Mozart's	Sweets	Tarrytown	Café	
9.6	Café Josie	Southwestern	Clarksville	Upmarket	$48
9.5	Eastside Café	American	French Place	Upmarket	$45
9.5	Vivo Cocina Texicana	Mexican	French Place	Casual	$28
9.4	Jo's Hot Coffee	Light American	South Congress	Café	$8
9.4	Green Muse Café	Light American	St. Edward's Area	Café	$9
9.4	Chez Zee	American	Northwest Hills	Casual	$35
9.4	Amy's Ice Cream	Sweets	Clarksville	Counter	
9.3	Magnolia Café	American	Tarrytown	Casual	$18
9.2	Clay Pit	Indian	Capitol Area	Upmarket	$33
9.2	Mars	New American	West Campus	Upmarket	$45
9.1	El Chile	Mexican	French Place	Casual	$31
9.1	Hyde Park Bar & Grill	American	Hyde Park	Casual	$28
9.0	Casa de Luz	Light American	Zilker	Counter	$13
9.0	Kerbey Lane Café	American	Seton Medical Area	Casual	$19
9.0	Ararat	Middle Eastern	North Central	Casual	$22
8.9	Taverna	Italian	Warehouse District	Upmarket	$48
8.9	1886 Café & Bakery	Light American	Congress Ave. Area	Upmarket	$31
8.9	Azul	Light American	East Austin	Counter	$11
8.9	Tèo	Sweets	Seton Medical Area	Counter	
8.8	Stubb's BBQ	Barbecue	Red River Area	Counter	$18
8.8	Bouldin Creek Café	Light American	Bouldin Creek	Café	$8
8.7	Mirabelle	Southwestern	Northwest Hills	Upmarket	$46
8.6	Vespaio	Italian	South Congress	Upmarket	$62
8.6	Aquarelle	French	Warehouse District	Upmarket	$91
8.6	Café Mundi	Light American	East Austin	Café	$11
8.5	Vespaio Enoteca	Italian	South Congress	Casual	$32

Vegetarian-friendly date places *listed in order of **experience** rating*

9.7	Zoot	New American	Tarrytown	Upmarket	$64
9.7	Mozart's	Sweets	Tarrytown	Café	
9.6	Café Josie	Southwestern	Clarksville	Upmarket	$48
9.5	Vivo Cocina Texicana	Mexican	French Place	Casual	$28
9.5	Eastside Café	American	French Place	Upmarket	$45
9.4	Amy's Ice Cream	Sweets	Clarksville	Counter	
9.3	Magnolia Café	American	Tarrytown	Casual	$18
9.2	Clay Pit	Indian	Capitol Area	Upmarket	$33
9.2	Mars	New American	West Campus	Upmarket	$45
9.1	El Chile	Mexican	French Place	Casual	$31
9.0	Ararat	Middle Eastern	North Central	Casual	$22
8.9	Taverna	Italian	Warehouse District	Upmarket	$48
8.9	Tèo	Sweets	Seton Medical Area	Counter	
8.9	1886 Café & Bakery	Light American	Congress Ave. Area	Upmarket	$31
8.9	Azul	Light American	East Austin	Counter	$11
8.7	Mirabelle	Southwestern	Northwest Hills	Upmarket	$46
8.6	Vespaio	Italian	South Congress	Upmarket	$62
8.6	Café Mundi	Light American	East Austin	Café	$11
8.6	Aquarelle	French	Warehouse District	Upmarket	$91
8.5	Vespaio Enoteca	Italian	South Congress	Casual	$32
8.4	Bistro 88	New American	Westlake	Upmarket	$49
8.0	Brick Oven on 35th	Italian	Seton Medical Area	Casual	$26
7.4	Cipollina	Italian	Clarksville	Counter	$18

Vegetarian-friendly, kid-friendly *listed in order of **food** rating*

8.2	Changos Taquería	Mexican	UT Area	Counter	$11
7.7	Dandelion Café	Light American	East Austin	Café	$8
7.6	A La Carrera	Mexican	Far Northwest	Casual	$21
7.1	Upper Crust	Light American	Burnet	Café	$6
7.0	Pyramids	Middle Eastern	North Central	Casual	$15
6.8	P. Terry's	Burgers	South Lamar	Take-out	$6
6.7	Hut's Hamburgers	Burgers	Warehouse District	Casual	$13
6.6	Mangia	Pizza	UT Area	Casual	$15
6.4	Freebirds	Mexican	Hyde Park	Counter	$9
6.3	Thundercloud Subs	Light American	Capitol Area	Counter	$7
6.2	Kerbey Lane Café	American	Seton Medical Area	Casual	$19
6.1	Frank & Angie's	Pizza	Warehouse District	Casual	$23
5.9	Nu Age Café	Light American	Tarrytown	Casual	$22
5.9	Magnolia Café	American	Tarrytown	Casual	$18
4.6	EZ's	American	Seton Medical Area	Counter	$20
4.4	Austin Pizza Garden	Pizza	Oak Hill	Casual	$17
	Amy's Ice Cream	Sweets	Clarksville	Counter	
	Paciugo Gelateria	Sweets	Warehouse District	Counter	
	Sticky Toffee	Sweets	Warehouse District	Take-out	
	Tèo	Sweets	Seton Medical Area	Counter	
	Central Market		Seton Medical Area	Grocery	
	Whole Foods		Clarksville	Grocery	

Vegetarian-friendly delivery *listed in order of **food** rating*

8.3	Pao's Mandarin House	Chinese	Lake Travis	Casual	$20
8.0	Hyde Park Bar & Grill	American	Hyde Park	Casual	$28
7.7	Mekong River	Vietnamese	Sixth Street District	Casual	$18
7.7	FoodHeads	Light American	UT Area	Counter	$8
7.6	Satay	Indonesian	North Central	Casual	$24
7.5	Taj Palace	Indian	North Central	Casual	$22
6.9	Bombay Grill	Indian	Westlake	Casual	$23
6.7	Austin's Pizza	Pizza	Capitol Area	Counter	$9
6.7	Star of India	Indian	North Central	Casual	$22
6.6	Peony	Chinese	Northwest Hills	Casual	$28
6.6	Mangia	Pizza	UT Area	Casual	$15
6.2	Hunan Lion	Chinese	South Lamar	Casual	$23
6.2	Sarovar	Indian	Burnet	Casual	$25
5.7	NeWorlDeli	Light American	Hyde Park	Counter	$13
4.4	Austin Pizza Garden	Pizza	Oak Hill	Casual	$17

BEST OF *THE FEARLESS CRITIC*

In what is sure to be the most controversial section of all, we hereby offer the Fearless Critic's best-of-Austin picks in several categories. Come disagree on www.fearlesscritic.com...

Best brisket
1 Kreuz Market
2 House Park BBQ
3 Louie Mueller's
4 Smitty's Market
5 Rudy's Country Store

Best brunch
1 Fonda San Miguel
2 Eastside Café
3 South Congress Café
4 Marco Polo
5 Green Pastures

Best chicken-fried steak
1 Hill's Café
2 Hoover's
3 Mesa Ranch
4 Shady Grove
5 The Frisco Shop

Best chopped beef
1 Ruby's BBQ
2 The Salt Lick 360
3 Green Mesquite
4 Stubb's BBQ
5 Bee Caves BBQ

Best dessert
1 The Driskill Grill
2 Café at the Four Seasons
3 Amy's Ice Cream
4 Aquarelle
5 Jeffrey's

Best enchiladas
1 Las Manitas
2 Polvos
3 Manuel's
4 Azul Tequila
5 Chuy's

Best game
1 Hudson's on the Bend
2 Mesa Ranch
3 Mikado Ryotei
4 Green Pastures
5 The Driskill Grill

Best margaritas
1 Fonda San Miguel
2 Guero's
3 El Chile
4 Nuevo León
5 Z' Tejas

Best Mexican martinis
1 Chuy's
2 Trudy's
3 Matt's El Rancho
4 Iron Cactus
5 A La Carrera

Best migas
1 South Congress Café
2 Trudy's
3 Las Manitas
4 Maria's Taco Xpress
5 Z' Tejas

Best mole
1 Fonda San Miguel
2 El Chile
3 El Borrego de Oro
4 Manuel's
5 Oaxacan Tamaleo

Best pizza
1 Mandola's
2 Tuscany
3 Asti
4 Vespaio and Vespaio Enoteca
5 Taverna

Best minimalist queso
1 Kerbey Lane
2 Taco Cabana
3 Z' Tejas
4 Juan in a Million
5 Trudy's

Best everything-but-the-kitchen-sink queso
1 Magnolia Café (Mag Mud)
2 Polvos (do-it-yourself queso)
3 El Chile (rajas con queso)
4 Salt Lick 360 (queso flameado with brisket)
5 El Arroyo (spinach queso)

Best ribs

1 The Salt Lick and the Salt Lick 360
2 Artz Rib House
3 Lewis' BBQ
4 Iron Works
5 The County Line

Best salsa

1 El Chile
2 Evita's Botanitas
3 El Mesón Taquería
4 La Mexicana Bakery
5 Angie's

Best sandwiches

1 Azul
2 Tâm Deli & Café
3 FoodHeads
4 Portabla
5 Delaware Sub Shop

Best tacos

1 Changos Taquería
2 El Mesón Taquería
3 Maria's Taco Xpress
4 El Taquito
5 La Mexicana Bakery

Best tortilla soup

1 Curra's Grill
2 Las Manitas
3 Polvos
4 Flores
5 Santa Rita Tex-Mex Cantina

Best value

1 The Salt Lick
2 Din Ho Chinese BBQ
3 Kreuz Market
4 Oaxacan Tamaleo
5 El Chile and El Chilito
6 El Borrego de Oro
7 Smitty's Market
8 Louie Mueller's
9 Castle Hill Café
10 Casino El Camino
11 Café Josie
12 Rudy's Country Store
13 Swad
14 House Park BBQ
15 Vespaio Enoteca
16 South Congress Café
17 T&S Chinese Seafood
18 Sunflower
19 Marco Polo
20 Phoenicia Bakery

Most overpriced

1 Kenichi
2 Truluck's
3 Maiko Sushi Lounge
4 Dan McKlusky's
5 Judges' Hill Restaurant

Best when somebody else is paying

1 The Driskill Grill
2 Aquarelle
3 Emerald Restaurant
4 Wink
5 Café at the Four Seasons

Lowest-rated food

1 Buffet Palace
2 Enchiladas y Mas
3 Rosie's Tamale House
4 Tree House
5 Jovita's

Lowest-rated experience

1 Maiko Sushi Lounge
2 Bee Cave Bistro
3 Buffet Palace
4 Dan McKlusky's
5 Wanfu

FIFTY BEST BITES OF AUSTIN

If you had just one month in the city, and 25 pounds to gain...

Austin, Texas Benedict, 1886 Café and Bakery
Baby back ribs, Artz Rib House
Barbacoa taco, La Mexicana Bakery
Barbecued chicken enchiladas, El Arroyo
Bob Armstrong Dip, Matt's El Rancho
Brisket, House Park BBQ
Chicken taco, Julio's
Chicken-fried steak, Hill's Café
Chile con queso, Chuy's
Chopped beef sandwich, Ruby's BBQ
Churrasco, Doña Emilia's
Cochinita pibil, Curra's Grill
Coffee, Jo's Hot Coffee
Cornbread, Z' Tejas
Crispy oysters, Jeffrey's
Food samples, Central Market
French fries, Hyde Park Bar and Grill
Frisco Burger, The Frisco Shop
Frojito, Habana Calle 6
Frozen custard, Sandy's Hamburgers
Zabaglione gelato, Tèo
Green chile macaroni and cheese, Roaring Fork
Guinness float, Alamo Drafthouse
Hamburger, Casino El Camino
Home-brewed root beer, Texicalli Grille
Hudson's Mixed Grill, Hudson's on the Bend
Hyde Park Fudge Cake, Texas French Bread
Mag Mud, Magnolia Café
Margarita, Güero's
Meatloaf sandwich, The Kitchen Door
Mexican martini, Trudy's
Mexican Vanilla ice cream, Amy's Ice Cream
Migas, Las Manitas
Miles of Chocolate, Grapevine Market
Mole enchiladas, Fonda San Miguel
O. T. Special, Dirty Martin's Place
Pancakes, Kerbey Lane
Peach cobbler, Hoover's
Purple Margarita, Baby Acapulco's
Roast duck, Din Ho Chinese BBQ
Salsa, El Chile
Schlotzsky's Original sandwich, Schlotzsky's
Serrano cheese spinach, Stubb's
Shack taco, Taco Shack
Shiner Bock during a 'Horns game, The Posse East
Smoked turkey, The Salt Lick
Sticky toffee pudding, Sticky Toffee Pudding Company
Taco al pastor, Maria's Taco Xpress
Tortilla soup, Polvos
Veggie burger, Shady Grove
Wild boar chile pozole, South Congress Café

REVIEWS

A La Carrera

Under the (queso) skin, this is one of
Austin's best Tex-Mex deals

food
7.6 **6.6**
10   10
experience

Mexican   **$21**   *Far Northwest*

Casual restaurant
Daily 7am-10pm. *Breakfast.*
Kid-friendly. Vegetarian-friendly.

11150 N. Hwy. 183
Austin
(512) 345-1763

Bar Full
Credit Cards Visa, MC, AmEx
Reservations Accepted

It is well known that many of Austin's most authentic taquerías and down-home regional Mexican spots are often found in the most unlikely, out-of-the-way locations. A La Carrera proves that that can sometimes be the case for Tex-Mex, too: this joint is difficult to find, but definitely worth the effort. Look for the restaurant in the Balcones Woods shopping center off U.S. 183 just south of the Balcones Woods intersection; the name is not listed on the shopping center sign, so if you blink, you could miss it.

With a silly '70s-looking rainbow sign and interior paint explosion, A La Carrera gives off a first impression that could potentially induce seizure, in which case your medical costs might potentially outweigh the benefits of the restaurant's low prices. Otherwise, though, the food is solid, and the value excellent. The staff is affable and extraordinarily family-friendly, if hardly speedy.

But who's in a rush when there's queso on the table? A La Carrera's version of this Austin Tex-Mex benchmark stays liquid and has a nice, smoky flavor—that is, once you get past the disconcerting cheese skin that initially gels along the surface, perhaps protecting the cheese from the elements (and the glare of those colors). Queso flameado is also good, sparing you from the grease that can often plague the dish. Fajitas are more heavily peppered than we like, but the beef strips are tender, and guacamole, pico de gallo, and sour cream all do their part to balance out the kick. Mole enchiladas aren't particularly complex, but at this price, these are just fine, rich and nutty with a hint of chocolate. The shrimp-filled chile relleno is for heat-lovers only, covered in a very spicy red sauce; melted cheese on top helps keep the fire under control.

Wash it all down with a Mexican martini, and if that doesn't knock you out, continue on to their sumptuous flan. It's creamy, dense, with deep caramel and just a drizzle of thin chocolate sauce on top. They might not do that in Mex, but this is Tex, after all. –MPN

Alamo Drafthouse

The films shown here are much livelier than the food

food

4.2
10

9.6
10

experience

American

$22

Warehouse, S. Lamar, N. Central

Movie theater
Depends on movie schedule. Shows most days 7pm and 9:45pm; "Weird Wednesday" (free show) Wed. at 11:45pm.
Date-friendly.

409 Colorado St.
Austin
(512) 476-1320
www.drafthouse.com

1120 S. Lamar Blvd.
78704, (512) 476-1320

Bar Beer/wine
Credit Cards Visa, MC, AmEx
Reservations Accepted

2700 W. Anderson Ln.
78757, (512) 476-1320

The Alamo Drafthouse is quintessentially Austin, home to the wackiest this city has to offer. There are several Alamos around town, but the classic venue is still the downtown theater, with its notched wooden benches and tables, and vaguely criminal air. Why, the Drafthouse seems to ask the world, aren't there more movie theaters that bring food and drinks to your seat?

This being Austin, though, the cinema does not rest at that mere gimmick. In addition to the first-run options, Alamo also shows the strangest stuff, from free midnight horror sexcapades on "Weird Wednesdays" to a wonderfully bizarre Michael Jackson sing-along. There are also various open-screen nights where Austin's movie-making masses can spin their reels.

First, a primer: Once you enter the theater, you peruse the menu using darkroom-style yellow lights that hide beneath the narrow bar in front of you. Next, you scrawl your order in freehand onto a piece of paper, which you then place in the notch along the back of the bar, carefully positioning it such that it sticks up and can be spotted by one of the servers, who will confirm your order with a flashlight. (The waitstaff is incredibly good-natured given their arduous task.)

As for the food, it's just okay, but would you expect eye-rolling creations? You can barely see the plate, and, anyway, you're busy watching the little green men. Alamo's menu items are a little more earthbound. Pizzas have a nice, tangy sauce but humdrum toppings and an overdone crust. Fries are crunchy but can come cold. Stay away from queso (strange, to put it charitably), avoid the mealy portobello sandwich, and opt instead for the chicken pesto, which is herby and moist. Beers on tap are lively and broad-ranging, and, of course, there's Amy's ice cream for dessert.

Some events pair more elaborate menus with films, such as a recent screening of all three Lord of the Rings movies with meals at all seven Hobbit eating times (elevenses: pan-seared sausage and tomatoes with cheeses, cabbage, and pickles; dinner: stewed coney with taters, carrot, and leek, with crusty bread). Now *that's* eatertainment. –RM

Alborz

Decent Persian cuisine with a bit of
ambition and an eclectic bent

food
7.2 **8.0**
10   10
experience

Middle Eastern   **$28**   *North Central*

Casual restaurant
Sun.-Thurs. 11:30am-9:30pm;
Fri.-Sat. 11:30am-10pm.
Vegetarian-friendly. Wireless Internet.

3300 W. Anderson Ln.
Austin
(512) 420-2222

Bar Beer/wine
Credit Cards Visa, MC, AmEx
Reservations Accepted

Located off Anderson Lane in an area filled with eateries, Alborz is a
welcome addition, helping to fill the gap in Middle Eastern restaurants
in this neighborhood. Alborz takes a stab at the upscale, with white
tablecloths, mirrors and windows swathed in wine-colored drapery, lots
of (fake) plants, twinkling lights, Persian music playing, and belly
dancing on Friday and Saturday nights. But Iranian travel posters and a
few knick-knacks bring it solidly back into the realm of the
neighborhood ethnic restaurant.

Dollar-wise, the à-la-carte menu strays dangerously into the high
teens, but the lunch buffet is more reasonable at around $9, with a
varied selection including several clearly marked vegetarian dishes.
Alborz has a way with details: tabbouleh is heavy on the parsley but
has tiny currants that give it a nice sweetness; the sour cherry rice is a
lovely dark pink and yellow and has a faint tart and sweet flavor that
compliments the mouthwatering, garlicky ground beef shish kebabs.
The rich, almost black gormeh sabzi is a stew of beef and black kidney
beans that lend it its dark color. An eggplant stew is weaker, soft and
watery, but the potatoes with cherry tomatoes have a lovely brightness,
and the sesame chicken has delicious crisp skin and aromatic lemon,
turmeric, and clove flavors. The buffet also sports a lively array of
salads, with such fresh ingredients as lentils and mint.

For dessert, there's thick rice pudding colored with saffron and
doused with way too much rose water. It has undertones of cardamom
and saffron, but is too soapy to finish. Regardless, we're glad that
Alborz has jumped into the Middle Eastern restaurant fray—a bit of
friendly competition never hurt anyone. –MPN

Amy's Ice Cream

Austin dessert classic, now and
forever—we have a crush on Amy

9.4
10
experience

Sweets

Clarksville, West Campus, South Congress

Counter service
Sun.-Thurs. 11:30am-midnight;
Fri.-Sat. 11:30am-1am.
*Date-friendly. Kid-friendly. Live
music. Outdoor dining. Vegetarian-friendly. Wireless Internet.*

1012 W. 6th St.
Austin
(512) 480-0673
www.amysicecreams.com

Bar None
Credit Cards Visa and MC
Reservations Not accepted

3500 Guadalupe St.
78705, (512) 458-6895

1301 S. Congress Ave.
78704, (512) 440-7488

For more than 20 years, Amy's Ice Cream has been Austin's favorite
place to get dessert. Having started out with a shop on Guadalupe,
Amy's now has stores all over Austin and even San Antonio and
Houston. It's a wonderful place to end a first date or take the kids, with
a fun, funky atmosphere featuring neon signs, a cow motif, and local
art for sale. One of Amy's main attractions is the friendly "scoopers"
with their eclectic headgear and behind-the-counter antics.

But let's get down to business. Amy's is the *sui generis* of ice cream.
At 14.9% butterfat, it's rich and creamy, and the flavors change often.
Then there are the "crush-ins"—candy, fruit, excellent cookie dough,
and dozens of other treats that are ruthlessly whacked and beaten into
submission—and into your ice cream—in a spectacular scoop-flipping
display that rivals the knife-throwing chefs at those Japanese teppan-
yaki steakhouses. The technique was invented in Massachusetts in the
1970s by Steve Herrell, of Steve's and Herrell's fame, but Amy's takes it
to the next level.

The subtly flavored "Just Vanilla" is always on the menu, as is the
sweeter, almost cinnamony "Mexican Vanilla," which can be cloying for
some tastes. Sweet cream is ideal for those that enjoy simplicity—it
places the focus on Amy's creamy base. Watermelon is as close to the
real thing as it gets—it actually tastes like watermelon, not like artificial
candy. We also love oatmeal raisin, with dense, chewy chunks of
cookies that taste freshly baked. A real surprise is the Shiner ice cream,
made with local Shiner Bock beer. It looks like vanilla but has a sweet,
delicate, fermented flavor that grows on you with each lick.

As fabulous as the ice cream is, here's the downside: this is not DQ,
and it ain't cheap. Also, Amy's is very popular and therefore often
crowded. But once you've spooned some, you'll forget the suffering.
–MPN

Andiamo

A pan-Italian restaurant with friendly
food and warm feelings

food
7.7 **7.6**
10 10
experience

Italian $**50**   *Far North*

Upmarket restaurant   2521 Rutland Dr.   *Bar* Beer/wine
Mon.-Fri. 11am-2pm, 5pm-   Austin   *Credit Cards* Visa and MC
9:30pm; Sat. 5pm-9:30pm;   (512) 719-3377   *Reservations* Recommended
closed Sun.   www.andiamorestaurant.com

Andiamo is a 2004 arrival that dubs itself "Northern Italian." Perhaps it
is one of the best amongst Austin's less-than-stellar Italian-restaurant
lineup. Perhaps it is a surprising touch of elegance along an unlikely
stretch of strip mall. And perhaps it is a satisfying way to spend an
evening in the hands of a warm, thoughtful, doting staff.

But whatever it is, Andiamo is not Northern Italian. The only
preparations on Andiamo's entire menu that seem distinctly connected
to Italy's North are one dish of gnocchi with fontina and a couple
appearances of polenta. Otherwise, the menu is composed of a few
typical pan-Italian dishes, such as seafood linguine and mixed fried
seafood, along with dozens of dishes that aren't even remotely Italian,
like grilled scallops with pesto. Given that "Vitello alla Sorrentina" (a
veal cutlet with prosciutto, eggplant, cheese, and tomato) is named
after Sorrento, a city in Italy's deep south, you might assume it to
actually be a *southern* Italian dish—if not for the fact that, like veal
parmigiana, veal sorrentina is an invention as American-born as the
double-skinny pumpkin-spice latte.

So if you come to Andiamo expecting Italian-American cuisine, not
Northern Italian, then you probably won't be too disappointed with the
kitchen, which is generally competent at what it does. Best are the
hand-formed filled pastas, like a sensational plate of ravioli with a
savory stuffing of mushrooms and delicate, homemade pasta dough.
But skip the tower of mozzarella with tomato and basil, whose tomato
doesn't contribute enough sweetness; and avoid the underwhelming,
mismatched fish mains, like tilapia mare chiara (with mussels and clams
in a tomato sauce).

And, above all, don't be fooled by the local media into thinking that
Andiamo is something truly special just because it's better than
Romeo's, Vinny's, or the Tree House. Austin has great Mexican food,
great Southern food, great barbecue, and even some great Asian
food—but with Italian, for the most part, we're still oceans away. –RG

Angie's Mexican

Mexican restaurants might get better
than this—but maybe not much cuter

food

6.6 | 8.0
10 | 10

experience

Mexican $**20**   *East Austin*

Casual restaurant   900 E. 7th St.   *Bar* Beer/wine
Sun.-Mon. and Wed.-Sat. 7:30am- Austin   *Credit Cards* Visa and MC
4pm; Fri. 7:30am-9pm; closed   (512) 476-5413   *Reservations* Not accepted
Tues. *Breakfast. Outdoor dining.*

It's easy to miss the driveway that leads up to this adorable, airy little
house atop a little knoll just east of IH-35, before you hit the main strip
of East Austin Mexican joints. The hallmarks of Angie's are uniformly
competent preparations—even if the menu doesn't do anything to
surprise you—and an irresistibly homey feel. There's a hodge-podge of
furniture, and windows, from some angles, overlook downtown from
afar. This combination has translated into extreme popularity, and on
weekend afternoons you can expect a wait.

The menu is cleanly divided between Tex-Mex (cheesy enchilada
plates and so on) and Mex-Mex (authentic taco fillings, meats that
rotate by the day, and hearty stews). We are suckers for barbacoa
(made from slow-cooked cow's head), and Angie's gamey version is no
exception, although a few chunks here and there, at our last visit, were
a bit dry. But you need not eat the head to get your kicks; simple
enchiladas, chicken or cheese, are also fairly well executed, if far from
the best in town.

Particularly strong here are the tortillas: corn tortillas are homemade,
and flour tortillas—when filled—are crisped on the griddle before being
served, which releases extra tortilla flavor. Migas are decent, with
enough cheese—which is far from a given in these parts—although the
eggs seem more like omelettes than scrambled. Chile con queso is
thinner than most, but its taste is ideal, with exactly the balance of chile
and onion that we look for. Angie's salsa is brighter than expected; if
you like your salsa *really* spicy, you can't do much better than this. The
only real weakness in the basic Mexican repertoire here is the refried
beans, which don't have enough seasoning, pork-fat flavor, or anything
else to add oomph. But such deficiencies are the exception, not the
rule. –RG

Aquarelle

Sophisticated French food that's right
on the money—and we mean *money*

food

9.0 / 10

8.6 / 10

experience

French

$91

Warehouse District

Upmarket restaurant
Tues.-Thurs. 6pm-8:45pm; Fri.-Sat.
6pm-9:45pm; closed Sun.-Mon.
Date-friendly. Vegetarian-friendly.

606 Rio Grande St.
Austin
(512) 479-8117
www.aquarellerestaurant.com

Bar Beer/wine
Credit Cards Visa, MC, AmEx
Reservations Essential

Aquarelle is a *serious* restaurant. We mean that in every sense of the word: chef-owners Teresa Forman and Robert Brady are serious about the food (dinner only, including multiple prix-fixe options), serious about the wine (more than 100 reasonably priced bottles, including 25 by the glass), and serious about the service (there are only occasional slip-ups). Although Aquarelle's old house feels almost cozy, with warm, yellow walls, this is not an informal place. There is black truffle, and there is foie gras imported from France. You must be psychologically prepared for what you're getting into, in terms of time (hours upon hours), money (set aside more than $100 a head, including wine), pomp, circumstance, and a certain amount of foof.

The menu rotates frequently, but at our last visit, an appetizer of soft-shell crabs with Meyer lemon beurre blanc, crispy onions, and caper berries, was worth every penny of its $14 price tag. The crabs were sensational, plump and meaty, fried carefully and judiciously. We like to order escargot in puff pastry to challenge a restaurant's kitchen, as it is a dish that can easily go horribly wrong. Not in these masterful hands: Aquarelle's Vol-au-Vent was deeply forgiving, with its pastry magically light and its snails exceptionally tender.

Unless you're in Philadelphia, the combination of steak and cheese can be difficult to pull off, but here, a pan-seared beef tenderloin took unusually well to its Forme d'Ambert blue cheese, and a port-wine reduction did not overwhelm the dish in spite of the meat's subtle flavor. Veal sweetbreads were gently fried and lovingly doused with truffle oil, although their accompanying arugula lacked seasoning. Desserts have generally been close to flawless.

Is this the best restaurant in Austin? Probably not, but it might be the most technically proficient. Comparing Aquarelle against the city's new fusion superstars is difficult—and, ultimately, perhaps pointless. There is a time and a place for haute French cuisine, and when that time comes, this is the place. –RG

Ararat

Concentrate on the warm romance, not
on the food or the prices

food
5.8
10

9.0
10

experience

Middle Eastern $**22**   *North Central*

Casual restaurant
Mon.-Fri. 11am-2pm, 5pm-11pm;
Sat.-Sun. 5pm-11pm. *Date-friendly.*
Live music. Vegetarian-friendly.

111 E. North Loop Blvd.
Austin
(512) 419-1692
www.araratrestaurant.net

Bar BYO
Credit Cards Visa, MC, AmEx
Reservations Recommended

Ararat is cozy and intimate, with just a few tables snuggled into a room lined in lovely kilims and knotted rugs. It has the pleasantly padded and patterned feel of a Persian rug salesroom, minus the haggling (and plus a few candles). Service is warm and attentive. The restaurant has accomplished the difficult task of making individual guests feel important—for this reason, Ararat is a terrific place for a date or special occasion.

But while the room has the look of Ali Baba's cave, the food lacks authenticity. Take, for example, the appetizers. Baba ganoush is rather sour and lacks any smoky eggplant richness. Tabbouleh has neither lemony zing nor herby green notes, though the Ararat version with dried fruit and nuts—while making it taste rather like gorp—adds interest. Most disappointing is the hummus, a basic test of any Middle Eastern restaurant. Ararat's has turmeric, which adds little flavor, but gives the dip the disconcerting appearance of French's mustard (it also shares its too-smooth texture).

Unsteady execution extends to the mains. A beef stew is tomatoey and uneventful; salmon is moist, but its accompanying rosemary tahini is bland and insufficient; the stuffed peppers are undercooked, so that the peppers themselves are still crunchy, with no softened sweetness, and their rice filling is too minty—it tastes of toothpaste. Only the roast lamb makes a better impression: it is tender and pink, with traditional but satisfying garlic and rosemary flavors. And presentations are bright and pretty.

In the end, Ararat is a destination that shines more in its atmosphere than its food. We suggest you go with that in mind: pick an occasion, dress up, BYOB, or choose one of their fancy fizzy pomegranate drinks, which are quite nice. Bat your eyes at your date, order dessert, and you won't be disappointed. –RM

Arirang Sushi

Feeling the fresh, happy tension
between Japanese and Korean

food

7.6 / 10   **6.4** / 10

experience

Japanese   **$23**   *Sixth Street District*

Casual restaurant   616 E. 6th St.   *Bar* Beer/wine
Mon.-Thurs. 11am-10pm; Fri. Sat.   Austin   *Credit Cards* Visa, MC, AmEx
11am-2am; closed Sun.   (512) 480-2211   *Reservations* Accepted

Despite the banner proclaiming its Grand Opening (just barely removed by the time we went to press) and the colorful Mexican tiles to the right of the entrance that still read "Bienvenidos a Esta Casa," Arirang Sushi has actually been settled comfortably in this location for a couple of years now, quietly serving up quality Japanese and Korean fare at affordable prices. The place is small and plain, pleasantly decorated with some Japanese lanterns and screens, and offers a nice respite from both the daytime and late-night heat of Sixth Street.

We recommend a lunchtime visit for one of their specials, many of which are accompanied by little perks, such as a bowl of wonderful miso soup (soft as clouds and just salty enough), gyoza, or vegetable sides. Dispense with any fear that you might harbor of ordering sushi at a Korean-Japanese joint: while Arirang's sushi lunch is hardly a steal by Austin standards, the price includes six varieties of well-executed nigiri (sushi pieces lightly pressed onto a pad of rice—gently yielding, beautifully striped salmon and crisp, salty eel were strong points at our last visit) and eight pieces of California roll, assembled at the bar, as well as a salad and a bowl of that delightful miso soup. For such a quantity of top-notch seafood, $10.95 is not bad.

Cheaper options on the Korean side of things include the bi bim bap, a tasty combination of egg (yolks pleasantly runny), rice, veggies, and agreeably lean marinated meat, although perhaps the "diet food" label on the menu serves as a warning that the serving of beef is a little stingy. The accompanying "Arirang Hot Sauce" lacks vigor. Bento boxes and a variety of noodle dishes round out the menu. All in all, it's a solid option for the downtown lunch crowd, with fresh, subtle ingredients.
–RM

[Editor's note: just before press time, Arirang had renamed itself Geisha and was preparing to phase out most Korean menu items.]

Arturo's

Funky American fusion with good
weather underground, but pale food

food
5.8 **7.9**
10   10
experience

American $**12**   *Capitol Area*

Counter service   314 W. 17th St.   *Bar* None
Mon.-Tues. 7am-2:30pm; Wed.-Fri. Austin   *Credit Cards* Visa, MC, AmEx
7am-10pm; Sat. 9am-1pm, 5pm- (512) 469-0380   *Reservations* Accepted
10pm; closed Sun. *Breakfast. Brunch. Live music. Outdoor dining. Wireless Internet.*

It is decidedly pleasant to escape the summer heat and head underground to Arturo's Underground Café. It has the (literally and figuratively) shady feel of an urban beatnik dive, with murals in deep, dark colors that look like Maurice Sendak might have penned them in a darker moment. All that's missing, in fact, is cigarette smoke—and that would be (gasp) illegal.

Arturo's serves mainly ambitious sandwiches with an ethnic bent, as well as Mexican-influenced breakfast fare. All would be fine and dandy, were it not that Arturo's suffers from the same malaise as so many small Austin restaurants with a funky vibe and fusion on their menus (Magnolia, the Omelettry, Bouldin Creek Café, Mr. Natural…sadly, the list goes on and on): cuisines that have so much life and heat cool down when they hit the neutralizing reagents of the American table. As such, quesadillas, though they come in bold variety, taste mainly of grilled cheese, and sandwiches don't quite live up to their exciting monikers. The "Amalfi" sandwich, thickly slathered with an olive-caper spread, is oddly sweet, and rather off-putting. Adobo chicken, which comes in both a quesadilla and a sandwich, is very mild. On the more traditional side, Arturo's "secret recipe" chicken salad is runny, and, despite the perky crunch of pickles, dull.

We recommend you go for breakfast—a meal that demands less kick. There are decent traditional American brunch items, such as pancakes and French toast, as well as some very good breakfast tacos (we like the spinach version, which is fresh).

Service is fast, funky, and friendly, and the crowd offers an unusual mix of grungy slackers and polished politicos from the nearby capital. On a scorching day at the end of summer, it is hard to ignore the draw of the dark. Who knows—you may even find your very own Deep Throat lurking in a shady corner. –RM

Artz Rib House

Ribs, burgers, beer, and bluegrass—this
place makes you proud of America

food

7.7 8.2
10   10

experience

Barbecue $**22**   *South Lamar*

Casual restaurant   2330 S. Lamar Blvd.   *Bar* Beer/wine
Mon.-Sat. 11am-10pm;   Austin   *Credit Cards* Visa, MC, AmEx
Sun. noon-9pm. *Kid-friendly.* (512) 442-8283   *Reservations* Not accepted
Live music. Outdoor dining.   www.artzribhouse.com

Ask an Austinite where to get the best ribs in town, and there's a good
chance the answer will be Artz Rib House. A frequent, and well-
deserved, winner in local rib contests, Artz is also known for its
scrumptious burgers; for its very South Austin atmosphere, slightly run
down but pleasantly laid back; and for its live music. In a sense, the
place also has the feel of the American South, with checkered
tablecloths, sweet and sultry service, and an eternally more-relaxed-
than-you feel.

Artz is mainly a barbecue joint, but besides barbecue plates and by-
the-pound meats, they also offer sandwiches, soup, and several
desserts. The sweet potato and pecan pie is very good except when the
pecans are stale, and we like the dense, sweet bread pudding as well.
There are some other attempts to distract you from the ribs—tortilla
soup, for instance, is spicy but uninspired, sprinkled with shredded
cheddar and soon-soggy corn chips—but don't be fooled. Order the
delicious baby back ribs, with their gently smoked flavor and distinct
smoke ring; the ribs are meaty and juicy, edged with lovely, charred fat.
Go whole hog with a mixed barbecue plate, served with three meats.
As the brisket can be underseasoned, we recommend you stick with
those ribs (they'll stick to you) and some of Artz's smoked sausage,
which has a fine texture and peppery taste, and is finished on the grill.
The moist, smoked chicken leg makes a nice third—it actually tastes like
chicken and not just like smoke. All barbecue plates are served with
creamy mashed potato salad, tart and attractive cole slaw, and pinto
beans that are spicy and cooked just right, as well as the requisite
onion and pickles.

As for the barbecue sauce, it's slightly sweeter and thicker than
traditional Hill Country barbecue sauce, but still with enough tomato
and vinegar to fit the bill. Perhaps as a nod to Austin's general health
consciousness, they serve wheat bread rather than the usual white. It's
kind of like drinking a Diet Coke with your mammoth plate of fatty
meat. –MPN

Asti

A good-looking Italian far more
authentic than most competitors

food
8.7
10
7.5
10
experience

Italian, Pizza   **$ 37**   *Hyde Park*

Upmarket restaurant   408C E. 43rd St.   ***Bar*** Beer/wine
Mon.-Thurs. 11am-10pm; Fri.   Austin   ***Credit Cards*** Visa, MC, AmEx
11am-11pm; Sat. 5pm-11pm;   (512) 451-1218   ***Reservations*** Recommended
closed Sun.   www.astiaustin.com

Asti, a relatively new arrival in Hyde Park, and sister restaurant of Fino
further south, has quickly gained a large and loyal following. The
modern restaurant appeals on a deep level to Austinites who don't
have much in the way of authentic Italian (as opposed to red-sauce
Italian-American) to choose from. With prices that aren't exactly cheap
but aren't through the roof, either, Asti serves the more complex dishes
that characterize Italian food outside these shores, and executes well on
many of them, even if a few don't have the delicacy that can make the
cuisine such a delight.

In general, the kitchen is careful and well-educated. Salt and other
spices are used with wild abandon—sometimes too wild—but some
dishes are grandly triumphant. A lamb shank that is braised osso-buco
style is lovely, its meat dark, rich, and slipping off the bone, even if the
effect is lessened by saffron risotto that drowns in too much spice and
heat. The problem is reversed with the smoked pork tenderloin: simple,
creamy risotto with sweet peas and crispy, flash-fried onions can't stand
up to the powerfully salty meat. Rigatoni all'amatriciana, the classically
balanced Roman dish of pasta with tomato sauce, pancetta, and
onions, is a success, although the sauce is relatively chunky rather than
being judiciously mixed and integrated. We love the deliciously thin,
authentic pizzas (particularly a white truffle variety), and a simple, dense
panna cotta with candied hazelnuts for dessert is wonderful when it's
on the menu (it wasn't at press time).

The tone of the place is airy, restrained, and very appealing. Trendy
people sit at the mod tables looking beautiful; the room sparkles in red
and silver and lights. It might be described as '50s diner meets modern
Italian chic. For the ultra-chill, there is even counter seating with a view
of the frenetic kitchen. But be warned—the general cool becomes
decidedly frigid in the air-conditioned summertime, so bring a sweater.

Service is also charming (it's nice to be greeted by the owner, rather
than a black-clad teenager—not that there's anything wrong with
black-clad teenagers). And keep your eyes out for beautiful Italian-
accented waiters. –RM

Austin Diner

It's just a diner—but maybe we should
stop and appreciate that fact

food

6.1
10
6.5
10
experience

American   **$12**   *Burnet*

Casual restaurant
Mon.-Sat. 6:30am-2:30pm,
5:30pm-10pm; Sun. 6:30am-
2:30pm. *Breakfast. Kid-friendly. Live music.*

5408 Burnet Rd.
Austin
(512) 467-9552

Bar None
Credit Cards Visa, MC, AmEx
Reservations Not accepted

Diner is a fun word. It conjures up a lot of images—barstools, funky
uniforms with little hats, the smell of hash browns frying, and "Alice."
There just aren't many places in Austin that really fit the description,
but the Austin Diner is one, and it's aptly named, with a blue-and-green
frog-themed décor that reminds us of what your estranged
grandmother's house might have looked like in the early '60s.
Everything feels a little grimy, but still homey. A welcoming mural near
the front door depicts Bevo and several armadillo buddies preparing to
chow down on a massive breakfast of pancakes. Service at the Austin
Diner is friendly but slow, and you get the feeling that there's no way
you could rush through a meal here. It's almost like eating in another
era, when we were allotted more than 30 minutes for lunch.

The menu strikes a balance between Tex-Mex and standard American
fare. For breakfast, we like the three-egg omelette served with two
sides, like hash browns, bacon, or toast. The omelettes are firm but not
overcooked, and filled with your choice of cheese and veggies—they're
quite hefty, and the price is right. Lunch specials include soups of the
day and comfort food like turkey meatloaf.

But this is Austin, and so in marches the Tex-Mex. Tortilla soup is mild
and cheeseless, but heavily garnished with chips, sour cream, and
guacamole. Other Tex-Mex offerings include a chile relleno in a spicy
gravy with lots of cheese. Cheeseburgers are huge and come in a
handy paper wrapper that will help you keep it all together; they're
garnished with delicious pickles that are extra dilly. We love the onion
rings—they're golden, crunchy, and come with just the right amount of
grease, if you're willing to wait a little. After all, this place has been
waiting for you, frozen in time, since the '50s. –MPN

Austin Java Company

A pleasant but thrill-less coffeeshop
expression of the new Austin

food
6.5 / 10 **8.0** / 10
experience

American

$**12** *Clarksville, Zilker, Far Northwest*

Café
Mon.-Thurs. 7am-11pm;
Fri. 7am-midnight; Sat.
8am-midnight; Sun. 8am-11pm.
Breakfast. Brunch. Live music. Outdoor dining. Wireless Internet.

1206 Parkway
Austin
(512) 476-1829
www.austinjava.com

Bar Beer/wine
Credit Cards Visa, MC, AmEx
Reservations Not accepted

1608 Barton Springs Rd.
78704, (512) 482-9450

12221 Riata Trace Pkwy.
78727, (512) 249-1508

The Austin Java Company, perhaps as much as the storied Whole Foods itself, represents the city's rapid transformation over the past decade into a tech-boom-inspired yuppieville. A product of the fat years in the mid 1990s, it was one of the first spaces in town to go wireless, and its breed of organic coffees and lightly ethnic American food is designed to appeal to Austin's growing imported population of Promising Young People.

On the surface, this is an appealing proposition. Austin Java's menu has more interesting flavors than many of its counterparts, and if the prices are a touch higher than elsewhere, you get some attractive frills for that extra dough. We like, for example, the "Black and Blue Burger," with cracked pepper and gorgonzola. It does not come as rare as ordered, but the meat has a nice steaky flavor, and the blue cheese isn't overpowering, pairing nicely with peppery mixed greens. Another unusual perk is the "African Peanut Soup," described as "soon to be award winning"—it's a pleasing mixture of the new and the comfortably familiar. The soup tastes like a spicy combination of Campbell's tomato mixed with crunchy Jif peanut butter, but we mean that in the best possible sense—the concoction embodies interesting-cozy, which is also the successful theme of the décor.

But take this happy compromise a step too far, and you've got the problem faced by so many casual yuppie restaurants—they lose their flavor and cater instead to the New Austinite: the other white meat. Thus Tex-Mex and Cajun menu items are on the bland side. Eggs "benedict" (sans meat) over spinach and artichoke have a tasteless hollandaise, though the eggs are nice and runny. We say, if you're doing white-bread, stick with white bread—we love Austin Java's pancakes, which are cooked until the outside is almost crisp, and come with sweet cinnamon butter and syrup. –RM

Austin Land and Cattle

Write it on your arm in permanent marker: steak

food
8.1 / 10
7.4 / 10
experience

Steakhouse

$**60**

House Park Area

Upmarket restaurant
Sun.-Thurs. 5:30pm-10pm;
Fri.-Sat. 5:30pm-11pm.
Date-friendly.

1205 N. Lamar Blvd.
Austin
(512) 472-1813
www.austinlandandcattlecompany.com

Bar Full
Credit Cards Visa, MC, AmEx
Reservations Accepted

The important thing to remember about Austin Land and Cattle is that it is a steakhouse. (Operative word here: steak.) Unfortunately, since the recently revamping of their menu, there is less emphasis on steak. Why are restaurants so often deceived, perhaps through overzealous perusal of restaurant-industry trade journals, into straying from their core competencies? Do they really think that someone with an irresistible urge for seared tuna is going to drive over to a place called Austin Land and Cattle?

The room goes for a half-assed attempt at a cowboy theme—still, it's warm and dim, with a less clubby feel than the other steakhouses in town, and there is a certain informality even amidst the high prices and great wine list. When in doubt about ordering, apply the cardinal rule and ask yourself a simple question: Is it steak? If the answer is "no," you're probably choosing the wrong thing.

Most appetizers should be avoided, as they break with the cardinal rule, having nothing to do with steak. "Oysters Tex'efeller" is a preparation that drowns the poor bivalves with cilantro, garlic, and lime. Buffalo-wing-style lamb chops are a total waste of good lamb. An ahi tuna appetizer is seared and happily rare, but lacks pizzazz. Salads are better—the warm spinach with portobello mushrooms and red onions has a wonderful, rich bacon flavor. And we do recommend the spicy, creamy sweet potato clam chowder.

Main courses span species, but don't forget that this is where you really need to focus. Say it with us: "steak." There are several cuts to choose from, and there's a fun primer explaining cooking temperatures like "black and blue" and side sauces like béarnaise, ALC steak sauce, and a wonderful jalapeño blue cheese. Cuts are tender and flavorful, and french fries are solid. But get distracted, and you could end up with dry pork chops in a painfully spicy honey-garlic sauce, or (wince) chicken. Service is helpful and friendly, but don't let them talk you into anything rash. Just remember you're here for the steak. Have we made ourselves clear? –MPN

Austin Pizza Garden

The best pizzeria in Oak Hill—not that
the field is particularly strong

food

4.4 **6.5**

10   10

experience

Pizza

$17   *Oak Hill*

Casual restaurant
Sun.-Thurs. 11am-10pm;
Fri.-Sat. 11am-11pm. *Delivery.*
Kid-friendly. Vegetarian-friendly.

6266 W. Hwy. 290
Austin
(512) 891-9980

Bar Beer/wine
Credit Cards Visa, MC, AmEx
Reservations Accepted

The Austin Pizza Garden in Oak Hill occupies the historic Old Rock
Store, a two-story limestone square built in 1898 now festooned with
green awnings and a bright neon "PIZZA" sign. Open since 1994, this
place may not be serving the best pizza in Austin, but it certainly serves
the best in Oak Hill, the only competition being the Gattiland and
Double Dave's down the road at the Y. The building itself is interesting,
with wood and stone floors, vaulted ceilings, an enormous fireplace,
and a small upstairs dining area. Spartan furnishings are offset by quite
an eclectic collection of art on the walls, from the usual Texas pastoral
scenes, to embroidered Indian elephants decked out in their festival
finest.

Pizza, in a myriad of odd varieties, dominates the menu, which also
includes calzones, salads, sandwiches, and pasta dishes. Austin Pizza
Garden's "signature" crust is described as thin and crispy, but we find it
cracker-like, and too brittle around the edges (there is a thicker crust
available). Toppings are fresh and plentiful, and there are over 20 pizzas
on offer including a quattro formaggi that seems to contain a
supermarket-sized wheel's worth of cheese, but gets a surprising flavor
boost from bacon and mushrooms.

There are also Cajun-inspired and vegan pizzas as well as an
encyclopedic list of toppings with which you can create your own pizza
including avocado, scrambled eggs, crab, almonds, and sour cream—
though we'll just stick to pepperoni, thank you. The sandwich menu
also has some unusual choices, alongside more traditional ones, but the
execution can be rather inelegant. The muffaletta, for example, is a
meaty salt lick—the combination of salts from the cold cuts, olive relish,
and mustard are enough to make your tongue prickle uncomfortably.
–MPN

Austin's Pizza

A ubiquitous in-town chain that's been
giving corporate pizza hell since 1999

food
6.7 /10   4.5 /10
experience

Pizza $ 9   *Capitol, W. Campus, S. Lamar*

Counter service   800 W. 12th St.   *Bar* None
Sun.-Thurs. 10am-11pm;   Austin   *Credit Cards* Visa, MC, AmEx
Fri.-Sat. 10am-midnight.   (512) 795-8888   *Reservations* Not accepted
Delivery. Vegetarian-friendly.   www.austinspizza.com

                                   2324 Guadalupe St.   1817 S. Lamar Blvd.
                                   78705, (512) 795-8888   78704, (512) 795-8888

Since opening in 1999, Austin's Pizza has been giving the big-name
pizza chains in town some much-needed competition. There are over a
dozen locations around Austin offering a variety of pizzas and a couple
of salads, as well as hot wings and cheese sticks. It's primarily a pick-up
and delivery operation; the restaurants themselves are very small and
not really designed for diners. Depending on the location, there are
usually a few booths or tables, and it's usually kept clean, but there's no
décor whatsoever, and no table service. Needless to say, there's no
lunch buffet, either. If you eat in, you'll receive your pizza in a box, as if
you were taking it to go, and then you can have fun with the plastic-
ware, paper plates, and paper towels on the tables.

The two available salads are the Greek and Zilker (the name is
typically, jubilantly local). The veggies are usually pretty fresh, though
the salads are pre-made and boxed. The Zilker has broccoli, carrots,
mushrooms, and more; the Greek comes with peppers, feta, olives, and
a tart dressing.

The pizza has a thin crust with a crisp bottom, the tomato sauce is
well seasoned, and for better or for worse (depending on your
outlook), they don't skimp on the cheese. There are plenty of toppings
to choose from, including gourmet ones like goat cheese, grilled garlic
chicken, portobello mushrooms, prosciutto, and artichoke hearts, and
also several different sauces such as pesto, alfredo, barbecue, and Thai.
Austin's Pizza also has a menu of signature pizzas, many with amusing
names like "The MoPac" ("bumper-to-bumper" pepperoni, Canadian
bacon, sausage, and veggies), the vegan Say Soy (with pesto, lots of
veggies and soy cheese), and the "Pesto A Go-Goat" (use your
imagination). All in all, though it's a little more expensive, Austin's Pizza
beats the snot out of all those national chains. –MPN

Avenue B Grocery

food

experience

The sandwich shop of generations past,
still in the heart of historic Hyde Park

Light American $ 9   *Hyde Park*

Counter service   4403 Ave. B   ***Bar*** Beer/wine
Mon.-Sat. 8am-6pm; closed Sun.   Austin   ***Credit Cards*** Visa, MC, AmEx
Breakfast. Outdoor dining.   (512) 453-3921   ***Reservations*** Not accepted

Austin is a young town, much of it built well within the memories of its youthful inhabitants. One notable exception to this is Hyde Park, the grand old neighborhood of craftsman bungalows and gingerbread Victorians north of the University. Hyde Park's grid formation seemed that of a much larger town than Austin was a century ago—as if in anticipation of the greater years to come. Walking its leafy streets, you get a sense not of the cattle town Austin once was, but rather of the old city it was. And confirming this long-time urbanism, tucked between the lovely homes, you'll find the Avenue B Grocery, quietly approaching its own centennial.

This worn little grocery has passed through many sets of capable hands, miraculously maintaining its purpose throughout. The current owner, Ross Mason, has run the place for the last 20 years, dishing out sandwiches and sarcasm in a friendly whir of conversation. Ingredients are fresh, and the sandwiches are lovingly constructed. There is little that is new or special about them, but they are thoughtfully and generously executed. The "Queen B" is particularly good—three kinds of cheese, ripe avocado, pickled jalapeños, mushrooms, lettuce, tomatoes, and thinly sliced onions, with mustard and mayo. The jalapeños transform this otherwise ordinary sandwich. The grocery also sells an excellent BLT, plus fresh-baked pies and brownies from the Texas Pie Company in Kyle.

But perhaps what is nicest about Avenue B Grocery is the grocery itself. It is one of those stores that, from tiny spaces, manage to serve up everything you could possible want, from toiletries to fresh produce to toy airplanes. In this sense it is truly local—Hyde Parkers have probably been "just popping out to the corner store" here for decades. Lucky them. –RM

Azul

Take your fusion sandwiches outside, please

food
8.0
10

8.9
10

experience

Light American $**11**   *East Austin*

Counter service
Mon.-Fri. 7am-10pm; Sat. 8am-
10pm; closed Sun. *Breakfast.*
Date-friendly. Outdoor dining. Vegetarian-friendly.

1808 E. Cesar Chavez St.
Austin
(512) 457-9104

Bar Full
Credit Cards Visa, MC, AmEx
Reservations Not accepted

Azul is an unassuming sandwich shop with a leafy back patio and a cheerful, decoratively painted interior. Small tables of diverse shapes, with mismatched retro chairs, complete the pleasant picture, and the kitchen counter is lined with an impressive collection of LPs. The owner frequently does the honors at the small counter, and seems to know most of her customers by name.

Azul is open three meals a day, and turns out a highly impressive collection of gourmet sandwiches, plus some perky sides and snacks. They also serve a variety of coffee drinks, with some uncommon flavor options, such as Ovaltine. This congenial mixture of low-brow and high-brow is evident in the food as well, which is executed with a vaguely Italian twist. A PB&J gets the panino treatment here (pressed), and the standard BLT becomes a PLT, made with prosciutto on grilled Italian bread. (Corny, but we kinda wish we had thought of that one.) Standouts include a gourmet tuna melt and an inspired pork tenderloin sandwich, with flavorful, herby pork; chêvre; and sprightly apple slices for crunch. This is accompanied by a superb, mustardy shallot vinaigrette, which graces several menu options.

Breakfast options include homemade waffles with commendable toppings such as prosciutto, poached eggs, and syrup. Dinner offers much the same as lunch, but dresses up the menu with a salmon burger and a ribeye sandwich. Smaller dishes are equally interesting. A green bean salad features nearly raw beans sliced crossways in little rounds, like spring onions, and complemented by toasted almonds—yummy. Each dish is generally well seasoned, fresh, and bright. Prices aren't low for sandwiches, but when every ingredient is given the star treatment and the cost rarely rises above seven bucks, it's hard to complain.

Pretty food in a pretty place—we approve. –RM

Azul Tequila

Quality interior Mexican food in an
unlikely strip-mall setting

food
8.3
10
4.1
10
experience

Mexican $**30**   *South Lamar*

Casual restaurant   4211 S. Lamar Blvd.   *Bar* Full
Sun.-Thurs. 10am-10pm;   Austin   *Credit Cards* Visa, MC, AmEx
Fri.-Sat. 10am-midnight.   (512) 416-9667   *Reservations* Accepted
Live music. Outdoor dining. www.azultequila.com

Azul Tequila is a very pleasant surprise hidden in a rather unpleasant
South Lamar parking lot in the shadow of U.S. Highway 71. It is one of
a small number of Austin restaurants (Garibaldi's, on South Congress, is
another) whose sophisticated interior-Mexican menus will remain
forever hidden behind a featureless, unstylish concrete-and-asphalt
exterior.

The bland, often empty, interior likewise belies the dynamism of the
cooking, but you'll quickly settle in as you munch on the blissfully warm
chips and lively salsa. We recommend you go directly to the part of the
menu labeled "Platos del Interior." Most of these dishes are worth
trying. Spicy enchiladas pipián, in a rich pumpkin-seed sauce, have an
unusually strong and nutty flavor. A Yucatán-style fish prepared on a
banana leaf, topped with a bright achiote sauce, is simple and light.
But our favorite dish here is the chile relleno en crema, filled with
savory shredded pork, almonds, tomatoes, onions, and raisins. It is
milder and mellower than the dish often is, and its creamy sauce has a
soft sweetness, comforting in its restraint. The kitchen's one weakness
seems to lie in all things bean—both the refried and charro versions are
as dreary as the parking lot outside on a rainy day. Generally, dishes
here are gentler versions of those found elsewhere—a trait which
prevents them, on the whole, from breaking new ground, but which,
aided by gracious service, assures a soothing supper.

It is perfectly fair, we think, to hold such restaurants' unfortunate
locations and décor against them—we dine out, after all, in part to *go
out*, to be someplace. But if all you're after is some interesting, low-
maintenance, flavorful cooking, Azul Tequila easily satisfies. A signed
photo by the door attests to the fact that the Dixie Chicks, at least,
know good Mexican when they taste it. –RM

Ba Le Bakery and Deli

A great place, if you can find it, for
sandwiches beyond the placidly familiar

food
6.1 **3.8**
10   10
experience

Vietnamese, Light American   **$ 8**   *Far North*

Counter service   8624 N. Lamar Blvd.   **Bar** None
Daily 8am-8pm.   Austin   **Credit Cards** Visa, MC, AmEx
Breakfast.   (512) 491-9188   **Reservations** Not accepted

This grubby little hole-in-the-wall north of U.S. 183 is part of a rapidly
expanding realm of authentic, inexpensive Asian restaurants and
grocers that cater to the growing immigrant population of North
Austin. Lucky Austin. Cheap, lively, and interesting Asian food (we're
talkin' not your grandma's take-out) is becoming readily available in this
town, especially concentrated along the 183 North corridor. We
recommend a thorough and enthusiastic field trip.

Ba Le will meet some of these expectations—and not others. Though
most of the clientele is Vietnamese, menus are helpfully translated, and
the staff, though a little distracted, is very good-willed. On offer are
fresh, savory sandwiches on newly baked French bread for around two
bucks (two bucks!). The bakery, however, is a little on the manky side
(the interior is a bit of a mess), and the preparation is not always suited
to the uninitiated palate.

Sandwiches are spread with lard in the classic Vietnamese style, and
then filled with some combination of meats and a bright array of
pickled vegetables, jalapeño peppers, and cilantro. The Ba Le Gourmet
Sandwich has a pungent pâté and a fatty pork deli meat, which,
combined with the lard, can be a little challenging, but the sandwich is,
on the whole, a satisfyingly flavorful meal. More familiar options, such
as the chicken sandwich, are equally tasty and less intimidating. Ba Le
also serves some greasy noodle dishes, which, again, are nice and
savory but a little too fatty for our taste. More intriguing is a variety of
oddly colored puddings on sale in a refrigerated case against one wall.
Don't be afraid to experiment. We heartily recommend, for example,
the che dâu, a rice pudding of a rather unsettling shade of green, with
perky sweet corn, stewed in creamy coconut milk. Go on—see what it
does to ya. –RM

Baby Acapulco

A jungle-themed Tex-Mex joint that
caters to Baby Alcoholics

food
2.6 / 10   **5.9** / 10
experience

Mexican

$23

Zilker, N. Central, Far Northwest

Casual restaurant
Mon.-Sat. 11am-midnight;
Sun. 11am-11pm. *Delivery.*
Live music. Outdoor dining.

1628 Barton Springs Rd.
Austin
(512) 474-8774
www.babyacapulco.com

Bar Full
Credit Cards Visa, MC, AmEx
Reservations Not accepted

5610 N. IH-35
78701, (512) 302-1366

9505 Stonelake Blvd.
78759, (512) 795-9000

You can tell a lot about a place by its menu. Baby A's sends off warning
flares faster than an Air Force One escort. Ignore, for a minute, the
menu's blithe claim to "proudly serve only Land-o-Lakes cheeses," and
the fact that cigarettes appear closer to the front of the menu than the
food. Several mistreated Mexican standards flaunt the use of American
cheese, which is like bragging that you bought your pasta sauce at 7-
Eleven. Much of the menu is taken up by a variety of specialty drinks
printed in bright party colors that correspond rather unnervingly to the
colors of the drinks themselves when they emerge. It is presumably this
Technicolored trick that draws the masses of college kids and youthful
cubicle escapees on Friday nights and into the weekend. Chief amongst
them is the disturbingly potent "Purple Margarita." A word of warning:
a happy hour spent at Baby A's is a crime that carries its own
punishment.

The IH-35 location of Baby A's looks like a strip club, with pink neon
lights; better known is the prominent spot on Barton Springs Road's
hallowed Restaurant Row, and its bright and pleasant service lightly
complements the bright and pleasant patio, but the food lives dutifully
up to the uncertain promise of its menu. Much of it is awful. A range
of appetizers, from mouth-clogging cream-cheese-stuffed jalapeños to
deep-fried spinach bites is anything but appetizing; chile con queso is
grossly underseasoned, without any chile kick; brisket tacos are dry and
thoroughly bland; a particularly low note is hit by the popular spinach
enchiladas, whose canned innards are doused in a gloop that will leave
you with gelatinous corn nightmares. We recommend you play it safe
and stay away from dishes that include cheeses or sauces. (We do
recognize that such a task might be a bit challenging.) Baby A's al
pastor is a rather bland example of its kind, with the meat tending
toward fat, but there are nice bits of caramelized pineapple in it, and a
squeeze of lime does it a lot of good. And the tortilla soup here
deserves its good reputation: its healing powers might even combat an
evening spent consuming strange purple beverages. *MOMMY! I'M
SCARED!* –RM

Bangkok Cuisine

A bland exterior conceals a colorful
array of Thai favorites

food **7.7** /10   **6.3** /10
experience

Thai   **$24**   *Far North*

Casual restaurant   9041 Research Blvd.   *Bar* Beer/wine
Mon.-Fri. 10am-3pm, 5pm-   Austin   *Credit Cards* Visa, MC, AmEx
10pm; Sat.-Sun. 5pm-10pm.   (512) 832-9722   *Reservations* Accepted
Vegetarian-friendly. Wireless Internet.

The Bangkok is one of the better Thai restaurants in Austin, its
particular attraction being an impressive and economical lunch buffet
which draws a regular crowd of business folk and other hungry
campers. They come for the yummy food, but have the added perk of
ogling the notable collection of gilded Thai dancing ladies on display,
sadly diminished of late (Why? Why? Bring back those buxom
beauties!). A gracious group of servers is never pushy, never lax, but the
lunch system is fend-for-yourself, which can be a challenge at rush
hour. Just pile it on—there's an astonishing variety, and it's all tasty.

The buffet generally sports at least two soups, with bright
lemongrass flavors, and a range of appetizers such as spring rolls,
tempura-style veggies, and oddly irresistible "Butterflies"—folds of
deep-fried pastry encasing a crab and cream cheese filling. There is an
accompanying range of tangy dipping sauces (combinations of sweet
and sour, peanut, and crunchy cucumber). The rotating selection of
mains always includes a couple of meat and a couple of vegetable
options; there is generally a good tofu alternative, a red curry, and a
yellow curry. Other stars are a basil chicken dish with fragrant hints of
anise, and a sweet, potato-laden massaman curry. There are also a
couple of noodle dishes on offer, including excellent, nutty pad Thai,
some tasty deep-fried fish, a salad bar and a couple of desserts (we
particularly like a salty-sweet black rice pudding, served with frothy
coconut sauce—an acquired taste, perhaps, but strangely pleasing). It
all makes for quite a spread!

The only drawback is the restaurant's location, which is in a faceless
strip mall north of U.S. 183. But by the time you roll out the door, you'll
appreciate the longer recovery period before returning to the old desk
job. –RM

Beck's on Congress

A hip bar to catch some tunes while
crunching something Texas-fried

food
6.6 | 8.3
10 | 10
experience

American $**34**   *South Congress*

Pub
Sun. 9am-10pm; Tues.-Fri. 5pm-
11pm; Sat. 9am-11pm; closed Mon.
*Brunch. Date-friendly. Live music.
Outdoor dining. Wireless Internet.*

1321 S. Congress Ave.
Austin
(512) 445-4441
www.becksoncongress.com

Bar Full
Credit Cards AmEx
Reservations Accepted

Formerly D & L's Texas Music Café, this restaurant was re-christened
when the D of the partnership left the business. Aussie L(eoni Becker)
has changed the name, but little else. It is, we reassure you, the same
place, with the same food, the same pleasant patio, and the same
wonderful Texas music.

The owner may be a foreigner, but the chefs aren't, and cooking
here is down-home Texan. This means migas, meatloaf, catfish, and a
breeze from the gulf carrying oysters and shrimp. The kitchen's main
weakness lies in its over-fondness for the deep fryer. They use it not
only too much, but inexpertly. Many items are fried darker than they
need to be—crunchy rather than crisp. The corn-chip-crusted catfish
po-boy presents a formidable challenge: how to get your mouth around
all those tough sharp edges. Some fried green tomatoes are less
scorched, but the underripe tomatoes haven't cooked well enough to
retrieve any sweet softness. They are helped by a lovely, simple pico,
with cabbage and spinach. In general, however, the kitchen flirts with
excess. Sandwiches are sloppy with too much sauce and goop, and the
"South Austin Burger" (which is only offered at weekend lunch) is all
out of proportion, with bacon and a thick, unmanageable slice of ham
on top of the patty. We love, however, the Magic Mushroom, a
marinated portobello burger with an herbed spread. Meatloaf, too, is
tasty, meatier than most Austin versions, and the fried okra, so often
stringy and tough, is a pile of delightful little bites.

The best reason to come here, however, is the nightly live music out
on an intimate, truly lovely patio shaded by majestic live oak trees,
which sparkle in white lights after dark. Happy-hour drinks at the
Continental Club next door, dinner at Beck's, and Amy's Ice Cream two
doors down for dessert—now that's one kickin' Austin evening. –RM

Bee Cave Bistro

Giving "Hill Country Cooking" a bad
reputation—and a bad attitude

food

experience

American $**37**   Bee Cave

Casual restaurant   11715 FM 2244   *Bar* Full
Tues.-Thurs. 11am-9pm; Fri.-Sat.   Austin   *Credit Cards* Visa and MC
11am-9:30pm; Sun. 10am-2pm;   (512) 263-1950   *Reservations* Not accepted
closed Mon. *Brunch. Outdoor dining.*

Located in an upscale shopping center in a posh and rapidly growing area of Far West Austin, Bee Cave Bistro is a terribly disappointing restaurant that seems to survive only on the strength of its loyal longtime customers. Its pale walls display art for sale, dried vines form loopy designs against the ceiling, and it all adds up to no personality. A sign above the bar proclaims this to be the home of "Hill Country Cooking," but between the sterile environment, droning elevator music, uninspired menu, and lackluster service, the Bee Cave Bistro feels more like your only option at the end of a lonely airport terminal.

Call Bee Cave Bistro only in the case of emergency—the attitude on the phone can be downright misanthropic. When two of our friendly interns called Bee Cave Bistro to collect some simple information about the restaurant, one was hung up on, the other actually *yelled at*. This was unprecedented in the history of our restaurant guide.

Unfortunately, this is not one of those places whose food is good enough to shrug off the rudeness as "quirky character." This menu has little do to with the Hill Country, or even Texas. Mediocre rolls with bland chile and honey compound butter start you off as you peruse the pricey selections. A house salad of lettuce and dried carrot shreds is dressed with an overly sweet balsamic vinaigrette that's for sale by the bottle (we can't imagine who's buying). Caesar salad is average. The daily quiche comes in huge slices, but doesn't have the right density—it's more like a light, flavorless egg pie. The Santa Fe turkey sandwich on a croissant is greasy and smushed thin, with just a smidge of guacamole for Southwestern flair. Burgers are better, cooked to temperature, though disturbingly dense and much too expensive. With this attitude and this food at these prices, the most impressive thing about the Bee Cave Bistro is that they're still in business. –MPN

Bee Caves BBQ

Is barbecue best when served out of a trailer?

food

6.7 10

8.2 10

experience

Barbecue

$ 7

Westlake

Counter service
Mon.-Thurs. 11am-7pm; Fri.
11am-3pm; closed Sat.-Sun.
Kid-friendly. Outdoor dining.

6220½ Bee Caves Rd.
Austin
(512) 306-9040

Bar None
Credit Cards No credit cards
Reservations Not accepted

It is a well-established principle in Texas that true barbecue is at its best in the most humble of surroundings. Bee Caves BBQ, you might say, tests the extreme limits of that principle. And while this barbecue-hawking trailer might not scale the heights of smoked-meat supremacy, it certainly reaffirms the theory. For what could be better than the downmarket glory of the people of the Republic of Texas, smoking meat in the most unlikely of all places? You can't stop barbecue—you can only hope to contain it.

The trailer, complete with smoker and such, is set up along a stretch of the zooming Bee Caves Road, west of downtown, that otherwise conceals little more than set-back gated communities, road signs, and cell-phone towers. Family packs of barbecue by the pound are fairly standard, but here, unlike at many other places, the chopped beef sandwich takes center stage. This is the wet, saucy kind of chopped beef, served in classic form: with pickles and onions, and on a basic burger bun, which absorbs every drop of juice and sauce.

Those that choose to eat in (or, rather, out) stay in the general woodsy vicinity of the trailer, only a couple of paces from the road, and sit on one of the tree stumps. (When was the last time you dined on a tree stump?) Prices could hardly be any cheaper, whether by the pound or by the extremely economical sandwich. It all makes for quite a pleasant stopover if you can't take the rush-hour traffic on Bee Caves—or if you just get hungry. –RG

Bellagio

Good calamari and mediocre veal
amidst suburban statuettes

food
6.7 **7.0**
10   10
experience

Italian   **$52**   *Far Northwest*

Upmarket restaurant
Mon.-Sat. 5:30pm-11pm;
closed Sun. *Outdoor dining.*

6507 Jester Blvd.
Austin
(512) 346-8228
www.bellagioitalianbistro.com

Bar Full
Credit Cards Visa, MC, AmEx
Reservations Accepted

When you enter Bellagio, be prepared to feel like you're not in Austin.
Nor in Italy, for that matter. This restaurant's strip-mall façade could be
part of any suburb in America, and it comes complete with a giant
horse statue out front (quite a photo-op). The outdoor patio is inviting
and warmly lit, but inside, a Venus de Milo-esque sculpture stands out
amongst other pieces of mass-manufactured art on the warm mauve
walls, which are evocative of an expense-account hotel room.

It is as if the restaurant selected every single one of its furnishings
from a catalog of faux objets d' art marketed to the money-without-
taste segment of Italophiles that, upon setting eyes on these plaster
statues of the gods, become immediately nostalgic for that day in Rome
when they demanded meatballs with their spaghetti in loud English
before elbowing their way through a sweaty picture-taking mass to
throw a 50-euro-cent coin into the Trevi Fountain. Fortunately, Bellagio
pipes in Frank Sinatra, crooning his way through a medley, and he saves
the day.

Bellagio's fried calamari have a textbook texture—soft within, and
just crispy enough—and they come with a pleasant, mild red pesto
sauce. Pizza is another good appetizer; a version with spinach,
gorgonzola, mozzarella, and parmesan cheeses is slightly heavy, but not
overwhelming. Chicken saltimbocca isn't bad, but the chicken breast
comes too thick—not pounded enough, if at all—and is overburdened
by caramelized onions, prosciutto, and marsala wine. A veal cutlet with
lobster and shrimp, touted as a signature dish, is an even bigger
letdown—it has arrived so tough as to be logistically challenging, and
it's poorly matched with in-your-face shellfish flavors. Desserts, however,
are consistently good; truffle with layers of moist chocolate and anise-
laced cannoli are strong choices. There is a decent wine list, with staff
that knows it well. But your best bet here is probably happy hour, when
you can sit outside and enjoy complimentary doses of the best fried
squid in town. –AH

Beluga

Spectacular sushi amidst Dellionaires in a Round Rock strip mall

food
8.8 / 10
6.5 / 10
experience

Japanese

$40

Round Rock

Upmarket restaurant
Mon.-Thurs. 11:30am-2pm,
5pm-10pm; Fri. 11:30am-2pm;
Sun. 5pm-10pm; closed Sat.

661 Louis Henna Blvd.
Round Rock
(512) 255-6454
www.belugasushi.net

Bar Full
Credit Cards Visa, MC, AmEx
Reservations Accepted

On an average day or night, Round Rock may only be a realistic restaurant destination for North Austin denizens, but the sushi at Beluga is so good that it might be worth the trip up from anywhere in town. It's a friendly place, popular for lunch, whose bar, perhaps surprisingly, turns into a big Dell after-work hangout; or maybe that fact is not so surprising, given Beluga's talent for good, dim mood lighting. Even if the tiled floors and white ceilings remind you that you are, after all, dining in a strip mall, the effect is offset by wavy lines, purple colors, recessed lighting, hanging lamps, and trance music. The designers of this place clearly understand that if you're working with a strip-mall space, you're not going to make it cozy, so you might as well go for modern. It's a respectable choice.

A jalapeño roll, suggested by the staff as a signature dish, is like a sushi version of a jalapeño popper: the chile is stuffed with cream cheese, yellowtail, and rice, and deep fried in a remarkably delicate manner. The effect is comfortable and satisfying, and the jalapeño roll's ponzu dipping sauce works too, even if the subtle taste of the yellowtail itself is lost amidst all the other flavors.

That last part is only a shame because Beluga's yellowtail, on its own (or atop a finger of rice, as in nigiri), is quite good. Ditto for the tuna, which is fresh and unusually light in color. The only downside to Beluga's sushi pieces is that the slabs of fish are sliced thinner than they are at other joints, increasing the rice-to-fish ratio. On the other hand, the vinegared rice is well nigh perfect, the best in town, so you might not view that as a problem. Best of all, though, is the uni (sea urchin). When available, it is sheer, almost sexual joy, melting across your tongue like the custard of a faraway fantasy. –RG

Ben's Longbranch BBQ

Old-fashioned barbecue in East Austin,
with some tough love on the side

food

6.0 / 10   **5.5** / 10

experience

Barbecue $**17**   *East Austin*

Casual restaurant
Mon.-Thurs. 10:30am-4pm; Fri.
10:30am-6pm; Sat. 10:30am-
8pm; closed Sun. *Outdoor dining.*

900 E. 11th St.
Austin
(512) 477-2516

Bar Beer/wine
Credit Cards Visa, MC, AmEx
Reservations Accepted

At the IH-35 end of a revitalized strip of East 11th Street, a draw to all those who want a half-hour's laziness in the middle of a hard day's work or an escape from the air-conditioned void of the offices just beyond the highway, sits Ben's.

The shabby wooden building is open mainly for lunch, served cafeteria-style (first meat, then sides, then dessert and drinks) from behind a long counter under the manful command of a series of tough-talking women. Even an early lunch hour will find them out of several meats and sides, and we advise you to keep up with the hand-scrawled signs updating the options, as these ladies quickly lose patience with those who don't follow directions. The dining experience recalls junior high cafeteria lunches, and a simple misstep can quickly revive that quaking 12-year-old, uncertain of what to do. Relax. The Longbranch ladies' bark is far worse then their bite, and we haven't heard as many "babies," "honeys," and "sweethearts" since winning over the lunch ladies as old-hand eighth-graders. (At least RM won them over...RG remains silent on the issue.)

This old-fashioned tough love is Ben's biggest draw, as the barbecue itself, while perfectly good, is easily outstripped by other nearby joints such as Sam's on East 12th. We recommend the "Big Ben Special"— brisket and sausage sandwich between two slices of sourdough, with a side and a drink, for five bucks. *Five bucks!* Both the sausage and the meat are tender and flavorful. Pork ribs are also good, the aromatic spice rub serving to lift the greasy flavor a little. The sauce is similarly spiced, with an interesting light fruitiness, though in the end we probably prefer the hotter, more tomatoey standard. Sides are uneventful, but we do like to complement our meal with one of the retro sodas, like A&W served in a glass bottle. Now *that's* old-school.
–RM

Bert's BBQ

No longer the best (or only) barbecue
near the UT campus, but still not bad

food

6.2 **7.1**
10   10
experience

Barbecue $ 8   *W. Campus, Oak Hill, NW Hills*

Counter service   610 W. MLK Blvd.   *Bar* None
Mon.-Fri. 11am-6pm; Sat.   Austin   *Credit Cards* Visa, MC, AmEx
11am-4pm; closed Sun. *Delivery.* (512) 474-2613   *Reservations* Not accepted
Kid-friendly. Wireless Internet.

                                  12005 W. Hwy. 290   3563 Far West Blvd.
                                  78737, (512) 288-7879 78731, (512) 345-2378

We have long been bothered by the striking lack of barbecue places near the UT campus; we once supposed that with the time it takes to smoke meat properly, not to mention the smoke itself, it was just too difficult to bring this highest of Texas cuisines into student reach. Ruby's barbecue now sits brightly atop the Drag, but John Mueller's, a shining star that had moved in just east of campus, has now sadly closed; we miss its tantalizing smoke smells wafting toward UT. Long before these two, though, there was Bert's BBQ on MLK, a lonely campus pioneer, with its bright orange and white sign. Bert's features the standard barbecue décor—the picnic tables in the dining room are heavily carved, hunting trophies and articles cover the walls—but UT sports memorabilia also studs the interior, with an entire area dedicated to the 1969-1970 season, when Bert's first opened its doors.

Counter service is friendly but not always fast, and you'll notice that Bert's offers much more than the usual sides—perhaps in concession to the rampant vegetarianism on college campuses. But it is clear what Bert's is all about from the cords of wood stacked out front (and taking up precious spaces in their small parking lot) and the heavy scent of smoke. What's less clear is the smoke ring on their brisket—a definite flaw—although the meat is nicely seasoned and adequately salty, if a bit dry. Turkey isn't dried out (a too-common problem with this most difficult of birds) and has a mild smoke flavor, but peppery, finely ground sausage is more tightly packed than we like. Sides change from day to day, but always available are the creamy but basic potato salad, chopped cole slaw, and beans. Avoid the bland, mushy black-eyed peas, and opt instead for Bert's cakey house-made brownies, 'cause what could beat a meat-and-sweets combo? –MPN

Bistro 88

Rattan dreams and often good Asian fusion in the suburbs

food
8.1 / 10

8.4 / 10
experience

New American, Pan-Asian $**49**   *Westlake*

Upmarket restaurant
Mon.-Fri. 11am-2pm, 5:30pm-
9:30pm; Sat. 5:30pm-10pm;
Sun. 5:30pm-9pm. *Date-friendly.
Vegetarian-friendly.*

2712 Bee Caves Rd.
Austin
(512) 328-8888
www.bistro88.com

Bar Full
Credit Cards Visa, MC, AmEx
Reservations Recommended

Bistro 88 is a hard nut to crack. First of all, it's not really a "bistro" in any sense of the word; but we do love its secluded environment, a world away from the strip-mall scene that surrounds it. Enter, and you are immediately transported into an Asian colonial fantasy: rattan chairs, hanging wooden birdcages with butterflies, and strange Anglo-Japanese paintings are amongst the Orientalist accoutrements. Chandeliers emit subdued lighting, buffering the reds, yellows, greens, and whites of the walls, while lots of live plants and a lively crowd—even at lunchtime—complete the scene.

That is not to say that all at Bistro 88 is transportative. While some of the pan-Asian preparations work well, others strike out. One of our favorites is a delightful, if chalky, carrot-jalapeño soup made with cream, coconut milk, and a lot of kick. Aggressive hot pepper masks the mid-palate, but this bowl of soup is a simple pleasure that grows as you eat. Pot-stickers are interestingly presented in a big pasta sheet—you have to cut them apart yourself—but in the end, they just taste like pot-stickers. Attempts at fusion sushi and ceviche are even less impressive, sometimes suffering from not-very-tender fish, and an avocado-crab salad is utterly uninspired. A baked, stuffed avocado, with similar ingredients, is more interesting, if shockingly mayonnaisey.

On most American restaurant menus, "sea bass," unmodified, has come to mean Patagonian toothfish (a.k.a. "Chilean sea bass"), a meltingly oily fish similar to black cod. Here, it's a signature main course, served "Hong Kong style," and even at "market price" (give us a break) it's a winner. The tender, pearly white fillet floats in a "sake soy sauce" that swirls with tastes of ginger, garlic, and fermented soybeans. Braised napa cabbage is a really nice addition, and Japanese eggplant is a stroke of side-dish genius: sweet, squishy, and irresistible.

Come expecting world-class pan-Asian fireworks, and you'll be disappointed. Come to escape the neighborhood for a light, refreshing Asian-themed evening, and Bistro 88 might even exceed expectations.
–RG

Black's BBQ

Worthwhile barbecue if you're in Lockhart, even just for historical interest

Barbecue

$11

Lockhart

Counter service
Sun.-Thurs. 10am-8pm;
Fri.-Sat. 10am-8:30pm.
Kid-friendly. Outdoor dining.

208 N. Main St.
Lockhart
(512) 398-2712
www.blacksbbq.com

Bar Beer/wine
Credit Cards Visa and MC
Reservations Not accepted

Even in the all-star barbecue town of Lockhart, Black's, which has been around since 1932, has quite a reputation. The place advertises that it is the "oldest family-owned barbecue restaurant in Texas," and touts its various citations from state legislators and such. Barbecue is a crowded market in Lockhart, though, and it can be tough to keep up with the local competition for hegemony.

There's the requisite smoke amidst brick as you come in, the secret recipes and storied history, the pictures of Ann Richards and Longhorns and Texas license plates sharing wall space with taxidermic wonders like deer heads. You stand in line in one room, where you buy tokens for your drinks, and the drink orders are filled in the other room, where you also get your hot and cold sides. This time-honored process just adds to the country charm.

But something seems missing from the meat itself. The brisket and pork loin, both well-seasoned and imbued with plenty of post-oak smoke, are the best options here. But the brisket isn't the moistest around. As for the sauce, the Black's folks comment that they added the sauce only after "a lot of people from the North came down. They'd ask for it." Fair enough—Black's remains part of the no-sauce school of Texas barbecue. That said, we're not big fans of the extremely sweet pumpkin-pie aspect of the sauce they do provide (they cite lemon and cumin as ingredients, but won't divulge the rest of the recipe; to us, it tastes more of clove or nutmeg).

Meats after brisket are even less impressive. Ribs can dry out; turkey is good, again quite smoky, and not too dry, but a far cry from the Salt Lick's moistness. Sausage, which is touted perhaps above all else, brandishes solid flavor; it's tightly packed (more tightly, perhaps, than our favorites). Black's has its high points, but if you've come all the way to Lockhart for barbecue, we think you can do better at Smitty's or Kreuz. –RG

The Bluebonnet Café

Come on in, y'all, we just took a pie
outta the microwave

food
4.4
10

8.0
10

experience

American

$**13**

Marble Falls

Casual restaurant
Mon.-Thurs. 6am-8pm; Fri.-Sat.
6am-9pm; Sun. 6am 1:45pm.
Breakfast. Kid-friendly.

211 Hwy. 281
Marble Falls
(830) 693-2344
www.bluebonnetcafe.net

Bar None
Credit Cards No credit cards
Reservations Not accepted

The service at this Marble Falls fixture is enthusiastic and astonishingly rapid; the food is plentiful and cheap; the crowds are large, chatty, and unpretentious. It is a place that reminds us that such clichés as "just down-home folks" have more genuine roots. Alongside homemade pie, the Bluebonnet Café serves up a very recognizable slice of a certain kind of Texas: the generally white clientele is middle class, middle-aged, conservative, and polite. Tables fall into brief pre-meal hushes for grace. In the summer, bluebonnets and stars 'n' stripes brighten T-shirts; in the winter, reindeer grin red-nosedly from sweaters and Christmas ornaments dangle from earlobes.

But such authenticity has an ironic flipside: the thoroughly middle-American embrace of the artificial. Thus tamale soup tastes of the Old El Paso taco seasoning packet, Country Crock replaces butter at the tables, mashed potatoes are reconstituted, salad dressing tastes store-bought, and microwaves have left their watery mark on all the food that emerges so speedily and steamingly from the kitchen. Dishes are prepared cafeteria-style, hours in advance (the price for that fast service), and suffer for it. Veggies are timid and overcooked, bread and pies spongy from high-tech reheating. Gelatinous gloop seems to be the consistency of choice here: gloopy dressings, gloopy pie fillings, gloopy cream gravy that's also bland. Brown gravy, too, glistens with a threateningly gloopy glow. The chicken-fried steak, always of dubious heritage, wilts somewhat in its old age. Only the fried okra, crisp and sweet, offers a pleasant surprise.

Yes, in some ways we applaud the Bluebonnet for keepin' it real, but just as we are singing to ourselves, "tastes like Texas, feels like ho-o-ome," we realize that this is simply a commercialized jingle, designed for that other, more corporate source for cafeteria-style southern comfort food, Luby's, and that the food here ain't really home cookin'. —RM

Bombay Bistro

One of the area's few date-worthy
Indian restaurants—and oh, what bread

food
7.3 /10   7.8 /10
experience

Indian $ 30   Arboretum

Upmarket restaurant
Mon.-Thurs. 11am-2pm, 5:30pm-
10pm; Fri. 11am-2pm, 5:30pm-
10:30pm, Sat. 11:30am-3pm,
5:30pm-10:30pm; Sun. 11:30am-
3pm, 5:30pm-10pm. *Vegetarian-friendly.*

10710 Research Blvd.
Austin
(512) 342-2252
www.bombay-bistro.com

Bar Beer/wine
Credit Cards Visa, MC, AmEx
Reservations Accepted

Newly opened Bombay Bistro is bringing a touch of elegance and a
more modern feel to Austin's Indian restaurant scene. Walking in one
would never know that just a few months ago this now attractive (even
for a strip mall) venue used to be a Souper Salad. Tasteful Tiffany-style
lighting and bronze and mahogany furnishings give Bombay Bistro a
subdued classiness, but the place still retains an allegiance to the South-
Asian-restaurant-décor paradigm. That is to say, there is that de-rigueur
art featuring elephants and subjects from Hindu mythology, but here,
it's less front and center than it is at many Indian restaurants. Another
thing that sets Bombay Bistro apart from the crowd is its wine list,
which, while hardly encyclopedic, does offer more than the usual house
red, white, and pink, including a few white varietals that are actually
well suited to the subcontinent's spicy palate.

At lunchtime, Bombay Bistro offers a buffet that has fewer dishes
than its competitors, but makes up for it in quality. Dishes are made in
smaller quantities and served in chafing dishes rather than on a heavily
laden steam table. Freshly made naan is brought to each table, and true
lovers of Indian cuisine will understand how rare and beautiful a thing
that is. Bread is one of the things that Bombay Bistro does well—there
are several to choose from, all light and crisp-edged with a delicate
chewiness. At dinner, savory, almost weightless papadum arrives just in
time to whet the appetite, accompanied by an almost ketchupy
tamarind and bright mint sauce. While tandoori chicken is nothing out
of the ordinary, its sister prawns are tender and juicy. Lamb korma can
be a little tough and salmon dried out, but the saag paneer is creamy
and rich with dense paneer cubes that give it an almost bouncy texture.
Finish up with delicious mango ice cream, a gentle finish after a meal
that may give your palate a workout. –MPN

Bombay Grill

Decent Indian food in Westlake—
nothing more, nothing less

food

experience

Indian $**23**   *Westlake*

Casual restaurant
Daily 11am-2:30pm,
5:30pm-9:30pm. *Delivery.*
Vegetarian-friendly.

3201 Bee Caves Rd.
Austin
(512) 329-0234

Bar Beer/wine
Credit Cards Visa, MC, AmEx
Reservations Accepted

Part of a minor empire of Austin Indian restaurants, Bombay Grill, located in a Westlake shopping center, feels very much like the other members of its family. Its color scheme is pink and burgundy, and the onion-domed silhouette windows are bedecked in beads and shells.

Bombay Grill's menu differs only slightly from that of its sister restaurant, Star of India. Mains are moderately priced, while the decadent "Maharaja's Dinner" bombards you with eight different dishes for about $25 (this is also available at Star of India). There are also lunch and dinner buffets, and here's where the differences between the two restaurants really make themselves known—they offer a nearly identical selection of dishes, but they are executed differently.

The Madras soup is thinner than Star of India's, but still spicy, with grated coconut adding a little texture. Samosas aren't nearly as spicy, but are still very good, and vegetable pakoras are much crispier, as they should be. The mushroom matar features a delicate curry that is correctly pureed. A mild chicken curry's sauce is thin, but still flavorful. Worse here is the saag paneer; it has an off taste—tinny, as if the spinach were canned. But the luscious lamb meatballs in curry are identical to Star of India's, and the tandoori chicken is good as well.

One of our favorite treats at Bombay Grill is the onion kulcha, which is never on the buffet. It's an onion-filled flatbread served hot, with a wonderful fluffy texture set off by its crisp, griddled edges. Another winner is the lamb shahi korma, with chunks of lamb simmered in a rich and creamy almond sauce. For dessert be sure to try the pistachio kulfi. This delicious Indian take on ice cream has a fine cardamom flavor, and is lowfat to boot. –MPN

Boomerang's Pies

One of the world's great comfort foods,
Oz-tin style

food
6.8
10

6.7
10
experience

Australian $ **10** *UT Area*

Counter service
Mon.-Thurs. 11am-9pm;
Fri.-Sat. 11am-10pm; closed Sun.
Kid-friendly. Wireless Internet.

3110 Guadalupe St.
Austin
(512) 380-0032
www.boomerangspies.com

Bar Beer/wine
Credit Cards Visa, MC, AmEx
Reservations Not accepted

Few comfort foods are more comforting than meat stuffed inside a portable pocket o' dough. The Australian meat pie was not the first of this genre: the Cornish pasty in Britain, for one, was documented by Shakespeare. Meanwhile, Italy has the calzone and the panzerotto, Brazil the pastelinho, the rest of Latin America the empanada; the Jamaicans have their beef patties, the Chinese their wontons, the Indians their samosa, the Moroccans their pastilla.

Australia's beloved Four 'n Twenty meat pie is the traditional snack at Australian Rules Football matches. In case you didn't watch much late-night ESPN in the 1980s, that game is played without pads on a giant, oval-shaped field up to 200 yards long. Writes Jim Caple: "ESPN owes an enormous debt to Australian Rules Football, which filled large segments of programming in the days before the network had contracts with the NFL, NBA, and baseball. There never was any explanation of the game's rules…leaving American viewers perplexed by the chaos on the field."

Half a world away, the same type of little pie enjoyed at Aussie football matches is now being served in a hip, modern, airy Austin space complete with WiFi, a flat-screen LCD, stained concrete floors, olive-green industrial ceilings, and delightfully giddy service. Boomerang's angle on the concept is multicultural, tolerant, and very Austin, with such versions as "Texas BBQ" and "Spicy Mexican Veggie." To us, these cute miniature pies, good for handheld consumption, would seem ideal for the post-bar crowd—that is, if the place didn't close at 10pm.

Taste-wise, these pies are all about the crust—an indulgently satisfying pastry shell that keeps the ingredients moist within. A Thai chicken pie is disappointingly dominated by ginger, with a cloying sweet-and-sour sauce evocative of cheap Chinese take-out. But the Traditional Beef Pie, with ground beef and onions, is delicious; while the Aussies may prefer ketchup, we love it with the Boomerang Sauce, a creamy, spicy concoction with Mexican flair. After all, we are in Austin.
–RG

Bouldin Creek Café

South Austin, how we love thee—
except the ill-inspired veggie fusion

food

3.8 **8.8**
10   10

experience

Light American $ 8   *Bouldin Creek Area*

Café   1501 S. 1st St.   *Bar* Beer/wine
Mon.-Fri. 7am-midnight; Sat.-Sun.   Austin   *Credit Cards* Visa and MC
9am-midnight. *Breakfast.*   (512) 416-1601   *Reservations* Not accepted
Live music. Outdoor dining.   www.bouldincreek.com
Vegetarian-friendly. Wireless Internet.

In theory, we are all in favor of this funky South Austin hangout. It has snagged a great location at the heart of the Bouldin Creek neighborhood, a shining example of what can be great about Austin, with its pretty, old houses that are modest enough to draw a nice mix of families and students. Many of these locals congregate regularly at this little coffeeshop to shoot the breeze and discuss left-wing politics. There is a pleasantly haphazard group of tables out front, a generous screened-in porch in back, and plenty more cozy nooks and crannies inside.

An easygoing, possibly pierced staffer takes orders from a vegetarian-friendly menu of sandwiches, salads, and omelettes, and sends you back out with a table number decorated with a photo of the Miami Vice guys, or something else suitably kitschy. There, you plop down at a table between an impossibly pierced customer in a "Catheters" T-shirt and a frenzied, cramming student. The clientele here is of the grungy-hip variety, accessorized with laptops and massive stacks of books—except Leslie, who is inevitably accessorized with much less than that.

So far, so good. It is only when you begin to sip the coffee, and the food arrives, that this entertaining mixture begins to spoil. The brew is hopelessly weak, and perhaps the long menu is too much for the small kitchen to handle: scrambled eggs are dry; grilled cheese, which apparently earns a "famous," is thoroughly uninspired; and soups, which appear periodically, are hit-or-miss. (On one occasion we were served some indecipherable goo that looked like something Yoda, in keeping with the college-cult atmosphere, might have tried to pull a spaceship out of. And failed.) And stay away from anything that combines vaguely Mexican ingredients, like a depressing bean salad, which uses bland salsa as an excuse for a dressing. That said, some of the lighter, vegetal options are agreeable: chips come with a nice, cuminy salsa; a marinated portobello taco is quite good. But you're just as cool here if you're not eating. And if at all possible, take yourself home a gaunt but hot South Austinite. –RM

Brick Oven

Good brick-oven pizza (and they've got some other stuff, too)

food

6.8 / 10   7.0 / 10
experience

Italian, Pizza   **$22**   *Red River Area, Arboretum, Far S.*

Casual restaurant
Mon.-Thurs. 11am-9pm; Fri.
11am-10pm; Sat. 11am-10pm;
Sun. 5pm-9pm. *Outdoor dining.*
Vegetarian-friendly. Wireless Internet.

1209 Red River St.
Austin
(512) 477-7006
www.brickovenll.citysearch.com

Bar Beer/wine
Credit Cards Visa, MC, AmEx
Reservations Accepted

10710 Research Blvd.   9911 Brodie Ln.
78759, (512) 345-6181   78748, (512) 292-3939

For years, we'd been baffled by what has become known as The Great Brick Oven Pizza Puzzle: why, when we would try to order our favorite pizzas from the Brick Oven restaurant on 35th street, would we be met with blank stares at the Red River branch? This agony of semantics only deepened as three more Brick Ovens opened, until finally, eureka, came the solution: it turns out that the Brick Oven on 35th Street is not in the same family of restaurants as the other four, despite the nearly identical pizzas and names. This review is not about the Brick Oven on 35th Street; it is about the other four Brick Oven locations. (See "Brick Oven on 35th" for the review of that establishment.)

Regardless, these Brick Ovens make some of the best thin-crust pizza in Austin. They call it "European style," referring to the fact that it's fired in actual wood-burning ovens that cook at nearly 700 degrees (pizza should ideally be cooked hot, hot, hot). The resulting crust is deliciously, and uniquely, crisp. There is a wide assortment of fresh toppings, and pizza is even available by the humongous slice for the kids. Our favorite is the European with spinach. The menu also has a selection of salads, calzones, and pastas, including the chicken formaggi, a baked pasta dish with roasted chicken, marinara, and five kinds of cheese, as well as desserts. The tiramisu has a nice espresso flavor, and is moist and spongy.

Service at Brick Oven varies, and is occasionally inattentive, but that hasn't stopped us from returning for the superlative pizza. Be sure to eat in, as these creations don't hold up well as carryout—no pizza preservatives here. And remember to eat your spinach, son. –MPN

Brick Oven on 35th

The closest Brick Oven to campus—and
unrelated to the rest

food

6.9 | **8.0**
10 | 10

experience

Italian, Pizza $**26**   *Seton Medical Area*

Casual restaurant   1608 W. 35th St.   ***Bar*** Beer/wine
Mon.-Fri. 11am-2pm, 5pm-10pm;   Austin   ***Credit Cards*** Visa, MC, AmEx
Sat. 11am-10pm; Sun. 11am-9pm.   (512) 453-4330   ***Reservations*** Accepted
Date-friendly. Vegetarian-friendly.   www.brickovenon35th.com

Listening to students on a nerdy college date can be downright
hilarious. Coos are interspersed with extracurricular-activity banter and a
discussion of the status of fellowship applications. Before ordering, a
cogent analysis of the price-to-quality ratio of each item on the menu is
undertaken. Discussion and debate of pizza toppings ensues. Iced tea is
the drink of choice. The check is inevitably split. And then, of course,
there is the slackerbation. Slackerbation, in case you're not versed in
the term, is the phenomenon whereby students try to one-up each
other with the incredible quantity of work that has been assigned to
them, the miniscule percentage of it that's done, and the
unprecedented level of procrastination that has taken place. Of course,
there is the underlying understanding that they'll get it all done the
night before it's due, and because of their innate genius, still manage at
least an A-.

Brick Oven Restaurant on 35th is, confusingly, unrelated—yet
incredibly similar—to the other four Brick Oven pizzerias around town.
In part because of its proximity to campus, the place tends to attract
the anti-Tex-Mex college-date crowd. There is a certain downmarket
romanticism here: warm lighting, cheap wine by the bottle, an
informality that doesn't take away from the intimacy of the tables. The
pizza is oily and cheesy but thin, with a soot-stained seared crust that
blows away much of the competition. Spinach is a good topping
choice, although more standard options like pepperoni seem somehow
ill-paired with pizza in this style.

There's also an array of unimaginative Italian-American mains like
cheesy baked lasagne, spaghetti and meatballs, and so on—their
comfort-foodiness can hit the spot on a certain night, but if you're
looking for good Italian dishes, you should look elsewhere. Come for
the great pizza and relaxed vibe, and theorize on whether both
members of the couple next to you are about to lose their joint
virginity—after their five-page papers are completed, of course. –RG

The Broken Spoke

Two-step the night away, perhaps with
an okay burger too

food

4.7 / 10

9.5 / 10

experience

American

$24 *South Lamar*

Pub
Tues.-Sat. 10am-1am; closed Sun.
Kitchen closes Tues.-Thurs.
10:30pm; Fri.-Sat. 11:30pm.
Live music.

3201 S. Lamar Blvd.
Austin
(512) 442-6189
www.brokenspokeaustintx.com

Bar Full
Credit Cards Visa and MC
Reservations Not accepted

The Broken Spoke opened in 1964, and today it's Austin's last great country dance hall. The place is hard to miss on South Lamar; an old tour bus and oil rig sit out front, and the barn-red building is decorated with old wagon wheels (watch the trees as you pull in to park—and, depending on your level of intoxication, watch out for the building itself, which was recently rammed by a runaway bus). Many country stars got an early boost here, from Willie Nelson to George Strait, but plenty of other local talent still fills the bill like Jimmie Dale Gilmore, The Geezinslaws, and Don Walser and the Pure Texas Band. Past visits by great country stars are immortalized in a museum-quality shrine that you pass on the way back to the dance hall; it's filled with photos, instruments, and a fair number of cowboy hats, swiped right off the performers' heads. (Our favorite feature is a ladies' rest room completely dedicated to George Strait.) Dim lights and pool tables, along with hunting trophies and a fancy saddle, complete the look.

Once inside, wallflowers beware—the Broken Spoke employs charming dancers to sweep the shyer ladies to their feet, and even the most cynical Northeasterner may soon find herself circling the floor.

The Broken Spoke is understandably known much more as a great place to hear country music than as a place to eat. The menu appears unchanged since 1964, with basics such as burgers, a selection of steaks, and a handful of Southern and Tex-Mex items, with prices that won't break the bank when you're more interested in spending your money on beer while catching the show. The Broken Spoke claims the best chicken-fried steak in Texas, and while we find it bland and chewy, it does have a nice light cream gravy. Burgers are a better bet: done in the thin style, with a butter-fried bun and loads of crisp veggies, they make fine two-stepping fuel. –MPN

Buenos Aires Café

Simple Argentine food that translates
well across cultures

food
8.2 | **6.7**
10 | 10
experience

Argentine   **$17**   *St. Edward's Area*

Counter service   2414 S. 1st St.   ***Bar*** BYO
Mon.-Thurs. 8:30am-9:30pm; Fri.-   Austin   ***Credit Cards*** Visa, MC, AmEx
Sat. 8:30am-10pm; closed Sun.   (512) 441-9000   ***Reservations*** Not accepted
Breakfast. Outdoor dining.   www.buenosairescafe.com

For centuries, a debate has been raging across Andean South America
over who lays claim to the empanada: the Argentines? The Chileans?
The Ecuadorians? It's a silly argument, because some version of a meat-
filled pocket of dough, baked or fried, has evolved in parallel on every
corner of the globe.

We'll take the empanada, though, over all the competition—and in
Austin, we'll take the beautifully executed version at the brand-new
Buenos Aires Café. Its (not-so-) "spicy ground beef" filling is balanced
with onions and olive slices that are restrained enough not to
dominate. The milanesa, meanwhile—a fried, breaded beef cutlet—is
another preparation with worldwide equivalents: the wiener schnitzel in
central Europe, the milanese in Italy, the katsu in Japan...or the
chicken-fried steak in Austin. In all cases, the key is taking all your
aggression out on the meat by pounding it hard before dredging it.
Here, too, Buenos Aires Café does it right, whether in a big, fresh-
baked baguette sandwich, or, for dinner, as a milanesa napolitana, with
tomato sauce, ham, and melted cheese—comfort food for the ages.

The café is located on a transforming block of a transforming South
Austin neighborhood that is, like Buenos Aires itself, on the border of
the hip with the run-down. It seems too plain a place for dinner, but
the simple, modern and cheery space is well suited to lunch or
merienda, as the Argentines call the late-afternoon break for coffee and
medias lunas (buttery croissants). Other sweets include alfajores
(cookies layered with dulce de leche and sometimes chocolate-coated),
an Argentine national obsession; and after dinner, panqueques (crepes)
de dulce de leche, which infatuate the palate with crispy, doughy
sweetness. –RG

Buffet Palace

The lowest-rated restaurant in the *Fearless Critic*—and a health hazard too

food

1.2 10

1.4 10

experience

Pan-Asian
Southeast

$14

North Central, Far South,

Casual restaurant
Mon.-Thurs. 11am-9:30pm; Fri.
11am-10pm; Sat. 11:30am-10pm;
Sun. 11:30am-9:30pm. *Kid-friendly.*

1012 W. Anderson Ln.
Austin
(512) 458-2999

Bar Beer/wine
Credit Cards Visa, MC, AmEx
Reservations Accepted

4608 Westgate Blvd.
78745, (512) 892-1800

2601 S. IH-35
78741, (512) 388-9600

There's so much debate these days about the American propensity for obesity and its causes—nutrition, culture, lifestyle, and so on. While there seems to be a self-control issue at the heart of the matter, there are also other factors at work: for instance, the all-you-can-eat buffet. While a generation ago this phenomenon was relegated primarily to weekend brunch and Las Vegas, today all-day buffets seem to be popping up all over. Take for example, Buffet Palace—an all-you-can-eat Asian buffet with locations in both North and South Austin, so you can gorge no matter where you find yourself. This utterly charmless establishment has no service to speak of—only the largest buffet you are likely to see in your life.

There are several soups, a variety of cold salads, massive quantities of seafood and sushi, do-it-yourself phô (Vietnamese noodle soup), and a myriad of hot dishes with all regions of East Asia ostensibly represented. None of the food is particularly good, but it is cheap (though less so on the weekends).

Korean jap chae noodles have the consistency of rubber fishing lures. The egg rolls are bland, and the Vietnamese soft spring rolls are too soft, though their cilantro is crisp and fresh. Sesame chicken lacks sesame, and you'll be hard pressed to find any chicken in the Japanese chicken salad. The beef bulgogi has good flavor, but the meat is very fatty. The boiled shrimp seems aged, and the sushi has a texture suggesting that the fish was previously frozen. The dessert selection includes candied bananas, cookies, and soft-serve ice cream—a big hit with the many families that eat here.

In case you're still pondering a visit to Buffet Palace, chew on this: at press time, the place had failed three health inspections in a row. Ick.
–MPN

BurgerTex

A Korean-influenced burger shack—
you'd better believe it

food

6.9 | 4.5
10 | 10
experience

Burgers, Korean   **$15**   *North Central, Pflugerville*

Counter service   5420 Airport Blvd.   *Bar* Full
Mon.-Sat. 10am-9pm;   Austin   *Credit Cards* Visa, MC, AmEx
closed Sun. *Kid-friendly.* (512) 453-8772   *Reservations* Accepted
                           www.burgertex.com

                           15803 Windermere Dr.
                           Pflugerville, (512) 990-9499

It is slightly hard to believe, glancing at the cheap little storefront and grim interior, that BurgerTex has earned its reputation for quality. But it doesn't take long for the easy warmth of the service and your first bite of juicy, charcoal-tinged burger to convince you that you came to the right place.

BurgerTex is run by a Korean family. Service is polite, genial, and efficient, and the menu, in addition to a line of standard options and embellishments (bacon and cheese, grilled onions and mushrooms), actually features a bulgogi burger: fine, almost crumbly strips of beef, marinated in a sweet soy-sesame-garlic sauce, and served burger-style on a bun. It is the Korean equivalent of the sloppy joe (only it's a lot less sloppy): salty-sweet and comforting, and reminiscent of a time when our intellect required less of our taste buds.

BurgerTex has several other strengths. The most obvious novelty is that you pick your toppings yourself from a salad bar (thus gaining the underappreciated advantage of choosing your own slice of tomato: you can avoid the dreaded hard, white end bit). You can heap on the pickles and jalapeños to your heart's content. Carbs, too, convince: buns are sizeable and sweet, with plenty of flavor and enough substance to stand up to a hearty patty; fries are crisp and show some skin; onion rings are especially tasty, thick and juicy, in a light and chewy tempura batter.

This isn't the best burger in town by any means, but when even the shabby décor—with its rough wooden counter and striped white and green awning—begins to take on the laid-back, sandy appeal of a beachside burger shack, you know they've won you over. –RM

Byblos

We wish all cafeterias were as good as
this northern Middle Eastern purveyor

food

7.3 **5.5**
10   10

experience

Middle Eastern   **$ 7**   *Far North*

Counter service
Mon.-Sat. 11am-9:30pm; Sun.
11am-6pm. *Vegetarian-friendly.*

13000 N. IH-35
Austin
(512) 490-1212

Bar None
Credit Cards Visa, MC, AmEx
Reservations Accepted

We find it a bit strange that for all the belly dancing and fancy décor, the best Middle Eastern restaurants in Austin seem to be the ones that aren't trying so hard. Byblos certainly falls into that category. A relatively new establishment in far northern Austin, Byblos is unassuming, with cafeteria-style service, a menu posted above the steam tables, and simple tables and chairs. There's not much in the way of ambiance. This the sort of place that would probably fit in well on campus: it's inexpensive, fast, and bare-bones, just right for a bite between classes. A few photographs of Lebanon make up the rest of the scenery, just to let you know where the food is from.

Byblos' kitchen crew is happy to tell you about the dishes and help you make up your mind, and we are pleased to see that not everything is pre-made—meat dishes and kebabs are grilled to order on grills visible right behind the counter, and all wraps are made fresh as well.

Our only real complaint about Byblos (besides its being practically in Waco) is that so many of the garnishes are pickled. It can get to be a bit too much, especially if you order a dish like fattoush, with similarly tart marinated vegetables. We like Byblos' simple "pies," which consist of soft pita bread smeared with meat, spinach, or cheese and quickly heated in the oven—they are satisfying in the most basic way. Kebabs, too, are tasty, if typically a little tough. Sides are the real stars here— tabbouleh is fresh and lemony, with lots of herbs but not too much parsley; baba ganoush is smoky and subtle; hummus has good flavor, spiked with lemon and not overloaded with tahini; and steamed potatoes with lemon and herbs are an excellent accompaniment for meat dishes. –MPN

Café 909

A creative, casually posh little
restaurant with frontier freshness

food

9.3 **8.0**

10 | 10

experience

New American $**60**   *Marble Falls*

Upmarket restaurant   909 2nd St.   *Bar* Beer/wine
Tues.-Sat. 5:30pm-9:30pm;   Marble Falls   *Credit Cards* Visa, MC, AmEx
closed Sun.-Mon.   (830) 693-2126   *Reservations* Essential
Date-friendly.   www.cafe909.com

Back in the day, residents of this little quarry outpost sent great slabs of granite to Austin for its gleaming pink Capitol in exchange for the railroad that would let them transport it there. Today, we find the inevitable offspring of that marriage of convenience: a new exchange of diligent suburban commuters for well-heeled urban weekenders. The old storefronts on Main Street have been reworked to display shabby-chic "collectibles" and boutique clothing.

But just off Main on Second Street, at Café 909, something of Marble Falls' pioneer spirit remains. Chef-owner Mark Schmidt calls himself a "rustic gourmet"—a phrase that sets off as many alarm bells as a breach of the LBJ Dam (the gastronomic equivalent of shabby-chic?). But we are happy to report that his Café beautifully executes the paradox.

We cannot tell you much about the restaurant's interior—from the moment you enter, the focus is fully on the food. Service is exceedingly attentive, and your first nibbles arrive just as you're easing into your drink, in the form of a bright amuse-bouche (perhaps a bit of immaculately seared salmon or scallops on a heap of scented couscous). Appetizers and mains arrive quickly on each other's heels, though never near enough to nip, and if the plates are beautiful, it is because of the beauty of the ingredients: as with the room, there are no distracting flourishes. The food, based on regional ingredients and served according to season, is hearty without ever sagging toward heavy. A rich golden borscht, flavored with foie gras, mushroom, and horseradish, glows both from without and within. Carolina flounder finds an excellent match in smoked ham, kale, and cannelloni beans, comfortably enveloped in the warm yellow of a poached egg. Hashes, squashes, bacon, and beans exemplify the strong and simple flavors on the menu.

There is hardly a false note; this food sings sweetly an old song of spacious skies, majestic purple mountains, and amber waves of grain. –RM

Café at the Four Seasons

food · 10 · experience · 10

A particularly delicious restaurant that
meets a particular set of demands

New American · **$73** · *Convention Center Area*

Upmarket restaurant
Mon.-Thurs. 6:30am-10pm; Fri.
6:30am-11pm; Sat. 7am-11pm;
Sun. 7am-10pm. *Breakfast.*
Brunch. Date-friendly. Outdoor dining.

98 San Jacinto Blvd.
Austin
(512) 478-4500
www.fourseasons.com/Austin

Bar Full
Credit Cards Visa, MC, AmEx
Reservations Recommended

Let's say you need a place to celebrate a birthday, a graduation, or a
promotion. Or perhaps you need a restaurant with just-so standards
where you can close a major deal. You seek the simultaneous
satisfaction of several specific conditions as to which, you may have
come to realize, achievement in Austin is rare:

You would like to be able to engage with others at your table
without anyone's having to shout. You would prefer enough distance
between your table and the rest for conversations not to travel,
unbidden, around the room.

You would like to dine in surroundings that bespeak unfussy
elegance, with just a touch of good fun. Indeed, you would very much
enjoy a choice of handsome settings, including al fresco dining—even
the possibility of eating Beverly Hills-style, beside a pool.

You would, of course, prefer to be well cared for from the moment
of your arrival through the time that you depart without being fawned
over, looked down upon (other than literally), or, in the obnoxious
tradition, having your captain consult his watch.

And you would prefer a marvelous menu that doesn't displace
reliable favorites but also offers, alongside them, new culinary
adventures that are neither silly or pretentious, but can serve to place
the chef's dynamic ambitions. That might mean subtle versions of the
flavors of the Southwest on your plate, from a loving treatment of veal
sweetbreads, to a smoky pork tenderloin with cheese grits that displays
remarkable subtlety, to a tasting of four meatless dishes that is one of
the city's best vegetarian mains.

And, of course, you want a wine list that is the equal of these
challenges, including a bevy of fine choices by the glass. Naturally, you
realize that having all of your demanding conditions satisfied is going to
come at a price that won't be a real steal (although you would
occasionally like to come just for civilized, excellent-value, small-portion
afternoon desserts). The Café at the Four Seasons, with a menu that
changes four times each day except Sunday—when there is a
resplendent and long-lived brunch—will distinguish itself on each of
these crucial scores. And it might be the only place in town that does.
—JC

108 / THE FEARLESS CRITIC

Café Josie

Delicious food with a tropical
inspiration and unparalleled warmth

food

9.3 **9.6**
10   10

experience

Southwestern $**48**   *Clarksville*

Upmarket restaurant   1200B W. 6th St.   *Bar* Beer/wine
Tues.-Thurs. 11:30am-2pm,   Austin   *Credit Cards* Visa, MC, AmEx
6pm-9:30pm; Fri. 11:30am-2pm, (512) 322-9226   *Reservations* Recommended
6pm-10pm; Sat. 6pm-10pm;   www.cafejosie.com
closed Sun.-Mon. *Date-friendly. Vegetarian-friendly.*

Some top restaurants win people over primarily with their personality,
style, and uniqueness. Others stress flavor and presentation above all
else, and let the food alone take center stage. What makes Café Josie
one of our very favorite places to eat in Austin is its ability to combine
the best of both of those worlds. Equal amounts of inspiration, it
seems, have informed the positioning of every light in the room, the
spices that emerge from every item on the plate, and every physical
movement on the part of the excellent, down-to-earth waitstaff. The
results are stunning.

It would be difficult to carve out a more convivial space in which to
dine casually and elegantly than this one, hidden a bit back from
Gallery Row on Sixth Street west of Lamar. Modern local artwork does
not seem stark here; rather, it sings in tune with the comfortable tables,
chairs, and the din of diners. Even on the nights on which no single
dish propels Café Josie into the stratosphere, consistently interesting
flavors will tickle your palate for the entire evening. It is this sort of
sensory-barrage style of cuisine that Austin does best.

Chef Charles Mayes dubs his cuisine "tropical," meaning that
ingredients are centered around the equator, whatever their longitude.
Excellent soups, which often integrate Mexican spices, change daily.
Most memorable are his sauces, from the lime-cilantro aïoli that adorns
fried oysters with a surprisingly delicate breadcrumb crust to a smoky
crawfish sauce that showed up in a recent fish special, elevating a timid
piece of grouper to greatness. Succulent, mesquite-grilled shrimp come
painted with a spicy honey chipotle sauce that sweet-talks the
crustaceans. Even the rice, so often an afterthought, bursts with bright,
herbal notes including poblano. Afterward, a blackberry crisp, like a
bubbly cobbler, covered with Amy's ice cream, is so good that it's
impossible not to appreciate the dish, however full you might be. And
impossible not to schedule a repeat trip. Soon. As soon as possible.
–RG

Café Mundi

Southern life is easy, especially when you're sitting out on a good patio

food
7.9 / 10
8.6 / 10
experience

Light American   **$11**   *East Austin*

Café
Mon -Thurs. 8am-10pm;
Fri -Sat. 8am-11pm; Sun. 8am-
5pm. *Breakfast. Date-friendly.*
Live music. Outdoor dining. Vegetarian-friendly. Wireless Internet.

1704 E. 5th St.
Austin
(512) 236-8634
www.cafemundi.com

Bar Beer/wine
Credit Cards Visa and MC
Reservations Not accepted

Café Mundi is tucked away alongside a silent line of tracks in an apparently abandoned industrial stretch of East 5th Street. Although a lively East Side scene is in fact just a few blocks away, this seeming isolation is part of Café Mundi's tranquil charm. The inside of the café is small and sleek, with some brushed steel furniture and Austin's ubiquitous wireless access, but it is really outside in the warm air that Café Mundi's little world springs to quiet life.

The generous patio space surrounding this spot is lovely, its hidden corners charmed by some mysterious spirit of Southern ease. Mosaic paths of bricks, half obscured, wind their way between the pinks and taupes of a thicket of crape myrtles, banana leaves wave overhead in graceful clusters, and the sculptures that rise out of the ground look so comfortable and settled that they seem like the remains of an older civilization. The abandoned Mexican mural on the El Lago Mexican Food warehouse across the street reemphasizes the effect of forgotten ease, and on most nights, the soft acoustic tunes of local musicians wander between the customers. Monday nights in warm weather bring outdoor movies. This is Austin at its best: natural, warm, unprepossessing, relaxed.

The food, too, echoes those qualities. Everything tastes resoundingly fresh, and, indeed, the proprietors sometimes pick up their produce from a local who swings by with the harvest from his couple of acres. Amongst the sandwiches, the "Easy Cheesy" is a highlight, with three kinds of cheese that ooze but never get chewy. Rotating soups are reliable—the gingery carrot and the spinach taste fresh-plucked from the earth.

Nothing truly flashes here but the fireflies, but if you go in the evening, when the blaze has gone out of the heat and the guitarist is just beginning to pluck his strings, you can really be transported. –RM

Cantina Laredo

Decent upmarket Tex-Mex, straight outta...*Dallas?*

food
7.3 /10   **7.7** /10
experience

Mexican $**37**   *Warehouse District*

Upmarket restaurant   201 W. 3rd St.   *Bar* Full
Sun.-Thurs. 11am-10pm;   Austin   *Credit Cards* Visa, MC, AmEx
Fri.-Sat. 11am-11pm.   (512) 542-9670   *Reservations* Accepted
Outdoor dining.   www.cantinalaredo.com

Cantina Laredo is one of the more ambitious restaurants to participate in the large-scale, city-subsidized development of the area dubbed the "Second Street District." Although this one is actually on Third Street, it looks and feels more connected to the yup-and-coming new row of boutiques and eateries on Second Street.

We must first disclose that Cantina Laredo is unfortunately a subsidiary of Consolidated Restaurant Operations (the name alone makes us shudder), of Spaghetti Warehouse and El Chico fame. However, designers seem to have done a nice job of avoiding that chain-restaurant feel; although furnishings are distinctly new, they're soothing and intimate. We are booth fans, and particularly like the cozy two-person booths here. Lighting is dim, and there's a certain pleasant bustle to the space.

Initial signs here have been mostly positive. Guacamole prepared tableside is a gimmick, and frankly, an impediment: we would have preferred a blended version, as showed up as a side dish with a main course later in the meal. Still, the guac's taste was fresh and cilantro-forward and the seasoning pleasant, if salt-hungry. At press time, the restaurant was still waiting on its liquor license, so it was generously giving away margaritas, which were strong, tasty, and not overly sweet. Service was as giddy and unpolished as one might expect for a new opening, but in a friendly way—they're clearly headed in the right direction.

Easily the most impressive thing we have tried so far has been the "Camarón Poblado Asada," a favorite of controversial Austin journalist Emma Graves Fitzsimmons, with sautéed shrimp, mushrooms, onions, and jack cheese all stuffed inside a grilled poblano pepper, which is itself wrapped in a tenderized carne asada steak. It sounds like overkill, but the combination is cheesy and harmonious. The steak was recommended medium-well, but ordered rare, it was juicy and delicious. Watery spinach enchiladas and fairly dry mole enchiladas were much less impressive, more in line with our chain-generated expectations. But we're pleasantly surprised with most of what we've seen so far. –RG

Capitol Brasserie

Simple, authentically delicious French food in Texas? Mais oui!

food
9.0 **9.3**
10   10
experience

French   **$48**   *Warehouse District*

Upmarket restaurant
Mon. 7am-10pm; Tues.-Thurs.
7am-1am; Fri. 7am-3am; Sat.
10am-3am; Sun. 10am-3pm,
5pm-10pm. Late-night menu only after 10pm Tues.-Thurs., after 11pm Fri.-Sat.
Breakfast. Brunch. Date-friendly. Outdoor dining. Wireless Internet.

310 Colorado St.
Austin
(512) 472-6770
www.capitolbaustin.com

Bar Full
Credit Cards Visa, MC, AmEx
Reservations Recommended

Capitol Brasserie, which opened in the middle of downtown in late 2005 in the space formerly occupied by Mezzaluna, recreates the feeling of a typical bustling Parisian brasserie as well as we've seen it done anywhere in America. Within a matter of days after opening, Capitol was boisterous even late on weeknights, and for good reason.

First of all, the space is spot on. Instead of going overboard with Disneyesque pomposities like mirrors painted with loopy French handwriting or wine served in quarter-carafes, Capitol decorates its white walls simply, with just enough Parisian posters to prevent the rooms from feeling sparse, and nostalgic lamps that emit a warm, inviting light. Better yet, a little outdoor seating area has round metal tables facing the sidewalk in ideal pedestrian-scoping position.

Back inside, the lively din might be too loud for some, but the noise forms an essential component of the brasserie vibe. Particularly welcome is the late-night menu; offered until 1am Tuesday to Thursday and 3am Friday and Saturday, it's no bar-food afterthought—you can get wee-hours steak frites, or a tremendous rendition of crôque madame (a rich, grilled ham-and-cheese sandwich with gruyère, indulgent béchamel, and a carefully fried egg) that surpasses many versions in France. There's also a classic prix-fixe Sunday brunch.

The dinner menu is reliable, from the bread (warm, soft, and superb) to onion soup gratin (acceptable, but without significant depth of flavor) to the classic mussels in one of four broths (best is the well-developed, winey "au Saffron," although we also like the garlicky "Basquaise"). We also like tender duck confit, whose only weak point is its bed of tough frisée. Skate, another classic brasserie plate, has the delicate nuttiness of brown butter drowned out by a thick, aggressive vinaigrette, but the fish is cooked flawlessly. Less memorable are the chocolate soufflé, which tends not to rise enough, and under-battered French toast. But such missteps are rare. This place is destined to be a downtown mainstay. –RG

Carmelo's

Overpriced Italian food that's outclassed
by the more modern competition

food

4.9 / 10
6.8 / 10
experience

Italian   **$56**   *Sixth Street District*

Upmarket restaurant   504 E. 5th St.   *Bar* Full
Mon.-Thurs. 11am-2pm, 5pm-   Austin   *Credit Cards* Visa, MC, AmEx
10:30pm; Fri. 11am-2pm, 5pm- (512) 477-7497   *Reservations* Accepted
11pm; Sat. 5pm-11pm; Sun.   www.carmelosrestaurant.com
5pm-10pm. *Date-friendly. Outdoor dining.*

Opened in 1985, Carmelo's was Austin's best Italian restaurant for
many years, with little other competition in town, but now with places
like Vespaio and Siena, it will have to work hard to earn back that
honor. Located downtown in a graceful 1870s hotel, the restaurant has
ivy-covered walls, an intimate outdoor seating area, and fun Carnevale-
inspired murals and sculptures of costumed revelers. Inside, the mood
changes; Carmelo's is well appointed, but the clichéd décor liberally
employs both Italian and Texan stereotypes—wine racks and trellises
line the walls, Laura Ashley-type floral draperies accent columns and
walls, and a longhorn head is mounted near the door. Service from a
mix of veterans and amateurs is hit-or-miss, but it is always friendly and
polite.

  We like to begin dinner with ruby-red carpaccio, served paper-thin
with a simple lemon, oil, parmesan, and pepper garnish—it's rich but
light, and won't ruin your appetite. Avoid the caprese salad—the
buffalo mozzarella is watery and grainy, and we can't figure out where
the kitchen is getting underripe tomatoes even in summer. Mains
extend well beyond the usual pastas, which tend to be tender yet
toothsome, though sauces run to the bland. Steaks are often
overcooked (ask for rare if you want medium-rare), but rich sauces will
make up for any dryness. We are particularly unimpressed by the
sautéed veggie sides, major components of which include canned baby
corn, and pre-peeled baby carrots of the kind you buy in the two-
pound bag for your kid's lunch box. But two things not to be missed at
Carmelo's are the fantastic dessert cart, stocked with at least a dozen
different cakes, and the equally well-stocked drink cart, laden with
Cognacs, Argmanacs, Grappas, and even Calvados. –MPN

Casa de Luz

A soothingly crunchy vegan café where "nature is the menu planner"

food
6.6 **9.0**
10 10
experience

Light American   **$13**   *Zilker*

Counter service
Mon.-Fri. 7am-9am, 11:30am-2pm,
6pm-8:30pm; Sat.-Sun. 11:30am-
2pm, 6pm-8:30pm. *Breakfast.*
Outdoor dining. Vegetarian-friendly.

1701 Toomey Rd.
Austin
(512) 476-2535
www.casadeluz.org

Bar None
Credit Cards Visa and MC
Reservations Not accepted

In a town that is alternifying with yuppies from both coasts—a town increasingly packed with granola restaurants—Casa de Luz is clearly the King of the Crunch. Tucked behind the Parkside Community School off Barton Springs Road, down a pleasant brick path lined in lush foliage, the restaurant feels like a Mexican villa that's a world away—even from the baseball field across the street. Casa de Luz serves vegan, organic, and macrobiotic food in a one-choice prix-fixe set menu every day, including all the soup and salad you can eat, to a dauntingly healthy clientele. The pleasant, airy communal dining room is filled with tinkling nature music, and the space encourages fellow feeling, serving as an informal marketplace for freelance yoga instruction, and, on certain days, maybe even a bit of a new-age pickup scene.

All of which begs the question: are you fit enough to face this food? We do not mean to imply that it is bad—rather, it's the fact that the food is so clearly *good* for you that makes us fidget. One leaves Casa de Luz feeling as if one's insides have been scrubbed by a very clean cloth, one's digestive tracts have been lovingly massaged, and all one's parts, head to toe, have been thoroughly anti-oxidized. And yet there are some extremely tasty sleights of hand coming from this kitchen, like a granular, deeply flavored sunflower-seed "cheese" (although they call it something else) that adds color to black beans.

In general, breads are less successful, and grains, as a rule, are rather weighty. Rice, though, is often adorned with the interesting crunch of seeds, and tamari is an omnipresent seasoning option. Casa de Luz has much better luck with vegetables, which are organic, locally grown, freshly prepared and flavorful. And the kitchen isn't afraid, vegan or not, to use lively flavors—a typical menu might include bright collard greens with a tahini, and mix sweet yams with nuts, caramelized onions, and raisins, thus neatly avoiding the refined-sugar dilemma.
–RM/RG

Casino El Camino

Expect a long wait in this dive bar for
some of Austin's best burgers

food

8.4 / 10

4.6 / 10

experience

Burgers

$12

Sixth Street District

Pub
Daily 4pm-2am.
Kitchen closes at 1:30am.

517 E. 6th St.
Austin
(512) 469-9330
www.casinoelcamino.com

Bar Full
Credit Cards Visa, MC, AmEx
Reservations Not accepted

Don't be deceived by this Sixth Street dive bar's haunted-house logo
and dark, grunge-rock atmosphere: a back window in the rockin'
hangout consistently turns out some of the best burgers in the city,
along with spot-on versions of other bar-food standards like fries,
wings, and chili-cheese dogs to boot.

First, a primer: don't expect speedy service. In fact, don't expect
service at all. You'll wait in line to sidle up to a little window in the back
of a bar. If you don't want to be humiliated, you'd better know what
you want by the time you get to the front. If all goes well, you'll be
handed a ticket that offers you admission to the privilege of a burger,
generally sometime between 20 minutes and an hour later. Don't
expect to be informed when it's ready—time management is left up to
you.

Thankfully, it's all worth it. The burgers, which belong to the big,
round, and thick school of thought—the sort that you can actually ask
for rare (and we recommend doing so)—are really just as they should
be. Juices are skillfully locked in by the molding and grilling processes,
and the result is a deliciously moist burger of imposing size. The
"Buffalo Burger," with hot wing sauce and blue cheese (not buffalo
meat), has its devotees, but we think the combination overwhelms the
excellent meat, rather than flattering it. These are relative statements,
of course; it's still a great burger, and the buffalo sauce is a good
version, doing right by the wings.

But even better—amazing, in fact—is the "Amarillo Burger," with
roasted serranos, jalapeño jack cheese, and cilantro mayo, a delicious
Southwestern combination whose heat does not interfere with the
taste of the burger's juices. Another success is the "Chicago Burger," a
more classic bacon-cheddar combination with equally impressive
execution. There are few, if any, better remedies for the midnight
munchies than this, and the late hours are yet another feather in
Casino El Camino's formidable, if grungy, cap. –RG

Castle Hill Café

Showstopping Southwestern creations
in a chic but calm environment

food

9.3 **9.5**

10   10

experience

Southwestern $**46**   *Clarksville*

Upmarket restaurant	1101 W. 5th St.	*Bar* Beer/wine
Mon.-Fri. 11am-2:30pm,	Austin	*Credit Cards* Visa, MC, AmEx
6pm-10pm; Sat. 6pm-10pm;	(512) 476-0728	*Reservations* Recommended
closed Sun. *Date-friendly.*	www.castlehillcafe.com	

It's hard to decide whether to get more excited about the food or the feeling at this sensational restaurant set in an unlikely house on Fifth Street, a block west of Lamar. The place achieves a striking balance between informal and upscale. Lighting hits exactly the right mood, while lots of booths and relaxed table settings put you at ease. The staff is as friendly and casual as it would be at a warm, fuzzy neighborhood joint, yet these folks also unpretentiously brandish considerable culinary expertise—from encyclopedic wine knowledge to an intimate familiarity with everything that comes out of the kitchen.

And some of those dishes have the power to be really special. At our most recent visit, Castle Hill was serving a thrilling plate of Gulf red snapper, expertly crusted and pan-seared, its white meat impeccably fresh—practically swimming. The snapper fillets were laid out atop a striped succession of sauces that reminded us of a Mexican flag: guajillo beurre blanc, coriander crème fraîche, and smoked poblano salsa, all set against the sweetness of an incredible roasted corn pudding and an exemplary pile of spiced kale.

Other impressive dishes in recent times have included "crab cakes" that also integrated crawfish and scallops, served with a creamy remoulade with a dazzlingly complex portfolio of vegetal flavors that somehow achieved unity. The kitchen also has a way with pork, as in smoked pork tenderloin flautas with sun-dried cherry chutney. Some dishes are less impressive, not because of particular flaws, but rather just a relative lack of complexity, as in a dark, slightly bitter duck gumbo or in the tasty, if not groundbreaking, shrimp enchiladas with so-called "tomatillo-poblano verde," whose huitlacoche (truffle-like corn fungus, a Mexican delicacy) was barely detectable.

The excellent wine list soars above and beyond the call of duty, and almost everything is available by the glass. This is the kind of place that Austin does best: imaginatively tweaked upscale Southwestern, at reasonable prices, without an ounce of pretense. Take your out-of-town friends here, and they'll start looking at Austin real estate. –RG

The Catfish Parlour

Fried fish with plenty of nostalgia but
not enough salt

food

5.7
10
6.6
10
experience

Southern, Seafood

$23 *Far NW, N. Central, Far South*

Casual restaurant
Mon.-Sat. 11am-10pm;
closed Sun. *Kid-friendly.*

11910 N. Hwy. 183
Austin
(512) 258-1853
www.catfishparlour.com

Bar Beer/wine
Credit Cards Visa, MC, AmEx
Reservations Accepted

111 W. Anderson Ln.
78752, (512) 454-2729

4705 E. Hwy. 290
78741, (512) 443-1698

As Austin has grown more cosmopolitan and culinarily sophisticated, fried fish houses like this one, once staples of the city's food scene, have dwindled. But this barn-like space, plastered with Burma shave ads and the like, has held on for over 30 years, and now, with two locations (not too many, not too few), seems admirably spry for its age.

The food served here is decidedly old-fashioned, to both its benefit and detriment. We like the restaurant's investment in large-family eating: like that other southern family fallback, KFC, the Catfish Parlour sells its fare by the bucketful, with bulk prices allowing a family of six to have a bountiful dinner for close to five bucks a person. We like that meals come with plenty of fixin's; the Catfish Parlour's slaw is particularly good—a bright green version with cabbage, thinly sliced green peppers, and herbs in a tangy vinaigrette. And we like that for a restaurant in which almost everything is fried, there is surprisingly little grease in evidence.

There is also, with the exception of the cole slaw, very little seasoning. Everything could do with a good salting, starting with the fish itself. The cornmeal crust has a good crunch, but it is a little thin, and quite bland, and the fish underneath seems entirely unseasoned. Signature cigarillo-shaped hush puppies are essentially empty fried shells. Onion rings are all crackle and no pop. In a concession to the more heath-conscious times, the restaurant serves a few non-fried options, but while the tuna steak *is* cooked rare to order, it, too, cries out for a sprinkling of spices.

Luckily, the lively house-made tartar sauces (jalapeño and regular) and spirited signage add some life to the party. Just beware of the posted Sturgeon General's warning: "Consuming too much fish may cause you to swim upstream and spawn." The fish themselves occasionally seem a little tired from the journey. –RM

Central Market

Quite simply one of the best gourmet supermarkets in America

Seton Medical Area, Far South

Specialty grocery
Sun.-Thurs. 7am-9pm;
Fri.-Sat. 7am-10pm. *Breakfast.*
Kid-friendly. Live music. Outdoor
dining. Vegetarian-friendly. Wireless Internet.

4001 N. Lamar Blvd.
Austin
(512) 206-1000
www.centralmarket.com

4477 S. Lamar Blvd.
78745, (512) 899-4300

Bar Beer/wine
Credit Cards Visa, MC, AmEx
Reservations Not accepted

Austin's two Central Markets are dazzling, world-class gourmet superstores. They are, first and foremost, candy stores for gourmet home chefs: every single hunk of cheese, jar of salsa, bottle of olive oil, or bin of shrimp is selected with a deep underlying commitment to "foodie" principles. Whatever the department, Central Market always seems in relentless pursuit of the best ingredients available, whether it's USDA prime dry-aged beef from our backyard or sultry, exotic sauces from Sicily. After a trip here, you may well find it difficult to return to your local corner grocery for anything at all.

The Central Market Café, which had just re-opened at press time, has long been not only a convenient place for hungry shoppers to stop by for a bite to eat while shopping, but also a worthwhile dining destination in its own right. The seat-yourself spaces are clean and well lit, with flowers on the tables and works by local artists for sale on the walls. There's live music on the patios on the weekends, and the North store has a wonderful tree-shaded playscape that's a huge hit with the mommy set. Food is reasonably priced and the portions are substantial. Strong points (again, before the major renovation) have included simply grilled salmon, rich and delicious pot roast, and fresh sautéed veggies. Selections for vegetarians and vegans are nothing less than excellent, and we expect this trend to continue with the exciting new opening.

If you're in a rush, Central Market's "Café on the Run," the in-store food counter, offers up freshly prepared main courses, soups, and sides, as well as sushi, and the sandwiches that are found on the Café menu, such as the always tempting roast beef and brie on croissant. The coffee counter also makes one of the best espressos in Austin—yet another feather in this legendary food store's delicious cap. –RG

Changos Taquería

A bright and upbeat source of top-notch tacos and trimmings

food
8.2
10

5.8
10
experience

Mexican

$11

UT Area, South Lamar

Counter service
Daily 7am-10pm. *Breakfast.*
Kid-friendly. Outdoor dining.
Vegetarian-friendly.
Wireless Internet.

3023 Guadalupe St.
Austin
(512) 480-8226
www.changos.com

3005 S. Lamar Blvd.
78704, (512) 416-1500

Bar Beer/wine
Credit Cards Visa and MC
Reservations Not accepted

Changos communicates, perhaps better than any other restaurant in town, what is great about Mexican food in Austin. It's fresh, it's friendly, it's cheap, it's unassuming, and most importantly of all, it is exceptionally good. The Guadalupe location, with its lime-green floor and beautiful counter of handmade cream tiles, is jollier than the newer spot on South Lamar, but both offer comfortable, bright surroundings and a friendly and efficient vibe that lets you focus on the food. The simple tacos and burritos prepared at this fast-food-style offspring of Manuel's so far surpass what most of America associates with those dishes that they seem a different cuisine.

Changos makes everything from scratch, from the delicate corn tortillas that are amongst the best in the city, to rotisserie-roasted adobo pork that is sweet, hot, and limey. Everything tastes sparkling-new, bright, and punchy. Tex-Mex isn't just heavy beans and rice, grease and starch. It can be a medley of lime, cilantro, and smoky chiles; it can be a fiesta of yellow and green and popping-red flavors.

People love the burritos here for their generosity and value, but we recommend you go for the tacos. The grilled "Del Mar Taco," with its tender marinated mahi-mahi, spicy pico de gallo, and creamy cheese, is our favorite; but close behind it is the al pastor, with that tangy rotisserie pork, roasted pineapple chunks, plenty of fresh cilantro, and a squeeze of lime. Each taco comes wrapped in one of those sweet corn tortillas, which has just been pressed and grilled the old-fashioned way, and moistened by one of five house-made salsas.

Two tacos make a meal, but go on—have three! Add to this some creamy corn soup, and a bottomless cup of fresh agua fresca (a fruit drink), and you've got yourself one helluva good time. –RM

Chapala

Cheap and cheery Mexican, en español,
por favor

food

5.2 **4.9**
10   10

experience

Mexican · **$ 5** · *East Austin*

Casual restaurant
Mon.-Sat. 7am-11pm;
closed Sun. *Breakfast.*

2101 E. Cesar Chavez St.
Austin
(512) 320-0308

Bar Beer/wine
Credit Cards Visa, MC, AmEx
Reservations Not accepted

We happily include Chapala in this book because, while it doesn't break
new culinary ground, it is an excellent example of the kind of likeable,
uncomplicated restaurant that often flies well below the radar of most
restaurant reviewers. Don't be turned off by the bars on the windows
and slightly down-and-out feel—Chapala is friendly as can be, and
despite catering to an almost entirely Spanish-speaking East Side crowd,
very accessible.

There are no frills in this sincerely authentic Mexican dive. Food is
incredibly cheap and on the whole reliable, though there are some
ordering pitfalls. Keep it simple and fresh, and you'll emerge satisfied.
Breakfast, served until 11am, provides the best deals. At press time,
three breakfast tacos with your choice of filling cost a dazzling $2.29,
and there is nothing above four dollars. For lunch, three bucks will get
you a hearty torta, or a Jalisco-style sandwich filled with avocado,
tomato, sour cream, and your choice of a wide range of meats.
Authenticity also has its advantages with respect to meats—amongst
the options are such Mexican standards as lengua (tongue). Other
offerings show a more delicate touch, augured by the light, warm
tortilla chips and fresh, garlicky salsa that greet your arrival. We
particularly like the enchiladas verdes, which are tart and clean flavored.

None of this food is particularly striking—at these prices, it would be
spectacular if it were—but the waitresses, who, by the way, speak
Spanish to all customers regardless of their honky-quotient, are so
indefatigably warm, and so patient with awkward mumbles through
Spanish-English cognates ("yo quiero el porko por favor") that they and
some music from the bounteous Tejano jukebox provide all the thrills
you'll want. –RM

Chez Nous

A healthy outlet for your romantic
Parisian fantasies

food

8.2 | **9.9**
10 | 10

experience

French

$**51**

Sixth Street District

Upmarket restaurant
Tues.-Fri. 11:45am-2pm, 6pm-
10:30pm; Sat.-Sun. 6pm-
10:30pm; closed Mon. *Date-friendly.*

510 Neches St.
Austin
(512) 473-2413

Bar Beer/wine
Credit Cards Visa, MC, AmEx
Reservations Essential

For almost a quarter of a century, Chez Nous has been one of Austin's best destinations for an intimate special occasion, and even the recent wave of New American cuisine that has splashed over the city has failed to dislodge it from this pedestal. By keeping it small, this authentic French bistro downtown has, appropriately enough, managed to maintain that our-house-is-your-house feel ("Chez Nous est chez vous," perhaps?).

The little interior of the restaurant is thoroughly transporting, with lace curtains, fresh flowers in old French liquor bottles, Toulouse-Lautrec posters, and lighting that is just dim enough. And despite the well-explored French theme, the décor never feels like a tourist shop.

Chez Nous' main selling point is a $22 three-course prix-fixe, which consists of a choice of terrific house-made pâtés or a salad (the salade Lyonnaise is outstanding); one of three mains; and for dessert, luxurious mousse au chocolat, crème caramel, or a brie plate. The kitchen has a real way with fish, which is always well cooked and simply dressed. Duck is another strength— it comes out reliably rich, pink, and tender. Preparations are traditional—the menu keeps a blissful distance from fusion—and mouth-watering. A veal chop, for example, just melted into its wild-mushroom and crème fraîche gravy when that preparation was on the menu; at press time, they were doing it with vermouth sage sauce and lemon-roasted asparagus. There are only a few, strangely incongruous, weaknesses. The bread served upon arrival is flimsy and a little stale, the butter pats too hard. We don't quite get their ubiquitous potato-puff side dish, and escargot, at our last visit, were chewy and disappointing. Perhaps most surprising of all, in a quality French restaurant, the brie is stiff and over-refrigerated.

But such bumps are quickly smoothed over by the classy service of the sexy French staff. They make a charming team, which is also, as it happens, a formidable force in the city-wide soccer league (trophies are proudly displayed at the counter). It is just this kind of laid-back cool that makes Chez Nous such a winner. –RM

Chez Zee

Sweet treats and pickles in one of
Austin's most romantic settings

food
5.8
10
9.4
10
experience

American $35   Northwest Hills

Casual restaurant   5406 Balcones Dr.   *Bar* Full
Mon.-Fri. 11am-10pm; Sat.   Austin   *Credit Cards* Visa, MC, AmEx
9am-12:30am; Sun. 9am-   (512) 454-2666   *Reservations* Recommended
10pm. *Brunch. Live music.* www.chez-zee.com
Outdoor dining. Vegetarian-friendly.

With its beautiful atrium seating surrounded by lush plants and
fountains, subtle lighting, and unobtrusive piano music, Chez Zee is the
kind of setting that could bring you to your knees (with a ring). The
menu features American, Southwestern, and Italian-influenced dishes,
with a particularly lively range of appetizers. The "Aztec" corn and
shrimp soup is light and tasty with a simple tomato base. Pecan-
encrusted brie is good, but the accompanying chutney lacks pizzazz.
Interestingly, Chez Zee still offers that disappearing Deep South delicacy,
the fried dill pickle: theirs is thin, crisp, nicely salted, not too pickley,
and absolutely delicious with the creamy chipotle dressing.

Mains offer fewer thrills, with a succession of dully sauced chickens.
The Caesar salad is average, but with shatteringly crisp, not crunchy,
croutons. Both chicken marsala and grilled chicken, served over angel
hair pasta with cream sauce, are bland. "Tuscan" chicken marinara is
good, but oversalted (and in absolutely no sense "Tuscan"). But we like
the filet mignon with a lemon-dressed salad and blue cheese. We
would normally avoid the dreaded low-carb menu (may this fad die
with haste), but they grill the filet to temperature, and the salad, with
its bright citrus flavor, is a nice, light foil to the steak.

Chez Zee promotes itself as a dessert destination, and the lengthy
dessert menu with assorted after-dinner drinks attests to this. The
"Maida's Cake" is rich and delicious. An intriguing rosemary-lemon
cake is also surprisingly tasty, with subtle rosemary and pronounced
lemon. Service at Chez Zee can be less than attentive, and lunch and
dinner items are inconsistent in quality. But the weekend brunch has
some wonderful choices, like the crème brûlée French toast, making
brunch an appealing option. –MPN

Chinatown

An unusually far-ranging menu of
Chinese cuisine in an office-park setting

food
7.2 **6.7**
10 10
experience

Chinese, Japanese $ **30**   *Northwest Hills*

Upmarket restaurant
Mon.-Thurs. 11am-10pm; Fri.
11am-10:30pm; Sat. 11:30am-
10:30pm; Sun. 11:30am-10pm. *Vegetarian-friendly.*

3407 Greystone Dr.
Austin
(512) 343-9307

3300 Bee Caves Rd.
78746, (512) 327-6588

Bar Full
Credit Cards Visa, MC, AmEx
Reservations Accepted

One of Austin's longer-established Chinese restaurants, Chinatown has been serving a variety of regional cuisines from the Middle Kingdom for well over 20 years in two Austin locations—Northwest Hills and Westlake. However, they are no longer under the same ownership. This review refers only to the Northwest Hills Chinatown, whose décor is elegant, with vibrant, red-and-black lacquer and racks of wine. Service is helpful and meticulous and they are usually happy to accommodate special requests.

The menu offers house specialties complete with wine recommendations, and a section featuring "Home Cooking Country Style"—styles of cooking specific to different regions of China. There's sizzling kan shao from Szechuan; kung pao with hot sauce and peanuts; black bean sauce from Hunan; and garlicky Yu-Hsiang-style dishes. Chinatown also has access to sushi, as it shares a space with Musashino, one of Austin's best Japanese restaurants. The sushi menu is limited, but everything is excellent and extremely fresh.

The egg-drop soup is peppery and very simple, with nothing in it but egg. Shanghai vegetarian spring rolls are crisp and light, filled with carrots and mushrooms. Pork dumplings have a subtle ginger and leek flavor, and the sauce is fiery hot with chili paste, but lacks that all-important vinegar punch. Amongst the mains, we recommend the Szechuan bean curd, with its soft texture and warm, lingering heat. The sizzling dishes are served in a sweet, thin sauce and arrive dramatically sizzling, as promised, on a cast iron plate. Amongst the Yu Hsiang dishes, which are rich with garlic and lots of crisp water chestnuts and green onion, our favorite is a combination of pork threads and julienned eggplant. The sauces at Chinatown also have a wonderful consistency—none of that cornstarch glueyness you so commonly find in Chinese food. And while this isn't the best in town, it's pretty good for Austin Chinese. –MPN

Chisholm Trail

Barbecue that lags sadly behind the
lofty Lockhart standard

food

5.8
10
7.7
10
experience

Barbecue $ **11**   *Lockhart*

Counter service   1323 S. Colorado St.   *Bar* Beer/wine
Daily 8am-8pm.   Lockhart   *Credit Cards* Visa, MC, AmEx
                         (512) 398-6027   *Reservations* Not accepted

Is Chisholm Trail, which has "only" been around since 1978 and sports
a drive-thru window, free-riding on the Lockhart legend? Hoping not,
we had high expectations when we first arrived at this simplest of
cafeteria-style environments. That simplicity is already a good sign in
Texas, as we all know, and the American flags and random Texas
memorabilia lend some character here, although the brown tables and
chairs look like they were recovered from the bank auction of a
spectacularly unsuccessful telemarketing operation. More to the point,
though, Chisholm Trail's 'cue falls well short of the heady *Texas Monthly*
hype, and certainly short of the local competition; the joint brings up
the rear of the Lockhart pack, by a fair margin.

As for the food, we'll begin with the brisket, as customers tend to
do. It's not exactly bad, but it's not much above average either, smoky
but decidedly on the dry side. Not as dry, though, as the crackly pork
ribs, whose meat requires significant effort to pry off the bone. The
barbecue sauce (heresy to some in these parts) is a gummy, sticky-sweet
concoction that tastes more like…dare we say…a bottled version.
Sausage, meanwhile, has a good grind and texture, but it's
underseasoned.

Worst of all, however, are the sides. Macaroni and cheese, at our last
visit, was a soggy, watery mess, the noodles cooked to virtual mush,
the cheese thin and runny with little seasoning. Cole slaw might as well
have come from the supermarket aisle, and potato salad was only
slightly better. If you truck it all the way out to Lockhart, it would be
foolish to waste your appetite on this. –RG

Chooby Doo

A quick, haphazardly eclectic lunch stop
with a stupid name and okay food

food

5.9   5.3
10   10

experience

American, Pan-Asian, Middle E. $ 7   Far South

Counter service
Mon.-Sat. 11am-9pm;
Sun. noon-8pm. *Outdoor dining.*
Vegetarian-friendly.

3601 W. William
Cannon Dr., Austin
(512) 891-9850
www.choobydoocafe.com

Bar None
Credit Cards Visa and MC
Reservations Not accepted

The Chooby Doo International Café is selling itself as a healthy and inexpensive alternative to the usual fast-food suspects. Beyond that, Chooby Doo is also much more pleasant than those spots: vividly painted walls and hanging paper lanterns are offset by gleaming metal furniture. Local artists display their works on the wall, and other handicrafts, such as hats and necklaces, are available as well. Service is friendly and pretty fast, with counter orders delivered to the table.

The eclectic menu centers around several variations on Southeast Asian dishes, but there are also many Mediterranean options and even Chicago-style hot dogs. Start with the savory Thai tom yum soup, slightly sour and aromatic from fish sauce and kaffir lime leaves, with glass noodles, veggies (including fresh chopped tomatoes), and chicken. If you are looking for a light meal, here it is. Substantial salads are simple, with fresh veggies and light dressings, like the black sesame-seed-studded Asian chicken salad. The chicken can taste old, though, so vegetarian salads are a better bet. Asian dumplings are cheap and plentiful, but also bland.

We have always been pleased, however, with Chooby Doo's sandwich menu and its myriad of possibilities. The French-Asian fusion sandwiches are particularly good; amongst them, we like the Chinese barbecued pork on soft French bread, whose meat has a sweet hoisin flavor that is set off by crisp shredded carrots, cucumber, and cilantro. We also enjoy the baba ganoush wrap—the warm, soft flatbread is garnished with the same set of fresh veggies, and the baba ganoush is pureed smooth and has a subtle, smoky flavor that manages not to overshadow the eggplant.

But if you think healthy fast food misses the point, and the mildly exotic sends you squealing, like Scooby Doo himself, into hiding, there's always the all-American hot dog with all the fixin's. –MPN

Chuy's

Good Tex-Mex in a finely realized, self-consciously retro environment

Mexican $**27**   *Zilker, Far Northwest, Far North*

Casual restaurant   1728 Barton Springs Rd.   *Bar* Full
Sun.-Thurs. 11am-10pm;   Austin   *Credit Cards* Visa, MC, AmEx
Fri.-Sat. 11am-11pm.   (512) 474-4452   *Reservations* Accepted
Live music. Outdoor dining. www.chuys.com

                           11680 N. Hwy. 183   10520 N. Lamar Blvd.
                           78759, (512) 342-0011   78753, (512) 836-3218

It's well established that Chuy's was the place where, in 2001, the Bush daughters got caught (Jenna for using somebody else's ID, Barbara for underage drinking) in a humorously well-publicized episode that vaulted Austin's Tex-Mex scene onto the front page of every newspaper in America. At least the Bush daughters had good taste: the margaritas at Chuy's are as reliable as any in town, and we have no doubt that the episode actually wound up boosting business at this well-loved 1950s-retro-themed Tex-Mex joint.

Even better than the 'ritas are the Mexican martinis—a true Texan invention. It's not just an excuse to order three martinis at once: we think the flavor mix is better, with less sweetness. The Chuy's version comes in a plastic shaker with that not-quite-attached lid that must be held down while pouring, as it's the only tenuous barrier between the drink and the outside world. Needless to say, somebody always forgets this fact, and the result is a sudden flash hailstorm of ice, tequila and Cointreau all over the table and, no doubt, somebody's lap—a natural check, perhaps, on the person who probably didn't need the rest of that drink anyway.

The rock 'n' roll, top-down cars, and other '50s paraphernalia work pretty well as a theme—it's carefully done up with Disneyesque detail. We also like the fish tank and the feisty servers. As for the food, it's better than you might think for such a studenty place. The queso is absolutely top-notch, with more seasoning than most, while hatch green chile enchiladas hit just the right balance of Tex with Mex, as do the tomatillo sauces, although we wish the chicken were somewhat less dry; nonetheless, the joint has a solid grasp on the essence of comfort food. Beef fajitas are well seasoned, remarkably tender, and come with tasty flour tortillas. The only real headache here is the wait: an hour or more on weekend nights. Sometimes fame has its costs. –RG

Cipollina

Great pizza and a little bit of everything else—even tango

food

7.8 | **7.4**
10 | 10

experience

Italian, Pizza $**18**   *Clarksville*

Counter service   1213 W. Lynn St.   *Bar* Beer/wine
Mon.-Wed. 7am-9pm; Thurs.-Fri.   Austin   *Credit Cards* Visa, MC, AmEx
7am-10pm; Sat. 8am-10pm; Sun.   (512) 477-5211   *Reservations* Not accepted
8am-9pm. *Breakfast. Date-friendly.*   www.cipollina-austin.com
Live music. Outdoor dining. Vegetarian-friendly. Wireless Internet.

Cipollina, put together by the owners of upscale Jeffrey's nearby, has charmed not only the residents of the ever-more-happening Clarksville neighborhood but also multitudes of yuppies from further afield, who descend on the place in beautiful, brightly-colored flocks. On Thursday and Friday nights, the restaurant plays host to tango and Latino jazz dance bands, respectively; tables are pulled aside, and the floor quickly fills with long legs and bodies swaying to the beat with enviable flair.

But on most afternoons and weekday evenings, you'll find this simple Italian joint a place to relax with a cup of coffee or a glass of wine. Tables are generously spaced, the flowers on the table are plain and wild, and counter service keeps both starchiness and through traffic to a minimum. Plus, if you come between 3:30pm and 5:30pm (or anytime on Sundays), Cipollina's excellent wood-fired pizzas are half price.

These are single-serving pizzas, with flavorful crusts and a variety of posh toppings. Tragically, they've removed our favorite from the menu—it was called the "Veggie Medley," and it starred roasted peppers and caramelized onions; happily, though, they'll still make it at quiet moments. There is also a range of pasta dishes and frittatas on display behind the deli glass, but much of it suffers from the usual out-all-day sag. For example, the overcooked squash and chewy cheese in the vegetable lasagna (or lasagne, if you're an Italophile) usually bear the marks of this treatment, but at least its tomato sauce is sweet and fresh. Salads have delicious, tangy dressings, and come adorned with homemade crostini and sharp peperoncini. There are well-executed sandwiches (we particularly like the fontina and mushroom, with a deep, winey porcini spread and oozing cheese; unfortunately, it was no longer on the menu at press time). Soups, such as a sprightly chilled mango-carrot, are also good bets. And don't leave without sampling the gorgeous baked goods. You'll leave nibbling and feeling like one of the cool kids. –RM

Cisco's

The Tex-Mex breakfast of presidents—
but can we trust our presidents' taste?

food

3.4
10

9.0
10

experience

Mexican

$11

East Austin

Casual restaurant
Daily 7am-2:30pm.
Breakfast. Brunch.

1511 E. 6th St.
Austin
(512) 478-2420

Bar BYO
Credit Cards Visa, MC, AmEx
Reservations Accepted

To call Cisco's an institution would be an understatement. This classic East Austin "bakery" is really a restaurant known far and wide for its hearty Tex-Mex breakfasts, particularly the migas. As a result, the place reliably draws in a crowd that's a cross section of all Austin: the East Austin Mexican-Americans, the old-school Texans, the sorority sisters, the emo-rock hipsters, and all the rest.

They come, first and foremost, for the ambience, which has changed little since Cisco's opened a half century ago—there's even wainscoting. Still, the feel is more timeless than time-frozen, perhaps because the crowd is so modern. Do take the time to gaze upon the articles and paraphernalia on the walls, which tell some fascinating stories, including LBJ's single-minded obsession with Cisco's tamales— apparently he wound up subcontracting with the tamale purveyor for private delivery to the White House.

Nowadays, though, the tamales have disappeared from the menu, and it's unfortunately possible that the kitchen has gone downhill since the sad passing of Rudy Cisneros, the patron saint of Cisco's, whose likeness is still featured (complete with cigar) in the restaurant's logo. The truth is that the migas are not really so impressive—slightly dry and tasteless scrambled eggs without enough chile character; rubbery, supermarket-style tortilla chips; and so on.

The highlights are a salty, well seasoned ranchero sauce that has a bit of kick to it, and refried beans redolent of smoky pork fat. Hot buttermilk biscuits, which appear in a basket at the beginning of a meal, are accompanied by squeeze bottles of honey and liquid butter; we challenge you to find someone who doesn't like *that*. But don't expect culinary fireworks here; come, instead, to soak in the atmosphere of a legendary Austin standby that still fits the city like a trusted old cowboy hat. –RG

Clay Pit

Romantic nouvelle Indian served in
what feels like a wine cellar

food
8.4 / 10
9.2 / 10
experience

Indian $**33**   *Capitol Area*

Upmarket restaurant
Mon.-Thurs. 11am-2pm, 5pm-
10pm; Fri. 11am-2pm, 5pm-11pm;
Sat. 11am-3pm, 5pm-11pm;
Sun. 5pm-10pm. *Date-friendly. Vegetarian-friendly.*

1601 Guadalupe St.
Austin
(512) 322-5131
www.claypit.com

Bar Full
Credit Cards Visa, MC, AmEx
Reservations Accepted

When a restaurant anoints itself a purveyor of "contemporary Indian cuisine," it can often mean nothing other than menu that adds a token Tandoori salmon dish to the standard lineup and charges slightly higher prices for the same stuff you could get at your corner curry house. Not so at the Clay Pit, a fusion restaurant that turns Indian cuisine into something completely unexpected and exciting. The romantic atmosphere, with dimly lit tables set beneath a series of stone arches for an old-wine-cellar effect, makes the Clay Pit another kind of rarity: an Indian restaurant in which you actually feel like drinking wine.

You might start with coriander calamari—a version of fried calamari whose heavy batter isn't subtle (it's sort of like a pakora batter), but conceals tender squid. The dish is served with an excellent version of cilantro aïoli. Goat curry is a strength amongst the mains. There's rack of lamb on the menu, shrimp with coconut milk and pomegranate seeds, and a delightful selection of vegetarian apps and mains. But best of all is a showstopping dish called "Khuroos-E-Tursh," which is chicken breast stuffed with spinach, mushrooms, onions, and cheese, with a sweet cashew-almond cream sauce. The preparation sounds heavy and elaborate, yet the ingredients come together with a rich but not overbearing sweetness that is deeply seductive.

A weak point of the Clay Pit is the requisite all-you-can-eat lunch buffet, which seems…well, requisite, serving up the Indian standards instead of bringing out the restaurant's fusion strengths. So go for dinner, for which the dimly lit room is more appropriate anyway. The location of the Clay Pit makes it a popular spot for UT student dates or visiting-parent dinners, but we recommend the place for any occasion or demographic at all. –RG

CoCo's Café

Mediocre Taiwanese fare with a bubbly upside

food

3.1	5.2
10	10

experience

Chinese $ **8**   *West Campus*

Counter service   1910 Guadalupe St.   *Bar* None
Daily 11am-11pm.   Austin   *Credit Cards* Visa, MC, AmEx
Kid-friendly.   (512) 236-9398   *Reservations* Not accepted

Ahh, the bubble tea, the Asian delight. Those funny little tapioca balls that pop up through oversized straws and make smiles spread sweetly over kids' faces. For many, these odd teas are what the Coke float is for mainstream America—that sweet treat from those childhood moments when parental approval turned into a special occasion.

But perhaps because of its inherent oddness, bubble tea has developed a decidedly grown-up appeal amongst Austinites, especially in this town that so celebrates the Weird. The teas provide a remarkable eating and drinking experience—the unearthly colors and unusual flavors; the glow of the balls and their sweet, slimy resistance; and the double-wide straws nestled into those specially sealed plastic cups (like the old Star Trek episodes, they're so hokey they're cool). And the best place in Austin to get these bubbly concoctions is at Coco's on the Drag.

This Taiwanese hole-in-the-wall is cute and perky, with a relatively authentic feel and a long list of bubble drinks. We particularly recommend the taro tea, which is not too sweet and delightfully unfamiliar to Western palates, and the sweet and milky watermelon cream version. But we encourage you to experiment. Coco's also sells a short menu of Taiwanese dishes that are very popular with the Asian UT crowd, but they aren't much to write home about. We like the green onion pie (more familiar as the scallion pancake), but veggie dumplings are disconcertingly fishy; tofu curry lacks subtlety; and a surprisingly horrid dish called sticky rice, at our last visit, arrived in a pool of gelatinous sludge with what appeared to be burlap on top.

Stick to the drinks; if, for some reason, the idea of gooey, slimy translucent pearls shooting up into your mouth doesn't appeal to you, don't worry: all drinks can be ordered bubbleless. Otherwise, beam us up, Scotty. –RM

Conan's Pizza

Cheap lunch specials and a chance to
revisit your childhood Frogger career

food

4.7	5.7
10	10

experience

Pizza $ **9**   *W. Campus, N. Central, Far South*

Counter service   603 W. 29th St.   *Bar* Beer/wine
Mon.-Thurs. 11am-11pm;   Austin   *Credit Cards* Visa, MC, AmEx
Fri.-Sun. 11am-midnight.   (512) 478-5712   *Reservations* Not accepted
Delivery. Kid-friendly.   www.conanspizza.com

                               2438 W. Anderson Ln.   2018 W. Stassney Ln.
                               78757, (512) 459-3222   78745, (512) 441-6754

Conan's Pizza was Austin's first specialty pizzeria when they opened
their deep-dish doors in 1976, and entering their restaurants, one feels
that time has barely passed. Wood-paneled walls, plants whose tendrils
span the ceilings and whose lives probably span decades, booths
decorated with years' worth of postcards, framed comic drawings of
Conan the Barbarian doing his thing, and priceless video games (okay,
those might have been updated in the 1980s), all give the space a retro
feel.

Service is pretty fast, though not overly friendly, with order and pickup at the counter. The menu at Conan's four restaurants is basic: pizza,
garlic and cheese breads, salad, soda, and beer. Elderly iceberg lettuce
comprises the bulk of the salad, with a smattering of black olives and
shredded mozzarella piled on top. The blue cheese dressing is thin, but
there are several others to choose from. Pizza is reasonably priced,
toppings are basic, and the sauce is pureed thin and a bit sugary.
There's thin or pan crust, with a choice of white or wheat dough. The
thin crust isn't particularly thin, but it does have a crisp bottom, while
the deep-dish crust is thick, but has a soft texture that reminds us of
Bisquick. But the pizza is actually pretty good for the price. Just be sure
you get it while it's hot—cold Conan's cheese turns into a substance of
which DuPont's best scientists would be proud.

Conan's big draw is the all-you-can-eat lunchtime buffet (not offered
at the location near campus) and the by-the-slice lunch specials that are
especially appealing to budget-conscious students. And then there's the
nostalgia factor. Conan's reminds us of eating out with the family when
the most exotic topping was pepperoni, and getting to play an arcade
game while you waited was still a novelty. –MPN

Cooper's

Classic, no frills barbecue at the biting
end of a snaking Hill Country drive

food

8.3 | **7.1**
10 | 10
experience

Barbecue $**14**   *Llano*

Counter service   604 W. Young St.   *Bar* Beer/wine
Sun.-Thurs. 10:30am-8pm;   Llano   *Credit Cards* Visa, MC, AmEx
Fri.-Sat. 10:30am-9pm.   (325) 247-5713   *Reservations* Not accepted
Date-friendly. Kid-friendly. Outdoor dining.

Cooper's is lodged deeply, snugly, into Red State Texas, complete with a
thank-you letter from W himself. It is staffed by terse old-timers, who
do their talking in squints rather than words, and look like they oughta
be chewing on something tough.

In fact, in spite of the gargantuan reputation of the place, the meat
here does, occasionally, creep surprisingly close to toughness. Cooper's
is generally listed amongst the top three barbecue spots in Central
Texas, but it provides a certain kind of manly meat that is very different
from the sweet, sauce-crusted 'cue served by most local smoke barons.
Cuts are massive and unadorned, except by a very basic salt-'n'-pepper
dry rub. This is a meat-lover's delight—all you get is the flesh, and
plenty of it. There's sometimes wonderfully gamey cabrito (baby goat),
too, which is an unusual treat. The barbecue sauce is thin, vinegary,
and peppery, in what many would describe as the correct, authentic Hill
Country style.

Still, the meat stands up well on its own. The most famous option is
the "Big Chop," an absurdly sized pork chop that is shockingly thick,
but can vary dramatically in tenderness. Sausage can also be leathery,
but has excellent flavor; chicken is far moister, and liberally peppered,
while brisket—the best choice of all—is bountifully cushioned by fat.
You pick your cut before you even enter the restaurant, from a great
steel pit that's manned by a laconic old man in a gimme cap. At your
request he'll dunk your choice into a vat of sauce before slapping it
onto a red plastic tray for you to carry in and enjoy.

Cooper's may not be for everyone, but if you like to travel, this joint
reminds us of the old tourism slogan: "Texas—it's like a whole other
country." –RM

Cosmic Café

This tame vegetarian Indian restaurant
is a sad replacement for West Lynn

food
5.0 | **6.4**
10 | 10
experience

Indian $**16**   *Clarksville*

Casual restaurant   1110 W. Lynn St.   *Bar* BYO
Tues.-Thurs. 11am-10pm; Fri.-Sat.   Austin   *Credit Cards* Visa, MC, AmEx
11am-10:30pm; Sun. noon-   (512) 482-0950   *Reservations* Not accepted
9:30pm; closed Mon. *Live music.* www.cosmiccafeaustin.com
Outdoor dining. Vegetarian-friendly.

We were as shocked as rest of you to find that our town's best
vegetarian eatery, the West Lynn Café, an Austin institution, had closed
down, disappeared seemingly overnight, and been replaced by this
vegetarian Indian restaurant. Apparently the West Lynn folks had long
been contemplating a retreat into the comforting arms of Mother's,
their other Austin business, and an eager long-time patron had only
been waiting for the final decision to pounce on their prime Clarksville
digs. He also pounced on the accommodating old staff (75% of whom
remained for the transition) and the veggie-craving clientele.

Everyone means incredibly well; optimism shines on the faces of the
staff as they do their best to sell the new place, and of the customers
as they do their best to enjoy it. Unfortunately, Cosmic doesn't hold a
natural beeswax candle to its predecessor. The dishes are less creative,
and less elegant, than were West Lynn's; what we have here, in the
end, is a slightly worse than average Indian restaurant.

Much of the food is simply too bland. An asparagus soup is peppery
but uneventful, and the dal (a classic Indian lentil stew), is more
flavorful but too runny. Naan bread is fine, but the chutney selection is
lifeless. Samosas are soggy and greasy, and filled with boredom.
Vegetable curry lacks imagination. Cardamom flavor is notably absent
from the kheer (rice pudding). Even dishes that in theory have some
fusion-inspired novelty, such as a mandala pizza on naan, end up
tasting like run-of-the-mill American fare. Only the rather irritating,
punning names show much inventiveness.

It's too bad, really, both because we mourn the loss of an old reliable
destination, and because vegetarian Indian food, with the lovely, fresh
dishes of the southern part of that country, can be otherworldly. But
Cosmic Café is decidedly terrestrial. –RM

Costa del Sol

A dive with friendly, Spanish-speaking
service and Salvadoran specialties

food

6.3 / 10   3.5 / 10
experience

Latin American $**23**   *Far North*

Casual restaurant   7901 Cameron Rd.   *Bar* Beer/wine
Daily 9am-9pm.   Austin   *Credit Cards* Visa and MC
Breakfast.   (512) 832-5331   *Reservations* Accepted

Costa del Sol is one of a handful of places in Austin that serves
Salvadoran food. That alone makes it more interesting than the
countless anonymous Mexican dives that flank the highways and fill the
strip malls all around this town. But like all of these, Costa del Sol is
really a local feeding hole, attractive mainly to those who live around
there, and who know they will be recognized and warmly greeted by
someone who speaks their native tongue and makes the food that they
grew up eating. As such, Austin's many little hole-in-the-wall Mexican
and Central American restaurants are invaluable fonts of culinary
heritage, even if they are not, in the end, the diamonds in the rough
that urban foodies are forever in hopes of finding.

Costa del Sol certainly has no sparkle to speak of. Housed in an old
fast-food joint, its tables have the laminate stickiness that comes after
years of being pawed by grubby kiddie fingers. Located way north on
Cameron Road, the restaurant offers diners a romantic view of U.S.
183. On a hot, landlocked day, we can only dream about the ocean
sunset depicted on its menus.

Costa del Sol may not cook up anything special, but it gives us tasty
new options that broaden our culinary scope. We like the pollo
encebollado, featuring browned chicken cooked in a pile of sweet
onions and tomatoes, served with rice, beans, and tortillas. Mojarra
frita (deep-fried tilapia) has a batter that's rather chewy and needs salt,
but beneath the crust, the fish is tender and moist, and, when
brightened with a squeeze of lime, wraps nicely with some grilled
onions and sliced avocado into a tortilla. Costa del Sol also prepares its
own pupusas. Hot off the griddle and oozing cheese, these little stuffed
masa pancakes make a very satisfactory snack, if not, perhaps, one
worth the trek all the way north. –RM

County Line

An Austin barbecue chain with high-flying views that don't merit the prices

food
5.9
10

8.9
10

experience

Barbecue $ **29**   *Westlake, Northwest Hills*

Casual restaurant
Mon. 11:30am-9pm; Tues.-Thurs.
11:30am-9:30pm; Fri.-Sat.
11:30am-10pm; Sun. noon-9pm.
Kid-friendly. Outdoor dining.

6500 Bee Caves Rd.
Austin
(512) 327-1742
www.countyline.com

5204 FM 2222
78731, (512) 346-3664

Bar Full
Credit Cards Visa, MC, AmEx
Reservations Accepted

Knock, knock. Who's there? Interrupting cow. Interrupting co…? Moo.

The cow interrupting in this instance is the large, stuffed longhorn variety that hangs from a wall at the County Line barbecue restaurant and occasionally blurts out insufferably bad jokes. She is an apt spokesperson for this oddly conflicted business that has fought hard to join the ranks of Austin's barbecue elite—it cannot quite decide between low-brow kitsch and pricier, high-brow ambitions. Although outposts now dot all of Texas and now even grace New Mexico and Oklahoma, Austin's two locations in the hills and on the lake are famous for their views; the former has a particularly nice terrace from which you can watch the stunning Hill Country sunsets. The interior décor, meanwhile, seems cribbed from a western-themed Vegas casino, complete with loud wall-to-wall carpeting, multi-colored lighting, and disco-ball-cum-wagon-wheel fixtures.

The food, for its part, more or less gets the job done. The County Line is not, in the end, one of the best spots for barbecue in (or outside of) town, but we do like their unspeakably enormous, unusually meaty beef ribs—there's a sleeping-bag-sized version hanging on one of the walls—and their tender, subtle sausage. Pork ribs are also decent, but the brisket is considerably drier than the humor of its wall-mounted cousin. Slaw is interestingly big and chunky, but beans are bland, and barbecue sauce is too vinegary and lacks complexity. The County Line does its less classic sides well, though: sugary bread costs extra, but it's worth it—you can't put it down. And side salads come well dressed (we particularly like a creamy pecan-herb vinaigrette).

The problem is, with its hilltop pretensions, this restaurant simply prices things too high. Dishes cost around one-and-a-half times as much as they do elsewhere, and the all-you-can-eat barbecue combos climb shockingly high into the $20s (the Salt Lick gives you the same for under $10). And that, friends, is a poor joke. –RM

Crown & Anchor Pub

Cold beer, hot fries, cold beer, darts,
cold beer, grad students, cold beer

food

5.6 **6.8**
10   10

experience

American   **$13**   *UT Area*

Pub
Daily 11am-2am. Kitchen closes
at 11:45pm. *Outdoor dining.*
Wireless Internet.

2911 San Jacinto Blvd.
Austin
(512) 322-9168

Bar Beer/wine
Credit Cards Visa, MC, AmEx
Reservations Not accepted

The first sign that this campus pub is a significant step above a frat-house watering hole is the vigilant dude perched at the door checking ID's. If Posse East, on the opposite edge of the San Jacinto strip, is the ultimate undergraduate dive—a pulsing pile of burnt orange—then the Crown and Anchor is its grad-student counterpart, composed, peaceful, and relaxed.

But let us be clear—this ain't the Library of Congress; it's a bar. Like many good hangout bars, it has a pool table, a couple of dartboards, and some well-placed TVs. The décor is far from elegant, with the predictable gestures toward the sea-life: oars; a ship's steering wheel; and oddly rigid, torpedo-sized hanging fish. Neon beer signs illuminate the window in a neat row. But there are also countervailing hints of a pleasant adult mellowness: natural woods abound, and lazy ceiling fans hover over a comfortable deck. We love the long narrow table that runs the length of this deck, welcoming a neighborly collectivity.

This friendliness is enhanced by a wide range of draft beers available in pitchers that encourage sharing (it's that kind of place), complemented by an impressive catalog of international bottles. The food menu is considerably shorter, and represents bar food at its most basic—e.g. burgers. These are thin but moist, amply spread with both mustard and mayo, plus all the regular fixin's, and you can add bacon, cheddar, mushrooms, jalapeños, and so on; we like the bacon and cheddar combination. Excellent, crispy, salty fries play a strong supporting role. While these are by no means the "best burgers in town" as bragged on the menu, they are tasty and cheap. This is probably because they're also small—and we must say it's nice leaving a bar meal without that rumbling note of burgerly regret. –RM

Cuba Libre

Sixth Street Cuban that's not bad—
especially after a couple of mojitos

food

6.8	7.9
10	10

experience

Latin American   **$33**   *Warehouse District*

Casual restaurant   409 Colorado St.   *Bar* Full
Daily 4pm-2am. Kitchen closes   Austin   *Credit Cards* Visa, MC, AmEx
Sun.-Thurs. 10pm; Fri.-Sat. 11pm. (512) 471-2822   *Reservations* Accepted
Live music. Outdoor dining.   www.cubalibreaustin.com
Wireless Internet.

This is not your average Sixth Street bar, but it's hardly the Cuba of Che and Fidel. Suffice it to say that the college prepsters who frequent this restaurant and bar are the furthest thing from commies. Cuba Libre has a pleasingly smooth and polished atmosphere, even if the immaculately Polo-shirted clientele has a little too brassy a sheen. The feel is more Fourth Street than Sixth Street. The curtains that part before you upon entering open with a dramatic swish onto a long, dark room, lit by little candles, luxuriously padded in dark leathers, and plated in glowing coppers. Cuba Libre promotes this high-end club feel to lure a crowd as interested in the endless list of rums for mojitos as in the Cuban-influenced menu.

The food, however, is actually pretty good. Some dishes are rather plain Tex-Mex—the chicken quesadillas have little to offer besides some lively guacamole—so we recommend you stick to the more obviously Caribbean options. We particularly like a smoky, creamy Cuban black bean soup (neatly finished with swirls of tangy sour cream). Amongst the mains, the hot and crunchy trout stands out: delicately crusted fillets are sweet and tender, topped with a fruity mango concoction that is beautifully balanced by a jalapeño sauce. And a mint-lime mojito sauce manages to turn inevitably blah grilled chicken breasts into something rummy and exciting. Go for dinner on a Tuesday evening, when two-for-one deals abound, but if you end up here on a Saturday night, the bar turns into a major drinking and dancing scene.

Cuba Libre's line of high-end cigars has been clipped short by Austin's brand-new smoking ban, but they do still have the classy-kitsch tradition of a $10 martini and manicure every Thursday night. So go for it, ladies; now, if only your partners could learn to be gentlemen. –RM

Curra's Grill

Unpretentious interior Mexican with a
lofty but well-deserved reputation

food
8.5 / 10   **7.5** / 10
experience

Mexican

$27   *St. Ed's Area, Burnet, N. Central*

Casual restaurant
Daily 7am-10pm. Breakfast. Brunch.
Delivery. Kid-friendly. Live music.
Outdoor dining. Wireless Internet.

614 E. Oltorf St.
Austin
(512) 444-0012
www.currasgrill.com

6801 Burnet Rd.
78757, (512) 451-2560

Bar Full
Credit Cards Visa, MC, AmEx
Reservations Not accepted

7604 Robalo Rd.
78757, (512) 220-6196

We love this pair of eateries for assertively proving what we already knew: that Mexican food isn't just cheap and satisfying but is also gourmet cuisine. The regional Mexican dishes served are complex, subtle creations far removed from the beans, grease, and rice of fame, and good enough to draw the crowds. The large, busy room is bright with colors, and there is also capacious deck seating outside, watched over by several spirits of Mexican legend. The décor is not particularly cohesive, but outdoor seating is nice, and the happy throng pulls it all together quite effectively.

The menu is packed with tasty choices. We recommend that you explore the less familiar regional options. Best in a strong field is the cochinita pibil, a traditional, spicy Yucatan dish in which marinated shredded pork is slowly cooked in a banana leaf, leaving it meltingly tender, and hinting of cinnamon. It comes with fried plantains, black beans, rice, and tartly pickled red onions that are a beautiful bright purple. The resulting mix of sweet and savory is new and delightful, and makes for one of our favorite plates in town.

On a more familiar note, the chile relleno here is also good; it comes in a lovely pecan cream sauce that mellows the bitter notes of the poblano. Queso flameado, with melted jack cheese, roasted poblano strips, and chorizo, makes for a flavorful appetizer; and tortilla soup is as good as they come. Not so, however, for "Curra's Molletes," which sound like unusual comfort food—French bread, chorizo, black beans, and melted cheese—but come out heavy and greasy. But such missteps are few and far between. And at roughly half the cost of the upmarket competition, Curra's is a wonderfully low-key way to get that interior Mexican fix. –RM

Dan McKlusky's

A laughable excuse for a steakhouse—
but you won't be laughing at the check

food

3.3 **1.6**
10 10

experience

Steakhouse · **$63** · *Sixth Street District*

Upmarket restaurant
Mon.-Fri. 11:15am-1:30pm,
5pm-10pm; Sat. 5pm-10pm;
Sun. 5pm-9pm. *Live music.*
Wireless Internet.

301 E. 6th St.
Austin
(512) 473-8924
www.danmckluskys.com

Bar Full
Credit Cards Visa, MC, AmEx
Reservations Accepted

Where to begin with this late-1970s-era steakhouse that time seems to have simply passed by? Perhaps we might start with the uninviting atmosphere, which tries to look classy and winds up just feeling dingy, with cheap, aging booths. Or perhaps with the terrible grilled steaks. Don't let the classically executed culinary-school quadrillage (the criss-cross pattern on the meat's surface) deceive you into assuming that there's technical prowess in this kitchen. When the meat not overcooked, grey, and lifeless—as it usually is—it's instead tough, sinewy, and relatively tasteless. (It's hard to say which of those options is less appealing.) Add to that an utter lack of seasoning, a gummy béarnaise sauce, and bland potatoes, and you have a colossally disappointing meal. The only thing more colossal than your disappointment, in fact, will be your check: several steaks on the menu break the shocking $40 barrier.

What about a simple burger, you ask? That, too, seriously underperforms, with unappetizingly congealed cheese, low-quality lettuce and tomato, a supermarket-quality bun, and so on. As for the seafood and lobster, we will leave them to your imagination, as we would like the *Fearless Critic* to be suitable for readers of all ages.

Even the service here is awful, with a waitstaff that seem to have no idea what they're doing. Servers disappear for what seems like ages, only to return with the wrong thing or the wrong sense of where your meal is, or ever was. Indifference is the best you can hope for—and this, in a town renowned for its cheery service?

We do understand that, even in the face of such negative forces, memory can be a powerful emotion, and we can only surmise that it is nostalgia that keeps a few regulars coming back often enough for Dan McKlusky's to stay in business. Maybe Dan McKlusky's was better back in that era. Or maybe this sort of thing passed for a good steakhouse in 1979. But either way, as things stand, there is no place in 21st-century Austin for this steak, with this service, at these prices. –RG

Dan's Hamburgers

Stick it to those corporate vultures; the
burgers are better here anyway

food

6.3 **5.1**
10   10

experience

Burgers

$ **7**

Far South, East Austin, N. Central

Counter service
Sun.-Thurs. 6am-10pm: Fri.-Sat.
6am-11pm. *Breakfast. Kid-friendly.*

4308 Manchaca Rd.
Austin
(512) 443-6131

Bar None
Credit Cards No credit cards
Reservations Not accepted

844 Airport Blvd.
78702, (512) 385-2262

5602 N. Lamar Blvd.
78751, (512) 459-3239

Dan's Hamburgers has been open since 1973, serving no-frills, fast-ish
food for breakfast, lunch, and dinner. (For those of you wondering,
Fran's is a maritally challenged split-off from Dan's, offering similar food
in a slightly more interesting environment.) With cash-only counter
service (there are ATMs available by the registers), food is made to
order, so you will have to wait a few minutes for your meal. There's no
décor to speak of—just blank walls, lots of windows, and tables and
booths crowded with families, workers, and teenagers.

The menu is simple: eggs, biscuits, and pancakes for breakfast, with
mostly hamburgers for lunch and dinner, though there are a few other
items, like chicken-fried steak, chicken and fish sandwiches, and grilled-
cheese sandwiches for the feisty vegetarians. Burgers come in small,
medium, and large sizes with multiple patty options. They are fried and
thin, and come with sliced tomato, pickles, chopped onion, and lettuce
that are fresher than what you'll find at McDonald's or Burger King,
with cheeseburgers fused to their buns with industrial-strength
American cheese.

Grilled cheese sandwiches come with chips and a multitude of pickles
slices we remember from high school when boys would fling them at
the windows in a bocce-like competition to see who could get the most
in a close grouping. Fries are thinly cut with skins intact, a little soft and
greasy, or you can have vivid orange curly fries with your burger. We
like to pay a little extra for Dan's crunchy and sweet battered onion
rings. Dessert includes excellent shakes, creamy and thick—order them
early, as they need a little time to melt before they slide easily up a
straw. In the end, it's still fast food, but if that's really what you want,
it's always good to support the little guy. And at least their heating
device of choice is the griddle, not the microwave oven. –MPN

Dandelion Café

Good food, kid-friendly, and just a little
bit like Les Amis—what's not to like?

food

| **7.7** | **7.6** |
| 10 | 10 |

experience

Light American $ **8**   *East Austin*

Café
Mon.-Fri. 7am-9pm; Sat. 8am-
3pm; closed Sun. *Breakfast.*
Kid-friendly. Vegetarian-friendly.
Wireless Internet.

1115 E. 11th St.
Austin
(512) 542-9542
www.dandelioncafe.com

Bar None
Credit Cards Visa, MC, AmEx
Reservations Not accepted

East Austin's Dandelion Café may be the last real link to Les Amis, one
of Austin's most loved, hated, and missed coffeeshops. The Dandelion
Café was opened by two longtime Les Amis amies, Mary Beth and
Stephanie, and while there are some similarities between the two cafés,
the Dandelion is not trying to be Les Amis at all (which is a good thing,
since nothing ever could be).

Unlike its moodier ancestor, the Dandelion is brightly painted, even
cheery; there's a comfortable sitting area, a cute kids' corner, and even
a section on the menu entitled "after-school snacks." But that
wonderful black-and-white party photo from Les Amis' New Year's Eve
Party, circa nineteen-seventy-something, lives at the Dandelion now,
and much of the menu reminds us of the glory days (though everything
is of a much higher quality here, and there's no need to wonder what
shenanigans might be taking place in the kitchen, affecting your food).

The Dandelion Café is up bright and early (with none of Les Amis'
late-morning hangover), serving cereal, bagels, toast and their
wonderful, ever-changing breakfast pie, which is filled with eggs,
cheese, and veggies. We are always drawn to the black beans and
brown rice, that necessity of college survival. Dandelion makes theirs
fresh, and garnishes it all with cool diced tomatoes and onions, chunks
of avocado and pickled jalapeño, cheddar, and sour cream. The house
soup is a spicy cream of jalapeño, better suited to the winter months,
so have fruit or chips with your sandwich when it's hot out. We love
the roast turkey and Swiss on wheat, which comes with baby greens
and slices of pear whose sweetness compliments the faint smokiness of
the turkey. If you are in the mood for more of a carb-and-sugar high,
don't miss the "Fancy" grilled cheese, a hot, buttery sandwich on raisin
bread with herbed goat cheese and lemon-fig preserves. Sweet. –MPN

Dario's

Tex-(yawn)-Mex in an East Austin with
much better to offer elsewhere

food

3.1 10   **3.3** 10

experience

Mexican   **$21**   *East Austin*

Casual restaurant
Tues.-Wed. 7am-4pm; Thurs.-Sat.
7am-10pm; Sun. 7am-3pm; closed
Mon. *Breakfast. Live music.*

1800 E. 6th St.
Austin
(512) 479-8105

Bar Full
Credit Cards Visa, MC, AmEx
Reservations Accepted

In an East Austin full of interesting places for Mexican food, Dario's is boring, boring, boring. Come in and you'll be seated at a nondescript table amidst dozens of others in a room that's like a big, dark, impersonal cafeteria. Things take yet another turn for the worse when the queso arrives: it's chunky and unappetizing. Nor do the mediocre chiles rellenos, or tacos with boring ground beef, improve things. Rice and beans are blah, and the salad just sits there on the plate with nothing to do.

You can try to look for high points, but there's little you can do when the menu could bore through solid rock. In fact, there is only one course of action when the menu is that dull. Here's a hint: it starts with an "e"…Enchiladas! The cheese enchiladas at Dario's drown in a chili con carne gravy that's brown like good ol' Tex-Mex from decades past. The gravy moistens the enchiladas, whose corn tortillas don't maintain a hint of dryness, while that yella' cheese does its part, oozing out everywhere—from above, from below, from without, from within. You know the drill, but sometimes that's exactly what you want. Get any more ambitious than cheese enchiladas, and you'll get yourself into trouble.

Apparently, Dario's has a certain following amongst cops, it's got live music on some nights, and it's been around for a while…at least that's something. Still, the question remains: why would you eat at Dario's if you happen to be in East Austin, in one of America's greatest Mexican-American neighborhoods, with so many tastier options just blocks away? –RG

Dariush

A new downtown Persian restaurant
with food worth avoiding

food

3.1 / 10

4.9 / 10

experience

Middle Eastern

$27

Capitol Area

Casual restaurant
Mon.-Fri. 11am-2pm, 6pm-10pm;
Sat. 6pm-10pm; closed Sun.

918 Congress Ave.
Austin
(512) 479-7979
www.dariushpersiangrill.com

Bar Full
Credit Cards Visa, MC, AmEx
Reservations Accepted

Opened in late 2005 on the north end of Congress, just south of the
State Capitol, this Middle Eastern restaurant is in an attractive, soaring
bi-level space in the former home of the 1920s Club, which was a fun
live music and cocktail venue. With wrought-metal chairs, Persian rugs
on the exposed brick, and an upright piano in the back of the room,
Dariush is a strange place to be eating dinner—it still feels more like a
music bar than a restaurant.

The menu has an air of exoticism, and the excitement builds as you
read about dishes you have probably never heard of before, like chelo
khoresht-e ghooreh bademjan (a beef stew with eggplant and sour
grapes)—which rather sharpens your disappointment when the
execution does not live up to the promise. That stew, for instance, at
our last visit, had tragically tough, overcooked beef without a trace of
the tenderness or moistness that one expects from slow cooking. While
the taste of its gravy was not terrible, the beef was a literal chore to
eat, and the white basmati rice accompaniment was utterly tasteless.

But we've been disappointed by almost everything we've tried at
Dariush, beginning with the boring pita bread and a mezze plate—
mixed appetizers whose only highlights are standard, acceptable stuffed
grape leaves and a tasty spinach and yogurt dip. The lowlights include a
tabbouleh sacked by excessive parsley; a "yogurt and wild shallot" dip
that just tastes like yogurt (and which, at our last visit, showed up again
next to our main course); completely flavorless hummus; and
uninteresting olives, feta, and tomato whose presence on the plate
doesn't add any value. The service at Dariush, meanwhile, is not quite
rude, but definitely distracted and unhelpful. Give us our 1920s Club
back! –RG

Delaware Sub Shop

Enormous subs that will change the way
you think about sandwiches

food

7.8	**5.8**
10	10

experience

Light American   **$ 8**   *UT Area, Westlake, NW Hills*

Counter service
Mon.-Sat. 10:30am-8pm;
Sun. 11am-8pm.

1104 W. 34th St.
Austin
(512) 458-8423
www.delawaresub.com

Bar None
Credit Cards Visa and MC
Reservations Not accepted

3654 Bee Caves Rd.
78746, (512) 347-1045

2121 W. Parmer Ln.
78727, (512) 836-7655

Since first opening in 1980, Delaware Sub Shop has been the best
place to get East Coast-style subs in Austin, and it has gradually
expanded to nearly a dozen locations. These don't have much
atmosphere to speak of, as there's only counter service and much of
the business is take-out, but some of the older locations are decorated
with University of Delaware memorabilia. Service is friendly but slow
during the lunch rush. These monster sandwiches take time to make, so
call your order in if you're pressed for time.

Delaware Sub Shop's motto is "No Bologna Here," and that's more
than true—all of the sandwiches are made with high-quality ingredients
and offer serious value. Of the 20 or so sandwiches they offer, our
favorites are the "Italian Gourmet" and the Philly cheese steak. The
Italian Gourmet includes three kinds of ham, salami, provolone, and
sweet and hot peppers, and is seasoned with oil and herbs. It's a spicy
feast, lush with meat, and crisp with fresh vegetables. The Philly cheese
steak is grilled hot to order; gooey with cheese, sautéed onions,
peppers, and mushrooms, it's a real treat.

Other sandwiches are delicious too—the "Deli Turkey" has a fresh
roasted flavor, and the "Italian Meatball" is a real East Coast grinder,
with a slight fennel taste to the meatballs that is complimented by
tomato sauce and tart, sliced onions. All sandwiches are available in
seven-inch and 14-inch sizes, and four of them are available as kids'
meals at a three-and-a-half-inch size along with chips, a drink, and a
cookie for about three bucks. And since it's not just limited to children,
it is truly a happy meal. There are also daily specials that are heavy on
taste, but light on the pocketbook—a good enough excuse to
eventually try everything on the menu. –MPN

Din Ho Chinese BBQ

Humble, authentic, delicious Chinese
cuisine, on a Lazy Susan if you please

food
8.8 **7.3**
10   10
experience

Chinese, Seafood   **$ 24**   *Far North*

Casual restaurant   8557 Research Blvd.   ***Bar*** Wine and beer only
Mon.-Sat. 11am-12:30am;   Austin   ***Credit Cards*** Visa and MC
Sun. 11am-9:30pm. *Kid-friendly.*   (512) 832-8788   ***Reservations*** Accepted

The handwritten note tacked on the wall at Din Ho Chinese BBQ is
written in English and Chinese: "If you would like chicken with head
on, please reserve with cashier." Clearly, these folks aim to please both
authenticity-craving Chinese families and scaredy-cat Westerners. But
come on, whoever you are: go for the head.

The menu offers a variety of options ranging from Chinese-American
standards like beef lo mein to the intriguing sea cucumber with duck
web (it's one of the best duck webs in the Austin area). It's hard to go
wrong here. Just about everything is tasty, with fresh ingredients and
tender meat, but the *pièce de resistance* is the corner of the restaurant
that purveys roast and barbecued meats. Pork is succulent and tangy,
while memorable roast duck is bursting with juice, one of the best
preparations of duck in the city. "Salt Chicken," another product of the
barbecue corner, is moist and delicious. Back in the kitchen, scallops
and shrimp with garlic sauce is a superb dish, with buttery seafood,
crisp vegetables, and a surprising, fruity sauce that, happily, couldn't be
further from the Szechuan-brown-sauce gloop that we dread so
intensely. And don't miss the Dungeness crab with garlic and onion,
which, like the whole fish preparations, comes straight out of the fish
tanks in back; the dish requires a bit of manual labor but is a succulent
fantasy.

Din Ho has done little to decorate this large, hallowed hall, but the
atmosphere comes from the guests and the food. There is always a
jolly, multi-colored crowd, with many families, and through the throng
weave carts of glistening red smoked ducks, their necks curved in neat
rows. Service is friendly and remarkably fast given the hordes, and there
is always an agreeable patron happy to translate the staff's halting
English. Best of all, Din Ho still sports that fast-disappearing standby of
family Chinese restaurants: the Lazy Susan. Hooray! –RM

Dirty Martin's Place

A UT favorite that still fries 'em up like they used to

food

7.7 / 10 **9.2** / 10

experience

American, Burgers $**12**   *West Campus*

Casual restaurant
Daily 11am-11pm. *Kid-friendly.*
Outdoor dining.

2808 Guadalupe St.
Austin
(512) 477-3173
www.dirtymartins.com

Bar Beer/wine
Credit Cards Visa and MC
Reservations Not accepted

Dirty Martin's is Austin's best impression of a greasy spoon, and by that we mean that they *really* spoon on the grease. Everything in the joint has a vague sheen to it. But we have to say that their "Kum-Bak Burgers" are some of our favorite guilty pleasures in town.

Burgers are of the soft, squishy, flat variety—asking for them rare misses the point—and come on sweet buns shiny with fat, in traditional plastic baskets. There are a variety of ordering options, but the best of the lot is the "O.T. Special," a cheeseburger with crispy bacon, and the standard lettuce, tomato, and mayo. As a slight concession to your arteries, we'd recommend the small O.T., with a side of onion rings. The rings here are big and juicy, with a flaky batter that has little to do with the artificial orange crumbs you see so often today. Another good order is the "D.H. Special," with extra cheese and grilled onions. Shakes and malts are popular, but we find them a little cloying. Dirty Martin's does, however, serve an appealing range of old-school fountain drinks, such as floats, ice cream sodas, and cherry cokes, and makes its own lemon and limeade. A range of sides only a Texan could love, such as deep-fried pickles and deep-fried, cream-cheese-stuffed jalapeños, are also available.

But what we really like about Dirty Martin's is the way it has, since 1926, loyally catered to the UT crowd. It is a proud college dive, the décor and T-shirts a faithful burnt orange, with signed photos of famous gridiron warriors on the walls. The staff is a superbly friendly mix of students and old-timers. Austin is rapidly outgrowing its college town feel, but little nooks like this one reassure us that it never really will. –RM

Doc's

A glossy new garage-turned-into-bar
with a bright, friendly attitude

food

4.2	9.2
10	10

experience

American, Mexican   **$22**   *South Congress*

Pub   1123 S. Congress Ave.   *Bar* Full
Daily 11am-midnight. Kitchen   Austin   *Credit Cards* Visa, MC, AmEx
closes Sun.-Thurs. 10pm;   (512) 448-9181   *Reservations* Not accepted
Fri.-Sat. 11pm. *Date-friendly.*   www.docsaustin.com
Outdoor dining. Wireless Internet.

Doc's is brand-spanking new, and is full of perky shine and enthusiasm.
The most recent addition to the South Congress strip, it's bright and
friendly, housed in an old mechanic's garage. A spacious front patio is
lined with smart, cactus-filled planters and packed with multicolored
bouncer chairs (those attractive pressed tin numbers familiar from the
fifties). It is impossible to imagine actually sitting in these in summer;
when your thighs shudder just at the thought of the touch of that hot
metal, and everything glows neon in the glare of the avenue's asphalt.
Of course, this jolly spot pairs ideally with the wonderful outdoor
climate that we enjoy for eight months of the year.

For the rest of the time, there is pleasant indoor seating as well, with
both tables and raised counters with bar stools, where you can watch
the game on pristine flat-screen TVs, or play some pool or shuffleboard.
Hub caps and license plates are nailed a little too liberally about the
place, which is very aware of its recent automotive history.

The servers are equally bright and perky, and perhaps also try a little
too hard. Everything shines with the enthusiasm of a new enterprise.
While we expect this will be mainly a place to grab a beer and a chat
with some friends (note that on Tuesdays that chat will take on a
decidedly Texan twang—all Texas beers are just two bucks a pint), Doc's
takes its kitchen fairly seriously. The menu includes bar appetizers as
well as decently executed pub grub and Tex-Mex. Queso is unusually
white and gloopy; you can ask for jalapeños and picadillo to add flavor,
but they won't stop the disgusting clumps from forming just minutes
after the queso is plopped down on the table. Burgers, though, are
particularly good (cooked honest-to-goodness medium-rare upon
request); enchiladas verdes aren't bad; fries and onion rings are crisp;
and there's a pretty good chicken-fried steak. But stay away from
fancier fare—the blackened tilapia, for example, is desperately
oversalted. Not all that glitters is gold. –RM

Dog Almighty

A jolly little joint that dishes out great dogs

food
6.4
10

5.7
10
experience

American

$ 5   *Burnet*

Counter service
Mon.-Sat. noon-8pm;
Sun. noon-6pm. *Kid-friendly.*
Live music. Outdoor dining.

6701 Burnet Rd.
Austin
(512) 300-2364
www.dogalmighty.com

Bar BYO
Credit Cards Visa, MC, AmEx
Reservations Not accepted

The hilarity of its name conveys much of this young hot dog purveyor's successful formula. It takes a simple thing, dresses it up with some childish fun, and sells a product that is, in the end, as much leisure as lunch.

Don't get us wrong, though: Dog Almighty takes its hot dogs very seriously. They are 100% beef, tender and flavorful, and grilled over an open flame. How nice it is to see those telltale blackened bits. Of course, we love the classic hot dog from a New York City stand to warm up a chilly autumn afternoon, but something about those pink, boiled dogs looks disconcertingly naked. The only nudity here is in the "Hippy Hollow Dog," named after the local nudist-swimming hole— these hot dogs come bun-less, for the Atkins-afflicted. But we recommend getting yours appropriately clothed, as the buns here are well toasted, warm, and crisp, and all the toppings, from chili to sauerkraut, are made in-house. The favorite order at Dog Almighty is the Classic, topped with chili, cheese, mustard and onions. The chili is pretty good—lean, thick, and minus any dreaded nubbly bits. There's also something to be said for simpler orders, though, which offer subtler flavors and fewer postprandial regrets. You can always get the chili on a frito pie.

Perhaps the nicest thing about Dog Almighty is the attitude of the little place. Service may be a little lackadaisical, but the atmosphere clearly encourages fun. Kids are welcomed (a few child-drawn thank-you posters decorate the walls), and foosball and ping-pong tables stand ready for use, free of charge. The latter even comes with a handy list of rules ("no sneaky serves") beneath a picture of Chairman Mao with a paddle. Who said lunch was all about the food? –RM

The Dog and Duck Pub

A stab at a corner pub that just misses
the mark; unlucky, as the Brits might say

food
5.9
10

7.4
10

experience

American   **$20**   *Capitol Area*

Pub
Mon.-Sat. 11am-2am; Sun. noon-
2am. Kitchen closes Sun.-Mon.
and Wed.-Thurs. 11pm, Tues. and
Fri.-Sat. midnight. *Outdoor dining. Wireless Internet.*

406 W. 17th St.
Austin
(512) 479-0598
www.dogandduckpub.com

Bar Full
Credit Cards Visa, MC, AmEx
Reservations Not accepted

The Dog and Duck is Austin's best attempt at an English pub, and in some ways it is successful. It manages to capture the feel of a place where you might go almost daily for a pint and a chat, with a nice, cozy array of tables both inside and out. It has a few dartboards, some games on a couple of TVs (sadly, not the footie), and a generous selection of brews on tap. Inside, it is dark, wood paneled, and cushioned; outside, airy and spacious. In other words, it's just what you want.

The food on offer here, however, is less of a success. The Dog and Duck tries its darnedest to serve up some classic pub fare, but what comes out has little to do with the original. In England, a ploughman's is a splendidly simple selection of top-notch local cheeses served with fresh bread and a (frequently homemade) pickled chutney of some sort. The Dog and Duck version, however, comes with a couple of lumps of processed cheese that would be more at home in a Lunchables box than a pub, and no pickle. But the bangers and mash, another English pub staple, are perfectly decent here—even if the bangers (sausages) remind one more of Elgin than England.

Less palatable are the fish and chips (the words "gag" and "yuck" spring unfortunately to mind), the soggy orange batter ineffectively concealing unevenly cooked fish. The chips (fries), at least those that have managed to dodge the grease dripping from the fish, are good, however—crisp and golden. Burgers are dry and a little chewy, but a chicken breast in gravy is miraculously moist. All in all, it's a mixed feedbag. We advise you to stick with the pints, if possible. –RM

Doña Emilia's

Revved-up, high-concept South
American food in an off-balance setting

Latin American   **$46**   *Convention Center Area*

Upmarket restaurant   101 San Jacinto Blvd.   ***Bar*** Full
Sun.-Thurs. 11am-2:30pm, 5pm- Austin   ***Credit Cards*** Visa, MC, AmEx
10pm; Fri. 11am-2:30pm, 4pm-   (512) 478-2520   ***Reservations*** Accepted
11pm; Sat. noon-11pm. *Brunch.* www.donaemilias.com
Delivery. Live music. Outdoor dining. Wireless Internet.

With its recent move to swankier downtown digs, Doña Emilia has entered Austin's high-end food scene with a swinging step and enviable panache. We are happy to see such a fresh face on the South American food scene.

The restaurant has an elegant bar that mixes good, strong, sweet caipirinhas and mojitos, but on the whole, the interior is disappointing. It has the bland feel of a rather suave hotel lounge, with dark wall-to-wall carpeting and upholstery. Clashing with this reserve is a messy open kitchen, lending clatter and discord but little interest to the atmosphere. People go out to eat, after all, in part to avoid the mess of their own kitchens.

Such wrinkles are smoothed away, however, by the arrival of the food, which is simple and scrumptious, often employing that pleasing Latin combo of sweet and savory. "I am a great eater of beef," says Shakespeare's Sir Andrew, "and I believe that does harm to my wit." But Doña Emilia's beef is prepared with great wit, and is light, bright, and flavorful. The best dish on the menu is the much-vaunted churrasco—a huge portion of delicate beef tenderloin, soft as cheese, smothered with vivid chimichurri sauce. Ceviche is fresh and powerfully limey, flavored with cilantro and a splash of tequila, but shrimp tends to be a bit tough, and its tostones (fried plantains) come undersalted and brittle in places, perhaps sliced too thickly for this sort of frying.

The rest of the menu ranges from the traditional (such as the extensive bandeja paisa, a combination of steak, fried eggs, red beans, fried pork skins, and more) to the more modern (such as a massive, meaty sea bass steak, beautifully grilled, but slightly overwhelmed by a salty soy-habañero sauce). Prices are very reasonable for such goodness, and the short lunch menu has many of the stars in smaller portions for under 10 bucks. How could you not go for that? –RM

Drakula

A Romanian restaurant in Austin—
welcome to the 21st Century

Romanian   **$23**   *Far North*

Casual restaurant   8120 Research Blvd.   *Bar* Beer/wine
Mon.-Fri. 11am-10pm;   Austin   *Credit Cards* Visa, MC, AmEx
Sat.-Sun. noon-10pm.   (512) 374-9291   *Reservations* Accepted
Delivery.   www.drakulaaustin.com

One of Austin's newest restaurants, and perhaps its most unusual
ethnic joint, Drakula is housed in a strip-mall space decorated with lacy
tablecloths and curtains, Romanian and American flags, and lots of
folksy knick-knacks. The chipper folk music can be a little grating after
an hour or more, but the service is eager and friendly, and they offer
cheap lunch specials.

The menu covers traditional Romanian fare (which is like a fusion of
Northern Italian and Russian food) with a few unorthodox touches, and
a short but standard kids' menu. Start with the appetizer assortment
(the plate for one is enough for two, or even three people) with
veggies, feta, mildly peppery salami, caviar spread, olives, and
meatballs. The caviar spread is creamy, cool, and cheese-based, with
icre (mild, bright orange roe) blended in. The small, handmade pork
and beef meatballs, called chiftelute, are highly seasoned and slightly
spicy like a sausage.

Stuffed cabbage (sarmale cu mamaliga) is excellent, filled with
ground pork and rice and seasoned with dill. It's a little salty and tangy,
delicious eaten with sour cream. Romanians traditionally eat a salad
with dinner, so try the typical white cabbage salad, finely shredded and
in a light vinaigrette.

The use of hot peppers is common in Transylvanian dishes, but a
heavy dose of chopped jalapeños makes the grilled fish in spicy broth
(peste saramura) unusually fiery. The kitchen also took some liberties
here by using catfish rather than the pike or carp you'd more
commonly find in this dish. But then, when in Austin…. Finish with a
cheese pie, a pastry filled with layers of lightly sweetened ricotta,
cottage, and cream cheese with raisins.

The food is good and so are the people—we recently spotted the
Drakula delivery van distributing food to the homeless. –MPN

The Draught House

A pub in a Tudor mansion—we only
wish the food were better

food
4.5
10

9.2
10

experience

American

$19

Seton Medical Area

Pub
Mon.-Thurs. 5pm-2am; Fri.-Sun.
3pm-2am. Kitchen closes at 9pm.
Outdoor dining.

4112 Medical Pkwy.
Austin
(512) 452-6258
www.draughthouse.com

Bar Beer/wine
Credit Cards Visa, MC, AmEx
Reservations Not accepted

We really love the Draught House. We love it so much we are actually
reluctant to write about it here. Located on the bottom floor of a
Tudor-style house in Rosewood, the Draught House serves a large
selection of beers on tap and a couple of cheap wines, but no liquor.
The furniture is made of dark, heavy wood with a myriad of deep scars
from carved graffiti, and polished to a shine by years of elbows and
bottoms rubbing across it. The interior is usually dark, smoky, and dimly
lit—there are no neon beer signs here, the walls are covered with
vintage Guinness and British World War II posters. There are few
distractions, just a couple of dartboards and an unobtrusive TV with no
volume. The Draught House is about visiting with your friends.

Another fun thing about the Draught House is the tailgating. There
isn't much in the way of outdoor seating, but patrons bring their own
lawn furniture or sometimes just sit on top of their cars and drink in the
parking lot. This is not a pickup scene, nor are there are any fratsters. In
fact, the place just doesn't seem to appeal to the twentysomethings at
all.

Although the Draught House has recently adopted a very short
menu, it is a pub, and not really a place to eat. The menu offers chips
with Kinky Friedman's salsa (why the hell not?), pizzas made with
Mangia's crusts, quesadillas, nachos, and greasy calzones all served on
paper plates with plastic-ware. On the weekend there are free
appetizers, but these are generally to be avoided. Service at the
Draught House has historically been at the bar, so food delivery is at
times delinquent. But like we said, this is a pub: approach it like a Brit,
and have the beer for dinner. --MPN

The Driskill Grill

food

9.4 / 10   9.9 / 10

experience

Fantastic food and atmosphere,
fantastically high bill

New American $105   *Congress Avenue Area*

Upmarket restaurant
Tues.-Sat. 5:30pm-10pm;
closed Sun.-Mon.
Date-friendly.

604 Brazos St.
Austin
(512) 391-7162
www.driskillhotel.com

Bar Full
Credit Cards Visa, MC, AmEx
Reservations Essential

The high-flying, high-priced Driskill Grill is located in the historic Driskill
Hotel, and warmly but sumptuously decorated in very masculine dark
woods, subdued lighting from tiny Tiffany lamps, and ornate copper
ceilings. So transportative is the experience is that you feel as if Billy the
Kid might just show up and plop down at the next table, perhaps
paying his check with notes peeled off a roll of spoils from this
afternoon's heist. You wonder how he'd react to the sashimi.

Service is courteous and exacting, and the constantly changing menu
full of possibility. We recommend the chef's eight-course tasting menu,
which offers the most bang for the (considerable) buck. It's also
available with wine pairings. The only other option is a four-course prix-
fixe; there is no à-la-carte menu, so come ready for a long dinner.

The constantly changing menu fuses New American and Texan
traditions, freestyling at times but still maintaining a focus on
impeccable, first-rate ingredients and careful presentation. A chop
salad, for instance, might be jazzed up by Maytag blue, bacon, and
fried plantains; bright ruby beef tartare, at one visit, was a study in
land-sea contrasts, with sea-scented oysters fried to crispiness, hot
oriental mustard, and tobiko caviar. But sometimes the simplest
preparations are the best; in a roasted beet salad, which each beet is a
vivid jewel—the sweet depth of the beets was paired with equally rich
but almost sour warm Camembert and an unexpected Amaretto crème
fraîche. On the heartier side, gamey, horseradish-encrusted lamb chops
with earthy trumpet mushrooms have also been excellent. Dessert
options are all tantalizing, but our favorite is the decadent chocolate
tasting, with crème brûlée, ice cream, and a toothsome candy bar using
various high-end chocolates.

We love the Driskill Grill—a dinner here is truly something special.
But if you want to do it right, plan on closer to two C-notes a head
than one. But this tasting menu might just be worth robbing a bank
for. –MPN

Eastside Café

Fresh-from-the-garden fare in a cozy
old house

food

8.2 **9.5**
10   10

experience

American $**45**   *French Place*

Upmarket restaurant
Mon.-Thurs. 11:15am-9:30pm; Fri.
11:15am-10pm; Sat. 10am-10pm;
Sun. 10am-9:30pm. *Brunch.*
Date-friendly. Outdoor dining. Vegetarian-friendly.

2113 Manor Rd.
Austin
(512) 476-5858
www.eastsidecafeaustin.com

Bar Beer/wine
Credit Cards Visa, MC, AmEx
Reservations Essential

Eastside Café is one of the best spots in Austin for brunch. Set in a rambling 1920s house with a large garden that provides much of the restaurant's produce, its shaded porches are cooled by lazy fans. Each of the rooms is filled with only a handful of tables, giving every space an intimate feel. The rooms are decorated with photos from the garden, which is open to the public to wander and explore.

The daily specials are posted on colorful chalkboards in each room. The complimentary cornbread is some of the best in town—warm and moist, flecked with mild chiles. Choose wheat or white for your French toast, which is crisp on the outside but soft in the middle with a nice cinnamon flavor. The cheese grits with green chiles are cheesy but not gooey, with a fluffiness reminiscent of scrambled eggs. Blueberry blintzes are sweet with a lovely thick, cream-cheesy filling, but lack the tang we expect from ricotta. Mixed field greens in the salad were probably still growing that morning; it is tossed in a light raspberry vinaigrette and crisp with large chunks of Granny Smith apples, toasted pecans, and almonds. It comes fabulously topped with a gorgeous disc of warm, breaded, fried goat cheese that is golden on the outside, but meltingly soft in the center. The grilled tuna in a sandwich is made tart with an orange and lime juice marinade, cooked to a still-moist medium, and served on a wheat or white bun with the usual veggies and a deliciously complex ginger-soy mayonnaise.

Dinner is fun too, when the gracious old house takes on a warm evening vibe. Pastas can disappoint; meats and fish mains are most appealing, and a rich but not oversweetened chess pie, when available, makes for a memorable dessert. But we still love the place most for brunch. Come on a warm day, take a walk through the garden and see what's growing, then order a mimosa. —MPN

Eddie V's

A clubby steak and seafood joint with
high prices and no compelling catch

food

7.3 / 10 **6.9** / 10

experience

Seafood, Steakhouse, American   **$63**   *Sixth Street District, Arboretum*

Upmarket restaurant
Lounge daily 4:30pm-10:45pm;
dinner daily 5:30pm-10:45pm.
Live music.

301 E. 5th St.
Austin
(512) 472-1860
www.eddiev.com

9400 Arboretum Blvd.
78759, (512) 342-2642

Bar Full
Credit Cards Visa, MC, AmEx
Reservations Recommended

Even if there are only three branches of Eddie V's, this restaurant
manages to feel a lot more like a chain than it really is. Eddie V's was
co-founded by the folks behind Z' Tejas, but bears little resemblance to
its laid-back Southwestern sisters. Here, instead, the atmosphere is
strange, dark, and clubby, with curvy banquettes, live piano, and Jazz
Age-style artwork with a distinct air of newness to it all. Still, Eddie V's
pulls off the old-boy shtick better than some of its local competition.
We prefer the informal atmosphere of the restaurant's bar area to the
more tricked-out parts of the restaurant; in fact, our favorite thing to
do at Eddie V's is to sit at the bar, slurp oysters, and down martinis
during happy hour—it's a certain version of the good life.

As for the regular menu, oysters are again a good choice; they can
be hard to find in downtown Austin, and they're reasonably priced
here. Not so for the $12.50 crab cakes, which are fine and
appropriately crispy but unremarkable. But that price point is nothing
compared with the lobster. The "market price" for the lobster plate
(two broiled tails), at our last visit: $52. What market, you have to
wonder, do they go to? The answer: none—the lobster, we were told,
was frozen.

A tuna steak with avocado and tomato is good, not great. A better
choice is any one of the prime steaks, which are juicy and cooked
appropriately to temperature; creamed spinach almondine works well
as a side. Still, if you want steak, why not choose the broiled, dry-aged
version at the similarly clubby and pricey but vastly superior Ruth's
Chris? And what to make of the failing 64/100 score—in the bottom
handful of restaurants in the city—on their 2006 health inspection? In
short, Eddie V's has a certain elitist charm, but unless you're an
absolute sucker for the nightly live piano music, it is unclear why, on a
given night, you would ever choose this place over the competition.
–RG

888

A dark, shabby Vietnamese joint that
gets the basics right

food

6.8 | **2.2**
10 | 10

experience

Vietnamese

$24   *Southeast, Far North*

Casual restaurant
Daily 11am-midnight.

2400 E. Oltorf St.
Austin
(512) 448-4722

12914 Meehan Dr.
78727, (512) 302-5433

Bar BYO
Credit Cards Visa, MC, AmEx
Reservations Not accepted

Step inside 888 (not to be confused with the upmarket Bistro 88), and
you will plunge into extraordinary darkness. This lighting has gone way
past dim into a whole new category. Even in the midday sun, the place
manages to impart a sinking feeling—especially when you sink deep
into the seats of the decrepit booths. Otherwise, you'll initially find little
to set 888 apart from Austin's other downmarket Vietnamese joints.
There is the obligatory fish tank holding a few fish swimming about as
if they know their days are numbered; apparently, the odd landscapes
on the walls don't delude them into thinking that they are swimming
through a mountain stream. In the unlikely event that the restaurant is
full, should you wish to wait outside for a table to open up, the
restaurant graciously provides a ripped-up couch for just such an
occasion.

888 offers a well-loved lunch buffet on weekdays. Otherwise, a look
at the staggeringly long menu reveals numerous varieties of phô,
vermicelli dishes, less interesting stir-fry dishes, and so on. Whole fish is
a good way to go; amongst soups, we like the Hu tiêu bò kho, a beef
stew with cinnamon that is served with a plate of basil leaves, bean
sprouts, a lemon slice, and jalapeños. The savory depth of its broth is
more notable than the beef chunks themselves; they're tougher than
you would expect (braised meat should be meltingly tender). Bun tom
thit nuong (vermicelli with grilled pork and sautéed shrimp) is less
impressive; while the pork benefits from the charred taste imparted by
the grill, and shrimp are succulent and flavorful, that's about it. It's
helpful to dump all available fish sauce upon the noodles to moisten
them.

So, nothing fancy here, in spite of how elaborate the menu is—but
the price is right. Just remember, it is dark in there, so unless you're a
Congress Bridge bat, we strongly recommend take-out. –AH

1886 Café and Bakery

A spot in Austin's famous Driskill Hotel
that's like a French café, minus smoke

Light American

$31

Congress Avenue Area

Upmarket restaurant
Mon.-Thurs. 6:30am-10pm;
Fri. 6:30am-midnight; Sat. 7am-
midnight; Sun. 7am-10pm.

116 E. 6th St.
Austin
(512) 474-5911
www.1886cafeandbakery.com

Bar Full
Credit Cards Visa, MC, AmEx
Reservations Accepted

Breakfast. Brunch. Date-friendly. Vegetarian-friendly. Wireless Internet.

The 1886 Café and Bakery is an elegantly appointed establishment in
the heart of downtown, with gorgeous dark wood paneling and
furniture, high ceilings, and leadlight windows. This grandeur is only
fitting, as the restaurant is attached to Austin's most historic and
distinguished hotel, the venerable Driskill. But it is also the little things
that set the 1886 apart from other small bakeries and cafés: the hat
rack at the door; the bar seating that allows a revealing look at the
immaculate kitchen; the gleaming copper pots that hang from the
kitchen ceiling; the beautiful pastry case; the *New York Times* available
for perusal at the bar; and the friendly and attentive service.

The breakfast menu is filled with fruits and cereals, pastries,
pancakes, and three variations on eggs benedict. Ginger snap
pancakes, topped with fresh blueberries and vanilla maple syrup, come
sprinkled with powdered sugar and mint leaves. Sadly, the pancakes are
not gingery at all, but they are delicious nonetheless. The croissants are
buttery and flaky, but served cold when they would certainly be better
warm or at least room temperature.

The "Austin, Texas Eggs Benedict" combines some of the best
poached eggs we have ever eaten—so round they look like scoops of
vanilla ice cream, and with thickened but still-runny yolks—with spicy
cornmeal and jalapeño biscuits for a South Texas touch. This is topped
by a mild but flavorful chorizo gravy and served with two pieces of
smoked bacon that are just crisp enough. It is a wonderfully local take
on a classic dish. The portion sizes are ideal: filling, but not so much as
to send you away in the dreaded mid-morning food coma. It is a lovely
way to start the day—the kind of meal that could actually turn you into
a Breakfast Person. –MPN

El Arroyo

Ditch your worries in favor of a warm, relaxed night of Tex-Mex

food
7.1 / 10
8.7 / 10
experience

Mexican

$**28**

Clarksville, Far NW, Bee Cave

Casual restaurant
Mon.-Tues. 11am-10pm; Wed.-Thurs. 11am-11pm; Fri. 11am-midnight; Sat. 10am-11pm; Sun. 10am-10pm. *Brunch. Kid-friendly. Outdoor dining. Wireless Internet.*

1624 W. 5th St.
Austin
(512) 474-1222
www.ditch.com

Bar Full
Credit Cards Visa, MC, AmEx
Reservations Accepted

17301 N. Hwy. 183
78750, (512) 918-2900

12432 FM 2244
Bee Cave, (512) 402-0007

The downtown branch of El Arroyo, a.k.a. "The Ditch," has a little bit of everything Austin. It's got the studenty vibe, with Texas football on the TVs, neon beer signs on the walls, and shorts and T-shirts on everyone. It's got the funky, alternative touches: mix-'n'-match patterned tablecloths, comical signs, yard art, and crystal chandeliers hanging from the gorgeous live oak on the patio. It's got expansive outdoor seating, with ceiling fans (some of which actually hang improbably from the live oak) and merry lights. It's got that relaxed, friendly, very Texan service from a staff that looks culled from the local sororities and frat houses—light-haired, sporty, and cheerful.

The other branches, particularly the one at Bee Caves, are less impressive, with chain-feeling furniture and less of a quirky vibe. At any branch, though, prices are very reasonable, and the queso is a top-notch representative of the genre: well seasoned, no skin, no tendency to congeal. We like to add the fresh guacamole. Spinach queso, too, will disappear at an alarming rate. Mains, like the queso, are amiably low-brow, and usually yummy (although the kitchen downtown would destroy Bee Caves in a cook-off). Barbecue chicken enchiladas are glorious spicy-tangy creations with tender smoky chicken, roasted peppers and onions, sour cream, and a barbecue sauce that, for once, tastes like the real thing (not like slightly sour ketchup)—a marriage of Austin's two great culinary traditions. Rice can be bland and dissociated, though, and beans barely average. But tortilla soup, with its judiciously cooked vegetables, creamy avocado, and tasty broth, is terrific. El Arroyo also quietly serves one of the best burgers in Austin. We can all be thankful that the fool who tried to burn down the downtown branch a few years back didn't close it for good.

The only thing this classic Austin establishment doesn't offer you is an empty belly—the staff T-shirts, which sport the slogan "Body by Queso," will attest to that. –RM

El Azteca

Friendly East Austin service and Mex
colorful enough to tickle you pink

food

5.6 **7.4**
10   10

experience

Mexican   **$23**   *East Austin*

Casual restaurant
Mon.-Sat. 11am-10pm;
closed Sun. *Outdoor dining.*

2600 E. 7th St.
Austin
(512) 477-4701
www.aztecarestaurant.com

Bar Full
Credit Cards Visa, MC, AmEx
Reservations Accepted

El Azteca has been a favorite of a wide range of Austinites since 1963. Despite its location relatively far down East Seventh street, it draws loyal customers from all over town, so that a visit to its colorful (okay, baby-pink) dining room will afford a view of something much closer to Austin's actual demographics than the one presented by the relatively segregated amusements toward which most of us tend. This pleasant picture is enhanced by remarkably open, warm, and chatty service, which makes even a first-time visitor feel like one of the old-timers.

It is most likely this friendly atmosphere that merits such loyalty. The food, while fairly tasty, does not immediately demand a second visit. The menu is relatively simple, with an emphasis on charcoal-grilled fare such as Mexican-style steaks and chops that come well-prepared in generous portions with a notably smoky appeal. There is also a respectable vegetarian menu, which is rather unusual for so bare-bones a Mexican joint.

All sauces are house-made, spicy, and clearly fresh. The salsa is bright, but some very dominant cumin obscures other flavors. Ranchero sauce is subtler than most; and a very spicy chipotle sauce, available over both cubed pork and enchiladas, is pleasantly sweet and tangy, if a little overpowering. Like many of the more authentic Tex-Mex places, El Azteca serves cabrito (a.k.a. baby goat), a fatty, stringy meat, baked in the oven with few adornments, though the ranchero sauce and lovely stewed charro beans add life to the plate.

On the whole, the food here is no better than average. But after the warmth of the service, the spice of the salsas, and the added heat of some rather racy depictions of Aztec legends that line the walls, you'll leave with an internal glow, even after some complimentary sherbet has cooled you down a little. –RM

El Borrego de Oro

A friendly, downmarket Mexican joint
with lamb that will leave you grinning

food
8.6 **6.4**
10 10
experience

Mexican   **$21**   *St. Edward's Area*

Casual restaurant   3900 S. Congress Ave.   *Bar* None
Daily 7am-9pm.   Austin   *Credit Cards* Visa and MC
Breakfast.   (512) 383-0031   *Reservations* Not accepted

Down South Congress—*way* down South Congress—lies this little-
known gem of a Mexican restaurant. A set of white walls hides two
rooms in which one of the best simple regional Mexican menus in
Austin is served. It is the kind of restaurant in which half of the lunch
patrons are dining alone, eyes closed, absorbing every molecule of the
tastes and smells as they inhale the enormous plates. It is these sorts of
unpretentious, downmarket gourmands around town, particularly in
South Austin, that often signal the best places to eat from a pure food
perspective, even if the surroundings are merely perfunctory, with basic
tables and chairs and little else.

And whatever else El Borrego is, it is certainly that. Sure, there are
the Tex-Mex classics—the combination plates with crispy tacos, the
cheesy enchiladas—but that is far from what El Borrego is about.
Borrego means lamb in Spanish, and that's where you should start—
whether with a caldo (soup) or the full plate, both of which burst with
chunks of slightly dry but rich, deeply flavored lamb. Inside the
homemade corn tortillas, perhaps with a smear of beans, a dabble of
rice, and a bit of salsa, the lamb is magnificent.

No less formidable is El Borrego's mole, which strikes a remarkable
balance between spicy and sweet. The flavor of dry-roasted chiles
emerges from deep within the sauce, lording over hints of sweetness
and saltiness and endowing the chicken with a remarkably noble flavor.
And don't fail to notice how close the beans and rice come to
perfection within their genres. Even the flour tortillas, though not made
in-house, are just what they should be.

Lost in the lamb and the mole, you may not even notice the service—
but it's informal and friendly. Even the guy that comes around to refill
the iced tea has a smile on his face. So will you. –RG

El Chile

Exciting Mexican food in a prize-winningly renovated East Austin house

food
9.2 **9.1**
10   10
experience

Mexican $**31**   *French Place*

Casual restaurant
Mon.-Sat. 11am-10pm; Sun.
11am-9pm. *Brunch.*
Date-friendly. Outdoor dining.
Vegetarian-friendly. Wireless Internet.

1809 Manor Rd.
Austin
(512) 457-9900
www.elchilecafe.com

Bar Full
Credit Cards Visa, MC, AmEx
Reservations Not accepted

El Chilito, 2219 Manor Rd.
78722, (512) 382-3797

This unpretentious spot on the up-and-coming Manor strip has burst onto the scene and quickly established itself as Austin's champion in the hip-but-moderately-priced-Mexican category. Its small house is brightly painted without being garish, and it's tastefully decorated with milagros, crosses, and Latin American art. A warm buzz pervades the room, while the covered porch area enjoys an equally chilled-out elegance. Few restaurants in Austin manage to achieve such a beautiful balance of hip and relaxed. (The El Chilito "taquería and café," a few doors up the street, serves a more basic menu.)

Fun drinks include a sweet, eye-catching prickly-pear frozen margarita (it's a hot-pink party in a glass), although we love the regular rocks margaritas. Dark, smoky house salsa, made from oven-roasted tomatoes and jalapeños, might be Austin's best. Guacamole has a nice lime kick, while queso flameado, made from jack cheese, a little grease-free chorizo, and a tart pico de gallo, is wonderful with El Chile's thick, warm homemade flour tortillas. Even better are the remarkable rajas con queso, with roasted poblanos, onions, and a truly creamy texture. Tilapia ceviche is yet another startling achievement, with a lovely acidity and fresh, melting texture.

Amongst mains, El Chile's carne asada has good flavor, although it can come out quite charred. Shrimp enchiladas are quite simply the best in town. Their filling is chunky with lots of peppers and corn, and the two sauces blend together beautifully—a mild chipotle and a lovely contrasted green cilantro cream sauce, neither of which overpowers the shrimp. And the list goes on. Oaxacan red mole is tremendous, subtle and smoky, one of the most unusual moles in the city. Chiles rellenos, stuffed with pork, are also best-in-class. Even the rice is tops. Much has been made of the fact that El Chile was opened by a group of Jeffrey's alums; frankly, if not for the long waits, we'd take a meal here over one at Jeffrey's, any night of the week. –MPN/RG

El Gallo

Horrible Tex-Mex food—and everyone
knows it but the food critics

food

2.2 **4.6**
10   10

experience

Mexican   **$25**   *St. Edward's Area*

Casual restaurant
Tues.-Thurs. 8am-10pm; Fri.-Sat.
8am-11pm; Sun. 8am-9pm;
closed Mon. *Breakfast. Kid-friendly.*

2910 S. Congress Ave.
Austin
(512) 444-6696
www.elgallorestaurant.com

Bar Full
Credit Cards Visa, MC, AmEx
Reservations Accepted

"When a restaurant has been around as long as El Gallo," writes
Brooke Townsend in the restaurant's Citysearch "editorial" review, "you
know it's got to be good."

Just who are these reviewers? Putting aside the flawed logic of Ms.
Townsend's statement, does CitySearch's parent company,
InterActiveCorp, demand positive "reviews" to entice advertisers? Can
we turn to the venerable *Statesman*, at least, for an honest account of
El Gallo? "Good food," it croons online. "Forks up." How about the
Chronicle? "Authentic Mexican and tasty Tex-Mex."

Even the 18-year-old St. Ed's freshmen know that's not true, which is
why they go to Curra's instead of walking right across the street to El
Gallo. In fact, just about everyone in Austin but the critics seems to
understand that this restaurant is terrible, which is why it's often empty.
Do the city's food writers simply fold under ad-sales pressure to turn
reviews into advertorials? Or are critics just scared, in this brave new
media world, to be critical?

At least El Gallo is bad in an interesting way. Picture the dusty Old
San Antonio Highway upon which the restaurant was born—a time
before IH-35. El Gallo, its walls painted with fake stones and pastoral
murals, is a time machine. A bizarre bullfight tapestry looks like a giant
rug, and holiday lights make every day Christmas.

While Austin's Tex-Mex cuisine has evolved since the bland 1950s, El
Gallo's has not—and it's not even cheap. If you must eat here, try to
catch the mariachis on Thursdays, Fridays, or Saturdays, and try the
mushy cheese enchiladas or the decent cabrito (kid). Beef tacos are
rubbery, comically hard to eat. Guacamole has no taste, salsa no chile
flavor, rice and beans no seasoning. A beef tamale swimming in a sea
of bland gravy somehow manages to remain dry. Margaritas are sickly
sweet. Even chile con queso is flavorless, worse than versions at
mediocre chains. Culinary nostalgia is more fun when the food is
tolerable. –RG

El Mercado

Mild-mannered Tex-Mex in a happy-go-lucky setting

food
4.9 **6.8**
10 10
experience

Mexican

$27

Capitol Area, Burnet, Far Northwest

Casual restaurant
Mon.-Thurs. 11am-10pm; Fri.-Sat. 11am-11pm; Sun. 11am-4pm. *Brunch. Kid-friendly.*

1702 Lavaca St.
Austin
(512) 477-7689

Bar Full
Credit Cards Visa, MC, AmEx
Reservations Accepted

7414 Burnet Rd.
78757, (512) 454-2500

13776 N. Hwy. 183
78750, (512) 219-0232

The headline of the newspaper clipping that hangs proudly by the door of El Mercado's South First Street location dubs it the Old Reliable, and in some ways this is an accurate moniker for this longtime Austin hangout. But sometimes old reliable can creep its tired way to just old—El Mercado can no longer really compete with the better Tex-Mex and interior Mexican options in town.

We have a hard time complaining, however, about a joint that dishes out satisfying food at such cheap prices (lunch specials are $5.50) with an unwaveringly friendly attitude. This is gringo Tex-Mex—spices are dulled down—and most of the servers, if funky, are as white as the clientele. But El Mercado makes up for this monochromatic theme by taking the colorful ambiance we know from most Tex-Mex joints and kicking it up a couple of notches. Bright multi-colored tiles pattern the walls, and a general atmosphere of frenetic good cheer pervades. This is family Mexican on steroids.

The food is much meeker. Fajitas are mild, with little spice or smokiness. Spinach and mushroom enchiladas have something reminiscent of the school lunch about them (perhaps it is the canned flavor in the ranchero sauce), and even the barbecue version has no real kick, the only barbecue flavor coming from a hint of store-reminiscent sauce; the plate is somewhat improved by sweet grilled onions, but they don't hold a dying candle to El Arroyo's punchy rendition. Boost the passion quotient with a "Hot Latin Kiss" (again, more an American fantasy than a Mexican one): shrimp-stuffed jalapeños wrapped in bacon.

As an easy place to grab a quick meal in a warm and welcoming atmosphere, we happily recommend this spot. They seem to live by their slogan "World Peace through Tex-Mex," and that is a concept we can respect. –RM

El Mesón Taquería

Mexico in a small, tasty package that's
known to the insiders

food

8.1 **5.6**
10   10

experience

Mexican $ **14**   *Southeast*

Counter service
Sun.-Thurs. 6:30am-3pm;
Fri.-Sat. 6:30am-3pm,
5:30pm-9pm. *Breakfast. Wireless Internet.*

806 Burleson Rd.
Austin
(512) 416-0749

Bar Full
Credit Cards Visa, MC, AmEx
Reservations Accepted

This little taco shop way down Burleson, by the airport, is a gem. It serves a lively array of authentic interior Mexican specialties that far surpass both in interest and in execution the options on offer at most taquerías. The only thing that has kept this revelation off the lists of many Austin foodies is its obscure southeastern location; nevertheless, a sneaky gang of insiders has been growing of late, and nowadays you might find lines of loyal customers out the door.

The secret to El Mesón's success is keeping it simple: service is limited to the Mexican-tiled counter, where the patron is faced with a short list of options, all available for the same low price, which includes beans, rice, and tortillas. Hooray for short menus!

And, in fact, any choice is good here. The pipian (chicken stewed in a pumpkin-seed sauce) is sweet and creamy; the classic taco filling of al pastor (spit-roasted pork) is a contender for best in town, with lean, flavorful pork and juicy pineapple, all of it glistening golden red. Barbacoa (stewed cow's head meat) is meltingly tender, and pairs perfectly with either of the house salsas (an unusual, creamy orange jalapeño salsa, when in season, is particularly good). Wrap any of these up with some beans (we prefer the pinto to the black) in steaming corn tortillas, and give in to the tender goodness. El Mesón also does a killer, limey guacamole, though chips can be thick and stale.

We particularly like the mixed crowd drawn to this unlikely spot. East Austinites mix happily with downtown businessmen and college students, and the occasional pilot, dropping in from the airport, adds class to the crowd with his stripes. Everything is obligingly labeled in both English and Spanish—what a delicious way to learn a language!
—RM

El Patio

Famously bad Tex-Mex with a mighty
Old-Austin rep

food
2.4 **5.6**
10   10
experience

Mexican $ **15**   *UT Area*

Casual restaurant   2938 Guadalupe St.   *Bar* Beer/wine
Mon.-Sat. 11am-9:45pm;   Austin   *Credit Cards* Visa and MC
closed Sun.   (512) 476-5955   *Reservations* Not accepted

Despite Kinky Friedman's insistence in his Austin guidebook that it is still "right up there at the top," El Patio has a well-earned reputation as the worst Tex-Mex joint in town. We say this with love. Any restaurant that has held it out in this town for over 50 years deserves a good deal of respect. And El Patio (pronounced to rhyme with cat-io, as befits a place distinguished by a neon sombrero) has plenty of old-school appeal, from extremely friendly service to a signed poster of UT's starting forward, ca. 1971, to the cheap margaritas that make the youthful crowd smile wider as the night draws on.

It is presumably this Old-Austin pedigree that endears it to the Kinkster, who tells an almost certainly apocryphal tale of a young Elvis taking a friend's mom here on a date in a lavender caddie in the early fifties. Pedigree will get you only so far, however (okay, we admit that 56 years and counting is reasonably far), and the food here is just about on par with the King's other passion: Twinkies. As might be expected of a Tex-Mex restaurant opened in the 1950's by an unequivocally un-Mex family, there is little south-of-the-border flair to this food. In fact, until a few years ago, El Patio proudly served crackers with its runny salsa (we kid you not).

This is Tex-Mex as it used to be: bare-bones enchiladas heaped with runny chili, topped with runny queso. Although we've got to admit that we actually rather enjoy El Patio's guacamole chicken enchiladas, the menu and kitchen are stuck back in an older, far more parochial Austin. What's nice is that that parochialism is accompanied by such open goodwill. Paul Joseph, whose family has run the joint since 1954, likes to say "our policy is very simple—merely to serve the best." There's something to this when applied to the clientele; it's way off base on the food. –RM

El Regio

This little rotisserie turns out some of
the city's best roast chicken

food

6.9 /10   **2.4** /10

experience

Mexican   **$10**   *Southeast, N. Central, Far North*

Counter service   1928 E. Riverside Dr.   *Bar* None
Sun.-Thurs. 10am-10pm;   Austin   *Credit Cards* No credit cards
Fri.-Sat. 9am-11pm.   (512) 326-1888   *Reservations* Not accepted

                           6615 Berkman Dr.   9405 N. IH-35
                           78723, (512) 933-9557   78753, (512) 836-5892

El Regio squats happily beside the pawn shops in a somewhat seedy
strip mall on East Riverside Drive, dishing out some superior Mexican-
style roast chicken. Don't be confused into going to La Regiomontana,
the associated restaurant next door; you want the little hut with the
drive-thru. You'll recognize it by the rather shocked-looking overgrown
chicken in the red apron and sombrero painted on its side.

The cars move quickly past the window, as the ordering is simple:
you ask for either a half chicken or a whole, both of which come with
Mexican rice, a grilled onion, a warm stack of corn tortillas, two
excellent salsas (avocado and roja), and a cut lime. We recommend you
also order the outstanding charro beans—smoky, creamy pintos stewed
with pork fat, onions, and cilantro.

The chicken is simply prepared. First, it's rubbed with red chiles and
other Mexican-influenced spices, giving the meat a little kick without
overpowering it. Then, it's roasted just as it should be. It is moist,
buttery, and comes through that little window piping hot. Wrapped in a
warm, tender tortilla with some tangy-sweet roast onion, a little of the
creamy avocado salsa, rice, those beans, and brightened with a squeeze
of lime, it makes for one satisfying bite. And the half-chicken with all
the fixin's provides a very generous meal for two for under 10 bucks.
There is also a sweet and bland mayo potato salad to round out the
meal, if you like that sort of thing.

You'll have to take your food to go unless you'd like to hunker down
in one of the sadder parking lots in town (the next-door restaurant's
seating area looks like a bus-station waiting room), but that's okay. This
food simply begs to be taken back to satisfy the hungry mouths at
home. –RM

El Sol y La Luna

Immensely popular Tex-Mex with
ambition—sometimes fulfilled

food
5.0 **7.5**
10   10

experience

Mexican

$19

South Congress

Casual restaurant
Sun.-Tues. 7am-3pm;
Wed.-Sat. 7am-10pm.
Breakfast. Brunch. Live music.
Outdoor dining. Vegetarian-friendly. Wireless Internet.

1224 S. Congress Ave.
Austin
(512) 444-7770
www.elsolylalunaaustin.com

Bar Beer/wine
Credit Cards Visa, MC, AmEx
Reservations Accepted

El Sol y La Luna, on the South Congress strip, serves Tex-Mex with all
the standard fixin's but sometimes perks them up with unusual,
upmarket touches. Thus you'll find a range of familiar dishes given new
life by their signature ingredient—smoked salmon. We recommend all
of these. The salmon, more flaky than moist, gives nice body to the
dishes in which it resides, and has enough flavor to stand up to the
Mexican spices (which the standard mahi-mahi and tilapia, though they
make nice canvases, don't). The salmon taco comes with the added
surprise of a sweet and sour balsamic reduction. How fancy.

Spinach and mushroom enchiladas are also good, but the mole and
chipotle enchiladas are decidedly greasy, even if their flavors are
appealing. The caldo, or chicken soup, is more interesting than the
norm, with sweet pumpkiny undertones (though the vegetables can
come badly overcooked), and migas for breakfast are satisfying, though
not the best around. El Sol y La Luna is, however, guilty of two of our
great restaurant pet peeves: the menu is far too long (what are whole-
grain bagels and tofu salad doing at a Tex-Mex place?), and the chips
and salsa *aren't free* (although when they do arrive, the salsa is fresh
and garlicky, and the chips are warm). And avoid at all costs the fake
margaritas (the restaurant doesn't have a full liquor license, so they
make their 'ritas with low-grade wine).

Sit outside on the brightly-colored, fenced-in patio, which manages
somehow to achieve, in a pokey corner under the low tile roofs, the
feel of a Mexican village square, enhanced by a few greedy winged
visitors. The inside feels a little more haphazard. Service is also
haphazard, friendly but unbearably slow—while the lunch specials
make this a popular office destination, we wonder how they ever get
back to work in time. Maybe that's the appeal: El Sol y La Luna offers
its customers a Mexican siesta. –RM

El Taquito

Taco treats for night owls with all the
noirish romance of a back-alley deal

Mexican $ **5**   *East Austin*

Take-out   1712 Old E. Riverside Dr.   *Bar* None
Sun.-Wed. 5pm-3am;   Austin   *Credit Cards* No credit cards
Thurs.-Sat. 5pm-4:30am.   (512) 441-8320   *Reservations* Not accepted

Folks, I think we've found it—that establishment of student-slacker-
Sixth-Street-maven legend, the cure for a bad dinner, a bad mood, a
bad date, and the excessive consumption of bad alcohol: the perfect
cheap, late-night taco stand. Rare is the Austinite who has not longed
for just such an insider tip, to say lightly "let's go to my favorite taco
stand" and lead an admiring companion to the promised land,
preferably in some cheap little strip, preferably on the East side of
town, where, preferably, Spanish is the lengua of choice.

El Taquito meets all these requirements. Here, for a buck and a half
tops, the taco world is your proverbial oyster. Just east of IH-35, on the
south side of Riverside Drive, in the darkened parking lot of a Pinky's
Wireless shop, you'll see a little taco stand. Ignore it. Harder to see, up
the sloping lot to the right, seemingly abandoned, is another. You'll
have to climb over some rubble and slip through a gap in the chain-link
fence to reach it, but El Taquito will sell you what you crave. Best is the
carnitas taco, tender and moist, with light, sweetly roasted pork. Ask
for a sliver of avocado—it's a little extra (at these prices, who's
counting) but the added creaminess is divine. The deshebrado taco,
with juicy shredded beef, and the al pastor (sadly pineapple-less) are
other good orders. Tortillas are homemade and delicate, and though
the taquitos are pequeñitos, they pack a flavorful punch.

Don't panic too much if your Spanish isn't up to the task—the lovely
ladies of El Taquito are patient, and all you've got to do is memorize
the sentence "tres tacos de carnitas con aguacate, por favor." Then
give your companion a streetwise, I-come-here-all-the-time smile. –RM

El Zunzal

Charming, straightforward Salvadoran
fare in East Austin

Latin American $**19**   *East Austin*

Casual restaurant   646 Calles St.   *Bar* Beer/wine
Sun.-Thurs. 11am-10pm;   Austin   *Credit Cards* Visa, MC, AmEx
Fri.-Sat. 11am-11pm.   (512) 474-7749   *Reservations* Not accepted

A nice change from Austin's myriad Tex-Mex and Mex-Mex eateries, El
Zunzal has been serving up Salvadoran food in East Austin for three
years. Though this is not the only restaurant in town offering
Salvadoran food, we do feel that it is the most authentic. Named for a
beach in El Salvador, El Zunzal unobtrusively educates newcomers with
maps painted on the walls and Central American travel posters. The
main dining room is bombarded by blaring music and the dramatic
chattering of Mexican soaps. Service is fast and friendly, but a working
knowledge of Spanish is certainly helpful here.

The menu is full of charming misspellings of breakfast items, a few
weekend-only offerings, Mexican standards, and even burgers for those
too chicken to try something new (we pity da fool). Start with pupusas,
a Salvadoran standard that's like a stuffed pancake made of masa. They
are filled with chopped-up chicharrones, cheese, or loroco—pickled
buds of a popular Central American plant that tastes a bit like broccoli
and kale. Pupusas can be topped with a tart pickled cabbage
condiment called curtido, but we like them on their own, crisply
griddled and oozing with cheese. Tamales de elote and tamales de
puerco come in a light masa and can be a little bland. We prefer the
elote, served with a thin sour cream that accentuates the corn's natural
sweetness. Plátanos fritos (fried bananas) are delicious—soft and
caramelized and served with more thin sour cream. The pastelitos de
carne remind us of crisp but greasy empanadas filled with ground beef
and rice.

Mexican offerings are less interesting: carnitas are tough, and tacos al
pastor have nice flavor, but could use some pineapple. Stick to the
Salvadoran food, as that's what El Zunzal does best. –MPN

Elsi's

Salvadoran with some shine but too much starch

food

5.2
10

5.2
10

experience

Latin American $**19**   *Burnet*

Casual restaurant   6601 Burnet Rd.   *Bar* Full
Mon.-Sat. 7am-9pm;   Austin   *Credit Cards* Visa and MC
Sun. 8am-9pm. *Breakfast.*   (512) 454-0747   *Reservations* Accepted
Brunch. Live music.

Recently moved from its previous spot 20 blocks further south on Burnet Road, Elsi's now has a home that's freshly painted cantaloupe orange and purple, with tile floors and a bar, and is looking shiny and new. Paintings for sale decorate the walls; with the open space and tile, the acoustics can be a bit noisy. Service can be downright sloppy near closing—rushed and brusque, with forgotten dishes and premature checks, so come earlier, if you are able.

Elsi's menu is largely Tex-Mex and Salvadoran, and inexpensive lunch specials are a real bargain compared to higher-priced ã-la-carte items. Chicken-filled enchiladas morenos are a good example of this—covered in a simple red sauce and topped with considerable quantities of fresh avocado and queso fresco with rice and beans, they are a sizeable lunch at a reasonable price, if somewhat underseasoned. Caldo de pollo is also on the mild side, but this clear broth is swimming with large-cut squash, corn, onions, and roasted peppers.

Pupusas, that Salvadoran specialty, are also on the menu here—these greasy cornmeal pancakes come stuffed with either heavy cheese, or finely shredded pork, and a not-quite-pickled cabbage condiment on the side. A more flavorful main is Elsi's garlicky shrimp dish—the shrimp are a little overcooked, but the sauce is zippy. Unfortunately, toward the end of the day, rice starts getting crunchy and salads start to look tired. That said, fried yucca still comes out crisp and attractive, with an excellent spicy salsa on the side. However, pieces are irregularly cut; you may get nice, crisp, thin ones or heavy, starchy, fat ones. After all the starch, we must suggest you go elsewhere for dessert—all the desserts here contain plantains, including plantain empanadas filled with a disconcerting white custard and topped with an equally unappetizing pink syrup. –MPN

The Emerald Restaurant

food

8.0 / 10

8.8 / 10

experience

Care to drink away your kids' college fund?

Irish, French, American   **$80**   *Bee Cave*

Upmarket restaurant
Daily 5pm-11pm.
Date-friendly.

13614 W. Hwy. 71
Bee Cave
(512) 263-2147

Bar Beer/wine
Credit Cards Visa, MC, AmEx
Reservations Essential

Château Lafite, Margaux, Petrus, Romanée-Conti, Haut-Brion—if these names mean anything to you, then you must visit the Emerald Restaurant and see a wine list that you'll think must be fiction (especially when you start ordering—the list isn't updated often enough as bottles are sold). Emerald's list is certainly one of the best in Texas. Many of the legendary vintages are represented, and if you have the means and the inclination, this may be your last chance to try some wines that are now nearly impossible to find outside of private collections.

Emerald's musty house on Highway 71 is familiar to many lake-goers for its large, lounging-leprechaun billboard, and to others for its romantic Valentine's Day dinner. They serve the kind of celebratory meals your great-grandparents might have eaten out, sort of like turn-of-the-century Delmonico's but with an Irish bent. Plates are huge, and there is no innovation here; while you wouldn't want to eat at Emerald all the time (unless you are drinking a 1928 Latour for dinner), we feel this type of food has a place—it helps us to see how upscale cuisine has evolved, and where it was for so long.

Formal service is slow but gracious, and dishes are well executed. Dense soda bread and sweet treacle bread arrive to start. Poached salmon is served cold with a horseradish sauce and buttery croutons, blending together for a spicy, crunchy, rich appetizer. Onion soup with melted cheese served in a whole onion is flambéed dramatically at the table. Mains cover fish, fowl, and game. We enjoy the savory stuffed quail topped with a lovely dark cherry sauce, as well as rare veal medallions with rich mushroom and truffle sauce. For dessert, try the "Boreen," a dense chocolate and marmalade tart, and if you can spare an extra few hundred, perhaps a bottle of Château d'Yquem, the greatest wine in the world. –MPN

Enchiladas y Mas

Sometimes Mas is not enough—here it's not even close

food

1.4 / 10

4.3 / 10

experience

Mexican $**18**   *North Central*

Casual restaurant   1911 W. Anderson Ln.   *Bar* Full
Tues.-Sat. 7am-9pm; Sun.   Austin   *Credit Cards* Visa and MC
7am-2pm; closed Mon. *Breakfast.* (512) 467-7100   *Reservations* Not accepted

"Never Trust A Skinny Cook," reads the menu at this longtime North Austin Tex-Mex joint. But the perpetrators lurking behind the kitchen doors at Enchiladas y Mas are fattening up their customers on a dire combination of grease and processed cheese that is far from encouraging—the enchiladas (y mas) served here make you think more of the guy on the couch who fires up the can of Cheez Whiz at halftime than of an expert chef with promising Emeril-style perky rotundity.

It is hard to imagine what keeps folks coming back (the restaurant is generally packed), unless it is that the almost entirely white clientele really does prefer that afore-mentioned cheese-in-a-can to anything more authentically Mexican. Aside from some pretty tiled tables, the space is drab and has a temporary feel, the only color coming from strings of beer pennants. However, a lively banter presides, and service is very friendly (though we must warn those protective of their personal space: some of the waitpeople have a decidedly hands-on approach).

The food, however, ruins any brief pleasantness. To put it gently, it's awful. Be particularly wary of the cheese enchiladas, which are filled with American-style cheese that has melted into a substance of considerable scientific interest. Doused in a "beef sauce" which is really just greasy brown gravy with a few stray grains of beef, they are a monumentally bad concoction. The sour cream sauce is Olympic-quality bland, and while you may be briefly fooled into liking the verde because its tartness cuts the processed flavor of the cheese, it is worse than most in town. Additional squares of cheese ornament the tops of the enchiladas, looking as if their handy plastic wrapping was just peeled off them. The only redeeming feature here is some very spicy salsa—chug the stuff like an old-school anesthetic, and you might just survive the meal. –RM

European Bistro

Cherry soup, stuffed cabbage, and the sweet smells of home...in Pflugerville?

food

8.3 / 10   8.5 / 10
experience

Hungarian $37   *Pflugerville*

Upmarket restaurant   111 E. Main St.   **Bar** Beer/wine
Mon.-Thurs. 5pm-9pm; Fri.-   Pflugerville   **Credit Cards** Visa, MC, AmEx
Sun. noon-10pm. *Date-friendly.* (512) 835-1919   **Reservations** Accepted
Live music. Wireless Internet. www.european-bistro.com

It is hard to imagine two places aesthetically further apart than Budapest and Pflugerville. Despite the Ye Olde Gifte Shoppes and Wilkommen signs, Pflugerville is distinctly New World, all strip malls and subdivision sprawl, its remnant of Old Main Street a mere blip in the obliterated landscape of access roads and cookie-cutter ranch houses.

And yet, improbably, in one of the few remaining older buildings, we find the impressively authentic European Bistro, serving high-end, well-executed Hungarian specialties. Old World pretensions sometimes lean a little heavily on a preponderance of doilies and embroidery, but there is definitely an old-fashioned charm to the place. The service, from a mostly Hungarian staff, is attentive and incredibly well meaning, if at times a little awkward. These folks are trying hard to succeed, and they deserve to. Everything on their menu is beautifully made from scratch. The soft, dense, gray-brown bread on its own will send a European into wheeling nostalgia; sausages and spätzle meet with equal success.

Hungarian food is, first and foremost, comfort food: stews, starches, and rich, creamy sauces. The European Bistro serves an excellent (if mild) goulash in both a soup and a stew form, accompanied by homemade dumplings. German influences are abundant and suitably solid, as seen in the veal bratwurst with hot potato salad, with salty bacon accents. It's pleasant to eat food prepared with such familial goodwill (behind all these dishes, in fact, one senses a mother urging her growing boy to eat more). Our favorite dish in this category is the stuffed cabbage, the leaves cooked sweet and soft, the ground pork filling scented with spices. And if you finish your plate, mama will let you have some apple strudel, not too sweet, crisp and steaming from the oven. –RM

Evangeline Café

Average New Orleans food, sublime onion rings

food
6.0 | 5.9
10 | 10
experience

Southern $23   Far South

Casual restaurant   8106 Brodie Ln.   *Bar* Beer/wine
Mon.-Sat. 11am-10pm;   Austin   *Credit Cards* Visa, MC, AmEx
closed Sun. *Live music.*   (512) 282-2586   *Reservations* Accepted
Outdoor dining.   www.evangelinecafe.com

One of the many restaurants to crop up along South Austin's Brodie Lane in recent years, Evangeline Café is different in that it is neither a fast-food restaurant, nor even a member of any of Austin's several local midrange chains. Named for the eponymous Longfellow poem about the Acadians' forced migration from Nova Scotia to Louisiana, Evangeline serves Louisiana cooking in a restaurant space that looks like a scrapbook. The walls are covered with a chaotic assortment of Mardi Gras costumes and memorabilia, photos, street signs, athletic gear, and hunting trophies. Service is friendly and relatively fast despite quite a few customers from around the neighborhood.

Evangeline Café's menu is filled with the usual Creole fare as well as a few interesting variations. Beer and wine are available, but if you don't want to drink, be sure to try Evangeline's sunny house-made lemonade. There are three different hot sauces on the tables, which is a good thing, as many dishes could stand to be revved up. We like our gumbo spicy, and while Evangeline's gumbo-in-a-mug has good flavor and lots of sliced andouille, it's not quite kicky enough for us. Same goes for the catfish po-boy—the fried fish is crunchy and not at all muddy, but the remoulade reminds us of supermarket-variety Russian dressing, and the whole thing could use a little more oomph.

Happily, accompanying onion rings are awesome, hand battered and thin cut, with a light coating and a good amount of grease. Attractive "Crawfish Evangeline" features a bland étouffée over linguine, without enough depth of flavor. It comes with a pistolette (a crisp, chewy fried roll). Which reminds us: don't miss the stuffed pistolette filled with shrimp or crawfish étouffée—the texture of the roll and étouffée blend to make a toothsome mess, just right with some of that hot sauce.
—MPN

Evita's Botanitas

Supercharged Mexican in a sweet-as-sugar setting

food
6.4
10

7.7
10
experience

Mexican $23   Far South

Casual restaurant   6400 S. 1st St.   *Bar* Full
Mon. and Wed.-Thurs. 9am-   Austin   *Credit Cards* Visa, MC, AmEx
9:30pm; Fri.-Sat. 9am-10pm; (512) 441-2424   *Reservations* Accepted
Sun. 9am-8:30pm; closed Tues. *Breakfast*.

This is one of those restaurants that's a pleasure to tell people about. You can feel like you're driving through a whole lotta nothing before you happen on this little spot in a strip mall below Stassney, but it's every bit worth the trek. The restaurant is scrappy and colorful, with pink walls, murals of Mayan temples, tables swathed in the colors of the Mexican flag, and piñatas hanging from the ceiling.

Your meal will start with the now-famous salsa wheel, a lazy susan of sorts that can tempt you to ruin. The chips are so plentiful, the salsas and escabeche so razor-sharp, that by the time you've drowned the heat with some beer and reached for more, you might well already be out of stomach real estate.

But leave space: next come gorgeous quesadillas, filled with grilled mushrooms, onions, and poblanos, and served with sour cream and a bright guacamole; or a greasy but delicious queso flameado, with spicy dried chiles, poblano rings, sliced mushrooms, and warm tortillas. Migas are a bit browned and need some salt, but they're otherwise sweet and flavorful, with plenty of cheese. Some tacos are bland, including picadillo (ground beef) and pollo (chicken). Carne guisada has a nice flavor, though the gravy is thin, while barbacoa needs salt and isn't chopped well enough for our taste. A tuna steak, though rather well done, simply dances in a peppery chile de arbol sauce, and enchiladas swim in any number of wonderful sauces (we like the verde, which you'll recognize as one of the stars from the salsa wheel). All come beautifully presented in rainbow of colors, with delicate sides of cilantro-lime rice or smoky borracho beans.

The folks at Evita's couldn't be friendlier, full of chatty advice and helpful suggestions. This restaurant should be called Evita's Bonitas, for as our man John Keats so admirably put it, a thing of beauty is a joy forever. –RM/MPN

EZ's

A popular retro-counter-service chain—
but beware the burgers and veggies

food

4.6 **5.7**
10   10

experience

American, Pizza   **$20**   *Seton Medical Area, Westlake*

Counter service
Daily 11am-11pm.
Kid-friendly. Outdoor dining.
Vegetarian-friendly.

3918 N. Lamar Blvd.
Austin
(512) 302-1800
www.ezsrestaurants.com

2745 Bee Caves Rd.
78746, (512) 329-0003

Bar Beer/wine
Credit Cards Visa, MC, AmEx
Reservations Not accepted

EZ's is a family-friendly Texas mini-chain with a checkerboard 1950s-diner theme. We can see the informal appeal, especially to kids. You order at the counter, and wait for your number to be called. The airy, retro dining room and shady outdoor seating can both be fun. Unfortunately, the food is a big disappointment, especially given the place's relative popularity.

There is definitely something to the highly-touted rosemary chicken. It's a half bird, delicately roasted—but not overcooked—in the brick pizza ovens; the result is moist, flavorful meat with crispy and well-seasoned skin (especially on the delicious thigh piece), and well-textured focaccia that's cooked in the pizza oven. Unfortunately, horrible sides practically ruin the whole plate. Rice has no distinguishable flavor, and essentially unseasoned carrots, zucchini, squash, and broccoli are like hospital food, an object lesson in blandness. At our last visit, the carrots were so dry that a white crust had formed on each slice. If you want your kids to eat vegetables, don't let them anywhere near these.

The pizzas have thick, pleasantly seared crusts but disappointing toppings, while burgers suffer from an identity crisis. Their size, weight, and price evokes the "gourmet burger"—the sort with meat high-quality enough that you might ask for it medium-rare—but EZ's doesn't ask how you'd like yours cooked. You'll find out why when you see the gristly, low-quality beef; it's a burger with neither the meatiness and flavor of the thick style nor the comfort-food goodness of the thin, greasy-spoon style. Add clumpy, congealing cheese and leathery, overcooked bacon, and you've put together one of the worst burgers in Austin. This is one of the few places when we actually prefer the vegetarian version (here, it's a "bean burger") to the real thing. Curly fries and onion rings are below average, too.

The best thing at EZ's is the vanilla milkshake, whose careful balance of Blue Bell ice cream, milk, and vanilla syrup is cookbook-worthy. We'd skip the whipped cream on top, but hey, we're grown-ups. –RG

Fadó

A warm Irish pub with food that's
mother superior to Mother Egan's

food
7.6 **8.6**
10   10
experience

Irish, American   **$26**   *Warehouse District*

Pub
Mon.-Fri. 11:15am-2am; Sat.-Sun.
6:30am-2am. Kitchen closes Mon.-
Thurs. 10pm; Fri.-Sat. 11pm.

214 W. 4th St.
Austin
(512) 457-0172
www.fadoirishpub.com

Bar Full
Credit Cards Visa, MC, AmEx
Reservations Accepted

Fadó, the cozy Irish pub in downtown's warehouse district, serves
perhaps the best pub grub in town—it's good enough to make you
wish Texas had a colder climate.

Sure, there are the requisite annoying affectations of most things
"Irish" on this side of the pond: the Guinness paraphernalia, the display
cases of artifacts from "Joyce's Dublin," and, for those inspired by his
spirit, some rather unforgivable drawers labeled "writing paper" and
"quills and nibs" (fortunately empty). Irish musicians perform the
obligatory U2 songs.

But there is a lot about the pub that feels genuine. It's the only place
in town that regularly shows live footie without a cover. The room is
comfortable (the interior is all at angles to create spaces that are private
without feeling cramped), and there is a warm patina to all surfaces,
from the lovely tile floor to the pressed-tin ceiling. Texas Hold 'Em poker
tournaments (for pride, not money) on certain nights of the week are
lots of fun.

Best of all, the food easily lives up to its Irish-pub-fare pretensions
(much more than can be said of Mother Egan's Irish Pub a few blocks
away). Chicken pot pie is a warm winner, with a delicate crust and
none of the gelatinous goo that so often sinks the dish. The Irish
breakfast is another good order, with baked beans, sunny eggs that are
beautifully runny, sausage that is appropriately bready yet still well-
seasoned, a couple of rashers of Irish bacon, fried tomatoes, and some
sweet brown bread to mop up leftovers. Corned beef is slow-cooked
on the premises, and there are some very respectable fish and chips.
And don't miss the delightful brown-bread ice cream for dessert.

Service is welcoming and chatty, with a wicked Irish warmth well
expressed on the menu:

May you have food and raiment.
A soft pillow for your head.
May you be forty years in heaven,
Before the devil knows you're dead. –RM

Farm to Market Grocery

All hail the return of the neighborhood grocery

South Congress

Specialty grocery
Daily 8am-8pm.

1718 S. Congress Ave.
Austin
(512) 462-7220
www.fm1718.com

Bar Beer/wine
Credit Cards Visa, MC, AmEx
Reservations Not accepted

This gem of a shop on South Congress is still in its infancy but already has proven to be a well-conceived grocery, supporting our local markets and still managing to offer customers a wide variety of items, despite the shop's tiny size. Inside, every inch of space is being put to use, yet the shop maintains a clean and uncluttered feel. Farm to Market's slogan is "Eat Locally," and the proprietors do an excellent job making this wish our command. They currently sell products from over 80 local growers and producers, and are bringing in more all the time.

All the usual suspects are represented like Tom's Tabooley, Pure Luck Dairy, New Canaan Farms, and Eastside Café, but there are many more that we're tickled to discover. Goat's-milk ice cream, from Water Oak Farms near Bryan, comes in myriad tempting flavors, including chocolate chip, with little bits of rich chocolate swathed in a vanilla ice cream that still maintains its goaty muskiness. Farm to Market doesn't have a seating area, but offers plenty of grab-and-go possibilities like dense French bread sandwiches filled with rich roasted eggplant and red peppers, or if you're feeling naughty, terrines and confits by Le Marseillaise. Note that this is not a meat and fish market—the spotlights here are on excellent local produce and packaged products. There's also a modest but extremely well chosen wine selection.

Happily, Farm to Market doesn't take itself too seriously, and still brings in key items on all of our shopping lists. We are pleased to find soy milk, baby food, and fish sauce, important pantry staples not always made in these parts, and the kind of items that makes Farm to Market the sort of place where we could shop every day. –MPN

Finn and Porter

Overpriced food in a fancy, weird
space—and we don't mean good weird

food
6.1 / 10

6.0 / 10
experience

Seafood, New American, Japanese   **$63**   *Convention Center Area*

Upmarket restaurant	500 E. 4th St.	*Bar* Full
Daily 5pm-11pm.	Austin	*Credit Cards* Visa, MC, AmEx
Outdoor dining.	(512) 493-4900	*Reservations* Accepted

Watching an upscale restaurant mini-chain inside an upscale hotel maxi-chain try its hand at cutting-edge design is like watching a Texas politician trying to rally the masses in broken Spanish: while on some level you have to admire the effort, it's sometimes hard not to wince at the bumbling execution.

So bizarre is Finn and Porter's décor that the attentive, deferential waitstaff seems almost lost in the stark glare of hanging lights that criss-cross the middle reaches of the soaring, two-story dining room. Metallic cords stripe the air like a network of circus tightropes—or the personal-rocket runways that 1950s sci-fi writers imagined would grace the 21st-century skies. Meanwhile, disturbingly bright color panels, monolithic columns in woodsy shades of brown and yellow, and translucent urns feel like the apocalyptic remains of a Frank Lloyd Wright house sacked by aliens.

The kitchen, like the design, has ambition but exercises it without grace. At our last visit, an amuse-bouche of mushroom consommé was overwhelmed by parsley. The sushi bar hawks some truly exotic—and truly expensive—pieces of fish, but they fall flat. O-toro, for example, the fattiest of the fatty tuna, tips the monetary scales at $15 for two pieces, but was disappointingly stringy at our last visit. Even worse were fishy chu-toro, and sea urchin sushi wrapped by seaweed so tough that it was a real challenge to chew.

Amongst the main courses, the $35 Finn and Porter "Trio" was recommended as the signature dish, but its three proteins seemed strange bedfellows: a delightfully tender lobster tail had gentle notes of vanilla and judiciously sautéed vegetables, but it paired poorly with a stodgy beef tenderloin with béarnaise sauce, and a crab cake, though meaty, was humdrum and out of place. A dessert of hot homemade donuts sitting on dulce de leche swirls, served with a cup of Amaretto-laced hot chocolate, was better, but for $100 a head, this restaurant leaves us scratching ours. –RG

Fino

A sleek, tasty tapas-and-more spot that
proudly extends the Asti empire

food

9.2 / 10   **9.3** / 10

experience

Spanish $**50**   *UT Area*

Upmarket restaurant
Mon.-Thurs. 11am-10pm; Fri.
11am-11pm; Sat. 5pm-11pm;
closed Sun. *Date-friendly.*
Outdoor dining.

2905 San Gabriel St.
Austin
(512) 474-2905
www.astiaustin.com

Bar Full
Credit Cards Visa, MC, AmEx
Reservations Recommended

One of Austin's high-flying relative newcomers, Fino arrived in 2005 to
take over the space previously occupied by the Granite Café. It's the
brainchild of Emmett and Lisa Fox, the couple behind Hyde Park's Asti.
The feel here is nouveau-retro with natural touches—small lamps
illuminate individual tables giving them an intimate feel, Asian-inspired
wood shelves blend nicely with shades made of thin branches, and the
warm lighting chips in to create an ideal date environment. Meanwhile,
a sleek outdoor lounge area evocative of Miami Beach makes a roomy
alternative to the packed bar. It doesn't seem to have taken long for
Fino to get off the ground, as business is flowing in the same place
where it was once all dried up. Perhaps part of the reason for this is the
staff's infectious enthusiasm—they are thrilled to show you around, and
everyone goes out of their way to be sure that their guests are
comfortable and well attended.

Fino's Spanish-influenced menu is full of tapas-like "small plates," the
new craze, and also offers several salads and mains, including paella
(for two), a rarity in Austin. It's easy to go wild with so many
scrumptious-sounding little bites to eat—breathe, and take things one
at a time. Try the Cabrales-stuffed dates—the salty robustness of the
cheese complements the sweet density of the dates, making for lush
and chewy mouthfuls. Skewered grilled pork with sea salt is smoky and
tender, though we find the chunky hummus and eggplant dishes
lacking in flavor.

Fried goat cheese with onion compote and honey works well, too.
However, on one visit, the cheese arrived below room temperature. For
dessert, try the palate-brightening lemon pot de crème. Prices, even for
the "big plates," are delightfully fair for what you're getting. In the
end, Fino is a tasty and romantic standby with an exciting concept and
a long, bright future ahead. –MPN

Flipnotics Coffeespace

A fresh, trendy coffee spot complete
with Pee Wee Herman alarm clock

food

5.1 / 10

8.4 / 10

experience

Light American $**12**   *Zilker*

Café   1601 Barton Springs Rd.   *Bar* Beer/wine
Mon.-Fri. 7am-midnight; Sat.   Austin   *Credit Cards* Visa and MC
7am-1am; Sun. 8am-11pm.   (512) 480-8646   *Reservations* Not accepted
Kitchen closes 1 hr. earlier.   www.flipnotics.com
Breakfast. Date-friendly. Live music. Outdoor dining. Wireless Internet.

Flipnotics is your local coffeeshop-cum-music-venue-cum-vintage-clothing-store for the Barton Hills and Zilker crowd. It is pleasingly punk, with a crazy-fun collection of clothes and knick-knacks. The upstairs café has less to offer; other than free-trade coffee from the Texas Coffee Traders, options are pretty limited. The Satellite Café in Oak Hill, run by the same folks, has a more extensive menu.

But Flipnotics does serve a series of salads, bagels, sandwiches, desserts, and, in the winter, soups. Sandwiches are on the whole unexciting, but the tuna is a nice surprise, on nutty toast with just the right amount of mayo and a pleasing, peppery kick. Wraps, such as the grilled chicken, have fresh vegetables and a notably generous helping of golden-green sliced avocado (an item that, let's face it, will make absolutely anything yummy), but they suffer from a lack of condiments. Salads also sport an appealing, crisp mix of vegetables (except for tinned black olives—the Cheerios of the olive world). These come clad in lively garbs, such as the peanutty Thai dressing; we recommend you ask for extra and anoint your sandwich with it. In addition to coffee, which is served in a mix-'n'-match set of mugs that you might have accumulated in your own cupboard, there are beers and fresh but runny smoothies (head down the road to the Daily Juice instead for the real, though costly, deal).

Service is relaxed and informal (be prepared to have some of your order be negged—they frequently run out of things). There is pleasant, intimate seating both indoors and out, and a stage inside that is host to an impressive nightly lineup of live music acts. We wouldn't eat here any day, but for a post-Barton-Springs swim snack, it might be just the ticket. –RM

Flip's Satellite Café

Overstretched diner food in a café
setting that's far, far out

food

5.0 | 5.2
10 | 10

experience

American $17   *Dripping Springs*

Casual restaurant   7101 W. Hwy. 71   *Bar* Beer/wine
Sun.-Thurs. 8am-9pm; Fri.-Sat.   Dripping Springs   *Credit Cards* Visa and MC
8am-10pm. *Breakfast. Brunch.*   (512) 301-1883   *Reservations* Not accepted
Live music. Outdoor dining. Vegetarian-friendly.

"I saw two shooting stars last night," croons Billy Bragg's boyish lover, "but they were only satellites...." Flip's Satellite Café in Oak Hill offers the same slightly manufactured disappointment. The more food-oriented sibling of Flipnotics Coffeespace, it has none of that venue's punky charm—the attitude here seems sedated by the location.

The first sign that this café has suffered at the hands of human innovation is its romantic setting "at the Y in Beautiful Oak Hill!" as the menu proudly states. That is, it sits in a vast parking lot between the Big Lots and the Blockbuster. The interior does little to alleviate the antiseptic feel, besides, perhaps, spreading a little grubbiness here and there.

The menu spans the wide gap between diner-style breakfast fare and highfalutin' items from the grill, such as pork tenderloin. Both sides of the menu suffer for the stretch. The simpler breakfasts are unsuccessfully dressed up. A good example is the "Mississippi Sun," which reworks eggs benedict with veggie cakes, chipotle hollandaise, and roasted-corn pico. But at our last visit, the poached eggs, having clearly spent too much time in the southern heat, crumbled at a touch, and while the veggie cakes had good flavor, the hollandaise had none, and the odd kernels of corn that dotted the plate were only partly defrosted. We recommend that you stick to the basics—vast pancakes are fluffy and acceptable.

On the other side, high-brow dinner entrees are dumbed down. Grilled items are prepared clichés, and the phrases "sautéed vegetable medley" and "rice pilaf" conclude almost every menu description. A portobello melt sports a dry, unmarinated mushroom, and while we like the feta dill sauce, it is barely scraped on to the bun. To make matters worse, food tends to arrive desperately late. Then again, it takes a while to hard-poach an egg. –RM

Flores

Sorry—did we just eat some Mexican
food? It was so mild we didn't notice

food
4.9 **6.2**
10   10
experience

Mexican   **$23**   *N. Central, Oak Hill, Lake Travis*

Casual restaurant   2700 W. Anderson Ln.   *Bar* Full
Mon.-Thurs. 11am-10:30pm;   Austin   *Credit Cards* Visa, MC, AmEx
Fri.-Sat. 9am-10:30pm; Sun. (512) 302-5470   *Reservations* Accepted
9am-5pm. *Brunch. Kid-friendly. Live music. Outdoor dining.*

                             1310 RR 620 S.,   6705 W. Hwy. 290
                             Lakeway   Oak Hill
                             (512) 263-9546   (512) 892-4845

The family-owned Flores Mexican Restaurants scattered around Austin
serve generally bland Mexican fare and an array of reliably strong
margaritas. Spaces differ widely in atmosphere, ranging from the
original Oak Hill restaurant's diner-like feel to Anderson Lane's more
festive Tex-Mex attitude. Service is okay—not particularly fast, but
certainly passable.

The menu covers all the bases, including weekend breakfast, and
some kid-friendly burger and chicken dishes. Aside from the salsa
served with the chips, very little of the food is spicy, which may be the
reason (beyond the margaritas) that our friends who can't handle the
heat well are so fond of Flores. Tacos come in house-made shells filled
with mildly seasoned meat, veggies, and cheese. Shrimp enchiladas are
filled with grilled onions and tiny bay shrimp, and slathered with a
tinny-tasting red sauce. Carne guisada is an unappealing shade of grey,
the lack of tomato in the gravy carrying over to the taste, and tough
beef tips are too large to be eaten in a taco. On the upside, the rice is
okay, the various beans on offer are well made, and tasty chicken
flautas are rolled with mild green chiles. The best dish at Flores is their
tortilla soup, which, beyond the necessary tortillas, is unlike any other
that we've had. Flores goes against the norm, making their soup with a
clear base and no tomatoes whatsoever. The broth is chock full of
large-cut veggies: carrots, onions, discs of corn still on the cob,
avocado, and chunks of chicken. Melted white cheese clings to the
veggies and tortilla bits, adding depth to this warm and simple bowl of
yumminess.

Flores serves sleepy Mexican fare in a town where the cuisine dances.
But if you're looking for the kind of comfort that comes with a great
nap, the margaritas and cozy tortilla soup may be just your thing.
—MPN

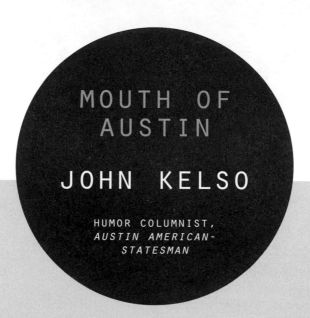

MOUTH OF AUSTIN

JOHN KELSO

HUMOR COLUMNIST,
*AUSTIN AMERICAN-
STATESMAN*

One thing you can say about Arkie's, a greasy spoon on the far eastern end of Cesar Chavez Street?

The cook is clairvoyant. He must have known I was coming, because the fried chicken I ordered tasted like it had been cooked the day before.

I don't think of Austin as a hotbed of fine cuisine. It's not San Francisco and it's not New Orleans. On the other hand, it's not Des Moines, either. Austin's strong point: you can get a whole lot of decent food here for not a lot of money. You can go to lunch for less than $10, and you can usually find dinner for less than $20. Even the expensive places have deals. At Eddie V's, a tony place, they've got a budget happy hour on Mondays. At that yuppie seafood place on the ground floor of the Frost Bank Tower—I call it McCormick and Schmuck, though that's not quite right—they have a happy-hour price break on oysters, too. And, of course, there is lots of Mexican food. And you just can't charge an arm and a leg when your sides are rice and beans.

Sadly, however, Austin is losing some of its traditional groceries to time and a lack of interest. This is a young town; young people would rather have sex than eat (not necessarily a bad choice). But, as a result, there really aren't any wonderful barbecue places left in the city limits. If you want great barbecue, you have to go to a town like Lockhart or Llano. And how many places in Austin still sell chili, the official state dish? It's easier to find Vietnamese soup here than a bowl of red.

Still, it beats the heck out of what you're going to find in downtown Keokuk. Now would somebody pass the chips and salsa before I get mad? –JK

Fonda San Miguel

Austin's premier interior Mexican
restaurant ages gracefully

Mexican $59 North Central

Upmarket restaurant
Mon.-Thurs. 5:30pm-9:30pm;
Fri.-Sat. 5:30pm 10:30pm; Sun.
11am-2pm. *Brunch. Date-friendly.*

2330 W. North Loop Blvd.
Austin
(512) 459-4121
www.fondasanmiguel.com

Bar Full
Credit Cards Visa, MC, AmEx
Reservations Essential

Fonda San Miguel is the grande dame of all Austin Mexican restaurants.
She has elegant lines in the style of a tiled Spanish mission, a deep
orange warmth, and an important Mexican art collection. For decades,
customers have been greeted by a classy, black-clad lady, her hair pulled
back in a tight silver bun that belies the warmth in her face. Even if you
aren't so lucky, her matriarchal manner will still grace your experience.
You will be offered a comfortable seat, a matchless margarita, and
impossibly thin tortilla chips in the airy, leafy atrium. After a while, you
will be led past the restaurant parrot into the beautiful dining room.
Yes, long before Uchi and Zoot, Fonda San Miguel was putting Austin
on the culinary map.

There have been whispers that La Fonda has been slipping in recent
years; whether due to rising prices or a slight decline in quality, there *is*
some truth to the reports. Seasoning, lately, can be erratic. But it's hard
to frown long at something so beautiful, from the setting, to the order-
memorizing, virtuoso waiters, to the immaculately displayed food. Start
with sopa del elote, enhanced by the vaguely metallic tang of poblanos.
Or try the queso flameado with sweet, fresh-pressed corn tortillas and
rich duck sausage. Perhaps the best dish on the menu is the justifiably
famous mole—a deep, subtle dish, more chocolaty than most (and
nobody is complaining). Another wonder is the pescado tikin xik—
tender fish in achiote sauce with bright pink pickled onions—but skip
the cochinita pibil, which can be dry at times, and the over-marinated
ceviche.

Better yet, come for the Sunday brunch buffet—$38.95 well spent:
comforting green enchilada casserole, escabeche and gently steamed
nopalitos, mole and migas, and gorgeous sweet corn pudding. It is all
laid out in hand-made Mexican pottery and dished out personally by
the maverick chef Miguel, the consummate host, the Restaurateur-King
who is, like most great civic figures, as comfortable cooing with babies
as cavorting with celebrities. –RM

FoodHeads

Simple, convenient, and delicious pan-American sandwiches

Light American $ **8**   *UT Area*

Counter service
Mon.-Fri. 8am-4pm; Sat.
8:30am-4pm; closed Sun.
Breakfast. Delivery. Live music.
Outdoor dining. Vegetarian-friendly. Wireless Internet.

616 W. 34th St.
Austin
(512) 420-8400
www.foodheads.com

Bar None
Credit Cards Visa, MC, AmEx
Reservations Not accepted

This small operation has provided catering services to Austinites and to local cafés for over a decade now, but they have recently expanded to an eat-in location just north of the University. Their trademark is fresh, creative sandwiches, and when they say "fresh" they mean it: everything, including their pickles, baked beans, mustards, and other spreads, is made by the FoodHeads food-heads from scratch. As a result, this little café turns out incredibly high-quality sandwiches to an enthusiastic lunch crowd culled from the nearby university and Seton Hospital.

Sandwiches are a combination of build your own (bread plus meat plus cheese plus condiment) and more adventuresome rotating specials. There is plenty to choose from, although soft cheeses like brie or chêvre are notably absent from their cheese list. A simple portobello sandwich, with plenty of bright green spinach, is very successful, but the menu also includes more ambitious combinations like the "Gypsy Grove," a combination of pork tenderloin, ham, Swiss cheese, cherry peppers, Tabasco slaw, and a fried egg. Most impressive is a commanding list of homemade spreads that includes everything from chipotle mayo to bagna caüda (butter, garlic, and anchovies). Daily soup specials are also notable, though often extremely substantial. On one visit, both a tomato soup and a sweet potato soup tasted just right, but were almost too thick to deserve the tag (the former reminded us of a well-executed pasta sauce).

Perhaps the nicest thing about FoodHeads is the setting: located in a nicely refurbished old craftsman bungalow, it still has something of the feel of a private home, with books lining the built-ins, a comfortable porch, and a pretty flower-garden in the front. Both in terms of the food and the ambiance, FoodHeads wipes the table with the neighborhood's other shift-key-trigger-happy sandwich shop, NeWorlDeli. –RM

The Fox and Hound

Celebrate the Horns' success, not the food

food
4.2
10

7.4
10
experience

American
$20
Capitol Area

Pub
Daily 11am-2am. Kitchen closes
30 min. earlier. *Live music.*
Outdoor dining. Wireless Internet.

401 Guadalupe St.
Austin
(512) 494-1200
www.shrg.com

Bar Full
Credit Cards Visa, MC, AmEx
Reservations Accepted

The Fox and Hound sounds like another of those Austin incarnations of English corner pubs, but in fact it is a less charming institution—a chain sports bar that rises somewhat bleakly out of one of the more wasted corners of downtown.

The inside is a dark and crowded stack of rooms, greenly lit by the flickering light of plasma TVs. On game days (particularly during UT's historic football and basketball runs of 2005-2006), the place turns into an absolute madhouse, in some cases closing its doors to anyone and everyone hours before games to prevent overcrowding. This is one of the best places to watch the Horns if you are in the "holler wildly after the coin toss" mold of sports spectator. You think that the number and size of TVs on the first floor is impressive—until you get to the second floor. There are even several televisions up on the roof, which offers a calmer game-watching experience (if you can stake out one of the precious tables, which is unlikely), and a fine view of the sun setting over downtown Austin's myriad sprouting parking garages.

The food is what it is. Stick to the burgers, which are pedestrian but fine, and come accompanied by crisp, salty fries with the skins still on. Buffalo wings, served in newsprint, have a slow, lingering burn and good crunch. It's hard to complain about bar food when it's nothing more, or less, than you'd expect. As a place to watch the Longhorns eating up the gridiron while you eat up some classic bar snacks and throw back a few cold ones, this does just fine. –RM

Fran's Hamburgers

food

6.2 **5.0**
10   10

experience

To the diner go the spoils—the burgers, that is

Burgers $ **8**   *South Congress*

Counter service
Mon.-Thurs. 10am-10pm; Fri.-Sat.
10am-10:30pm; Sun. 11am-10pm.
Kid-friendly. Live music. Outdoor dining.

1822 S. Congress Ave.
Austin
(512) 444-5738

6214 Cameron Rd.
78723, (512) 458-6007

Bar None
Credit Cards No credit cards
Reservations Not accepted

Fran won her little corner of South Congress from Austin's Hamburger King Dan in a divorce settlement, and the large plastic lady on the roof of the establishment holds up the prized burger in a celebratory salute. Inside, the mood is a little tamer, but classic. Everything is red and white, from the checkerboard floor to the coca-cola paraphernalia decorating the walls. A hideous jukebox rules from a corner, offering a wide selection of CDs (beware when it falls into the wrong hands). The restaurant would be quite pleasant if the low ceilings didn't make the large room feel a little buried.

Counter service is friendly, accommodating, and fast. The food is cheap, and perfectly fine, though we wouldn't recommend it past the occasional hamburger when a craving hits. Patties are thin but still moist, and the standard accoutrements are generously piled on. We like the jalapeño burger, because, while the peppers show no sign of heat, they do add a little extra pickle. The hickory burger, doused in a ketchupy barbecue sauce, is also a decent choice. Pad this with a side of fries or onion rings. The fries retain their skins, which both add a little crispness and reassure the eater of their original potato identity; onion-rings are pleasantly sweet and crunchy, and not too greasy, though they can be a little over-battered. Resist the temptation to finish off your meal with a shake—they're made with soft serve rather than real ice cream, resulting in a thick and cloying disappointment.

Fran's also serves some Texas classics, like a chicken-fried chicken doused in heavy cream gravy, but we hardly need to tell you to stick to the burgers. They're certainly better than Sandy's 'round the corner, and cheaper than Magnolia next door. –RM

Frank and Angie's

Good lunch specials and better pizza on
the West Sixth Street strip

food

6.1 | 6.5
10 | 10

experience

Pizza, Italian   **$23**   *Warehouse District*

Casual restaurant   508 West Ave.   ***Bar*** Beer/wine
Daily 11am-10pm. *Kid-friendly.*   Austin   ***Credit Cards*** Visa, MC, AmEx
Live music. Outdoor dining.   (512) 472-3534   ***Reservations*** Accepted
Vegetarian-friendly.

Frank and Angie's is a family-friendly Sixth Street pizzeria that pays
more than passing homage to Frank Sinatra. Photos of Old Blue Eyes
adorn the walls around the entryway, and there are at least two dishes
on the menu named for him (as well as many named for other Italian
celebrities like Sophia Loren, Joe DiMaggio, Federico Fellini, and more).
The restaurant is small and cute, with a mural depicting an Italian
neighborhood in mid-20th-century New York City on one wall,
supplemented by movie posters, a map of Sicily, and the Italian flag.
Lace curtains dress the windows and mismatched tablecloths give Frank
and Angie's a homey feel. Friendly staff and quick service are especially
good given the volume of business that this pizzeria does (and quite a
surprise compared to the woeful service at neighboring sister restaurant
Hut's).

Frank and Angie's no-frills menu is comprised of pizza, sandwiches,
pasta, calzones, salads, and a few appetizers. Presentations are equally
frill-free—pizza is served on metal trays, and other dishes come in
baskets. Minestrone soup is thin and tomatoey with lots of
vegetables—basic but good. Most of the non-pizza fare is plain. Salads
are pre-made; pasta dishes are cooked al dente with simple sauces.
Sandwiches, such as a dried-out chicken marinara, fail to impress. What
does shine at Frank and Angie's is the pizza. The sauce is made daily,
the crust is thin and crisp, toppings are fresh, and the cheese blend is
delicious, a bit salty, and caramelized beautifully at the edges. These
pizzas range from the traditional margherita to cheeseless vegan pies
like the "Mona Lisa," to the unconventional, like the Cajun-influenced
"Ennio Morricone" (named for the Italian film composer). Don't miss
the cannoli for dessert; it's one of the best in town, with a nice, creamy
filling that isn't too sweet. –MPN

Freddie's

A backyard party every afternoon —and you're invited

food
3.9 **9.4**
10   10
experience

American, Burgers $**21**   *Bouldin Creek Area*

Casual restaurant
Daily 11am-midnight. Kitchen
closes 10:30pm. *Date-friendly.*
Live music. Outdoor dining.
Wireless Internet.

1703 S. 1st St.
Austin
(512) 460-3014
www.freddiesplaceaustin.com

Bar Full
Credit Cards Visa, MC, AmEx
Reservations Recommended

Despite the sleazy ring of the ads inviting you to "come play with Freddie in his big backyard," this South Austin burger joint is just the kind of new neighbor you'd want. Freddie's is part restaurant, part live music venue (an act gets going twice a week at 6pm), part movie theater (classics are shown outdoors on Tuesday nights), and part sports bar (utilizing that same outdoor screen to show Monday Night Football or the Longhorns), but in part because of its verdant tract of land on the banks of Bouldin Creek, the place still manages to maintain the casual vibe of a friend's get-together. With multi-colored Christmas lights strung up on the trees, conversations buzzing through the air, and the warm, happy-go-lucky attitude of the staff, it's hard not to feel at home here.

Whether or not your own backyard buddy would have been a skilled chef, Freddie's food gets just a passing grade. Burgers and sandwiches take the spotlight, but it's unusual for a place that does such elaborate burgers, and so many of them, not to ask customers about cooking time. When your burger comes, you'll understand why: these square, thin patties are not the sort you'd cook rare. But neither do they have the buttery, indulgent goodness of those little short-order burgers. Thumbs down for the beef (and thumbs down for the failing score of 54/100 in their 2006 health inspection). Still, Freddie's has a decent seasoning mix: jack cheese and banana peppers are reliable accoutrements, and Texas toast works well for structural support. Fries are homemade in the skin-on, thick-cut style, but they're underseasoned.

For many people here, though, the food's not the point. Folks tend to come more for the drinks, sights, and sounds; there are games of washers at all times, and happy hour specials from 4pm to 7pm. On Tuesdays, Wednesdays, and Thursdays, they even throw in free smoked brisket beginning at 6pm. Although the beef can sometimes disappear within minutes. It's hard to argue with free food. –RG

Freebirds World Burrito

The burritos aren't free, but there's
freedom of choice

food

6.4 **6.3**
10   10

experience

Mexican $ 9   *Hyde Park, South Congress,*
Westlake

Counter service   1000 E. 41st St.   *Bar* None
Sun.-Thurs. 11am-10:30pm;   Austin   *Credit Cards* Visa, MC, AmEx
Fri.-Sat. 11am-11pm. *Kid-friendly.*   (512) 441-5144   *Reservations* Not accepted
Live music. Outdoor dining.   www.freebirds.com
Vegetarian-friendly. Wireless Internet.

                              515 S. Congress Ave.   2765 Bee Caves Rd.
                              78704, (512) 462-3512   78746, (512) 330-0040

We must admit, hesitantly, that something good did come out of that lair of maroon madness known as College Station. Putting football rivalries aside for the moment (yes, you can do it) when Freebirds migrated southwest to Austin, local Longhorns quickly realized that it was worth swallowing their Aggie hatred for long enough to swallow a bite or two of those famous burritos.

The Freebirds burrito is a simple thing, made in the assembly-line style popularized by Subway, but decidedly better than fast food, and spiked with local flair. The formula: take an enormous tortilla (flour, wheat, cayenne, or spinach), stuff it to the bursting point with anything and everything (chicken, steak, or roast veggies, plus beans, pico de gallo, guacamole, jalapeños, cilantro, and so on), drench it in sauce, and then wrap the whole mess in a tidy aluminum package so that you can actually eat it without bringing a change of clothes.

This is more Tex than Mex, but the taste is fresh, the toppings perky, the mood affable. Odd little aluminum-foil sculptures pop out of the walls for a peek (you can add your own creation when your aluminum wrap is done with its other duties), and a mad Statue of Liberty, having crashed through a wall, soars overhead on a motorcycle wielding a particularly large burrito. Freebirds is veggie-safe (they never use lard, which creeps silently into so many Tex-Mex dishes), but for carnivores, we recommend the steak burrito. Although the barbecue sauce is a signature option, skip it—it's too sour to complement the fillings.

Freebirds' burritos come in a variety of sizes, from the "half-bird," which is bigger than half a standard burrito and a good deal, to the "super monster," which weighs a pound and a half—and, in the right hands, well aimed, could take the legs out from under a large Longhorn (we're not naming names). –RM

Fresh Plus

Mellow shopping, and don't miss the single-beer to-go case

Hyde Park

Specialty grocery
Daily 8am-9pm.
Breakfast. Kid-friendly.

408 E. 43rd St.
Austin
(512) 459-8922

Bar Beer/wine
Credit Cards Visa, MC, AmEx
Reservations Not accepted

Austin's family-owned Fresh Plus grocery stores have been in operation in one capacity or another in their current locations since the 1920s, though the original Hyde Park Store was founded on Guadalupe Street in 1906. The Clarksville and Hyde Park stores actually became "Fresh Plus" in 1985, with previous incarnations as differently named small groceries. Today, these stores offer convenient shopping for neighbors on foot in their respective ever-walkable enclaves. It's a pleasant look back at the era of the neighborhood grocery.

We are particularly fond of the outdoor mural depicting jovial farmers amongst their produce that adorns the much-loved Hyde Park location. The shelves are filled with a well-balanced mix of standard groceries as well as their organic competitors, and Fresh Plus is also good about stocking locally-made products. The stores themselves are on the small side, but you'll have no trouble procuring your everyday needs here.

While Fresh Plus does not have seating areas for its patrons to enjoy a snack and the view, they do offer lots of items for meals on the run. Local favorites like Tom's Tabooley, Turbo Falafel, and Lana's are well represented, but there are also house-made delicacies that should not be overlooked. Fresh-sliced deli meats and sandwiches are also tempting, and the 98% lean mesquite-smoked chicken is so moist, you can probably hold the mayo. So delicious are many of Fresh Plus' options that perhaps, on a nice day, they might do some lunch business with patrons who would rather not wait to be seated at neighboring restaurants. –MPN

The Frisco Shop

Harry Akin's Night Hawk empire lives on
in this time-frozen spot

food
6.9 **8.0**
10 10
experience

Steakhouse, American $**16**   *Burnet*

Counter service   5819 Burnet Rd.   *Bar* Beer/wine
Daily 7am-10pm. *Breakfast.* Austin   *Credit Cards* Visa, MC, AmEx
Kid-friendly. Live music. Outdoor (512) 459-6279 *Reservations* Not accepted
dining. Wireless Internet. www.thefriscoshop.com

A meal at the last remaining outpost of Harry Akin's old Night Hawk
empire is a trip back in time. The Frisco Shop is a classic joint that gets
at the very essence of what Burnet Road—Austin's old Miracle Mile—
was, and still is, all about. Although the first branch of Akin's famous
Austin chain was a little burger joint that he opened on South Congress
in 1932, the Frisco Shop on Burnet was his fourth Night Hawk
restaurant. This one got going in 1953, still before Akin became mayor
of Austin. (He served one term from 1967 to 1969.) The time-frozen
atmosphere could hardly be any more transportative, from the moment
you plop down at one of the fake wood tables and are greeted by one
of the ladies, pen and pad in hand, in a "What'll it be, hon?" kind of
way.

The best part of the Frisco Shop is that here, unlike at certain other
historic food venues, experiencing the living history of American cuisine
doesn't have to taste bad. The focus of Akin's restaurants has always
been beef, and for a long time he raised his own. "There's nothing
accidental about quality," he declared in the restaurants' motto. Amen
to that.

Beef takes many forms, but we encourage you to go straight for the
"Frisco Burger," with cheese, lettuce, and relish, or the "Down South,"
which adds tomato and mayo. It's not often you see a burger made
from USDA Choice, but here you go. You can skip the cut steaks;
though they're not bad, and the beef is good, they can come
overcooked. If you want to really taste a piece of history, though, try
one of the "chop't" steaks—they're chopped and then re-formed.
Chicken-fried steak is another good option. Slaw is good and fresh, if
without much tang; fries are too soft for our taste. Pies are a knockout,
a very popular choice amongst the (generally older) clientele. –RG

Galaxy Café

When the food catches up with the
ambience, this place will really take off

food

6.1 / 10   **7.9** / 10

experience

American   **$15**   *Far South*

Counter service   9911 Brodie Ln.   *Bar* Beer/wine
Daily 7:30am-10pm.   Austin   *Credit Cards* Visa, MC, AmEx
                           (512) 233-6000   *Reservations* Not accepted
                           www.galaxycafeaustin.com

A recent addition to the growing number of restaurants gracing South
Austin's Brodie Lane, the Galaxy Café has a lot of character. Galaxy
Café might be wedged in between longtime local faves Brick Oven and
Maudie's at the Slaughter Lane intersection, but it's not totally
overshadowed by its better-established neighbors. This place has its
own thing going on, and it seems to be doing just fine.

We love the interior, for starters; with its vibrant red and black color
scheme and wood accents, Galaxy is striking at the first glance. The
curved surfaces and circular mirrors that cluster the walls give the room
a tricky, hole-punched optical effect that is eye catching and fun. The
overall atmosphere works toward an updated take on '60s modern
design, with a Jetsons kind of spin. Service at the Galaxy Café is friendly
and attentive, with counter service followed by table delivery. The menu
consists primarily of breakfast items and sandwiches, with a few dinner
specials showing up in the evening. Galaxy offers an inexpensive weekly
wine list by the glass or bottle especially chosen to complement menu
items.

We're sad to say that Galaxy Café's food is not quite on par with
their marvelous décor, but it is inexpensive, and you'll be hard pressed
to find an item that isn't okay. Breakfasts are actually quite good, with
basics like scrambled eggs, spicy sausage, and home fries festively
strewn with red and green bell peppers. Later in the day, there's a light
cilantro-lime soup that lacks the lime kick that its name implies. Turkey
burgers are served on a wheat bun and have good flavor, but are a bit
on the dry side. Thin chipotle-apricot pork is also dry, even though
moistened by a sweet jam that lacks punch, but it's accompanied by
whipped sweet potatoes we'd be proud to serve at Thanksgiving.
–MPN

Garden District

A cute and friendly South Austin coffee cabana

Light American $ **9**   *St. Edward's Area*

Café   2810 S. Congress Ave.   *Bar* None
Mon.-Fri. 7am-6pm;   Austin   *Credit Cards* No credit cards
Sat.-Sun. 8am-6pm. *Breakfast.* (512) 462-2473   *Reservations* Not accepted
Outdoor dining. Wireless Internet.

This coffeeshop, adjacent to the grounds of the Great Outdoors Garden Center, could hardly be any cuter—or any more South Austin. On the little stone patio, you can sit under a little green awning and gaze out upon rows of flower pots being ogled by a rotating cast of gardeners-to-be. Inside, the vibe gets down to the very essence of Weird Austin, with the concrete walls painted in alternating shades of yellows and oranges, a couple of couches and comfy chairs, local artwork for sale, and of course, wireless Internet. The folksy staff is completely at ease making small talk with every brand of South Congress hipster.

As for the coffee itself, it's from Ruta Maya, and it's full flavored. The various incarnations, with a vague Cuban theme, include the Tres Leches Café, which is a fantasia on the famous Latin dessert cake. Here, the three milks are whole milk, condensed milk, and evaporated milk, and they're all fluffed up with the steamer in the cappuccino style. The resulting sweetness has a complexity that blows away that of your standard sugar-filled cappuccino. Smoothies, too, get high marks, with a vegan soy milk option and a bevy of fresh fruit possibilities, including "Amazon Cherry."

The food isn't really the main event here, but the chalk-scrawled, veggie-friendly menu includes sandwiches (the Boca Burger is a veggie burger with cheese, lettuce, tomato, pickles, and onions), beef and chicken empanadas, and a vegetable sandwich with hummus and avocado. Baked goods include that Tres Leches cake in its original form. If you are hungrier, try the hot, pressed Cuban sandwich; it could use a little more zing, but it's moist, crisp, tasty, and really hits the spot.

The name of the place is a nod to New Orleans, which is also a subject of some of the wall art. Don't forget to toast to the speedy rebirth of the legendary food scene in that greatest of all American port cities. –RG

Garibaldi's

Sophisticated interior Mexican food in a
far from sophisticated setting

food

7.4 **4.3**
10   10

experience

Mexican

$21

Far South

Casual restaurant
Mon.-Thurs. 8am-9pm; Fri.-Sat.
8am-10pm; Sun. 9am-3pm.
Breakfast. Brunch.

4201 S. Congress Ave.
Austin
(512) 326-9788

Bar Beer/wine
Credit Cards Visa, MC, AmEx
Reservations Accepted

It's surprising that Garibaldi's isn't better known. Perhaps it is the name, which reeks a little of white-bread Family Italian in the style of the Olive Garden. But in fact, Garibaldi's belongs to an elite and short list of Mexican restaurants in Austin (Curra's, Manuel's, and of course Fonda San Miguel are others) that serve intense, complex, and delicious regional cuisines of Mexico. The strip mall location south of Ben White doesn't help it any, but the inside of Garibaldi's is bright and warm (warning: it can be a little too warm on hot summer nights), and the service, though vaguely dopey, is friendly.

The kitchen serves cosmopolitan Mexico City fare that is a little unexpected in the low-brow setting. The standard interior dishes are reliable here. The chile relleno, though fried, is excellent, the batter much eggier and lighter than usual (more Eastern than Western in its consistency). It can pool in parts and become soggy, but on the whole it adds a sweet, nutty flavor to the dish, amplified by raisins and pecans. Other typical standouts include a sweet and spicy cochinita pibil (pulled pork cooked in a banana leaf with plantains), though this dish lacks the depth and style of the exceptional Curra's version up the road. A more unusual standout, hard to find in Austin, are the albóndigas: meatballs stewed in a spicy chipotle-tomato sauce. Ceviche is simple and fresh, and comes in a healthy portion; sides are made with care on the premises, and chips and salsa are lively and satisfying.

All these are very reasonably priced, and a pleasure to consume. Still, something about Garibaldi's just feels a little flat—it desperately needs some attention to force it to wake up a little. –RM

Gene's Po-Boys

A genial spot that takes it easy, New
Orleans-style, with some deep-fried fun

food
7.1 **7.9**
10   10

experience

Southern   **$13**   *East Austin*

Casual restaurant   1209 E. 11th St.   *Bar* None
Mon.-Sat. 11am-8pm;   Austin   *Credit Cards* Visa, MC, AmEx
closed Sun. *Live music.*   (512) 477-6600   *Reservations* Not accepted
Outdoor dining.   www.generestaurant.com

Gene's has both some of the grit and some of the charm of the Big
Easy, but it lacks that great and grimy city's deep, dark side. Everything
about Gene's is laid-back, friendly, and open. Although it was actually
opened by Gene and Claudia Tumbs in 2000, the restaurant has the
feel of a place that has been around a lot longer: the bric-a-brac of
years of friendly service has gathered along the shelves that line the
walls, brightening up, along with the requisite Mardi Gras posters, a
space that could really use a lick of paint.

But mostly it is the openness that creates the atmosphere here.
Gene's is frequented by a happy mix of Eastsiders and Westsiders, and
after Hurricane Katrina, the restaurant provided a welcome and familiar
home to musicians displaced by the storm. (New Orleans jazz and blues
frequently mingle here with smells of deep-fried chicken, catfish,
shrimp, and oysters.)

Warm as it is, the service can sometimes be glacial, and we warn you
that the Easy attitude can be somewhat at odds with the half-hour
lunch break. When it does arrive, however, food is piping hot and crisp.
Fried chicken is liberally peppered and salted (so important when deep-
frying) and catfish has a flavorful cornmeal batter that is crisp without
being crunchy, so that the delicate texture of the fish isn't buried in the
crust. Po-boys come with simple lettuce, tomato, and pickle, and plenty
of mayo; the bread is fresh and chewy, and the portions huge. Sides,
such as smoky, creamy red beans and rice, and bacon-studded, vinegary
green beans, are thoughtful and flavorful. It's no wonder the place has
been a hit since the day it opened. Gene may make po-boys, but
Claudia smiles like she's got diamonds on the soles of her shoes. –RM

Grape Vine Market

Excellent Mediterranean-style lunches in
an impressive wine-and-more store

North Central

Specialty grocery
Mon.-Fri. 10am-2pm; Sat.
10am-3pm; closed Sun.
Vegetarian-friendly.

7938 Great Northern Blvd. *Bar* None
Austin
(512) 323-5900
www.grapevinemarket.com

Credit Cards Visa, MC, AmEx
Reservations Not accepted

Austin's Grape Vine Market is one of the very best wine shops around, and whether you are a true oenophile, or just someone who really likes to drink, this is a place you just have to see for yourself. The 18,000-square-foot shop has far and away the biggest wine selection in town as well as an astounding variety of beer and spirits, cigars, and gourmet foods. It's hard to think of caviar as a bargain, but Grape Vine has extremely reasonable prices, as such prices go, all the way to the top of the line. Olive oils and vinegars, amongst other products, are world class.

Grape Vine also offers wine classes, gift baskets, catering, and has recently opened its deli counter for lunch, with a few tables by the windows and fireplace for diners. All of the menu items are made simply and with impeccably fresh ingredients. We love the dense dolmas, seasoned with lots of dill, mint, and lemon. The sandwiches are served on wonderful fresh-baked bread and come with a side of fruit. Chicken pesto panini are filled with grilled chicken, hot capicola, melting Montasio cheese, and pesto with a fresh, green basil flavor. The pizzas come on a crisp and chewy thin crust. Amongst them, don't miss the "El Guapo," topped with prosciutto and drizzled with truffle oil, with Parmigiano-Reggiano caramelized at the edges; its subtle blend of saltiness is sublime.

For dessert, there's goat's milk ice cream or the local delicacy known as "Miles of Chocolate." If you are a chocolate lover, you must try this decadent, creamy, too-good-to-be-a-brownie creation, made by a man who is as sweet as his confection. Come for the wine, and you might go home with a lot more than that—whether in your shopping bag or your stomach. –MPN

Green Mesquite

Well-loved, well-located, famously friendly barbecue

food

7.3 / 10   8.7 / 10
experience

Barbecue, Southern $21   *Zilker, Oak Hill*

Casual restaurant
Daily 11am-10pm. *Delivery.*
Kid-friendly. Live music.
Outdoor dining. Wireless Internet.

1400 Barton Springs Rd.
Austin
(512) 479-0485
www.greenmesquite.net

7010 W. Hwy. 71
Oak Hill, (512) 288-9135

Bar Beer/wine
Credit Cards Visa, MC, AmEx
Reservations Not accepted

Restaurant row's purveyor of "BBQ and More," Green Mesquite is the third incarnation of a shop that's been serving up food in its locale for well over 50 years. Opened in 1988, Green Mesquite survived a fire several years back, and has continued on without breaking stride, serving Southern favorites and hosting live music on the patio. The atmosphere is relaxed, and the décor like a big scrapbook, with pictures of friends and family, flyers from past shows, and autographed photos everywhere. Service at Green Mesquite is some of the friendliest you'll find, which is saying a lot in a city renowned for easy smiles and genuine neighborliness.

The menu offers daily specials, barbecue by the pound, sandwiches, tacos, chicken-fried steak, catfish, and so on. And the food is consistently good. Barbecue is slightly above average, which in this part of Texas means it's pretty darn good. Pork ribs have occasionally come a little dry, but the brisket is reliable and juicy, and we love the tangy, smoky chopped beef. Sausage has a nice medium grind, and the turkey is moist and not overly smoky. The sauce is tart, peppery, and tomato based, and barbecue comes with all the fixin's: pickles, onions, and soft, white sandwich bread. Potato salad is creamy, slightly yellow with mustard, and has nice bits of pickle, and cole slaw is chopped and tangy. They also do a good job with Southern classics like chicken-fried steak; burgers are done in the thin style, and come with crispy fries or savory onion rings. Try the rich, tomatoey jambalaya, with nice persistent heat and lots of chicken, ham, and sausage.

Keep in mind that the Oak Hill branch has far less atmosphere, although the service and food are still on par. But the Barton Springs Green Mesquite is a local tradition, and the patio is a nice place to sit with kids—just watch out for Zorro, the cheeky resident squirrel and barbecue lover. –MPN

Green Muse Café

As the name implies, go here to write
(or just to pretend to)

food

6.0 | 9.4
10 | 10
experience

Light American   **$ 9**   *St. Edward's Area*

Café
Mon.-Fri. 8am-midnight;
Sat.-Sun. 9am-midnight. *Breakfast.*

519 W. Oltorf St.
Austin
(512) 912-7789

Bar Beer/wine
Credit Cards Visa, MC, AmEx
Reservations Not accepted

Date-friendly. Live music. Outdoor dining. Vegetarian-friendly. Wireless Internet.

From the outside, the Green Muse Café looks like any number of Austin's privately owned coffeeshops—kind of funky, with murals, benches out front, and half of a giant coffee cup that looks like it's been built into the wall. Once inside, it's apparent that there is something different about the Green Muse—it has class. While many Austin businesses display art for sale on their walls, the Green Muse goes a step further, with walls that are themselves works of art. Each surface is painted a different color and made of a different material—brick, textured cement, wood. While this may sound haphazard, the effect on the eye is not.

The Green Muse consists of two smallish main rooms and a lovely outdoor area. Tables are not crowded together, so seating is limited, and as in Europe, singles are likely to share a space. Even better then the interior is the shaded porch and garden. It's an absolutely spectacular retreat from the city, a spacious and romantic space with a little pond.

Order your drinks and food at the bar from the extensive drink list or very short menu. They sell coffee, tea, Italian sodas, and a few other drinks, as well as beer and wine—another rather European touch (and one we've missed around here since Les Amis' tragic closure). Be sure to try the delicious rose lemonade, which is floral without being cloying. The menu offerings consist of a few baked goods (while they last), panini and cold sandwiches, and some Middle Eastern sides. In the morning, muffins are a good choice—they are big and moist. For lunch, we like the crisp prosciutto panino with melted mozzarella and a thin layer of well-balanced pesto with just enough garlic kick. After dinner, drop by for a late-night glass of wine on the porch with someone special, or a quiet chat with friends. –MPN

Green Pastures

Austin's Haunted Mansion—plus
peacocks and fresh-baked rolls

food
8.7 / 10
9.1 / 10
experience

American $**67**   *Bouldin Creek Area*

Upmarket restaurant
Daily 11am-2pm, 6pm-10pm.
Brunch. Date-friendly.
Outdoor dining.

811 W. Live Oak St.
Austin
(512) 444-4747
www.greenpastures.citysearch.com

Bar Full
Credit Cards Visa, MC, AmEx
Reservations Recommended

How could a restaurant founded in 1948 in the mansion of a family named Koock *not* be haunted? But this is not your average haunted house. First of all, there is the proliferation of live peacocks; at night, they can actually be found sleeping on the branches of the glorious live oak trees that cover Green Pastures' stately seven-acre lawn. Look for the two bright-white albinos amongst them. What is perhaps more surprising than all that plumage, though, is the fact that, to this day, this beloved South Austin icon of civilized dining still holds its own with the city's culinary elite.

But first, back to the history. The house belonged to Chester Koock and his wife Mary Faulk Koock, sister of John Henry Faulk, the noted humorist and politician that was blacklisted during the McCarthy era. Step inside, gaze upon the faded grandeur of Green Pastures' somber old portraits, and you will be positively spooked. Apparently, even the staff is afraid to wander the upstairs bar alone at night. Continue upstairs, and you'll find the room in which John Henry Faulk died.

Even if the food plays second fiddle to the spooky spirits, it is well above average. The old-world details are all done just right, like dinner rolls, which are sweet, satisfying, and freshly baked from homemade dough. Caesar salad is prepared tableside with verve, as is the legendary Bananas Foster. The seafood is just so; redfish is delightfully prepared with a lobster nage (a cream sauce made with reduced stock) that is, as the French might say, correct. A game sampler of smoky sausage, delightfully rare venison, and tender quail has no weak points. Neither does bread pudding.

Not only is this the South of your antebellum dreams, you can even rest assured that the restaurant's history is politically correct. So relax, and enjoy the extensive Sunday "Plantation Brunch"—without even a twinge of historical guilt. –RG

Güero's

It's hipped and hyped—if only the food
were good

food

experience

Mexican $26   *South Congress*

Casual restaurant   1412 S. Congress Ave.   *Bar* Full
Mon.-Sat. 11am-11pm;   Austin   *Credit Cards* Visa, MC, AmEx
Sun. 8am-11pm. *Brunch.*   (512) 447-7688   *Reservations* Not accepted
Date-friendly. Live music.   www.guerostacobar.com
Outdoor dining. Wireless Internet.

As a patron once said, Güero's is where thin people go to eat fat. Hip
and hot as ever, this is still *the* watering hole for many an Austin metro-
texmexual, the favorite of celebrities from pop to politics. A weekend
night will almost always hit you with an hour's wait, so the first
question is: Does Güero's live up to the hype?

The answer, perhaps unsurprisingly, is no, though the atmosphere is
something of a self-fulfilling prophecy—people who come for the crush
will keep coming, making the bar and back room absurdly loud. A
roaming mariachi only adds to the effect; you may find yourself
ducking rapid-fire "olés" as they ricochet off the walls. But the jangle
is mellowed by one of Güero's margaritas—tart and limey delights
without any trace of cloying sweetness.

But although Güero's has recently rectified its omission of the right to
free chips and salsa, which is guaranteed in the state Constitution, the
food underperforms against the Austin Tex-Mex standard. Queso is
runny and bland, and what the heck is the "Güero's Dip"—with its
cold, bland layers of beans, guac, and plain shredded cheese—if not an
excuse for the kitchen to get rid of some leftovers? While the chicken al
carbón (marinated in achiote and orange juice) has lively flavor, it's also
dry, and has come overcooked to the point of crunchiness. Even the
adventurous-sounding Santa Fe enchiladas (topped with a fried egg)
wind up boring. Smoky-sweet fajitas are probably your best option.

Service at Güero's is friendly but distracted, while prices, though
reasonable to begin with, are riddled with hidden charges (add a
comically random $1.15 extra, for instance, for fresh mole—and
apparently, for a two-enchilada plate, this "cost is reflective per
enchilada"). In short, it's a high-maintenance approach to a low-
maintenance cuisine in an easygoing town. If you enjoy being jostled
physically by the crowds and mentally by the prices, then go to Güero's.
But Austin knows how to treat you much better. –RM

Gumbo's

A clubby, hit-or-miss homage to New Orleans

food

7.4 / 10

7.7 / 10

experience

Southern

$51

Capitol Area, Round Rock

Upmarket restaurant
Austin branch Mon.-Thurs. 11am-2pm, 5:30pm-10pm; Fri. 11am-2pm, 5:30pm-11pm; Sat. 5:30pm-11pm; closed Sun. Round Rock branch Mon.-Fri. 11am-2pm, 5-10pm; Sat. 5pm-10pm; closed Sun. *Date-friendly.*

710 Colorado St.
Austin
(512) 480-8053
www.gumbosaustin.com

901 Round Rock Ave.
Round Rock, (512) 671-7925
www.gumbosroundrock.com

Bar Full
Credit Cards Visa, MC, AmEx
Reservations Accepted

It's nice that Austin has so many restaurants that honor New Orleans cuisine. True, we're not that far from the Big Easy, but the number of places around town where you can get gumbo, jambalaya, and shrimp creole is considerable. That's not to say that places like Gumbo's, the downtown version of which is in the old Brown Building (the other one is in Round Rock), are quite there yet. Compliments, however, for the finely realized décor: ornate but dark, clubby but relaxed—like a faux-century-old bastion of luxury dining for New Orleans' best-established country club members.

The first disappointment, however, is that the eponymous gumbo is not necessarily a strong point here. It's dark and deeply flavored, but lacks complexity. It's still better, though, than the oysters Rockefeller, which are full of sound and fury. People rave about these; we have no idea why, other than the fact that, in an unusual twist, the oysters double up, with a fried oyster placed on top of each baked one. But such tricks don't compensate for the flaws of the baked oysters beneath: precious little creaminess, dissociated spinach, little detectable Pernod. That said, fried oysters are one of the better things to order at Gumbo's.

Not so for dry tilapia, or underseasoned dirty rice, just one amongst various uninspiring side dishes. We do, however, like the steak, which comes as rare as you order it, and we love even more an flawlessly conceived dish of blackened catfish, which is crispy, fresh, and spicy; and it's impossible to complain about the impeccable bread pudding with bourbon butter sauce. Afterward, you might want to catch a drink at the Brown Bar next door—it's a slice of refurbished Austin, with Turkish marble and a yuppie pickup scene. –RG

Habana Calle 6

food

6.8 / 10

6.7 / 10

experience

Home of a delicious mojito—and its
frozen twin, the frojito

Latin American

$**34**

Sixth Street District

Upmarket restaurant
Sun.-Thurs. 11am-11pm; Fri.-Sat.
11am-midnight. *Date-friendly.*
Delivery. Outdoor dining.
Wireless Internet.

709 E. 6th St.
Austin
(512) 443-4252
www.habana.com

Bar Full
Credit Cards Visa, MC, AmEx
Reservations Accepted

Habana Calle 6 seems to have truly found a home at its latest digs on
Sixth Street. It has plenty of space inside, including two bar areas, and
patio seating in a grotto-like setting overlooking Waller Creek where
they have live Caribbean music on the weekends, but not in the
wintertime. They can also help book a band for you if you wish to hold
a party there. Many people come just for mojitos (or frojitos, the frozen
version—of the two, we recommend the former). But happily, the food,
too, is decent.

In case you're a Cuban-food novice, the cuisine is dense, filling, and
meat-and-starch-heavy, but rarely spicy. A good place to start is the "Un
Poco de Todo" appetizer, with yuca frita (yucca-root french fries), fried
plantains, a crisp empanada filled with picadillo (a ground beef
mixture), and alitas de pollo (crunchy fried chicken wings). This
assortment is served with three sauces: a glorious hot and sweet
mango sauce; a garlicky mojo; and a spicy roasted-tomato salsa (to
please the inner Austinite).

The "Tamal Cubano" is a Cuban version of the tamale, a bit sweet
and lighter in texture than what we are used to here. The "Plátano
Loco" is a dense shredded pork, ham, and Swiss cheese sandwich
made tart with dill pickles and served on a chewy, deep-fried plantain
that's been sliced lengthwise, instead of bread. Habana's version of ropa
vieja is a real mass of meat; this traditional Cuban dish reminds us of
pot roast, with slow-cooked beef that's so tender that it falls into
"rags," as the name, which translates to "old clothes," suggests. It's
excellent.

For dessert, try Habana's delicately moist tres leches cake, topped
with whipped cream and powerful cinnamon. Service at Habana is
friendly, but not always quick, and can also be a bit scattered, so be
sure to come with your patience prepared—or, better yet, with your
mojito-drinking shoes on. –MPN

Habanero Café

A relaxed South Austin Mexican joint
where smoky fajitas are good fajitas

food
7.3 **6.9**
10 10
experience

Mexican $ **9**   *St. Edward's Area*

Casual restaurant   501 W. Oltorf St.   *Bar* None
Sun.-Mon. 7am-3pm; Tues.-Sat.   Austin   *Credit Cards* Visa, MC, AmEx
7am-5pm. *Breakfast.*   (512) 416-0443   *Reservations* Not accepted

"Fajitas al mesquite," tout the hand-painted letters on the outside of this cute building, which sits in the heart of South Austin, near the intersection of Oltorf and South First. The fajitas are exactly as advertised: the beef (and you should order beef) is smokier than the norm, with a deep, dark crust blessed with lots of spice, and—in the case of the "fajitas rancheras," which we favor—welcome heat. It is a pleasure to eat fajitas for which particular care has been taken in the marinating and preparation of the meat; this is far from a foregone conclusion in Austin.

Other dishes, though, are also well conceived. Enchiladas rojas are exactly what they should be, and better yet are the enchiladas verdes, with the acidic bite of tomatillo balanced well by a dose of white cheese. Beans have a well-developed flavor, and yellow rice is well dissociated. Delicious, too, are the various meats that fill tacos or hard-to-resist gorditas (with lettuce, tomato, and pico de gallo inside grilled corn cakes made from masa, thicker than tortillas). Lengua (tongue meat) comes in bigger, leaner chunks, with a less assertive taste than usual, but it's satisfying. Better yet are tacos or gorditas al pastor, with a depth of flavor to support the depth of red color in the chunks of pork.

Habanero (they spell it without the "ñ") also has a way with morning foods, from breakfast tacos to migas. We're delighted, too, with the we're-so-glad-you're-here attitude, the relaxed feel of the place, and the light that pours onto the tables that sit in the front of the little restaurant for an atrium-like effect. This is not a date place, nor is it a fun place to chug margaritas (in fact, there's no liquor license)—it's just a neighborhood Mexican restaurant that is as reliable for a solid, authentic lunch as just about any in town. –RG

Hai Ky

At this little Vietnamese spot,
everything's happenin' but the food

food

4.1 **6.7**
10   10

experience

Vietnamese   **$13**   *Southeast*

Casual restaurant
Daily 11am-10pm.
Vegetarian-friendly.

1931 E. Oltorf St.
Austin
(512) 693-2464

Bar Beer/wine
Credit Cards Visa and MC
Reservations Not accepted

This popular hole-in-the-wall Vietnamese on East Oltorf is another of Austin's *Chronicle*-y overrated restaurants. Despite the three gushing reviews from three highly esteemed publications that hang in the window, the food here is actually quite bad. It's a pity, because we like everything else about Hai Ky: it has a sense of fun, it's tremendously cheap, portions are huge, service is friendly, and the restaurant strikes no poses. In fact, until chopstick hits mouth, it is precisely the sort of place we would want in our neighborhood as the go-to haunt.

And that's what it clearly is for the lively mixture of guests who frequent it. They must be there for the prices and the company, because Hai Ky's pan-Asian mix of dishes is uniformly unsatisfactory. Tough spring rolls, filled with iceberg lettuce and chewy vermicelli, are overpowered by bitter, anisey basil, and the peanut sauce they come with has arrived disconcertingly fizzy. The phô soups are bland and fatty, with blubbery meat (though they come in massive, brimming bowls—the small feeds about 40). Other dishes lack subtlety: lemongrass chicken, usually so bright a dish, is overwhelmed by a heavy soy sauce, and the satay beef, which bears no resemblance to the familiar tangy skewers, has an exaggerated, syrupy brown sauce. Even rice comes overcooked and clumpy. Slightly better is a tofu rice-noodle dish with peanuts. It isn't very interesting, but the tofu is well prepared and flavorful.

Everything arrives lickety-split, however, and it's hard to hold a grudge when the staff and the atmosphere are so lighthearted. Rotating art hangs on bright orange walls, next to a poster that invites you to display your own, regardless of talent, and the facilities sport the sign "Hai's restroom of delight: maximum capacity 2." Just don't stray too far from their door. –RM

Hangtown Grill

Kid-friendly dining in not-always-kid-friendly Westlake

food

5.9 /10   **5.9** /10

experience

American, Pizza $**14**   *Westlake*

Counter service
Sun.-Thurs. 11am-9pm;
Fri.-Sat. 11am-10pm. *Delivery.*
Kid-friendly. Outdoor dining.

701 S. Capital of Texas
Hwy., Austin
(512) 347-1039
www.hangtowngrill.com

Bar Beer/wine
Credit Cards Visa, MC, AmEx
Reservations Not accepted

After opening in the mid '90s just off the Drag, Hangtown Grill seems to have reconsidered its target clientele and moved to Westlake, where the place have since been a popular lunch spot for the mom-and-tot crowd, local high school students, and even the occasional office worker. The large open space has a Western theme, which is easy to overlook with the energy and din of the noisy lunch crowd, not to mention the line of TVs that hang from the walls. Service is rapid and courteous once you make it to the counter, but during peak hours, the line can trail right out the front door (which reminds us: parking in this shopping center borders on nightmarish at certain times of day). If you don't mind the heat and want to escape the noise, outdoor seating is available, but the few immature trees aren't providing any shade yet.

Hangtown's menu is very basic, featuring mostly burgers, pizza, and salads at reasonable prices (not always the case in Westlake). Burgers come in an array of combinations, like barbecue and Southwestern varieties, and include turkey, chicken, and fish variations. Portions are big with generous toppings, but these burgers tend to get soggy pretty fast. Curly fries are crisp, and not overseasoned—they're a popular item with the kiddos. Salads are uninspired but fresh, and certainly a lighter choice than the drippy burgers.

Pizza, too, comes in several variations, many of them chicken. There's ample cheese and ingredients are fresh, but the flat, not-quite-thin crust is not the best. After lunch, there's ice cream, as well as floats and other concoctions—another reason why so much of their clientele is so young. Still, there are better places in town for this type of food, with far less noise and hassle. –MPN

Hao Hao

Uneven Asian fare in an uninspiring place

food
5.8
10

4.0
10
experience

Chinese

$16 *Far S., W. Campus, Round Rock*

Casual restaurant
Tues.-Fri. 11am-2:30pm, 5pm-9:30pm; Sat. noon-9:30pm; Sun. noon-9pm; closed Mon. *Delivery. Wireless Internet.*

1901 W. William Cannon Dr., Austin
(512) 447-8121
www.haohaoaustin.com

Bar Beer/wine
Credit Cards Visa, MC, AmEx
Reservations Not accepted

Dobie Mall,
2025 Guadalupe St.
78705, (512) 505-0155

1235 Round Rock Ave.
Round Rock, (512) 388-3322

Hao Hao's Chinese and Vietnamese cuisine has garnered a pretty decent reputation in this town, based mostly on a large and lively hot-and-sour chicken soup that is packed with vegetables. The Dobie Mall branch, strangely renamed "Hoa Hoa" after a renovation, enjoys a cult following amongst UT students; before catching a movie at Dobie, they come to spend their Bevo Bucks, eat sesame tofu, and hang out with the friendly staff and their boisterous kids.

These perks make it disappointing that the menu is so unreliable. Soup is a strong suit—we also like their simpler wonton soup, which is salty and flavorful, with lean chunks of pork and plenty of ginger and scallions. While we are pleased by Hao Hao's inclusion of traditional dishes left off of many cheaper Asian menus, they don't often live up to their potential. The duck in a clay pot, still on the bone, is exceedingly fatty (a frequent flaw in our flabbiest of feathered friends, but here there is little of the rich meat to compensate), and chopped into small, splintery pieces that seem to muddy up the broth instead of swimming in it. Sweet green leeks go a little ways toward redeeming the dish. The lemongrass chicken, a more standard Vietnamese option and generally a good restaurant yardstick, is equally indelicate, with a heavy brown sauce in which the lemongrass has to shout to be heard. From the Chinese corner (which offers fewer surprises than the Vietnamese menu), the sweet-and-sour pork emerges punchless and even more fluorescent than normal.

Hao Hao isn't helped by a drab atmosphere that survives even the liveliest of crowds (and the place is often busy). The décor is cheap, and the room is too large to feel charming. And while the owner makes friendly chit-chat as he wanders the room, some of his staff are less amiable. We like drawing attention to hidden gems—Hao Hao just isn't one of them. –RM

Hickory Street Bar & Grill

food **4.5** **8.4**
10   10
experience

New Orleans-themed food that's
friendly and fun, but not so good

American $**23**   *Congress Avenue Area*

Casual restaurant   800 Congress Ave.   *Bar* Full
Mon.-Fri. 6:30am-10pm; Sat.-Sun.   Austin   *Credit Cards* Visa, MC, AmEx
11am-10pm. *Breakfast. Brunch.*   (512) 477-8968   *Reservations* Not accepted
Kid-friendly. Live music. Outdoor dining. Wireless Internet.

We want to like the Hickory Street Bar and Grill—we really do. It's in a great downtown location, with a shaded, leafy patio that's unexpectedly sheltered, offering a nice mix of the urban and the rustic to this busy corner of Congress Avenue just south of the State Capitol. Most days, this patio features live musical acts on a pleasant outdoor stage in front of a rushing waterfall. It has a fresh and friendly attitude (a sign above the register reads "Keep your Copper. We got no Cents here. Hickory Street Bar and Grill—always one step ahead of the Federal Government").

The rag-tag bunch of servers, meanwhile, are outstandingly friendly, perhaps learning from their employers, who offer them a scholarship program which helps with the cost of tuition and books—an admirable salute to the college-town appeal of this city. And the restaurant serves up no-fuss food with a range of all-you-can-eat food bars. It all sounds so good.

Yet something about Hickory Street doesn't quite come together. The inside space doesn't match the patio, and is strangely cavernous and disorganized. And at its best, the food is fine, but rather boring; at its worst, it's pretty bad. Best is the "Truck Stop Chili," which comes in various forms with a well-developed flavor and pleasant bite—but not an overbite. The weekend "New Orleans brunch buffet," though offering a wide selection for the blanket price of about 12 bucks, shows no sign of the verve for which that city is famous. The burgers, though they come pleasingly medium-rare as ordered, are smothered in a gob of chewy cheese, underseasoned and floppy, while fries are overseasoned and floppy. The salad and soup bars are barely above the level of cafeteria fare, and the migas are just terrible.

We understand why Austinites have become so loyal to this place—in many ways it has earned their support. But support doesn't always mean good food. –RM

Hill Country Dining Room

food	
8.6	**6.2**
10	10
	experience

Creative, if overdressed, cuisine in the
Barton Creek Resort's stuffy restaurant

Southwestern $**68**   *Westlake*

Upmarket restaurant
Sun.-Thurs. 6:30am-2pm,
6pm-9pm; Fri.-Sat. 6:30am-2pm,
6pm-10pm. *Breakfast. Brunch.*
Live music. Outdoor dining.

Barton Creek Resort
8212 Barton Club Dr.
Austin, (512) 329-7924
www.bartoncreek.com/restaurant_hill.asp

Bar Full
Credit Cards Visa, MC, AmEx
Reservations Accepted

It can sometimes be entertaining just to sit back and contemplate all
the things that a very expensive restaurant does to make itself seem
worth the money. Champagne in the lobby before you're seated, and
an amuse-bouche once you are. Live piano music on weekends, and a
sommelier who compliments your wine choice—whatever it is. While
the service isn't our style—so courteous as to border on patronizing—
we do recognize that some people enjoy being fawned over when
they're paying this much.

Still, it's particularly amusing when a restaurant goes so far out of its
way to pull all the little isn't-this-a-fancy-night-out perks, and then gets
them all wrong. Consider, for instance, the sorbet that was brought
between our appetizers and main courses on our last visit to the Hill
Country Dining Room. Mid-meal sorbet is already a pomposity, but at
least it's one with an ostensible purpose: to cleanse the palate. Yet
instead of the acidic citrus that can do so, they whisked us out a
cloying chocolate-and-banana sorbet. Who wants dessert before
dinner? (Okay, maybe some of you. But still.)

Nonetheless, the flagship restaurant of the Barton Creek Resort and
Spa is putting some good food on the plate: luxuriantly seared foie gras
sits proudly atop ideally balanced toast quarters, even if a "spiced apple
compote" evokes average applesauce. Better are char-broiled lamb
ribeyes, delightfully rare, with smooth smoked cheddar grits that
sinfully serenade the Southwest. Chipotle-glazed quail is another
showstopper, with an unusual jalapeño cornbread stuffing.

But much less convincing, at our last visit, was a 13-dollar lobster-tail
appetizer, in which the advertised coconut was hard to taste. And table
arrangements leave a lot to be desired. Few tables allow couples to sit
caddy-corner—inexcusable for a purported date place. And the
furnishings and lighting just add to the stuffiness, reminding you that
you're in a hotel. The place is known for its Sunday brunch, with
cracked crab claws and good eggs benedict (unless they've been sitting
around too long). Regardless, there are many better ways to spend this
much money. –RG

Hill's Café

Chicken-fried steak and nostalgia in
evocative old South Austin

food
7.6 **9.0**
10 10
experience

American, Steakhouse, Barbecue **$27** *Far South*

Casual restaurant
Mon.-Thurs. 11am-10pm; Fri.-
Sat. 11am-10:30pm; Sun.11am-
9:30pm. *Kid-friendly. Live music.*
Outdoor dining. Wireless Internet.

4700 S. Congress Ave.
Austin
(512) 448-4878
www.hillscafe.com

Bar Full
Credit Cards Visa, MC, AmEx
Reservations Accepted

It's hard to get more Austin than Hill's Café. Rows of booths are decked
out with Willie Nelson paraphernalia and plaques honoring the
governor of Texas; drinks are brought out in enormous tumblers by the
couldn't-be-any-friendlier staff; and the menu proudly proclaims that
the chicken-fried steak is "the last of a kind" and that the restaurant is
"the home of the First Sizzlin' Steak in the United States." Bold boasts
indeed. And yet what's more Austin than boasting?

South Congress was once Old U.S. 81, the Old San Antonio Highway.
In 1947, the Goodnight family—that of the legendary cattle breeder
Charlie Goodnight—opened a 20-seat coffeeshop next to their
Goodnight Motel. Floods and fires ensued in the years since, but Hill's
Café is now reopened under the ownership of radio personality Bob
Cole. Live music is offered many nights, but these ain't no indie emo
crooners—you're more likely to see cowboy hats and double chins than
faux-vintage T-shirts concealing anorexic stomachs.

The fun doesn't end with the music and the scene: the food delivers
exactly as promised. Whether or not this was the first steak to sizzle, it's
flavorful beef, cooked properly as ordered. Better yet is the barbecue—
brisket is tender with smoky red edges, ribs more resilient but not a bit
dry, crusted with salt and dark spice. Winning sides include fried okra
and a great potato salad, but not a wimpily-dressed side salad.

The tour de force, however, is the sweet, luscious, indulgently crispy
chicken-fried steak. The gravy is thicker and gloopier than most,
allowing it to more or less sit atop the meat, but it works. This dish is
art: not a hint of greasiness, not one sinewy bite on the plate—just the
dreamy texture overlay, creamy upon crispy upon tender, flavor upon
flavor upon flavor, fat upon fat upon fat. –RG

Hill-Bert's Burgers

A burger joint straight from the '70s—
we hope you like yellow

food

5.2 **6.9**
10   10

experience

Burgers $**10**   *UT Area*

Casual restaurant   3303 N. Lamar Blvd.   *Bar* None
Daily 10am-10pm.   Austin   *Credit Cards* Visa, MC, AmEx
Delivery. Outdoor dining.   (512) 452-2317   *Reservations* Not accepted
                                www.hill-bertsburgers.com

                                5340 Cameron Rd.
                                78723, (512) 371-3717

Hill-Bert's Burgers has been around for more than 30 years—long enough for Austin to forget, if it ever knew, who Hill-Bert was; long enough for the cheapo diner-style décor and old-fashioned friendly service to acquire a great deal of charm; and long enough, sadly, for Austinites to learn what a good, properly cooked burger can be—and that there's a good deal better to be had elsewhere in town.

Still, we're awfully fond of this burger joint. First and foremost, you've got to admire the place for its brazen use of the color yellow. The crayon-bright shade is spread all around the restaurant like so much French's mustard. And while there is a certain amount of decay and grime to the space—which has barely changed since the Maldonado family opened shop in 1973—it is undeniably jolly.

This atmosphere is aided by unflaggingly friendly service. There is little seating besides some yellow vinyl swivel chairs flanking a window counter, but unless you live nearby, we don't really recommend the drive-thru, as Hill-Bert's burgers have a very short shelf-life. They are the thin variety, and the meat is only marginally better than that at McDonald's, albeit with good flavor and plenty of toppings, especially when you add jalapeños. We recommend the crispy, sweet onion rings over the fries (which can be a little mealy). Hill-Bert's also serves some pretty decent Dallas wings, accompanied by the requisite blue cheese and celery sticks.

You probably already know that there's not much to write home about in this food. But burgers are cheap, and children's scribbled thank-you notes line the counter. Plus, Hill-Bert's is one of the few places in town that can pull off selling gimme caps and brown-and-yellow logo T-shirts without seeming "That 70's Show" gimmicky. And that's worth quite a bit. –RM

Hoffbrau Steak House

A dingy but classic Austin steakhouse, circa 1934—vegetarians not welcome

food
4.8
10

8.7
10
experience

Steakhouse

$24

Warehouse District

Casual restaurant
Mon.-Fri. 11am-2pm, 5pm-9pm;
Sat. 5pm-9pm; closed Sun.
Outdoor dining.

613 W. 6th St.
Austin
(512) 472-0822

Bar Beer/wine
Credit Cards Visa and MC
Reservations Not accepted

Eating at the Hoffbrau Steakhouse is a little like time travel. Open since 1934, there's little to indicate that over 70 years have passed. The feeling is that of a 1940s roadhouse: there's a handful of ugly orange tables with benches and metal folding chairs, and some old photos and boxes of arrowheads displayed on wood-paneled walls. While it's not exactly date-friendly, there's just something special about the Hoffbrau.

They are busy, and people wait for tables, soaking in the *je ne sais quoi* and the smell of sizzling fat from the flat-tops and fryers visible on the other side of the front counter. We would have thought that a place like the Hoffbrau would appeal to a certain type of diner— perhaps truckers and frat boys—but everyone is there: older gentlemen dining alone, groups of college kids, families, and so on. Once, we even sat next to Larry Gatlin.

There is no real menu at the Hoffbrau; the waitress just comes to your table and tells you what they've got. There are no frills. The Hoffbrau's tired-looking salad is served only with the very garlicky house dressing. Onion rings are greasy but heavenly, and the steak fries are enormous—the size of small bananas. The steaks include a 14-ounce T-bone and a 12-ounce or 17-ounce sirloin, bathed in what the waitresses refer to as "sauce"— about 1/3 cup of melted butter and grease with a touch of lemon juice. These steaks are old-school—thin cuts that fill an entire plate. Their thinness makes the steaks easy to overcook, so the cooks may get the temperature right, or not. To be safe, order one temperature less than you want. While we couldn't eat there every day, or even monthly, there's just something about the Hoffbrau. We are even moved to haiku:

Greasy potatoes
   Giant steak with limp salad
Eat the onion rings.

—MPN

Home Slice Pizza

East Coast pizza has arrived...well...it'll be out any minute now...

food

7.0 / 10
9.1 / 10
experience

Pizza $18   *South Congress*

Casual restaurant   1415 S. Congress Ave.   ***Bar*** Beer/wine
Mon. 11:30am-11pm; Wed.-Thurs.   Austin   ***Credit Cards*** Visa, MC, AmEx
11:30-11pm; Fri.-Sat. 11:30am-   (512) 444-7437   ***Reservations*** Not accepted
midnight, window open until 3am; www.homeslicepizza.com
Sun. noon-10pm; closed Tues. *Date-friendly. Wireless Internet.*

East Coasters who've spent the years since that promising job landed them in Austin working on their y'alls and earning their Tex-Mex and barbecue credentials finally have their chance to boast local knowledge. The latest addition to the South Congress Strip is Home Slice: a true-to-its-word New York-style pizza joint.

Now, a few places around town claim New York-style pizza, but this trendy gem, all bright and shiny and comfortable with its sweet collection of tables and jazzy décor, comes about as close as any, with truly thin crusts and traditional toppings. Even amidst the rush of pizza-tossers, the crisscrossing routes of the hip and beautiful waitpeople, and the swish of excellent draft beer being poured into pitchers, the warmly lit environment manages to maintain a certain low-key, almost romantic vibe, especially at the booths, and most of all in the back room. This might be the best pizza atmosphere in Austin.

Pizzas are divided, in the grand tradition, into whites (no sauce) and reds (sauce). In an homage to New Haven, Connecticut—home of Wooster Street and the world-famous Frank Pepe's and Sally's pizza joints—there is even a white clam pizza on the menu. Unfortunately, Home Slice's version doesn't even approach the crispy, charcoaly, sweet-'n'-oily glory of New Haven; this one is underseasoned and covered with tasteless, shriveled-up clams. Skip it.

We do like a white pie with garlic, tomato, basil, and ricotta, which pairs well with Kalamata olives. Home Slice's subs are also an underappreciated delight, with the judicious kick of hot cherry peppers. Otherwise, we recommend that you stick with the basic red pizzas, whose cheese and tomato sauce are well above average. The crust could use more salt, as well as more time in the fire—they're not quite seared to New York deliciousness. Where they do spend their time is something of a mystery, however—the pies sometimes take nearly an hour to arrive. But as the garlicky oil drips slowly from the sagging tip of a truly thin-crust pizza, who are we, we humbly ask, to complain?
–RM/RG

Hoover's Cooking

Comfort cooking in every sense of the word

food

8.3 /10   **9.2** /10

experience

Southern

$25

French Place, Far Northwest

Casual restaurant
Mon.-Fri. 11am-10pm;
Sat.-Sun. 8am-10pm.
Brunch. Kid-friendly.

2002 Manor Rd.
Austin
(512) 479-5006
www.hooverscooking.com

13376 N. Hwy. 183
78750, (512) 335-0300

Bar Full
Credit Cards Visa and MC
Reservations Recommended

Three cheers for Hoover Alexander. With his sunny disposition, his welcoming restaurant, and his down-home comfort cooking, he's made Austin a happier, more contented place. Hoover's status as a beloved family restaurant, like that of a hand-me-down teddy bear, glosses over its somewhat shabby edges, and the restaurant deserves every ounce of blind affection it can get. You leave Hoover's feeling just plain good.

Despite outstandingly warm service, Hoover's is always about the food, first and foremost. There is a certain kind of loving, especially in the South, which is communicated mainly through the kitchen. Such meals are sweet, warm, creamy, and, most importantly, filling (we are reminded of a certain Jewish father, eagerly dishing out seconds). Hoover's cooking does this kind of talking. The meal begins with a hot basket of sweet rolls and cornbread. From there, almost all options are good. The creamy artichoke dip has a serious following. We love the meatloaf, coarsely grained and beefy, smothered in a thick sauce of tomato, green peppers, and onions. It has a hearty, peppery kick, to which Hoover's buttery mashed potatoes are an ideal match. Chicken-fried steak is spectacularly well seasoned and dreamily crispy—if occasionally gristly in places—with a pleasant cream gravy. Or try the punchier jerk chicken, with its crisp skin and salty bite. All meals come with multiple choices of sides (we particularly like the okra, although we've had bland mac and cheese, underseasoned grits, and overly liquidy creamed spinach). And even after that, it'll be hard to refuse your waiter's suggestion of some sweet peach cobbler à la mode for dessert.

Alexander started his culinary career under the tutelage of the legendary Harry Akin, founder of the Night Hawk chain. Akin was the man responsible for the desegregation of Austin restaurants, and Hoover's Cooking is one of the few places, even (sadly) today, that black and white Austinites enjoy together in equal numbers.

For he's a jolly good fel-*low*…which nobody can deny! –RM

House Park BBQ

Brisket so tender that you can leave
your dentures at home

food
8.5
10

8.3
10
experience

Barbecue
$ **7**
House Park Area

Counter service
Mon.-Fri. 11am-2:30pm;
closed Sat.-Sun. *Outdoor dining.*

900 W. 12th St.
Austin
(512) 472-9621

Bar BYO
Credit Cards No credit cards
Reservations Not accepted

Located just down the street from House Park Field, House Park BBQ has been serving 'cue from its tiny house since 1943. With just a few tables inside, but several umbrella-topped picnic tables out front, House Park does a good business each weekday during lunch—the only time that they are open—attracting suits, students, and just plain ol' folks.

This is one of the few places in Austin where you can really get a feel for old-time Texas barbecue; it seems they're smoking not just meat, but the whole restaurant—walls are tinged grayish brown; the photos, hunting and fishing trophies, and news clippings that collage the walls are yellowed; and everything smells of smoke, making the posted "No Smoking" sign seem a little silly. Even the clock's face is a yellow-brown color. Cash-only counter service is quick and friendly, and customers help themselves to bread, jalapeños, pickles, and onions from a side table.

House Park's offerings are limited to very basic barbecue and rudimentary sides. Their wonderful motto, "Need no teef to eat my beef," is apt—their brisket is perhaps the most tender we've had. It has excellent charring and a lovely brown and red-edged color; it's moist and tender through and through; and it tastes divine. Sadly, the sausage, while having a good, coarse grind and mild, peppery flavor, has a tough casing that is quite a lot to chew. House Park's sauce has tart vinegar and tomato flavors, and a nice thin nap. Sides are simple, to put it mildly—potato salad is chunky with a creamy mustard base, cole slaw is light and coarsely chopped, and beans have a nice firm texture but are otherwise bland.

Come to House Park for the fabulous brisket, and to get a feel for what barbecue—and Austin—was like before things got so danged fancy around here. –MPN

Hudson's on the Bend

A high-priced, high-flying riverside
restaurant that honors the Southwest

food
8.8
10
9.1
10
experience

Southwestern   **$82**   *Lake Travis Area*

Upmarket restaurant
Sun.-Mon. 6pm-9pm,
Tues.-Thurs. 6pm-10pm,
Fri.-Sat. 5:30pm-10pm.
Date-friendly. Outdoor dining.

3509 RR 620 N.
Austin
(512) 266-1369
www.hudsonsonthebend.com

Bar Full
Credit Cards Visa, MC, AmEx
Reservations Essential

Even the name of this restaurant sounds venerable, old-school Austin, old-money Texan. And indeed, although owner Jeff Blank's restaurant has only been around since 1984, there is probably no culinary address more revered by the old Austin guard. It is a warm and lovely place, whether you're by a roaring fire and colorful paintings inside the old house, or out on the patio, whose rows of little white lights give off that rich country wedding-tent feel.

Some people might still deem Hudson's too fat-old-boy for their tastes, but it's hard not to appreciate its singular culinary focus. Rather than trying to do the generic pan-New-American that dominates other expensive menus in the area, this restaurant demonstrates a deep and longstanding devotion to what Mr. Blank dubs "Texas Hill Country cuisine," located at the exciting intersection of Southwestern and rural game-farm fare. Executive chef Robert Rhoades (who's in with our controversial president) does best in that arena, as in the "Hudson's Mixed Grill," a canonical dinner main of game meats grilled over hardwood that transcends the seasonality of the menu: axis venison, rabbit tenders, spicy game sausage, achiote-marinated buffalo, and sensational quail, whose glaze is bright with cilantro. Hot and crunchy ruby trout in mango habañero aïoli, with ancho sauce and herb polenta soufflé, is another righteous homage to Southwestern fusion. Good, too, if slightly less interesting, are rattlesnake cakes in a pistachio nut crust, though their tomatoey, smoky, spicy sauce dominates any unique snake flavor.

Hudson's falters when it strays from that genre. An amuse-bouche shooter of lobster bisque, on a fall visit, had spice but not much else (lobster is clearly not a Hill Country ingredient), while the cheap pyrotechnics of Parmesan crisps couldn't rescue a pedestrian Caesar salad with no detectable trace of anchovy. "Chili-Accented Lime, Scallop, and Shrimp Ceviche," meanwhile, was overwhelmed by an olive flavor that doesn't belong. So stick to the Hill Country fare, settle in, and come ready to *spend*. The good news is that, even when it misfires, Hudson's is ambitious and evocative enough to justify the high prices. –RG

Hula Hut

A festive, heavy-drinking waterside spot
where you may be pelted by pineapples

food
5.1 **7.8**
10   10
experience

American, Mexican, Pan-Asian $ **31**   *Tarrytown*

Casual restaurant
Sun.-Thurs. 11am-10pm; Fri.-
Sat. 11am-11pm. *Kid-friendly.*
Outdoor dining.

3826 Lake Austin Blvd.
Austin
(512) 476-4852
www.chuys.com

Bar Full
Credit Cards Visa, MC, AmEx
Reservations Not accepted

There are those that have risked their lives for the Hula Hut. One naïve
boater, in particular, was so dedicated to get there for an afternoon
margarita and a tubular taco that when his engine gave out, he tried to
paddle in—only to get sucked into the Dam, where his boat was
shredded to bits. He survived unscathed. You might not be so lucky,
however, if you drink your margaritas as fast as the fratty local crowd
tends to at the Hula Hut.

Clearly, this restaurant, right on the banks of Lake Austin, owned by
the Chuy's empire, is doing something right: you might have to wait up
to two hours to be seated on a weekend evening. The place is decked
out with bamboo, surfing supplies, and grimacing carved wooden
masks, and the menus, too, embrace theme cuisine. Although there's a
lot of traditional Tex-Mex—queso, fajitas and such—you'll also find
pineapples showing up almost anywhere (we'd recommend giving your
clothes a good shake upon leaving, to make sure they don't follow you
out). Vinaigrettes become "Hawaiian," and a Polynesian plum sauce
glazes everything within reach.

While motifs may have you racing through a novel, they can be less
welcome in the kitchen, and at Hula Hut, the plot, along with the
sauces, thickens a little too much. Burgers are coarse-ground and
chewy; in the Hawaiian version, a thick slice of pineapple adds little.
Mango quesadillas wallow a little in their dense cream cheese. Tortillas
are freshly made, but oddly thick and floury. Salmon tacos are dry and
occasionally a little fishy.

But the Hula Hut doesn't pretend to be about delicate food. It's a fun
place to drink a lot, and an even more wonderful place to sit—if you
get a table on the deck, on the side that doesn't overlook the hideous,
water-spitting mechanical fish (which is definitely worth a quarter to
see in action), and the service is easygoing. Now, drink up!
–RM/RG/VGC

Hunan Lion

Overpriced but decent Chinese-
American in South Austin

food

6.2 | **7.0**
10 | 10

experience

Chinese   **$23**   *South Lamar*

Casual restaurant   4006 S. Lamar Blvd.   *Bar* Beer/wine
Mon.-Thurs. 11am-2:30pm,   Austin   *Credit Cards* Visa, MC, AmEx
5pm-10pm; Fri. 11am-2:30pm, (512) 447-3388   *Reservations* Accepted
5pm-11pm; Sat. 11:30am-11pm;
Sun. noon-10pm. *Delivery. Vegetarian-friendly.*

Hunan Lion is one of Austin's better-known Chinese restaurants south
of the river, probably because it's been in business longer than most.
The décor is somewhat more upscale than you normally see in Austin's
Chinese restaurants, featuring the usual sorts of wall art, fake flowers,
and white tablecloths, but also several aquariums and a collection of
pretty white and blue teapots. Also prominently displayed is a four-star
review of the Hunan Lion written by the *Austin American-Statesman* in
1987. Is that, we wonder, why Hunan Lion believes itself justified
charging such high prices for generally good, but hardly fabulous, fare?

Service is extremely courteous and prompt, while still relaxed, and no
table goes neglected. Spring rolls are average, while hot and sour soup
is peppery but uninteresting. Crispy walnuts (an unusual menu offering
for Austin Chinese) are definitely crispy, and a little sweet, but are
otherwise not particularly compelling.

There are brighter spots, though: pan-seared dumplings require a 15-
minute wait, but are very tasty, filled with subtly seasoned ground pork,
and served with a gingery black vinegar and soy dipping sauce. Pork in
hot garlic sauce is delicious, with a spicy and well-balanced sauce.
Orange beef is also good, sweet and spicy with pieces of dried orange
peel; however, the slices of beef are so large that they cry out for a
steak knife to bring them to order.

Open all afternoon on the weekends, Hunan Lion is an okay place to
stop if you are seeking a mid-afternoon meal, but this is certainly not a
four-star venue—whatever that is, or was, supposed to mean (truth be
told, we have no idea). Its faded glory is a hangover from when there
weren't better options in town. –MPN

Hut's Hamburgers

The best burgers in town seem to come and go, but Hut's is always here for us

food

6.7 **7.3**

10 10

experience

Burgers

$13

Warehouse District

Casual restaurant
Daily 11am-10pm. *Kid-friendly.*
Vegetarian-friendly.

807 W. 6th St.
Austin
(512) 472-0693

Bar Beer/wine
Credit Cards Visa, MC, AmEx
Reservations Not accepted

Hut's Hamburgers has been open in Austin since 1939, although they only moved to their current Sixth Street location in 1969. The restaurant's motto, "God Bless Hut's," was coined in 1981 by *Texas Monthly* after the disastrous Memorial Day Flood washed away nearly everything else on the block, but spared Hut's entirely. The place still has a vintage feel, with its soda bar, old team pennants, and walls barely visible behind photos, articles, longhorn and buffalo heads, and other bric-a-brac. Service can be slow, and there's often a wait in the crowded entryway.

The menu's focus is on burgers, though there are other sandwiches and blue plate specials. Burgers are where it's at, though, and they can be made in dozens of permutations, beginning with the choice of meat: regular hamburger, all-natural beef, moist veggie burger, chicken breast, or ground buffalo. The "Wolfman Jack" is excellent—the gaminess of the buffalo meat pairs well with spicy green chili, crisp smoky bacon, jack cheese, and cool sour cream. There is, however, a moment when you worry it'll wolf you. The "All-American Buddy Holly Burger" comes with lettuce, tomatoes, onions, pickles, and American cheese, and is delicious with a side of spicy chipotle mayonnaise (also an option for other burgers).

Skin-on french fries are skinny and limp, and not even a much-needed and liberal salting can resuscitate them. Onion rings are monstrous, almost the size of the burgers themselves, and breaded with lots of cracked black pepper. Other menu items are okay, but not nearly as good as the burgers. Meatloaf topped with bland tomato sauce is moist and lighter than normal, which is good given the huge portion size. Side veggies are often items like okra, a vegetable medley, or underseasoned mashed potatoes. Don't miss the milkshakes at Hut's—they are just the right thickness for slurping through a straw and come topped with whipped cream and a cherry. What would go better with your burger? –MPN

Hyde Park Bar and Grill

The fries are to die for at this friendly
pan-American cult favorite

food

8.0 / 10

9.1 / 10

experience

American $ **28**   Hyde Park

Casual restaurant
Daily 11am-midnight. *Brunch.*
Delivery. Vegetarian-friendly.

4206 Duval St.
Austin
(512) 458-3168

Bar Full
Credit Cards Visa, MC, AmEx
Reservations Not accepted

The Austin staple with the funky, formidable fork and its ever-changing sign (at press time, french fries were masquerading as birthday candles), Hyde Park Bar and Grill has been serving up solid American fare for well over two decades. Located in trendy Hyde Park and with a simple décor that accentuates the art for sale that's on display, this place is a neighborhood favorite for everything from brunch to a late-night snack. There's a full bar that offers room to wait with a drink when they're busy.

We like to start with the steamed dumplings which are filled with turkey, peas, and other veggies and served with a peanutty sauce. Clam chowder is a little thin, but it has good flavor and is thick with chunks of clam and vegetables, and the macaroni and cheese has all the complex, golden hallmarks of a homemade version. Burgers and sandwiches are huge and generally delicious. Hyde Park is now offering a Texas-raised "Kobe" beef burger (this term, which originally referred to special beer-fed and tummy-massaged Japanese beef, seems to be getting thrown around more and more these days). Our favorite, though, is the Horseshoe sandwich. This open-faced burger is served on Texas toast, covered with cheddar cheese sauce and a tower of their wonderful fries. Now *that's* comfort food. Now, about those fries: they are the best in Austin and possibly the world. The fries are delicately buttermilk battered, ideally peppered, and served with "The Sauce," a mayonnaise-based, spicy concoction with a bit of pickle (although it's not to the taste of some of our Contributing Editors). Be sure to order extras; we have never found anything like these fries anywhere else, and we just can't get enough of them.

Brunch features great drink specials like two-dollar mimosas. We like the "Southwestern Omelette," which is a sunny yellow, moist, and filled with a warm, gardeny mixture of poblanos, tomatoes, onions, and cheese. But the best part is that you can get it with a side of fries.
–MPN

Ichiban

Another entry into the Austin sushi arena, with an unusually laid-back vibe

food

7.2 10   **7.3** 10

experience

Japanese, Korean

$**23** *Burnet*

Casual restaurant
Mon.-Thurs. 11am-10pm;
Fri. 11am-10:30pm; Sat.
7pm-10:30pm; Sun. 1pm-9pm.

7310 Burnet Rd.
Austin
(512) 452-2883

Bar Beer/wine
Credit Cards Visa, MC, AmEx
Reservations Accepted

Sometimes we wonder how much Austin's burgeoning sushi scene is about the food, and how much it is about seeing and being seen. The trendiness of certain new downtown Japanese restaurants (Kenichi and Maiko are two of them) certainly does beg the question, particularly when the wait times we endure are neither proportional to the quality of the food nor indicative of a good bargain.

All this brings us to one of Austin's longest-running Japanese restaurants, Ichiban, and its total lack of trendiness. Even with Ichiban's stylized blue roof and roaring, river-scaped courtyard complete with koi (which we suspect are deaf by now), it's easy to get the feeling that this must originally have been to home to a Mexican restaurant. Inside, that fear is allayed by a sushi bar, a dining room decorated with Japanese prints and gongs, and an aquarium, ringed by nearly private Japanese-style dining areas complete with tatami lanterns, mats to sit on, and shoe shelves.

The menu is filled with Japanese standards as well as a short selection of Korean dishes with pictures and English descriptions to help you through. Service is friendly and very helpful, so don't be shy if you have any questions. One of our favorite things about Ichiban is the variety of combination plates, like the makunouchi, served in compartmentalized lacquered trays.

But do try the sushi, which is fresh, reasonably priced, and comes artfully arranged with vegetable carvings. Crunchy tempura is also a good choice, with huge slices of vegetables and shrimp. We have been less impressed by the poached chicken teriyaki in a thick, sweet sauce that overwhelms the meat, and the grainy, overcooked salmon butteryaki. On the Korean side, we like the pork bulgogi, which is presented here as a light stir-fry with bright green onions and sprinkled with sesame seeds—a much lighter version than we are accustomed to. Sometimes, Ichiban teaches with a wise man's nod, less is more. –MPN

Indian Palace

Hit-or-miss Indian food, but they make
the neighborhood more interesting

Indian

$**21**   *Northwest Hills*

Casual restaurant
Daily 11am-2:30pm,
5:30pm-9:30pm.
Vegetarian-friendly.

3616 Far West Blvd.
Austin
(512) 241-1732

Bar Beer/wine
Credit Cards Visa, MC, AmEx
Reservations Accepted

Northwest Hills newcomer Indian Palace has entered uncharted waters
as the first really exotic restaurant to grace this neighborhood. (In our
not-too-distant youth, pizza and cheap barbecue were about all you
could find in this part of Austin, and the addition of fast food chains
hardly improved things.) Perhaps the proliferation of student-oriented
housing in this neighborhood in recent years is beginning to lure some
less-traditional business at last.

Unfortunately, Indian Palace is average at best by Austin standards,
but it certainly is a colorful addition to this area, where a gentle tan
would stand out like hot pink. The décor at Indian Palace is a little odd,
with leadlight lamps hanging at odd junctures, leaving you wondering
who the previous tenants were. The buffet table seems to creep
uncomfortably close to the kitchen. Service is helpful and attentive, but
rather cold.

Most of the food is passable, with a few real standouts, like thin but
spicy matter paneer with peas and dense cheese cubes. We also like
the savory, veggie-full aloo bangan, highly spiced with tender potatoes
and silky eggplant. Crisp samosas are highly seasoned, and served fresh
from the fryer, still glistening with oil. Fried flatbread, onion kulcha, are
crisp edged while still elastic and moist on the inside. On the other
hand, tinny saag paneer should be avoided, and the tandoori chicken is
worse still, with miniscule pieces that have a distinctly off-putting
metallic flavor. Chicken curry is safe, though a little dry, while chana
masala has tender but firm chickpeas in a subtle curry. If you are
looking for a dessert beyond the usual kheer (rice pudding), you might
want to try gulab jamun, a dish not unlike donut holes bathed in a light
rose water and cinnamon syrup; they make a pleasant surprise on an
Indian buffet. –MPN

Iron Cactus

A downtown Tex-Mex throbber with yuparitas and a nice terrace

food
6.2 | **7.3**
10 | 10
experience

Mexican — $**35** — *Sixth Street District*

Pub
Mon.-Fri. 10am-11pm,
Sat. 10am-midnight,
Sun. 10am-10pm. *Brunch.*
Date-friendly. Outdoor dining.

606 Trinity St.
Austin
(512) 472-9240
www.ironcactus.com

Bar Full
Credit Cards Visa, MC, AmEx
Reservations Accepted

Sixth Street, even at its most upscale, tends, first and foremost, to be about the alcohol. Iron Cactus, one of the only joints on the strip with any pretensions of being upscale, is emblematic of this theory: design is ultra-modern (okay, 1990s modern), there's a Sunday brunch, and there's seating at dinner tables for hundreds—but the star of the show is really the tequila list.

If you're the sort of person that can imagine spending upwards of $10 on a shot of tequila, this is the place to do it. The most impressive tequila list in Austin includes Cuervo Reserva de la Familia, El Tesoro Paradiso, and, to celebrate your sketchy Internet company's IPO, Herradura Selección Suprema at $39 per shot. For those without offshore accounts, we recommend a tequila flight, which offers you the chance—for 10 or 12 bucks—to compare and contrast three cactus liquors. Margaritas and Mexican martinis are also good: no sour mix here, just tequila, triple sec or Cointreau, and simple syrup.

Otherwise, this is just a predictable Tex-Mex joint. Chile con queso is solid, and fajitas and enchiladas are just as expected—well executed, if lacking creativity. As for the sleeked-out décor, we can't quite sign onto the program. The lines are curvy, the walls exposed brick, and the lighting done up like a movie set, with a sleazy red glow emanating from hidden nooks. Even the windows are trendified floor-to-ceiling showpieces. Perhaps unsurprisingly, this is fast becoming a Texas-based chain.

In the end, it is the lovely rooftop terrace that elevates Iron Cactus from the "okay if you're on Sixth Street" category to the "worth going to Sixth Street for" category. Although you might have to wait for a table up there, the space is a revelation on a warm night; you can watch as the world passes by beneath the twinkling lights of the Austin skyline, and refill your Mexican martini. And refill it. And refill it again.
–RG

Iron Works BBQ

The space couldn't be any more
evocative—but the brisket could

food

6.5 **9.3**
10 10
experience

Barbecue $**14**   *Convention Center Area*

Counter service   100 Red River St.   *Bar* Beer/wine
Mon.-Sat. 11am-9pm;   Austin   *Credit Cards* Visa, MC, AmEx
closed Sun. *Outdoor dining.* (512) 478-4855   *Reservations* Accepted
                           www.ironworksbbq.com

The tin building that houses Iron Works BBQ, opened in 1978, was
once the ironsmith workshop of Fortunat Weigl. Fortunat was a
German iron worker who arrived in Ellis Island in 1913. Along with his
sons, Lee and Herbert, he founded a workshop that went on to
become one of the most notable in Texas, creating iron pieces for the
State Capitol, museums, and so on. Not only is Iron Works' space
steeped in history, it does justice to that history, like a living museum.
Exposed beams reveal the framework of the building, while fans (no
A/C) make it feel like a real, live iron workshop.

Iron Works has also become one of the most beloved places
downtown for barbecue. From a food perspective, this reputation is
only partly deserved. You sidle up to the line, cafeteria-style, to partake
in barbecued meats including hearty beef ribs, which are formidable,
tender, and satisfying. Sausage is also above average. The brisket,
however, is bimodal: some pieces are quite dry, while others are more
tolerable; still, in this brisket-happy town, those results are
disappointing. This is partially compensated for by Iron Works' excellent
spicy barbecue sauce, which is preferable to their deep, dark, thick
regular version. (Barbecue sauce is most desperately needed, after all,
when meat is dry, and here it comes to the rescue.) Sides and the salad
bar are no better than average. The beans taste Mexican—we're not
sure if that's a good thing or not—and potato salad is fine, albeit with
too much egg.

A combo plate, for $11.95, easily feeds two normal appetites, so that
price point is right on. And even if there's better barbecue to be had in
town, we keep coming back here for the singular atmosphere. –RG

The Jackalope

Beckoning you into a Sixth Street lair of
drinks, food, and more drinks

food

7.0 / 10

6.3 / 10

experience

American, Burgers　　　　　**$12**　　*Sixth Street District*

Pub
Daily 11:30am–2am.
Kitchen closes at 1am.
Date-friendly.

404 E. 6th St.
Austin
(512) 469-5801
www.jackalopeaustin.com

Bar Full
Credit Cards Visa, MC, AmEx
Reservations Not accepted

However drunk you are, as you scan the blurry faces of dangerously
beautiful roller girls and tattooed love-boys in skinny jeans that
populate the Jackalope, it can be hard not to notice the velvet nudes
on the wall. It can be equally hard to reconcile the Bastille-turned-
opera-house-meets-'50s-diner quality of the interior with the taxidermic
masterpiece that is the bar's namesake, mounted proudly above the
gaudily back-lit rows of liquor bottles.

　Yet just beyond that smug antlered rodent lies one of the best bar
kitchens in Austin. The Jackalope offers a variety of sandwiches; a
champion amongst them is the juicy wood-grilled chicken with melted
brie, bacon, and Caesar dressing on a wheat bun. The Philly cheese
steak sandwich features a giant cut of meat with mountains of
peppers, onions, and cheese—eminently shareable—and the fried
catfish in a po-boy is satisfying and crispy, if undersalted.

　No self-respecting bar is going to get off without serving wings, and
our vote for best of the Jackalope's three flavors is the honey jalapeño.
Subtle. Sweet. Spicy. Brilliant. The hot wings, though tasty, are labeled
"porno hot," but in fact they boast little more than Skinemax-grade
spice. No sweat on the brow here—and nothing below the waist.

　For vegetarians, there are several salads and a superb portobello
mushroom sandwich with a large, thick cap—not dry and diminutive—
garnished with a chunky, light pesto without too much oil; roasted red
peppers; and caramelized onion. Less successful are the waffle fries,
with a decidedly funnel-cake quality to their flavor that seems to betray
the freshness of the frying oil. So skip the fries, and buck up. Ignore the
eau de PBR. Grab a tall boy (or girl), and indulge in all this dark den has
to offer, which, contrary to appearances, is a great deal more than
velveteen breasts, cheap beer, and billiards. –SEF

Jaime's Spanish Village

It's the oldest Tex-Mex in town—and that's about it

food
4.4 / 10
5.8 / 10
experience

Mexican $**24**   *Red River Area*

Casual restaurant
Mon. 11am-2pm; Tues.-Thurs.
11am-9pm; Fri.-Sat. 11am-
10pm; closed Sun. *Outdoor dining.*

802 Red River St.
Austin
(512) 476-5149

Bar Full
Credit Cards Visa, MC, AmEx
Reservations Accepted

Austin's longest-lived Tex-Mex restaurant, Jaime's Spanish Village has been open since 1931. Entering through their stone gate into the uneven courtyard, you'll have to duck, and it won't be the last time, as Jaime's may have the lowest ceilings in the city. Stone walls and small rooms contribute to the feeling that the restaurant was built inside a cave. If you are at all claustrophobic, we strongly suggest that you sit outside.

The far dining room has small windows lining Red River Street, and sitting at those tables under the encroaching ceiling is reminiscent of riding in a dining car, especially with the red vinyl upholstery on the chairs. Jaime's décor represents its long tenure in Austin, with some old, bullfight-themed artwork overshadowed by decades of photos. Service can be slow and unenthusiastic, but they are willing to make changes to lunch specials, so it's not too hard to create your own mix—and, at under six bucks, a pretty good deal for downtown.

Jaime's is known for strong margaritas that come in several varieties and by the pitcher at a reasonable price. They also sell jarred versions of their thin, super-spicy salsas (which are full of chile seeds) and their surreally smooth queso at local groceries. Most options on the short menu at Jaime's, though, are pretty mediocre. Thick chalupas with bland refried beans and ground beef are topped with piles of shredded iceberg lettuce. Guacamole is fresh, with lots of chopped tomato and onion, but also underseasoned, lacking lime. Enchiladas filled with chunks of chicken are tender, but mole tastes of peanut butter and chocolate with a heavy dose of cumin, making up for a lack of complexity with a smothering of cheddar cheese. There is certainly better Tex-Mex in town, but few other spots have the kind of history Jaime's does, filled as it is with so many Austinites' fond memories.
–MPN

Java Noodles

Sort-of-Indonesian food at a popular
but disappointing lunch hotspot

food

3.5 **5.3**
10   10

experience

Indonesian $**19**   *Southeast*

Casual restaurant   2400 E. Oltorf St.   *Bar* Beer/wine
Mon.-Fri. 11am-2:30pm,   Austin   *Credit Cards* Visa, MC, AmEx
5pm-10pm; Sat. 6pm-10pm;   (512) 443-5282   *Reservations* Not accepted
Sun. noon-3pm.

East Oltorf is becoming something of a haven for inexpensive purveyors of world cuisines that, a few decades ago, you would never have imagined would be represented in Austin. Unfortunately, Java Noodles, which claims to serve Indonesian food, is not on that list. Instead, most of the food here is just the same disappointing brand of bland curries, noodle dishes, and stir-fries that you'd find at a discount corner pan-Asian joint. Word has it that Java Noodles has gone downhill since a change of ownership in the early 2000s, which could partly explain our disappointment.

Popular lunch specials include a self-service "soup bar," where you can fill up on awful chicken wings, egg rolls no better than lowest-common-denominator Chinese greasy-spoon versions, slightly more interesting fried bananas, and of course the soups. Amongst those, the coconut curry soup, though hardly innovative, is warm and sweet, easily defeating the hot-and-sour soup in a battle of minor-league flavors.

We wish we could continue on to some fascinatingly authentic Indonesian favorites, but unfortunately, there's not much to say. We do like a combination plate that features braised meat with curry and fried egg, but chicken satay—the Indonesian signature—is gummy and peanutty, nothing special. Rendang—a sort of beef stew in coconut milk—is probably the best thing on the menu, but it's not available at lunch, when the underwhelming stir-fry dishes, made with tough meat, dominate the offerings. Pad Thai is too sticky, too sweet, without enough shrimp or peanut flavor—and anyway, isn't Pad Thai Thai?

All of this is frustrating, because real Indonesian food can be wonderful. Why do places like this feel the need to pursue every culinary tentacle of Asia, cramming in Chinese-American common denominators like fried dumplings and generic stir-fries, rather than focusing on what's unique about their own purported culinary focus? You might call it a lack of culinary self-esteem, and until Java Noodles gets over it, don't expect any surprises—or much of any interest. –RG

Jeffrey's

George W. loves this upmarket classic—
but can you trust him?

food
8.6 8.3
10   10
experience

New American $**84**   *Clarksville*

Upmarket restaurant   1204 W. Lynn St.   ***Bar*** Full
Mon.-Thurs. 6pm-10pm;   Austin   ***Credit Cards*** Visa, MC, AmEx
Fri.-Sat. 5:30pm-10:30pm;   (512) 477-5584   ***Reservations*** Essential
Sun. 6pm-9:30pm.   www.jeffreysofaustin.com

Talk about food in Austin, and people will start talking about Jeffrey's. You'll hear about 40-dollar beef tenderloins, about Chef David Garrido cooking at Presidential inaugurations, and about all the everybody-who's-anybodies coming back to this steadfastly elegant, fancy-but-not-quite-stuffy, see-and-be-served restaurant for more than a quarter-century.

Everybody seems to have a strong opinion about Jeffrey's, and not all of them are positive. One thing that seems to come up is a nagging sense that maybe people have been spending a little too much of their money here through the years. Is $13 too much for the crispy oysters with habañero honey aïoli?

Well, not if you're the President, who apparently swears by this "signature" dish. The creamy mollusks come perched atop yucca crisps that are like a fuller-bodied version of potato chips; they're correctly fried, well paired with the aïoli and spill of tomatoes, and easy to enjoy. Even better is a silky, sherry-laced chipotle crab bisque, whose well-reduced stock practically jumps out of the bowl and dances across the palate. Equally good is a main course of appropriately rare duck leg and prawns, the honey-ginger-saffron glaze a bright amusement, its peanut scallion rice a long-lost soul mate.

Unfortunately, there are too many miscues at Jeffrey's to justify the prices: the taste and texture of duck spring rolls is just okay, their flavor too restrained, the counterpoints of chayote slaw and "spicy dipping sauce" too wimpy. Ginger beef dumplings are another underwhelming attempt at Asian fusion. And king salmon with tomato ancho butter, at our last visit, showed up overcooked to the point that the quality of the fish hardly mattered anymore, and its seasoning was weak—an even greater offense when salmon is dry. What's truly offensive, though, is the bill. All told (three courses, wine, tax, tip), $120 per person should buy something a lot closer to perfection—and we don't mean our waiter's affected, faux-British accent. –RG

Jerusalem Gourmet

A dive, but some of the best Middle Eastern in Austin

food

7.6 /10

5.2 /10

experience

Middle Eastern

$ 9

Southeast

Counter service
Mon.-Fri. 11am-8pm; Sat.
noon-7pm; closed Sun.
Vegetarian-friendly.

1931 E. Oltorf St.
Austin
(512) 444-4344

Bar None
Credit Cards Visa and MC
Reservations Not accepted

It may be hard to believe, but despite the pseudo-fancy décor and weekend belly dancers with which the other places are trying to lure you, some of the best Middle Eastern food in town is being served at a hole in the wall on Oltorf, three blocks east of IH-35. Jerusalem Gourmet is a tiny Middle Eastern grocery and deli housed in a dingy strip mall. Or maybe it's not such a surprise; this neighborhood actually conceals some of Austin's most exciting ethnic culinary finds.

There are only a handful of tables, and the décor is minimal—a wall full of dry goods and hookahs, and a few travel posters of Middle East locales to put you in the mood. But beware: during the lunch hour, Jerusalem Gourmet fills up fast, and you may find yourself taking your lunch to go, or else cozying up to strangers.

Counter service, if mostly friendly, is not terribly fast, but portion sizes are decent and prices reasonable. Many items are offered à la carte, and there are also several combo plates so you can try much of what Jerusalem Gourmet has to offer. We like the combination of tangy pieces of lemon chicken and savory chopped souvlaki heaped over rice and served with a salad. Deep-fried, fist-sized kibbeh—seasoned ground beef with a side of spiced tahini—is also a tasty and inexpensive main.

Herbivores will be very happy here—the vegetarian plate features dense dolmas; creamy, smoky baba ganoush; small, crunchy falafel; rich eggplant stewed in tomato sauce; and hummus that we are sad to say is a little bland. We do recommend the moist, tart tabbouleh, lemony but well balanced, as well as crisp, buttery spanikopita. For dessert, try a ma'moul: it's a dry cookie filled with sweet, chopped dates so rich that they initially taste like chocolate. We also like the buttery, light baklava, which is topped with vivid green ground pistachios. –MPN

Jim Bob's BBQ

A smoky, stewy, sultry escape from the city

food 6.5 / 10

7.4 / 10 *experience*

Barbecue

$**12**   *Bee Cave*

Counter service
Mon.-Sat. 10am-6pm,
Sun. 10am-2pm. *Breakfast.*
Kid-friendly. Outdoor dining.

12701 W. Hwy. 71
Bee Cave
(512) 263-3041
www.jimbobsbbq.com

Bar Beer/wine
Credit Cards Visa, MC, AmEx
Reservations Not accepted

It's amazing how certain 15-minute drives from downtown Austin can make you feel that you've suddenly embarked on a temporary vacation in the hilly countryside. The modest, barn-red Jim Bob's BBQ, which is actually in the village of Bee Caves, Texas, at the intersection of Highway 71 and FM 2244, is an example of this phenomenon. The joint comes complete with chipping paint and the feeling that you've seen this place before in an old Western.

The interior resembles that of a typical small-town barbecue shop, with neon beer signs gracing the walls, a chalkboard menu behind the counter, and family-sized picnic benches. The outdoor patio has more pleasant seating with a view of the hills dotted with rooftops in the distance. Although you might not have come prepared to eat your barbecue with a spoon, don't pass up Jim Bob's Bad-Ass Stew, a tasty combination of sausage, pork, and cabbage in a deeply developed broth with a spicy kick. The excellent chopped-beef sandwich on a standard white hamburger bun is packed with wet, saucy beef, much of which plops onto your plate after the first bite. The smoky brisket and turkey are decent, not too dry, but best teamed up with barbecue sauce. Breakfast tacos also have a serious following here.

You may be curious, just as we were, about Jim Bob's "Purple Pig," but we regret to admit that the name is much more exciting than the wrap itself, whose tough, dry chunks of pork topped with raw purple cabbage just isn't appetizing. A thin, tangy mustard sauce could improve the Purple Pig by livening up the pork, but there isn't enough of it, and the surrounding unheated tortilla is below average. Avoid the Purple Pig, though, and Jim Bob's is worth the trip. As we overheard one satisfied patron putting it at our last visit: "This is definitely worth your money, pops." –AC

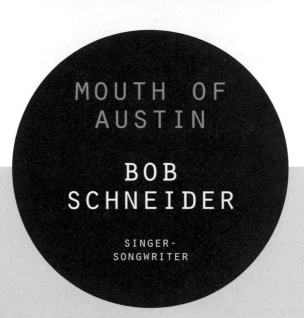

MOUTH OF AUSTIN

BOB SCHNEIDER

SINGER-
SONGWRITER

My favorite and most oft-visited eating locale in Austin is Jim Bob's BBQ. They serve, without a doubt, the finest breakfast tacos in the country. They are huge and freshly made every morning with fresh ingredients. Everything is made fresh, including the salsa, which is what really sets these babies apart from the rest. My recommendation: the egg and bacon. –BS

[MUSICIANS

COME STRAIGHT

TO THE

POINT]

Jo's Hot Coffee

Remember when "coffeeshop" meant
something other than "laptop outlets"?

food

6.8 / 10   **9.4** / 10

experience

Light American, Sweets   **$ 8**   *S. Congress, Warehouse District*

Café
Mon. 7am-6pm; Tues.-Wed. 7am-
9pm; Thurs.-Sat. 7am-10pm; Sun.
7am-9pm. *Breakfast. Date-friendly.*
Live music. Outdoor dining. Vegetarian-friendly. Wireless Internet.

1300 S. Congress Ave.
Austin
(512) 444-3800
www.joscoffee.com

242 W. 2nd St.
78701, (512) 469-9003

Bar Beer/wine
Credit Cards Visa and MC
Reservations Not accepted

The original Jo's is a true South Congress icon—a welcome rest stop for everyone from foot-sore shoppers to old-school hipsters to big-wig out-of-towners staying at the adjacent Hotel San José. Everybody who's anybody in Austin—and everybody who's nobody too—has stood in line for a cup of coffee at Jo's.

Aside from the small hut that sells a range of drinks, sandwiches, and baked goods, it is an entirely open-air establishment, roughly framed by a wooden-roofed porch and counter. It would be wrong to say that Jo's has the feel of a European sidewalk café; this is a deeply Austin joint, from the rusty metal chairs and tables to the sunset views of downtown right to the Capitol. But Jo's does perform many of the same roles as its Euro-equivalent. For instance, tables are covered more in newspapers than laptops, adding a cosmopolitan feel to the good company, the cars zooming by, and the bands that sometimes play in the parking lot.

Sandwiches have fresh and decent ingredients, but they're not made to order. A tuna salad sandwich is a little dry and lacks zing, while a hot pepper beef version is too fatty and skimpily filled. The more classic roast beef, with horseradish aïoli, is much tastier, however; and don't miss the sensational chocolate-chip cookies and "fried pies" stuffed with cheese—some of the finest sweet snacks in the city.

The notice board is a clearinghouse for all kinds of Austin events, large and small—a reminder that Jo's has developed something of that ineffable neighborhood importance that, in a former era, belonged to the local newsstand. It is perhaps for this reason, above all, that there has been some grumbling amongst purists that the new downtown outpost of Jo's—amidst the new stretch of yuppie boutiques on Second Street—is sacrilege. The new branch, done up in a postindustrial minimalist style, adds indoor seating, a more substantial food menu including burgers, and shorter queues. The horror! The horror! –RM/RG

Jorge's Tacos Garcia

Funky atmosphere and cheap
margaritas—you'll forget it's a chain

food

4.8 / 10   **6.5** / 10

experience

Mexican

$**24**   *North Central*

Casual restaurant
Mon.-Tues. 11am-9pm; Wed.-
Thurs. and Sat. 11am-10pm;
Fri. 11am-11pm; closed Sun.
Outdoor dining.

2203 Hancock Dr.
Austin
(512) 454-1980
www.jorgesaustin.com

Bar Full
Credit Cards Visa, MC, AmEx
Reservations Accepted

Jorge's is one of a loose-knit family of restaurants that stretches across the Panhandle and Permian Basin, from Amarillo to Midland-Odessa all the way down to Austin. The house Jorge's occupies is brightly painted with a nice patio, and lots of plants. The décor is more than eclectic, with aquariums built into the walls, kitschy folk art, beaded curtains, and sequined chandeliers. A verdant patio and inexpensive margaritas make Jorge's a happy-hour hot spot, with the only nearby competition coming from Fonda San Miguel, where margaritas and appetizers are far from cheap. Service at Jorge's can be slow, making this a better place for a casual drink than a lunch-hour bite.

The menu offers basic Tex-Mex à la carte and an array of combo plates. The food itself is far from spectacular, but there are a few good picks here. Most unimpressive in our minds are the so-stale-you-might-lose-a-tooth chalupas and the clichéd plasticky queso. Why go out when you can make this so much better at home? Also, the guacamole lacks both lime and salt—absolute necessities—and has a distinctly pre-packed flavor.

Chicken flautas are better, wrapped in chewy, toasted corn tortillas, though they are served in a thin, yet chunky red sauce that merits no further discussion. The cheese enchiladas are made with a heavy dose of grease, but the accompanying rice is well seasoned and the refried beans taste fresh. Beef tacos are more interesting: the meat is tomatoey, simply seasoned, and not too spicy, and served in handmade shells that are delicious and roasty, offset with fresh shredded lettuce and tomatoes; they taste homemade. We also like the tamales, which are made with lots of shredded pork and a spicy white corn masa—just the kind of thing you'd want for the holidays. –MPN

Jovita's

A South Austin live music joint full of
quirky character—but not good food

food

2.0 **7.4**

10   10

experience

Mexican   **$15**   *Bouldin Creek Area*

Casual restaurant
Tues. 11am-10:30pm, Wed.-
Thurs. 11am-10pm, Fri.-Sat.
11am-11:30pm, Sun. 11am-9pm;
closed Mon. Kitchen closes at 9pm. *Live music.*

1617 S. 1st St.
Austin
(512) 447-7825

Bar Full
Credit Cards Visa, MC, AmEx
Reservations Not accepted

It was a tough decision whether or not to include Jovita's in *The
Fearless Critic.* Clearly, the place is not really about the food. What it is
about is the endlessly amusing, kitschified live music that happens in
the back room, which comes complete with a stage; think Don Walser,
Ponty Bone, and Cornell Hurd. It's a lot of fun to hang out in the back
room, sip a good Mexican beer, and immerse yourself in just the sort of
illustriously edgy environment that makes Austin deserve the title of
Live Music Capital of the World.

But "Mexican Restaurant and Cantina" *is* painted on the outside of
the building, and there *is* plenty of mediocre Tex-Mex on offer. The
place is right along a hip stretch of South First, in the middle of the
South Austin scene, and inexplicably, there are even people who come
in just for lunch or dinner, ordering the Mexican combo plates to wash
down their margaritas.

We pity those fools, because everything we've tried here has been
terrible. Dry, stringy chicken ages inside even worse corn tortillas with
the consistency of cardboard and crackly, tasteless sauce. Possibly the
only items less appealing than the bland, improperly prepared Tex-Mex
dishes are the soapy-sweet margaritas, which, to us, are
indistinguishable from glasses of pure sour mix on the rocks. The dining
room (separate from the back room where the live music happens) is
plain, save for wall art that features revolutionaries. After tasting this
food, you might want to stage a kitchen coup of your own. –RG

Juan in a Million

Lots of character, but we're picky about our migas

food
6.0 **8.9**
10   10
experience

Mexican   **$17**   *East Austin*

Casual restaurant
Sun.-Wed. 7am-3pm;
Thurs.-Sat. 7am-8pm.
Breakfast. Brunch.

2300 E. Cesar Chavez St.
Austin
(512) 472-3872
www.juaninamillion.com

Bar Full
Credit Cards Visa, MC, AmEx
Reservations Not accepted

On a strip of Cesar Chavez Street in East Austin that is famously lined with row after row of Mexican restaurants, this is Juan in a Million—at least as far as the local press is concerned. For much of its two-decades-plus lifespan, the joint has been showered with accolades and flooded with patrons. Above all, they come for the migas, the breakfast tacos, and other breakfast specialties. So does it live up to the hype?

Yes and no. To call Juan in a Million disappointing would be a stretch, but we will say that there are dozens of other Austin places with better migas. Here, the chile flavor is good, but the scrambled eggs themselves can come dry and underseasoned. Not so for the delicious refried beans, with a wonderfully unexpected smokiness, or for the soft little cubes of fried potato, whose savory balance is nearly perfect.

The most impressive achievement of all, though, is the sensational chile con queso. Thinner than many versions, it's also far more flavorful, with an explosive and salty blend of cheese and pepper flavors. As is so often the case with chile con queso, it's also superlative as a sauce—moistening the migas, say, or adding another dimension to the already formidable breakfast tacos of machacado con huevo (a version of machaca, the dried shredded beef that is the most popular burrito filling in northern Mexico).

The unassuming atmosphere—white walls, daily lunch specials scrawled on a sign, a gentle but constant bustle—is part of Juan in a Million's charm. So is the legendary personality of Juan himself, who greets virtually every customer that enters his restaurant. It's unlikely that you'll forget Juan. But you'd better do something memorable yourself if you hope to be anything but another of his million admirers.
–RG

Judges' Hill Restaurant

Whose idea of an anniversary date
is *this?*

food
6.0 / 10   **5.5** / 10
experience

New American $ **65**   *West Campus*

Upmarket restaurant
Mon.-Fri. 6:30am-10am, 5:30pm-
10pm; Sat. 7am-10am, 5:30pm-
10pm, Sun. 7am-10am, 11am-
2pm, 5:30pm-10pm. *Breakfast. Brunch.*

1900 Rio Grande St.
Austin
(800) 311-1619
www.judgeshill.com

Bar Full
Credit Cards Visa, MC, AmEx
Reservations Recommended

The drapery's red and aloof.
  The chandeliers glitter with foof.
You can't help but think, as you order your drink,
  Is this some sort of State Dinner spoof?

The servers are far from the rudest;
  But their knowledge is not the astutest.
And no one who dines while they're dressed to the nines
  Wants a silence that's practically Buddhist.

The menu is big and deluxe.
  You start with foie gras, liking ducks.
Its Bing cherries are spry, but its brioche is dry—
  Not bad, but not worth 15 bucks.

Your quail's a horseradishey loss.
  Your tuna's too orange with sauce.
Your scallops are chewy, your gnocchi are gooey—
  Just who, in the kitchen, is boss?

The big, stuffy room is defeating
  The one other table that's eating.
They're resigned to their fate: a dystopian date,
  Where the man is reluctantly treating.

You proclaim, while digesting the thrill
  Of the staggering size of your bill:
"Only if I smoked crack would I ever come back
  To the Mansion at Judges' Hill."

–RG

Julio's

Go a little James Brown eating the
chicken tacos at this warm taquería

food
7.1
10

7.5
10
experience

Mexican $**19**   *Hyde Park*

Casual restaurant   4230 Duval St.   ***Bar*** Beer/wine
Daily 8:30am-9pm. *Breakfast.*   Austin   ***Credit Cards*** No credit cards
Live music. Outdoor dining.   (512) 452-1040   ***Reservations*** Not accepted

Julio's rounds out the little community of restaurants in Hyde Park by
providing a satisfying Mexican option, and it's nice to see it hold its
own amongst such Austin big-shots as the Hyde Park Bar and Grill,
Mother's, and Asti.

More than any of these places, it has the feel of a spot the locals
might come to every day. There is pleasant, myrtle-shaded outdoor
seating, and the interior is quiet and surprisingly classy for a little
taquería, with stained-wood booths and chairs, and powder-blue walls.
This smooth surface is reassuringly ruffled by loyal through traffic, and a
late-afternoon visit will find a dining room littered with the lingering
leftovers of a lunchtime's worth of local habits: newspapers lie
scattered, and dishes pile up on some tables (service is friendly but a
little lax).

Julio's claim to its limited fame is its roast chicken. They rotisserie-grill
whole flocks of fowl behind the counter, and serve the results in tacos,
enchiladas, and salads, as well as in the standard quarter-, half-, or
whole-bird portions. These have crisp, fiery skins, but the inside meat
can be disappointingly dry. We like the tangy enchiladas verdes with
chicken and cheese, and the spicy fajita tacos, but the imperative order
here is Julio's famous chicken taco. The key to its success is that the
kitchen melts the cheddar cheese onto the tortilla before piling on the
pollo, so that the gooey, cheesy flavor combines with the chicken fat
into a buttery delight. With garden-fresh salsa and perky lettuce,
cabbage, and tomato on top, and the juices from the roast meat, salsa,
and cheese blending into a velvety broth, a hot Julio's chicken taco can
be a surprisingly nostalgic culinary experience. It is oddly reminiscent of
a cross between rich chicken soup and cheesy pizza—two of the
ultimate feel-good foods. –RM

Katz's

Jolly waiters dish the goods all night
long at this Austin deli institution

food
6.7 | **8.6**
10 | 10
experience

Light American, Jewish Deli   **$23**   *Warehouse District*

Casual restaurant
Daily 24 hrs. Breakfast. Brunch.
Kid-friendly. Wireless Internet.

618 W. 6th St.
Austin
(512) 472-2037
www.ilovekatzs.com

Bar Full
Credit Cards Visa, MC, AmEx
Reservations Not accepted

"We can't help it...we gotta tell ya," Katz's sure is korny. Marc Katz,
who learned the kosher deli business on his father's knee in Queens,
has been lording over the memorabilia-plastered dining room of his
Sixth Street establishment (and over much of the rest of this town),
bald head shining, grin flashing, 24 hours a day since 1979. All the
while he's been helplessly telling kustomers all about it, with his brassy
ads, his bright yellow kaddy (license plate 24 HRS), and even his
mayoral kampaign.

So what's all the talk about? Katz's serves up some pretty tasty
kosher-*style* deli food (but this is *not* a cheeseburger-free zone). Skip
the underwhelming bagel with cream cheese and lox, but the Reuben
sandwich is thick, buttery, and juicy, piled high with peppery pastrami
and/or corned beef. House-made pickles are tart and crisp, while potato
pancakes are sweet and crunchy, served with a diminutive dot of
applesauce. Breakfast anytime includes some lovely challah French toast
that has achieved that chimera of restaurant French toast—the still-soft-
and-gooey center—and creamy scrambled eggs.

Katz's, of course, never kloses, and its Sixth Street location can invite
a pretty mixed crowd in the wee hours. Good thing the night shift
always sees plenty of cops chowing down, as well as cabbies,
musicians, college kids, and even Austin's blues king Clifford Antone.
All of them are apparently willing to dish out excessive amounts of cash
($10.99 for a veggie omelette!?) for some yummy, but in the end fairly
standard, deli fare.

However, we gotta hand it to Katz—he certainly knows how to
market. And we have to applaud a guy for having the chutzpah to
open a Jewish deli in Austin, Texas, in 1979. There is something deeply
enjoyable about seeing all those Texans eating pastrami on rye. –RM

Kebab Palace

An unpretentious dive that's just like home—if home is Skopje, Macedonia

food

7.0 / 10   4.3 / 10

experience

Macedonian   **$11**   *Far North*

Casual restaurant
Mon.-Sat. 8am-10pm;
closed Sun. *Breakfast.*

1314 Rutland Dr.
Austin
(512) 836-8668

Bar BYO
Credit Cards Visa, MC, AmEx
Reservations Not accepted

Despite the insipid name, Kebab Palace is a unique entity: it is Austin's only purveyor of Macedonian food. The restaurant bills itself as a "fancy hole in the wall"—well, it's a hole, anyway. The bare room is decorated only with some postcards from Macedonia and a fuzzy television continually playing Fox reruns. Mix-'n'-match, fruit-patterned dishes and the predominantly Slavic accents of staff and clientele add to one's sense of being at one's Eastern-European granny's house for dinner.

The food matches this atmosphere. Many places brag of home cooking—advertise that their food is "just like mama used to make it"—but food that actually tastes homemade is a rarity in the restaurant world. Kebab Palace hits the proverbial household nail squarely on its head. This is definitely comfort food, plain and simple—moussaka, stuffed peppers, goulash. The latter is a thick, oniony stew of tender beef, with winey back-notes and plenty of mushrooms, and it is excellent. Sarma, a Macedonian variation on the dolma, features cabbage leaves stuffed with seasoned ground beef and cooked in a tomatoey broth. The little packages are a trifle too salty, but full of flavor. And to the gentlemen of the house, Kebab Palace offers the "Hungry Man's Special" ("no offense, ladies, for the 'hungry man's' remark, but I make the menu")—a generous helping of spicy kafta kebab sausages, served with onions and french-fries. Now that'll put some hair on your chest. The house "pita"—a fluffy round of bread that is very pleasant but is in fact, to borrow from the great Douglas Adams, a substance almost, but not entirely, unlike pita—accompanies mains.

Service, as befits the homely surroundings, is chatty and relaxed—as the menu proudly boasts, Kebab Palace is a spot where "everything is homemade, and almost everybody knows your name." –RM

Ken's Donuts

For 20 years, this little shop has run
rings around the competition

7.5
10
experience

Sweets   *West Campus*

Take-out	2820 Guadalupe St.	*Bar* None
Daily 24 hrs. *Breakfast. Kid-friendly.*	Austin	*Credit Cards* No credit cards
Live music. Wireless Internet.	(512) 320-8484	*Reservations* Not accepted

We include Ken's in our book, well, because, dammit, we can, and
because this upstanding establishment so wonderfully, achingly conveys
the Austin of old, the stoned-out, weirdo, carelessly friendly slackerville
that it was, that we just can't leave it behind. Plus, they make some
serious donuts.

Ken's sits in a cluster of old-Austin stalwarts at the north end of the
Drag (ahh, Toy Joy, Vulcan Video, Taco Shack—what joys). It is a plain,
enticingly fragrant bakery, heralded by a dark green awning. Inside, the
only adornment is a large, indecipherable mural that covers one wall
(perhaps, under the appropriate chemical influence, it comes magically
together), unless you count the body art of the employees. Of these,
there is usually only one in sight, generally a lonely, lanky young man
with spacey eyes and a good-natured grin.

If you like this type of donut, these remain unbeatable. Though
Krispy Kreme has wound its popular way down south, we find that
their little candy-like rings live up to the hype only when they are truly
hot off the presses—otherwise, they're too sweet. Ken's takes a purer
approach: its plain-glazed donuts are large, gooey, yeasty pleasures—
the challah of donuts, if you will—and only ever-so-lightly frosted. A
dozen are a steal at just four dollars. Even better, get a dozen mix-'n'-
match donut holes for just a buck (a little secret: the staffer behind the
counter will usually just grab a bunch and stuff 'em in the bag—we've
made off with a glorious 24 on one occasion). There are also
unconfirmed rumors that free donuts are, or once were, doled out to
young ladies who flash the donut boys. We chose not to test this rumor
ourselves (the "fearless critic" moniker has its limits).

Other greats include the rich, not-too-sweet glazed chocolate-cake
donuts, and the old-fashioned sour-cream-cake variety. But in the end,
we're purists—go for the good old plain glazed, tip generously, and
wind your way down the Drag munching the chewy, golden goodness.
–RM

Kenichi

Hip doesn't have to be pretentious in
Austin—but it is at this sushi bar

food

7.4 **7.5**
10   10

experience

Japanese   **$83**   *Warehouse District*

Upmarket restaurant   419 Colorado St.   *Bar* Full
Sun.-Thurs. 4:30pm-10pm;   Austin   *Credit Cards* Visa, MC, AmEx
Fri.-Sat. 4:30pm-11pm.   (512) 320-8883   *Reservations* Recommended
Date-friendly.   www.kenichiaustin.com

With its zigzagging sake bar, 80-dollar Kobe steaks, and spectacularly
attractive staff and clientele, this downtown Japanese fusion joint might
well be Austin's pinnacle of pomposity. Kenichi has clearly taken the
"warehouse district" moniker seriously, with a post-postmodern ceiling
that billows with what looks like exposed insulation nestled between
the bare beams, stories above. The sushi bar is a lively solo-dining scene
and a fun place to flirt over 15-dollar glasses of sake and delicate bites
of sashimi, especially if you can handle the trendier-than-thou
yuppiness, and especially if your company has just gone public.

It's not even close to worth the money—if you're counting—but
that's not to say that Kenichi is *all* style over substance. We have had
several truly formidable pieces of raw fish here. At our last visit, we
liked a gentle halibut ceviche, bathed in coconut milk and served with
plenty of cilantro in a martini glass. Perhaps we would have been
happier if the price had been closer to $10 than $20 (details, details).
Good amongst mains is the five-spice seared sika deer sirloin, with a
pretty little squash purée and deliciously subtle "prickly pear jus."
When they say "seared," they mean it—ask for it rare, and you're
basically eating raw venison, not even warmed through; in a rare
departure from our norm, we prefer this one at least medium-rare.

We also enjoy tender strips of Kobe beef that you cook yourself on a
rock. Chicken teriyaki is sweet and bold, but not nearly worth the
money. Amongst sushi options, we've been deeply impressed by
swordfish sashimi and consistently excellent yellowtail and salmon.
We've tried uni (sea urchin) on two occasions, and once it was
amazing, the other time middling. Toro, at our last visit, was an oily,
fishy waste of $18 for two pieces. One distinguishing feature of Kenichi
is its delightful willingness to serve dinner later than most places
around, especially on Sundays. But at normal hours of the evening,
there are other places we'd choose before Kenichi for *our* high-priced
sushi therapy. —RG

Kerbey Lane Café

Breakfast (and Tex-Mex) all night, pajamas optional

food
6.2 / 10 **9.0** / 10
experience

American $**19**   *Seton Med., W. Campus, S. Lamar*

Casual restaurant
Daily 24 hrs. Breakfast. Brunch.
Kid-friendly. Outdoor dining.
Vegetarian-friendly.

3704 Kerbey Ln.
Austin
(512) 451-1436
www.kerbeylanecafe.com

Bar Full
Credit Cards Visa, MC, AmEx
Reservations Accepted

2606 Guadalupe St.
78705, (512) 477-5717

2700 S. Lamar Blvd.
78704, (512) 445-4451

Kerbey Lane Café has long been a favorite with Austin's sizeable night-owl contingent, students included. With several locations, all open 24 hours, they've been serving reasonably priced Tex-Mex, sandwiches, vegetarian food, and most notably breakfast, since 1980, rivaling Magnolia Café in the all-night arena. (It's like the Horns and the Aggies: everyone must prefer one or the other, but not both.)

The atmosphere and attitude are very Austin—artsy and laid back, art for sale on the walls, flyers and local rags available to read in the waiting area. The original branch, actually on Kerbey Lane, is the most atmospheric, set in a cute little house. The South Lamar branch, with its bland booths, feels more like a Denny's. Still, there's a latent romance to these places; on one 2am meal at Kerbey Lane, the couple next to us had come to celebrate their engagement—one hour earlier.

There are the pan-veggie-fusion tacos that you would expect at such an Austin place. One taco, for instance, combines moist, lemony tabbouleh; tasty hummus; and sunflower sprouts. The tortilla, of course, is whole wheat, and the result is warm, fresh, and really pretty good. Other winners include the legendary queso, which is unusually white-colored with remarkable depth of flavor, and the Cobb salad, elevated to tastiness by juicily marinated grilled chicken. Unfortunately, as is so often the case at hippieish joints, more traditional Mex fares worse. Carne asada, for example, has meat flecked with cracked pepper, but it's still tasteless—and so tough it's practically inedible.

But most people come for breakfast. Buttery migas are fine, but the grilled breakfast sausage, though spicy, can be overly salty. The short stack of gingerbread pancakes is enormous. Sadly, they come a bit dry, although they have good flavor. Skip the cakes, such as carrot cake, which can sit out air-drying. The servers are friendly, and sometimes even a colorful part of the experience (the dress code seems to require showing your tattoos). –MPN

Kismet Café

A pleasing little Middle Eastern spot in
the heart of campus

food
6.9 **4.8**
10   10
experience

Middle Eastern	$ **9**	*West Campus*

Counter service	411 W. 24th St.	*Bar* None
Mon.-Sat. 10am-9pm; Sun.	Austin	*Credit Cards* Visa, MC, AmEx
11am-8pm. *Outdoor dining.*	(512) 236-1811	*Reservations* Not accepted

"Kismet" means "destiny" in Arabic, Turkish, and English, and while
that is a rather grand name for this Middle Eastern restaurant off the
Drag, the little place does seem intended for its particular location,
where it has been stuffing students for some years now. It has the feel
of the many kebab shops that clutter Europe's cities. Despite the plastic
dinnerware, Kismet plays its role with some aplomb, and the interior
space, with its bright murals and high ceilings, is airier and more
elegant than the initial small, shabby counter promises. Customers are
also greeted with a smile—and, sometimes, familiar chit-chat—by the
friendly owners.

The food is exactly what one would expect from an informal Middle
Eastern joint, and is very enjoyable. We particularly like the vegetarian
sampler platter, with soft-stewed eggplant and zucchini with sweet
tomato notes; bright tabbouleh; light, lemony hummus; a tender,
savory stuffed grape leaf; and deep-fried cauliflower that looks brown
and horrid but tastes divine. Nothing is particularly fancy or innovative,
but it's all yummy, and pleasantly comforting. Best of all, every order
comes with the Phoenicia Bakery's glorious pita bread, which Kismet
has the good sense to import (along with the somewhat tough baklava,
a less glorious shipment). Other highlights include the smoky, powerful
baba ganoush (eggplant dip) and Kismet's crunchy falafel, its golden
interior flecked with flavorful herbs. We prefer the plates to the wraps,
which, despite the presence of that pita bread, tend to be dry and
include iceberg lettuce rather than the lovely salads and dips.

Kismet does excellent business during term—if we were students,
we'd have lunch here all the time. Its appropriate, relaxed vibe
welcomes the young, flannel-shirt and backpack crowd. So go on in,
Luke, it is your kismet. –RM

The Kitchen Door

The meatloaf sandwich, taken to the next level

food

6.9 / 10   4.2 / 10
experience

Light American $ **9**   *Tarrytown, Northwest Hills*

Counter service
Mon.-Fri. 8am-7pm; Sat. 8am-
6pm; closed Sun. *Breakfast.*
Delivery. Outdoor dining.

2504 Lake Austin Blvd.
Austin
(512) 236-9200
www.thekitchendoor.us

3742 Far West Blvd.
78731, (512) 794-1100

Bar None
Credit Cards Visa, MC, AmEx
Reservations Not accepted

The single reason to come to the Kitchen Door is to order their marvelous meatloaf sandwich. Be forewarned: this is a serious eating endeavor. To borrow from the friendly folks at Lipton, this ain't no sippin' sandwich. So either wear those old baggy jogging pants, or bring the family for backup. When you arrive, don't let the posters advertising the chicken salad sandwich distract you—it's really just a decoy to lure you into culinary mediocrity. Neither should you let your gaze wander to the oddly outdated and slightly crusty items on display behind the deli counter (who knows how long those plastic-wrapped deviled eggs have been sitting there?)—you'll only get discouraged. Trust us: get the meatloaf.

Every element of this sandwich is made from scratch. The Kitchen Door is a bakery as well as a sandwich shop, and all of the bread is homemade. Get your sandwich on the whole-grain bread, which is sweet, dense, and chewy. When you order, a genial fellow behind the counter will slice off a mammoth piece of beefy meatloaf, nicely seasoned, and slap it on the griddle along with a generous helping of onions. These then crisp and sweeten in front of your eyes and your tantalized nose; after a few minutes, upon request, he'll add a slice of the cheese of your choice to bubble over the meat. When the whole lot is finished, piled onto thick wedges of bread, and slathered with a kind of three-mustard blend, your sandwich will probably weigh in at close to a pound, and be an irresistibly gooey, oozy, sweet and savory delight.

Take it to go. Wrapped in aluminum foil, its flavors blend nicely in the heat of its steam, and the Kitchen Door has no décor to speak of, aside from a spectacular collection of useless kitchen gadgets for sale. –RM

Korea Garden

Funky Asian fusion that flip-flops
between the raw and the overcooked

food

6.7 / 10   **7.2** / 10

experience

Korean, Japanese $**33**   *North Central*

Casual restaurant   6519 N. Lamar Blvd.   *Bar* Beer/wine
Daily 11am-10pm.   Austin   *Credit Cards* Visa, MC, AmEx
Date-friendly.   (512) 302-3149   *Reservations* Accepted

Korea Garden forms an attractive proposition: an extensive sushi menu, traditional grill-at-the-table Korean barbecue, and a funky, Asian-minimalist interior. Who would we be not to get excited about that, not to swallow our doubts about pan-Asian food and dive in with our hopes held high?

And in many ways Korea Garden satisfies these hopes. The service is supremely polite and attentive, the atmosphere is pleasant, and the seemingly authentic low-lying tables surrounded by pillows have hidden dugouts beneath them so that even long-limbed fellows who have forgotten how to cross their legs can comfortably join the trendily bendy.

The food, too, is quite satisfying. Sushi is Korea Garden's greatest strength—it is attractive, buttery, and fresh, elegantly prepared at a bar that spans the non-barbecue half of the restaurant. There is a long list of specialty options, but we strongly recommend you keep things basic. Yellowtail nigiri (sushi pieces) are lovely and supple, and easily outclass nouvelle preparations involving ingredients like mango.

On the barbecue end of things, we are less satisfied. It is hard to go wrong with soy-marinated meat freshly grilled and served with a variety of pickles, and Korean barbecue is inevitably tasty. But in some ways the process here falls well short of the ideal. Instead of grills with open flames at the tables, which bring crucial smoke and searing heat to the meat, Korea Garden has griddles, which lack essential oomph. Pork, beef, tongue, and chicken cook up drier and with less caramelization than we've found elsewhere, and the marinade also lacks punch. And while the accompanying dips and pickles are tasty, they are rather stingily distributed.

Still, to a large group of friends alternately singeing their fingers at the grill and retreating to the comfort of the raw, Korea Garden can present an uproarious night out. –RM

Korea House

Cheap, tasty Korean food and bad
sushi, all served with a scowl

Korean, Japanese $**31**   *North Central*

Casual restaurant   2700 W. Anderson Ln.   *Bar* Beer/wine
Mon.-Thurs. 11am-10pm; Fri.   Austin   *Credit Cards* Visa, MC, AmEx
11am-11pm; Sat. noon-11pm;   (512) 458-2477   *Reservations* Accepted
Sun. noon-10pm.

Korea House's popularity has really taken off in the last decade along
with the tech boom in Austin. This once-quiet restaurant, tucked away
in the back of a rather pleasant shopping center with its own man-
made stream and koi pond, is a real hot spot for the high-tech lunch
bunch. The main draws are the cheap, fast lunch specials, and the sushi
bar that was added later in the restaurant's life, perhaps to try and milk
the computer nerds for all they're worth.

The strain of all this business is starting to show. The waitstaff tends
to be harried, curt, and occasionally even bordering on nasty. On a
recent visit, the front dining area and sushi bar were like a scene out of
Sartre—there were flies everywhere, with diners flapping their arms so
violently, it looked like the entire restaurant was in the throes of a
seizure. Come before 11:30am or after 1:30pm on weekdays, or be
prepared to wait along with everyone else and their cube-mates.

The Korean food is good—with every order you receive the
traditional noodle soup in clear broth with several bowls of condiments
and sides, such as boiled yam, spicy vinegared cucumbers, and kimchi.
Each dish also comes with a choice of rice, and an appetizer, such as
the boring, cabbage-beleaguered yaki mandoo. We particularly like the
pork bulgogi, with their sweet, hot sauce, that you somehow keep
munching in the vain attempt to quell the heat. At dinnertime, Korea
House offers a wider range, such as the fun traditional Korean
barbecue, grilled tabletop.

If you are a sushi connoisseur, don't eat here. The sushi lunch specials
are certainly inexpensive, but there's a reason for that. The sushi is
served much too cold, and the fish isn't fresh. Have we made ourselves
clear? –MPN

Koreana

Pricey, decorative Asian food whose
quality is mainly skin deep

food
4.4 | 6.8
10 | 10
experience

Korean, Japanese $**31**   *Far North*

Upmarket restaurant   12196 N. MoPac Expwy.   *Bar* Beer/wine
Mon.-Fri. 11am-2pm, 5pm-10pm;   Austin   *Credit Cards* Visa, MC, AmEx
Sat.-Sun. 5pm-10pm.   (512) 835-8888   *Reservations* Accepted
                             www.koreana.citysearch.com

Koreana has been widely praised both for its sushi and for its upscale
pan-Asian cooking. The restaurant is located in an unpromising site off
the Mopac access road way north at Parmer Lane, but the room that
opens up upon arrival has a surprisingly spacious opulence. The doors
closing behind you shut out any memory of the roar of the traffic
outside.

After a few moments, however, the effect wears a little thin. The
dining room is the kind of space that might be called "elegantly
appointed," its walls and furniture "burnished," but it takes part in all
the sham pretensions tied up in such decorator-speak. From the faux-
finished copper walls and chairs, to the soft-jazz soundtrack, to the
parsley that garnishes the desserts, the details at Koreana seem to fall a
little flat.

And these deflated pretensions extend to the food, which looks, like
the room, exceedingly elegant at first glance. Pepper-crusted, seared
tuna in a white wine cream sauce is slightly chewy and somehow
unsatisfying, the sauce pairing oddly with the heat of the pepper and
obscuring any natural sweetness in the raw fish. Worse still, the shrimp
that rests ornamentally on the edge of the avocado kama has arrived
with a strange, metallic tang, and the avocado's seafood stuffing is
bland at best. All across the menu, the details have been flubbed. Sushi
seems vaguely refrigerated, and though the fish is tender and fresh, the
rice can come overcooked to the point of mushiness. A broiled red
snapper in Thai chili sauce is pleasant, but was a little overdone at our
last visit, and the sauce is syrupy and overpowering. In the bi bim bap,
the egg—a crucial, unifying ingredient—is hard boiled, obliterating all
of its binding properties.

Yes, the plates are pretty, the service gracious, but that, as the saying
goes, don't feed the bulldog. –RM

Koriente

This new arrival has a natural warmth,
but the food tastes rather reheated

food

6.1	7.2
10	10

experience

Korean $ **9**   *Sixth Street District*

Casual restaurant
Mon.-Sat. 11am-10pm;
closed Sun. *Outdoor dining.*
Wireless Internet.

621 E. 7th St.
Austin
(512) 275-0852
www.koriente.com

Bar None
Credit Cards Visa and MC
Reservations Accepted

This new arrival on East Seventh Street is trying with a sweet and winning energy to draw attention to itself. A parking lot (accessed from Sixth Street) and a colorful bed of flowers make it an unusually user-friendly downtown lunch option, and the friendliness continues inside the little spot. Service is remarkably eager and attentive (on one visit, we were brought water alongside our ordered bubble tea because the server thought it would better complement our sweetish main course), and food arrives scant seconds after it was ordered.

This, however, is the first sign of trouble. Dishes at Koriente are either served cold or in a form that can be rapidly nuked back to life, and both the flavors and the textures suggest such energy-sapping treatment. The signature dish, for example, a kind of Korean-influenced pot roast, is a mush of textures, and all the taste has been zapped out of the carrots and Korean radishes. A pleasant sauce of wine and apple juice is overpowered by the cloying sweetness of Chinese dates. The dish, in fact, raises ghosts of Passovers past, and Aunt Ethel's Jewish (over)cooking.

Another popular and less inventive order is the bulgogi. But here, too, flavors are weaker than elsewhere, and we can't help but miss the added egg that makes bi bim bap such a pleasure at some other restaurants. Is this an ill-inspired concession to Texan tastes? What do they take us for? We prefer the cold dishes, which are well executed. The summer rolls, for example, are crisp and fresh, with the lovely addition of avocado, and wrapped in tender rice paper (so often too chewy elsewhere). Still, the dish leans heavily on its soy dipping sauce for flavor.

But the welcoming attitude and light Asian décor are hard to resist, and you might want to give it a try—if only to sit in their funky, wiggly insect-like chairs with independent suspension. –RM

Kreuz Market

The granddaddy of Texas barbecue, still smoking along

food
9.1
10

9.1
10
experience

Barbecue

$**12**

Lockhart

Counter service
Mon.-Fri. 9am-6pm;
Sat. 9am-6:30pm.
Kid-friendly.

619 N. Colorado St.
Lockhart
(512) 398-2361
www.kreuzmarket.com

Bar Beer/wine
Credit Cards Visa and MC
Reservations Not accepted

It is fair to say that Kreuz Market put Lockhart, Texas on the map as the barbecue capital of the state, if not the world. While there are several barbecue joints in this small town, Kreuz Market (pronounced "krites") has been around since 1900, a more-than-respectable tenure. Like its contemporaries, Kreuz Market originally opened as a grocery, smoking meat to preserve it in the days before refrigeration—that's how the Texas barbecue tradition started.

In 1999, Kreuz Market moved a short distance up the road from its original spot to a huge barn-like structure that could, in a pinch, probably seat the entire town population. Antique scales and cash registers, photos, and signs line the hall where customers wait in line to order. A dozen pits fill the back walls, and heat and smoke envelop you as you walk in. Meats are sold by the pound, cut to order, and, as ever, given to customers on butcher paper.

Drinks and sides are available in a separate room with picnic tables, its walls still lined with old Kreuz memorabilia and hunting trophies. Of the available meats, sausage is the star here, with beautiful smoke and pepper, the loose coarse grind has a fabulous texture, wonderful on saltines with a bit of avocado and a dash of hot sauce. If you feel the need for a side, don't miss the German potato salad, a hearty diversion from the usual creamed style. Kreuz offers no sauce, and never has, allowing the meat to speak for itself. We can see both sides of the sauce-versus-no-sauce debate; regardless, Kreuz offers onion, pickles, jalapeños, and avocados to spruce things up. Brisket can be dry on the end pieces, so specify that you want it cut from the center, and ask for it fatty. These days it can be a crapshoot, but on a lucky day, or at a lucky hour, this brisket is juicy, profoundly seasoned, and utterly spectacular. –MPN

Kyoto

Above-average fish in an improbable
second-floor office-building space

food
7.8
10

6.3
10
experience

Japanese

$**37**

Congress Avenue Area

Upmarket restaurant
Mon.-Thurs. 11:30am-2pm, 6pm-
10:30pm; Fri.-Sat. 11:30am-2pm,
6pm-11pm; closed Sun.

315 Congress Ave.
Austin
(512) 482-9010
www.kyotodowntown.com

Bar Beer/wine
Credit Cards Visa, MC, AmEx
Reservations Accepted

The first thing that will strike you upon entering this second-floor space
in office-building country is the strange, hushed atmosphere. A
deferent, eminently Japanese formality accompanies the process of
being seated, even though the restaurant is casual in many other ways
(paper napkins, catalog furniture, glossy photo-illustrated menus). Still,
there's a certain charm to the place—warm, low, lighting; exposed
brick; and a set of screens dividing the conventional part of the
restaurant from another room of low Japanese tables with floor
seating.

Kyoto may be best known for the bargain-basement sushi happy
hour, which runs 6pm to 6:45pm Monday through Saturday. However,
deals aside, Kyoto is quietly serving some of the better sushi in Austin.
Equally impressive are freshness and consistency; it's virtually impossible
to get a piece of fish here that is anything less than very good. But
there are also superstars, beginning with the ama ebi (sweet shrimp),
whose texture approaches perfection; the kitchen will deep-fry the
delectable shrimp head, where the most flavor of all is hidden, and
serve it to you on a separate plate.

Notable amongst other nigiri sushi are the beautifully cooked unagi
(eel), which has a less overbearing sauce than most; a deliciously
buttery sake toro (fatty salmon); soft and comfortable tuna; a sprightly,
well-textured red snapper; and salmon roe just as it should be, a pile of
fresh and resilient little balloons that pop streams of savory fishiness
into your mouth at the slightest application of pressure. Only toro has
been a disappointment, soft but not the freshest around. Don't
underestimate the non-sushi dishes, either—even the miso soup is top-
notch—but with fish this good, it's hard to resist the temptation to
have it all raw. –RG

La Cocina de Marybel

South American cuisine meets Luby's, with some success

Latin American $15   East Austin

Casual restaurant   1411 E. 7th St.   *Bar* BYO
Mon.-Tues. 7:30am-4pm;   Austin   *Credit Cards* Visa and MC
Wed.-Fri. 7:30am-9:30pm;   (512) 542-9717   *Reservations* Accepted
Sat. 9am-9:30pm; Sun. 9am-5pm. *Breakfast.*

A newcomer to East Austin, La Cocina de Marybel has added itself to the growing list of local restaurants serving Latin American food other than our standard Tex-Mex. This small but bright little spot doesn't have a liquor license (it's BYO), but doesn't seem to be having any trouble drawing a lunch crowd, which may be due to their inexpensive all-you-can-eat lunch buffet. Service is friendly but inexperienced, and the restaurant seems to be understaffed.

The kitchen's claim to be both South American and "international" is a bit of a stretch, and we wish Cocina de Marybel would focus on what they're good at, make like the song, and lose the spaghetti and proverbial meatball; unfortunately, meatloaf and the like comprise much of the menu, and even more of the buffet.

Most of the South American food is Venezuelan, like the authentic arepas—cornmeal disks the size and shape of English muffins, sliced in half and filled with a cheese sauce and queso de mano, a grainy, dry, handmade farmer's cheese. We love even more the cachapas, which remind us of omelettes made with soft, pudding-like polenta, filled with queso de mano, griddled, and then topped with a tart Salvadoran table cream. They are an excellent comfort food. Cocina de Marybel's savory beef-and-potato-filled empanadas are made with a deep-fried corn crust that is dense and crunchy, but strangely served with a side of ranch dressing. Another authentic taste of traditional Venezuelan food is offered by the hearty pabellón—tender, fork-shredded beef and onions served with black beans, rice, and sweet fried plantains.

On the more "international" side of the menu, crunchy coconut-encrusted shrimp makes for a tasty appetizer, served with a thin, gingery sauce that isn't a bad match with the South American dishes. We can't help humming, "tastes like Venezuela, feels like ho-o-ome." –MPN

La Dolce Vita

A fancy gelato-and-cordials stop that
has separation anxiety from Italy

8.1
10
experience

Sweets

Hyde Park

Café
Daily 9am-midnight. *Date-friendly.*
Outdoor dining. Wireless Internet.

4222 Duval St.
Austin
(512) 323-2686

Bar Full
Credit Cards Visa, MC, AmEx
Reservations Not accepted

Austin, like Italy, is an ice cream place: the heat just begs the spooning of cold goodness. Thus, it didn't take long for this relatively recent arrival to Hyde Park central to win the city's attention with dizzying selection of Italian-style gelato, along with baked goods and even some deli sandwiches and such at lunchtime.

But the place is really about dessert and drinks. The style of La Dolce Vita gets you away from the kid-focused atmosphere of other ice cream vendors in town. In the elegant, harlequin-patterned room, you can sit with your scoop and a sweet, boozy upscale coffee concoction and eat your ice cream like a grown-up. There is an enormous and impressive display of liqueurs and after-dinner drinks, including the city's best selection of amaro (the Italian herbal digestif). There's also a selection of cigars—if you want to take it to the next level—and you can enjoy all of this out on the patio.

While American ice cream relies heavily on butterfat to provide that irresistible sweet creaminess, gelato has lower fat and is denser, drawing more from the underlying flavors for its taste. Unfortunately, it can also become a grainy, drippy failure. Some of La Dolce Vita's gelato sits separating sadly in its bin; some, in keeping with the café's name, is too sweet for our tastes; and some flavors are ill-inspired gelato-maker flights of fancy, like peanut butter (better as fattier ice cream) and Coca-Cola (if we wanted frozen Coke, we'd go to 7-Eleven and get a Slurpee!). Tèo takes this place to town. Still, vanilla is light and creamy, chocolate is strong and interesting, espresso is dark and rich, lemon is bright and summery without being mouth-puckeringly tart, and powerful cinnamon combines well with the graininess of the form. Pastries in the window are a mixed bag: though the ricotta tart is dry and mealy and an almond tart too sweet, we like the dense, nutty pistachio tart (ask for it warmed). And don't forget those after-dinner drinks—they're a lost art. –RM/MPN

La Feria

Mediocre Tex-Mex and margaritas in an unattractive restaurant

food
2.7 **2.0**
10   10
experience

Mexican $**22**   *S. Lamar, Lake Travis, Cedar Park*

Casual restaurant
Mon.-Fri. 11am-10pm; Sat. 9am-10pm; Sun. 9am-10pm. *Brunch. Live music. Outdoor dining.*

2010 S. Lamar Blvd.
Austin
(512) 326-8301
www.laferiaaustin.com

Bar Full
Credit Cards Visa, MC, AmEx
Reservations Accepted

2303 RR 620
Lakeway, (512) 263-8888

315 N. Bell Blvd. (Hwy. 183)
Cedar Park, (512) 275-0916

The branch of La Feria on South Lamar is difficult to miss; its spacious parking lot surrounded by palm trees makes it look a bit like a desert oasis at an intersection—plus neon. Inside, it's hardly an oasis, though: red brick walls, tile floors, low ceilings, mismatched oilcloths on the tables, and dim lighting accentuated by a few beer signs make the place feel like nothing so much as an outdated diner. The patio is a small improvement, but overall, La Feria totally lacks personality. Microscopic pictures highlight dishes on their extensive menu, and advertise evening mariachi music and margaritas. Most days and nights, the place is startlingly empty, and at those times, even the patio loses its potential appeal amidst the echo of space and the whiz of South Lamar automobiles. We can't help but wonder how they stay in business.

Lunch specials are cheap and include a vat of iced tea, and service is distant but friendly and fast enough. Unfortunately, brittle chips and thin salsa do not start the meal off right, and matters improve little when the mains arrive. The best thing we've found at La Feria is a plate of tacos al pastor—the pork has a nice chile flavor without being hot, and it's topped with a fresh pico de gallo, though we would prefer the traditional pineapple, onion, and cilantro mixture. But the menu is a minefield. Avoid grilled fish tacos, which are composed solely of muddy-tasting catfish. Flautas are crisp and chicken-filled, served with underseasoned guacamole and sour cream—they would benefit from a sauce. Enchiladas suizas are bland, their chicken filling dry, and the stark whiteness of the dish cries out for a sprinkle of chopped cilantro—or something. Anything.

La Feria is open all day, and cheap margaritas may make this a worthwhile happy-hour stop, if you happen to be driving by. But if you end up here for any other reason, the joke's on you. And it's a bad joke. –MPN

La Mexicana Bakery

A tiny tienda and taquería offering
cheap sweets in the wee hours

food
6.1 / 10   **3.8** / 10
experience

Mexican $ **6** *Bouldin Creek Area*

Counter service
Daily 24 hrs. *Breakfast.*
Live music.

1924 S. 1st St.
Austin
(512) 443-6369

Bar None
Credit Cards Visa and MC
Reservations Not accepted

The longtime South First Street favorite with the glaring neon sign, La
Mexicana Bakery is a popular stop for Hispanic émigrés with growling
stomachs or insatiable sweet teeth. It's packed on weekends and even
hoppin' on weekday mornings; the plentiful bakery selections and taco
offerings are cheap and keep the crowds clamoring for more. Lengthy
kitchen hours are alluring as well—La Mexicana is open 24 hours.

Service is quick and amiable, but be ready to order in Spanish, or
point and grunt—don't worry, they'll understand you. With tacos
ranging from one to two dollars apiece, it's hard to go wrong—but you
can, so watch out. The barbacoa is dreamily moist and flavorful without
being overly fatty; it's glorious with a squeeze of lime and some onions
and cilantro. Equally good are the deeply flavored, carefully charred
carnitas. Both work well in tacos or tortas. Much less convincing are
carne guisada, with underseasoned gravy overwhelmed by tomato, and
tacos al pastor, which are oily, salty, and chewy. Beware of the huevo
con chorizo; we've actually discovered melted plastic (overlooked
chorizo casings?) within that mix. Tortas (Mexican-style sandwiches) are
generally well prepared, the bread home-baked and properly toasted,
the lettuce, tomato, and mayo well balanced. We enthusiastically
recommend the salsa verde, but the smoky, delicious roja is for fire-
eaters only—it will leave your mouth tingling for a half hour.

There's a definite south-of-the-border atmosphere at La Mexicana;
Spanish is the language of choice, and a detailed wall mural depicts a
baker, a burro, and a beauty gleefully toting the Mexican flag. There are
a large number of posters of Latin American soccer teams, portraits of
the Virgin of Guadalupe, and family photos. There's also an in-house
florist and a small grocery selling Mexican pantry staples such as
piloncillo, Jumex juices, and masa. And if you need to wire money to
Latin America while awaiting your huevos rancheros, this is your place.
—MPN

La Michoacana

A transportative Mexican grocery
offering cheap eats at a basic counter

East Austin, Far South

Specialty grocery
Daily 7am-9:30pm.
Breakfast.

1947 E. 7th St.
Austin
(512) 473-8487

512 W. Stassney Ln.
78745, (512) 916-9938

Bar None
Credit Cards Visa, MC, AmEx
Reservations Not accepted

Austin's two La Michoacana groceries cater mainly to Latin American immigrants, offering dry good staples from Mexico and Central America, cheap prices on meat and produce, as well as in-house taquerías and panaderias to satiate immediate hunger. The East Austin locale is painted with murals of huge vegetables and cuts of meat on the outside. Inside space is at a premium; aisles allow only one small cart at a time, and every wall and surface is there for the selling of product. The meat department is particularly interesting, with cases stacked a foot and a half high with every cut imaginable, including ones you might prefer not to imagine (trotters, anyone?).

When you're done browsing and are ready to eat, figure out what you want and head over to the registers to pay—you pay for everything in advance here. The cashier will give you a ticket with your order to be presented at the counter. A working knowledge of Spanish is a good thing here, as they might take some liberties with your order if they believe that a gringo wouldn't really order *that*.

If you choose to eat in, there are counter seats and a few booths and tables that could certainly stand to be wiped. Menu choices vary from simple breakfast items to tacos, tamales, stews, and more. Slightly soggy chiles rellenos are filled with mild asadero cheese. Beef fajita tacos are strangely tough, so we prefer the garlicky chicken fajitas with rajas and onions, wrapped in La Michoacana's thin, tasty tortillas. If you are a tamale fan, try the hoja de plátano, a Oaxaca-style tamale steamed in a banana leaf that's uncommon in these parts. The masa has a light texture; and, with its large chunks of tender, roasted chicken, the tamal is big enough on its own to be a meal that's light on the tummy—and your wallet. –MPN

La Reyna

Mediocre Mex in a town with so many
better options

food

3.6 **4.8**

10 · 10

experience

Mexican · **$19** · *Bouldin Creek Area*

Casual restaurant
Mon.-Thurs. 7am-9:30pm; Fri.-Sat.
7am-10:30pm; Sun. 8am-9pm.
Breakfast. Outdoor dining.

1816 S. 1st St.
Austin
(512) 447-1280

Bar Full
Credit Cards Visa, MC, AmEx
Reservations Accepted

La Reyna is one of a row of Mexican restaurants spread out along
South First Street, without much to help it stand out from the crowd.
The building, at least, is easy to spot, with its large sign and red roof,
but its interior is decorated in the standard cheap cantina style with
sarape tabletops, beer signs, the same oil paintings that seem to hang
in a third of the restaurants in town, fake flowers, and so on. Even
without customers, La Reyna is loud from the noise of competing TVs
and Conjunto music. Friendly and attentive service (and stiff margaritas)
may be La Reyna's strong suit, but it is not enough to make up for
mostly uninspired fare.

As is to be expected, chips with flaming hot salsa arrive with the
menu, but don't eat too fast, because a second basket will cost you.
Appetizers are underwhelming: queso is a bland bowl of gloop, while
thick tostadas with globs of refried beans and sparse cheese comprise
the nachos; meanwhile, basic quesadillas might be fine if it weren't for
a slight fishiness. In fact, we detect fishy flavors in lots of unfortunate
places at La Reyna (do they need some new spatulas?), including the
mole, which would otherwise be decent, with its deep-roasted tones
and back-of-the-palate burn. Taco salad comes in an enormous fried
flour tortilla bowl, and is simple but tasty and filling. Not so for a
disappointingly bland, undersimmered menudo that can only be
rescued by squeezing in copious amounts of lime juice.

The big winner at La Reyna is certainly the carne guisada, which is
tender and rich, with a potato brunoise helping to thicken the gravy.
Oh, and portions are large enough that you can skip the bland rice and
beans without fear of going hungry. But sometimes the food is so bad
that you don't *want* big portions. –MPN

La Traviata

This lady's no tramp, but rather one of
Austin's better Italian restaurants

food
8.5 / 10   **7.1** / 10
experience

Italian $**51**   *Congress Avenue Area*

Upmarket restaurant   314 Congress Ave.   *Bar* Full
Mon.-Thurs. 11:30am-2pm,   Austin   *Credit Cards* Visa, MC, AmEx
5:30pm-10pm; Fri. 11:30am-2pm, (512) 479-8131   *Reservations* Recommended
5:30pm-10:30pm; Sat. 5:30pm-
10:30pm; closed Sun. *Date-friendly.*

For a restaurant whose name recalls both the glitz and glamour of
opera and the illicit pleasures of a lady of the night, La Traviata is
surprisingly plain—and, were it not for the amplified roar of many mild-
mannered conversations echoing off rough-hewn stone, tame. The only
aspect of the restaurant that sets a slightly racier tone is the deep-red
color of the one painted wall. There are no pretty patterns here aside
from that formed by the clustered little tables and their well-heeled
occupants.

But we rather wish, on the whole, that the kitchen would take the
same homey approach. When it does, the food it turns out is excellent,
the quality of a dish apparently inversely proportionate to the number
of ingredients that went into it. Amongst the appetizers, for example, a
simple, hot, crispy polenta square, sitting in a plain and creamy blue
cheese sauce, is lovely. And the Traviata salad, featuring arugula in a
surprisingly rustic buttermilk dressing with a few crumbs of mellow
gorgonzola, is a treat.

Mains include a short list of pastas and meatier options, and here,
again, less is more, more or less. We love, for example, a mild but
wonderfully subtle roasted fennel risotto, made with a slightly salty
asiago cheese, and lightly adorned with mint, chard, and julienned
spring onion. A hearty rigatoni dish in a red sauce with delicious lamb
meatballs would be wonderful if there weren't so much going on that
your palate is spinning dizzy, a heavyweight dose of garlic quickly
delivering the knock-out punch. Similarly, the duck confit becomes a
saltwater bird, its meat tender but briny (though a sweet fig sauce
helps balance it).

Service is courteous but can run a little ragged in the noisy, crowded
space. In general, La Traviata sings sweetest when it sings softly. –RM

Las Manitas

Legendary authentic Mexican, right in your face

food
7.6 **9.0**
10 / 10
experience

Mexican   **$16**   *Congress Avenue Area*

Casual restaurant
Mon.-Fri. 7am-4pm; Sat.-Sun.
7am-2:30pm. *Breakfast. Brunch.*
Outdoor dining.

211 Congress Ave.
Austin
(512) 472-9357

Bar Beer/wine
Credit Cards Visa, MC, AmEx
Reservations Not accepted

You are not the first to wander through the three-ring circus of this enormous open kitchen, not the first to gawk in awe at the masa-patting frenzy of the jovial, tortilla-making Mexican women, to marvel at the unbridled refried-bean chaos that envelops the space from wall to wall, from floor to soaring ceiling, to feel that you have just been beamed from the financial district of downtown Austin to the kitchen of a bustling lunch joint in downtown Guadalajara.

Nor will you be the last. Like many of Austin's most beloved eateries, Las Manitas is so much about who has been here, and for how long they will continue to come: the Mayor, the Drummer, the President, the Kinkster. None of which takes the least bit of thunder away from Las Manitas' relentlessly authentic preparations of Mexican classics: soups that change by the day, for instance. Wednesday brings a wonderful sopa tarasca, made with ancho chiles, onions, beans, chicken stock, tortilla strips, and Mexican cheese.

Avoid crispy tacos and the like; keep in mind that this is not a Tex-Mex place (ask for "queso" and you'll get a bowl of cold shredded cheese). But do try the enchiladas, with those homemade corn tortillas smothered with deep, dark sauces, and pork-fat-kissed refried beans that approach perfection. Creamy-egged migas are extraordinarily good—amongst the city's elite. On a pleasant day, try the trendily shabby outdoor garden in the back; the passage takes you through that amazing kitchen.

Still, there are people that just don't get Las Manitas' popularity: why would you wait in line to cram into an overcrowded restaurant with rushed, indifferent service, whose Mexican fare is hardly the best in town? Order wrong, or look for the flaws, and you might see it their way. Lose yourself in the experience, hum along to the rhythmic culinary symphony of plate clanks, Spanish shouts, and tortilla pats, and you will find yourself in a place that is unmistakably Tejano, unmistakably Austin, and unmistakably spectacular. –RG

Las Palmas

Fairly standard East Austin Tex-Mex-
meets-Interior, with a pleasant porch

food
5.1 | 4.7
10 | 10
experience

Mexican $26   *East Austin*

Casual restaurant   1209 E. 7th St.   *Bar* Full
Mon.-Thurs. 11am-10pm;   Austin   *Credit Cards* Visa, MC, AmEx
Fri.-Sat. 11am-11pm; closed (512) 457-4944   *Reservations* Accepted
Sun. *Breakfast. Outdoor dining.*

This East Austin Mexican joint, in the space formerly occupied by Nuevo
León, delivers well on the basics. The front porch is a pleasant place to
sit with your food and margaritas and while away the time, although
the interior is unremarkable—standard for downmarket Mex.
Nonstandard, though, is the option of playing lotería (Mexican bingo)
on Friday evenings from 5:30pm to 7:30pm.

Chile con queso has a good flavor, but it shows too much skin. (This
is a common problem around Austin, but Las Palmas has a particularly
bad case of it.) Catfish ceviche, amongst starters, is just okay; it has a
lot of avocado, but at our last visit, it suffered from not enough lime
and perhaps not enough time to marinate to allow the acid to "cook"
the fish. As a result, the fish, while tender, tasted raw, which was a
particular problem with catfish (there's a reason we don't eat catfish
sushi).

On the brighter side, enchiladas rojas are above average, with good
corn tortillas and some serious spice to them. Chiles rellenos are
winners too, stuffed with juicy beef, potatoes, and onions (like an
unusual, but successful, beef-stew version of the dish). Flour tortillas,
too, are good, sweet, and appropriately charred. Carne guisada is salty
and fully developed, and rice is above average, but beans are just okay.
There are also some more interesting coastal Mexican fish specialties,
like huachinango (red snapper) a la Veracruzana (with tomatoes,
onions, and capers) or al mojo de ajo (in garlic sauce), but enchiladas
and rellenos might still be the safest choices. Keep it simple, and you'll
do well here. –RG

Las Palomas

Sweet-tempered Tex-Mex and Mex-Mex
in a Westlake strip mall

food
7.0 | 7.4
10 | 10
experience

Mexican $29 Westlake

Casual restaurant
Tues.-Thurs. 11am-2pm, 5pm-
9:30pm; Fri.-Sat. 11am-2pm,
5pm-10pm; closed Sun.-Mon.
Kid-friendly. Live music. Outdoor dining.

3201 Bee Caves Rd.
Austin
(512) 327-9889
www.lospalomasrestaurant.com

Bar Full
Credit Cards Visa, MC, AmEx
Reservations Not accepted

"Palomas" means "doves" in Spanish, and that image aptly evokes the gentle appeal of this longtime Westlake favorite. It is a little hard to find, tucked far into a strip mall, but the interior is not at all what one expects. The serene, peach-toned dining room is dotted with wicker furniture, giving the place the look of a sunroom in a senior home that quite suits the genteel atmosphere and the somewhat older clientele that frequents the restaurant.

The food here takes the same mild-mannered approach, with soft flavors incorporated into rather elegant Tex-Mex and interior Mexican dishes. A cup of the corn soup to start the meal exemplifies this technique. The soup is light—milky rather than creamy—and sweet, with none of the salt or heaviness that the addition of cheese so often brings to the dish. Many of the dishes on the menu seem influenced more by French than by fiery Mexican cooking. Cream, butter, and wine sauces abound. But this characteristic twist makes for some unusual options.

There are, however, plenty of spirited Mexican dishes to choose from. The traditional Yucatan dish of cochinita pibil (spiced, shredded pork slowly cooked in a banana leaf) is less richly flavored than usual, but tender and very satisfying, especially when combined with the tart marinated onions that accompany it. Las Palomas' mole sauce is a little muddy, but we like their tangy, lively enchiladas verdes, and a fillet of orange roughy (somewhat unfortunately the restaurant's fish of choice) is awakened by a spicy, smoky chipotle sauce.

The pleasant picture at Las Palomas is completed by exceptionally friendly, attentive service. Only a classy mariachi band breaks the calm; we must admit, though they're very good, that we've wished them away from our mellow meal. –RM

Le Soleil

This North Austin Vietnamese shines
more in its food than its service

food

7.9 **4.5**
10   10

experience

Vietnamese $**26**   *Far North*

Casual restaurant   9616 N. Lamar Blvd.   ***Bar*** Beer/wine
Daily 10am-10pm.   Austin   ***Credit Cards*** Visa and MC
Vegetarian-friendly.   (512) 821-0396   ***Reservations*** Accepted

Way up north on Lamar, past the highway and hidden amidst miles of
strip malls, lies Le Soleil, a Vietnamese restaurant in the capable hands
of Tommy Le. Mr. Le left the excellent Sunflower for sunnier climes after
splitting with his wife and co-owner; of the two, Le Soleil is slightly
more ambitious, with a longer menu and many more tables.

Perhaps it is these ambitions, perhaps just stubborn loyalty, but
something about Le Soleil fails to satisfy quite as Sunflower does. The
mirrors and ugly décor, oddly cheerful in the latter's small dining room,
are vaguely depressing in the vast, pinkish hall of the former. What
seems a charming informality of service at Sunflower feels irksome and
harried in the larger room.

And the food, while still very good, suffers a little from the changes
as well. Some dishes feel rushed, others slightly overcooked. Food
comes out when it's ready, or when the server has time, so that rice can
stand for 15 minutes, cooling and hardening, before the accompanying
curry arrives. We don't want to complain too much, however, as much
of the same delicious Vietnamese fare is on offer here as at Sunflower.
One of Le Soleil's menu additions is a selection of traditional hot clay
pots, with rice plus meat or seafood baked in earthenware, so that the
edges are crusty and sweet, and the meat stays moist and tender. They
are simple but decided pleasures. There is also a selection of soups on
offer (the traditional hot and sour is sweeter and less lively than the
more familiar Thai version), excellent seafood, and a variety of
interesting Vietnamese drinks.

Only the pleasure is somewhat spoiled when the staff begins packing
away chairs and sweeping the distant corners at 9:45, though the
restaurant ostensibly serves 'till 10. –RM

Lewis' BBQ

We don't know what they're doing to
those ribs, but it sure is good

food

7.1 **5.8**
10   10

experience

Barbecue $ **8**   *East Austin*

Counter service
Mon.-Thurs. 11am-8:30pm;
Fri.-Sat. 11am-10pm; closed
Sun. *Outdoor dining.*

1814 Harvey St.
Austin
(512) 473-2225

Bar None
Credit Cards No credit cards
Reservations Not accepted

Lewis' BBQ on East MLK may seem off the beaten path, but it is worth
the drive. You shouldn't have any problem spotting the small house: it's
done up in a shade of Pepto-Bismol pink, with a difficult-to-read Coca-
Cola sign out front. Lewis' is mostly a take-out spot, but barbecue, at
its heart, is a take-out food. If you do feel like eating right away, there
are three picnic tables under the porch just for that purpose. Order at
the window, and be sure to have cash on hand.

It may take them a few minutes to assemble your plate, so if you're
waiting in the heat, be sure to ask for a soda from their freezer—we
swear, a near-slushy Coke never tasted better than it does at their
picnic tables when it's 100 degrees out. Most patrons seem to prefer to
wait in their cars, but with a cold drink, the porch is much nicer—the
area is permeated by smoke that reminds us of a campfire, and with so
much less traffic on MLK since the old airport closed, you can hear the
trilling crescendo of the cicadas again.

Lewis' menu consists of plates, sandwiches, and by-the-pound
barbecue, including pork chops and mutton. The meat here is milder
than you usually see in this part of Texas, and the sauce thicker and
sweeter, more like it is in other parts of the barbecuing world.
Everything is tender and juicy, with gentle smoke, and sweetness
dominating rather than spice. Lewis' serves Elgin sausage, peppery and
moist; it's the hottest thing on the menu. The brisket, by comparison, is
fairly bland. But pork ribs are a must here—give them a gentle shake,
and the meat falls right off the bone, with an astonishing, succulent
tenderness that's rarely seen. Sides are basic, but we like the chunky
potato salad filled with pickles and onions. After all, what would
barbecue be without all that stuff? –MPN

Little Mexico

food 7.5 / 10 5.8 / 10 experience

Above-average Mexican with some authenticity in a little South First house

Mexican $25   *Bouldin Creek Area*

Casual restaurant   2304 S. 1st St.   *Bar* Full
Daily 7am-9:30pm.   Austin   *Credit Cards* Visa, MC, AmEx
Breakfast.   (512) 462-2188   *Reservations* Not accepted

This small, brightly lit restaurant might look like just another Tex-Mex joint along South First Street, but it's been around for a while, and its food is much better than the haphazard exterior might suggest. The unexpected charm of this place begins with the extraordinarily friendly service (speak Spanish, and they'll speak Spanish back) and the extraordinarily spicy salsa, which brandishes serious heat—the stuff will set you ablaze. Although chips are garden-variety, chile con queso is better than average, if thin, while "Jerry Jeff's Dip," named after local country-rock-outlaw singer Jerry Jeff Walker, adds watery picadillo and decent guacamole to the mix.

You might have to amuse yourself at the fast-food-style tables by looking at the depressing grab-a-stuffed-animal game—this isn't exactly an atmospheric spot, although it has a certain homey feel. Regardless, the food is good enough to distract attention away from that. In short, this is a place to come for distinguished Mexican food on a night that's just like any other.

Excellent menudo and pork in adobo lead a list of interior Mexican options, but even the standard enchiladas are well above average, with a sauce that's red and tastes of real chiles instead of that dreaded brown gravy. Beans are well seasoned, with a notable depth of pork-fat flavor, and rice has better texture and taste than most. On the other end of the authenticity spectrum, there's "Antonio's Taco," which integrates potato, bacon, and brisket. Interior Austin, perhaps? –RG

Longhorn Po-Boys

Not bad for a quick lunch, but if you want Creole food, look elsewhere

food
4.3 / 10   **5.1** / 10
experience

American, Middle Eastern $ **7**   *UT Area*

Counter service
Mon.-Thurs. 7:30am-10pm; Fri.
7:30am-5pm; Sat. 8:30am-6pm;
Sun. 9am-10pm. *Breakfast. Delivery. Live music. Outdoor dining. Wireless Internet.*

2901 Medical Arts St.
Austin
(512) 495-9228

Bar None
Credit Cards Visa, MC, AmEx
Reservations Not accepted

In some ways, Longhorn Po-Boys is exceedingly comfortable in its own skin. It is a popular student hangout with a loud and loyal clientele, augmented by the traffic from the coffee shop that shares its space. But in other ways this campus sandwich spot is suffering somewhat from an identity crisis.

For one thing, the fare served here has nothing to do with the Louisiana sandwiches that inspired its name. Instead, it is more or less a Middle Eastern restaurant, serving falafel, shawarma, and other regional standards, alongside an unadventurous menu of American sandwiches. But the Middle Eastern food served here falls a little short of the desirable mark: as far as that goes, Longhorn Po-Boys is inferior to Kismet on the Drag, and to Tom's Tabooley just north of it.

The chicken shawarma, for instance, is not well marinated, and only partially cooked on the traditional rotisserie before being finished on the griddle. Dolmas are absurdly small, with very little rice hiding between the rolls of grape leaves; falafel balls, meanwhile, are dry and crunchy, although they have a nice heat and toasty flavor. Kafta does not have any marked parsley freshness, and the spinach pie has arrived suspiciously icy inside. What we do like about the cooking here, however, is that it gives lemon juice the enthusiastic respect it deserves. The flavor is widely in evidence, and seldom fails to perk up the drabber options. Plus, like most Middle Eastern spots in town, Longhorn has the good sense to use that superior Phoenicia pita bread. American-style sandwiches are of the uneventful Subway variety, but taste good.

Service is Austin-style laid back and friendly, and the long line moves quickly, making Longhorn Po-Boys a reasonable lunch destination. It is also right next door to Kinko's, so you can sit and eat something restorative after finally printing out that blasted term paper. –RM

Lotus Hunan

Somewhat better than average Chinese
food...zzz

food
6.0 **6.5**
10   10
experience

Chinese $**22**   *Westlake*

Casual restaurant   3201 Bee Caves Rd.   *Bar* Beer/wine
Daily 11am-10pm.   Austin   *Credit Cards* Visa, MC, AmEx
Delivery.   (512) 327-7776   *Reservations* Accepted

Although Lotus Hunan Chinese restaurant has been serving food at the
same Westlake location for 20 years, the establishment has changed
owners, and the food has largely improved as a result. The usual red
lanterns, aquarium, and Chinese wall art make the décor typical, but a
fresh-cut bamboo arrangement up front is a nice touch. Ballad-style
Chinese music doesn't cover the sounds of the happy staff laughing
and singing in the back.

Lunch specials are reasonable, but dinner mains come at a heftier
price. (This is Westlake, after all.) Appetizers like bland pork, carrot, and
cabbage-filled egg rolls are so boring that your dining companion might
have to nudge you when you start snoring. Velvet corn soup might
wake you up with its frightening shade of yellow (egg and canned
corn)—but not with its faint flavor.

Scallops in hot garlic sauce are firm yet tender, with crisp water
chestnuts and lengths of punchy green onion. There's a lingering heat
from the spicy sauce, but Lotus Hunan is happy to adjust the
seasonings in all their dishes for those unfortunates with wimpy taste
buds. Try the "Young Duck with Ginger Root" stir-fry—the duck is a
little tough at the edges from a previous roasting, but the strong ginger
flavor is a nice foil to the slight gaminess (or should we say duckiness?)
of the duck. Slivers of duck skin and fat are rich and chewy, and the
brown sauce has a gentle sweetness punctuated by green onions. This
dish isn't available as a lunch or dinner special, so be sure to seek it out
on the à-la-carte menu.

Business seems to come mostly from the neighborhood, so Lotus
Hunan is rarely crowded. Service varies, sometimes detached, other
times friendly and attentive. Teapots are closely watched, so you'll rarely
have to ask for a refill. But do yourself a favor and drive to a better
place—Austinites no longer have to settle for Chinese-American food
this dated. –MPN

Louie Mueller's BBQ

One of Texas' barbecue palaces—it's not to be missed

food

9.0 | **8.5**
10 | 10

experience

Barbecue   **$10**   *Taylor*

Counter service
Mon.-Sat. 10am-6pm;
closed Sun. *Kid-friendly.*
Wireless Internet.

206 W. 2nd St.
Taylor
(512) 352-6206
www.louiemuellerbarbeque.com

Bar Beer/wine
Credit Cards Visa and MC
Reservations Not accepted

Opened as a grocery in 1946, Louie Mueller's has been a standard-bearer of Texas barbecue since the Muellers began cooking up their meats in 1949. Now owned by Louie's son Bobby and his wife Trish, the place still cooks everything up fresh each day. Louie Mueller's occupies what was once an old basketball court, but it has been their home for nearly a half century, and it shows: the high ceilings and once-green walls are varying shades of greasy brown and black from all the smoke. Dim lighting and the tap of feet shuffling against hardwood floors almost give Louie's the feeling of a chapel. But there's nothing fancy here—just picnic tables, old scales, beer signs, a collection of magazine articles, and most interestingly, a corkboard of business cards that are never removed and therefore range in color from pale tan to deep sepia from the years of smoke.

Food is served up on butcher paper, as it should be in an old-school Texas barbecue joint, with help-yourself iced tea and plastic-ware; they'll always cut you a chunk of brisket to sample while your food is being weighed. When choosing between moist and lean brisket, don't ponder your waistline; moist and fatty is always the way to go—tender and juicy, it has a textbook red smoke ring, and an oaky flavor. Don't miss the jalapeño sausage, made of 100% beef, with a wonderfully grainy but juicy texture that falls apart when cut into; it's hot, though, so keep your iced tea handy.

Louie's sauce, meanwhile, is one of the best we've had: it's thin, spicy, and vinegar-tart, without a bit of sweetness to mask any of the meats' subtle nuances. Sides are made fresh daily; chopped cole slaw is a little too salty, but mashed potato salad is better, heavy on the mustard. But the sides are just that—simple textural counterpoints that serve merely to refocus attention on Louie's main, deservedly legendary attraction: spectacular smoked meat. –MPN

Louie's 106

Tapas and more for the business-casual
set on Sixth Street

food
7.7 | **8.2**
10 | 10
experience

New American, Spanish $**50**   *Sixth Street District*

Upmarket restaurant
Mon.-Thurs. 11:30am-10pm; Fri.
11:30am-11pm; Sat. 6pm-11pm;
Sun. 6pm-9:30pm. *Date-friendly.*

106 E. 6th St.
Austin
(512) 476-1998
www.louies106.net

Bar Full
Credit Cards Visa, MC, AmEx
Reservations Recommended

Austin's original tapas bar, Louie's 106, has a menu that includes dishes
that have ventured far from any Mediterranean roots. Located on Sixth
Street just off Congress, Louie's has a beautiful open space with very
high ceilings that accommodate balcony seating overlooking the main
dining room as well as tall paintings. The kitchen is open, giving a
partial view of the action, and the restaurant also has downstairs rooms
that are available for parties and meetings.

The tapas menu (tapas are Spain's traditional bar snacks) offers a
variety of simple and typical hot and cold plates such as fried olives
with romesco sauce, melon with prosciutto, herbed goat cheese
crostini, duck pâté, and fresh mozzarella with tomatoes. The regular
menu is largely Mediterranean, with the exception of a handful of
Asian-inspired dishes that we find misguided and out of place.

The basic rule is that you should stick with what's simple (if not
necessarily Spanish), like a delicious beef carpaccio, served with fresh
grated parmesan, olive oil, shallots, and Dijon mustard. The carpaccio is
also available with ahi tuna. Crispy fried calamari come with an aïoli
and a roasted-red-pepper rouille. But uncomplicated does not always
mean flawless. Prince Edward Island moules marinière are simple and
flavorful, but at one visit, too many of the mussels were closed,
suggesting that they were either under undercooked or bad specimens.
The New York strip steak with cracked black pepper, on the other hand,
comes nicely grilled, and we like its rich green peppercorn demi glace
and caramelized garlic butter.

Louie's 106 is no longer unique for its tapas, and certainly better and
more interesting can be had in Austin. But when it comes to service
and atmosphere, few are up to Louie's high standards. –MPN

Lucy's Boatyard Grill

A lakeside spot with boats and buoys
sailing overhead, but so-so food

food

5.3 | **9.0**
10 | 10

experience

Seafood, American   **$33**   *Tarrytown*

Casual restaurant
Sun.-Thurs. 11am-10pm;
Fri.-Sat. 11am-11pm.
Date-friendly. Live music.
Outdoor dining.

3825 Lake Austin Blvd.
Austin
(512) 651-0505
www.lucysboatyard.com

Bar Full
Credit Cards Visa, MC, AmEx
Reservations Not accepted

Owned by the successful folks behind Chuy's, Lucy's Boatyard takes
advantage of some of the best real estate this city has to offer. It is
spread luxuriously over a series of decks along Lake Austin, all of which
afford glorious views of the lake and the dam, and of the hills of
Westlake behind them.

The building does look rather like an old boatyard all tarted up:
rough-hewn boards and warehouse-like spaces are painted the
appropriate lighthouse red and white. But it was in fact built as a
restaurant, and throughout the course of an evening it is hard to shake
the effect of a theme park. The buoys, rowing standards, and marine
doodads are clearly imported, and while the vast crowds of young
prepsters who frequent the place on weekend evenings might look like
they've just stepped in off the yacht, they haven't.

The food suffers from the same overdone role-playing as the décor.
The menu is a Louisiana-and-Texas-themed surf-and-turf affair, but little
of it is well executed. We do rather like the 7-Up rolls that open the
meal—fluffy, crunchy little things with a gentle, sweet tang. But the
much prized Maryland crab cake goes from the "Un-Cola" to just plain
uncool: no self-respecting restaurant should be serving an innocent
customer who just consented to paying $14 for her dinner so heavy,
drab, and soggy a thing.

On the turf side of things, Lucy's pork chop, served with peach and
green chile sauce, is better, but the sauce is a bit of a cliché and doesn't
do much for the meat. Only when it departs from the script does the
Boatyard fare better: its wood-fired pizzas, with their paper-thin crusts,
are justifiably respected, though they need some spice, and can sag a
little at the center. Ultimately, Lucy's is best for lunch and happy hour,
when the lake views are more visible, and the prices lower. –RM

Madam Mam's

More like Madam Mediocre's, though
the noodles are quite comforting

food

6.8 5.3
10   10

experience

Thai $16   West Campus

Casual restaurant   2514 Guadalupe St.   Bar None
Daily 11am-9:30pm.   Austin   Credit Cards No credit cards
Vegetarian-friendly.   (512) 472-8306   Reservations Not accepted
                               www.madammam.com

Austin holds an unshakeable affection in its heart for Madam Mam's,
the large Thai noodle house that stakes its claim on a significant part of
the Drag. Perhaps it is its convenient campus location that sucks in the
students at a rate that is directly proportional to the rate at which the
students suck in its noodles. Perhaps it is because, at a time when the
Drag was surrendering its final few spots to the shiny veneers of Barnes
and Noble (now, sniff, no more) and Jamba Juice, Madam Mam's
sprang up with some of the old ramble and ramshackle, slight disorder,
and local feel. It's not so much that the restaurant has the successful,
homey atmosphere of so many truly Austin venues—it doesn't—but
rather its simple refusal to manufacture one that is appealing. But
whatever it is, this shop remains packed until its doors close, at an
unconscionably early 9:30pm (in a college town!), with an obdurate
click.

In fact, the room feels a little too large, the tables too small, and the
odd imported embroidered bags on the wall too scattered for Madam
Mam's to be properly comfortable. But for the masses of Longhorns
who frequent the place, the food is properly comforting, though little
goes beyond the ordinary. Soups are spicy, sour, and ample; pad Thai, a
student favorite, is warm, sweet, and tasty—neither too dry nor too
runny. Curries, too, are satisfying though humdrum, but the sautéed
eggplant with jalapeños is livelier, the eggplants soft but still
appropriately purple. The pad see ew (stir-fried rice noodles) is a low
point, greasy and thoroughly bland.

All in all, we feel Madam Mam's does not quite deserve the loyalty it
has won. We'd love to frequent it as a late-night, post-party campus
comfort-food dive; unfortunately, by then its doors have been closed
for hours. –RM

Madras Pavilion

A vegetarian, kosher Indian dive with
yummy dosai, but avoid the bathrooms

food
7.2 **5.2**
10   10
experience

Indian   **$15**   *Far North*

Casual restaurant   9025 Research Blvd.   *Bar* BYO
Mon.-Thurs. 11:30am-3pm,   Austin   *Credit Cards* Visa, MC, AmEx
5:30pm-9:30pm; Fri. 11:30am- (512) 719-5575   *Reservations* Not accepted
3pm, 5:30pm-10pm; Sat.-Sun.
11am-10pm. *Vegetarian-friendly.*

Madras Pavilion serves primarily South Indian specialties, presenting an interesting alternative to the majority of Austin's Indian restaurants, which are focused on other parts of India and Indian-American food. This reasonably priced spot in a North Austin shopping center feels a little like a work in progress—a buffet steam table takes up one wall, the rest is mostly unadorned, and an odd bear in a top hat occupies the entryway. Service can be a bit gruff, and English speakers difficult to find.

The menu is entirely vegetarian and has a section of kids' offerings, as well as a lunch buffet. Much of the food is fried, as evidenced by the appetizer combo plate, which is served with five condiments—a curry, the standard tamarind and mint chutneys, a grainy coconut sauce, and something boring and unidentifiable. Bland, donut-like medhu vada has a light fennel flavor, and paneer pakoda, a battered and fried cheese, is chewy and uninteresting. We like the bonda, a fried potato concoction with a creeping heat, and the very similar veggie cutlet: mashed and fried vegetables seasoned with coriander, curry, and lemon.

Madras Pavilion is known for two things: it is the one of the few truly Kosher restaurants in town, making for a lively mix of saris and black suits, and it has tremendous dosai—foot-and-a-half-long rice-and-lentil-flour crêpes rolled like burritos around a variety of fillings. They are deliciously light, served crisp and hot, again with a variety of condiments, like chutneys and strong lime pickle. We love the creamy butter masala dosa, filled with curried potatoes, onions, and nigella seeds. Curries are also a good choice—palak paneer has an unusual nutty flavor to its spinach, and the paneer (homemade cheese) comes in nice, big cubes. Spicy malai kofta has sliced almonds and is so rich, you might not even realize that the "meatballs" are vegetarian. L'chaim. –MPN

The Magic Wok

Campus Chinese take-out with cheesy
name? Well, what did you expect?

food
2.2
10
3.6
10
experience

Chinese $ 7   West Campus

Counter service   2716½ Guadalupe St.   *Bar* None
Daily 11am-2:30pm,   Austin   *Credit Cards* Visa and MC
4:30pm-2am. *Delivery.*   (512) 474-7770   *Reservations* Not accepted
                                www.themagicwok.com

Sometimes cheap and plentiful just isn't enough, and nobody teaches
this lesson better than the poor-quality campus Chinese takeout joint.
We're telling you, folks, this is one classy establishment, complete with
flimsy plastic cutlery and Styrofoam plates, and an electronic "sex
reactor" of the kind found in some movie theaters. For a small fee, the
device will answer the question: "How sexy are you?" After a decidedly
un-magical meal here, "cold fish" will be by far the likeliest result.

Ugly seating, borrowed from waiting rooms, sits on a gray linoleum
floor, bleakly confirming that this is essentially a take-out joint. The
service falls in with the general attitude: it is quick and efficient, but
doesn't waste time with simple friendliness. The main selling point of
the Magic Wok, particularly for its student clientele, is that it is open
until 2am (note that delivery service ends a little earlier). But you should
know better than this.

There are no surprises on the menu, whose food is as passionless as
the décor and more or less identical to that found in thousands of
campus take-out spots, with the three meats, accompanied by anemic
veggies, doused in a sticky Szechuan brown sauce. This is thick and
syrupy, with no more subtlety than the stuff that comes in the plastic
squirt bottles shaped like log cabins. Breaded, deep-fried chicken is
chewy and tough, and we distrust those meats that are hidden from
view by their casings (the wonton's innards, for example, do not fare
well in the light of day). Ignore any "hot and spicy" stars next to menu
items—there's no heat here. Even generally reliable bland items, such as
fried rice and lo mein, manage to be unusually uninteresting. The only
customers who seem pleased with the place are the odd bugs scuttling
across the floor. –RM

Magnolia Café

24-hour queso and fusion, with a side
of funky: we're not sorry they're open

food
5.9 **9.3**
10   10
experience

American   **$18**   *Tarrytown, South Congress*

Casual restaurant
Daily 24 hrs. Breakfast. Brunch.
Date-friendly. Kid-friendly.
Vegetarian-friendly.

2304 Lake Austin Blvd.
Austin
(512) 478-8645
www.cafemagnolia.com

1920 S. Congress Ave.
78704, (512) 445-0000

Bar Beer/wine
Credit Cards Visa, MC, AmEx
Reservations Not accepted

Not everyone here is a true, wild-eyed weirdo. But to many Austinites, Magnolia Café, with its "Sorry, We're Open" slogan and 24-hour schedule, is a lingering icon of everything that's still wacky about the city. Even if you're tempted to dismiss Magnolia (along with the "Keep Austin Weird" motto) as a contrived attempt to commercialize the slacker fetish, try making that argument after late-night hunger strikes and you find yourself in front of a bowl of irresistible queso. As such, the restaurant is often packed at the most unlikely times, when a queue can trail out the door and into the moonlight. But don't be discouraged—seating is efficient. Service is fast and quirky, often delivered by a harried waiter passing by in a blur and a twinkle of studs and piercings. But would we have it any other way?

Magnolia's menu fuses Austin's diverse culinary traditions: comfort food, Tex-Mex, and pan-vegetarian. Sometimes they try to do it all at once, transporting you right back to the infancy of American fusion in 1988, when something like a "tropical turkey taco"—with smoked turkey, jack cheese, avocado, pico de gallo, and pineapple in a whole-wheat tortilla—still seemed daring. Nowadays, even your mom's salsa is spicier than Magnolia's, but the tropical turkey taco is still tasty. So is the unique curried stuffed squash.

Much less successful are Magnolia's attempts to replicate cuisines like Mexican (timid enchiladas have no south-of-the-border flair) and Italian (pasta dishes are bland and ill conceived). But Magnolia's queso is deservedly legendary, whether you prefer the comfortable, well-textured plain version or the immensely popular Mag Mud, packed with black beans, avocado, and pico de gallo. After all this eclecticism, though, Magnolia's greatest strengths lie in its simple, American home cooking, like warm brownies topped with rich vanilla ice cream, and above all, their wonderful pancakes. But maybe that's only fitting, for home is where the heart is, and sooner or later, in the wee hours of two remarkable decades, many Austinites have left their hearts at Magnolia Café. –RM/RG

Maiko

Pretentious, uneven downtown sushi
with an offensively bad attitude

food

6.3
10

1.0
10

experience

Japanese   **$77**   *Warehouse District*

Upmarket restaurant   311 W. 6th St.   *Bar* Full
Mon.-Wed. 11:30am-2pm, 4:30pm-   Austin   *Credit Cards* Visa, MC, AmEx
10:30pm; Thurs.-Fri. 11:30am-2pm, (512) 236-9888   *Reservations* Accepted
4:30pm-midnight; Sat. 4:30pm-   www.maikoaustin.com
midnight; Sun. 4:30pm-10:30pm. *Live music. Wireless Internet.*

It's rare when the service at a restaurant is so horrible that it completely
ruins an otherwise okay meal. Stand at the front of the restaurant
waiting for a table, and you're actively ignored by the staff, even when
the restaurant is empty. Ask your server what he recommends, and he
shrugs: "It's pretty much the same as what you could get at any sushi
place."

We found that statement particularly funny, because that's exactly
what Maiko, with its hipper-than-thou, exposed-brick interior and
spectacularly pretentious menu, is trying *not* to be. Recent specials, for
instance, have included an Aizamo-tamari-soya-braised duck breast
with sweet soya milk, eggplant, and ginger emulsion; also making
appearances have been a green-soybean-paper roll of salmon,
yellowtail, and tuna with mango; bluefin toro sushi purportedly shipped
in from the Tsukiji fish market in Tokyo; and, on one evening, a steak of
diamond Kobe beef priced at $70. You'd think that a restaurant with
one of the most expensive main courses in Texas would not slap the
check down next to you, start sweeping around your table, and actually
turn off the lights before you've finished your main course. You'd be
wrong.

If you haven't walked out in disgust from being ignored before you
even get a menu, there are some gastronomical highlights: aji, for one,
which is a variety of horse mackerel that Maiko ships in from Japan. It's
mild and melting, artfully served. Sushi rolls (with prices up to an
incredible $18) are also reliable, as is wagyu beef that you sear yourself
on a hot rock, and a well-executed bowl of udon noodles, nicely
doughy without being pasty. But the sushi bar can be erratic, with
stringiness and fishiness everywhere. Even the toro (fatty tuna), at our
last visit, was a fishy disappointment. Cost? Eight dollars *per piece*.

And how about Maiko's failing score of 60/100 on their 2006 health
inspection, placing it in the bottom 15 in all of Austin—and this for a
place serving *raw fish*? Charging up to $125 a head in a city otherwise
full of good Japanese food at fair prices, Maiko is a not just a shocking
rip-off—it is a sore on the face of Austin. –RG

Málaga

Trendy tapas and interesting wine
flights in a trendy location

food
8.4
10

8.8
10
experience

Spanish

$**47**

Warehouse District

Upmarket restaurant
Mon.-Wed. 5pm-midnight; Thurs.-
Sat. 5pm-2am; closed Sun. Kitchen
closes Mon.-Wed. 10pm; Thurs.
11pm; Fri.-Sat. midnight. *Date-friendly.*

208 W. 4th St.
Austin
(512) 236-8020
www.malagatapasbar.com

Bar Full
Credit Cards Visa, MC, AmEx
Reservations Recommended

Undoubtedly Austin's best stop for tapas, Málaga is a noisy and trendy
mecca for those 21 and up. High ceilings are accentuated by floor-to-
ceiling wine racks, mirrors, and intricate hanging Moorish lamps.
Wrought-iron accents (including tiered tapas trays), Picasso prints, and
photos of Flamenco dancers complete the Spanish-influenced (or, better
stated, Spanish fetishist) décor.

Málaga has a substantial wine list, featuring wine flights and an
unusually impressive list of wines by the glass; once open, the bottles
are preserved with a special vacuum system, enabling you to try high-
end selections in small tastes. The menu consists solely of tapas, but
there's so much variety there, you won't miss the presence of mains.
The tiny, artful food seems to reflect the youthful and polished clientele
that packs Málaga on weekends and keeps them busy throughout the
week. Even so, the service generally remains friendly and helpful, if at
times harried.

Start with something simple to whet your appetite, like assorted
Spanish olives or warm roasted piquillo peppers filled with salty, slightly
grainy goat cheese and a side of herbed bread slices drizzled with olive
oil. Málaga has several tempting seafood tapas, from spicy raw salmon
in adobo with cucumber slices (use them like crackers as a vehicle for
the salmon), to luscious sea scallops and basil wrapped in jamón
serrano and seared, the melted fat from the ham giving the scallops a
buttery mouth feel. Heavier tapas include lomo a la plancha—seared
strips of tender beef cooked medium-rare and served with warm pita
triangles and aïoli.

Some dishes are not up to snuff—the chintzy cheese plate has come,
on occasion, with oxidized fruit, and while the cordero cacereño is
delicious, with medium-rare strips of grilled lamb tasting faintly of
rosemary, the curried yogurt sauce is a bit of a stretch—it just doesn't
go well with the rest of the heavily Iberian menu. Be sure not to miss
the watermelon, Serrano ham, and Garroxta cheese salad, which is
drizzled with balsamic vinegar, microgreens, and pine nuts—it's a bold
dish with fascinating textures that would be suitable for dessert. –MPN

Mandola's

An excitingly authentic Italian gourmet
grocery-and-counter-service-restaurant

food

8.5   6.2
10   10
experience

Italian, Pizza   **$19**   *Hyde Park*

Counter service
Daily 6:30am-10pm.
Breakfast. Outdoor dining.
Vegetarian-friendly.

4700 W. Guadalupe St.
Austin
(512) 419-9700

Bar Beer/wine
Credit Cards Visa, MC, AmEx
Reservations Not accepted

"Thrilling" is not a word that you'd usually want to use when describing the new arrival of a specialty grocery store. But in the case of Mandola's, which opened in Hyde Park in March, 2006, we're pretty close to that point. Where else around here can you get homemade mozzarella? Imported truffle oil and mushrooms? Reasonably-priced, thin-sliced prosciutto di Parma that seems to have come straight off the airplane? (Okay, fine, Central Market. But still.)

The Italian wine selection is small but remarkably careful. Instead of the mass-marketed Chiantis and Pinot Grigios, you'll find the work of smaller producers from Piemonte, Abruzzo, and Sicily. Of course, there are also the Brunellos and such—and their prices are relentlessly reasonable. Quality seems valued over quantity, selectivity over selection. That's not to say there's not selection, though: at last count, there were eight different Proseccos in the fridge.

Aside from the grocery side of the business, Mandola's has also ambitiously entered the restaurant market (you order at the counter). Initial signs have been quite promising indeed—especially with respect to the thin-crust pizza, which comes in two sizes (for one or two people, more or less). Although it's not wood-fired or made of bricks, the pizza oven is capable of reaching extraordinarily high temperatures, and as such, the razor-thin crusts are delicately and beautifully seared. We have loved the margherita, with fresh slices of real mozzarella and a gorgeous tomato sauce. It's exciting stuff.

This may be the only place in town that spells everything right in Italian, including "lasagne," which even Microsoft Word incorrectly corrects (that dish is authentically baked with béchamel but underseasoned). Other varieties of homemade pasta and sauces are equally authentic, such as a wonderfully executed tagliatelle alla Bolognese (thin, flat noodles with meat sauce). The indoor-outdoor space is pleasant enough, with warm lighting, although you won't quite forget that you're sitting in a grocery store. But in this case, that's not a bad thing. –RG

Mangia

A popular local pizza chain that's a little too full of its fillings

food
6.6 | 5.2
10 | 10
experience

Pizza | **$15** | *UT Area, Tarrytown, NW Hills*

Casual restaurant
Sun.-Thurs. 11am-10pm; Fri.-Sat.
11am-11pm. Mesa Drive location
closes 30 min. earlier. *Delivery.*
Kid-friendly. Outdoor dining. Vegetarian-friendly.

3500B Guadalupe St.
Austin
(512) 302-5200
www.mangiapizza.com

Bar Beer/wine
Credit Cards Visa, MC, AmEx
Reservations Not accepted

2401 Lake Austin Blvd.
78703, (512) 478-6600

8012 Mesa Dr.
78731, (512) 349-2126

There is a small contingent of Austinites that insists Mangia serves by far the best pizza in town. We can only say, with our best Jon Stewart ironic head tilt, "eh." The restaurant serves a familiar thin-crust pizza, along with some Italian-American pasta dishes; but its claim to fame, aside from the huge green dinosaur with the big claws and genial grin who looms from the Guadalupe location (and on all Mangia paraphernalia), is the stuffed pizza. This consists of a thick layer of cheese and fillings sandwiched between two thin layers of dough, the upper one covered in an excellent tomato sauce.

There are certainly some very tasty specialty options. The spinach pizza is justly the most popular, with an almost pesto-like filling of spinach, cheese, and spices, and fresh mushrooms thrown in for good measure. It is thick and flavorful. In general, we recommend you order the more strongly flavored options on the menu (such as the Chicago special, with sausage, peppers, mushrooms, and onions), in order to cut the masses of cheese that necessarily accompany the thick layer of filling.

But we don't quite get the point of this elaborate construction. Perhaps the idea is to combine the substantial feel of deep dish with the crispness of thin crust pizza, but if so, the plan backfires a little. The result is two layers of crust that are in fact dry and a little too crunchy, with the all-important topping-to-dough ratio thrown all out of whack. Pizza dough should be allowed to rise a little so that the outside is crisp but the inside still has some fluffy chew to it. Mangia's doesn't.

Pizzas are served with the same relaxed grin that's on Dino, but we've had to wait 45 minutes for a pie, and who needs fast food served slowly? –RM

Manny Hattan's

A pricey New York deli that feels a little lost

food
4.9 **6.1**
10   10
experience

Light American, Jewish Deli $**27**   *Arboretum*

Casual restaurant
Sun.-Thurs. 7am-8:30pm;
Fri.-Sat. 7am-1am. *Breakfast.*
Brunch. Delivery. Wireless Internet.

9503 Research Blvd.
Austin
(512) 794-0088
www.mannyhattan's.com

Bar Beer/wine
Credit Cards Visa, MC, AmEx
Reservations Accepted

We got to give credit where it's due: Manny Hattan's certainly tries hard. Herring, lox, and whitefish are all flown in from New York, along with cheesecake from the Carnegie Deli and bagels from the immortal H&H. But the exiled New Yorker, munching a reheated bagel in a restaurant with a gimmicky name, watching the highway across a parking lot studded with Best Buys and Container Stores, deep in the heart of urban sprawl, might never feel so far from home. This is off-off-*OFF* Broadway, folks.

And there is such a thing as trying too hard. At last count, the menu featured eight independent uses of the dreaded "famous" tag, ending, of course, with the "World Famous Reuben," of which Manny Hattan's claims to be the "home." Call us crazy, but we'd have placed it somewhere a lot closer to the New Jersey Turnpike.

While little on the menu is actively bad, there are few thrills. If Grandma had made that chicken broth in the matzo ball soup, we'd advertise for a better Grandma (come *on*, it's a basic job requirement). It is dull and watery. Sandwiches, such as that Reuben, are decent but undistinguished and could use more dressing. The aforementioned bagel is predictably reliable, with barely acceptable lox and whitefish, but it isn't anything like the sweet and chewy beautiful rounds that one hopes for with such a pricey choice. Awful knishes are featureless mashed-potato lumps, dry and crackly, with barely any trace of seasoning. French toast is impossible to ruin, but even that's a little heavy here, its challah a little dry in the center. On the whole, Manny Hattan's takes a distant second place behind Katz's in the Jewish deli department. –RM

Manuel's

Classy interior Mexican cuisine in a
flashy setting—bring your pink sequins

food

8.9 / 10   **7.0** / 10

experience

Mexican   **$39**   *Congress Avenue Area, Arboretum*

Upmarket restaurant
Mon.-Thurs. 11am-10pm; Fri.-Sat.
11am-1am; Sun. 10am-10pm.
Kitchen closes Fri.-Sat. midnight;
appetizers only 11pm-midnight. *Brunch. Live music. Outdoor dining. Wireless Internet.*

310 Congress Ave.
Austin
(512) 472-7555
www.manuels.com

Bar Full
Credit Cards Visa, MC, AmEx
Reservations Recommended

8012 Mesa Drive
78731, (512) 349-2126

Manuel's has long had an excellent reputation in this town, and for good reason. Its only current rival in the battle for the casually upscale, moderately priced, interior Mexican championship is El Chile. But Manuel's also carves out a distinct niche of its own with a clean, streamlined feel and some fascinating nouvelle takes on Mexican classics.

Take, for example, Manuel's famous caldo. It is a stark and exciting dish, sharp in flavor, with a deep red-brown color—almost black—gained from the dried chiles that form its base. The predominant flavor is the ancho pepper, which has interesting, smoky back notes that blend beautifully with the bright, creamy avocados sliced into the bowl.

Other appetizers are more approachable, and equally tasty. We like a very spicy, tart ceviche of ahi tuna, although it's sometimes—not always—a little chewy. Manuel's "gorditas" depart completely from their genre: they are deliciously soft, almost the texture of mashed potato cakes, with sweet fresh corn. Amongst mains, you should stay away from the bland, terribly overpriced camarones a la plancha—just a few sautéed shrimp and some okay rice, really—but we recommend the excellent, dynamic mole, lighter and fruitier than most, and the chile relleno en nogada, filled with shredded pork, almonds, and raisins, and enveloped in a walnut cream brandy sauce. Its rich, sweet, spicy cinnamon flavor tastes just like Christmas.

The funny thing about all this culinary elegance is its setting. The downtown branch, a favorite business lunch spot, is stuck firmly, luxuriantly in the '80s, complete with granite, mirrors, black leather, heaps of pink neon light, and a jazz brunch on Sundays. The Arboretum branch is more expansive with less character, but it boasts outdoor tables in an atmospheric garden. Still, we stick to downtown. With sultry service from black-clad, slightly unbuttoned waiters, we are reminded of the last days of disco, when the living was fast and loose. All that's missing is the soundtrack. –RM

Marakesh

A downtown Middle Eastern restaurant
with something for everyone

food
6.5 / 10   **7.2** / 10
experience

Middle Eastern $**18**   *Capitol Area*

Casual restaurant
Mon.-Sat. 11am-10pm;
closed Sun. *Outdoor dining.*
Vegetarian-friendly.

906 Congress Ave.
Austin
(512) 476-7735

Bar Beer/wine
Credit Cards Visa, MC, AmEx
Reservations Accepted

Marakesh Café and Grill occupies a charming 19th-century storefront near the capitol that is attractively painted with murals depicting bazaar and oasis scenes, and dimly lit by heavy iron chandeliers hanging from the high ceilings. The resulting atmosphere is much more interesting than what you find in so many of Austin's shopping-center ethnic restaurants. Speedy, friendly service and plentiful lunch specials make Marakesh a popular lunch spot for the suited downtown crowd, but on weekend evenings, the place lets its hair down, and belly dancers wiggle their wares to the delight of diners.

The menu covers a wide array of Mediterranean and Middle Eastern specialties, along with easily avoided American-style sandwiches (Veggie D-Lite?!). Happily, the Middle Eastern food is veggie-friendly. Falafel is fried to a crunch, but it's nicely soft-centered and a little spicy, with lots of lemon flavoring the ground chickpeas. Tabbouleh is heavy on the parsley, and a refreshing Turkish salad is spicy, with jalapeños, tomatoes, onion, and cucumbers in vinegar. The hummus is lovely, light, and creamy, with lemon and sesame back-notes from the tahini. We also love the smoky baba ganoush—you can scoop both up with crunchy thyme bread. Soft, lemony dolmas are available vegetarian, or filled with rice and ground lamb. Grilled chicken is moist, seasoned with coriander and accompanied by delicate couscous or aromatic yellow rice. Stay away from the tough lamb kebabs served with a soggy romaine-lettuce salad.

There are so many good appetizers at Marakesh, we sometimes like to make a meal of just them (the $20 mezze plate feeds five), and then finish with a bit of dessert. The baklava is chewy and the nutty filling has lots of sugar and cinnamon, but we hold out for the hareesah, a dense cake made with semolina flour and subtly flavored with a hint of rosewater. –MPN

Marco Polo

Very genuine Malaysian-Chinese that's
worth seeking out for the dim sum

food
8.1
10

5.8
10
experience

Chinese, Malaysian, Seafood   **$24**   *Southeast*

Casual restaurant
Sun.-Thurs. 11am-2:30pm, 5pm-
10pm; Fri.-Sat. 11am-2:30pm,
5pm-11:45pm. Dim sum Sat.-Sun.11am-2:30pm.
Brunch. Delivery. Live music. Outdoor dining.

2200 S. IH-35
Austin
(512) 445-5563

Bar Full
Credit Cards Visa, MC, AmEx
Reservations Accepted

This no-frills restaurant hidden in a Clarion Motel off South IH-35 is—
improbably—one of the most genuine options for dim sum and
Southeast Asian seafood in town. The large numbers of Asian-
Americans who frequent the place seem to confirm that notion, so we
didn't let it throw us too much when, on one visit, our moo shu pork
came with pancakes that were, without a doubt, bona fide, authentic
tortillas.

But you should bypass the moo shu and other such standard
Chinese-American chicken, beef, pork, and uninspired egg rolls, and go
straight for the unusually authentic family-style Chinese dishes and
stews with ingredients like preserved egg—or the equally interesting
Malaysian curries and rice dishes like nasi lemak (made with dried
anchovies). There's even Singapore-style chili crab on the menu, and
delicious steamed whole fish, which you can choose from amongst the
variety of fresh catch on offer daily.

But many people know Marco Polo best for its tops-in-town dim sum
brunch, when a profusion of dumplings and tidbits are served the
traditional way: drive-by style from little carts stacked high with platters
and bamboo steamers. Prices are low, making this a great option for
students on a hungry Sunday. The only unorthodox aspect of dim sum
here is the friendly waiters' amusing Hawaiian shirts.

If you're a dim sum virgin, come in a group of at least three to
maximize tasting opportunities, and don't be intimidated by the
unfamiliar. Dish names, poorly translated and mumbled hastily, aren't
very helpful anyway—just point, taste, and learn. Puffy white
barbecued pork buns are outstanding, eminently wolfable creations
with a dough that manages to be both light and gooey. Fat, slippery
rice noodles and sweet-meets-savory turnip cakes are experiments in
soft textural counterpoints. Aromatic, tea-steamed sticky rice and
sweetly caramelized pot-stickers are other highlights, but avoid the
horrid vegetable rolls. They only push the carts around weekends from
11am to 2:30pm, with no reservations; go early to avoid a long queue.
But even with a wait, Marco Polo is well worth it. —RM/RG

Maria's Taco Xpress

A lovely taco joint under the watchful
eye of South Austin's Patron Saint

food

8.0
10

9.0
10

experience

Mexican $ **8**   *South Lamar*

Counter service
Mon. 7am-3pm; Tues.-Fri.
7am-9pm; Sat. 8am-9pm;
Sun. 9am-2pm. *Breakfast.*
Live music. Outdoor dining.

2529 S. Lamar Blvd.
Austin
(512) 444-0261
www.tacoxpress.com

Bar Full
Credit Cards No credit cards
Reservations Not accepted

Like the figurehead of a majestically deteriorating ship, the open arms
of the Taco Goddess beckon from above Maria's Taco Xpress, one of
Austin's most beloved neighborhood taquerías. South Austinites came
out in force to support this icon of eclecticism when a developer tried
to purchase the property for an apartment complex a few years back.
But Taco Xpress stands strong, still an eloquent expression of everything
south of the river, stuffed full of kitsch of the highest order and
patronized by a scruffy mix of South Austinites, who represent the city's
increasingly outnumbered breed of Linklater-memorialized slackers.

A recent expansion of the patio means that there's now room for
everyone, even on the busy weekend mornings when people drag
themselves out of bed at the crack of noon to munch some griddled
goodness to the tunes of a spirited gospel-blues band. This outdoor
space is a mix of the worn-out, the wacky, and the warm, with
higgledy-piggledy tables and hidden corners, presided over by a
gloriously tacky "Patron Saint of South Austin"—a fairy-godmother-ish
figure in a massive, puffy dress, gilded head to toe, framed against the
wall. It's almost impossible to be grumpy under her spell.

The tacos here are not the freshest and brightest in town, but we like
many of them. Our favorites are a moist, flavorful pollo guisado taco, of
pulled, stewed chicken; a delicious al pastor, tender, fatty, and well
seasoned; and the migas taco, with griddle-cooked eggs that pick up a
nice blackened flavor from the rest of the food. Gorditas are sliced in
half to form greasy but yummy sandwiches with any number of fillings.
However, avoid the much-vaunted barbacoa—we find it bland and
dry—and skip the chewy grilled veggie options. Drown everything in
Maria's chimichurri sauce; it looks suspect, with prickly, wilted cilantro,
but it's in fact a magical elixir that wakes everything up with its spicy,
tangy kick—including you. –RM

Marisco Grill

Strangely flat seafood at high prices—
sometimes authenticity isn't enough

food

3.8 **4.7**

10 10

experience

Mexican, Seafood

$33

Sixth Street District, Burnet

Casual restaurant
Mon.-Thurs. 9am-10pm; Fri.-Sat.
9am-midnight; Sun. 11am-10pm.
Breakfast. Outdoor dining.

211 E. 6th St.
Austin
(512) 474-7372

Bar Full
Credit Cards Visa, MC, AmEx
Reservations Not accepted

6444 Burnet Rd.
78757, (512) 458-9440

There is a certain genre of authentic Mexican seafood restaurant that feels both upmarket and downmarket at the same time. It's upmarket in the sense that, in addition to the tortilla-based standards, the menu includes a range of pricey seafood mains. But it's downmarket in the sense that the atmosphere still feels like a Tex-Mex dive, and that the higher prices are justified merely by the more prestigious ingredients, not creativity.

When the seafood really sings, we love this sort of place. When it doesn't, it just feels like a rip-off. Unfortunately, it's the latter at Marisco Grill, whose two branches totally fail to deliver on their promise of fresh, tasty fish. Everything we've tried has been disappointing, beginning with bag-esque chips and jar-esque salsa. We wish the fish in the ceviche tasted as fresh as its avocado slices; instead, it has off-notes. In a 13-dollar plate of camarones al mojo de ajo (shrimp in garlic sauce)—which is meant as a simple stage on which big, fresh crustaceans can shine—the shrimp are instead the miniscule sort you'd find in Chinese take-out. In a strange twist, the dish comes with rice plus a mix of corn, zucchini, and carrots instead of refried beans. The vegetable mix is actually fresh and well seasoned; it's just out of place.

The service is friendly and feels very Mexican in every way, but even that can't rescue this food. And people seem to know it: the Burnet branch is often empty, while the joint along the main Sixth Street strip has far fewer patrons than you'd expect for such a prime location—though perhaps in part because of its bizarre, brightly illuminated dinginess. The conclusion is a little bit ironic: This is a Mexican seafood restaurant authentic enough to be along the strip of eateries along the main street of a midsized town in northern Baja California. It's just not the one on that strip that you'd want to go to. –RG

Mars

A fantastical world of starry skies and
pan-Asian flights of hit-or-miss fancy

food
6.5 **9.2**
10   10
experience

New American, Pan-Asian $**45**   *West Campus*

Upmarket restaurant
Mon.-Wed. 5pm-10pm; Thurs.
5pm-10:30pm; Fri. 5pm-11pm;
Sat. 5:30pm-11pm; Sun.
5:30pm-10pm. *Date-friendly. Vegetarian-friendly.*

1610 San Antonio St.
Austin
(512) 472-3901
www.marsaustin.com

Bar Full
Credit Cards Visa, MC, AmEx
Reservations Recommended

Mars is a cutting-edge fusion restaurant, circa 1992. It opened during an era when "eclectic" was still a kind of cuisine, a moment in American culinary history when integrating Asian spices into menus at vegetarian-friendly establishments other than brown-sauce Szechuan restaurants or downmarket curry shops was still a novelty. It was a time when the idea of fusing elements of Thai, Indian, Chinese, and Japanese food on one menu was still exciting rather than disconcerting.

As a result, Mars is a frustrating restaurant to write about. You want to salute and honor a restaurant that broke new culinary ground in Austin at a time when it was desperately needed, but our duty is to our readers, not the restaurants, and we would be dishonest not to admit that Mars' kitchen seems dated, and that the lack of focus of its menu takes away from the magical potential of the dining environment. Still, it is hard not to fall in love with the place's dim, mystical atmosphere from the moment that you step inside its doors. Reds, blacks, golds, and a complete indoor firmament give the place an intergalactic, Zen-like quality.

The most successful dishes are the ones that are bold and aggressive, like a marinated flank steak with mustard, kimchi, and sticky rice, or tea-smoked duck à l'orange. But the menu is a minefield. Hummus is bland; dishes with lo mein noodles, paired with tofu, chicken, and so on, are tired; baby back ribs are sticky-sweet and poorly paired with roasted garlic mashed potatoes. Vegetarian mains, often underseasoned, are so much less than they could be. Worst of all are the dry, overcooked fish mains, like salmon and halibut. And while servers are generally friendly, the attention can be spotty. Nonetheless, we fully understand Mars' longevity and continued appeal. If only they would update the cuisine by a decade and a half. –RG

Matt's El Rancho

Half a century of Tex-Mex history
swimming in Mexican martinis

food
4.9 **8.8**
10   10
experience

Mexican $**29**   *South Lamar*

Casual restaurant
Mon., Wed.-Thurs., and Sun.
11am-10pm; Fri.-Sat. 11am-
11pm; closed Tues. *Kid-friendly.*
Outdoor dining.

2613 S. Lamar Blvd.
Austin
(512) 462-9333
www.mattselrancho.com

Bar Full
Credit Cards Visa, MC, AmEx
Reservations Not accepted

It's hard to get much more classic, old-school Austin than Matt's El Rancho, the consummate Tex-Mex hangout with a bar that rages with people downing delicious Mexican martinis. Half of the loyal clientele might have been drinking and eating here since former pro boxer Matt Martinez opened the place in 1952 as one of the first handful of Tex-Mex restaurants in the world. Parents seem to begin taking their kids to Matt's El Rancho at the exact moment when their own parents stop taking them. But aside from the families and the golden oldies, you're also likely to run into local politicians, community figures, and Austin legends like Shayne and Courtney Wade.

The meal must start with a "Bob Armstrong Dip," known to regulars simply as a "Small Bob" or a "Large Bob," which features well-executed queso tastily decked out with ground beef and guacamole. A tortilla soup isn't bad, although it's not one of the better versions in town; a chile relleno is best with the full option package (pecans, raisins, and onions, which, as insiders know, you can request on just about anything). Tamales drowning in brown enchilada sauce aren't bad, but enchiladas themselves are boring. If you must, choose green, not red. In short, this isn't the most thrilling Tex-Mex.

Aside from the history, the most staggering thing about Matt's El Rancho is the size of the place. The parking lot alone takes up the better part of a city block on South Lamar. Inside are three enormous rooms, each seemingly bigger than the last, plus outdoor seating in good weather. You're guaranteed to see enormous family gatherings, long tables with big groups celebrating birthdays, and so on. And it's not hard to see why: the queso and Mexican martinis just keep coming, the service is informal and real, the prices are reasonable, and you're experiencing a slice of living Texas history. –RG

Maudie's

Gringo Tex-Mex, where, unfortunately,
Elvis has *not* left the building

food

2.9 / 10   **7.8** / 10

experience

Mexican, American

$22   *Tarrytown, South Lamar, Westlake*

Pub
Daily 9am-10pm.
Breakfast. Outdoor dining.
Wireless Internet.

2608 W. 7th St.
Austin
(512) 473-3740
www.maudies.com

Bar Full
Credit Cards Visa, MC, AmEx
Reservations Not accepted

1212 S. Lamar Blvd.
78704, (512) 440-8088

3801 N. Capital Of TX Hwy.
78746, (512) 306-8080

Ask many Austinites where they'd eat their last meal in town, and
Maudie's will make the short list. Why, we do not know. The Tex-Mex
fare served here is thoroughly mediocre, and neither the atmosphere
nor the service compensates for it. No, Maudie's is one of those places
where people go because they've always gone, and they've always
gone because that's where people went.

Plus, the fajitas aren't bad. Both the beef and chicken have sweet
caramelized edges and plenty of onions and peppers. We recommend
you stick with them. Maudie's popular enchiladas, topped with
"famous" chili con carne sauce, are an item from the Tex end of the
cuisine that you could only love if you're in a truly altered state. The
Tex-Mex equivalent of the Manwich, these enchiladas don't just swim in
grease—they do laps and the backstroke. In a similar vein, Maudie's
popular queso reminds us distressingly of ranch dressing. If we were
Mexican food, we would turn our backs on this stuff and pretend we
didn't know it—like the brash American cousin in the Hawaiian shirt at
the family reunion.

Even more authentic options aren't great. Fish tacos feature great
hulks of tilapia completely buried in a peppery rub, but are otherwise
dry and uneventful.

Perhaps one other reason that people come is that most Maudie's
locations are family-friendly without going Disney (they remain
appealingly gritty); at the more upmarket "Maudie's Milagro"
Davenport Village location, there is even a well-ventilated patio
overlooking the Hill Country. Perhaps they come, too, for the mango
margaritas, a standout in the difficult-to-pull-off frozen-fruit family.
Perhaps they come because the service, though a bit intense on busy
nights, can be quite amiable. Or perhaps they make the pilgrimage to
sit in the small, hot pink room on South Austin Boulevard and bask in
the rosy glow under countless images of Elvis. Maudie's does, in fact,
seem to serve the kind of low-brow gringo-Mex that the King would
have liked. –RM

Mekong River

Lively Vietnamese and Thai fare wakes
up a dead downtown afternoon

food

7.7 **6.6**
10   10

experience

Vietnamese $**18**   *Sixth Street District*

Casual restaurant
Sun.-Thurs. 10:30am-10pm;
Fri.-Sat. 10:30am-11pm.
Delivery. Vegetarian-friendly.

215 E. 6th St.
Austin
(512) 236-8878
www.mekongriveronsixth.com

Bar None
Credit Cards Visa and MC
Reservations Not accepted

Mekong River should be appreciated more. It takes advantage of a
great Sixth Street location, with its tall ceilings and windows and
elegant dimensions, and the Vietnamese and Thai cuisine offered here
is well above average. The menu is long and varied, and though prices
are occasionally a buck or two above average as well, the portions are
routinely ample enough for two. Only the service seems a little
maladroit, particularly during busy lunchtimes.

Dishes are served in huge bowls, generally with your starch of choice
already mixed in. Some items disappoint—beef spring rolls, for
example, contain mainly chewy vermicelli—but for the most part things
are nicely seasoned, with that sweet-tart-savory combination that
makes this region's food so appealing. Fresh vegetables and herbs
abound. We can recommend the pineapple curry (though you'll have to
hunt a bit for the pineapple) and a lemongrass vermicelli dish called
"Spicy Landlord," something we can all relate to.

The menu, peopled with many such lively characters, makes for an
imaginative lunchtime escape. Located as it is within spitting distance of
so many offices, Mekong's menu offers the dreary cubicle inmate an
outlet into his or her fantasies, simply by ordering. Thus we find a
"Spicy Boss" keeping the "Spicy Landlord" company, as well as a
"Secretary Holiday," "R-rated Shrimp," "Saigon Mistress," and
"Ambassador's Daughter." We'd like to see that soap.

But what we ultimately recommend is for you to bypass all these
temptations and order the Vietnamese phô, which is really Mekong's
specialty. So often that dish is a murky soup—like dirty bathwater, the
unappealing reminder of a meat's questionable past. But here, the
various phô are clean-flavored and complex. Anisey notes of Thai basil
and green hints of celery brighten the broth. Plenty of veggies and a
spicy kick can break you out of the dullest afternoon. –RM

Mesa Ranch

A newcomer with unpretentious
modern variations on country cookin'

food

7.5 / 10 **6.8** / 10

experience

Southwestern $**44**   *Northwest Hills*

Upmarket restaurant
Mon.-Thurs. 11am-2pm, 5pm-9pm;
Fri. 11am-2pm, 5pm-10pm; Sat.
5pm-10pm; Sun. 5pm-9pm.
Brunch.

8108 Mesa Dr.
Austin
(512) 853-9480
www.mesaranchaustin.com

Bar Full
Credit Cards Visa, MC, AmEx
Reservations Accepted

We love when a restaurant goes out of its way to honor Texan cuisine
and ingredients, and for that alone, this newcomer wins a blue ribbon.
Its aesthetic is rural Texas to the core, if somewhat contrived, with
horse-themed wall art, saddles here and there, and even a case of guns
on the wall. The bar area is nicely set off and perhaps more
atmospheric than the rest of the restaurant itself, but it all achieves a
pleasant feel, especially for a brand-new strip-mall restaurant, with
warm, yellow walls, cozy place settings, and a staff that is
extraordinarily friendly and helpful.

If not for Mesa Ranch's relatively remote location (at least with
respect to downtown), near the Anderson Lane/Spicewood Springs
Road exit off MoPac, this restaurant would be an excellent standby as a
place to take out-of-towners hoping for a taste o' Texas. And we don't
just say that because of the menu's ambitions: the kitchen follows
through well in most cases, above all in a thrilling preparation of grilled
quail, whose glaze features jammy dabs of preserved fruit without
overpowering the beautifully textured meat. Great, too, are grilled
shrimp, tender, juicy, and thoughtfully seasoned.

Other dishes can be hit-or-miss, but there are more hits than misses,
and Mesa Ranch shows great potential. An appetizer of fried cactus
with Shiner Bock beer batter is a clever idea, even if the cactus strips,
though properly crispy, don't have an inspiring taste. The strips come
with a pedestrian ranch dressing plus Shiner Bock-laced chile con queso
whose beer flavor really comes through—almost too much, if you relish
that traditional queso taste. The queso also suffers from that queso
disease in which it forms a skin and thickens too quickly. But we salute
the concept. Steaks and mesquite-grilled pork spare ribs, meanwhile,
are a treat, and even Austin classics like chicken-fried steak have an
edge: this one's chicken-fried venison, and the gravy boasts poblano.
Here's to Texas. –RG

Mexico Lindo

A surprisingly authentic sea-Mex find on
South Lamar

food
7.5 **4.4**
10 · 10
experience

Mexican · $**25** · *South Lamar*

Casual restaurant
Daily 6am-10pm. *Breakfast.*
Outdoor dining.

1816 S. Lamar Blvd.
Austin
(512) 326-4395

Bar Full
Credit Cards Visa, MC, AmEx
Reservations Accepted

It can be really hard for a new restaurant to spread the word about its existence, especially when it's a squat, easy-to-miss building along a zooming strip of South Lamar without foot traffic. But it can be even harder when such a restaurant isn't even new—just under new management. For a long time, there was little to distinguish this place from the next one along the strip.

But now they should stop, because the new incarnation of Mexico Lindo, with a renewed focus on seafood, has rendered it a well-kept secret in the authentic Mexican realm. The pleasant, pale-yellow patio melds the sounds of outdoor-speaker mariachi music and the rush of cars in a competition for auditory supremacy. Inside, the space isn't quite as charming, with a sad-looking bar and crinkly yellow walls that look vaguely like the skin formed atop a bad batch of chile con queso. But don't let that scare you away from the seafood-centric menu, which might as well come straight outta northern Mexico or Baja California.

Chips and red salsa are standard-issue stuff, but green salsa brandishes some serious heat. Margaritas are sweet and bright orange, not bad if not the best around. Things start to get really interesting with a spot-on shrimp cocktail spot on (if spicy), whose sweet, fruity sauce is the most authentically Mexican we've had in town, with tomato, cilantro, avocado, and the requisite saltines. It's not everyone's thing, but this one is a paradigm. Amongst mains, fried seafood is fine, but we prefer the succulent shrimp al mojo, butterflied and coated in a slightly spicy red sauce that doesn't overwhelm their taste. Barbacoa is even more impressive, tender and not too gamey, with an ideal meat-fat balance; and moist rice and porky beans are nearly perfect. We hope that this eminently Mexican establishment is headed for neighborhood-legend status. But this is the free market, and it is up to the customers to decide. –RG

Mi Colombia

Yuppified South American food in a
gentrifying East Austin neighborhood

food
6.4 / 10

6.7 / 10
experience

Latin American $**16**   *East Austin*

Casual restaurant
Tues.-Thurs. 11am-3pm, 5pm-
10pm; Fri.-Sat. 11am-3pm, 5pm-
11pm; Sun. 11am-6pm; closed Mon. *Brunch. Kid-friendly.*

1614 E. 7th St.
Austin
(512) 391-0884

Bar BYO
Credit Cards Visa, MC, AmEx
Reservations Accepted

It's a cultural anthropologist's wet dream: this East Austin newcomer is bringing eclectic, modern dining to the Mexican neighborhood of East Austin—yet the inspiration for its food is a poorer part of Latin America than Mexico. The fonts, for starters, give Mi Colombia away as a place that is reaching out to yuppies in a traditionally working-class neighborhood. Located in an attractive house, the restaurant is formed by two long rooms separated by a window-filled wall. The color scheme is yellow and green with tropical plants, and dozens of postcard-sized paintings of butterflies line the top of the walls—Mi Colombia does not fall into the tacky decorating trap.

The restaurant is BYO, but if your aims are non-alcoholic, you can get a dizzying array of batas, cool and refreshing treat drinks popular in Venezuela and Colombia, made by pureeing fruit with either water or milk. On weekends all of the flavors are available including guava, guanábana, and blackberry, though there are usually only two or three choices on weekdays. Service is friendly and knowledgeable, but still lacks polish (sorry, dressing them nicely won't hide their mistakes...). Perhaps with a little time.

Mi Colombia's menu is heavily South American with a decidedly Caribbean influence, and while most things we've tried are tasty and authentic, there are a few items to be avoided. Number one in that arena is Mi Colombia's overpriced Cuban sandwich. Bland, with sliced pork rather than pulled, it has no cheese, and no flavor. Also bland are the buñuelos, deep-fried cheese bread that is spongy and dense, but not very cheesy here. On the other hand, we enjoy the patacones rellenos—deep-fried cups of slightly chewy green plantain filled with shredded pork and topped with melted cheese, then served with a pleasantly kicked-up salsa; their flavors and textures are delicious. Whole tilapia is beautifully served, crisp-skinned and golden, topped with translucent sliced onions and limes. The fish is flaky and moist, but watch out for bones. There are ups and downs, but you certainly can't deny that it's an interesting development. –MPN

Mikado Ryotei

Follow those in the know to this
Research Boulevard Japanese standout

food
9.1
10
6.6
10
experience

Japanese $**47**   *Far North*

Upmarket restaurant
Sun.-Thurs. 11am-10pm;
Fri.-Sat. 11am-10:30pm.
Live music.

9033 Research Blvd.
Austin
(512) 833-8188
www.mikadoryotei.com

Bar Beer/wine
Credit Cards Visa, MC, AmEx
Reservations Accepted

Sometimes it seems like greater Austin's best sushi places are shrouded in a veil of insider mystery. On most evenings at Mikado, for instance, the sushi bar fills up with regulars, many of whom seem to be on a first-name basis with the management. These insiders know exactly what to order, they're treated just right, and they wind up eating what can sometimes be spectacularly good sushi and Japanese fusion food. If you play it right, you could too.

Mikado is a strip-mall Japanese restaurant with a certain trendiness to it—not that that's necessarily a bad thing. The waitstaff is cute, the lighting is low, there's a big wine rack in the middle of everything. Although we don't mean to suggest that you must be a regular to enjoy the best of Mikado, we do recommend sitting at the sushi bar to strike up a conversation about what the freshest fish on offer is—or even just to schmooze. Wherever you're sitting, though, don't just stick to sushi: a starter of grilled quails on skewers is a knockout, rubbed with plenty of sea salt and spiced with crushed yuzu pepper. This is some of the best quail we've had in Austin, and Austin's a quail town.

So, too, for the sushi: on a good night, it can really floor you, and you might not be expecting that from a restaurant on Research Boulevard. Go for the nigiri (sushi pieces): hirame (fluke), suzuki (sea bass), sake toro (fatty salmon), hamachi toro (fatty yellowtail), uni (sea urchin), escarole, and simple maguro (tuna) meet with virtually equal—and considerable—success. The only weakness has been relatively tough octopus. Meanwhile, fusion permeates the cooked dishes. "Nagano Duck VSOP" is marinated in French cognac, brushed with black pepper and shoyu, and served with sautéed Asian greens; delicious steaks are oak grilled. This is one of the few restaurants this far from downtown that's worth the trip even for downtowners, and we don't say that lightly. –RG

Milto's

Good Greek-American food is hard to
come by, but try this one on for size

food

7.1 / 10   **8.1** / 10

experience

Greek, Pizza $**11**   *UT Area*

Counter service   2909 Guadalupe St.   *Bar* Beer/wine
Mon.-Thurs. 11am-10:30pm;   Austin   *Credit Cards* Visa, MC, AmEx
Fri.-Sat. 11am-11pm; Sun. noon-   (512) 476-1021   *Reservations* Not accepted
10:30pm. *Delivery. Outdoor dining. Wireless Internet.*

Milto's prime draw is its location, which is on a particularly splendid
corner at the north end of the Drag, surrounded by such fine company
as Toy Joy, Antone's Records, Taco Shack, Vulcan Video, and Ken's
Donuts. The setting is undeniably unattractive except to the fondest of
gazes, but along the wide sidewalks people lope comfortably, enjoying
the sun, passing time as easily as a frisbee, and even the traffic seems
lazy. Such spots represent the best of the Austin college-town scene;
they seem to have taken a nap a few decades ago and never quite felt
the need to wake up, stretch, and join the rat race.

   Milto's offers a cool, dark retreat to those who want to slip out of
the sun for a while. It serves up New York-style pizza alongside Greek-
American food at reasonable prices. In fact, this is some of the better
pizza in town, with a slightly sweet, crunchy crust and just the right
amount of sauce and cheese. Good toppings include the marinated
artichoke hearts, but we like a slice of plain pie accompanied by their
signature Greek salad, which isn't particularly authentic but is nice and
perky, with salty feta, real Kalamata olives, and a delicious, creamy,
garlicky dressing. Ask for an extra roll—they're made of the pizza
dough, and dipped in the dressing they are irresistible. In certain moods
(and budgets—it ain't cheap) these and a bottomless iced-tea make the
perfect lunch.

   Milto's also serves gyros, basic pastas, and the like. Most of these
options are good. There's nothing spectacular, but Milto's doesn't
pretend to anything more. It would rather just sit back, relax, and
watch the traffic flow. –RM

Mirabelle

A sexy suburbanite that executes well in
modern Southwestern style

food
8.9 **8.7**
10   10
experience

Southwestern $**46**   *Northwest Hills*

Upmarket restaurant   8127 Mesa Dr.   *Bar* Full
Mon.-Thurs. 11am-2pm, 5:30pm-   Austin   *Credit Cards* Visa, MC, AmEx
9:30pm; Fri.-Sat. 5:30pm-   (512) 346-7900   *Reservations* Recommended
10:30pm; closed Sun.   www.mirabellerestaurant.com
Date-friendly. Vegetarian-friendly.

Like an oasis—not a mirage—Mirabelle, sister of the downtown Castle
Hill Café, rises out of a middle-of-nowhere strip mall with mood
lighting, romantic flair, and exciting nouvelle Texas fare. It's not just the
trendified hanging lamps, not just the walls in hues of orange and
yellow, that take this atmosphere to the next level. It's something
ineffable, something about the combination of service and customer
base, that whisks you a world away from big parking lots and
Starbucks branches and into a zone of culinary immersion for the
evening.

Not every dish rises to the occasion. Smoked salmon with caviar is
cleverly paired with pancakes—a sidelong Southern scoff, perhaps, at
the aristocrats' blini—but the fish itself is no better than supermarket-
package stuff, and the accompanying potato salad isn't nearly good
enough to rise above the fact that it's just potato salad (actually, it's
below-average potato salad). No worries, though: the pork tenderloin
flauta with sun-dried cherry chutney picks up the slack, and seared sea
scallops are well executed, even if their "Thai coconut cream" is heavy
on the cream and light on the Thai.

Even better, by a fair margin, is the sensational bacon-laced corn
pudding that comes with espresso-rubbed venison, itself a formidable
piece of meat served with a correctly prepared brandy reduction.
Roasted duck breast with fennel-Merlot jus is pleasant, and grilled
shrimp are acceptable, but their show is stolen by a rice dish that is like
the illicit love child of jambalaya and risotto. Main-course salads,
perhaps predictably, aren't as impressive, but the wine list is solid.

What's more, prices are eminently reasonable. Mirabelle sports a
winning combination of casually elegant atmosphere and upmarket
Texican flair that makes it hard to beat as a place to take out-of-
towners, or as a place for a date, if you happen to be within reach of
this particular corner of Northwest Austin suburbia. –RG

Mongolian Barbecue

There is a flaw at the heart of the
Mongolian Barbecue game plan

food
2.8 | **4.0**
10 | 10
experience

Pan-Asian   **$17**   *Convention Center Area*

Casual restaurant   117 San Jacinto Blvd.   *Bar* Beer/wine
Sun.-Thurs. 11am-9:30pm;   Austin   *Credit Cards* Visa, MC, AmEx
Fri.-Sat. 11am-10:30pm.   (512) 476-3938   *Reservations* Accepted
                              www.mongoliangrille.com

If you design your own food, chances are it won't be as good as if it
were prepared by someone with, you know, *training*.

The basic concept here is that you go up to a kind of salad bar, pack
as many ingredients as you can (mostly vegetables, but also thinly
sliced, sometimes-still-frozen meats) into a bowl, pile pre-cooked
noodles precariously on top, douse it all with ladles-full of various
liquids (soy sauce, vinegar, coconut, and so on), and bring it to the
chefs who then cook it on a huge circular griddle. Fresh cilantro and
basil, a bowl of peanuts, and some eggs are available to perk things up.

There are guidelines to help you out, particularly when it comes to
the saucy bit; a poster spells out a series of formulas for hot and sour,
spicy garlic, satay sauce, and other sauces (one ladle soy, half a ladle
rice vinegar…). Unfortunately, when you counterbalance bad
ingredients with each other, and use too many of them, even the most
meticulous results can be a shade on the wrong side of nasty. Stay well
away from the hot and sour formula, for example, which can become a
vinegary, soggy mess. Satay is better, as it is redeemed by the nuttiness
of peanuts. A chicken soup, some below-par pot-stickers, and rice puffs
reminiscent of the leather tongues of shoes accompany your stir-fry.

There is a certain sick pleasure in seeing your creations mutilated on
the griddle by chefs wielding what appear to be sabers. They slash
away, tossing and chopping your food with manic aplomb in a musical
racket of metal on metal. But this music only echoes hollowly in the
cavernous, mirrored space on San Jacinto, which can be quite dead at
night (lunchtime is livelier). Food quickly turns cold in the unnatural
chill, and a lonely waiter wanders around with sadly little to do.
Perhaps he should instead perform a great public service by going
outside and warning pedestrians: "keep walking, folks, nothing to see
here." –RM

Moonshine

A warm, inviting space perhaps best for drinks and dessert

food
6.4 **9.5**
10   10
experience

American $36 *Convention Center Area*

Upmarket restaurant
Mon.-Thurs. 11am-10pm;
Fri.-Sat. 11am-11pm; Sun. 10am-
2:30pm, 5pm-10pm. *Brunch.*
Date-friendly. Kid-friendly. Outdoor dining. Wireless Internet.

303 Red River St.
Austin
(512) 236-9599
www.moonshinegrill.com

Bar Full
Credit Cards Visa, MC, AmEx
Reservations Recommended

Moonshine is serving souped-up down-home cooking in the downtown space formerly known as (sniffle) Emilia's. Moonshine has toned down the space—walls are hung with large mirrors accentuating its roominess, and Ball jar glasses and popcorn are subtle touches for a place that is trying to be homey and trendy at the same time. It really works, though, as does the magical outdoor garden. Business is brisk, and service is friendly but can be a little off, with food sometimes arriving out of sync.

The menu is made up of homestyle classics with an upscale twist. A chaotic Sunday brunch offers Southern favorites, breakfast standards, pastas, and more. House-made potato chips with a warm brie and sour cream dip need salt, but are addictive nonetheless. Baby spinach salad garnished with strawberries, sliced almonds, red onions, and goat cheese is lightly dressed, bright and delicious. A much-talked-about appetizer takes shrimp on the stick and does it up just like a corn dog. It's a fun concept…at least for a few bites, and then not so much. A hearty meatloaf is more than competent, but a highly touted marinated pork chop falls flat—or, better said, dry.

A chicken and artichoke BLT has contrasting textures from crunchy bacon and dense meat, with the artichoke hearts giving slightly salty and sour undertones. Chicken-fried steak has a lovely crunch—except where it is smothered by bland chipotle gravy that makes the breading sadly soggy. Mains come with veggies of the day—we especially like the brown-sugar carrots and pimento macaroni and cheese, which remind us of childhood dinners. This is one of the best mac and cheeses in town, but Moonshine's best work of all is their stellar peanut-butter pie, drizzled with caramel and chocolate in an Oreo crust—its delightful airy texture may help you feel less guilty about eating the whole enormous piece all by yourself. Ultimately, though, this place is all about the truly romantic feel, a rare find downtown. –MPN

Mother Egan's

Proof that a good reputation and the
luck of the Irish aren't always enough

food
3.3 **7.1**
10 | 10
experience

American   **$24**   *Warehouse District*

Pub
Sun.-Thurs. 11am-11pm;
Fri.-Sat. 11am-midnight. *Brunch.*
Live music. Outdoor dining.

715 W. 6th St.
Austin
(512) 478-7747
www.motheregansirishpub.com

Bar Full
Credit Cards Visa, MC, AmEx
Reservations Not accepted

An Irish pub was always going to be a somewhat dicey proposition
deep in the heart of Texas. Put it down to the sunny weather. Mother
Egan's has picked up something of a reputation for its food, but as far
as we can tell, they haven't earned it. The food available here, despite a
brave attempt at some Irish favorites, is thoroughly ordinary, and
sometimes worse. The shepherd's pie is a sad version of the hearty
classic, with dank, grayish mashed potatoes, and bland, fatty ground
beef that lacks vigor. Even the peas are mealy. Salads and dressings
taste like they're fresh from the packet.

Mother Egan's serves a Sunday brunch, but here, too, there are often
disappointments. On one occasion, eggs benedict came essentially
hard-boiled, which simply misses the point of the dish: yolk mixing with
hollandaise and together coating the English muffin. Even the bread
pudding with "Mother's whiskey sauce," with all due respect to Mom,
looked and tasted like it had had the worst of an unexpected
encounter with a rapid, low-maintenance heating device—it was a
heavy, mushy clump. The pub does, however, serve some perfectly
acceptable sandwiches and fish and chips.

Service here is friendly, if somewhat vague. The comfortable décor
consists of wood paneling and mirrors with the predictable Irish
accoutrements: whiskey bottles, Guinness signs, and so on. There is, in
fact, a fairly impressive collection of whiskeys available behind the bar.
A generous, plain deck spreads outside, facing a parking lot. Not quite
the romance of the Emerald Isle.

Mother Egan's is the kind of place worth going to during a wild night
on Sixth Street, if you need some fried appetizers to absorb the fumes.
But not even the luck of the Irish will help you with the crapshoot that
is this menu. –RM

MOUTH OF AUSTIN

JJ HERMES

EDITOR-IN-CHIEF,
THE DAILY TEXAN

The average undergraduate is an anathema to the restaurant scene: a stingy-tipping, check-splitting, water-only customer. We tend to honor the all-you-can-eat buffet, the happy hour, the 24-hour establishment, the pizza delivery. But the more erudite student, if I may ooze such pretension, can find a haven of healthy, quality meals a little more than a dozen blocks north of the University of Texas campus at Mother's Cafe and Garden.

The atmosphere exudes this sort of youthful warmth, especially befitting the Hyde Park neighborhood and the restaurant's connected, climate-controlled "garden." Even to an omnivore (as I am), their menu of vegetarian and vegan dishes is well worth discovering. Certainly try their cashew tamari salad dressing. As for entrées, I have never had a bad batch of spinach lasagna, capellini marinara, spinach-mushroom enchiladas, or their "Bueno Burger." And their vegan apple pie is quite delicious.

But for a uniquely proletariat meal right up any budding academic's alley, there's nothing more idealistic than ordering the Peasant's Meal—brown rice, beans or black-eyed peas—and a soup or salad. No fancy parsley decorations, no sun-carved oranges: simply sustenance.

I fondly recall Michael Birmingham, an Irish volunteer with Voices in the Wilderness fresh from spending several years helping poverty-stricken Iraqis in Baghdad, order a Peasant's Meal without hesitation. There's just something pleasing about skipping the dressings and getting right to the meat and potatoes—or in this case, just the potatoes. –JJH

Mother's

A veggie paradise, where the process doesn't always match the produce

food **6.6** / 10 **7.4** / 10 experience

American $**20**   *Hyde Park*

Casual restaurant
Mon.-Fri. 11:15am-10pm;
Sat.-Sun. 10am-10pm. *Brunch.*
Live music. Outdoor dining.
Vegetarian-friendly.

4215 Duval St.
Austin
(512) 451-3994
www.motherscafeaustin.com

Bar Beer/wine
Credit Cards Visa, MC, AmEx
Reservations Not accepted

A favorite of vegetarians (and those who admire them) throughout Austin, Mother's serves food not so much like Mom used to make, but rather like Mother Earth might. Mother's is one of a series of hopping spots that cluster around 43rd and Duval at the heart of Hyde Park, and its main selling point is the "garden," which is really more of a pleasant atrium packed with verdant tropical plants (you'd half expect a toucan to come winging through the growth). A pool of running water, live harp music on certain nights, and strings of white Christmas lights add sound and sparkle to the festive picture, which lacks only adequate lighting—poorly aimed spotlights mean that some diners have to eat out of their own shadows.

Service here is standard Austin-friendly, but it is sometimes somewhat vacant, and occasionally infuriatingly slow. When it does arrive, the food at Mother's is really pretty good—they make far more concessions to flavor than most restaurants whose menus prominently sport the word "vegan." Their fresh salsa is thick and garlicky, and a "Garden Patch" salad of perky vegetables (including winners like sunflower sprouts and shaved jicama) comes doused in Mother's special cashew-tamari dressing, if you choose (do it!). It's nutty, sweet, and wonderfully salty. The popular spinach lasagna is also a success; though it lacks structure, it is full of flavor, with the pleasant crunch of pecans.

But dishes that are more ethnically ambitious fare less well. A vegetable coconut-milk curry, at one visit, was muddy and over-spiced, the vegetables too hard (a frequent fault in vegetarianist cooking—perhaps it encourages asceticism). The artichoke enchiladas taste more Italian-ish than Mexican (they seem to share the marinara from the lasagne). Enchiladas verdes are better, but accompanying beans and rice are examples of the granola-crunching approach to starches (rice cakes, anyone?). Mother Earth may do well on the raw ingredients, but that doesn't always mean she knows how to cook 'em. –RM

Mozart's

Coffee and computers by the lake

Sweets   *Tarrytown*

Café   3825 Lake Austin Blvd.   *Bar* Beer/wine
Mon.-Thurs. 7am-midnight; Fri. Austin   *Credit Cards* Visa, MC, AmEx
7am-1am; Sat. 8am-1am; Sun.   (512) 477-2900   *Reservations* Not accepted
8am-midnight. *Date-friendly.* www.mozartscoffee.com
Live music. Outdoor dining. Vegetarian-friendly. Wireless Internet.

Sit down at one of the outdoor tables at Mozart's, and you enter a fantasy Lake Austin world, a place that it is impossible to imagine really lies less than a five-minute drive down Lake Austin Boulevard from downtown. Calm, crystalline waters and rolling hills spread out before your eyes. Swans swim by. All this, you ask yourself, for the price of one bottomless cup of (unfortunately somewhat watery) coffee?

Then the sun sets, and as party sounds begin to emanate from Lucy's Boatyard and the Hula Hut next door, Mozart's turns into a romantic dessert place. Lovey-dovey couples grab dishes of Amy's ice cream or plates of the decent cakes, pies, and cookies that are served out of the big glass case by the cash register. They sit by candlelight with the twinkling stars reflecting across the lake.

During the day, though, Austin's most scenically situated coffeeshop maintains a somewhat serious vibe, as if oblivious to the beautiful views. On weekdays, solo caffeine hounds with laptops, textbooks, or problem sets, outnumber groups by at least two to one, although logistical discussions of the just allocation of laptop power outlets can evolve into quite the informal pickup scene: "No, that's fine, I have plenty of battery power. So, are you a grad student?"

And sometimes it seems as though a lot of people at Mozart's are really using the place as their office. You'll overhear job interviews ("Well, first of all, I really like working with people"), business-plan pitch sessions ("But it's still not clear to me what the exit opportunities are"), and office hours ("What would be an example of a *good* argument?")—all on the agenda of an average Mozart's afternoon. There are other college towns and other state capitals and other tech boomtowns, but only in Austin would this all happen to the faint rhythms of Johnny Cash, along the shores of a shimmering lake. –RG

Mr. Gatti's

Austin's longest-lived and most
successful fast-food venture

food

4.9 10   **3.5** 10

experience

Pizza

$ **8**   *West Campus, S. Lamar, Oak Hill*

Casual restaurant
Hours vary by location. UT branch
open daily 11am–midnight.
Delivery. Kid-friendly.

503 W. MLK Blvd.
Austin
(512) 459-2222
www.mrgattis.com

Bar None
Credit Cards Visa, MC, AmEx
Reservations Not accepted

2614 S. Lamar Blvd.
78704, (512) 459-2222

7101 W. Hwy. 71
78749, (512) 301-8614

Founded in Austin in 1969, Mr. Gatti's has spread over much of the
southern United States. They offer consistently decent pizza, reasonable
delivery times, and an affordable buffet. Then there are the infamous
Gattitowns—buffet-only establishments with game rooms, TVs, and
battalions of wheeled high chairs for navigating your and your toddler's
way through their vast expanses. These are understandably popular
with kids—and even some parents.

The restaurants themselves are pretty short on ambience, most of
which comes from whatever is playing on the closest TV (usually
cartoons or sports). We prefer the regular Mr. Gatti's to the Gattitowns,
if only because they seem to smell better (fewer little people, perhaps?).

The buffet includes salad, pasta, a variety of pizzas, and dessert
pizzas as well, with larger buffets at the Gattitowns. The pizza crust is
fairly thin but chewy, with a texture reminiscent of smashed white
bread, sprinkled with fresh toppings and ample cheese (which comes in
slightly unfortunate pellets). There are usually a half dozen types of
pizza to choose from including a vegetarian sampler and a barbecued
chicken pizza with an overly sweet sauce that is balanced with plenty of
red onions. The pastas are sticky and served with a choice of bland
sauces.

The salad bar is full of pickled items as well as the usual offerings,
not always at their freshest. There's also fruit, Jell-O, and sometimes
pudding, all of which helps with feeding the little ones. There's no
reason to try most of the buffet, so we recommend that you stick to
the pizza, which, while not terribly memorable, is actually kind of
yummy, in an ashamed-to-admit-it kind of way. Mr. Gatti's is usually
heavily populated by families, and while it's not the best pizza in town,
it's certainly one of the easiest places to go for a meal with the kids.
–MPN

Mr. Natural

A mysteriously popular, somewhat grim
vendor of maltreated vegetables

food

3.7 / 10

4.5 / 10

experience

Light American   **$12**   *South Lamar, East Austin*

Counter service   2141A S. Lamar Blvd.   *Bar* None
Mon.-Sat. 8am-7pm; closed Sun.   Austin   *Credit Cards* Visa, MC, AmEx
Breakfast. Outdoor dining.   (512) 916-9223   *Reservations* Not accepted
Vegetarian-friendly.   www.mrnatural-austin.com

                                 1901 E. Cesar Chavez St.
                                 78702, (512) 477-5228

Mr. Natural, Austin's preeminent dealer in vegetarian and vegan foods,
is a thorough disappointment. Walk into the large, ungainly dining
room of the chain's South Austin branch, and you'll be struck by the
surprisingly *un*natural feel of the place. It has none of the crunchy,
hippy, homegrown warmth you might expect from a health-food store.
Instead, there's the antiseptic look of a school cafeteria, complete with
fake-veneer tables (you know you're in trouble when they're faking
something that is itself fake) and stained Styrofoam ceiling tiles. Even
the hanging plants, despite the restaurant's name, are plastic.

The food, unfortunately, recalls the same cafeteria, and while it
presumably does pass the various required "natural" tests, it tastes
none the better for it. Much of it has a hazily Tex-Mex bent, but shows
no sign of the lively spices that characterize the cuisine in Austin. Beans
of all varieties lack salt and flavor. Gorditas are dry and boring, the
black bean and crumbly tofu version particularly bad. Even some of the
more obviously vegetarian items are poorly executed, and sometimes
taste tinned. A carrot salad, enlivened by coconut flakes, is ruined by
dry, bitter carrots and tough, canned pineapple chunks. Some sautéed
potatoes, mushrooms and peppers remind us of a meal we had at
37,000 feet on Continental (to Mr. Natural's credit, at least we didn't
say American Airlines). Other vegetables fare better—some green beans
are well cooked, well seasoned, and buttery, and a garden salad with
cucumber is tasty enough. These look like triumphs by comparison.

Mr. Natural also sells natural and vegan baked goods in a variety of
brown shades; bottles of nutritional supplements and other health
goods peer somewhat disapprovingly down at patrons. Spelt cookies?
Mega-Flax digestive? Aloe Vera juice in a plastic bottle that resembles
bathroom bleach, anyone? Yeah, that's what we thought, too. –RM

Ms. B's

Slow service and phenomenal soft-shell
crab po-boys

food

6.9 | **6.0**
10 | 10

experience

Southern   **$27**   *Northwest Hills*

Casual restaurant   8105 Mesa Dr.   *Bar* Beer/wine
Mon.-Sat. 11am-3pm,   Austin   *Credit Cards* Visa, MC, AmEx
5:30pm-10pm; closed Sun.   (512) 372-9529   *Reservations* Accepted
Outdoor dining.   www.msbscreole.com

Ms. B's "authentic Creole cuisine" is a small restaurant that is big on
taste. The N'awlins-themed décor is purple and aqua, with checked
floors, jazz-inspired paintings, and comically grotesque fish sculptures
hanging above the bar. Service is slow, but the sassy waitstaff will keep
you entertained and be sure you clean your plate before you get
dessert.

Louisiana staples abound, and choices can be hard to make. There
are daily lunch specials as well as a variety of appetizers like crab cakes,
shrimp cocktail, and salad topped with blackened catfish. Breads baked
in-house are dense and filling; amongst them, cornbread and biscuits
are good, but save yourself for the zingy jalapeño cheese bread. Creole
dishes are classic, but on the whole beautifully executed. Seafood
gumbo is dark and spicy with lots of shrimp and crawfish. Red beans
and rice with andouille sausage are mildly spicy with an even
consistency, pairing wonderfully with crisp, juicy fried chicken. Peppery
crawfish étouffée is rich, but the dark sauce is a little thin.

Po-boys are wonderful, filled with catfish, oysters, shrimp, crawfish,
or vegetables. Don't miss the soft-shell crab po-boy—the whole
battered crab looks ready to defend, perched atop sliced baguette with
tomatoes and lettuce. But a highly seasoned batter and the crunch of
the fried blue cheese guarantee that she won't stand a chance against
the lucky diner who gets her for lunch. Accompanying fries are bright
orange with chili powder, greasy but good. For dessert, there's cobbler,
sweet potato pecan pie, and warm cinnamon-spiked bread pudding
filled with raisins and topped with Chantilly cream.

Prices here are a little high, and this is not a good place for a quick
lunch, but if you've got plenty of time, and a love of Louisiana
cooking—especially po-boys—Ms. B's will keep you very happy. –MPN

Musashino

It's trendy and you'll wait, but this is
some of the best sushi around

food

8.9 / 10

8.9 / 10

experience

Japanese

$**58**

Northwest Hills

Upmarket restaurant
Tues.-Thurs. 11:30am-2pm,
5:30pm-10pm; Fri. 11:30am-2pm,
5:30pm-10:30pm; Sat. 5:30pm-
10:30pm; Sun. 5:30pm-10pm;
closed Mon. *Date-friendly.*

3407 Greystone Dr.
Austin
(512) 795-8593
www.musashinosushi.com

Bar Full
Credit Cards Visa, MC, AmEx
Reservations Not accepted

Walking in the door at Japanese restaurant Musashino, you might think
you've arrived at a hot new club that caters to fishermen. Between the
net-and-puffer-fish décor and the cute, trendily clad waitresses in their
matching black baby-doll T-shirts, the atmosphere hovers just below
over the top. But the lighting is good, the crowd is vibrant, and the fish
is impeccably fresh, some of it flown in daily from Japan. Options
include rarely seen treats like monkfish liver. Unfortunately, such high-
flying sushi comes at a price, both financially and temporally—sushi is
not cheap (all those little plates add up fast), and before you even get a
glance at a menu, you might have a lengthy wait, even after you get all
the way out to the Anderson Lane exit off the MoPac, and even on
weeknights.

At lunchtime, Musashino offers Japanese street food: enormous
noodle and rice bowls brightly garnished with pickled radish and red
ginger that will fill you up without emptying your wallet. We love this
stuff. But it is ultimately the sushi that draws the crowds. While the
place may not have the cuisine-fusing pizzazz of Uchi (whose executive
chef happens to be a Musashino alum), its traditional fish is still
excellent.

When ordering, we recommend sticking to à-la-carte nigiri (sushi
pieces); we have been underwhelmed by the pricey omakase and chef's
selection sashimi (including, at one visit, inexcusably sinewy toro), even
if their presentations are pure art. A negitoro hand roll features ideal
rice, but the fish's delicate flavor is overwhelmed by shiso leaf. Basic fish
like salmon and yellowtail shine most brightly at Musashino. Mackerel,
however, is easily the best in town; and sweet, eggy uni (sea urchin)
approaches slimy perfection.

If you're looking for a quick bite at suppertime, try the sushi bar.
Otherwise, adopt a siege mentality and expect service to be slow. It will
be. Still, it's all worth the wait, worth the drive, worth the trouble, and
worth the money. –MPN/RG

Nau's Enfield Drug

A burger-and-ice-cream shop straight
out of the Andy Griffith Show

food
5.7 | 7.5
10 | 10
experience

American, Burgers $ **5**   *Clarksville*

Counter service
Mon.-Fri. 7:30am-4:15pm;
Sat. 8am-2:30pm; closed Sun.
Breakfast. Kid-friendly.

1115 W. Lynn St.
Austin
(512) 476-1221

Bar None
Credit Cards Visa, MC, AmEx
Reservations Not accepted

Walking in the door at Nau's Enfield Drug is like stepping back in time.
It appears that not much has changed here since the Nau brothers
opened their doors in 1951, and the effect is downright charming. Low
wooden shelves allow you to see around the shop, though that won't
help you find anything. It's all here, those little things you buy at the
drug store—cards, aspirin, small gifts, batteries, magazines, snacks,
shampoo—but the organization can be a bit haphazard, and there
aren't any signs to direct you; just friendly folks who'll show you what
you need. But the thing that smacks the most of the '50s is the lunch
counter in the back, with swivel stools, small booths, and a box of
newspapers for entertainment. More entertaining, though, is Nau's wall
of fame, covered with autographed 8-by-10 glossies of stars from
Governor Schwarzenegger to Don Johnson to local boy Lukas Haas.

Nau's menu is based on three ingredients: eggs, bread, and ice
cream. Breakfast items include tacos, omelettes, and lots of other egg
variations. Lunch is all about sandwiches, from pimento cheese, to
chicken salad, to Nau's old-fashioned hamburgers. These burgers are
what fast-food joints only wish they could make. Served hot with a side
of smiles by the friendly ladies behind the counter, they are thin and
basic, topped with tomato and lettuce that's actually fresh and crisp.

Nau's doesn't have a fryer, so chips are the only accompaniment, but
with all the wonderful ice cream desserts, you won't leave hungry.
Malts, shakes, floats, and sundaes are creamy and delicious, made in
front of you with an array of dated soda-shop equipment. These ice
cream dreams are also some of the cheapest in town, making them all
the more sweet. You'll leave whistling that familiar tune.... –MPN

NeWorlDeli

Another cute, quaint, up-and-coming deli

Light American   **$13**   Hyde Park

Counter service
Mon.-Fri. 7am-7pm; Sat. 8am-
5pm; Sun. 9am-4pm. *Breakfast.*
Delivery. Vegetarian-friendly.

4101 Guadalupe St.
Austin
(512) 451-7170

Bar Beer/wine
Credit Cards Visa, MC, AmEx
Reservations Not accepted

NeWorlDeli is the kind of eatery that neither adds much nor detracts much from the restaurant scene. It serves up perfectly fine sandwiches and soups in a location that is just a little too far north of campus to develop a studenty vibe. Some relatively pleasant window tables overlook the traffic on Guadalupe Street, but there's not much going on with the décor, and despite some vaguely hippy aspirations, the restaurant doesn't succeed in setting itself apart from the potted-plant, waiting-room air of the small shopping center in which it is located.

The food is similarly lacking in attitude. NeWorlDeli sells the kind of gruyère-and-ham deli food that you can find behind the counter of a decent supermarket. Any items that attempt to escape from this category demurely turn back at the gate. Thus we have failed to detect anything like a curry flavor in the incredibly mild curried chicken salad sandwich, and the tuna salad sandwich, though reasonably tasty, is of the variety any picky four-year-old would happily eat. Fresh ingredients bring a little more life to the soups—the cream of spinach soup and a tomato-laced chicken soup are good, but the tomato and basil tastes like nothing more than a top-of-the-line Campbell's competitor. A half sandwich and cup of soup lunch special is available for a reasonable price. The deli also serves some decent warm subs and breakfast tacos, wraps, bagels, and baked goods (some of them homemade, and some, well, made elsewhere).

Counter service is delivered with a smile and a chatty conversation, which always perks up a meal, however drab. Although NeWorld's menus proudly proclaim "Where Bland is Banned," we can only say that they seem to have been lax on the law enforcement. –RM

Noodle-ism

food

5.0 **6.3**
10   10

experience

A lot of shiny pan-Asian packaging
wrapped around nothing much at all

Chinese $**19**   *Congress Avenue Area*

Counter service   107 W. 5th St.   *Bar* Beer/wine
Mon.-Thurs. 11am-9:50pm;   Austin   *Credit Cards* Visa, MC, AmEx
Fri.-Sat. 11am-2:50am; Sun. (512) 275-9988   *Reservations* Accepted
noon-9pm. *Wireless Internet.* www.noodleism.com

There's a lot of hype surrounding this sleek noodle shop from the folks
behind Bistro 88. It has an ambitious menu of Asian-based fusion
dishes with hints of Italian, and a shiny red and black look, complete
with paper parasols and bamboo accents. But we find that Noodle-ism,
like many -isms, is essentially unappealing at heart. It offers watered-
down pan-Asian fare at beefed-up prices to a well-heeled, well-suited,
well-starched downtown business crowd. To make matters worse, the
service, from a staff of distracted teenagers, is shoddy (and we don't
mind counter service, but at those prices?).

Somehow Noodle-ism has managed to sponge off the reputation of
its much-vaunted big brother—the food here is, as they say, acclaimed.
That's where the *Fearless Critic* comes in: in this case, we don't see it.
Miso soup is meek—as the accompaniment to many of the dishes, it
seems the culinary equivalent of the nervous giggle. The noodle soups
are better—the Malaysian variety, for example, with a coconut-milk-
and-lemongrass-flavored shrimp broth, is fairly tasty, with the bold,
fresh crunch of nearly raw edamame. Many soups also come with
plentiful meat and/or seafood—but these, too, despite their noble
heritage, lack interesting complexity.

Outside of the soups, things really start to fall apart. "Petite Spicy
(Why 'Spicy'? Why?!) Wontons" are just appalling, their wrappers
watery and limp, the pork inside them completely lacking in salt or
flavor, the syrupy sauce they sit in so tasteless that you wonder how
they did it. Other noodle dishes are adventurous failures. The three-
cabbage ravioli lurks under a floury, cloyingly sweet butter sauce that
tastes like Olive Garden alfredo. A Kobe burger is decent, but not
worth the extra cash, and in general, bland dishes, like the Malaysian
soup, rely on the crunch of fresh vegetables to redeem them. Folks, we
hate to tell ya, but a poor, lone red pepper can only do so much. –RM

Nu Age Café

Vegetarian and vegan cooking that
traverses too many continents

food

5.9 / 10   **5.9** / 10

experience

Light American, Pan-Asian $ **22**   *Tarrytown*

Casual restaurant
Daily 11am-9pm. *Brunch.*
Kid-friendly. Vegetarian-friendly.
Wireless Internet.

2425 Exposition Blvd.
Austin
(512) 469-9390
www.nuagecafe.com

Bar BYO
Credit Cards Visa, MC, AmEx
Reservations Accepted

Austin newcomer Nu Age Café is trying to bring vegetarian and vegan cuisine to an unexpected level of elegance. Located in an upscale shopping center in Tarrytown, Nu Age is decorated in a confusing manner, with pink, tasseled curtains, floral upholstery, grey linoleum tiles, and photo murals of enormous fruits and vegetables. It's like Granny's bathroom meets the Whole Foods produce section.

Nu Age's thorough menu covers basics like veggie burgers and includes soups, salads, Asian dishes, and pastas. Between the Italian and Asian dishes here, we recommend the Asian. The sushi platter is substantial, with vegan rolls filled with avocado, pumpkin, asparagus, spinach, and cucumber that have nice contrasting textures and are served with soy sauce and such, along with a spicy red pepper coulis.

"Basiled Eggplant" comes with crunchy green beans, an attractive cone of brown rice, and a rich brown sauce, but the eggplant itself is overdone, leaving the skin tough while the flesh is too soft. The "Nu Pad Thai" noodles are sticky and overcooked, but otherwise have a nice flavor (despite being served with lemon wedges rather than lime). Mushroom linguine features more overcooked noodles in a bland cream sauce. Butternut squash is an unappealing shade of boarding-school oatmeal grey, with chunks of squash, crushed almonds, and fried sage for interest.

Nu Age does offer an interesting drinks menu, with different teas and fresh-squeezed juices. We like the "Kiwi Spritzer"—it's a lemon-lime soda with large chunks of frozen kiwi that eventually melt to create a tasty, kiwi-soda slurry. And there's a dessert menu with items like a hazelnut napoleon that pairs hazelnut-dusted phyllo sheets with a vanilla soy pudding and a berry coulis. It would be better with dairy, but when you're trying to appeal to hardcore vegans, what are you going to do? –MPN

Nubian Queen Lola's

Good Samaritan, good Louisiana cooking

food
7.9
10

4.3
10
experience

Southern   **$10**   *East Austin*

Casual restaurant
Mon.-Sat. 6am-midnight; closed
Sun. Hours are variable week to
week. *Breakfast.*

1815 Rosewood Ave.
Austin
(512) 542-9269

Bar None
Credit Cards Visa, MC, AmEx
Reservations Not accepted

There are a lot of really good things to say about Nubian Queen Lola's. The proprietress, Lola Stephens, opened the little restaurant as way to feed the homeless (which she does every Sunday when they are officially closed), and also helps students from low-income families with inexpensive lunches at an area school. When Katrina hit, Nubian Queen Lola's was one of the first places in town to hold a benefit, and the restaurant has shelves of photos, religious items, and souvenirs from grateful New Orleans evacuees.

In fact, Lola's seems more a charity than a business. From the outside, the building looks nearly condemned, with boarded up windows and spray paint, but a little purple trim and a small sign tips you off to what's inside: a cozy room with only two tables where a dozen or so diners eat family style. The room is decorated with purple sponge-print paint, Mardi Gras beads that hang from the ceiling, a mish-mash of art, and the occasional sermon playing loudly over the speakers (reminding you of the multiple meanings of "soul" food).

In addition to such redemptive fare, Lola's menu offers barbecue and sandwiches, but the best plan is to ask what's available, because the menu isn't a very good guide. And if there are more than four customers already there, and they aren't eating yet, we must suggest you go elsewhere, or you could be in for a very long wait. The kitchen is small and understaffed, and backs up quickly. When the food finally arrives, though, it's pretty good as well as cheap. Thin, but moist, bone-in pork chops, for instance, are served on Texas toast. A simple cheeseburger is given some oomph with a hearty dose of Creole seasoning, and red beans and rice are divine—beautifully seasoned with chunks of tender stewed meat and lots of onions, they're some of the best we've ever had. And that's saying something in the South. –MPN

Nueva Onda

There's heart in this little Mexican place,
but unfortunately you can't taste it

food **4.4** / 10   **7.6** / 10
experience

Mexican   **$17**   *St. Edward's Area*

Counter service   2218 College Ave.   *Bar* Beer/wine
Mon.-Sat. 7:30am-3pm;   Austin   *Credit Cards* Visa, MC, AmEx
Sun. 8am-3pm. *Breakfast. Brunch.* (512) 447-5063   *Reservations* Not accepted
Outdoor dining. Wireless Internet.

There is much to enjoy about Nueva Onda—the pleasantly slipshod
atmosphere; the family vibe of the business; the long, lazy brunches on
the leafy patio. Unfortunately, the food just doesn't cut it; in fact, it
bears an unfortunate resemblance to a national "Mexican" fast-food
chain that shall remain nameless.

Your order is taken at the little counter inside the restaurant by one
of the family, and all the service suggests a clear investment in your
enjoyment. There are other nice touches which make the place feel
personal: an indie movie written by a brother is on sale at the register,
and there are racks of games and pulp fiction for patrons' use on the
patio. That fun space sports a small stage for occasional live music,
twinkly Christmas lights, and some colorful Mexican garden
decorations. Large groups tend to congregate here to shoot the breeze,
which is surprisingly present, even in the summer, in this shaded little
spot.

The food is less lively. The migas (mysteriously lauded by local media)
are dry, with soggy tortilla chips and tinned tomatoes; accompanying
corn tortillas are tough and cracked. The quesadillas have cheese and
meat, but nothing else to perk them up. A chicken taco involves limp
shredded lettuce and chewy shredded chicken; the ground-beef version
tastes like Hamburger Helper, and doesn't deserve to be served this far
south, where folks know the difference. Refried beans are thoroughly
bland, and the rice is mushy. Some more authentic options include
decent fajitas and a chicharrón (traditional fried pork skins) taco. The
little things, like the fresh salsa and bright, chunky guacamole, can be
quite good (the chips are also light and warm). But most of the food....

Sorry—where were we? We were distracted by the big bell ringing in
our heads. –RM

Nuevo León

Warm food, warm service—and a good
time had by all

food
6.7
10

7.4
10
experience

Mexican $**24**   *East Austin*

Casual restaurant   1501 E. 6th St.   *Bar* Full
Mon.-Sat. 11am-10pm;   Austin   *Credit Cards* Visa, MC, AmEx
Sun. 11am-9pm. *Delivery.*   (512) 479-0097   *Reservations* Accepted
Live music. Outdoor dining. www.nuevoleoninaustin.com

Don't be fooled by the grab-the plastically-hideous-stuffed-animal-with-the-iron-claw game in the entrance hall: Nuevo León is actually a very classy establishment. The restaurant's posh new quarters are enormous, with several different dining spaces, the most striking of which is a large room with an endlessly high, vaulted ceiling. Everything in it is a uniform shade of terra cotta, from the stucco walls to the floor tiles—a little too self-consciously Mission, perhaps, but still pleasantly trippy. There is also a very nice back patio with views over Saltillo plaza and the downtown skyline.

But what really gives Nuevo León its air of aplomb is the service. Everyone is chatty and attentive, from the charming and radiant owner, so obviously house proud, to the experienced waitstaff. Nowhere are there upscale pretensions—just the kind of attention often missing from pricier joints, the sort that notices a dropped napkin, points out hidden costs, and inquires with convincing concern about an unfinished plate.

Any such leftovers are due to the portions' size, not the quality of the food. While there are few innovations at Nuevo León, the general know-how of the staff extends to the kitchen. The queso, for one, has a serious following. Particularly good is the tortilla soup, fat and flavorful, with a nice mellow heat, plenty of tortilla sticks, mounds of avocado, and the pleasant surprise of hominy. It comes with little bowls of rice and fresh cilantro, which you can pile on to your heart's content. Other standouts include the "Shrimp Saltillo"—generously sized shrimp that are a touch rubbery, but have a rich flavor, paired with bean-and-cheese flautas and creamy cheese enchiladas, both of which show surprising flavor and complexity for such low-brow items. Old-fashioned tacos are another favorite; the beef filling has nice charcoal hints that pair beautifully with roasted jalapeños, though the fried tortillas can be a little stiff. But the famous margaritas oughta loosen you right up.
–RM

Nutty Brown Café

food
5.0 | 7.6
10 | 10
experience

Hit-or-miss and overpriced, but where else are you going to eat out here?

American $ **29**   *Dripping Springs*

Casual restaurant
Sun.-Tues. 11am-10pm;
Wed.-Fri. 11am-midnight;
Sat. 11am-1am. *Brunch.*
Kid-friendly. Live music. Outdoor dining.

12225 W. Hwy. 290
Dripping Springs
(512) 301-4648
www.nuttybrown.com

Bar Full
Credit Cards Visa, MC, AmEx
Reservations Accepted

On Highway 290 West on the way to Dripping Springs, the Nutty Brown Café is trying hard to embrace a wide clientele. With live music Thursday through Sunday, the frequently posted "Bikers Welcome" sign, and an outdoor play area for the kids, they are doing a good job. On weekend evenings you'll find the parking lot *thrumming* with choppers, the play area swarming, and we've even spotted a certain local celebrity musician watching his daughter play from behind his dark glasses. The restaurant is comfortable inside and out with an enormous, oak-shaded deck that makes for an inviting place to sit, even in the summer, and service is fast, friendly, and accommodating.

The menu is on the pricey side and consists of basic Southern and Tex-Mex items ranging from salads, to sandwiches, to mains. The house salad is unexceptional, and the "Nutty Shrimp Wontons" (a Tex-Mex concoction of shrimp, bacon, cheese, and jalapeños enclosed on a wonton wrapper and deep fried) are chewy but acceptable, made somewhat more interesting by the chipotle dressing that accompanies them.

Other Texas standards are similarly mediocre: the chicken-fried steak's cream gravy is floury and the dish itself average, which makes us wonder about both the veracity and wisdom of using the "Kobe beef" mentioned on the menu; mashed potatoes have a hint of garlic, but a gluey consistency; baby back ribs are tender, with a sweet, uncomplicated barbecue sauce. The jalapeño creamed corn is tasty even though the corn used is not fresh, but avoid the unappetizing roasted whole button mushrooms—they're just too ugly to eat. Stick with the delicious, juicy burgers and fajitas served with all the fixings, and save room for dessert. The house specialty is their yummy "Skillet Apple Pie," served piping hot, à la mode, on a flat iron skillet. –MPN

The Oasis

Toast strong margaritas to a gorgeous
sunset, and you won't mind the food

food

5.6
10

8.8
10

experience

Mexican

$**32**   *Northwest Hills*

Casual restaurant
Daily 11:30am-10pm.
Date-friendly. Kid-friendly.
Live music. Outdoor dining.

6550 Comanche Trail
Austin
(512) 266-2442
www.oasis-texas.com

Bar Full
Credit Cards Visa, MC, AmEx
Reservations Accepted

Despite the rather Olympian wrath wielded by a lightning bolt against
the Oasis in summer 2005, it seems to be thriving as it always has.
We're pleased to see it. Whatever our thoughts about the food, Oasis
owner Beau Theriot earned a lot of goodwill after that fire destroyed
much of the building, particularly when he promised to hold those
weddings that had been scheduled to take place on the Oasis'
spectacular decks in his own home, in front of the same views. It did
not prove necessary. The restaurant's real draw—the Starlight Terrace,
450 feet above Lake Travis—has remained open since day one.

From here, the sensational sunsets really are worth the long drive
down FM 2222. Saturated oranges and bruised purples hang above the
lake, sinking slowly into the water and behind the hills, and as it gets
darker, the lights on the opposite shore, and their counterparts in the
sky, begin to prick through the deepening pink. We suggest you come
early, to enjoy more of the sunset and increase the chances of a deck's-
edge table. Also, try a peaceful weekday night—weekend sunsets are
somewhat marred by garishly loud covers from the live band.

The atmosphere at the Oasis is generally jolly, and generally packed
(neither the waitstaff nor the kitchen seems able to handle the crowds).
It's a decidedly white-bread crowd, and the homogeneity is reflected in
the food. Tex-Mex offerings are unreliable (you should particularly avoid
a chili-powder-drenched fish taco), though we quite like their beef
fajitas. Chile con queso is good, smooth with a little bite, although it
doesn't quite succeed in taking your mind off the stale, thick chips that
you're coating with it. In general, you should stick with the all-
American options: burgers are tasty, on a pleasantly sweet sourdough
bun, although they have arrived drastically undercooked. A Monterrey
chicken sandwich with sweet onions is another decent order. On the
whole, though, the fare seems a feeble accompaniment to the glorious
light. Perhaps Zeus is a food critic. –RM

Oaxacan Tamaleo

The lesson of the tamale: good things are often hidden in drab packages

food

8.1 **3.9**
10 10

experience

Mexican $ **7**   *North Central*

Counter service   1300 W. Anderson Ln.   *Bar* None
Mon.-Sat. 8am-8pm;   Austin   *Credit Cards* No credit cards
Sun. 9am-3pm. *Breakfast.* (512) 289-9262   *Reservations* Accepted
Live music. Outdoor dining. www.tamaleo.com

Anyone who has seen Leonor Baños-Stoute dance with a ceramic pot balanced atop her frizzy mop, her eyes rolling in mock dramatics, her hips swinging to the music, will know that her cooking has to be assertive and spicy. It is something of a surprise, then, to find her little restaurant tucked in complete anonymity inside a shoddy little shopping mart on Anderson Lane. You may well have to drive by twice before you see it—although there is a sign in the parking lot, the building itself is marked only with the food mart's name, and the words "Mexican food" scrawled in the window. You'll have to look past the rows of Doritos, motor oil, and other truck-stop necessities to find Oaxacan Tamaleo—a restaurant that is quietly serving up some of the best and most authentic Mexican food around.

Leonor's specialty, of course, is the tamale, which she prepares in the traditional Oaxacan way, in a banana leaf rather than a cornhusk. The result is a tamale that is moister and denser than the more familiar variety. But it is the fillings that really make Oaxacan Tamaleo stand out. All three varieties of tamale are good, but our particular favorite is a chicken in red mole sauce, which is fiery hot with a delicate chile flavor underneath. This is one of the seven traditional moles of Oaxaca, all of which are different from the brown, chocolaty mole poblano that you might be used to. The black bean and cheese tamale has a nutty, creamy taste that is easy to like, but while we like the tangy salsa verde in the pork tamales, the meat can be a tad dry.

Besides the tamales, Leonor serves traditional mains (again, the chicken in red mole is a star), including a rotating roster of weekday specials, for an impressive $4.98. Quench the flames of the food with a fresh, powerful jamaica (hibiscus) tea, the shriveled flower still floating in the deep red liquid—it tastes as if it has mystical healing powers. Leonor's delightful dance certainly does. –RM

Old Alligator Grill

We had no idea you could do such things to Twinkies

Southern $**30**   *South Lamar*

Casual restaurant
Sun.-Wed. 11am-2am; Thurs.-Sat.
11am-2am. Kitchen closes Sun.-
Wed. 10pm, Thurs.-Sat. 11pm. *Kid-friendly. Live music. Outdoor dining.*

3003 S. Lamar Blvd.
Austin
(512) 444-6117

Bar Full
Credit Cards Visa, MC, AmEx
Reservations Accepted

The Old Alligator Grill has long been popular in Austin as a family-friendly spot for Louisiana-style cooking. The restaurant is large, with a bar, billiards, outdoor seating, and an impressive stage for live music (they just don't use it much). It is decorated with vintage advertisements, neon beer signs, and an enormous stuffed alligator that appears to be creeping across the ceiling toward unwary victims. Service is friendly, enthusiastic, and timely when the place is not packed.

Heavy on fried foods, the menu is a lengthy collection of Cajun and Creole specialties. We like the "Cajun Kisses," which are jack-cheese-and-shrimp-stuffed jalapeños wrapped in bacon; they're chewy and spicy, with great bacon flavor. Spicy blackened 'gator tail tastes like dense (what else) chicken. The three kinds of gumbo on the menu have a nice, dark roux, but are shy on spice.

Finding a truly spectacular burger in Austin is like finding someone who thinks Dallas is cool, but the Alligator Grill is on the right track with theirs. Thick patties are cooked to temperature, and you can get them topped with those fun Cajun Kisses. Tasty fries are subtly battered and crispy. Crawfish étouffée is light but has a nice kick to it, and is served with dirty rice (unusual here—most Cajun places prefer to serve their étouffée over white rice). Red beans and rice also have good spice. Have your meal with a side of cornbread—it's airy and moist, and breaks into sweet crumbs.

Desserts include banana-bread pudding, beignets, and Blue Bell, as well as deep-fried Twinkies. These Twinkies are a heart attack on a plate—fried crisp, the center gooey, on top of strawberry sauce with whipped cream and cherries, and so sweet our teeth ache just thinking about them. The Old Alligator Grill might not quite transport you to New Orleans, but it's so much better than its cheap neon signs might suggest. Here's to not reading a book by its cover. –MPN

Old Pecan Street Café

food
6.4 **8.4**
10   10
experience

A leftover hideaway from a quieter
Sixth-Street past, with food to match

Southern   **$29**   *Sixth Street District*

Casual restaurant   310 E. 6th St.   *Bar* Full
Mon.-Thurs. 11am-10pm;   Austin   *Credit Cards* Visa, MC, AmEx
Fri.-Sat. 11am-midnight;   (512) 478-2491   *Reservations* Not accepted
Sun. 9am-3pm. *Brunch.*   www.oldpecanstreetcafe.com

The name of the Old Pecan Street Café gently recalls an earlier Austin.
An Austin of bountiful pecan trees and lazy streets, buzzing flies and
rocking chairs. An Austin in which the frenetic Sixth Street, where the
restaurant stands, was still the stately thoroughfare known as Pecan
Street. You can still slip into the quiet dark of the old building, once a
hotel, and escape the crush—it is one of the few entrances along the
strip that doesn't emit the fumes of air-conditioned beer.

Within, the place is indeed a throwback to the old days, with all the
advantages and disadvantages that accompany that distinction.
Bentwood chairs and white tablecloths give the joint a classy feel, and
ceiling fans circle slowly overhead, sending the hanging plants, on their
long chains, into idle circles. A few booths hug the wall beneath old
maps of the city.

The food, too, is of an earlier era. Slightly French, slightly Creole,
slightly Cajun, it is, in fact, distinctly middle-American. A chicken soup
is nicely spicy, but old-school saltines in a plastic packet keep it
company. Most of the fare is reassuringly bland, supplemented by the
classic sautéed veggies and lifeless fruit garnishes. Crêpes and quiche
are menu standards and take no chances. The crêpes poulet, for
example, with chicken and mushrooms in a tarragon cream sauce,
tastes like the pancake version of a chicken pot pie. A blackened
redfish is mild and a little too well done—the kitchen seems to cook for
a group of regulars that faded away years ago.

Still, when thrills are the last thing you seek, there is something very
pleasant about slipping away to the quiet calm of a younger town,
listening to Sinatra croon, and enjoying the ministrations of a modestly
attentive waiter in an apron and rolled-up shirtsleeves. –RM

The Omelettry

You should probably just stick to the omelettes

food
5.6 **7.1**
10   10
experience

American $**10**   *Burnet*

Casual restaurant   4811 Burnet Rd.   *Bar* None
Daily 7am-5pm. *Breakfast.*   Austin   *Credit Cards* No credit cards
Brunch. Vegetarian-friendly. (512) 453-5062   *Reservations* Not accepted

The Omelettry feeds its hordes of fans—a youthful bunch of North-Austin hipsters and hippies—with unflinching goodwill. Although you'll run into the occasional rude staffer (such as the one who preferred to hang up on our fact-checker than provide the restaurant's weekly opening hours), the trendy staff is generally laid back: slight mishaps are shrugged off with a smile, offending tabletop grime swept coolly off onto the floor. The result is an establishment that, though pleasantly relaxed in atmosphere, you cannot help but feel is letting itself go a bit. Things are a little sticky, and a lax ceiling tile or two slips lazily from its post. Somewhat odd local art spruces things up a little.

The Omelettry is popular for its neighborhood feel, and for its breed of fusion cooking that easily wins the hearts of Austinites: call it Hippy-Tex-Mex (enchiladas with sprouts on top—that kind of thing). You find something very similar at Kerbey Lane and Magnolia Café, as well as on the limited menus of many of Austin's studenty cafés, padded by burgers and breakfast specialties. Frequently, the result is a blander, less appealing version of what is inherently a lively cuisine—but one can't help appreciating the inventive attitude.

The Omelettry's food reaches just this mild-mannered compromise. Quesadillas, which upsettingly include limp lettuce, come with lifeless guacamole. Huevos rancheros lack pizzazz; gazpacho reminds us of V8. Predictably, all-American options are better, including some pleasingly plain sandwiches (the avocado BLT is a crispy winner); pancakes, though a little too soda-y for our tastes, are fluffy and good (particularly the gingerbread version, which we prefer to those at Magnolia). And, of course, omelettes are a strong suit, with interesting fillings such as a lemon sour cream sauce and winey sautéed mushrooms. The egg creations are light and cheesy, though they could be a touch moister.

On the whole, the Omelettry neatly echoes some of the laid-back strengths and white-bread weaknesses of some of the city's most popular establishments. —RM

Opal Divine's

A relaxed bar that's dog-friendly—but don't come for the food

food
4.5 **8.2**
10   10
experience

American

$21

Warehouse District, S. Congress

Pub
Daily 11am-2am. Kitchen closes
at 1am. *Brunch. Live music.
Outdoor dining. Wireless Internet.*

700 W. 6th St.
Austin
(512) 707-0237
www.opaldivines.com

Penn Field, 3601 S. Congress Ave.
78704, (512) 477-3308

Bar Full
Credit Cards Visa, MC, AmEx
Reservations Not accepted

The downtown branch of Opal Divine's Free House occupies a lovely two-story stone building that has been home to many failed bars—until now, that is. With a large deck overlooking the milder side of Sixth Street, and several small rooms which offer, in turn, a TV, darts, or, pleasantly, no distractions, Opal Divine's seems to have beaten whatever curse plagued the previous establishments. Patrons are encouraged to bring along their canine best friends (indeed, nowhere have dogs been so welcome since the tragic demise of Les Amis—a moment of silence, please…), and laughing groups with dogs take over the porch. There's also a Penn Field branch in South Austin that's popular amongst St. Ed's students—and that one, too, has a great outdoor space.

The menu features standard pub grub including substantial burgers, sinful cheese fries, and Austin's usual Tex-Mex basics. If your needs aren't being met in a timely fashion, you may be sitting in a "server-free zone" (these areas are clearly marked), in which case you'll need to go to the bar to place your order.

The vegetarian vegetable soup is ideal on a rainy day, with a hearty tomato base, lots of veggies, and just a little heat. The nachos seem to use canned-style refried beans, but they don't skimp on the cheese, and come with jalapeños, sour cream, and fresh-tasting salsa. You can also add beef or chicken to make them more of a meal. The fries are flecked with lots of black pepper, and they come out chewy and a little greasy, but pretty good. Quesadillas, though, are tragically bland.

We like Opal Divine's—the atmosphere is fun and relaxed and it's not so loud that you can't have a conversation. The food is just pub grub, but this is a cool place to hang out, and the menu isn't bad should you suddenly find yourself ready to chow down. That's the purpose of bar food, after all. –MPN

P. Terry's

An anti-fast-food burger shack that's
open late and well located

food
6.8 **4.8**
10   10
experience

Burgers $ **6**   South Lamar

Take-out   404 S. Lamar Blvd.   *Bar* None
Sun.-Thurs. 11am-11pm;   Austin   *Credit Cards* Visa and MC
Fri.-Sat. 11am-1am.   (512) 473-2217   *Reservations* Not accepted
Kid-friendly. Outdoor dining.   www.pterrys.com
Vegetarian-friendly. Wireless Internet.

"The whole idea for opening a hamburger stand," writes Patrick Terry
on his web site, "started as a reaction to reading the book Fast Food
Nation." Amen to that. The recent arrival of the delicious P. Terry's
hamburger shack on South Lamar near Barton Springs was welcomed
by almost everyone in the neighborhood. It's a good location, near the
bustle of South Austin but also within a couple minutes' reach of
downtown.

The service concept is simple: it's like a drive-up window without the
eat-in facility. You line up in your car—and in the wee hours, especially
on weekends, you will by no means be the first in line—and you bark
your order into a microphone. There is also a walk-up window and a
little patio with picnic tables at which to sit outside with your burger,
but most people here never leave their cars. Check your order before
you leave, as mixups are common.

Mr. Terry knows what he's doing: the price is right, and these freshly
grilled burgers are thin but great, in the ketchupless Austin style.
Cheeseburgers strike just the right cheese-melting balance. One burger
might be too small for most appetites; we recommend two, or the
"Double." Either way, the "special sauce" is mayonnaise-o-licious, and
you can ask for your burger with jalapeños and/or grilled onions (don't
forget!). There's also an unlisted grilled cheese available, and a veggie
burger, which the menu refers to as a "South Austin Addition." Fries
are cut by P. Terry's, with the skins still on (as if just to say "screw you"
to McDonald's); they're golden and aggressively seasoned. However,
their crispiness varies from day to day.

Keep in mind that P. Terry's closes at 11pm sharp (1am on weekends),
or sometimes even a few minutes early. Miscalculate and you could end
up in a burgerless traffic jam, with a dangerous backward maneuver
onto South Lamar as your only escape route. But there are certain
times, on certain nights, when you're willing to risk everything for a
good cheeseburger. –RG

Pacific Star

Decent fried seafood in a themed
environment

food
6.7 | **6.6**
10 | 10
experience

Seafood, American $**24**   *Far Northwest*

Casual restaurant   13507 N. Hwy. 183   *Bar* Beer/wine
Sun.-Thurs. 11am-10pm;   Austin   *Credit Cards* Visa, MC, AmEx
Fri.-Sat. 11am-11pm. *Kid-friendly.*   (512) 219-5373   *Reservations* Not accepted
Outdoor dining.

If Pacific Star only overlooked water and not the U.S. 183 access road,
you would think you were on the coast. Pacific Star is a picture-perfect
replica of the seafood restaurants that dot the Gulf coast, from the
neon beer signs, rope-strewn dock posts, and nautical theme, right
down to the chilly, A/C-cooled, 65-degree ambient temperature. If it's
too cold inside, Pacific Star has picnic tables under a pleasant covered
porch surrounded by tropical palm trees and visited by a profusion of
fish-glutted, semi-feral cats—another attribute that reminds us of the
coast. Service is casual, and food is generally served in baskets; most
items are relatively inexpensive, considering that Austin is a solid 200
miles from the Gulf.

Pacific Star serves mostly seafood (they do offer a chicken dish), and
is heavy on fried items, though they also make broiled fish and gumbo.
Standards include variations on crab, shrimp, oysters, crawfish, catfish,
and snapper, although specials often include fancier preparations such
as pecan-encrusted trout or salmon. Start out with "Oysters Diablo,"
which are oysters and jalapeños wrapped in bacon and broiled; they're
nice and spicy though a bit chewy, and it's just hard to go wrong when
there's bacon involved.

Another possibility is deep-fried jalapeños stuffed with a crab and
shrimp mixture. On their own they're a little dry and bland, but
surprisingly, tartar sauce improves them immensely. Baskets of fried fish
with hush puppies and soggy crinkle-cut fries are the norm here—
shrimp is particularly good, butterflied but still tender. We are also
impressed with thin fillets of catfish, fried crisp in a cornmeal crust, and
without any muddiness. Po-boys are also a good choice; simply
prepared with tomato and lettuce on the side, they are served on
buttery garlic bread that complements whatever deep-fried critter you
chose to fill it with. And there are plenty of such critters. –MPN

Paciugo Gelateria

A chain gelateria that fails to fulfill its
shiny Italian promise

3.9
10
experience

Sweets

Warehouse District

Counter service
Sun.-Thurs. 11am-9pm;
Fri.-Sat. 11am-10pm.
Kid-friendly. Outdoor dining.
Vegetarian-friendly.

241 W. 2nd St.
Austin
(512) 474-7600
www.paciugo.com

Bar None
Credit Cards Visa,MC,AmEx
Reservations Not accepted

The owners of this Italian gelateria may have just arrived in Texas from
Turin, Italy, in 2000, but that hasn't stopped them from pursuing
immediate dreams of a megachain in the Promised Land. For Paciugo
(pronounced "pa-choo-go"), these freeways were indeed paved with
gold: 24 Texas branches and kiosks will be open by 2007, a Mexico City
branch is already in place, and Chinese branches are soon to follow.
The appearance of Paciugo in downtown Austin has also increased
public fears that the city-dubbed "Second Street District" is being
secretly infiltrated by Dallas spies (Taverna and Cantina Laredo are also
Dallas-based). What's next, imitation Mustangs of Las Colinas galloping
across Zilker Park?

The good news: Austinites can breathe a sigh of relief, because
Dallas hasn't won yet—for gelato, at least. Paciugo, which suffers from
systematic problems with iciness, falls far behind our own Tèo in almost
every way. Still, sweet brown concoctions like hazelnut and tiramisu do
relatively well here, and cinnamon is surprisingly creamy. Chocolate
chocolate chip gelato, with the deep fudginess of Belgian chocolate, is
good, as is mixed berry (a version of the Italian frutti di bosco). Not so
for a slushy strawberry-balsamic sorbet; a banana flambé ice cream
overwhelmed by an unappealing alcohol taste; German chocolate
unimpressively paired with coconut; or a chocolate chip cookie dough
ice cream with bits of dough so sparsely scattered you'd think they
were as valuable as beluga caviar.

The most interesting offering at Paciugo is a mixture of extra-virgin
olive oil, black pepper, and sugar that tastes exactly as described. It's
appealing, although we're not sure we could get through a full dish of
it. And we won't be back here anytime soon. From the mass-market
fonting of the menus in the back to the antiseptic modern room in
which a few minimalist tables and chairs have been set up, Paciugo
frustrates its promise—and its product is just too Dallas for Tèo-trained
taste buds. –RG

The Paggi House

Stunning outdoor seating and a good
bar scene, plus hit-or-miss small plates

food

6.0 **5.0**
10 | 10

experience

American $**36**   *South Lamar*

Pub   200 Lee Barton Dr.   *Bar* Full
Mon.-Thurs. 11am-2pm, 5pm-   Austin   *Credit Cards* Visa, MC, AmEx
10pm; Fri 11am-2pm, 5pm-   (512) 499-8835   *Reservations* Not accepted
midnight; Sat. 6pm-midnight; Sun.   www.paggihouse.com
11am-3pm. Kitchen closes at 10pm. *Brunch. Date-friendly. Outdoor dining.*

There is hardly a more transportative outdoor atmosphere in Austin
than that found at the Paggi House. Step into this restaurant-bar just
steps from Lamar, and you enter a fantastical Gatsbyesque fête,
drinking martinis or a bottle of wine beneath tents, twinkling lights,
and gently glowing orbs. Most spectacular are the tables out back,
which overlook the river and city skyline. Come by around sunset, and
it's hard not to be convinced that Austin is the one and only city in
which you were meant to live and die.

Until you encounter the atrociously un-Austin service, that is. Just
finding a host or hostess to seat you is like winning the Urban
Challenge. When you finally do, the staff makes you feel like your
presence has imposed upon them terribly. Once you're seated, you'll
likely wait so long to order a drink, or even locate a server, that you'll
begin to wonder whether Paggi House is even a table-service
restaurant. You might even become tempted to sneak over to Taco
Cabana next door for an interim beer.

Although the Paggi House makes a big deal about its food, it's more
successful as a bar than as a restaurant. The menu consists entirely of
"small plates" (a growing trend), amongst which the best choice is
sugar pork. It's not a subtle dish, with hot sesame peanut sauce and
white chocolate butter, but it's beautifully textured, its meat not a
second overcooked, its sweet-salty mix alluring. Cream of crab soup
isn't bad, made with a refreshingly generous amount of crabmeat and
crunched up by fried shallots, but the soup overwhelms the palate with
salt. Less successful are bland, underseasoned hummus, with a texture
neither creamy nor appealingly chunky; and a smoked duck "nacho,"
with caramelized onions, black beans, gruyere, and barbecue sauce, a
confusing combination without much synthesis.

Still, our interpretation is that the restaurant service is really meant to
complement the drinks, and not vice versa. When a bar is this
enchanting, it's hard to justify leaving just because you get hungry. And
at that point, to be able to choose from a menu this creative—rather
than the bar food you might find elsewhere—is a joy. –RG

Pao's Mandarin House

food

8.3 **6.2**

10   10

experience

Chinese food with some authentic
touches in Lakeway, of all places

Chinese   **$20**   *Lake Travis Area*

Casual restaurant   2300 Lohman's Spur   *Bar* Beer/wine
Daily 11am-2:30pm,   Lakeway   *Credit Cards* Visa, MC, AmEx
4:30pm-10pm. *Delivery.*   (512) 263-8869   *Reservations* Accepted
Vegetarian-friendly.

Longtime local favorite Pao's Mandarin seems to have maintained its
loyal following despite its move from downtown Austin to the relatively
distant golf resort community of Lakeway. The new shopping center
location at RR 620 and Lohman's Crossing is decorated with predictably
cheap "class": koi-pond-themed stained glass, rosewood furniture with
vinyl-covered seats, and a huge, ornate jade ship. A sushi bar is open in
the evening, but Chinese cuisine is the main attraction here.

On daily lunch specials, and on the regular Chinese-American menu,
you'll find uneventful standards like bland, cabbage-filled egg rolls, and
well-executed but predictable options like spicy hot and sour soup
that's dense with tofu, pork threads, and tree-ear mushrooms. Sizzling
dishes made with oyster sauce are served crackling hot on special cast-
iron plates. Beef dishes are especially good—the meat is always tender
and flavorful. Don't miss the hearty beef and scallops in rich oyster
sauce with bright snow peas and water chestnuts. Beef fried rice is
more a meal than a side, with huge chunks of moist meat.

But if you have a more developed (read: daring) palate, you should
ask for the traditional Chinese menu. Amongst the exotic offerings are
cold shredded pig's ear, jellyfish, braised sea cucumber, duck tongues
with basil, and pig blood with winter chives. Less intimidating are lovely,
toothsome pan-fried pao tze dumplings filled with gingery ground pork
and served with a tart black vinegar dipping sauce. We also like the
shredded pork hoisin, served moo shu style with pancakes, but with a
drier texture and deeper flavor. Still authentic, but very tame, is a
chicken dish with winter chives, stir-fried in a white sauce and mild
enough for even a toddler.

Service is hurried, but efficient, and brusquely friendly. We were
shocked to find some of Austin's most authentic Chinese food all the
way out in Lakeway; so, probably, were the golfers. –MPN

Paradise Café

Mix-and-match cuisine in a tasteful
setting that rarely rises above the norm

food
6.5
10

6.6
10

experience

American, Mexican   **$25**   *Sixth Street District*

Casual restaurant   401 E. 6th St.   *Bar* Full
Mon.-Fri. 11:15am-2am; Sat.   Austin   *Credit Cards* Visa, MC, AmEx
11:30am-2am; Sun. noon-2am.   (512) 476-5667   *Reservations* Accepted
Kitchen closes at midnight.   www.paradiseonsixth.com
Wireless Internet.

Despite the plentiful parrots, the plant life, and the sailboard soaring gracefully over some tables, this name is a bit of an overstatement. Fortunately, the attempt to create a tropical haven on the Sixth Street strip doesn't go much further than those touches. On the whole, Paradise Café takes advantage of the scale and elegance that come naturally to this prime stretch of real estate: pretty facades, high ceilings, exposed stone walls, and grand, floor-to-ceiling windows.

Paradise's feel and food is a grand departure from the skankiness you might expect on this strip. Service is graceful, and the food, a slightly jumbled assortment that travels from Thailand (e.g. "Thai sticks," like satay skewers) to Texas (chicken-fried steak) by way of Mexico (tacos), is carefully prepared and satisfying. Still, it's hard to find many big winners on the menu; as is the case with many restaurants that serve global cuisine under the label "American," dishes here are often smoothed out to neutrality (look at what happened to "American" cheese), eliminating the peaks. Perhaps they subscribe to a view of culinary Paradise in which "Every valley shall be lifted up, and every mountain and hill be made low; the uneven ground shall become level, and the rough places a plain" (Isaiah 40:4).

At the same time, the kitchen demonstrates a pleasing attention to detail. The sesame chicken salad, though the dressing is essentially just teriyaki sauce, shows off delicately sliced, moist chicken on which the taste of the grill clearly lingers. Crisp quesadillas have a pleasant, fresh pico de gallo and smoky meat; guacamole is nice and garlicky, salsa fresh. Beef caldo (soup) is particularly good, with a flavorful broth and falling-apart-tender beef. Garlic toast is herby and sharp, meatloaf soft and meaty with buttery mashed potatoes (though slightly hindered by a dense tomato sauce), and hamburgers have appetizing toppings such as blue cheese and avocado slices. Prices, unfortunately, are a little too high for food that's all been made low. –RM/RG

Peony Asian Cuisine

food

6.6	8.3
10	10

experience

Mediocre Chinese and decent sushi in a
pleasant central Austin locale

Chinese, Japanese   **$28**   *Northwest Hills*

Casual restaurant
Mon.-Thurs. 11am-10pm;
Fri.-Sat. 11am-10:30pm;
Sun. 11am-9:30pm. *Delivery.*
Vegetarian-friendly. Wireless Internet.

5308 Balcones Dr.
Austin
(512) 459-3341
www.peonyasiancuisine.com

Bar Beer/wine
Credit Cards Visa, MC, AmEx
Reservations Accepted

Peony (which also contains Yoshi's Sushi Bar) is amongst the more
elegant of Austin's Asian restaurants. The exterior is hung with rusted
cut metal lanterns, the interior painted sea green and red. In a sleazy
touch, a bottle of wine stands at attention on each table (corkage and
setup are $8 if you want to bring your own). And naturally, the tables
are decked out with peonies too. Who would guess that just a few
years ago this was a pizza place? The menu is artfully crafted of
cardboard and richly hued papers. There are lots of vegetarian options,
a selection of Filipino dishes (unusual for Austin) as well as a page that
gives detailed descriptions of the available teas. The service is not
particularly quick, but it is Austin friendly.

Given the choice between the sushi bar and the regular menu, sushi
is by far the better choice. The fish is fresh, and served at the proper
temperature, and while the slices on nigiri (sushi pieces) are a little thin,
the price is right. We especially like the ama ebi—sweet raw shrimp
with a dense texture and a dollop of tobiko caviar for a burst of
sodium. The sushi plates are attractively garnished with deep-fried
prawn heads and shiso leaves. Miso soup is like a cumulus cloud in a
bowl, with sliced raw mushrooms, and a shock of slivered scallions.

The regular menu, however, is not up to snuff. Complimentary
sesame bread is bland, pot stickers are rubbery, and the pork in garlic
sauce is pretty but boring. The Filipino lumpia (similar to spring rolls) are
nicely crisp and served with an extremely strong garlic sauce, but the
chicken adobo is dry and virtually tasteless, despite being served amidst
a sea of garlic cloves. The daily lunch specials offer a variety of both
regular menu items and sushi plates, making this a worthwhile stop for
a sushi lunch date. –MPN

Phô Thai Son

Cheap Vietnamese basics in several
similarly bland rooms

food

5.7 **2.6**
10   10
experience

Vietnamese   **$ 9**   *W. Campus, Far N., Southeast*

Casual restaurant   1906 Guadalupe St.   *Bar* None
Daily 11am–midnight.   Austin   *Credit Cards* Visa and MC
Delivery.   (512) 892-8777   *Reservations* Not accepted

                           2501 W. Parmer Ln.   Phô Oanh, 2121 E. Oltorf St.
                           78717, (512) 482-0146 78741, (512) 443-4232

With its antiseptic interior, half decorated with photos of bucolic
Southeast Asian pastoral scenes, Phô Thai Son is much like the rest of
the myriad phô houses in Austin—large portions, cheap food,
perfunctory service, and middling quality. Other branches that belong
to this chain (including Phô Oanh, on East Oltorf) are essentially similar
to Phô Thai Son, with generic, office-style ceilings and white walls. The
food at these joints, while fundamentally about good value, is not bad;
you just need a tour guide to navigate the lengthy menu, and hey,
that's what we're here for. First of all, look to the name of the place,
skip the vermicelli and rice dishes, and go straight for the phô, which
comes in 22 subtly different combinations.

For those unfamiliar with this most basic of Vietnamese dishes, phô is
a gingery beef broth with rice noodles and generally some sort of meat.
It comes with a plate full of raw veggies and herbs that you add
yourself, including cilantro, mint, and sprouts. Some versions come with
a meat combination: phô tái, nâm, gâu, gân, for example, includes
steak, flank, tendon, and tripe. Of these, we prefer the deep-flavored
brisket. Tripe can be chewy, and flank gristly. Avoid also the chicken
and seafood; we like to keep it simple with the brisket, whose
tenderness pairs nicely with the fresh veggies. Things improve with the
addition of hoisin and much-needed hot sauce. The well-seasoned
broth absorbs the meat flavors; it's rich and very filling, especially given
the portion size.

Vermicelli dishes tend to be sticky, but the lemongrass pork is spicy
and laced with kicky slivered onions. Sliced vegetables in the salads are
often tired, but razor-thin grilled beef is sweet and chewy against cool
lettuce in a light gingery dressing. Avoid at all costs the spring rolls—
whether fried (overcooked and mostly carrots) or fresh (huge, rubbery,
and sparse, filled almost entirely of vermicelli). Like we said, cheap is
the draw here. –MPN

Phoenicia Bakery

A Middle Eastern deli with all the
yummy bits and bobs you could want

food

7.5   6.0
10   10
experience

Middle Eastern, Greek $ 6   *South Lamar, Burnet*

Take-out
Mon.-Fri. 9:30am-7pm; Sat.
9:30am-6:30pm; closed Sun.
Vegetarian-friendly.

2912 S. Lamar Blvd.
Austin
(512) 447-4444

4701A Burnet Rd.
78756, (512) 323-6770

Bar None
Credit Cards Visa, MC, AmEx
Reservations Not accepted

A proudly international establishment, Phoenicia produces a quality
lineup of Middle Eastern and Greek nibbles, from olives and feta to the
best fresh-baked pita we've had anywhere in Austin. It also does a brisk
lunchtime business in sandwiches and pita wraps (worth it just to hear
the salesperson shout "mas shawarma, por favor" over her shoulder)
and sells a wide variety of imported goods.

In fact, despite its slightly ungainly appearance both inside and out,
Phoenicia can feel like a home away from home to expats from all over
the globe. Its cluttered shelves accommodate just the right articles from
every country—stout, middle-class Tetley's tea and digestive biscuits
from England, sour cherries from Hungary, dried fish flakes from
Ghana—and familiar names peek amiably around the jars and cans at
the far flung.

The Middle Eastern products, of course, are the stars of the show.
Many varieties of olives lie marinating in big vats in the counter. Several
different feta cheeses are stacked in their salty brine (we find the
Bulgarian particularly creamy and good). Phoenicia makes its own
delicious hummus; smoky baba ganoush (an eggplant dip); terrific,
lemony tabbouleh with a fresh parsley punch; and less impressive, too-
hard dolmas (grape leaves stuffed with rice).

The sandwiches are cheap and terrific, herby, and fresh-tasting,
wrapped in that amazing pita. It is often still warm when it arrives, and
it is delicate, sweet, and chewy. The gyro is packed with tender beef
and lamb shawarma, and perked up by a tangy yogurt dressing. Grilled
zatar bread contains salty Kalamata olives and feta, marinated onions,
and a symphony of herbs. The chicken kebab sandwich is another
favorite.

A small picnic table sits uninvitingly on a bright strip of AstroTurf by
the parking lot. We recommend you take your food to go. It's made it
this far, after all. –RM

The Pit BBQ

A smoky hole-in-the-wall that serves up
cheap basics with a familiar nod

food

4.4
10

5.9
10

experience

Barbecue $ **8**   *Burnet*

Counter service   4707 Burnet Rd.   *Bar* None
Mon.-Sat. 11am-8pm;   Austin   *Credit Cards* Visa, MC, AmEx
closed Sun.   (512) 453-6464   *Reservations* Not accepted

"The Pit" barbecues, their names spelled out in rough wooden planks,
used to abound in Austin, leading to the vague impression of a family
of hammer-wielding barbecue czars (the Pits?) spreading their doctrine
of cheap, no-thrills smoked meat throughout the city. Not true. Each Pit
Barbecue, despite the familiar wooden logo, is owned and operated
independently, and quality fluctuates dramatically from place to place—
a fact that, perhaps, accounts for the way these spots have gradually
faded away from the face of the city over the past decade or two.

This review, however, covers the friendly, steadfast territory of The Pit
at Burnet and 47th. In the typical Burnet Road spirit, this little
restaurant has refused to change one since the days when Austin was
more slack than slick. We were raised on this stuff, and were happy to
love it without question.

Don't get us wrong. This is hardly the best barbecue this town has to
offer. But it is easy eatin', and the place is such a sweet little corner of
good cheer that it's worth a stop. It's just a hut, really, with a few worn
vinyl booths inside, but sit in them once, and you already feel like a
regular, and from a cheap little joint, that's not a bad offer.

We wouldn't recommend you order any bigger cuts of smoked
meat—they're not bad, but they also can't compete with the stronger,
truer smokiness and depth of flavor found at many an Austin meat-
shop. Instead, go for the Pit's specialty—the chopped beef sandwich. It,
too, isn't great as barbecue, but it does make for a very tasty sloppy
joe, neat, sweet, and free of questionable rubbery bits. Plus it's dirt-
cheap—you can get three of them for under five bucks. Heap on the
pickles and onions, and it's a nice little treat for you and two friends.
–RM

Players

A campus burger joint with loyalty and
the game on TV to recommend it

food

4.6 10 **5.6** 10

experience

American $**15**   *West Campus*

Pub
Sun.-Thurs. 11am-3am;
Fri.-Sat. 11am-3:30am.
Outdoor dining.

300 W. MLK Blvd.
Austin
(512) 478-9299

Bar Beer/wine
Credit Cards Visa, MC, AmEx
Reservations Not accepted

After the Posse East, Players is the most likely campus dive at which to
watch the Longhorns play. It has been serving cheap burgers to
students for decades, and, if it survives a recent land dispute with the
University of Texas, will presumably serve them for decades more.
Players is the kind of place that will always get business: its location at
the south end of the Drag is unbeatable, allowing it to supplement the
student business with some grown-up money from the Capital; and its
look is just grubby enough, just cheap enough, and just rough enough
'round the edges, to allow college kids to feel that kind of
possessiveness for it that comes only during "the best four years of
your life" (or five, or six, or seven…).

All that having been said, there is nothing so special about a Players
burger. It is perfectly adequate, nothing more. Burgers are grilled hot to
order, which is a perk (though not over charcoals, so they don't have
that distinctive smokiness). Their main distinguishing feature is a thick
slathering of mayo, which makes these burgers taste quite a lot like
Whoppers—if you're a Burger King person rather than a McDonald's
person, you'll probably like them. We like to order jalapeños on our
burger—they're unusually spicy here, and they cut the mayo and the
American cheese (that's your only choice) quite nicely. We quite like the
onion rings, which are crunchy and quite large, but fries are average at
best, and need to be consumed very hot. One Contributing Editor, who
will go unnamed (she should thank us for that), recommends dipping
the fries in your milkshake.

On the whole, however, we'd still recommend going up the road to
Dirty Martin's, where the burgers are a whole lot tastier, the rings, fries
and shakes more authentic, and where a recent expansion means you
can watch the game there, too. –RM

PoKeJo's

A rapidly expanding Austin barbecue
chain with extraordinary smoked birds

food

6.7	5.7
10	10

experience

Barbecue $15   *Clarksville, Hyde Park, Westlake*

Counter service   1603 W. 5th St.   *Bar* Beer/wine
Daily 11am-9pm.   Austin   *Credit Cards* Visa, MC, AmEx
Breakfast. Kid-friendly. (512) 320-1541   *Reservations* Not accepted
Outdoor dining.   www.pokejos.com

                           1000 E. 41st St.   4109 N. Capital of Texas Hwy.
                           78751, (512) 388-7578   78705, (512) 440-0447

In some senses, even run-of-the-mill barbecue is just better than other
kinds of foods. The smoking process is simply a superior way of
cooking tough meats: it caramelizes meats, melts their connective
tissue, keeps them moist, and adds that incomparable dimension of
smokiness that gives even the blandest meat so much character. Texas
is most famous, of course, for its smoked beef brisket, but barbecue's
golden influence is just as redemptively apparent in poultry. And
nowhere in Austin can you find such well-smoked poultry as, believe it
or not, at PoKeJo's.

We sound surprised because PoKeJo's is not generally ranked
amongst Central Texas' elite barbecue venues. This is partly because
their sauce—usually a benchmark of quality 'cue—is unimpressive and
ketchupy. Their brisket, though tasty, is loose and lacks structure; bland
chopped beef, oddly crumbly sausage, and mediocre sides round out
the bill.

But try their poultry, and PoKeJo's takes on a whole new flavor. The
wizards at the pits have managed to discover the elusive flavor in a
chicken. Theirs is moist, soft, and buttery, and practically falling apart.
Better still is their peppery turkey—a bird that is famously impossible to
cook so that it retains flavor and moisture. Calvin Trillin, that most
epicurean of food fans, has even launched a very sensible campaign to
replace the ever-disappointing turkey on Thanksgiving with the much
yummier dish spaghetti carbonara. We would respectfully direct Mr.
Trillin toward this barnlike space just west of downtown, plastered in
chicken wire and rusty old signs. Not only do they sell whole turkeys
during the holidays, but they also let you bring your own bird in to be
smoked, which means you can control the quality. Alternately, about 65
bucks will buy you five pounds of meat and four quarts of sides and
sauce—enough to feed quite a large family gathering. Happy holidays
indeed. –RM

Polvos

See and be seen with a great bowl of queso

food
8.3 / 10

9.2 / 10
experience

Mexican

$24

Bouldin Creek Area

Casual restaurant
Sun.-Fri. 7am-10pm;
Sat. 7am-11pm. *Breakfast.*
Brunch. Outdoor dining. Wireless Internet.

2004 S. 1st St.
Austin
(512) 441-5446

Bar Full
Credit Cards Visa, MC, AmEx
Reservations Not accepted

Polvos is the heady beacon of a South First Street revolution. The place is simple, almost downmarket, yet it has skillfully cultivated a magical vibe—with arrays of outdoor tables, heat lamps, live music, festive, friendly servers, and good, cheap happy hour margaritas—that seems to transcend the half-Tex-Mex, half-interior-Mexican menu. On many nights, the neighborhood streets are crowded with cars from Polvos' parking lot overflow, and youthful diners loiter there waiting to be seated.

Patio seating is in high demand, and the interior is typical Tex-Mex, with knick-knacks, Christmas lights, and a round salsa bar front and center that includes a good, smoky dark ahumada and a hot, gummy green version. The joint has a self-consciously humorous inability to label things properly; at the salsa bar, you might be confronted with ladles labeled for "blue cheese." But that's part of the charm.

Begin with delicious queso, one of Austin's best, with do-it-yourself accoutrements (picadillo, onion, cilantro, and such). Ceviche is attractively strewn with bright tomatoes, onions, and cilantro, and tart with lime, but fish is sparse. Shredded chicken within enchiladas is underseasoned and average, but the "exotic" sauce options are unusually interesting, including delicious pipian (made with pumpkin seeds) and smoky chipotle. Mole is excellent, and carne guisada is tender, with an acceptable, if mild, flavor. Tortilla soup is a winner, as are tacos, including an al pastor version made with good pork, fresh pineapple, and cilantro, and served with pummeled avocado. Rice and beans, however, could use more salt, while Polvos' breakfasts include passable eggs but dishwater coffee.

In the end, almost nobody seems to strike such a pleasant balance between good, low-key Mexican food and an easy environment in which to enjoy it. These phenomena seem to melt together on an average night—or Sunday brunch—to form a magnetic tractor-field grip on your steering wheel, and turn your car into the Polvos parking lot, whether or not it was in your plans for the evening. –MPN/RG

Portabla

Packing it all up to go—it's the
American way, even for upscale Italian

Light American $ **9**   *Clarksville*

Counter service   1200 W. 6th St.   *Bar* BYO
Mon.-Sat. 8am-9pm;   Austin   *Credit Cards* Visa, MC, AmEx
closed Sun. *Breakfast. Outdoor*   (512) 481-8646   *Reservations* Not accepted
dining. Vegetarian-friendly.   www.portabla.com
Wireless Internet.

Portabla represents a useful addition to the Austin food scene—well-
prepared, family-style food to go, with a vaguely Italian influence. They
also do a brisk lunchtime trade in their popular location on West Sixth,
with its gleaming aluminum tables each displaying a single rose
propped in a minimalist square vase.

   Matched with this kind of clean, modern look, the food is
surprisingly comforting, beginning with an excellent meatloaf of the
soft, bready variety, which is even better in a panino. The meat is sweet
with sun-dried tomatoes and gooey with mozzarella that merges with
crisp focaccia in a very satisfactory way. All the sandwiches on offer
show thoughtfulness—the veggies are roasted with dill, a tomato
condiment is stewed into a pleasant confit, and there are cranberries
and toasted almonds in the chicken salad. Portabla also produces an
excellent honey-and-wine-glazed roast chicken and fires its own, fancy-
topped pizzas.

   At its heart this is a deli, with a series of salads and entrees behind a
glass counter that changes daily—an arrangement that lends itself to
somewhat suspiciously tired-looking food that always tastes
considerably better than it promises. Austinites are taking to these delis
these days in a way that they began taking to sushi a few years ago
(Cipollina, around the corner in Clarksville, also springs to mind).
Perhaps as the population continues to get busier, the so-called
"gourmet deli" will, for better or for worse, become increasingly central
to our daily lives, as it is in other, bigger cities. Portabla may not quite
have the warmth and the charm of some of the city's shabbier
institutions, but we'd gladly bring their fare home to our table. –RM

The Posse East

The food ain't much, but there's no better place to watch the Horns

food
5.2
10

8.3
10
experience

American $**14**   *UT Area*

Pub
Daily 9am-2am. Kitchen closes
at 11pm. *Breakfast. Live music.
Outdoor dining. Wireless Internet.*

2900 Duval St.
Austin
(512) 477-2111

Bar Full
Credit Cards Visa and MC
Reservations Not accepted

The Posse East, just north of campus on San Jacinto, is the unofficial headquarters of Operation Orange, the ultimate undergraduate sports bar, offering pretty much everything the undemanding college kid could ask for. It has cheap food, cheap drinks, chatty bartenders, Daily Texan editors on Fridays, some board games and trashy reads inside, big-screen action outside, and a whole lotta Longhorn loyalty. Saturdays in the fall will find everyone in burnt orange, and if you plan to watch an away game here, come early, or you'll never find a spot. (Helpful hint: your chances of a table improve if the game is being broadcast on network television or has an early kickoff.)

This is one of those local spots that has become popular through years of just being there, rather than through any inherent qualities of its own, so don't expect fireworks. This warning absolutely extends to the food, which would not be out of place in one of the dorm cafeterias—an extension of which, after all, the Posse East essentially is. The menu covers burgers, simple sandwiches, and "Mexican food," which here means a hard taco shell with bland ground beef piled on top of it. The guacamole is a bad joke: a sizeable pile of wilted iceberg lettuce is concealed under a diminutive dollop of green mush. Burgers are relatively tasty, but nothing special, although we do rather like the fries. And at press time, only one item on the menu (the double-meat burger) broke the five-buck barrier; the prices are quite a boon if you're on a student budget.

In any case, you're not here for the food. You're here to scream like a maniac when Vince(anity) Young runs 30 yards for a touchdown on third and long, to groan in pain when Mack Brown makes a horrible sideline decision, and to be right there at operation headquarters when the Longhorns finally, beautifully, cream Oklahoma 45 to 12. –RM

Pyramids

A handful of excellent dishes and belly
dancers make this place worthwhile

food

7.0
10

7.6
10

experience

Middle Eastern, Greek $**15**   *North Central*

Casual restaurant
Mon.-Thurs. 11am-10pm; Fri.-Sat.
11am-11pm; Sun. 11am-9pm.
Kid-friendly. Outdoor dining. Vegetarian-friendly.

6019 N. IH-35
Austin
(512) 302-9600

Bar BYO
Credit Cards Visa, MC, AmEx
Reservations Accepted

One of a growing number of Middle Eastern restaurants popping up
across Austin, Pyramids serves up an enormous number of mezze, small
dishes found around the Mediterranean, as well as main dishes that are
representative of the region as well as of Greece. The atmosphere is a
bit more subdued than many of its counterparts, with yellow and
orange walls; only embroidered, tasseled kerchiefs serve as wall
decorations. Middle Eastern music plays, and belly dancers entertain on
weekends. Service is friendly and knowledgeable, but dishes come out
in a scattered fashion, which fortunately suits the mezze method just
fine.

If you are dining with a group, we certainly recommend this
approach. Order the mezze for two as an appetizer plate, which will
easily feed two for a whole meal, or a group wanting starters. This
appetizer is composed of about eight little dishes, including garlicky,
smoky baba ganoush; crunchy kibbeh, deep-fried ground beef balls
that are simple but satisfying; savory shaved gyro meat; and garlicky
chicken shawarma that is delicious with creamy garlic sauce mixed with
chili sauce. The accompanying spinach pies taste tinny and are wrapped
in a Bisquicky dough, but that's really our only complaint. Another
appetizer not to miss is lebne, a thickened yogurt with lots of lemon
that is both creamy and quite tart. Gyros and shawarma appear again
as main courses, but there are also more hearty dishes, like a simple
braised lamb shank sprinkled with parsley and served over rice. The
meat is tender and a bit fatty, with a strong lamb flavor, and makes a
nice meal for cooler weather.

For dessert, don't miss Pyramids' house-made baklava. Moist and
dense, but with flaky phyllo dough still crisp on top, it exudes notes of
orange. This is the best baklava we've found in Austin; in fact, it alone
justifies the trip to Pyramids, wherever you're coming from. –MPN

Quack's on 43rd

Slackers get a job at this decent Hyde Park bakery

food

5.0 /10   **8.1** /10

experience

Light American $ **6**   *Hyde Park*

Café   411 E. 43rd St.   *Bar* None
Mon.-Fri. 6:30am-midnight;   Austin   *Credit Cards* Visa, MC, AmEx
Sat.-Sun. 8am-midnight. *Breakfast.* (512) 453-3399   *Reservations* Not accepted
Outdoor dining. Vegetarian-friendly. Wireless Internet.

Captain Quackenbush's Intergalactic Dessert Company and Café was once the heart and soul of a rag-tag Drag, and perhaps the best embodiment of that strange and straggling Austin attitude that was so recognizable in the '70s and '80s. Peopled by strung-out students and amateur philosophers, Quack's had a smoking lounge that faced out onto the campus strip, where folks would spend hours drinking coffee and vigorously discussing nothing much at all. It was here at Quack's that one of Richard Linklater's city-defining slackers asked the characteristic question "who's ever written the great work about the immense effort required *not* to create?"

Sadly for Quack's, for the Drag, and in some ways for a booming Austin as well, the question received the obvious answer: Quack's on the Drag, that slacker's haven, is no more, gone the way of Les Amis, which also made an appearance in Linklater's film. They have been replaced Jamba Juice and Starbucks, those emblems of American productivity; today's Austin slacker is Urbanely Outfitted.

We are left with Quack's on 43rd, in the Hyde Park restaurant cluster. Even if it's an inadequate consolation prize, it is perfectly pleasant, with plenty of seating and the ubiquitous WiFi connection, and surely some of the same conversations echo, somewhat tamely, around its walls. Quack's also remains one of the three or so most popular UT studying lairs in town (along with Spider House and Little City). The café serves sandwiches that have been sitting in the fridge far too long (we suspect the muffaletta, for example, would be quite good, if it had a chance to defrost), and a completely unacceptable selection of pasta salads and the like. We recommend instead that you go for tea, and sample the baked goods, of which there is a wide variety. We particularly like the banana nut bread, the huge éclairs, and some salty oat cookies that offer the perfect combination of sweet and salty. Still, it looks little different from a chain—American "creativity" won in the end. –RM

Quality Seafood

Old-fashioned fishmongers, old-fashioned friendly service

food

7.1 / 10   **6.5** / 10

experience

Seafood   **$12**   *North Central*

Counter service   5621 Airport Blvd.   *Bar* Beer/wine
Mon.-Sat. 8am-7pm; closed Sun.   Austin   *Credit Cards* Visa, MC, AmEx
Breakfast. Wireless Internet.   (512) 454-5827   *Reservations* Not accepted

Officially named "Eaves Brothers Quality Seafood," this establishment on Airport Boulevard has been Austin's fishmonger since 1938. "Selling [its] Sole Six Days a Week," it is no longer the largest fish counter in town, with weighty competition from the likes of Central Market and Whole Foods, but it's still a friendly stop for some fresh seafood to go, or even for a meal in.

Quality Seafood's playful interior distracts from their lengthy cold case, with blue, mural-painted walls of ocean creatures in costume; life-sized replicas of sharks, dolphins, and various fish suspended from the ceiling, some adorned with sombreros; and a wood and metal seafood bar made to look like a stand you might find on a tropical beach.

Counter service is fast and friendly, making this a good stop if you are pressed for time, though you may find yourself awash with indecision as you peruse the menu, which lists a few appetizers but consists mainly of a wide assortment of fried seafood. Cool, ocean-scented oysters on the half shell are a breezy way to start at a very reasonable price. We love Quality Seafood's shrimp and corn chowder; thick and garlicky, with large tender shrimp, tiny scallops, and bits of potato and corn; it's a meal unto itself.

Po-boys are served simply, with remoulade and fresh veggies on toasted hoagie rolls, filled with lightly fried catfish, shrimp, oysters, blackened catfish, or (inexplicably) tuna salad. Family packs are available, and they're a convenient way to feed the whole clan—they include fish, sides, and that all-time Southern kid favorite, the hush puppy. One word of warning: wear solid shoes when you go—the trek past the walk-in coolers back to the bathroom is a wet one (we're hoping due to all the melting ice). –MPN

Ranch 616

A wacky joint that sticks a gourmet
Southwestern kitchen into a diner

food

7.8 **8.9**
10   10

experience

Southwestern $**43**   *Capitol Area*

Upmarket restaurant
Mon.-Thurs. 11am-2pm,
5pm-10pm; Fri. 11am-2pm,
5pm-11pm; Sat.-Sun. 5pm-11pm. *Date-friendly. Live music. Wireless Internet.*

616 Nueces St.
Austin
(512) 479-7616

Bar Full
Credit Cards Visa, MC, AmEx
Reservations Accepted

If you make it inside Ranch 616, and on busy nights that can be
something of an epic struggle, you'll find Austintatious kitsch paired
with a little of the well-heeled glitz and glamour of Dallas—country-
club bottle-blonds chat with trendy musician types. These folks are at
home in Texas, and they can afford to enjoy it.

The food suits these ambitions—it is upscale, inventive Southwestern
fare. But one senses that one of the reasons the crowd here seems to
be having such a riotous good time is that they're slumming it. Beneath
the reflected shine of their collective affluence and delight, under the
sparkle of the many lights, lies a surprisingly scruffy little restaurant.
This is kitsch at its cheapest (the prevailing theme is the plastic glitter of
Catholic charms from Mexico), often used to odd effect. Beer is served,
for example, in glasses saved from old prayer candles, which also light
the tables. These, in turn, are stolen from 50's dinette sets with
glorious, squiggly-patterned Formica tops. It all sits on a grubby
linoleum floor.

The whole grand mess is a lot of fun, but it's a little unsettling when
paired with the highfalutin' fare and matching prices. The kitchen
produces some fabulous details, but the complete dish is rarely an
unmitigated success. Frogs' legs, a typically adventurous choice, sit atop
beautiful poblano mashed potatoes, but they themselves are chewy, the
accompanying cocktail sauce boring. A much-lauded quail main course
has a lively beef picadillo stuffing, bright sautéed spinach, and those
same mashed potatoes, but the bird itself lacks flavor. Beef tenderloin is
tasty but usually overcooked, and some fish tacos, while served with
wonderful salty onion rings, are thoroughly dull (you'll find better at
almost any local taquería).

Service is friendly and attentive, but reaches you only dimly through
the rampantly loud music issuing from both a roaring band and
booming speakers. It's a high-maintenance game for the high-
maintenance set. –RM

Reale's Pizza and Café

A renowned, overzealously decorated
North Beach pizza-and-pasta temple

food

7.6
10

4.9
10

experience

Italian, Pizza   **$27**   *Far Northwest*

Casual restaurant
Mon.-Thurs. 11am-9:30pm;
Fri. 11am-10pm; Sat. noon-10pm;
closed Sun. *Kid-friendly.*

13450 N. Hwy. 183
Austin
(512) 335-5115

Bar Full
Credit Cards Visa and MC
Reservations Accepted

It's no secret that good Italian food is hard to come by in Austin. Good Italian food at reasonable prices is a veritable unicorn—but we do believe we've found the mythical creature. Reale's Pizza and Café serves real, East-Coast-style Italian food. Signs on the strip-mall storefront proclaim Reale's "your home away from Rome," and the restaurant takes that claim pretty seriously.

The kitsch factor inside is high: columns and arches lead from one room to the next; cherubic angels drift across the ceiling; and fake flowers, plants, and Chianti bottles are everywhere. The walls are decked out with photos of Roman tourist sights, and unfortunately the dim lighting isn't enough to hide the shabbiness of the red carpet.

But the silliness of the décor is not what's important here (who would complain of a cheesy soundtrack and superimposed rainbows while being shown a unicorn?). The food is the real deal, simple but well made. Pasta e fagioli is rich and tomatoey with lots of beans and elbow macaroni. Calamari are tender and crisp, and come with a red sauce that is actually good—thick and a little spicy with lots of garlic. Pastas are also excellent; "Chicken Genovese," in a creamy pesto sauce, has large pieces of chicken, not the anemic ones we're so used to here. And the hearty dish of spinach lasagne is a winner as well, with more of that good, spicy red sauce.

Reale's has begun to build up a reputation for their pizzas, though we think they could stand to be fired a minute or two longer. Their crusts are tender and elastic, with toppings like an array of roasted vegetables that are finished with a glistening drizzle of olive oil. For dessert, Reale's serves fairy-tale-worthy cannoli that are creamy and crunchy with a hint of orange offset by chocolate chips. This place is a real find. –MPN

Red River Café

A longtime Austin diner with just about what you're looking for

food
6.5
10

4.5
10

experience

American, Burgers

$**14**

UT Area

Casual restaurant
Mon.-Fri. 7am-8pm; Sat.-Sun.
8am-5pm. *Breakfast. Brunch.*
Outdoor dining. Wireless Internet.

2912 Medical Arts St.
Austin
(512) 472-0385

Bar None
Credit Cards Visa, MC, AmEx
Reservations Not accepted

One of the nice things about Austin as a college town is that there is relatively little town-gown friction. Students and townies intermingle happily, a comfortably grungy feel prevails, and everyone roots for the Longhorns. The Red River Café has been one of the favorite meeting grounds for this fortunate mix for almost 25 years, both because of its affordability and its proximity to campus. (Note that the café is not actually on Red River, but rather Medical Arts, which bends off it to the southwest.)

You'll recognize the café by the two large fried eggs that stare rather bleakly out at passersby. The interior is a contented, sloppy assortment of booths; a counter with stools; local art; and a colorful whirl of laid-back servers and patrons. And while everyone enjoys a formal occasion every now and then, we like that interactions with the friendly waiters here are perfectly natural, with neither the proper politeness nor the mad grin that often characterize attentive service—that said, the attitude can occasionally take a nasty turn; the Red River Café was one of only three establishments of 390 in Austin to hang up on our personable interns, who were merely collecting basic information.

The food remains similarly within the bounds of the familiar. Red River serves standard diner fare, focusing on brunch, with the Austin flavor of Tex-Mex and vegan-friendly options. Pancakes are probably the best order—they are tender and light, and though the berries in the blueberry version aren't fresh, they are pleasant and plentiful. Omelettes are a touch dry, and again, the ingredients could be fresher (the spinach in the Mediterranean, for example, tastes like it's been a while since it's seen sunlight), and eggs benedict have come overcooked. There are also some more adventurous specials, such as rich mango-cream-cheese French toast. But the real reason to come here is the presence of cheap, satisfying weekday breakfast specials, served all day, which offer hearty full meals for about six bucks.

Meet a buddy, eat some pancakes, and relax. –RM

Richard Jones Pit BBQ

Old-school barbecue, South Congress
style, Texas execution

food
6.4 **5.4**
10 10
experience

Barbecue   **$11**   *St. Edward's Area*

Counter service   2304 S. Congress Ave.   *Bar* None
Mon.-Sat. 6am-9pm;   Austin   *Credit Cards* Visa, MC, AmEx
Sun. 7am-9pm.   (512) 444-2272   *Reservations* Not accepted
Breakfast. Kid-friendly. www.rjbbq.com

Brisket like this makes you happy to be a Texan—or even a Texan transplant. It might not be the smokiest in town, but its tenderness is transcendent, forcing you to contemplate, for the hundredth time, the magical ability of barbecue to transform a tough piece of meat into a meltingly soft one. Richard Jones Pit BBQ honors that tradition in the most unassuming of surroundings.

Men and women, old and young and neither—you'll find them all amongst the illustrious South Austin clientele here. All sit unassumingly in a bunch of brown plastic booths beneath brown Venetian blinds that remain in a perpetual limbo state, somewhere between open and closed. Amidst the office-building walls and ceilings, the color brown turns out to be a serious motif; it informs almost every inch of restaurant space, from the cartoon artwork to the menu. Table service is perky without frills, although many people frequent the take-out window instead.

It bears mention that RJ's style of brisket is not for everyone. It's more about a soft, moist, almost gelatinous texture (which some dislike) than a strong meaty or smoky flavor. If you do subscribe to this school of brisket thought, then you'll enjoy it equally on a platter with sides or on a wimpy little hamburger bun, with pickles and onions. Barbecue sauce is mild but tangy, ketchupy but aromatic, neither runny nor gloopy.

Good ribs and fried chicken still play second fiddle to the brisket, and chicken-fried steak is decent, even if Hill's, down the road, takes it to town. Macaroni and cheese, meanwhile, is like chile con queso without the chile—an American-cheese soup with floating noodles so overcooked that many of them have fallen apart into two or three pieces. Still, we vastly prefer this school of mac-and-cheese thought to the dry, over-baked version that tends to proliferate at barbecue joints; here, it's unambitious, timeless, and utterly successful—just like RJ's itself. –RG

Ringers Sports Lounge

The food is bland, but you gotta love a
sports bar with a map

food

5.2
10

7.5
10

experience

American

$24   *Warehouse District*

Pub
Mon.-Fri. 4pm-2am; Sat.-Sun.
9am-2am. Kitchen closes at
midnight.

415 Colorado St.
Austin
(512) 495-1558
www.ringerssportslounge.com

Bar Full
Credit Cards Visa, MC, AmEx
Reservations Not accepted

Ringers is the sports bar to end all sports bars, the ultimate in Sunday,
Sunday, Sunday madness, proudly displaying 20 sparkling high-
definition flat screen TVs along with two massive theater-sized
projection screens. Nowhere in Austin will you find as many different
games on at one time as here, and if you're one of the city's countless
immigrants from other cities and other states—a city, say, where T.O.
isn't a dirty word (wait a minute, he's a Cowboy now!...)—then Ringers
presents your best chance of getting to see your team in action. Ringers
is *not*, however, the spot to watch the home team. Sure, there's plenty
of burnt orange here on Saturdays in the fall, and it gets pretty hoppin'
when the Spurs are in the finals, but this place does not have the hard-
earned atmosphere of a hometown joint. If you really want to watch
the Red River Shootout in local style, go to the Posse East or Players,
don't go to Ringers.

Nor should you really go to Ringers for the food, which is mediocre
at best. The kitchen makes the predictable bar food, which tries, and
fails, to match the venue's upmarket flashiness. Burgers come with
fancy toppings, such as a mush of guacamole, and each is topped with
one of Ringers' decent onion rings, but the thick, strangely regular
patties are dry and overcooked, regardless of how you order them,
making them reminiscent of hockey pucks (and you reminiscent for the
days when people cared about the NHL). The brisket sandwich is
stringy, and quesadillas involve nothing more exciting than jack cheese.

Still, when you walk in the door on a Sunday and are handed a map
of the games (the staff is surprisingly attentive for so loud and busy a
place), and the room spreads before you in a multi-colored sea of
jerseys, it's hard not to feel a little thrill. –RM

Roaring Fork

Wild West meets white tablecloth at the Stephen F...

Southwestern $52   *Congress Avenue Area*

Upmarket restaurant
Mon.-Thurs. 11:30am-2pm,
5pm-10pm; Fri. 11:30am-2pm,
5pm-11pm; Sat. 5pm-11pm;
Sun. 5pm-9pm. *Date-friendly. Wireless Internet.*

701 Congress Ave.
Austin
(512) 583-0000
www.roaringfork.com

Bar Full
Credit Cards Visa, MC, AmEx
Reservations Accepted

Even if it's the second in a two-restaurant chain that started in Scottsdale, Arizona, the Roaring Fork in the Stephen F. Austin InterContinental hotel seems to be making a point of being as Texas-centric as an upscale eatery can be. The bar and dining room are furnished in rustic wood with barbed-wire-patterned etched glass, and humongous antler chandeliers that only a hunter could love. The menu is heavy on game and Southwestern flair, with a wine list that is entirely domestic, though sadly lacking in Texas wines.

The bread basket is a treasure, with crisply crusted baguettes and currant-laden cornbread muffins. The locally grown Bluebonnet hydroponic mixed-green salad has contrasting hues from the arugula and baby red leaf. It's crisp with pecans and bacon bits, with bursts of sweet dried cranberries and smooth blue cheese. Don't pass up the New Mexico fondue appetizer—the cheese sauce is spicy and thin enough to lightly nap the grilled lamb chops, chunks of potato, and bread. Our favorite main, the mixed grill, sports subtly smoked Elgin sausage, luscious smoked pork shoulder, and grilled lamb chops with a demi-glace-like barbecue sauce that is rich and complex. Unfortunately, at our last visit, the chipotle cole slaw was gooey and the potatoes pasty. Chile-rubbed salmon is also problematic—it tends to have an overcooked, mealy texture—but the Israeli couscous with sweet corn and cheese is tasty and pops on the palate.

The ups and downs go on. Duck breast can come overcooked, but the chile and sugar-cured duck leg is slightly sweet, moist, and rich. And spicy green chile macaroni and cheese is extra cheesy, served sizzling in its very own cast iron skillet. Service at the Roaring Fork is friendly and accommodating—send overcooked items back and they will be happy to oblige. Most Sunday evenings, main courses are two for one, making it a great time to sit under the antlers and eat some good game. –MPN

Rockin' Tomato

One of the better pizzerias in the cheesy-American old school

food
5.4
10

6.5
10
experience

Pizza, American

$17   *S. Lamar, NW Hills, Far Northwest*

Counter service
Daily 11am-midnight.
Delivery.

3003 S. Lamar Blvd.
Austin
(512) 447-3351
www.rockintomato.com

Bar Beer/wine
Credit Cards Visa, MC, AmEx
Reservations Accepted

3563 Far West Blvd.
78731, (512) 231-1210

13729 N. Hwy. 183
78750, (512) 275-1777

As its name suggests, the Rockin' Tomato Pizza Company is a pizzeria with a rock-and-roll atmosphere. Wooden floors, black booths, and dim lighting remind us a bit of a bar, and billiard tables, karaoke nights, and a big screen TV complete the feel. Warhol-esque tomato-themed art, beer signs, and posters decorate the walls, while loud rock music can make conversation challenging. Still, counter service is friendly and engaging, and the restaurant does its best to make families feel welcome, with free buffet meals for small children, which is more than many of Austin's other pizzerias offer.

The buffet is quite a bit smaller than most competitors', but still has a good selection of pizza as well as rolls, a couple of soups and pastas, and the standard salad bar. On the regular menu you'll also find calzones, hoagies, burgers, and a selection of appetizers in case not everyone in your crew is in the mood for pizza. But we recommend that you stick to the pizza and pizza-related items.

Pastas are overcooked and come with uninspired sauces, and while soups are better—like the thick and chunky "Southwest Chicken," with black beans and corn—they are often underseasoned. The pizza, however, has got some good things going for it. Rockin' Tomato's crusts have a good thickness (chewy but not too doughy), toppings are fresh, and the cheese blend is judicious. We are particularly fond of the pizza rolls, oozing with cheese and full of garlic salt; best of the bunch are the steak-filled rolls—the garlic salt, meat, and cheese come together to form a savory treat. We can easily see losing the kids, chasing these rolls with a few beers, and shooting some pool—as long as it's not on karaoke night. –MPN

Romeo's

Stick to the calamari at this Chuy's-owned Italian-American formula joint

Italian $**28**   *Zilker*

Casual restaurant
Sun.-Thurs. 11am-10pm; Fri.-Sat.
11am-11pm. *Brunch. Kid-friendly.*
Live music. Outdoor dining.
Wireless Internet.

1500 Barton Springs Rd.
Austin
(512) 476-1090
www.austinromeos.com

Bar Full
Credit Cards Visa, MC, AmEx
Reservations Accepted

Romeo's is the Chuy's empire's Italian-American effort. The restaurant itself is cute, with dark wood and red walls, grape bunches and vines hanging from the ceiling, lots of mirrors, and live piano music each evening. It all adds up to a vibe with a certain kitschy romance to it, especially if you're a sucker for the Disneyesque. Romeo's welcomes families, but it's more commonly a youthful date destination, as is indicated by their motto, "Fall in love, again...."

The common denominator in Romeo's food seems to be lots of garlic, so pack some after-dinner mints, because the Hershey's Kisses that come with the check won't cut it (and might be all the kissin' you'll be gettin'). The first things to arrive are some un-Italian dinner rolls and a dish of olive oil with a heavy dose of raw, minced garlic. A Caesar salad is fresh, but the light dressing lacks that anchovy bite (a gap filled by the garlicky croutons, which could kill at 20 paces). We do love the delicious calamari, with their light, crisp batter and accompanying tart tomato sauce and spicy aïoli; and the five-cheese pizza with goat cheese has a nice wood-burning oven flavor, though the crust can be undercooked and soggy.

There are some even less successful dishes. Rosemary (really?) chicken ravioli with mushroom cream sauce is a winter dish in a summer town: they're bland and heavy, the pasta a few minutes past al dente. The braciola, meanwhile, should really be called "Meatloaf with Cheese"—this garlicky ground beef slab completely overwhelms its delicate bell pepper sauce. Good cannoli are hard to come by in Austin, and Romeo's are no exception. They're dry and overloaded with golden raisins and chocolate chips that, along with the strawberry jam topping, give them a disconcerting texture. Prices are a bit higher than they ought to be set, although the limited wine list is reasonable, and they have a full bar. But in spite of the evocative setting, in a town with mostly mediocre Italian, Romeo's is just running with the pack. –MPN

Ronnie's Real Food

A BYO restaurant speakeasy in the middle of the woods

American $**24**   *Westlake*

Casual restaurant
Hours vary. Service generally on
weekends. Call ahead to get
menus and schedules. *Date-friendly.*

205 S. Commons Ford
Rd., Austin
(512) 402-9900
www.ronniesrealfood.com

Bar BYO
Credit Cards Visa, MC, AmEx
Reservations Essential

You think *you're* in the know? You should see the customers at
Ronnie's Real Food. How do people find out about this place? It took
the sleuthing genius of two of our inner circle of well-trusted restaurant
confidants to clue us into this hidden gem.

To some, Ronnie is known largely as a commercial baker of vegan
cookies and such; Whole Foods is one of his major resellers. But that's
only the tip of the iceberg: in what feels like a house buried in the
woods—you're guaranteed to get lost on your first trip to Ronnie's—is
a word-of-mouth restaurant speakeasy, a man that cooks for the lucky
few on a lucky few nights per week, an enterprise at the very core of
all that's good about small business in Austin. The price is right, too—at
press time, it was $25 prix-fixe for a three-course meal.

Calling days in advance is a must—after all, Ronnie won't cook if
nobody's coming, so there's no guarantee that he'll be open on any
given day unless you reserve. When you do call, you can find out the
upcoming menus and choose from amongst them (once you're there,
only one set menu is offered per evening, so you'll have no decisions to
make—and we like it that way). We've enjoyed, for instance, a chunky
homestyle vegetable soup, a rustic loin of pork, and an excellent
gingery cake with whipped cream. The best way to describe the cuisine,
perhaps, is as lovingly prepared Texas home cooking—appropriate, after
all, given the setting. We can't describe or evaluate anything that you're
likely to eat, as the menu varies so much day to day. But we can tell
you that it's a charming, intimate, and above all, utterly unique Austin
experience. –RG

Rosie's Tamale House

We hear Willie likes it. Guess there's no accounting for taste...

food

1.6
10

3.9
10

experience

Mexican

$**22** *St. Ed's, Bee Cave, Dripping Spr.*

Casual restaurant
Mon.-Sat. 11am-9pm;
closed Sun. *Outdoor dining.*

102 E. Oltorf St.
Austin
(512) 440-7727

Bar Beer/wine
Credit Cards Visa, MC, AmEx
Reservations Accepted

13303 Hwy. 71 W.
Bee Cave,
512) 263-5245

28501 RR 12 N.
Dripping Springs,
(512) 858-4254

A small chain, Rosie's Tamale House can feel much like a pre-industrial fast-food joint, especially at its Highway 71 trailer, which offers counter service in a cave-like atmosphere. The posted menu is full of cryptic abbreviations for their various Tex-Mex combos (BR for beans and rice, CCQ for chile con queso); they also serve "broasted" chicken and previously frozen crinkle-cut fries.

Rosie's scattered sit-down establishments are decked out with photos, tacky velvet paintings, beer signs, and out-of-season Christmas décor, with service that ranges from curt and rushed to nonexistent. Rosie's claims to offer the "Best Mexican Food Around," which we suppose is true if you define "around" as "on the premises." Queso is a gluey, Velveeta-ish blend, while small tacos are full of wet, cumin-dominated ground beef topped sparsely with diced tomatoes, some lettuce, and a few shreds of cheese. Guacamole needs lime and salt, but the refried beans are okay, and the Spanish rice is better than many we've had. Enchiladas and tamales come drowned in a sweet, red sauce blended with gooey molten cheese. The contents of both the enchiladas and tamales are difficult to discern beneath all the sauce and cheese-food product. What we can tell is that the tamales are moist and the enchiladas tender with sticky tortillas. Flan is heavy and sticky sweet, with no subtleness whatsoever, and overcooked sopapillas are only marginally better.

Though beer is advertised on outdoor signs at the Highway 71 trailer, indoor notices firmly assure guests that it's a misdemeanor to consume alcohol on the premises. Rosie's remains firmly in the Stone Age, accepting only cash and checks with nothing as modern as an ATM to be found at some locations. Keep your cash and find better Tex-Mex elsewhere. –MPN

Rounders Pizzeria

These sweet pies are one of Austin's deep, dark secrets

food
7.9
10

8.4
10
experience

Pizza

$15 *Clarksville*

Counter service
Sun.-Thurs. 11:30am-10pm;
Fri.-Sat. 11:30am-11pm.
*Date-friendly. Delivery. Outdoor
dining. Wireless Internet.*

1203 W. 6th St.
Austin
(512) 477-0404
www.rounderspizzeria.com

Bar Beer/wine
Credit Cards Visa, MC, AmEx
Reservations Not accepted

Rounders serves one gratifying pizza. The dough is chewy, light, and sweet, with a crisp underside; the sauce is fresh and well seasoned; and the toppings are thoughtfully prepared and plentiful. It is, in fact, one of the best New York-style pizzas in town, and its reputation is rapidly spreading.

Families and friends flock to this little West Sixth Street pizzeria despite, or perhaps because of the air of debauchery—no doubt intentional—that hangs about the innocent little craftsman bungalow. They order a couple of sultry pies and a few brewskies (Bass, Shiner, Dos Equis, and Lone Star come by the cheap pitcher-full, and there is a nice selection from the smaller breweries). And they relax into their sinful pleasure.

There *is* something about the vaguely creepy dark green carpeting, deep aubergine walls, and faux leather tables that works, in a den-of-iniquity kind of a way. Perhaps its is the friendly, sexy, and somewhat hard-bitten waitresses who help pull it off. Their combination of brass and benevolence is certainly charming. Perhaps it is the old-school appeal of the Tron and Galaga video games by the door that draws 'em in (they've recently added Frogger to their collection).

But we think it is probably the superb pizza. You start with a red "pizza pie" or a white (sauceless) "Casablanca" base, and pile on the homemade toppings. The latter comes with sweet ricotta cheese, and we absolutely love it with fresh basil and Roma tomatoes added. In fact, add the ricotta onto anything—it is ambrosial. Other great toppings are the roasted red peppers, salty Kalamata olives, and peppery house-made meatballs. The only weakness is that these pies don't come by the slice, but that means more for lunch tomorrow. So enjoy the guilty pleasure of Rounders—just sit outside on the pleasant deck if you want a cleaner conscience. –RM

Roy's Austin

Behold the dangers of culinary imperialism

6.7 10

6.9 10

experience

New American, Hawaiian

$**66**

Convention Center Area

Upmarket restaurant
Daily 5:30pm-10pm.
Live music. Outdoor dining.

340 E. 2nd St.
Austin
(512) 391-1500
www.roysrestaurant.com

Bar Full
Credit Cards MC, AmEX
Reservations Recommended

It's hard not to be skeptical of the prospect of upscale Hawaiian fusion food from an Iron Chef TV star, Roy Yamaguchi, whose gaudy dining chain now dubs itself an "empire" on the web site. Still, once you wade through all the self-congratulatory rhetoric, there is some substance behind this well-lit, casually romantic space with an open kitchen, all plopped right in the middle of the downtown scene.

Before enjoying the cuisine, though, you'll have to translate the irritatingly pompous menu into English. "Yellow Fin Ahi Poketini" is really just a tuna poke (like a tartare) in a martini glass, with cubes of soft, fresh raw fish served in a fusion bath that integrates yuzu soy sauce, wasabi aïoli, flying fish roe, and truffle oil. It's good. The St. Louis pork ribs are another winning starter; whatever Chef Roy means by "Mongolian style," these slabs of meat bear explosive flavors of molasses and mesquite wood, with a sauce so thick and fully seasoned that it's almost too much for your palate—but not quite. Lobster pot-stickers, too, are crisp and successful.

Less convincing are the pricey main courses, whose flowery adjectives are often unrelated to the tastes themselves. At our last visit, a "Jalapeño Thai Basil Provencal Gulf American Red Snapper" was overcooked, without the least hint of basil or anything Thai, while a 31-dollar "Chipotle and Hawaiian Sea Salt Crusted Ribeye" was really just an average steak, tough in places—wherever the salt came from—and its "chorizo and jalapeño natural pan sauce" tasted more like a standard reduced brown sauce. Mashed potatoes, greens, and baby squash have arrived underseasoned and completely mismatched with Roy's bold flavors, and identical veggies often come with different dishes—an embarrassingly unsophisticated move for such an expensive restaurant. When you're paying a $75-a-head tribute to Emperor Roy, you should expect more than this outpost of his kingdom is currently providing. –RG

350 / THE FEARLESS CRITIC

Ruby's BBQ

A wonderful relic of the old rockabilly
Austin, serving up all-natural barbecue

food
8.1 **8.7**
10   10
experience

Barbecue $ **17**   UT Area

Counter service   512 W. 29th St.   *Bar* Beer/wine
Daily 11am-midnight.   Austin   *Credit Cards* Visa and MC
Delivery. Outdoor dining. (512) 477-1651   *Reservations* Not accepted
                            www.rubysbbq.com

The folks at Ruby's know how to treat a cow right. Everything smoked
at this gutsy little spot at the north end of the UT campus is free-range,
hormone-free, antibiotic-free. Unfortunately, the food isn't free—in
fact, it's on the pricey side by Austin standards, perhaps in order to
support the restaurant's environmentally and culinarily sound habits. But
that's probably a good thing: if we could eat as much as we wanted of
this artery-challenging stuff, it might be a short-lived pleasure.

A free spirit, however, happily prevails. Ruby's is unabashedly Austin.
The very walls sing the blues, papered as they are with autographed
posters from Austin's world-renowned blues hall Antone's (a former
neighbor). Siren smells lure customers from blocks away. Tables are
patterned in the notches of the years, servers patterned with tattoos,
and the place and the staff share a winning, laid-back charm.

Substance is added to this charm when the food arrives, as it should,
on a sheet of brown wax paper. Ruby's was once amongst the top
places in town for barbecue; sadly, the quality has gone downhill
slightly in recent months and years, particularly with respect to the
long, curving, crusted beef ribs, which are deeply smoky but can come
chewy. Flavorful brisket, these days, is generally moist, but not always,
and barbecued chicken has little flavor. However, the smoky chopped
beef, doused in a tangy barbecue sauce, is the best we've had
anywhere, far surpassing the duller and more peppery versions available
at competing joints.

Sides are full of surprises. Ruby's prepares two versions of almost
everything. Their creamy cole slaw smacks smartly of celery seeds, and
the sour vinaigrette slaw, which you can add to a chopped beef
sandwich, is one of the happiest accompaniments to the sweet fat of
barbecue we've found. Spicy beans have a creamy kick. A mustardy
potato salad, though standard, is also decent; we wish we could say
the same thing for the embarrassing macaroni and cheese (a dry,
caked-over disaster). Stick to the basics, however, and even a vegetarian
will be happy here (a pleasant surprise from a joint that takes its
barbecue seriously).

Now as ever, we salute Ruby's and their philosophy of "better living
through barbecue." –RM

Rudy's Country Store

The best gas-station chain barbecue around

Barbecue

$15 *Westlake, Far NW, Lake Travis*

Counter service
Mon.-Thurs. 6:30am-9:30pm;
Fri.-Sat. 6:30am-10:30pm;
Sun. 8am-9:30pm. *Kid-friendly.*
Outdoor dining.

2451 S. Capital of
Texas Hwy., Austin
(512) 329-5554
www.rudys.com

Bar Beer/wine
Credit Cards Visa, MC, AmEx
Reservations Not accepted

11570 N. Hwy. 183
78759, (512) 418-9898

7709 FM 620
78726, (512) 250-8002

It sure doesn't look like a barbecue joint—never mind a barbecue *chain*. It doesn't even look like a "Country Store." Really, Rudy's just looks like a gas station complete with convenience store. And yet it is a growing barbecue-and-gas empire that has proliferated not only across Texas, but even into New Mexico. Rudy's had long been a small store in Leon Springs on the outskirts of San Antonio when its owners decided to start selling barbecue in 1989, and today they are trying to claim a catering business on top of their in-store service. Barbecue breeds big appetites, we suppose.

Rudy's facades hardly seem corporate, though, with their rough-hewn logs, red paint, and bright yellow signs. Long tables, some picnic-style, others with folding chairs, remind us a bit of a church supper, and red-checked oilcloths lend a down-home feel. Other accoutrements include the requisite neon beer signs and trophy deer heads. Despite bold signs advertising "The Worst BBQ in Texas," long lines are a frequent thing at lunchtime, but service is still relatively fast, and often so in-your-face friendly that can border on uncomfortable if you're an introvert. Barbecue is sold exclusively by the pound.

Breakfast consists of sausage wraps and barbecue-based breakfast tacos, and lunch continues the barbecue focus. Notwithstanding their claims to the contrary, Rudy's serves up some darn fine 'cue. We are especially impressed with the tender, moist smoked turkey breast, with flavor that doesn't overwhelm. Extra-moist, fatty brisket is also a tender, nicely seasoned choice, though it's better with a dash of Rudy's "sause," a tomato and vinegar concoction that is somewhat thicker than the Hill Country standard, but still within range (and is also available for sale—Rudy's ships worldwide). Sausage is finely ground and peppery, with a jalapeño version that has a lot more fire. Sides are the usual assortment, but Rudy's does make a whole-kernel creamed corn that is, with its sweetness, a nice change of pace –MPN

Russo's Texitally Café

It's worth the drive to this pan-American spot for the lake view alone

American $**31**   *Marble Falls*

Casual restaurant   602 Steve Hawkins Pkwy.   *Bar* Beer/wine
Tues.-Sat. 10am-10pm;   Marble Falls   *Credit Cards* Visa, MC, AmEx
closed Sun.-Mon. *Kid-friendly.*   (830) 693-7091   *Reservations* Accepted
Outdoor dining.   www.texitally.com

Russo's Texitally Café is the ideal place to grab a bite in Marble Falls if you are absolutely mesmerized by water (as we are). Perched high above Lake Marble Falls, the comfortable and partially shaded patio has a spectacular view of the boats on the water and the surrounding Hill Country. The interior feels a little crazy, with baskets and a wine-themed décor as well as a line of burlap coffee sacks hanging along one wall, Texas flags, and an etched glass swordfish. While this may all be a little much, service is small-town Texas-friendly (read: *very* friendly), and the menu offers something for everyone.

Russo's claims "Texas Fare with an Italian Flair," and it certainly lives up to this claim, no matter where it leads. Lunchtime offerings lean toward pasta, burgers, and salads, but dinner-hour mains focus on meat. Overambitious "Beef with the Blues" tops a fresh salad with delicious slices of tenderloin cooked to order, but covers it with a mixture of sautéed mushrooms, tomatoes, pine nuts, and blue cheese that is just too overwhelming. Avocado and garlic cream sauces blend without clashing over penne and fried veal cutlets, but aren't quite enough to moisten the dry veal.

Keeping it simple seems to work better, like the Caesar salad garnished with crisp strips of fried onions and jalapeños. After dinner, don't miss Russo's specialty coffee drinks or bubble teas. Marble Falls is still a small town with just over 5,000 people, but sadly, the outside world has found it, and corporate chains like Chili's have made inroads here. In light of that, we hold out a particular hope that the town will be able to hold on to the sort of character that is found in homegrown businesses such as this family-run restaurant. –MPN

Ruta Maya

Free-trade coffee, free music, and free
classes for the college-activist crowd

food

experience

Light American, Sweets $ 6   *St. Edward's Area*

Café   3601 S. Congress Ave.   *Bar* Beer/wine
Daily 7am-1am. *Breakfast.*   Austin   *Credit Cards* Visa, MC, AmEx
Date-friendly. Live music. (512) 707-9637   *Reservations* Not accepted
Outdoor dining. Wireless Internet. www.rutamaya.net

Ruta Maya got its start in 1990 importing Fair Trade coffee from Latin
America, but the operation has since expanded into a community
coffee house with a lot more than just coffee. One is lured to Ruta
Maya by the intoxicating scent of coffee beans being roasted on the
premises. Their huge South Austin space is soaring in a postmodern
industrial way, with colorful walls and art exhibits, a huge stage for live
music, Sunday children's shows (as well as a kids' area with toys, books,
and pint-sized furniture), and lots of room for an assortment of tables,
uncomfortable folding chairs, and couches that can be moved when it's
time for yoga, informal classes, or weekend salsa dance lessons.

The place really comes alive at nighttime, when the beer drinkers join
the coffee drinkers on the couches, and some really fun live bands take
the stage—that's when the place feels most classically South Austin,
and when you can best understand its legendary reputation. College
kids come in on antiestablishment alterna-dates, and everyone generally
has a blast.

Food-wise, Ruta Maya supports more than just Latin American farms
and villages in its business—they buy much of their food ready-made
from local vendors such as Phoenicia Bakery, Quack's, and Solar Falafel.
Fresh sandwiches are made in-house between 11:30am and 1:30pm
(with wrapped ones available at the counter all day), but otherwise
most of the food is brought in. Unfortunately, much of it doesn't travel
well. On the other hand, it is cheap. Aside from sandwiches (like pulled
pork from Garden District, which we recommend you eat at the
source), there are breakfast tacos, bakery items, empanadas, salads,
bagels, pizza, and more. Avoid the pizza, with its overly thick, doughy
crust. Empanadas are microwave-warmed, so their crusts aren't crisp
enough, but fillings are tasty and well seasoned. Baked goods from
Quack's are decent and generous, such as enormous scones that are
brimming with currants and chocolate chips. Even if Ruta Maya doesn't
serve the best food, they certainly serve us in other ways. –MPN

Ruth's Chris Steakhouse

Why does the best steak in town have
to be found at a chain?

food
8.6
10

7.2
10
experience

Steakhouse $**74**   *Congress Avenue Area*

Upmarket restaurant
Sun.-Thurs. 4:30pm-10:30pm;
Fri.-Sat. 5pm-11pm.
Date-friendly.

107 W. 6th St.
Austin
(512) 477-RUTH
www.ruthschrissteakhouse.com

Bar Full
Credit Cards Visa, MC, AmEx
Reservations Accepted

There's something very specific about the pleasures of a good
steakhouse. You walk in knowing exactly what you want. A shrimp
cocktail, perhaps, or an iceberg wedge with blue cheese dressing. An
expensive steak, aged and buttery, with a big California Cabernet. It's
self-indulgent capitalism, and for a long time, it was impossible to find
at a chain. Enter Ruth's Chris, which got started in New Orleans in
1965, and in the years since, daringly challenged the notion that a
chain restaurant had to be mediocre—and, in the process, added a
nuance to the Great Chain Debate that simply could not be ignored.

The Austin branch is no exception, with a dark, clubby feeling and
impeccable service. It's one of the only places in town where
businesspeople can waltz in at 10pm on a weeknight and have a
proper meal. And they *pay* for it: with appetizers up to $17.95 and
mains into the $40s, is this the most expensive restaurant in Austin?
Does anybody who comes here care?

Bread comes fresh and well heated. The chopped salad, touted as a
classic, sports a little spill of fried onions on top that adds texture but
steals thunder from the tasty blue cheese. Steak arrives as refreshingly
rare as ordered, with a bewildering, peppery sizzle, and extra melted
butter on request (do it!). Creamed spinach is like a dream, with the
pepper and béchamel and spinach leaves all blending together into an
irresistible pile of fatty goodness.

National chains do not generally qualify for inclusion in *The Fearless
Critic*, but this exception is due to the fact that (wince) this is the best
place in town for steak. That's right: the best steak in the capital of the
great cattle-roaming state of Texas is found at a Louisiana-based chain
restaurant. Is that props for Ruth's Chris, or a demerit for Austin?

Maybe both. –RG

Saba Blue Water Café

Jekyll: appetizers and happy hour.
Hyde: mains and the late-night noise

food

6.4	**6.1**
10	10

experience

New American   **$47**   *Warehouse District*

Upmarket restaurant
Mon.-Wed. 4pm-midnight; Thurs.-
Sat. 4pm-2am; Sun. 6pm-midnight.
Kitchen closes Mon.-Tues. 11pm;
Wed.-Sun. midnight. *Wireless Internet.*

208D W. 4th St.
Austin
(512) 478-7222
www.sabacafe.com

Bar Full
Credit Cards Visa, MC, AmEx
Reservations Accepted

Saba Blue Water Café, like its Fourth Street neighborhood, is a hip, sleek and chic slice of the city. At least, that's what they want you to think. Part bar, part lounge, and part Latin-Caribbean fusion restaurant, Saba seems to lack atmospheric focus. Dark lighting, wooden beams looming overhead, and a tan brick wall give a down-to-earth urban feel to the place. At the far end of the café is a bright blue glass panel and paintings of dark-skinned islanders frolicking, occasionally baring it all. All the while, blaring music makes the place resonate like the bar that it is, rendering dinner conversation quite a task. As you shout to your dinner companions, a Saba staff member brings over a sexy blue bottle of iceless tap water (it's supposed to be elegant, but it's mostly just lukewarm) and a plate of delightfully crispy, multi-colored shrimp chips that pair well with chile oil and balsamic vinegar.

Appetizers are the highlight of Saba—in "Tuna Tempura," meltingly soft tuna chunks with a soft green shell are layered on top of a sweet honey-like sauce that has an overwhelming wasabi punch. Ceviche is made well, and fried oysters on yucca chips, topped with cilantro and ranchero sauce, are a good exercise in flavor and texture counterpoints. Main courses, however, can be disastrous. Mahi-mahi comes in a dry and tasteless hunk with bland sauce atop a hill of dry, clumpy rice. The dish is only rescued, in part, by sweet grilled bananas that slide off of their peels.

Things get better with dessert. A key lime crème brûlée, beneath its crisp, sugary top, has hints of the pie, with the same creamy texture. Cocktails are another strength here—a caipirinha is unusually well balanced—and food service is surprisingly friendly and attentive given the bar atmosphere. But there is nothing the servers could do to make Saba feel much like a dinner place. –SF

Salt Lick 360

What took them so long to hit the
suburbs? This is America, after all

food

9.0 | 7.0
10 | 10
experience

Barbecue $30   *Westlake*

Casual restaurant   3801 N. Capital of Texas   *Bar* Full
Sun.-Thurs. 11am-9:30pm;   Hwy., Austin   *Credit Cards* Visa, MC, AmEx
Fri.-Sat. 11am-10pm. *Delivery.* (512) 328-4957   *Reservations* Accepted
Live music. Outdoor dining.   www.saltlickthreesixty.com

Driftwood's Salt Lick, out in the Hill Country, is a longtime Texas legend.
Its suburban sequel, off Route 360, is not: instead of a country picnic
vibe, there's a modern interior with recessed lighting, and the outdoor
tables overlook a big, zooming road. Salt Lick 360, in Westlake's
Davenport Village, draws more of a business-lunch crowd than a
country-music crowd; to claim that this branch shakes a stick at the
original Driftwood standard would be a serious stretch. But that's not to
take away from number two, which in many ways maintains Salt Lick's
culinary reputation: the ribs are great, the brisket tender, the turkey
outstanding—wonderfully smoky and inexplicably moist.

The menu is much more expansive and sophisticated here than at
Salt Lick's original outpost, branching into "contemporary Texas
cuisine." For example, there's a tasty queso flameado layered with
chopped brisket and mushroom rajas. Then there's the "Baja Taco
Plate," and a 10-dollar "Burger 360" that combines ground beef and
smoked brisket, along with roast peppers, mushroom relish, and chile
con queso. The kitchen even tries its hand at grilled salmon.

None of this is offensive (although the salmon comes the closest). But
as you can probably guess, you're best off with what made Salt Lick
famous. Sandwiches are popular with the business lunch crowd, and
the chopped beef version is fantastic, but two dollars more gets you a
combo of ribs, turkey, and brisket; don't forget to ask for pickles and
onions. It's all smothered in that Salt Lick sauce that answers the cry of
the barbecue to "balance me with acid," and does so with an elegant
meld of mustard, vinegar, and sugar. Mop it all up with that spongy
mini-loaf of curiously irresistible, thick-cut white bread.

Don't think of this as an attempt to copy the original. Instead, just
enjoy the fact that you no longer have to go to the Hill Country to
smell the Salt Lick smoke and to taste that impossibly moist turkey. –RG

The Salt Lick

A famously rustic Hill Country barbecue
whose giant reputation is deserved

food
9.1
10

9.8
10

experience

Barbecue   **$17**   *Driftwood*

Casual restaurant   18300 FM 1826   *Bar* BYO
Daily 11am-9:30pm.   Driftwood   *Credit Cards* No credit cards
Date-friendly. Kid-friendly.   (512) 858-4959   *Reservations* Not accepted
Live music. Outdoor dining.   www.saltlickbbq.com

The Salt Lick is probably the most famous barbecue joint in the Austin
area, and the place deserves its reputation. The quick trip west on 290
to the romantically named Driftwood, Texas, is worth it for the half-
hour escape into the Hill Country alone. Plop down at a table in the
Salt Lick's spacious, barn-like pavilion, and you're surrounded by miles
of ranchland, cacti, wildflowers—and sometimes, on weekend
evenings, live country music that makes it all feel like a big party. On
Sundays, cowboy boots stand on every table, filled with some of those
flowers.

The servers are outstandingly helpful in that polite, relaxed Texan
way. Prices aren't low, but portions are huge; lunch is cheaper and just
as big. The classic order here is "Family Style," though all-you-can-eat
beef, sausage, and pork ribs, with endless sides, is the only way to go if
you feel like eating a cow and a couple of pigs for dinner. Brisket is
well-smoked and incredibly moist—most of the time—although the
beef captains tend to throw out a lot of the precious fat unless you ask
for it fatty. Pork ribs are subtly flavored, lean and moist on the inside,
with the ideal reddish halo around the outside of the cut edge—a sign
of expert smoking—and a crunchy, caramelized crust (mmm...meat
candy). And turkey is always a masterpiece; it's like a showcase for
smoke, a moist, juicy, neutral medium that allows the smoke flavor to
sing more clearly than it does on any other meat. We also love the
vinegary, mustardy barbecue sauce, which adds acidity.

Relative weaknesses are the sausage, which is less impressive than
other meats; and the sides, which are generally uninspired: cole slaw is
bland and watery, warm potato salad bland and over-buttered. But no
matter how full you might be, don't miss the pecan pie, less sweet than
usual and rich with the golden flavor of roasted nuts. You leave
Driftwood feeling like you've eaten twice, but thinking that both meals
were excellent. –RM

Sam's BBQ

Locals, celebs, and smoked sheep meet
at this local legend

food
8.2 **9.1**
10   10
experience

Barbecue $**11**   East Austin

Counter service
Mon.-Thurs. 10am-2am; Fri.-Sun.
9:30am-2am. *Outdoor dining.*

2000 E. 12th St.
Austin
(512) 478-0378

Bar BYO
Credit Cards No credit cards
Reservations Not accepted

A fair distance down East 12th Street, tucked into a crumbling clapboard house, sits an Austin institution: Sam's BBQ. Sam's has been serving its particular brand of southern comfort to East Austinites for quite a few decades now, and it doesn't look like it's changed much in that time. It still has the feel of the old South to it, on its dusty strip of road dotted with unsteady wooden houses and faded lots. While a few white faces (Bill Clinton's, among others) now appear amongst the clientele, especially in the drunken wee hours (Sam's serves till 2am), the regulars are still a predominantly East Side crowd of African-Americans.

Whatever you do at Sam's, you must not miss the mutton—Sam's serves a wonderful version of the rare barbecue treat. It is the best thing on their menu, a powerful eating experience, the meat tender and juicy, almost pungent, between protective skins of fat. The brisket is also good, and the chicken moist and smoky, but we find the house-made sausage, which is quite popular, disconcertingly mushy. You'll get the typical Wonder bread with your order, along with a barbecue sauce that's unlike any other in town, more like pureed tomato than spicy condiment; it's a little disappointing. Sides, too, are weak—but on the whole, the meat doesn't need them.

The best reasons of all, perhaps, to come to Sam's are the always friendly welcome, and the sensation you get when sitting in the small room that is plastered floor to ceiling with countless photographs—an indiscriminate mix of family Polaroids, traveling musicians, celebrity testimonials, and noteworthy African-Americans (Dr. Martin Luther King smiles beneficently down at a poster of the Lady Longhorns basketball team)—the powerful feeling that you're somewhere unquestionably, authentically American. –RM

Sambet's Cajun Deli

food

7.9 | **8.0**
10 | 10

experience

The best Cajun food in Austin, if pricey
given the counter service and décor

Southern   **$12**   *Northwest Hills, Cedar Park*

Counter service   8650 Spicewood   *Bar* BYO
Mon.-Sat. 11am-8pm; Sun. 11am-   Springs Rd., Austin   *Credit Cards* Visa, MC, AmEx
6pm. *Live music. Outdoor dining.*   (512) 258-6410   *Reservations* Accepted

                                   251 N. Bell Blvd. (Hwy. 183)
                                   Cedar Park, (512) 249-6411

Sambet's Cajun Deli is a North Austin dive (two now, actually) that
cooks up some of the best Cajun food we've had outside of Louisiana.
The deli doubles as a dim and dusty grocery, selling hot sauces and
Louisiana dry goods. The feeling is truly evocative: many of the seats
are plastic lawn chairs, tables are outfitted with empty Abita six-packs
that hold condiments, and dried gators and loud blues complete the
décor. Counter service is friendly and quick when Sambet's isn't busy,
but at lunchtime it usually is.

   The menu consists mostly of sandwiches and sides in various
combinations including the larger "Lagniappe Lunch," which includes
pint-sized sides. Seafood gumbo is well salted, dark, and rich, with lots
of crawfish. Jambalaya is chock full of andouille sausage, and it's spicy
and thick, not watery like some. We love the Texan drawl in the
crawfish-poblano chowder; it has a thin but creamy base, good heat,
and lots of corn, potatoes, and crawdads. Garlicky, deep-fried crab
cakes are crunchy with a fine texture, kicked up a notch, as Emeril
would say in his irritating way (you love him or you hate him), by a
delicious house-made cocktail sauce with a serious horseradish bite.
Bam!

   Sandwiches on offer are mostly po-boys and muffalettas, but there's
also a "Boudin" sandwich filled with a dense ground pork and rice
sausage. Seafood po-boys are slathered with a spicy mayo and the
fillings are battered and lightly fried until crisp. We're all about the mud
bugs, but po-boys also come with catfish, shrimp, oysters, roast beef,
or even alligator. (Now *there's* a Cajun treat.) Muffalettas also come in
several varieties, including veggie, but we like the original with melted
provolone, sliced ham and salami, and salty-tart olive salad on crisply
grilled bread. Wash it all down with real Southern sweet tea or a bottle
of our favorite—Abita root beer. –MPN

Sampaio's

A brand-new—and old—Brazilian
restaurant out on Burnet

food

6.4 **7.9**

10 10

experience

Brazilian $**42**   *Burnet*

Upmarket restaurant   4800 Burnet Rd.   ***Bar*** Full
Mon.-Thurs. 11am-10pm;   Austin   ***Credit Cards*** Visa, MC, AmEx
Fri.-Sat. 11am-10:30pm.   (512) 469-9988   ***Reservations*** Accepted
Outdoor dining.   www.sampaiosrestaurant.com

It's easy to laugh at new restaurants, even if just for their newness. But
Sampaio's, opened in an unlikely Burnet Road location in February
2006, is giving it the old college try. They're on the right track, with a
beautiful outdoor patio that boasts flowing brown awning drapes, oil
torches, and jasmine vines, all of which redeem the ridiculous
artificially-rough-edged checkerboard stone tables, which seem shipped
straight from the restaurant catalog. Inside, things have more of a turn-
of-the-21st-century tech-bubble aspect: low-hanging blue minimalist
lamps, a big faux-Mexican-mosaic column, and multiple levels of
recessed ceiling glow. But banquettes and booths score intimacy points,
the lighting's not too bright, and service is so friendly it's almost over
the top.

You might know Sampaio's by its former location on San Jacinto, but
that's now São Paolo's, run by the former partner of the Sampaio's
owner. So it shouldn't be too surprising that their menus share a lot,
including the drink selection. Here, caipirinhas are well balanced, not
too sweet but still seductive. Not so for the mojitos; drinking them is
like snorting sugar.

Bolinhos de arroz, the staff-recommended appetizer, are like Italian
arancine (deep-fried risotto balls), but these are stuffed with herbes de
Provence, jack cheese, and potatoes—maybe not nature's most star-
crossed ingredients, but an okay combination. The creamy rice balls
have a crispy enough batter, and the accompanying rosemary-tomato
cream sauce is symbiotically comforting. Good amongst mains is the
peixada nordestina, wherein a creamy coconut broth cures all ills—even
fishy (though not overcooked) salmon. Shrimp, though, are juicy and
well treated, and clams are snappy. We aren't as enthralled by the
peixada's side dish of pirão de farinha de mandioca, sort of like gummy
grits made from yuca flour and studded with pedestrian bell-pepper
cubes. Top-notch Brazilian food still hasn't arrived in Austin, but in the
meantime, these killer caipirinhas and satisfying plates will do. –RG

Sandy's Hamburgers

A wee budget outlet known for frozen custard, but the burgers don't deliver

food
4.6 **5.0**
10 | 10
experience

Burgers $ **5**   *Zilker*

Take-out   603 Barton Springs Rd.   ***Bar*** None
Daily 10:30am-10:30pm.   Austin   ***Credit Cards*** No credit cards
Kid-friendly. Outdoor dining.   (512) 478-6322   ***Reservations*** Not accepted

Sandy's is a holdover from a time when Austinites asked less of, and gave less for, their food. The tiny shack is usually swamped by the long circle of cars full of folks eager for some cheap eats and loyal to the drive-thru; unless you want to eat in a parking lot swarmed by flies, with a view of the open toilet, you should follow their lead. And cheap is right—a bi-weekly special offers a burger, fries, and soda for well under three bucks. Who said the dollar doesn't buy anything these days?

Satisfaction with Sandy's depends on your tastes and expectations. If you treat your visit like a trip to McDonald's, minus the megalomaniacal über-chain effect, you'll be happy here. The service is a little terse—you order at the window and move on, quickly please, if possible. The patties, like at Mickey D's, are of the hammered-thin variety, which can satisfy certain carnophobes' burger cravings (if the thought of a fat, juicy red-meat burger makes you quiver, Sandy's crunchy thin, fairly dry patties are just for you). There's plenty of bright yellow mustard (skip the nasty processed "cheese"), limp shredded lettuce, and a healthy helping of pickles. You can even add respectable bacon. And the fries, despite a somewhat anemic first impression, are actually very good—skinny, crisp and sweet.

By all means avoid the chili dogs: when the greasy mass touches the bun, all turns into a congealed orange mess—a fitting welcome for the "cheese" that then jumps on board, happy to mingle. Instead, round out your meal with Sandy's tasty, old-fashioned "Frozen Custard." The vanilla version is like a vanilla milkshake in soft-serve form, an interestingly tasty dessert. The chocolate frozen custard, though, tastes more like standard chocolate soft serve. Regardless, a mixed swirl of chocolate and vanilla will keep the kids, big and small, very happy. –RM

Santa Rita Cantina

Tex-Mex, cleaned up and taken shopping

food

6.2	**6.2**
10	10

experience

Mexican

$**29**

Seton Medical Area

Casual restaurant
Sun.-Thurs. 11am-10pm;
Fri.-Sat. 11am-11pm.
Brunch. Outdoor dining.

1206 W. 38th St.
Austin
(512) 419-7482
www.santaritacantina.com

Bar Full
Credit Cards Visa, MC, AmEx
Reservations Not accepted

Santa Rita, the relatively recent foray into Tex-Mex from the folks at the upscale 34th Street Café, is a little bit of a puzzling proposition. Why that whitest of establishments felt inspired to answer this city's desperate need for yet another Tex-Mex venue is anyone's guess. But answer it they did, with a restaurant in the new, high-end 26 Doors shopping center on West 38th Street. The Tex-Mex spot fits in strangely well with the boutiques and home-décor stores that surround it—it was rather revealing that a Thursday night "high-heel happy hour," which was held until late 2005, involved discounts for those customers shod in purchases from the fancy shoe shop next door.

Inside, however, Santa Rita feels just like any other Tex-Mex joint, if perhaps one given a little spit and polish. The walls are the requisite limes and mangoes; the atmosphere is relaxed, there is an extensive outdoor patio, and a couple of TVs show the soccer match—if it happens to be on the Deuce (no Spanish-language television here, and the TVs are flat-screen, natch).

The food leans predictably toward the Tex side of Mex, but it, too, is attractively cleaned up. There are crispy-shell beef tacos (those of the school-cafeteria variety), but here they actually taste quite nice, without any congealed, fatty residue. Beef enchiladas with "Tex-Mex" sauce (i.e. chili gravy) are similarly tidy, lacking the death-defying grease that can often accompany the dish.

There are also more authentic options, which are generally simple and tasty. We like the spinach and mushroom chile relleno, in a light ranchero sauce. The poblano, characteristically, is not battered and fried, but rather roasted, and the vegetable filling has a nice buttery creaminess. Best of all is a healing tortilla soup, with a toasty flavor, plenty of lime, and the unusually prominent tang of mild green chiles. There may be far better Tex-Mex in town, but it doesn't go so well with those new green pumps. –RM

São Paulo's Restaurante

Brazilian comfort food for the young people

food
6.0 / 10   6.0 / 10
experience

Brazilian   **$32**   *UT Area*

Casual restaurant   2809 San Jacinto St.   *Bar* Full
Mon.-Thurs. 11am-10pm;   Austin   *Credit Cards* Visa, MC, AmEx
Fri.-Sat. 11am-10:30pm; closed (512) 473-9988   *Reservations* Accepted
Sun. *Live music. Outdoor dining.* www.saupaulosrestaurant.com

Students just *flock* to this locale just north of campus. Perhaps it's for the extended happy hour and South-American-themed drinks, or perhaps for the Brazilian cheese rolls, poppable little baked spheres. But São Paulo's, formerly Sampaio's (which reopened, at least by name, on Burnet), is not the cheap student dive that its small storefront and green plastic awning, tucked into a scruffy strip on San Jacinto, might suggest. Inside is a cool, cushy, and quite proper little restaurant that serves up a mix of Brazilian and Tex-Mex comfort food.

The food *is* comforting, like warm milk (or, rather cream). The Brazilian half of the menu sports a coconut cream sauce, a parmesan cream sauce, an ancho cream sauce, a tomato cream sauce, and a Brazilian cream sauce, and they all taste pretty much the same: sweet, mild, and pleasant. But there are no thrills and too many disappointments, given the hopes we had for a rare Brazilian joint in Austin. Some dishes are oversalted, the fish is overcooked, and the service, though friendly, lacks focus (on one occasion the wrong dish was brought out three times). A few bizarre green lamps give corners of the otherwise pleasant room a fishy glow that matches the flavor of the seafood, and the blinds on the room-length window are inexplicably drawn down, leaving no natural light.

São Paulo's offers some dishes you can't find elsewhere in town, as well as some perfectly good versions of ones you can (the big burritos are very satisfying), but unless you're hankering for some warm and creamy consolation, you'll be underwhelmed. –RM

Sarovar

Lots of mediocrity offset by modern
décor and some truly scrumptious dishes

Indian $**25** *Burnet*

Casual restaurant
Mon.-Thurs. 11am-2:30pm,
5pm-10pm; Fri. 11am-2:30pm,
5pm-11pm; Sat. 11am-3:30pm,
5pm-11pm; Sun. 11am-3:30pm,
5pm-10pm. *Delivery. Vegetarian-friendly. Wireless Internet.*

8440 Burnet Rd.
Austin
(512) 454-8636
www.sarovar.net

Bar Full
Credit Cards Visa, MC, AmEx
Reservations Accepted

Walking into Sarovar is not like entering most of Austin's Indian
restaurants: the faint scent of incense and Indian music is there, but the
predictable décor is not. Instead, the walls are hung with abstract art
and the tables attractively swathed in blue and cream. The menu spans
the whole Subcontinent, and there are a lot of dishes available at
Sarovar that you are unlikely to see elsewhere in town. Unfortunately,
the quality of food is somewhat inconsistent, with some dishes
excellent but others merely humdrum.

On the latter side is a thin, tart tamarind soup with scattered lentils
and scarce flavor. There are a couple of unusual South Indian rice
dishes, but idli (rice cakes) are bland, reminding us of patties of pureed
packing peanuts. Slightly more interesting is upma, a sort of rice
porridge flavored with mustard seed and a few lentils. Yellow dal is
thin, almost watery, and potato and pepper curry is mild and
uninteresting. Tandoori chicken is dry and the pieces are small.

Better dishes include curries and kormas, which shine in both
carnivorous and vegetarian varieties. Curried spinach is creamy, with a
nice flavor; chana masala is rich and spicy, the chickpeas tender yet
firm. We also like the navratan korma, a dish like matar paneer (with
peas and homemade cheese), but with a creamier, lighter sauce, and a
faint taste of almonds. Our favorite dish at Sarovar is the curried goat,
which is meaty and tender with a slight caramelized flavor that is
wonderful. Scoop up your goat with batura—a naan-like bread that is
puffy and deep fried, but a fun change from the usual.

Desserts are nothing special, although the usual kheer (rice pudding)
has been beefed up with tapioca. Since that's not to our liking, we help
ourselves to more goat. Maaaaa. –MPN

Sasha's

An afterthought of an eatery in Austin's only Russian grocery

food

6.0
10

5.8
10

experience

Russian

$17

Northwest Hills

Casual restaurant
Mon.-Sat. 10am-7pm;
Sun. noon-5pm.
Vegetarian-friendly.

5523 Balcones Dr.
Austin
(512) 459-1449
www.sashasmarket.com

Bar None
Credit Cards Visa and MC
Reservations Not accepted

Austin's only Russian restaurant, Sasha's comprises a couple dozen seats in the front of a sizeable Russian store. The atmosphere is that of an ethnic grocery; all of the wall space is filled with merchandise such as CDs, T-shirts, matryoshki (Russian dolls), jewelry, and the like. Imported goods in the grocery are authentic, but sometimes seem quite pricey, especially if you've been to Russia ("45 rubles for *this?*").

The menu is limited and authentic, made up of basic Russian dishes that can easily be prepared behind the counter. It includes hot borscht, salads, pelmeni, and blintzes, as well as a few rather American sandwiches. The service can be slow, as there is only one person on duty, but it's fun to poke around the shop and check out the folk art while you wait.

The Russian dark bread with butter is served cold, but the bread is dense and chewy, with a pleasant hint of caraway. The pirozhki (small stuffed dough buns) have a nice texture and are filled with a peppery but otherwise bland filling of ground beef and potatoes. We like the warm eggplant salad, cooked to a soft consistency with onions, bell peppers, and lots of tomatoes. Try the authentic, beef-filled Siberian pelmeni—dumplings that are boiled and served with sour cream. There are also several blintzes on offer. Some have a dilled-up version of the pirozhki filling; another blends the eggplant salad with feta. Sliced smoked salmon is simply rolled in a crepe and served cold, with a drizzle of sour cream. The chicken sandwich is served on a French roll with Havarti and tastes fresh but plain, although a side of pickled cabbage gives it a Russian touch.

Sasha's does not serve alcohol but does have a wide variety of beverages including Russian drinks such as black tea, birch juice, black currant juice, and beer-like kvas. The menu prices are a little high, but stuffed with good Russian starches, you won't go away hungry. –MPN

Satay

A family-friendly restaurant serving
food from all over Southeast Asia

food

7.6 /10 **8.2** /10

experience

Indonesian, Pan-Asian **$24** *North Central*

Casual restaurant
Mon.-Thurs. 11am-2:30pm,
5pm-10pm; Fri. 11am-2:30pm,
5pm-11pm; Sat. 11:30am-11pm;
Sun. 11:30am-10pm. *Brunch. Delivery. Outdoor dining. Vegetarian-friendly. Wireless Internet.*

3202 W. Anderson Ln.
Austin
(512) 467-6731
www.satayusa.com

Bar Full
Credit Cards Visa, MC, AmEx
Reservations Accepted

One of Austin's first Thai restaurants, Satay has been around for 20 years, serving consistently well-prepared food in a pleasant atmosphere. The décor is simple, with Southeast Asian puppets, elephants, and art, and well as kitschy photos of the Thai royal family. Service is prompt but not rushed, and always friendly to families, but the food is what sets Satay apart. This is all the more impressive given the ambitious, pan-Asian scope of the menu, and nearly every dish can be made vegetarian. There's also a full bar, with house specialties to suit every meal.

The tom kha gai is a mouthwatering galangal-based soup with coconut milk and enough heat to clear the sinuses. The eponymous satay is offered with chicken, beef, pork, or tofu, marinated in a light curry, grilled, and served with a sweet and spicy peanut sauce, hot vinegared cucumber salad, and toast points to help kill the burn. Massaman curry is rich, hot, and a touch sweet, with mouthfuls of potato, onion, meat (or tofu), and the occasional peanut. Pad Thai noodles are cooked al dente with a nice, tart tamarind sauce and served with lime quarters, shredded cabbage, bean sprouts, and crushed peanuts, while a dish called "DWI" (pad kee mao) features toothsome wide noodles, beef and tomatoes, and stir-fried vegetables in a tart and spicy sauce. Note that we do not condone driving while intoxicated. For dessert, we recommend a lush chocolate Thai silk pie. The only dish we can complain about is the Bangkok spring rolls, which are light and crisp but lack flavor.

In recent years, Satay has expanded with pantry products for sale to the public, along with Satay Express, which offers quick Thai food to go. And while we welcome being able to buy their products for home consumption, it's never as good as being at Satay. –MPN

Sawadee Thailand

Warm, fuzzy Thai beloved for its lunch buffet

food
7.1
10
7.5
10
experience

Thai $**24**   *Far South*

Casual restaurant   5517 Manchaca Rd.   *Bar* Beer/wine
Mon.-Sat. 11am-9pm;   Austin   *Credit Cards* Visa, MC, AmEx
closed Sun.   (512) 383-9908   *Reservations* Not accepted

It would be hard not to love this relative (2004) newcomer, even if the food were terrible. Happily, it's not. The reception you get, upon entering the simple establishment, is memorable. It is as if you have stopped by the home of a family of Thai Austinites who are having a few friends over for a meal and are happy to have you join in the fun. The décor, though, is quite standard, with white walls, assorted Thai-related posters that aren't quite kitschy enough to be amusing, and very basic furniture.

You'll be treated with almost overzealous care for the duration of your meal, which might include such hard-to-find-in-Austin delights as a whole, fried, spicy red snapper, stir-fried squid with chili and Thai basil, or a duck breast cooked in five-spice seasoning. Sawadee has a way with larb, one of our favorite Thai dishes; it's a minced chicken salad infused with a delightful intermingling of lime, mint, and fish sauce.

Even a quick glance at the inexpensive lunch buffet, which runs from 11:30am to 3pm, gives away the fact that this is not your average Austin Thai. In addition to the usual red and green curries, the buffet table (depending on the day) might brandish beautiful curry soups with shrimp and pineapple, steaming vats of ground pork with chili peppers, and "Thai Toast," deliciously rich slices of deep-fried Texas toast studded with pork and garlic. As such, you can afford to skip the more mundane items like egg rolls and chicken wings. Don't overlook the pad Thai, though—it's an unusually well balanced version. Sipping the bright orange Thai hot tea (it's also available iced), with condensed milk, is like shooting up sugar. Not that there's anything wrong with that. –RG

Schlotzsky's

Austin's own has gone national—but
the sandwiches are still decent

Light American $ 8   *S. Lamar, W. Campus, N. Central*

Counter service
Hours vary by location. S. Lamar
branch open Mon.-Fri. 7am-
10pm; Sat.-Sun. 8am-10pm.
Breakfast. Kid-friendly. Outdoor dining. Wireless Internet.

218 S. Lamar Blvd.
Austin
(512) 476-2867
www.schlotzskys.com

Bar None
Credit Cards Visa, MC, AmEx
Reservations Not accepted

1915 Guadalupe St.
78705, (512) 457-1129

2545 W. Anderson Ln.
78757, (512) 419-0031

In 1971, in a little shop on South Congress Avenue, the first ever
Schlotzsky's sandwich shop was opened. It sold only one sandwich—a
muffaletta-inspired combination of meats and cheeses, an olive
tapenade, fresh veggies, and mustard. It was known as the "Original."
It's been quite a ride since then. Schlotzsky's grew into an international
force 6,000 shops strong—only to surprise everyone by filing for
bankruptcy in 2004.

Still, with a new start in the works, Schlotzsky's seems to be hanging
in there. You'd never know they were suffering from the swanky looks
of their several Austin locations, which tend to have more the feel of a
high-end hotel lounge than a floundering fast-food chain. Computers
sparkle in the aisles, reminding us that back in 2002, an Austin location
pioneered the WiFi thing, offering free access not only to customers but
to anyone within as many as four miles of the restaurant. But as recent
history shows, new has become a little old.

Take, for example, the company slogan: "Funny Name, Serious
Sandwich." Back in 1971, the sourdough deli sandwich was as strange
a breed in Texas as the Jewish immigrants who had made deli food so
ubiquitous in the northeast. Today, the name would strike only the
most parochial of Austinites as funny. Authentic deli sandwiches are
readily available, and, of course, the Schlotzsky's Original is far from
authentic.

Your feelings about Schlotzsky's, in fact, are entirely dependent on
how you feel about the least authentic aspect of its composition: the
sourdough bun. This is in fact a spongy, oily dough that has more in
common with the English crumpet than with real sourdough. We must
admit, sourdough or not, that we quite like it. Toasted, it adds interest
and texture without dryness, and its holes nicely soak up the mustard
and tapenade. And we gotta salute any fast-food chain that so
flamboyantly employs olives. –RM

Scholtz Garten

A historic gem of a German restaurant
whose food falls short of the concept

food
4.8
10

7.5
10

experience

German, Barbecue   **$20**   *Capitol Area*

Casual restaurant   1607 San Jacinto Blvd.   *Bar* Beer/wine
Daily 11am-2am. Kitchen closes   Austin   *Credit Cards* Visa, MC, AmEx
at 9pm. *Kid-friendly. Live music.*   (512) 474-1958   *Reservations* Not accepted
Outdoor dining. Wireless Internet.   www.scholtzgarten.net

Scholtz Garten may be Texas' oldest operating restaurant. Built by a
German immigrant and Confederate vet in 1866, the original Scholtz
was a boarding school that was turned into the bar and café that still
stands. To give you a sense of what this means, in 1866 the state of
Texas was just two decades old, Austin's roads were unpaved, and the
railroads that were to turn the town into a buzzing metropolis of
15,000 by the 1880s had not yet arrived. Scholtz, then, was a little
enclave of civilization in a dusty cattle town.

All this history does quite a lot for the place—a graceful brick
building with high, beadboard ceilings, stone walls, and a massive and
grand old mirror with beautifully beveled glass backing the entire
length of the bar. There is something refreshing about a place that,
when going for the time-worn look, can use its own old signs and
photos.

But it is a great pity for the Austin restaurant scene that this region,
so widely settled by German immigrants, has failed to produce any
great German food. Scholtz hunkers in the middle of a mediocre list.
The wiener schnitzel exemplifies such failures: it is dry, tasteless, and
lost in its watery breaded casing. The restaurant also smokes its own
barbecue, which is equally uninspired. A smoked turkey po-boy, for
example, has little flavor beyond a vaguely chemical aftertaste. We
recommend, rather, the German sides, which are far more authentic
(stewed red cabbage and a warm, sour, bacon-studded potato salad are
excellent). Scholtz does much better as a pleasant live music venue, and
as the home of many large gatherings, from political rallies to bar
mitzvahs.

Service is friendly, but can be frustratingly slow (where's that famed
German efficiency?). In conclusion, we quote Texas House Resolution
#68: "A gathering place of Texans of discernment, taste, culture,
erudition, epitomizing the finest tradition of magnificent German
heritage in our State." But were we legislators, we might propose an
amendment: "But you can skip the food." –RM

Sea Dragon

Authentic Vietnamese food with more
than just phô

food
7.5 **5.9**
10   10
experience

Vietnamese, Chinese   **$24**   *Far North, Far Northwest*

Casual restaurant   8776 Research Blvd.   *Bar* Beer/wine
Sun.-Thurs. 11am-9:45pm; Fri.-Sat.   Austin   *Credit Cards* Visa, MC, AmEx
11am-10:30pm. *Vegetarian-friendly.* (512) 451-5051   *Reservations* Accepted

13945 N. Hwy. 183
78717, (512) 219-5054

Sea Dragon makes some of the best Vietnamese food in Austin, and
some truly mediocre Chinese food as well. The two locations, both on
U.S. 183, are sparsely decorated with a few Chinese paintings and
neon beer signs, though they somewhat surprisingly host frequent
wedding receptions.

Sea Dragon's exhaustive menu offers nearly 300 dishes, including an
extensive selection of seafood. The weekday lunch buffet, while pretty
cheap, consists mainly of uncompelling Chinese dishes. We strongly
suggest that you order instead from the Vietnamese side of the menu.
Our favorite dish there is number three—cha gio (shrimp imperial rolls).
These authentic Vietnamese fried spring rolls, filled with minced shrimp
and wrapped in rice paper, have a satisfying crunch, and are served
with lettuce and mint leaves (which you wrap around the outside of the
roll—it's messy but delicious, trust us), and chili sauce and fish sauce for
dipping. Soft spring rolls are also good, made fresh so they aren't
tough, and offered with different fillings. Other winners are the
lemongrass and hot-pepper stir-fries available in many variations—
chicken, shrimp, lamb, beef, and so on. They're fiery and complex, with
crisp onions that contrast nicely with the meat.

On the Chinese side, there isn't much to recommend. The egg rolls
taste like the same stuff you find frozen at the grocery store. The tofu
dishes have the texture of diced kitchen sponge, and the noodle dishes
are sticky. Batter-fried dishes such as General Tso's and sesame chicken
are gummy. The better dishes seem to be the vegetable ones, like crisp
green beans in black bean sauce and the fresh and bright baby bok
choy in garlic. Table service at Sea Dragon is average, but to-go service
is very efficient, making it a great spot for Vietnamese take-out. –MPN

Seoul Restaurant

Passable Korean and Japanese food in
an unlikely neighborhood

food
4.6 **5.8**
10   10
experience

Korean, Japanese   **$30**   *Far South*

Casual restaurant
Mon.-Fri. 11:30am-9:30pm;
Sat. 4:30-9:30pm; closed Sun.

6400 S. 1st St.
Austin
(512) 326-5807
www.dksushi.com

Bar Beer/wine
Credit Cards Visa, MC, AmEx
Reservations Not accepted

Located in an unassuming strip mall in Way South Austin, "Seoul Restaurant and DK's Sushi Bar"—that's the full name—is not a bad option for diners south of Ben White looking for a decent Korean meal. The restaurant itself is surprisingly attractive for its location—aside from the sushi bar and a few nearly private booths, Seoul has a Japanese-style dining area with low tables enclosed within tatami-paneled walls. The walls are decorated in a fishing theme, and although TVs are liable to distract during dinner, Asian dance music provides a lively beat. Service varies between friendly and attentive and borderline surly, so be ready for a crapshoot in that arena.

Seoul's menu is split pretty evenly between Japanese and Korean dishes. Japanese dishes are good for the most part—we are particularly fond of the tempuras, which are attractively plated and well executed. The batter is sweet and light, shrimp is cooked through without being rubbery, and veggies, which are shredded and fried together in sort of a nest, still come out tasty and crisp.

Sushi is another story. While pieces are served at the correct temperature, the rice is dry and fish slices are thin and not always at their freshest. Granted, sushi isn't terribly expensive here, but then again, those savings come at a price. Korean dishes come with the mandatory assortment of condiments, from pickled vegetables such as the standard kimchi to plain boiled yams. The best of the bunch is a bowl of sticky and addictive boiled peanuts in a thick soy-sauce syrup (condiments often change). There are lots of noodle dishes, such as jap chae bab, a savory vegetable and beef stir-fry with gummy vermicelli and too much pepper. Just remember the airline-food lesson: you can always ask for more peanuts. –MPN

Serrano's Café

If nothing else, this is a reliable chain
for straightforward Tex-Mex

food

7.2 **6.7**

10 10

experience

Mexican

$28

Red River, Oak Hill, Arboretum

Casual restaurant
Mon.-Thurs. and Sun. 11am-
10pm; Fri.-Sat. 11am-11pm.
*Date-friendly. Delivery. Outdoor
dining. Wireless Internet.*

1111 Red River St.
Austin
(512) 302-1400
www.serranos.com

Bar Full
Credit Cards Visa, MC, AmEx
Reservations Accepted

5030 W. Hwy. 290
78735, (512) 891-7592

10000 Research Blvd.
78759, (512) 250-9555

Probably Austin's most successful mid-priced Tex-Mex chain, Serrano's
offers reliably mediocre-plus fare in a nicer-than-usual cantina
atmosphere. Serrano's many locations and margarita varieties make it a
popular place for business luncheons and after dinner drinks. The
crowd here varies, from business types to families to college kids. Of all
the Serrano's locations, the one standout is their Symphony Square
restaurant on Red River. With its relaxed and charming patio, it's a good
stop for pre-gamers on their way to the bars downtown—or to the
Horns game uptown. The tree-shaded limestone patio looks over a
small amphitheatre and a classically arched stone bridge crossing Waller
Creek, toward the ivy-covered building beyond—it's one of the nicest
outdoor restaurant spots in the city, and certainly the best thing
Serrano's has to offer.

Serrano's menu holds no surprises, touting the same Tex-Mex
standards you'll find all over town. The food is somewhat overpriced
given the quality, but it must be said that they don't skimp on portion
size. Nachos are huge, with half-moon chips the size of a halved 45 (or,
for you bright young things, larger than half a CD). They don't have
much cheese, and are utterly swamped with bland refried beans. Queso
is a perfectly acceptable version, just what you'd expect, but stuffed
jalapeños are to be avoided—flavor isn't the problem, but something
about their frying technique demands an inordinate amount of
chewing.

Quesadillas are another dish with texture issues—simply filled with
white cheese and pico de gallo, they taste bright and salty, but stale
tortillas make them tough. Mains fare about the same—ground beef
tacos are bland, but big; cheese enchiladas are covered with a mild,
thin, cumin-seasoned chile gravy; the verde and chipotle versions are
much better, almost good. Beef fajitas, too, are better—the meat isn't
as well seasoned as we'd like, but the texture is fine, and with all the
toppings, you probably won't notice anyway. –MPN

Shady Grove

Great burgers, a good patio, and you gotta love those Airstreams

food

6.1 / 10

9.1 / 10
experience

American $**23**   *Zilker*

Casual restaurant
Sun.-Thurs. 11am-10:30pm;
Fri.-Sat. 11am-11pm. *Kid-friendly.*
Live music. Outdoor dining.

1624 Barton Springs Rd.
Austin
(512) 474-9991
www.theshadygrove.com

Bar Full
Credit Cards Visa, MC, AmEx
Reservations Not accepted

A busy spot for down-home cooking, Shady Grove is located on Austin's "restaurant row" just east of Zilker Park on Barton Springs Road. Though it's only been open since 1992, Shady Grove has a much older feel—the stone building with its Austin-meets-Western décor was previously used as a grocery and a liquor store. Shady Grove offers live music in its shaded patio area, including the Thursday night KGSR broadcast. There's often a wait during peak hours, but they'll be happy to bring you a margarita or beer at the benches and tables that sit outside just for that purpose.

Main courses aren't fancy, but they are inexpensive at five to 10 bucks each. The house salad is a boring mixture of lettuce, tomatoes, and cucumbers, but the zippy cilantro-lime vinaigrette really livens it up. Hamburgers are made in the old-fashioned thin style with the usual veggies and a soft bun that can become soggy quickly, especially if paired with the spicy green chile. The chicken-fried steak, available with cream gravy or green chile sauce topped with jack cheese, has a crunchy crust that is a wonderful foil to the tender meat. It's refreshing to find an Austin restaurant that isn't touting its use of "Kobe beef" in dishes that really won't benefit from it.

The tortilla-crusted catfish has a crunchy coating that's not too spicy, and is smothered in queso, while the spicy Cajun meatloaf will give your mouth that extra kick. French fries are skin-on and delectably crisp with just the right amount of salt. Service at Shady Grove is done in Austin's standard quick, smiley style, and is particularly tolerant of children; they have a lengthy kids' menu with games and puzzles on the back, as well as crayons. This is a good stop for a cheap, filling meal and a leisurely margarita under the trees. –MPN

Shalimar

Authentic Indian and Pakistani catering
to our growing South Asian community

food
6.8 / 10   **4.4** / 10
experience

Indian $**11**   *Far North*

Casual restaurant   9310 N. Lamar Blvd.   ***Bar*** None
Sun.-Thurs. 11:30am-10:40pm;   Austin   ***Credit Cards*** Visa, MC, AmEx
Fri.-Sat. 11:30am-11:30pm.   (512) 719-3700   ***Reservations*** Not accepted
                             www.shalimaraustin.com

For a long time, the kind of cuisine that Austin's more cosmopolitan
residents most sorely missed was Indian food. Sure, there were a few
buffets here and there, but they were always rather disappointing, the
curries somehow lacking that authentic intricacy of spicing and
ingredients.

Over the past decade, that need has been neatly satisfied (Now, for
the next item in our culinary wish list—African food: why did Aster's
and World Beat Café close? Surely we were ready for it!). A bright array
of Indian restaurants and buffets has opened up across the city,
concentrated in the rapidly expanding Asian neighborhoods north of
U.S. 183. And while it is not as exciting as Swad, its neighbor to the
north, Shalimar does have an extensive and tasty buffet that includes a
variety of refreshingly foreign options.

Shalimar's most immediately obvious asset is a long and varied menu.
In addition to the familiar tikkas, kormas, masalas, and dals, there is
grilled fish, goat curry, cabbage, and beef. The buffet displays various
names that will be new even to those diners who consider themselves
rather old hands at the aloo gobi game. We recommend that you just
dive right in—Shalimar's best dishes involve vegetables that even the
friendly waitress—who spoke, we were relieved to find, not Hindi but
Spanish—could not identify for us. We particularly like the pound
tandura, which involves strange objects that look like smooth okra or
jalapeños, but have no heat; the doodhi dal, which mixes squash with
the conventional lentils; and the choley, a sweet stew involving corn
and chickpeas. Goat curry—not on the buffet but worth a try—
combines the fatty, rich meat with a tomato ragout, and is a little
greasy. But you can wash it down with some of the best mango lassi
this city has to offer. –RM

Shoal Creek Saloon

A bar that's a little more Monday Night
Football than High Noon

food

6.0 **7.2**
10 / 10

experience

American   **$23**   *House Park Area*

Pub
Mon.-Sat. 11am-midnight; Sun.
11am-11pm. Kitchen closes Sun.-
Wed. 10pm; Thurs.-Sat. 10:30pm.
Live music. Outdoor dining. Wireless Internet.

909 N. Lamar Blvd.
Austin
(512) 474-0805
www.shoalcreeksaloon.com

Bar Full
Credit Cards Visa, MC, AmEx
Reservations Not accepted

The Shoal Creek Saloon sounds like an old-school honky-tonk full of beer-swillin', gun-totin' outlaws. But the only bandit in sight is the one painted squatting down on the door of the men's toilet, and the only ones firing are the mosquitoes, who are apparently as fond of the bar's extensive outdoor deck as we are.

Instead, what Shoal Creek Saloon offers its customers is a quiet, tree-shaded meal on that deck, which does, indeed, overlook the pleasant scrappy tumble of Shoal Creek, and the park beyond it. It also offers a satisfying number of sharp new TVs on which to watch the big game, whatever shape that might take, and some fairly tasty bar food to snack on while you do so.

The food doesn't rise much beyond that distinction. Shoal Creek's menu has a slightly Cajun flare, sporting such Big Easy standbys as crawfish, gumbo, and étouffée—the last is watery and a little bland. A tuna sandwich, which you must order rare if you want it rare, is equally boring, with little to perk up the rather drab fish. Burgers are fine—we rather like the caramelized jalapeños on the "Reynaldo"—but the patties are dull and on the dry side, and fries were of the crinkle cut variety that always seems suspiciously reconstituted.

What does stand out here is the chicken-fried chicken, which is crunchy and blessedly grease free on the outside, moist on the inside, and enlivened by peppery cream gravy. The Saloon also serves a changing roster of bargain dinner specials, and half-price appetizers during "happier hour." There's not much more to report on; aside from somewhat lackadaisical service, the Shoal Creek Saloon neatly fills the sports-bar-cum-beer-garden role required of it. –RM

Shoreline Grill

Casually elegant New American in a
setting that almost justifies the prices

food

8.4 **8.8**
10   10

experience

New American   **$64**   *Convention Center Area*

Upmarket restaurant
Mon.-Fri. 11am-10pm; Sat.
5pm-10pm; Sun. 5pm-9pm.
Outdoor dining. Wireless Internet.

98 San Jacinto Blvd.
Austin
(512) 477-3300
www.shorelinegrill.com

Bar Full
Credit Cards Visa, MC, AmEx
Reservations Accepted

Power lunch. Those two words perhaps best epitomize the Shoreline Grill, a downtown eatery that was opened in 1989 by the owners of Jeffrey's. The place caters to the elite while studiously avoiding excessive formality, with an atmosphere of effortless elegance, integrating subdued modern art and light jazz. During daylight hours, the sunlight exposes views of bright greenery and a glimmering Town Lake that almost feel like part of the room. The lunch crowd is particularly businesslike, while the dinner crowd includes more tourists from the nearby hotels (the Four Seasons, for example, is a stone's throw away). In season, there's a spectacular view of Austin's famous bats at twilight.

On to the food: the crab cakes with chipotle mango sauce are touted by the staff as a top choice—and at $17 for an appetizer, they'd better be. They're made from lump meat that's slightly stringy but resilient, gently crisped, and generally satisfying—competent crab cakes, to be sure—but *$17?* "Cravado" is a crab-and-avocado creation, again employing real lump crabmeat, this time with a "cucumber tomato coulis" that is like a pureed gazpacho. Good, but no fireworks here, and you're another $14 poorer—and this all before the mains arrive.

Fish tacos, with a mixture of aïoli and avocado, are just average; the fish within is well crisped, although its flavor, at our last visit, was slightly metallic—not the freshest. Prime rib enchiladas are made with very well-done meat, almost like stewed tips, and served with grilled shrimp that, while juicy and not cooked a second too long, are also underseasoned. The prime rib dinner (up to $34 for a large serving) tends to come less rare than requested, and the salsas in various dishes seem to be strangely similar to each other. Dessert options include a "Chocolate Intemperance" that echoes the version at Jeffrey's. It's all good, and pretty, but these prices are hard to justify, even with the bats. –RG

Siena

An Italian-food setting lovelier than any
other in town

food
8.5 / 10 **9.2** / 10
experience

Italian $**55**   *Westlake*

Upmarket restaurant
Mon.-Thurs. 11:30am-2pm,
6pm-9:30pm; Fri. 11:30am-2pm,
6pm-10pm; Sat. 6pm-10pm;
Sun. 5:30pm-9pm. *Date-friendly. Outdoor dining. Wireless Internet.*

6203B N. Capital of
Texas Hwy., Austin
(512) 349-7667
www.sienarestaurant.com

Bar Full
Credit Cards Visa, MC, AmEx
Reservations Recommended

Austin's loveliest Italian restaurant is located in an expansive villa done
up to look like a Tuscan farmhouse, a Disneyesque creation hidden
behind a lonely stretch of Westlake strip mall. Siena's service is friendly
and knowledgeable, and the restaurant also has an impressively
extensive wine list with some pricey regional Italian gems. Happy hour
drink and appetizer specials are available on weekdays from 5pm to
7pm—they're best enjoyed in the cozier space by the bar and kitchen,
not in the vast dining room.

Even if Siena doesn't serve the very best Italian food in Austin—it's
easily surpassed by the sisters Vespaio—we salute the place for its
above-average authenticity. Among starters, we like roasted figs
wrapped in prosciutto, which are chewy and sweet, with a hint of salt
from pecorino, and acidity from a viscous balsamic vinegar. Mussels
steamed in white wine and Sambuca are fresh and light with a touch of
butter. In cooler weather, you might try the bruschetta, which piles a
dense but somewhat dry and tough Chianti-cooked ragù of wild boar
over giant slices of grilled bread, whose flavor completely absorbs the
smoke of the wood-fired grill.

That grill also makes key contributions to meat mains such as a sliced
grilled steak served simply with olive oil over greens, but with a less
meaty flavor then expected. Lamb osso buco is tender, served with a
bright mint gremolata and sweet, soft polenta with mascarpone and
pine nuts. Pasta dishes are available in smaller "primo" and larger
"secondo" portions; the idea is that, as in Italy, you can have a pasta as
a first course and then move on to your meat course. Some sides come
à la carte, so don't miss the heavenly sformatino di patate—a smooth
potato and chive flan scented with white truffle oil. Tempting desserts
include panna cotta with berries, and vanilla gelato with sliced
strawberries and a balsamic reduction that makes the berries sing—
even if its notes are still drowned out by the loud serenade of the
transportative atmosphere. –MPN

Silhouette

Expensive, hit-or-miss sushi in a warm,
sleek space with no video cameras

food
6.1 /10   **6.8** /10
experience

Japanese   **$41**   *Congress Avenue Area*

Upmarket restaurant
Sun.-Thurs. 11am-2pm, 5pm-
11:30pm; Fri.-Sat. 11am-2pm,
5pm-1:30am.

718 Congress Ave.
Austin
(512) 478-8899
www.silhouetteaustin.com

Bar Full
Credit Cards Visa, MC, AmEx
Reservations Accepted

This is the space formerly inhabited by Pango Tea Bar, which met a
rather bizarre end in January 2004, when its owner was arrested for
having planted a hidden camera in a basket near the toilet of the
women's bathroom, which was wired to a video system in his office.
When this news came out, all of the women in the Austin area that
had ever dined at Pango let out a collective shriek of horror.

Silhouette, which replaced Pango in its Congress Avenue location,
updated not just the moral fiber but also the space. It's a warm
environment, with modern artwork along its dark red walls, a big bar in
front, and a little sushi bar in back; cozy booths line the walls in
between, and tables are intimate and well placed. Although the
lighting seems brighter on some days than others, Silhouette has a
trendier and more romantic vibe than most sushi joints in town, but its
trendiness does not feel forced or irritating (à la Maiko).

The sushi basics are done well: salmon is rich and buttery, and
hamachi (yellowtail) has a fresh taste without a hint of fishiness. We
have tried uni (sea urchin) once, and were happy with the results,
although it doesn't stand up to Austin's uni giants. Unagi (eel) has been
reliable as well. Not so for suzuki (sea bass), which has been
consistently tough and inappropriately paired with a bitter, shredded
red root. Pricey toro (fatty tuna) has been neither particularly fatty nor
particularly good; in fact, it has given us that not-so-fresh feeling. Rolls
are creative but unspectacular, and suffer from mediocre, grainy sushi
rice.

We like the bubble tea options (an Asian specialty, with tapioca balls
resting on the bottom of sweet tea concoctions), and Silhouette also
does the traditional tea ceremony. Ultimately, though, the place is all
about the intimate atmosphere and the fun, creative cocktails, even if
the prices are too high and the sushi doesn't quite stand up to the best
of the competition. –RG

Smitty's Market

How can one small town have so much awesome barbecue?

food
9.0
10
8.0
10
experience

Barbecue   **$12**   *Lockhart*

Counter service
Mon.-Fri. 7am-6pm; Sat.
7am-6:30pm; Sun. 9am-3pm.
Kid-friendly.

208 S. Commerce St.
Lockhart
(512) 398-9433
www.smittysmarket.com

Bar Beer/wine
Credit Cards Visa and MC
Reservations Not accepted

The infamous family feud of the 1990s that had many of us fearing that barbecue in Lockhart was doomed has actually turned out to be a good thing for barbecue lovers. The Schmidt family duked it out, and in the end, one side got to keep the name Kreuz Market, while the other side got to keep the original building from 1900. Meanwhile, everyone has continued to make top-notch barbecue. It must have been a real blow to lose the Kreuz name, and along with it the reputation, but perhaps that has kept the crew at Smitty's working extra hard to maintain quality.

The pit room of the old red brick building doesn't seemed to have changed a bit, and the heat and smoke from the fire that is *right there*—watch your children, please—can be a bit overwhelming initially. Once your eyes adjust to the dark (the greasy, smoke-infused black walls make this room darker then you might expect), you can hop in line and order your meats by the pound right at the scales, and then adjourn to the dining room to get your drink and sides.

The small dining room certainly has changed some since the old days, although it's as bright and plain as ever, in stark contrast to the more done-up, and vastly bigger, Kreuz Market. Smitty's has a TV on the wall, and new tables and chairs; sadly, the knives that were once chained to the walls have disappeared. (Was the health department involved here?) But you shouldn't miss them too much, as the brisket at Smitty's is tender as can be. There is barbecue sauce available here, unlike at Kreuz, and although its use is shrugged off by the purists, it's well executed. Sausage is excellent, too, slightly finer in texture than it used to be, but still loose packed and delicious. Knives or no knives, Smitty's is a real part of our national barbecue heritage, a shining Texas star.
—MPN

Snow Pea

A popular, strategically located Asian take-out spot off 35th Street

food
5.3 / 10 **6.3** / 10
experience

Chinese, Korean, Japanese   **$24**   *North Central*

Casual restaurant
Mon.-Fri. 11am-2:30pm,
5pm-10pm; Sat.-Sun.
noon-10pm. *Delivery.*

3706 Jefferson St.
Austin
(512) 454-3228
www.snowpeaaustin.com

Bar Beer/wine
Credit Cards Visa, MC, AmEx
Reservations Not accepted

Snow Pea, a Chinese-Korean restaurant and sushi bar, does a good business in take-out but seems to be less popular as a place to dine in. The food at Snow Pea is mostly palatable, but it's quite average—nothing you'd ever find yourself craving. But it's no surprise that the only Chinese restaurant in a neighborhood that is both a densely populated residential area, as well as a thriving business district with much of Austin's medical community practicing within a few blocks, would wind up as such a mainstay for take-out.

The main dining room has an attractive waterfall built into a corner; otherwise, it's simply decorated with Japanese-style rice-papered windows, but the vinyl-covered chairs seriously detract from the décor. Service is friendly, but not always attentive. The sushi menu features the usual items as well as several house specialty rolls, and it's reasonably priced overall. During happy hour, nigiri (sushi pieces) are only a dollar apiece, so this is a good time to come in for a bargain, and the sushi itself is good, the fish slices thin but fresh, although the rolls can be overly soft.

On the Chinese side of the menu, appetizers are nothing special. Hot and sour soup has a nice consistency, but not much else going on, and egg rolls are just average. Mains, though, fare a bit better. There are some interesting seafood dishes on offer, including fried shrimp with deeply caramelized walnuts—a crunchy combination in a red sweet-and-sour sauce. Moo shu pork is also very good, with crisp veggies and a rich flavor. We have been less wild about the dan-dan noodles that have been offered in the past (they weren't on the menu at press time), which were served in a sweet peanut sauce with anemic-looking pieces of poached chicken. Unfortunately, as Snow Pea proves, the three secrets to great Chinese and Japanese cuisine are not location, location, and location. –MPN

The Soup Peddler

Soup's on—or, actually, it's in a plastic bag

food
6.3 / 10   **7.0** / 10
experience

American $ **10**   *Bouldin Creek Area*

Take-out
Mon.-Thurs. 11am-1pm, 5pm-7pm.
Closed Fri.-Sun. Food by reservation
only. *Vegetarian-friendly.*

501 W. Mary St.
Austin
(512) 373-7672
www.souppeddler.com

Bar None
Credit Cards Visa, MC, AmEx
Reservations Essential

The Soup Peddler is a unique concept in our food-service industry, even in a town full of unique concepts. Driving by the South Austin storefront, upon seeing the sign, you might think that it would be possible to enter the establishment and purchase some soup. But you'd be wrong. That privilege is reserved for the portion of the Soup Peddler's loyal clientele that has taken the time to reserve soup the week before. Those without reservations are cursed to a soupless existence—at least until next week.

Enter the web site, and you'll figure out how it works: you reserve ahead and pay by credit card. Although you're asked to specify which day of the week you want your soup, they're flexible on that point. When your week arrives, you can choose to pick up the soup yourself (in which case, when you actually enter the Peddler, you'll feel more like you've got a meeting at an office than a take-out restaurant), or you can choose delivery. Either way, the soup will be presented to you in a plastic bag. That's right, not a plastic bowl or container—they put the soup directly into a plastic bag.

Prices aren't cheap, though: $14-plus-tax worth of soup is only about enough to feed two hungry people, which isn't much less than you'd pay in a decent restaurant; add to this the hassle of breaking open the bag, heating the soup in a pot, dirtying dishes, and so on, and you're left a bit befuddled as to the value proposition, especially when it's good but not great. Duck gumbo, for instance, has a deep, dark, rich stock, but you have to add liberal quantities of salt to release its flavors. Potato-leek soup is decent, but so, probably, is yours; why not do it yourself if you're going to all this trouble? We appreciate the cute concept and salute the Soup Peddler for its quirky charm and contribution to Austin culture, so we feel kind of bad admitting that we're not particularly tempted to order again. –RG

South Congress Café

An idyllic slice of Austin's hip strip with
endlessly satisfying Southwestern fusion

food

9.1 / 10

9.3 / 10

experience

Southwestern

$42   *South Congress*

Upmarket restaurant
Daily 10am-10pm.
Brunch. Date-friendly.

1600 S. Congress Ave.
Austin
(512) 447-3905
www.southcongresscafe.com

Bar Full
Credit Cards Visa, MC, AmEx
Reservations Not accepted

We may not be fans of yuppification, but the South Congress Café, a recent arrival to the heart of this chic strip, though owned by the Trudy's chain, does much to redeem the upmarket trend that some old-time Austinites gripe is threatening the city's scrappy, eccentric appeal. The food and the décor are equally bright and attractive, and, more importantly, the prices are surprisingly cheap given the posh feel. The décor is inspired by mod Danish designs from the fifties, and a long, sloped window graces the length of one wall, brightening the room and offering views of the eye candy on South Congress Avenue.

The food is equally pleasant to look at, served on dishes with a cheeky slant to their edges, as if a fresh wind has just blown over them, leaving them slightly askew. The menu covers Texas, Louisiana, and the Southwest, but always with a twist. Blackened tuna tacos come with a delightful mix of condiments and salsas, each interesting, while pork tenderloin has a blue corn chorizo stuffing, and meatloaf gets a Texan kick, with jalapeños, venison, and a poblano demi-glace.

The café is open daily for a popular brunch, which comes with a bottomless basket of sweet, crunchy cornbread muffins—it's a pleasant way to spend a late morning, beginning with a delicious wild boar pozole that is sinus-clearingly spicy. Served with neat little piles of chopped red onion, oregano, and perky, crunchy raw cabbage, it'll cure the most hung-over and wilted of Sunday morning souls. Amongst the other brunch options, which are refreshingly served until 4pm every day, are terrific migas with an unusual creaminess—they, like some other dishes, are spectacularly paired with homemade flour tortillas, which are some of the best in town.

There are some weak spots in the cooking: the smoked chicken in one dish was greasy and over-spiced, while the New Mexico chile sauces that accompany many brunch options suffer from the opposite affliction—they're bland and starchy. But whether for the judicious prices or the lively drinks list, we think this is a comfortable place for a classy night—or morning—out. –RM

The Spider House

The punks are on the patio, the music's in the air

food

5.5 | 9.6
10 | 10
experience

Light American $ **7**   *UT Area*

Café
Daily 8am-2am. *Breakfast.*
Date-friendly. Live music.
Outdoor dining. Wireless Internet.

2908 Fruth St.
Austin
(512) 480-9562
www.spiderhousecafe.com

Bar Beer/wine
Credit Cards Visa and MC
Reservations Not accepted

The outdoor patio at Spider House is one of the nicest places to sit in all of Austin. If we wanted to communicate to some visiting out-of-towner just what it is we love about this hip, hot, higgledy-piggledy town, we'd take them here. Crazy-paved terraces, in a bright mix of bricks and flagstones, spill down the slope to the street, the many levels and odd tree or two creating an abundance of intimate spaces for friendly chatter. Seating is a hodge-podge of pressed tin gliders, their flaking paint singing of the South. Christmas lights crisscross overhead, though we miss the bizarre collection of pill bottles and decapitated baby dolls that once covered the bulbs.

The predominantly student clientele is pure punk and pizzazz. Austin's vast population of the young gathers here to finish term papers, take a stab at that Russian novel, play one of the many board games on offer inside, make up, break up, or talk sex, drugs, and rock 'n' roll. A walk through the tables yields a strange mix of snippets: "…and then *he* said…you sunk my battleship…dude, that trip was on a whole *other* level…aw, Leno sucks." Anonymous forms hunker immobile over their laptops and long-since-cold coffee.

Few people come to the Spider House for the food, but there are some decent options. Vegetarian chili, despite its meat substitute, is very good, with a lively mix of beans and plenty of heat. Avoid the astonishingly bland veggie burrito. Mostly, folks come to kick back with one of the many beers on offer, or a specialty coffee such as the Spanish cortado or Vietnamese café sua da. We also like the cremosas—Italian sodas with a touch of cream—and the thick, quality milkshakes (banana is particularly good). A hot summer night, live music or perhaps an outdoor screening of some cult classic, the chirrup of crickets, and you've got Austin. –RM

Star of India

Predictable Indian food with a substantial buffet

food
6.7 **6.5**
10   10
experience

Indian $**22**   *North Central*

Casual restaurant
Sun.-Thurs. 11am-2:30pm,
5:30pm-10pm; Fri.-Sat. 11am-
2:30pm, 5:30pm-10:30pm. *Delivery. Vegetarian-friendly.*

2900 W. Anderson Ln.
Austin
(512) 452-8199

Bar Beer/wine
Credit Cards Visa, MC, AmEx
Reservations Accepted

Walking into Star of India is much like entering many of Austin's Indian restaurants—there are arched windows, Persian rugs, and artwork depicting scenes from Hindu mythology. What helps Star of India stand out is the shrine just inside the front door. It's an elephant statue (an Asian good-luck symbol), wearing a garland of garlic (a Latin American charm for luring business), topped with a small statue of the Virgin of Guadalupe and a postcard of Pope Benedict XIII, and strewn with flowers, rosaries, and Spanish-language missionary pamphlets. It is an intimate mingling of disparate cultures and beliefs.

The restaurant offers lunch and dinner buffets as well as a regular menu. The buffet is pretty typical—cold sides are your standard assortment of chutneys, melon, basic salads, and peppery, turmeric-tinted pickled onions. Appetizers include spicy vegetable samosas and somewhat soggy vegetable pakora redeemed by a nice curry flavor. The "Madras Soup," made with curried tomatoes and coconut, is thick, creamy, and piquant—the ideal take-out soup if you have a cold. Many of the offerings are fairly average—some veggies lack luster, and the matter paneer, a curried tomato and pea dish that is often a favorite of ours, is particularly unappealing

Saag paneer is much better—the spinach is creamy and flavorful and there's plenty of that homemade cheese. Other standouts are a lovely, subtle chicken curry and the excellent bengan masala, which, with its stewed eggplant, okra, tomatoes, and peas, makes a delicious mélange of flavors. And lamb meatballs in curry are seared, moist and rich. For dessert, there's rice pudding and two painfully sweet, artificially flavored puddings. That said, the service at Star of India is quick and unobtrusive, and the buffet, if somewhat uneven, is a good value. Plus, you're sure to find good luck under that shrine. –MPN

Starlite

A still-delicious upscale favorite that has
moved downtown and trendified

food

9.0
10
8.5
10
experience

New American $65   *Warehouse District*

Upmarket restaurant   407 Colorado St.   *Bar* Full
Mon.-Fri. 11:30am-2:30pm,   Austin   *Credit Cards* Visa, MC, AmEx
5:30pm-11pm; Sat. 5:30pm-   (512) 374-9012   *Reservations* Recommended
11pm; closed Sun. *Date-friendly.* www.starliteaustin.net
Wireless Internet.

Starlite has left behind the cozy confines of its childhood home—a
sweet craftsman bungalow just north of the UT campus—and moved
downtown with the grownups. We must say we rather miss the old
digs, which could well have been rustic, if not for a trick which any
teenaged girl will tell you can jazz up an evening: add a little glitter.
Candle-spangled and sparkling, the homey corners of the house
combined all that was best of dark and bright for an enjoyable night
out.

The posh new digs downtown show the same talent for design:
ceilings are lofty, with sleek minimalist paneling and bricks rising up the
walls, and lighting is soft without feeling dark. Surrounded by such easy
elegance, it is hard to complain—perhaps these new harder edges just
need a little breaking in. Service, after all, retains that carefree formality
familiar from the old spot, and if a little cleaning up rubbed some of
the charm from the décor, it did the cooking, which had been a little
uneven, a favor. On the whole, the kitchen seems more accomplished
and the dishes, like the atmosphere, dressier than before. Classic
upmarket recipes like a warm spinach salad with bacon and blue
cheese are overshadowed by more elaborate concoctions sporting
strong, seasonal ingredients like pumpkin, sweet potato, and chestnuts.

But if, in the past, Starlite's strength was in its simplicity (we
remember fondly a beautifully clean white wine and pea risotto), there
is now a slight tendency to overdo it. A massive pork ribeye will defeat
even intrepid diners, while some initially lovely chestnut gnocchi
dissolve too quickly into mush. And there is often a little too much
going on in the construction of the dishes. Food rises in teetering
towers from the plates. A pungent goat-cheese tiramisu has included,
bizarrely, a stiff and unchewable baton made from what can only be
described as a strawberry fruit roll-up. Starlite may be all grown up, but
we feel someone should remind the chefs not to play with their food.
—RM

Starseeds

Dull diner food under the freeway, not the stars

food
5.2 / 10
6.7 / 10
experience

American   **$18**   *French Place*

Casual restaurant
Daily 24 hrs. *Breakfast.*
Brunch. Vegetarian-friendly.

2101 N. IH-35
Austin
(512) 478-7107

Bar Beer/wine
Credit Cards Visa, MC, AmEx
Reservations Not accepted

Well, the seedy part, at least, they have down. Starseeds inhabits an almost intentionally run-down diner tucked right under the roar of the IH-35 upper deck, on the east end of campus, like an ugly little duckling under the wing of a very noisy and aggressively protective mother. It joins Magnolia and Kerbey Lane in the ranks of 24-hour restaurants, and has that vaguely grimy feel of a place whose doors don't close long enough for someone to swab the surfaces. Still, there is some style to the place, which has a checkerboard floor, vinyl booths, a pleasantly disreputable air, and, in the wee hours, a lively and very Austin clientele of students, musicians, and bikers.

The menu is one we've all seen many times before, with the familiar brunch and lunch items augmented by Texas standards such as chicken-fried steak, migas, and tacos. All these are blandly ordinary versions of their kind, executed well within the bounds of competence. We recommend that you reject the always-weak Austin diner fusion fare (e.g. dry veggie tacos on stiff whole-wheat tortillas) in favor of more classic diner food. Pancakes are fluffy and fine, and come in comically different sizes depending on the orderer's luck; French toast is bounteous, and liberally dusted with defrosting berries. Neither does honor to its heritage. But we quite like an egg, cheese, and crispy bacon sandwich, especially when we add avocado and salt; the eggs are nicely runny.

In the end, we find that the Red River Café just a few blocks to the west is cheaper, warmer, and tastier, while for 24-hour service both Kerbey Lane on the Drag and Magnolia (farther away) are livelier. But you'll miss the all-night truck driver off the highway prying open his eyes with some coffee and a toothpick. –RM

Sticky Toffee Pudding

Little British treats elevated to the sublime

Sweets

Warehouse District

Take-out
Farmers' market only open
Sat. 9am-1pm. *Kid-friendly.*
Vegetarian-friendly.

Austin Farmers' Market,
W. 4th and Guadalupe
(512) 472-0039
www.stickytoffeepuddingcompany.com

Bar None
Credit Cards No credit cards
Reservations Not accepted

Okay, we admit it: this is not, technically, a restaurant. It is a small operation that sells superb baked goods from a stall in the Austin Farmers Market in Republic Square downtown, as well as through the higher-end grocers such as Central Market and Whole Foods. But the sweet wares sold are so irresistibly fine that we feel they deserve our attention. Baked by an imported Brit with a warm and chatty smile, these pastries have that innate goodness which graces the tables of the snuggest B&Bs in the spectacular English Lake District, from which she hails.

The company sells delicious scones and puddings, as well as some savory items such as an artful blue cheese and caramelized onion tart. Everything is made from scratch. But the true artwork, unsurprisingly, is the sticky toffee pudding itself. A fluffy, delicate deep brown, light as a sponge cake, it gains its complex flavor and sweetness from dates that have been soaked in coffee and vanilla. And, of course, it contains enough butter to fill Lake Windermere. Each pudding is baked individually in a special ramekin, and sits happily in a pool of toffee, topped by nuts, in a tidy box next to five identical mounds. The more you buy, the cheaper they are, so go on—get as many as you can. Heated, with a dollop of whipped cream, the pudding has a thick molasses sweetness from the dates, with a sugary crunch within its softness.

There are few things more difficult in the cooking world than the balancing act required in baking, and this dessert delicately pulls off the combination of rich and light that is such a delight to eat. The Sticky Toffee Pudding Company sells core-warming fare straight from the heart of the stormy, chilly highlands. –RM

Stubb's BBQ

Legendary for music and sauce, but
good for barbecue too

food

7.4 **8.8**
10   10

experience

Barbecue   **$18**   *Red River Area*

Counter service
Tues.-Sat. 11am-2am; Sun.
11am-9pm; closed Mon. Kitchen
closes Tues.-Wed. 10pm; Thurs.-
Sat. 11pm. *Brunch. Live music. Vegetarian-friendly.*

801 Red River St.
Austin
(512) 480-8341
www.stubbsaustin.com

Bar Full
Credit Cards Visa, MC, AmEx
Reservations Not accepted

Stubb's is perhaps more beloved in Austin for its live music—this is one
of the preeminent venues in the city—than for its good barbecue (and
its national barbecue sauce empire). Who *hasn't* played at Stubb's?
Willie Nelson is a regular, and the calendar is an international who's
who of rock, blues, folk, and so on. When a show is going on in the
venue below, though, it's hard to see from most tables in the
restaurant; instead, you'll dine to muffled loudspeaker sounds.

Nonetheless, the food, which is served up at the counter only, is
worthy of considerable praise. Serrano cheese spinach is sensational:
imagine the creamed spinach of your dreams, then add a judicious chile
pepper kick, and balance it with the tang of cheese. This is the best
spinach dish in Austin, but it's not even the best thing at Stubb's; that
honor goes to the world-class fried green tomatoes, which are crusted
in cornmeal and maintain a masterful, ineffable lightness even after
deep-frying. Considering these two dishes, plus the good onion rings,
cheese fries (done with jack cheese and pico de gallo), soupy black-
eyed peas, and potato salad, a vegetarian can have a great meal here.
It's hard to say that about almost any other barbecue joint in town.

There's a notable Sunday gospel brunch, which combines Southern
and barbecue dishes in a grand buffet. Competent, if not on the same
level as the starters and sides, are the barbecued meats. Fatty brisket
has a good smoke flavor, but it can come unusually, and distractingly,
spongy. Ribs are solid performers, while chopped beef has a twinkle of
brown sugar, and pulled pork is excellent, surprisingly tender and a bit
vinegary. And they may bottle the sauce and sell it all over America, but
that doesn't take away anything from the sauce's delicious power and
elegant balance; needless to say, it's best at the source. –RG

Sun Harvest

The well-appreciated underdog of
Austin's specialty grocery scene

South Lamar, North Central

Specialty grocery
Daily 8am-9pm.
Breakfast. Kid-friendly.

4006 S. Lamar Blvd.
Austin
(512) 444-3079
www.sun-harvest.com

2917 W. Anderson Ln.
78756, (512) 451-0669

Bar None
Credit Cards Visa, MC, AmEx
Reservations Not accepted

Sun Harvest is the Texas branch of the Wild Oats Markets, a nationwide chain of natural and organic-foods stores that reminds us of the midsized groceries that were so common in the '70s and early '80s before the megastore elephants began stomping them out of business. Sun Harvest has some advantages: the stores are easier to negotiate, carts are smaller, and while Sun Harvest doesn't carry as many items as some of its competitors, the natural and organic brands are well represented. Perhaps surprisingly, the bulk section, too, is well stocked, and you are likely to find what you need, assuming it isn't too obscure.

The main benefit of Sun Harvest, though—aside from supporting the little guy—is the calmness of the overall shopping experience; it's a good option when you need only a few items or are shopping on the weekend, when crowds and chaos reign at the competing giants. Eating at Sun Harvest is also relatively trouble-free, with a small selection but a lot of peace and quiet. There's a coffee and smoothie bar, and a modest seating area decorated with art for sale. Food options include pre-prepared foods wrapped and ready to go; some are made in-house and others by local producers like Out to Lunch and Kala's Cuisine, which is nice to see. A microwave is available to heat things up.

Roasted chickens are small but moist, and along with a side of potato salad, they make an easy lunch for two. Sun Harvest is a nice quiet place to sit and read while you snack, so don't forget, in the spirit of yuppie-grocery crunchiness, to buy a *Mother Jones*. –MPN

Sun Hing

A great bet for hungry students with a craving for take-out

food
6.7 **4.4**
10 10
experience

Chinese $**20**   *West Campus*

Casual restaurant   2801 Guadalupe St.   *Bar* Beer/wine
Sun.-Thurs. 11am-10pm;   Austin   *Credit Cards* Visa, MC, AmEx
Fri.-Sat. 11am-10:30pm. *Delivery.*   (512) 478-6504   *Reservations* Not accepted

Sun Hing doesn't look like much from the outside, and it doesn't look like much from the inside either. It seems a perfectly average, run-of-the-mill Chinese joint, which has the fortunate advantage of being significantly better than average. We wouldn't say more than that about Sun Hing, but no more is really needed: in its excellent location at the north end of the Drag, it is, in fact, what every true New Yorker would want—a local place from which you can order particularly good versions of the standard Chinese-American take-out dishes. Sun Hing even offers delivery within a limited area (and a wider territory, when they aren't too busy).

Thus the orange-flavored chicken here is crunchy but not overly battered and fried, with a subtle, natural citrus taste. The jalapeño chicken with black bean sauce is sharp, salty, and satisfying, and the beef with broccoli lean and tender, with crunchy vegetables and a superior brown sauce. There are weak spots on the menu—the dumpling appetizers are on the undercooked and mushy side—but on the whole this is a restaurant from which you can safely satisfy that take-out comfort food hole in your soul. Don't expect much more than brown-sauce Szechuan from the menu, though.

Eating in can be a less satisfying experience. A few Chinese charms hang somewhat randomly around the room, but aside from those it is rather drab, and service can be haphazard. The atmosphere varies between sadly quiet and annoyingly noisy, depending on whether the local frat house has decided on a night out or not. These distractions aren't enough to spoil the pleasures offered by the food, but we think take-out service is what Fortune intended for this little place. –RM

Sunflower

A surprisingly good Vietnamese joint
that even serves up fondue

food
8.5 | 5.8
10 | 10
experience

Vietnamese $22   Far North

Casual restaurant   8557 Research Blvd.   *Bar* Beer/wine
Wed.-Mon. 10am-10pm;   Austin   *Credit Cards* Visa and MC
closed Tues. *Vegetarian-friendly.*   (512) 339-7860   *Reservations* Accepted

Sunflower, an unprepossessing little Vietnamese restaurant almost
swallowed up by the strip malls just north of U.S. 183, boasts some of
the best bang for your sensory buck in Austin. And that's saying
something. One would hardly think, glancing around the blank little
room, with its cheap furnishings and tattered mirrors, that they could
get things so right. But the dishes that issue from the kitchen here are
almost uniformly first-rate, with great ingredients expertly handled. Take
a second look at those bare little tables—there are fresh-cut flowers in
the vases.

One scarcely knows where to begin with the recommendations.
Everything is good. Start with some vegetable spring rolls—of the fresh,
not fried, variety—wrapped in rice paper that's far more delicate and
alluring than usual, filled with veggies, rice noodles, soft tofu and
bright mint, and accompanied by a creamy peanut dipping sauce. Or
choose an eggy Vietnamese crêpe, with mushrooms and bean sprouts.
Cabbage-heavy salads are interesting—like Vietnamese slaw—with juicy
shrimp, fatty roast pork, and (when available) jellyfish. Lemongrass
chicken and beef have fine flavorings and the crunch of crisp green
beans. Shaken beef—cubes of grilled, marinated beef with onions,
tomatoes, and salt-and-pepper seasoning—is simple and very satisfying.
Sunflower also serves Vietnamese fondue: customers cook delicate
slices of raw beef in a bubbling, savory broth and wrap them in paper-
thin pancakes. Best of all is steamed California sea bass—a meltingly
buttery fillet covered in a soy, miso, and ginger sauce and finely
julienned scallions. It is one of the finest fish dishes in town.

Some complain of poor service, but we have never experienced it.
We find the longtime staff polite and welcoming, and the food arrives
quickly. One note to keep in mind: come early, or be prepared to miss
out on some dishes. When a small establishment serves such fresh, high
quality food, this sort of shortfall is predictable. We can only be
thankful that Sunflower's prices tally more with the atmosphere than
the cuisine. –RM

Sushi Niichi Express

A cheap, competent, and inexplicably empty Japanese lunch spot off the Drag

food
6.8 /10 4.9 /10
experience

Japanese **$17** *UT Area*

Casual restaurant
Mon.-Fri.11am-10pm;
Sat.-Sun. noon-10pm.

705 W. 24th St.
Austin
(512) 469-0499
www.sushiniichi.com

Bar Beer/wine
Credit Cards Visa, MC, AmEx
Reservations Not accepted

From the value-priced lunch meals, to the simple, stark, bright interior, to the close-to-campus location, just off the Drag, Sushi Niichi Express demonstrates, in every way, a clear sense of who its audience is: bargain-hunting UT sushi hounds.

As such, don't expect raw-fish fireworks from the sushi bar, although the value proposition is notable. Miso soup is salty and soothing. Bright red tuna and unusually soft, fresh red snapper are the most reliable of nigiri (sushi pieces) from the kitchen. Crab stick also boasts exactly the sweetness that it should. We have been less convinced by lean, slightly stringy pieces of salmon and a white tuna slab without much flavor. The California roll, which is usually pretty predictable, is surprisingly well below average here, with too much rice and an unstable structure. Amongst non-sushi options, vegetable tempura is judicious, as delightfully crispy as we've seen it; squash and eggplant pieces are also notable. Chicken katsu—a fried cutlet—is satisfying Japanese comfort food, although the tangy brown sauce often served with katsu is absent from this version.

It is a bit hard to explain the noticeable lack of customers that so often characterizes Sushi Nichii Express, especially given its bargain prices. Is the place situated just one block too far from the Drag to get the all-important foot traffic that even the most boring chain joints on Guadalupe enjoy? Are there just not enough sushi fans at the University? Or is the word just still not out? Whatever the explanation, we think this place deserves better, if only because of its bargain prices. –RG

Sushi Sake

Order wisely, and truly wonderful raw fish can be had out here

food
8.4 **6.0**
10   10
experience

Japanese $**45**   *Arboretum*

Upmarket restaurant
Mon. 11am-2pm, 5pm-10pm;
Tues.-Fri. 11:30am-10:30pm; Sat.
noon-10:30pm; Sun. noon-10pm.

9503 Research Blvd.
Austin
(512) 527-0888
www.sushisakeaustin.com

Bar Full
Credit Cards Visa, MC, AmEx
Reservations Accepted

"What's best today?"

Very few people sidle up to the sushi bar instead of the table, and even fewer start questioning the sushi chefs about what to order. The fact is, there's some good fish flopping around Austin, but get the sushi combination lunches or dinners and you can go sushi-bar-hopping to kingdom come and never see any of it. Sushi Sake is a classic example of the sort of place where curiosity is rewarded. A blackboard at the front of the restaurant, and another at the end of the sushi bar, will announce such specials as benisake (river trout) or sawala (Spanish mackerel).

Those are both great choices, when available—the latter has a milder flavor than the mackerel you're probably used to—but Sushi Sake's most impressive achievement is the uni (sea urchin); supplies are limited, but if they haven't run out when you show up, you'll be treated to a remarkably fresh, intensely flavored version of that most sublime of all orange slimes. The basics, too, are winners; yellowtail tends to be impressively fresh, with a completely submissive texture; salmon is squeaky-clean and resilient; and a fire-breathing wasabi tobiko, if you can handle it, is like freebasing wasabi.

Sushi fares better than other things on the menu; a seaweed salad, for instance, has some kick and good texture, but it's too salty. Stick to the sushi, and remember, don't fall into that bargain-combination trap. Sushi Sake is not a particularly memorable place to look at, but the environment is definitely pleasant, and as the day wears on, the vibe eases from lunch into dinner effortlessly, with lighting that's dim enough to mask your date's facial blemishes and shift focus onto the fresh fish. –RG

Suzi's China Grill

This classic Chinese-American spot gets
the Westlake treatment

food
6.9 / 10
7.4 / 10
experience

Chinese, Japanese

$**31**

Westlake, North Central

Casual restaurant
Mon.-Thurs. 11am-10pm; Fri.-Sat.
11am-11pm; Sun. 11:30am-10pm.
Vegetarian-friendly.

2745 Bee Caves Rd.
Austin
(512) 347-7077
www.suzischinagrill.com

7858 Shoal Creek Blvd.
78757, (512) 302-4600

Bar Full
Credit Cards Visa, MC, AmEx
Reservations Accepted

Suzi's China Grill is another in a rapidly expanding list of restaurants
owned and smoothly managed by Suzi Yi. Suzi seems to know what
Austin likes, and her recent ventures have revealed an attentiveness to
this city's evolving culinary interests. Despite being essentially a Chinese
restaurant, Suzi's China Grill has leaped onto the raw-fish bandwagon.
Its menu, too, is notably more ambitious than the essentially brown-
sauce Chinese served at the original China Kitchen. Crucially, there are
more non-breaded meat options, and a few dishes even show up free
of that signature sticky syrup.

The décor, like the menu, has been modernized. Clean linens and
muted colors still set the quietly genteel tone, but there is a notable
minimalist aesthetic that is mirrored on the plate, where arrangements
tend to exploit symmetry and lines.

Yes, you ask, but how does it taste? Quite good, actually. While we
are instinctively nervous about sushi at Chinese restaurants, Suzi's fish is
fresh and tender, and preparations are sound and flavorful. On the
more traditional menu, we particularly like the spicy ground chicken
and eggplant with its sweet, soft purple rounds, and the beautifully
green poached baby bok choy. And while there is nothing here that
truly surprises, even the wholly conventional kung pao chicken is solid,
with plenty of crunchy celery and a pleasant spiciness.

But what really draws in loyal customers is Suzi's trademark: the
attentive waitstaff. There is nothing flashy about the service here, but
as soon as a fallen fork rings against the floor, another is brought to
replace it. We've even been warned, on occasion, against ordering
certain subpar dishes. We deeply respect such honesty, and, as Suzi has
found, it is well rewarded. –RM

Suzi's China Kitchen

Brown-sauce Chinese with a good spit and polish

food
5.5 | **7.4**
10 | 10
experience

Chinese   **$23**   *South Lamar*

Casual restaurant
Mon.-Thurs. 11am-10pm; Fri.
11am-10:30pm; Sat. 11:30am-
10:30pm; closed Sun.

1152 S. Lamar Blvd.
Austin
(512) 441-8400
www.suzischinagrill.com

Bar Beer/wine
Credit Cards Visa, MC, AmEx
Reservations Not accepted

Suzi's China Kitchen is your average local Chinese restaurant, all cleaned up for Sunday morning. Suzi's dining room is genteel and muted. It goes for that mellow Asian thing: tinkly music, a fish tank or two, a quiet palette of beiges and whites, and large Chinese prints of landscapes with cranes and mountains. There are the vague middle-brow pretensions of a prominently displayed wine case and white linens. All of which, of course, add a buck or two to the bill.

The kitchen similarly tries to kick its otherwise run-of-the-mill preparations up a notch. Food arrives with cheesy but pretty garnishes of radishes and oranges. Colors on the plates are lively. Everything looks exceptionally clean. Behind all this is fine, but ordinary, Chinese food. Almost every dish comes doused in some version of a brown sauce. Orange-flavored chicken is in a brown sauce with orange zest; garlic beef in a brown sauce with extra garlic; red snapper in spicy sesame sauce comes doused in—you guessed it—another brown sauce with a few dried chili peppers and sesame seeds sprinkled over it. There is a remarkable sameness to almost all options.

That having been said, many brown-sauce Chinese joints are a little grubby. But at Suzi's, vegetables are crisp, meat lean and well-cooked, and nice little touches well executed (the nuts that are in various menu items have the sweet richness that comes with pre-roasting). Service, too, is polite and attentive (waiters notice, for example, if you seem to be ordering vegetarian items, and take care to warn of hidden meats; glasses are promptly refilled).

Plus, there is the pleasure of Suzi's nightly company—her queenly presence keeps many a full-grown man coming back. –RM

Swad

Bare-bones Indian without the bones—
some of the best vegetarian in town

Indian $**14**   *Far North*

Counter service   9515 N. Lamar Blvd.   ***Bar*** None
Daily 11:30am-2:30pm,   Austin   ***Credit Cards*** Visa, MC, AmEx
5pm-9:30pm. *Outdoor dining.* (512) 997-7923   ***Reservations*** Not accepted
Wireless Internet.

Sometimes a little novelty is all it takes to turn a simple meal into a great one. Swad, the extremely plain little restaurant in an Indian-dominated strip mall way north on Lamar, capitalizes on this. It serves no-frills Indian "vegifood" (the term is proudly displayed in neon on the building's exterior) that is such a fresh face in this neck of the woods that it seems almost extravagant. The secret is an authentic array of fried breads, yogurt dishes, and South Indian specialties that we have found nowhere else in town.

If the food is simple, to the uninitiated Westerner the dining experience can be distinctly high-maintenance. Counter service is preceded by a long and occasionally slow-moving queue, which is, in fact, a boon to the boggled patron staring at an indecipherable Indian menu. There are a few terse English menus floating around—make sure you grab one. Even then, there's not much help, but we encourage you to plunge right in. The vegetarian nature of the restaurant provides a kind of safety-net for the nervous orderer—don't worry, you won't end up eating any body parts you're not accustomed to. We can, however, make a few recommendations to ease you through the process.

The dahi poori—crisp pastry shells filled with chickpeas and spices and splashed with yogurt—are absolutely gorgeous. The Thali Special provides a nice sample of different specialties, including a flavorful but very thin dal; a variety of curries; some pickles and raita; chole bhatura (sweet, beautiful deep-fried bread); and kheer for dessert. Other good orders are the chickpea curry with fried bread and huge, architectural dosai—the thin pancakes typical of southern India that are extremely difficult to find in the area. And for the more terrestrially inclined, there is the masala rice—a spicy, comforting concoction.

Who knew a little drive up Lamar could take you so far? –RM

Sweetish Hill Bakery

food

7.3 | 5.1
10 | 10

experience

An upmarket bakery with excellent
sourdough and good sandwiches

Light American, Sweets $ **9**   *Clarksville*

Café
Mon.-Sat. 6am-7pm;
Sun. 6:30am-3pm.
Breakfast. Outdoor dining.

1120 W. 6th St.
Austin
(512) 472-7370
www.sweetishhill.com

Bar None
Credit Cards Visa and MC
Reservations Not accepted

Since opening in 1975, Sweetish Hill Bakery has been a favorite in East
Clarksville for pastries and lunches; these folks also make Austin's best
sourdough bread (which is no small feat, since the cultures that give
sourdough its distinctive bite prefer the cool humidity of the West
Coast to our hot, dry climate). The atmosphere is casual with lots of
outdoor seating and a few indoor tables. The décor is pretty sparse, but
there are a few fun photo portraits of people posing with their favorite
baked goods.

Sweetish Hill sells numerous pastries and breads as well as simple, à-
la-carte breakfast fare in the mornings such as scrambled eggs, mini
quiches, and bialy sandwiches. Dip into their chocolate offerings: pain
au chocolat is nicely layered and buttery without being at all oily or too
sweet, while éclairs are lovely, filled with a thick, semi-sweet chocolate
cream and topped with more meltingly good chocolate. Sweetish Hill
offers an extensive selection of sandwiches at lunchtime, as well as a
to-go case. The simply named "Hoagie" is quite large, served on chewy
ciabatta; amongst other choices, it can come neatly filled with ham,
salami, aged provolone, and veggies. Even when purchased pre-packed,
it's fresh and delicious. We find the pesto on the pasta primavera salad
a little meek (don't be so shy with the garlic!), but it is still very good.
Chicken salad with walnuts, though overpriced, has an unusual hint of
rosemary (it's not offered every day).

Sweetish Hill also sells house-made jams, sweet breads, and cakes.
Our favorite is the wonderful "Prinz Tom Torte," a chocolate cake
layered with a lightly mocha-flavored buttercream and edged with
crunchy toasted almonds. If you find yourself downtown feeling
puckish—and not too thrifty— Sweetish Hill isn't a bad choice for a
relaxing bite. –MPN

T&S Chinese Seafood

Authentic Chinese fare, dim sum, and
seafood—straight from tank to plate

food

8.7
10

7.1
10

experience

Chinese, Seafood

$**22** *Far North*

Casual restaurant
Wed.-Mon. 11am-2:30pm, 5pm-
1am; Tues. 5pm-10pm. Dim sum
Sat.-Sun. 11am-2:30pm. *Brunch.*

10014 N. Lamar Blvd.
Austin
(512) 339-8434

Bar Beer/wine
Credit Cards Visa, MC, AmEx
Reservations Accepted

At first glance, there's nothing special about T&S Chinese Seafood—it's nondescript and sparsely decorated. But it's also filled with the chest-buzzing hum of several huge fish tanks, aswim with your future dinner. It is rumored that many Austin chefs dine here on their nights off, or after their own kitchens have closed, to indulge in some of the freshest seafood in town. (T&S's own kitchen is open to a bleary-eyed 1am six nights a week.)

Despite the sleep deprivation, T&S's staff is friendly and helpful, glad to help you navigate your way through their voluminous menu, which is filled with practically any type of ocean critter you might find in a tank. Dim sum carts only roll around on weekends from 11am to 2:30pm, while not-as-much-fun à-la-carte dim sum is available on weekdays. Otherwise, T&S's menu covers the Chinese-American basics; gingery pot stickers really are delicious, but these standards are not what this place is about. Instead, you should sure to order seafood. Deep-fried shrimp toast, for instance, is hot with shrimp that's so tender you might think it's been pureed—but it hasn't. Rich and crisp, it doesn't need the accompanying sweet-and-sour sauce that's the color of FD&C Red Dye #5. Razor-thin fillets of sea bass are delicately fried and topped with tangy shredded leeks and ginger in a light soy sauce—eat quickly before they become soggy, but watch out for the occasional bone.

Don't miss the salt-and-pepper shrimp, deep fried and topped with minced garlic, with the scent of pepper slightly searing your nose upon its arrival but somehow not so strong as to harm the palate. The shrimp are crispy yet once again tender—in fact, they're some of the most delectable shrimp we've ever eaten. Nothing rubbery here, and it comes with the shells optional, for those with stronger teeth who prefer a more authentic experience (if you dare, suck the guts out of the head, where the greatest shrimpiness lurks). –MPN

MOUTH OF AUSTIN

MARK STRAMA

TEXAS STATE
REPRESENTATIVE

To Texans, "queso" is not just Spanish for cheese. In this state (and inexplicably, only in this state), queso is something close to religion.

Queso is the essential cornerstone of all Tex-Mex restaurants. For those of you visiting Austin from out of state, here's what to do: order a large queso appetizer, and use it as a dip for your chips while waiting for your meal. When your meal arrives, your server might try to clear the queso appetizer from the table. Do not allow this. You want to keep your leftover queso and pour it on your tacos, enchiladas, burritos, or whatever you are eating.

Everybody has their favorite restaurant for queso, but the truth is, all queso is good queso. So instead of getting into the "best queso in Austin" debate—typically featuring Maudie's vs. Guero's vs. Nuevo León—I want to turn you on to two places where you might not otherwise go looking for great queso.

The first is the Texicalli Grill on Oltorf. What's great about Texicalli is that they put queso on non-Mexican food—like their queso waffle fries or their fried yams. The other great place for queso is, conveniently, a drive-thru. Believe it or not, Taco Cabana's queso competes with any queso in Austin, as do their flour tortillas—and the two together are the best fast food in town. –MS

Taco Cabana

Think Taco Bell rivals this purest of fast-food chains? Get real

food
5.8 **3.0**
10   10
experience

Mexican   **$ 9**   *W. Campus, S. Lamar, Southeast*

Counter service
Daily 24 hrs. *Breakfast.*
Kid-friendly. Outdoor dining.

517 W. MLK Blvd.
Austin
(512) 478-0875
www.tacocabana.com

Bar Beer/wine
Credit Cards Visa, MC, AmEx
Reservations Not accepted

211 S. Lamar Blvd.
78704, (512) 472-8098

2507 E. Riverside Dr.
78741, (512) 462-2236

You gotta love "Taco C" (or "The 'Bana," depending on whom you ask). Founded in 1978 just down the highway in San Antone, this 24-hour fast-food Tex-Mex joint does a surprising number of things right. The ingredients are fresh and simple, the flavors spicy and limey, and there is a certain thing of beauty known as the salsa bar that seals the deal: this place kicks Taco Bell's a...ctually—let us put it this way: it takes that repugnant establishment's signature stuffed taco-gordita-fajita-crispy-chewy-cheesy-chalupa, and stuffs it up its bell.

This food is cheap, it's fast, and some of it is even good. We don't make any claims beyond that, but what more do you need? Certainly college students aren't looking for much more in the middle of the night, which is why they absolutely adore the place. Perhaps the most impressive thing about Taco Cabana is that tortillas are freshly pressed on-site at each restaurant, all day long. What's more, nothing is reconstituted or defrosted, and along with the variety of salsas (pico de gallo, mild, and en fuego), there are plenty of pickled jalapeños, fresh cilantro, and lime and lemon wedges on offer. The best order of all—especially at the 3am hour, when Taco C reigns supreme and the line winds out the door—might be queso (it's a simple, creamy, much-better-than-average version, and the *only* respectable fast-food rendition), along with a bunch of those freshly pressed tortillas.

Otherwise, we particularly like the quesadillas, in their crispy tortillas, and the chicken fajitas (beef can be tough). Burritos are the old-school kind, but avoid the fast-foody ground-beef filling; and skip the enchiladas entirely. Best of all is the roasted chicken "flameante"—it has a spicy, tangy skin and juicy, smoky meat. With charro beans and fresh tortillas, that's some tasty fast food. Taco Cabana's spaces, too, are much better than the norm, generally clean and bright, with hand-painted Mexican tiles and metal tables made out of bent beer signs add that faux-old-Mexico touch. A fast food joint that serves cold beer? Respect. –RM

Taco Shack

Good things can come in small
packages, even when they're chains

Mexican $ **5**   *Seton Medical Area, W. Campus*

Counter service   4002 N. Lamar Blvd.   *Bar* BYO
Hours vary by location. N. Lamar   Austin   *Credit Cards* Visa, MC, AmEx
branch open Mon.-Sat. 6:30am-   (512) 467-8533   *Reservations* Not accepted
9pm; closed Sun. *Breakfast.*   www.tacoshack.com
Outdoor dining. Wireless Internet.

                                 2825 Guadalupe St.   4412 Medical Pkwy.
                                 78705, (512) 320-8889   78756, (512) 300-2112

This family-run business has been keeping Austin's breakfast eaters
happy for a decade now. The tiny shacks are conveniently dotted
around town like raisins in a pudding, and people gather around them
with the same conviction that these are the good bits. Service varies
from dinky interior counters to drive-up windows (these are essentially
take-out joints), and is always approachable, whether the smile behind
the till belongs to owners Orlando and Yoli Arriage or to one of their
growing staff. There is something pleasantly ramshackle about these
spots that offers a much-needed, though brief, vacation from the heavy
concrete masses of the morning commuter's life.

Order the classic "Shack Taco," which is delectable, with buttery
scrambled eggs, spicy chorizo, potatoes that are beautifully caramelized
and sweet at the edges, plenty of cheddar cheese, and a fresh house
salsa. It might be the ideal breakfast food, and arrives in the blink of a
bleary eye. For those who like it hot, the "El Niño" has beans, chorizo,
cheese, and jalapeños, and is also exceedingly tasty.

Stick with the breakfast menu, which is dirt-cheap. There are other
options, but they lack luster (chicken tacos, for example, are tough and
dry). Plenty of places around town serve preferable lunch tacos, which
are a more ambitious art form. (Try, for example, Changos, which is just
down the road from a couple of Taco Shacks, and is immeasurably
better on this front.)

But for friendly service, cheap, satisfying breakfasts, and a truly local
approach, Big O and the gang can't be beat. The original location on
Medical Parkway right next to Riley Park, for example, has summer park
specials at allowance-friendly prices, so that that the neighborhood
kiddies can pop out of the pool and run barefoot down to the corner
for a snack. We heartily approve. –RM

Taj Palace

Some of Austin's best Indian food in an
unlikely spot

food

7.5 **7.7**
10   10

experience

Indian **$22** *North Central*

Casual restaurant
Mon.-Thurs. 11am-2pm,
5:30pm-10pm; Fri.-Sat. 11am-
2pm,5:30pm-10:30pm; Sun.
11am-2pm, 5:30pm-10pm. *Delivery. Vegetarian-friendly.*

6700 Middle Fiskville
Rd., Austin
(512) 452-9959
www.tajpalace.citysearch.com

Bar Beer/wine
Credit Cards Visa, MC, AmEx
Reservations Accepted

Despite its strip-mall location, Taj Palace is one of Austin's nicest Indian restaurants, slightly more tastefully decorated than most of its competition, decked out in navy and cream, with the expected artwork and pictorial beaded window coverings. Lighting is nicely dim and sitar music plays, but glass cases display Indian clothing and music for sale, which knocks it all down a notch. But Taj Palace quickly revives the cool factor with its window into the tandoor, allowing you to watch the chefs as they prepare food in the very hot brick oven (though we do think they could label it with something less gaudy than neon).

Taj Palace offers the requisite lunch buffet, as well as Monday and Tuesday dinner buffets that completely outclass the competition with attractive small chafing dishes and artfully displayed cold buffet tables rather than the steam tables you find everywhere else. A word of warning: be careful with your soup, as the metal bowls get really hot and you may find yourself playing the soup version of hot potato (an ill-conceived game). Samosas are lovely with a crisp crust and light filling. Don't worry about the naan; your server will bring it to the table, assuring that you get a fresh batch rather than the puffy cardboard wedges familiar from most buffets (another touch that we really appreciate here).

Lamb shish kebabs are highly spiced with a subtle gaminess, and curried meatballs in a light sauce are rich and smoky. Saag paneer is more leafy than creamy, with big pieces of paneer that have been lightly seared to a golden shade. And the huge chunks of tandoori chicken are wonderfully tender and moist. Finish up with cardamom-scented rice pudding—certainly one of the best buffet desserts we've found. –MPN

Tâm Deli and Café

Freshly made French-Vietnamese
specialties

food

7.9 **6.3**
10   10
experience

Vietnamese, Light American $**10**   *Far North*

Counter service
Wed.-Mon. 10am-8pm;
closed Tues.

8222 N. Lamar Blvd.
Austin
(512) 834-6458

Bar None
Credit Cards Visa and MC
Reservations Accepted

There isn't much to help the Tâm Deli and Café stand out in its
unassuming North Austin strip mall. The space is small and spare, done
up in a pleasant shade of green, with a few plants and Asian art
posters on the walls. The dessert case up front, though, hints of good
things to come, and service is friendly and helpful.

Tâm's menu is an interesting mix of Vietnamese basics and
Vietnamese-French fusion fare. This combination is not as surprising as
it may sound: the French colonization of Indo-China left a very deep
impression on the region's cuisine, and French influences blend into
dishes that are easily recognized by the Western palate, yet still exotic.
Tâm's selection of Vietnamese sandwiches is an excellent example of
this fusion. Beginning with baguettes spread with mayonnaise, the
sandwiches bear fillings such as curried chicken, char-grilled pork,
shrimp, and pâté, and are garnished with crisp pickled carrots,
cucumber, spicy jalapeño, and cilantro. They're a bright Asian twist on a
French lunchbox standard.

Huge crêpes that remind us of paper-thin omelettes are wrapped
around sliced pork, onions, shrimp, and lots of sprouts. Of the more
traditional dishes, we love the fluffy steamed buns filled with peppery
ground pork and hard-boiled egg, with some added zip from a dab of
chili sauce. Shrimp-and-yam cakes are fried to a good crispiness, slightly
sweet, and authentic. Tâm Deli offers several desserts, spanning both
Vietnamese and French cuisines, like sweet, sticky rice dishes that are
central to Vietnamese cooking. French cream puffs are especially good
and light, with toothsome pastry and a sweet, thick filling.

Tâm's menu is livelier and more sophisticated than Ba Le, the
Vietnamese deli up the road. It may be it a touch pricier, but it's still
cheap. And Tâm sells to-go items at less than the menu price, making it
a bargain for lunches on the run. –MPN

Taquería Arandas

Cheap, tasty, and open late—what's not to like?

food
7.0 **5.1**
10   10
experience

Mexican   **$ 8**   *St. Edward's Area, Burnet, Far N.*

Casual restaurant
Hours vary by location. S. 1st St. branch open Mon.-Fri. 7am-midnight; Sat.-Sun. 7am-1am. *Breakfast. Kid-friendly.*

2448 S. 1st St.
Austin
(512) 707-0887

Bar Beer/wine
Credit Cards Visa, MC, AmEx
Reservations Not accepted

6534 Burnet Rd.
78757, (512) 452-9886

834 E. Rundberg Ln.
78753, (512) 835-4369

If you find yourself looking for a good meal but with only a few bucks in your pocket, look no further than Taquería Arandas, and with branches scattered all over Austin, you won't have to look far. The restaurants themselves are no frills—a few pictures on the wall (such as out-of-place English pastoral scenes at the South First Street location) and basic furniture. Service is average, but with low prices, solid food, and great hours, Taquería Arandas is busy, and deservedly so.

Taquería Arandas does not serve much Tex-Mex; they make mostly Jalisco-style Mexican food, and it is the real deal. There's nothing fancy on the menu—just all-day breakfast tacos, other tacos, tortas, and assorted caldos; although Tex-Mex-ish burritos and enchilada plates do make appearances, they're not the way to go. The price is right here: nothing exceeds seven bucks (in fact, many items are well under two), portions are substantial, and the food is certainly worth the cost of admission.

Breakfast tacos come in the usual combinations with good texture all around: the eggs are well cooked, potatoes aren't mushy, and sausage has good spice. Be sure to add their thin, fresh salsa with roasted tomatoes and lots of cilantro. Barbacoa is flavorful, served with lime, onion, and cilantro to brighten up the richness, which is neither greasy nor fatty. And we love Taquería Arandas' moist tacos al pastor, with their unusual hint of clove, and a sweet, citrusy achiote flavor.

If you are in the mood for something more substantial, we highly recommend the soups—caldo de res, menudo, and pozole—which are more than enough for two and are clearly made with attention and skill. Pozole is a particular favorite, with rich stock, smoky roasted chiles, and tender mouthfuls of stewed beef, onions, and hominy given a crunch by fresh shredded cabbage and some acid from lime. Trust the mother of all Austin taquería chains to know how to make comfort food. –MPN

Taquería Las Cazuelas

A late-night pan-Mex purveyor whose
promise is lost in haphazard execution

food 2.8 /10

3.7 /10 *experience*

Mexican **$22** *East Austin*

Casual restaurant
Mon.-Thurs. 7am-midnight;
Fri.-Sun.7am-3:30am.
Breakfast. Delivery.

1701 E. Cesar Chavez St.
Austin
(512) 479-7911

Bar Full
Credit Cards No credit cards
Reservations Not accepted

Weekend food at three in the morning. That's the most redeeming
feature of this typical East Austin pan-Mexican joint, which otherwise
underperforms against the neighborhood competition. Although signs
proclaim a regional focus on San Luis Potosí, the offerings most highly
touted by the abundant writing on the walls—which seems to draw
inspiration from the discount-warehouse school of design—are solidly
Tex-Mex. Culinarily, they're also a minefield. Chiles rellenos, for
example, taste more like a three-egg omelette in barbecue sauce,
without a hint of crispiness to the tough, undercooked pepper; even
the cheese within is tasteless, and it's pretty hard to mess up melted
cheese. Rice and refried beans, too, are unusually bland.

Avoid the Tex-Mex classics and $4.95 lunch specials, and you'll do a
bit better. Search out the more obscure pockets of the menu—and the
painted walls and windows—and you'll find interior Mexican conceits
like a passable menudo, chewy patitas de puerco (pig's feet), tacos al
pastor, and hígado encebollado (liver and onions). Flour tortillas, while
not homemade, are at least sweet and satisfying. Another refreshing
touch is the healthy infusion of heat into the two excellent salsas that
start things off—one green and creamy, one red and chunky—but even
here there's a catch: the accompanying chips might as well have come
from a convenience-store bag.

The dark room is enlivened a bit by the Mexican music and the
colorful local conversation; unfortunately, aside from the obligatory
sombreros hatting random patches of wall, the dominant décor theme
is the cardboard beer ads strung across the ceiling. Service is friendly,
but not particularly engaging or helpful. Not that you'll care much in
the wee hours after a long night of drinking, which is the only time this
place should figure into your Mexican-food framework. –RG

The Tavern

Typical bar food—old-world charm costs extra

food
6.6 **8.1**
10   10
experience

American   **$26**   *House Park Area*

Pub
Mon.-Tues. 11am-2am; Wed.-
Sun. 7am-2am. Kitchen closes
Sun.-Thurs. 10pm; Fri.-Sat. 1am.
Breakfast. Outdoor dining. Wireless Internet.

922 W. 12th St.
Austin
(512) 320-8377
www.austintavern.com

Bar Full
Credit Cards Visa, MC, AmEx
Reservations Not accepted

The Tavern is a relic from another era, an old timber-framed arts-and-crafts house borrowed from rural fin-de-siècle Bavaria and plopped down at the busy intersection of 12th and Lamar, where it floats in a sea of cars and parking lots. You might half suspect the Technicolor hand of Walt Disney behind those quaint timber-crosses, until you walk in and begin to appreciate the pleasant mix of natural materials. Bricks, coppers, and woods, plenty of windows trimmed in a warm brick red, and human-scale dining spaces with cozy nooks and crannies make for a sweet little pub-restaurant. But the Tavern hasn't let tradition go to its head—service has a wry Texas humor, there are plenty of sports-event-focused TVs, and the pokey upstairs has a couple of pool tables and an appealingly used feel.

The prestige of the place does slip in a little with its prices: Most things cost a buck or two more than you would expect for what they are, and that's particularly bothersome when you're talking about a mostly congealed, nacho-cheese-from-a-metal-spout-tasting version of chile con queso—this ain't no Austin queso!—or a sweet, Tostitos-esque salsa. But burgers are charcoal-flavored and quite good, with fresh, crisp toppings, and are served on substantial kolache buns that add an agreeable sweetness. For those more vegetally inclined, there's a substantial veggie melt, though the meeker veggies are overpowered by a heaping mound of marinated mushrooms. Our favorite sandwich is the "Texas Cuban," with ham and turkey in reasonable proportions, made great by a generous helping of roasted tomatoes and onions, both nicely caramelized.

If you go light and get the peppery tortilla soup, you may have room for the luxurious bread pudding, finished with ice cream *and* whipped cream *and* chocolate sauce. Despite all that, it isn't too sweet, and the texture is the ideal combination of soft and chewy. All that's missing is a roaring fire in the hearth and snow falling on the Alps outside. –RM

Taverna

New, exciting, and sexy Italian—
"interior" Italian, if you will

food

8.8 **8.9**
10   10

experience

Italian, Pizza   **$48**   *Warehouse District*

Upmarket restaurant   258 W. 2nd St.   *Bar* Full
Mon.-Thurs. 11am-11pm; Fri.-Sat.   Austin   *Credit Cards* Visa, MC, AmEx
11am-midnight; Sun. 11am-10pm.   (512) 477-1001   *Reservations* Recommended
Brunch. Date-friendly. Outdoor dining. Vegetarian-friendly.

If "interior" has become a euphemism for "authentic" with respect to Mexican food in Austin, here's one Italian joint to which it might be equally applied. This December 2005 arrival to a hot corner of Austin's redeveloping Second Street District focuses on unusually authentic Italian preparations from Italy's northern regions, including some with which you might not be familiar. The loud bustle of the restaurant is appropriate to the district's buzz, too: the space is big and soaring, always packed yet somehow still intimate. The shaded outdoor tables are great; and the waitpeople, though hurried, are just plain sexy. Before we go any further, though, there is something we need to tell you: Taverna is (gulp) part of a Dallas-based chain. At least it's not a very big chain: this is the third branch.

Now that their skeletons are out of the closet, we can go on raving about the food, because it deserves to be raved about, beginning with the pizzas—they're done in wood-fired ovens, which makes all the difference. The basic margherita shines because of its thin, crisp crust, although we would have preferred less cheese to reduce the amount of moisture, which can interfere with that crispness.

The restaurant also dubs itself a "risotteria"—risotto specialist—and the moniker is justified by a brilliant risotto ai frutti di mare (with mixed seafood), yellow with saffron, its shrimp wet and succulent. Even more impressive is the "Lasagna Verde," which is one of the only versions of baked lasagne in Austin that includes creamy, indulgent béchamel, as the dish does in Italy. Good, too, are the other pasta dishes—we have yet to try a Taverna dish that did not impress us. Call it a pizzeria, call it a risotteria, call it an after-work drink hotspot. Call it one of Austin's best Italian restaurants. –RG

Tèo

Gelato heaven—and one more good
reason to boycott Batali the Buffoon

8.9
10
experience

Sweets

Seton Medical Area, Far North

Counter service
Mon.-Thurs. 7am-10pm; Fri.
7am-midnight; Sat. 8am-
midnight; Sun. 9am-10pm.

1206 W. 38th St.
Austin
(512) 451-9555
www.caffeteo.com

Bar None
Credit Cards Visa, MC, AmEx
Reservations Not accepted

Breakfast. Date-friendly. Kid-friendly. Outdoor dining. Vegetarian-friendly. Wireless Internet.

HEB, 500 Canyon Ridge Rd.
78753, (512) 293-4306

Tèo offers us a little sip and scoop of Italy—it's an espresso bar and
gelato shop in one that aspires to nothing more than doing these
things well. There's a new storefront in the Canyon Ridge Road HEB,
but the classic Tèo is located in the well-heeled 26 Doors shopping
center. The small storefront has just a few well-spaced tables inside,
and is simply decorated with bright polka dots, a clean line painting of
the Leaning Tower of Pisa, and an old black and white photo. Outside,
there's a partially covered porch with wrought-iron furniture and a
fireplace to counteract your brain freeze.

Tèo was once called Babbo's, but in 2004, lawyers for the obese,
megalomaniacal TV chef Mario Batali sent a cease-and-desist letter,
claiming that Batali's overrated New York restaurant, Babbo, entitled
him to nationwide ownership of the Italian word for "dad." Although
that claim would never have held up in court, the Austinites cowered
and changed their name to Tèo.

At least they stayed open. If standing before the gelato case fills you
with giddy indecision (as it does us), Tèo's friendly staff is happy to let
you sample the wares. The gelatos don't just form drippy, scooped-out
craters in their tubs; they overflow the containers in lazy waves and
swoops, vividly colored and enticing. Fruit flavors abound, like lush
strawberry, or deep, dark, red-berry-flavored "Fruits of the Forest" (a
literal translation of the Italian frutti di bosco). Lemon sorbetto is light
but very tart; a simple, creamy vanilla makes a nice foil for the lemon's
brashness. Hazelnut gelato is intensely creamy, with scattered ground
nuts. We are especially fond of the organic peanut butter and Nutella
gelato, which is slightly salty, the fresh-ground peanut flavors swirled
with loops of chocolaty Nutella. With so many tempting options, we're
delighted that Tèo will allow you to mix multiple flavors all in one
cup—otherwise, we'd do a gelato Ophelia in our desire to try it all.
–MPN

Texadelphia

Beer, not-so-great cheese steak, and a
decent chance the game is on

food

4.0 / 10

4.9 / 10

experience

American
Capitol

$**13**   *W. Campus, Congress Ave.,*

Counter service
Daily 11am-9pm. *Kid-friendly.*
Outdoor dining.
Wireless Internet.

2422 Guadalupe St.
Austin
(512) 480-0101
www.texadelphia.com

Bar Beer/wine
Credit Cards Visa, MC, AmEx
Reservations Not accepted

619 Congress Ave.
78701, (512) 236-1700

501 W. 15th St.
78703, (512) 391-9189

Texadelphia has been a part of student life since they opened their doors in 1981, serving relatively cheap sandwiches on campus to the poor and hung-over. Since then, they've spread across Austin and indeed, Texas, and are now trying to woo the almighty corporate buck with catering, delivery, and special corporate accounts. They've also set their sights on families—kids' meals and three-times-a-week kids-eat-free nights attempt to lure the fruitful multitudes. Once inside, though, it's obvious where Texadelphia's true customer base still lies. Generally dimly lit, with the comforting glow of beer signs, the restaurants around Austin are decked out with UT paraphernalia and the occasional Stevie Ray poster. All sandwiches are made to order, but service is fast, friendly, and laid back—you can bet the buck you just saved eating here that the guy behind the register is wearing flip-flops.

Texadelphia's menu is still just as basic as it was when we were in college—sandwiches, fries, salad, and brownies, of course, with all sandwiches coming with the omnipresent chips and salsa. As you may have gleaned from their name, the specialty of the house is the cheese steak. The "Founder's Special" is a souped-up Texas version with queso and a mess of jalapeños, spicy and flavorful; the queso helps to make the slivers of dried-out, griddled beef a bit more moist and a lot more palatable.

The Italian sub is served on their soft white roll, and the meats and veggies are fresh, but mustard and mayo overwhelm their flavors. We prefer the turkey on dark, sweet wheat bread; it has lots of meat, and its simplicity is quite satisfying. Overall, these are not the best sandwiches in town—you'd do better going to Delaware Sub Shop for the same amount of money—but then, Delaware Sub Shop doesn't serve beer, and they are nowhere near campus. –MPN

Texas Chili Parlor

Sticking it to The Man, and to your ribs, since 1976

food

6.8 /10

8.0 /10

experience

American

$**17**   *Capitol Area*

Casual restaurant
Daily 11am-2am. Kitchen closes
Mon.-Sat. midnight; Sun. 11pm.

1409 Lavaca St.
Austin
(512) 472-2828
www.cactushill.com/TCP

Bar Full
Credit Cards Visa, MC, AmEx
Reservations Not accepted

I wish I was in Austin
  In the Chili Parlor Bar
Drinkin' Mad Dog Margaritas
  And not caring where you are…

So begins Guy Clark's "Dublin Blues," which laments the loss of the devil-may-care, take-the-heat attitude that comes, apparently, with a move from Texas to Ireland—especially if you happen to meet a girl there (be forewarned, romantic travelers). The operative question concerning the Texas Chili Parlor, however, is whether you can take the heat. Chili ranges from "Mild (X)" to "Hot, Hot, Hot (XXX)," and we advise you to treat their rating system with respect. The habañero and pinto bean chili is not rated, so we'll go ahead and dole out a "Heck, No!" ranking. It is are-you-kidding-me spicy—the kind of hot that wipes out any memory of what flavor is. To add insult to injury, it is served, like all chili-bowls here, with some extra jalapeños on the side.

The regular spicy version, however, is terrific. It, too, should be taken seriously, but the spice is neatly moderated and slides into your stomach with a warm volcanic glow that stays with you for the rest of the evening. Thick, flavorful gravy and some incredibly tender, melting chunks of steak add authenticity and texture. On the mellower side, we like the green chili enchiladas. The restaurant also serves sandwiches and burgers, but it's not called the Texas Burger Parlor, is it? No. So stop being silly.

The restaurant seal showing a vulture bearing a banner stating "E Pluribus Chili" initially seems a little worrisome (from what ragged collection of meats are they mixing their stew?), but fears quickly subside: these folks know what they're doing. Perhaps, instead, the slogan refers to the scruffily laid-back and welcoming atmosphere of the place. It is comfortably Texan, with rusty old signs, biker-dude service, and rough-hewn charm. –RM

Texas French Bread

Texas meets France—and we like the
results

food

7.4
10

8.0
10

experience

Light American   **$ 8**   *UT Area, South Congress*

Counter service   2900 Rio Grande St.   *Bar* None
Mon.-Fri. 6:30am-6:30pm;   Austin   *Credit Cards* Visa, MC, AmEx
Sat.-Sun. 7am-5pm. *Breakfast.* (512) 499-0544   *Reservations* Not accepted
Outdoor dining. Wireless Internet. www.texasfrenchbread.com

                              3213 Red River St.   1722 S. Congress Ave.
                              78705, (512) 478-8794   78701, (512) 440-1122

Texas French Bread, while not particularly French, may well be Austin's
greatest connection to that country outside of the man in the yellow
jersey—and, happily, this relationship is less tortured than the latter.
This local favorite knows how to prepare excellent food from simple,
quality ingredients, which is, after all, the formula behind the success of
many a little Paris delicatessen. Texas French Bread, though, prefers to
concentrate on more homegrown fare—there are no Frenchy soft
cheeses here, and the croissants (a lone weakness) are heavy and
mealy—but practically all the pastries sold at the bakery are admirable.

The legendary Hyde Park Fudge Cake is a chocolate lover's dream
with gooey, bitter-sweet icing and just the right kind of crystallized
crunchy hints in the dough. The Lemon Pound Cake is an equally grand
achievement, immensely lemony with a wonderful moist texture. A
golden, cinnamon-veined sour cream coffee cake is another highlight,
as are crunchy currant scones. And be sure to try the superb ginger
cookies. Sandwiches are fresh and tasty—the ham and cheese is
particularly good, and we also like the well-executed "Tuna Niçoise,"
with a lemony vinaigrette. Chicken soup, too, is excellent. Even the
salsa accompanying the sandwiches is interesting and herby, although
we're not thrilled with the tortilla chips, especially at a bakery. A lunch
special includes soup, a sandwich, and a cookie, but it's on the pricey
side.

The small chain was threatened a few years back by over-expansion,
but they've pared down again to four convenient locations, and, as
Austin heaves a collective sigh of relief, it appears they are here to stay.
Most locations are plain and pleasant, with small wooden tables, and
the service relaxed and friendly. On one occasion, for example, we were
given a loaf of bread for free when the variety we had originally
wanted was unavailable. "You'll come back," the cheerful young fellow
behind the counter said. He was right. –RM

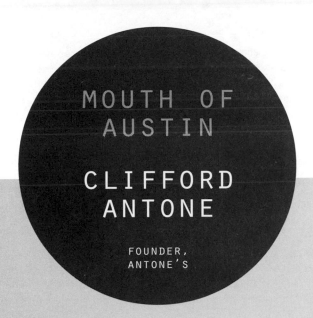

MOUTH OF
AUSTIN

CLIFFORD
ANTONE

FOUNDER,
ANTONE'S

Virginia's on South First Street was the best restaurant in the
history of Austin, by far. Anyone who's a real Austinite can tell
you that. It was just great home cooking. She did everything
herself: she bought the groceries, she was a butcher, she did all
the clean-up, she did all the serving herself. She took real good
care of you. She was the best lady I've ever seen and the
hardest worker I've ever met. She was like a mother to me.
When I got here in 1970, it was 99 cents a plate. 20 years later,
it was $2 a plate. Virginia's had the best chicken-fried steak,
bone-in, and just the best food.

Eddie Wilson got a lot of the ideas for his recipes at
Threadgill's from Virginia, and so did Danny Young for his
Texicalli Grill. When you walk in to the Texicalli, you'll see
Virginia's old sign hanging right there. Danny's another great
guy—the Mayor of South Austin. He's a scholar. Rob Lippincott,
too. Man, these people make your life better just knowing
them. It's just real Austin, this is the real scene.

There are so many, many great Austin restaurants. The Broken
Spoke, there's Texas tradition there too. Mr. James White, he
runs the oldest club in Austin, and he's serving food all the time.
I teach a class at UT and when I get students from out of town,
I take them over there. I like the barbecue. And I like the
chicken-fried, and the real french fries. But you can't eat them
every day.

And there are new places. There's Gene's on Eleventh Street.
He's a hard-working man, a hero, with a great story about how
hard work and perseverance can make it. Now he's done real,
real well, and he's got a great place. (Continued on p. 414)

And there all sorts of ladies following in Virginia's footsteps. Charlotte at Iron Works took care of so many musicians through the years it's unbelievable—she's today's Virginia, just a great lady who does everything herself. Pat at Ruby's is the same way—all these places, they cater to musicians, and when the musicians need help, they've got them covered. There's a long, wonderful relationship between music and food, musicians and restaurants in this town. Back in the day, Antone's was up there on 30th and Guadalupe, and Pat was opening up Ruby's Barbecue right next door. On the weekends, she'd stay open until 4am. I helped them get started—I'd just say "the party's at Ruby's," and we'd all head on over there after a show.

Musicians are late-night people, and we sure got a lot of late-night people here. And I guarantee you, outside of Las Vegas, of course, that Austin has the best all-night dining in the country. People say New York and LA have great food at night. They'll say, "Oh, New York's open all night," but every time I go there I never find any place open later than three or four in the morning. Aside from Vegas, you won't find a city with the kind of 24-hour menu that Austin has. Mainly I go to Katz's and Kerbey Lane and the Magnolia out there on Lake Austin. Late at night after a show at the club, I just head over to one of those places, and there's always something for me there. –CA

[ESPECIALLY

IF YOU'RE

A BLUES

LEGEND]

Texicalli Grill

Lively sandwiches, old-school Austin
charm, and a kickin' juke box

food

7.7 **9.3**
10   10

experience

American $**17**   _St. Edward's Area_

Casual restaurant
Mon.-Sat. 10am-9pm; closed
Sun. _Live music. Outdoor dining._
Wireless Internet.

534 E. Oltorf St.
Austin
(512) 442-2799
www.texicalligrille.com

Bar None
Credit Cards Visa and MC
Reservations Not accepted

Off South Congress Avenue, tucked in next to Curra's, deep in the heart of Austin, sits the Texicalli Grill—one of the most concentrated doses of this city you'll find. The tiny restaurant is plastered thick and fast with the musical, the liberal, the funny, and the flat-out wacky. Old posters from the Armadillo World Headquarters paper the walls and ceilings, aided by signed T-shirts from rock bands, an old ouija board, a pin-ball machine stuck sideways to the wall, a bumper sticker that reads "Somebody Else for President," the decapitated head of a Teenaged Mutant Ninja Turtle, and countless other odds and ends.

Long-time Austin musician and washboard player extraordinaire Danny Young (a.k.a. the Mayor of South Austin) is synonymous with the little place, and which is frequented by the many musical insiders he counts amongst his friends; on a recent visit, Clifford Antone reclined regally in a booth, discussing a local beauty pageant. Texicalli is luxuriously friendly, relaxed and odd, an unadulterated capsule of Austin. Sitting at a rickety little table here, you get the feeling that even if the rest of the city were to disintegrate into corporate yuppiedom, dissolve into suburban sprawl, one drop of Texicalli in the water would bring it wriggling right back.

The food here inevitably plays second fiddle to the rock-and-roll atmosphere, but there is a lot to like in it. The bulk of the menu is made up of a number of musically-named novelty sandwiches. These are inventive and well executed—never dry, and cushioned within sweet, soft rolls, along with plenty of spice and juice. We like the "Texicalli"—a lively cheese steak with mushrooms and jalapeños and less grease than usual—and the "Ruby Q," with onions, tomatoes, peppers and red cabbage, all grilled soft and sweet, paired with gouda and a tangy sided sauce; the sandwich just oozes juices.

The restaurant also brews its own spicy root beer. Now _that_ oughta cure what ails ya. –RM

Thai Kitchen

A campus Thai that turns up the heat,
but you may leave feeling a little dirty

Thai

$15   *UT Area, Far South, Westlake*

Casual restaurant
Daily 11am-midnight.

3009 Guadalupe St.
Austin
(512) 474-2575
www.thaikitchenaustin.com

Bar None
Credit Cards Visa, MC, AmEx
Reservations Accepted

803 E. William Cannon Dr. 3437 Bee Caves Rd.
78745, (512) 445-4844   78746, (512) 328-3538

Madam Mam's is easily the most popular Thai spot on campus, but a restaurant that closes its doors at 9:30pm cannot possibly satisfy a largely nocturnal student population. Something else must crop up to still the hungry hoots of the night owls, and that something is Thai Kitchen. This jovial, family-run establishment is open till midnight on most nights, with a laid back, if rather plain, atmosphere that is friendly to both students' personalities and their pockets.

Thai Kitchen has one of those inexcusably long menus listing a good eight pages of dishes that could easily be condensed into two. The owners also exhibit that hot naming passion that seems to lead so many area Asian menus into dirty pillow-talk, dubbing seemingly tame concoctions with monikers like "Never, never again," "Tiger Cry," "Just Say No," "Hurts so Good," and—take a deep breath—"Spontaneous Combustion." Whew.

And the dishes do seem to pick up a little of this smutty flavor. Thai Kitchen's cooking has a generally dirty, over-seasoned quality. The vegetable dumplings, for example—usually so light a dish—are odd and powerful pockets of spice. Curries tend to be hot (they'll adjust the heat to your taste), with pungent curry seasoning, and quickly separate into their oily and creamy components, the latter taking on a decidedly grainy texture. Flavors aren't exactly bad, but this is not the light, aromatic, fresh-tasting fare that we generally look forward to with Thai food. We quite like the soups here, however, which taste cleaner than other dishes, and are served traditionally in the flame-heated aluminum pots.

But if you're feeling adventurous, come in late, pick up an order of "Love Connection," and remember that for the youthful, the night is always young. –RM

Thai Noodles, Etc. House

food
6.8
10

5.5
10
experience

Campus Thai from the owners of
Satay—it's good, clean eating fun

Thai $**14**   *West Campus*

Casual restaurant   2602 Guadalupe St.   ***Bar*** Beer/wine
Daily 11am-10pm. *Outdoor*   Austin   ***Credit Cards*** Visa, MC, AmEx
dining. Vegetarian-friendly. (512) 494-1011   ***Reservations*** Not accepted

Every campus needs a noodle house. Noodles, Etc., hidden just off the north end of the Drag, behind 7-Eleven, satisfies the slurp-and-soup urge of hungry Longhorns. While it does not perfectly fit the role of college noodle stop—after all, there's no ramen, the undisputed heavyweight champion of dorm-room dinners—it easily satisfies that most basic of urges for something with creamy coconut, tangy lemongrass, a little bit of heat, and a healthy helping of starch.

Noodles, Etc. seems like the polar opposite of its main competition on campus, Thai Kitchen (Madam Mam's having run well away from the pack). While Thai Kitchen is something of a dirty pleasure—curries are greasy, grainy, spicy, and ready to absorb a considerable quantity of late-night alcohol—Noodles, Etc. instead provides, amiably, for the more sober lunchtime crowd, or for the cozy night spent at home with a book or a rented vid. Like any good mother behind a steaming pot of chicken-noodle soup, this place appeals to our healthier instincts.

All the dishes here are packed with veggies, which are a substantial strong suit. They are nearly always carefully cooked, the carrots crunchy but not raw, the green beans retaining their snap but no bitterness, the peppers tender and sweet, the eggplant soft and mellow. Even meat curries, which so often skimp on the vegetables, come piled with generous helpings of them. The only things to avoid are the tough, bland soft spring rolls and dry, sour pad Thai. We like the chicken with basil, with its anisey back-notes, and the rich red curry. Mango sticky rice is a good way to go for dessert. And all of the food is remarkably cheap, so eat up. –RM

Thai Passion

Staying open until 3am is genius, utter genius

food

6.3
10

6.8
10

experience

Thai $ **27**   *Congress Avenue Area*

Casual restaurant   620 Congress Ave.   ***Bar*** Beer/wine
Daily 11am-3am.   Austin   ***Credit Cards*** Visa, MC, AmEx
Vegetarian-friendly.   (512) 472-1244   ***Reservations*** Accepted
                             www.thaipassion.com

Thai Passion can be a little tricky to find—the entrance is just off Congress downtown at Seventh Street, and it feels a bit like you're sneaking into the back door. Once you're inside, though, that feeling dissipates—the restaurant is housed in an old limestone-brick building, and they've done a beautiful job creating décor that incorporates the building's architecture to full effect. Hardwood floors and navy accents add depth to the room, and bas-reliefs of Buddhas and dancers in limestone and red bricks blend naturally with the walls. A second dining room with high, slanted glass ceilings and tall potted trees adds that outdoor feeling. Service is Austin friendly and relatively quick, even on busy weekend nights.

The menu is shorter than most Thai menus we've encountered, but includes all of the curries, stir-fries, grilled dishes, and noodles that you'd expect. "Vegetarian Passion" rolls are bland, but filled with mushrooms and the crunch of shredded cabbage and carrots, and redeemed by a tangy sauce. Tom kha soup is thin and underwhelming. The flavors are all there—kaffir lime, galangal, chili pepper—but only in a supporting role to watery coconut milk. Rice balls are more fun, a little crunchy on the outside and chewy in the center, they're flavored with red curry and served over salad with sweet peanut dressing. Pud kee mow features wide noodles and vegetables sautéed together with tasty sugar and chili-marinated beef slices. The house curry is garee, a medium-hot yellow curry with potatoes and onions and a choice of meats or tofu. Avoid it with rubbery shrimp, and try it with chicken or beef instead.

While Thai Passion's cuisine tastes more passive than passionate, they do have one enormous plus: they are open until 3am every night. The convenient downtown location offers grateful clubgoers a viable late-night sobering-up option beyond the usual tacos and pancakes. –MPN

Thai Tara

Decent downtown Thai cuisine served
by prescient ninja waiters

food
7.6 10
7.4 10
experience

Thai $**23**   *Warehouse District*

Casual restaurant   601 W. 6th St.   *Bar* Beer/wine
Mon.-Thurs. 11am-3pm, 5pm-   Austin   *Credit Cards* Visa, MC, AmEx
10pm; Fri. 11am-3pm, 5pm-11pm; (512) 236-0856   *Reservations* Accepted
Sat. noon-11pm; Sun. noon-10pm. www.thaitara.com
Outdoor dining. Wireless Internet.

This Sixth Street eatery promises "exquisite cuisine." While we might
not quite use that adjective, it's more than adequate as a neighborhood
standby with an array of Thai standards and the occasional touch of
exoticism. The place has an easy atmosphere with subdued lighting and
lots of greenery, along with a pleasant outdoor patio that sparkles with
Christmas lights in the evening.

Thai Tara's appetizer sampler includes deep-fried cream-cheese rolls
with honey mustard sauce—hardly traditional Thai fare, but they're
strangely satisfying to some (if incongruous to others). Soft spring rolls
come with a punchy tamarind sauce that's spiked with peanuts, but the
shrimp within is barely average, with off notes. The real star of the
show is a tom ka soup so thick and full of chicken and veggies that it's
practically a stew. The base is a rich blend of coconut milk, galangal,
and kaffir lime leaves that is lush with sweet and tart complexities—
we'd even eat it for dessert. The basily po-tak fish soup, chock full of
mussels and crab, is another winner amongst starters.

Duck curry, with its roasted chile flavor and shreds of gamey meat, is
balanced by the tartness of whole cherry tomatoes and grapes as well
as chunks of pineapple. We are also fans of the larb, a Thai salad in
which the meat (here it's chicken) is minced, mixed with peanuts and
sliced red onions, and tossed with a chile-lime vinaigrette that's given
real depth by the addition of toasted rice powder; however, some bites
of chicken can be gristly. Fried fish mains are another appropriate way
to go. One disconcerting factor was the failing 54/100 score on their
October 2005 health inspection.

Thai Tara is wonderfully flexible with its menu, and nearly everything
can be made vegetarian (we recommend the pad kee mao with tofu).
Keep in mind that if you get there too late, they may not have any
desserts left. But you probably won't have room—the portions are
huge, which is just another reason why this joint seems to have such a
loyal following. –MPN/RG

34th Street Café

A hit-and-miss, upmarket café whose
minimalist aesthetic includes portions

food

7.5	**5.3**
10	10

experience

New American $**44**   *UT Area*

Upmarket restaurant   1005 W. 34th St.   *Bar* Beer/wine
Mon.-Sat. 11am-4pm,   Austin   *Credit Cards* Visa, MC, AmEx
6pm-9:30pm; closed Sun.   (512) 371-3400   *Reservations* Not accepted
Date-friendly. Delivery.   www.34thstreetcafe.com

We don't know what to make of the 34th Street Café. Captained by a
hot young chef out of the Texas Culinary Academy, it has that strange
mix of bright successes and resounding failures that perhaps comes
with youthful enthusiasm. We like experimentation, but this sort of
unreliability isn't acceptable in a restaurant that charges as much for
rather pretentious cuisine as this one.

Emblematic of the Café's weaknesses is the Chinese Hack Salad, a
big bowl of lettuce and shredded cabbage topped with grilled chicken
and drizzled with a combination of what they call "soy sesame
dressing" and "sweet chili sauce." Folks, let's be honest here—these
sauces are borrowed from the McDonald's repertoire, are they not? We
swear that sesame dressing is special sauce, and the sweet chili is
decidedly reminiscent of McNugget dip. The over-chopped vegetables
droop under all that slop. Along similar lines, the gazpacho tastes just
like V8.

These disappointments make the successes of some of the fancier
menu items quite surprising—and welcome. We very much
recommend, for example, roasted pork loin served with luscious chêvre
gnocchi and wonderful maple-sweetened kale. Salmon, in one
preparation, is beautifully cooked and simply but appealingly paired
with roasted fennel, orange couscous, and a light coconut green curry.
Unfortunately, the restaurant has the yuppie habit of serving diminutive
portions on huge white plates (you leave feeling as though you've
eaten only an appetizer), which is especially irritating at these
exaggerated prices. The room, too, suits the café moniker more than
the upmarket menu; avocado and raspberry tones prevail, along with
some pastel artwork, giving the restaurant a decidedly white-bread
atmosphere. Service is haphazard at best, and that's inexcusable in such
a situation: food takes an unconscionably long time to arrive, and the
stale dinner rolls sporadically on offer do little to tide over the famished
diner. It's not so much fun when food takes 25 minutes to arrive and
five minutes to eat. –RM

Thistle Café 360

Shiny but unexciting pan-American fare
with an unclear focus

food

5.8 | 5.8
10 | 10

experience

American   **$22**   *Westlake*

Counter service
Mon.-Sat. 11am-9pm;
Sun. 10:30am-3pm. *Brunch.*
Kid-friendly. Outdoor dining.

3801 N. Capital of Texas
Hwy., Austin
(512) 347-1000
www.thistlecafe.com

Bar Beer/wine
Credit Cards Visa, MC, AmEx
Reservations Accepted

Many casual restaurants have cropped up along Loop 360 in recent years, but we are hard pressed to explain why upscale restaurants can't seem to get a foothold here. This neighborhood is ripe for something special. Unfortunately, Thistle 360 is not it. From the spare décor and small pieces of abstract art to the window boxes that garnish the porch, Thistle Café has the sort of groomed simplicity that is Westlake to the core. The midday crowd is made up of the local work force and a large number of Westlake ladies-who-lunch, dressed in their finest casual wear without a hair out of place. Lunch service is at the counter, with food delivered to your table somewhat tardily, but dinnertime offers full table service.

Thistle Café's fare is decent, but nothing terribly special. Tortilla soup has a dark, roasted flavor with large pieces of chicken and no cheese. Pizzas are small, with a medium-thick crust and lots of fresh ingredients to choose from, but don't dilly-dally, or you may find pools of grease beginning to congeal on top. A chipotle chicken wrap is made with wheat tortillas and filled with lots of chicken, black beans, crisp veggies, and shredded cheese. It's not very spicy, served only with a mild dollop of an attempt at chipotle mayo. This hearty wrap really doesn't require a side, as big as it is, but all sandwiches come with one, so we suggest the bow-tie pasta salad with lots of basil, fresh carrots, and roasted red peppers.

One of the best things on offer is Thistle's Reuben: the rye has a great caraway taste, and melted cheese makes a nice salty combo with corned beef, served with thin, salty fries that would do any fast-food joint proud. But a fast-food joint this is not, and we are left thirsting for something more. –MPN

Thistle Café on Sixth

It's nouvelle naptime at the silent
downtown Thistle branch

food

7.1 / 10   **6.1** / 10

experience

American $**34**   *Warehouse District*

Upmarket restaurant   300 W. 6th St.   *Bar* Full
Mon. 11am-3pm; Tues.-Fri.   Austin   *Credit Cards* Visa, MC, AmEx
11am-9pm; Sat.-Sun. 5pm-9pm. (512) 275-9777   *Reservations* Accepted
Delivery. Live music. Outdoor www.thistlecafe.com
dining. Wireless Internet.

The Thistle Café is mired deep in an identity crisis. The inside is sleek
and minimalist, with such self-conscious design elements as twisting,
artfully arranged branches in the wall recesses, and light fixtures in
which myriad bulbs writhe at the ends of their wiry stalks like some
mechanical Medusa. The menu makes similar stabs at New American
minimalist chic: meats are paired with berries and wine reductions, the
local Mexican influence creeps into many dishes, and there is a
profusion of salads with blue cheeses and fruits.

But, somehow, their heart isn't in it. Despite a Sixth Street location
that has brought many such trendily clad spots into its limelight, Thistle
is a graveyard at night. On weekend evenings, the restaurant seems as
locked up as the suave office building that houses it. Its bar, which
should be its primary selling point, given the location, is hidden in the
back, beneath a few TVs.

No, deep down, we get the feeling that Thistle wants to be a
different kind of place—the kind of comfortable spot where a couple of
guys go to watch the game. Dishes that seem nouvelle in print turn out
to have a winning old-fashioned familiarity. For example, we really
enjoy the pork loin in a chipotle-berry sauce with baked beans. There's
no sign of the smoky, spicy peppers; instead, the dish is a kind of
gentleman's pork 'n' beans, with buttery mashed potatoes, a homely
apple-and-cranberry sauce, and sweet, barbecue-flavored beans. A soft,
pleasant meatloaf in a simple tomato sauce is another example of the
form. Even some dressed-up chicken-and-corn chimichangas arrive
tasting of chicken pot pie.

The kitchen's main flaw is that the saltcellar seems to have gone
missing, but every now and then (for example, in the pork loin—so
often an oversalted cut) we are reminded that quiet can also be a nice
kind of spice. –RM

Threadgill's

An Austin legend that sounds better
than it tastes

food
5.5 | **8.7**
10 | 10
experience

Southern   **$24**   *North Central, Zilker*

Casual restaurant
Mon.-Sat. 11am-10pm; Sun.
11am-9pm. *Brunch. Kid-friendly.*
Live music. Outdoor dining.

6416 N. Lamar Blvd.
Austin
(512) 451-5440
www.threadgills.com

301 W. Riverside Dr.
78708, (512) 472-9304

Bar Full
Credit Cards Visa, MC, AmEx
Reservations Accepted

Threadgill's first opened as a filling station back in 1933, but after getting hold of Travis County's first beer license, it quickly became the favorite watering hole for local musicians. Soon it became the world headquarters for a new style of music that merged Southern sounds of country, rock, and blues music. Janis Joplin jammed here in the '60s.

In 1970, inspired by the friendly, rockin' scene, Threadgill's regular Eddie Wilson opened the legendary Armadillo World Headquarters south of the river, which quickly put Austin on the music map for good. When that great eatery closed in 1980, Wilson reopened Threadgill's, which neatly took over the mantle of Austin's home for southern sounds and southern cooking. More recently, a second location has opened next door to the old Armadillo, and both spots now have regular live music.

For this splendid history, and for the thousands of posters and photos of Janis, Willie, and Jimmy Dale Gilmore, of Kinky Friedman political ads and old Armadillo flyers—and of countless more recent stars in Austin's grand musical firmament—we gotta love this place. But for the cooking, we have little affection. Texan culinary instincts in 1970 were not quite on par with the musical progress of the region, and the execution of the Southern comfort food served here is decidedly dated. Fried chicken cutlets are dry and overdone, as is a buffalo chicken sandwich, the buffalo sauce no more complex than Tabasco. Vegetable sides are bland and watery, and the mac 'n' cheese runny and under-salted. Threadgill's burgers are better, and come nicely smoky and medium-rare to order, but the buns are puny and not up to their task. Desserts, however, are generally good and not too sweet. Peach cobbler is buttery and makes the best of frozen fruit, and the buttermilk pie is a pleasure. While you eat them, you can hear the old echoes mingle with new ones. –RM

Thundercloud Subs

A run-of-the-mill sandwich shop with some old Austin charm

food
6.3 / 10 **4.7** / 10
experience

Light American $ **7** *Capitol Area, UT Area, Tarrytown*

Counter service
Hours vary by location. Many branches open Sun.-Thurs. 11am-10pm; Fri.-Sat. 11am-11pm.
Kid-friendly. Outdoor dining. Vegetarian-friendly.

1608 Lavaca St.
Austin
(512) 478-3281
www.thundercloud.com

Bar None
Credit Cards Visa, MC, AmEx
Reservations Not accepted

3200 Guadalupe St.
78705, (512) 452-5010

2308 Lake Austin Blvd.
78703, (512) 479-6504

With reluctant honesty, we must say that food-wise, Thundercloud subs are nothing to write home about. But for a certain group of Austinites—that select group that, like Thunderclouds, has been hanging around this town since the '70s—this ubiquitous sandwich chain defines home. The staff at each of the myriad locations around town is remarkably jovial, chatty and laid-back, and the sandwiches produced, while far from remarkable, are tasty, and old-Austin cheap. Listen—anywhere you can get a summer special egg salad sub for a buck and a half (the ingredients alone must cost that much!) wins, however qualified, our approval.

And, while hardly innovative, Thundercloud subs offer you plenty of reasons to grin and relax. They have the toppings you like—fresh avocados, crispy bacon, veggies that, unlike at most sandwich shops, you can believe were alive once. They have tempting pairings—the "Office Favorite" has house-made egg salad, bacon, and cheese, there is a roast beef and avocado, and an avocado turkey club. Plus, the sandwiches are free of what we like to call "the nasties"—you never regret a meal here, as everything tastes fresh and healthy. Particularly good on this front is the "Veggie Delight," which loads cream cheese (or hummus) with olives, sprouts, mushrooms, tomatoes, lettuce, onions, and, if you like, jalapeños (sounds a little crunchy but it's actually very nice).

The olives taste a bit tinned, the cheese options don't venture beyond American or Provolone, and the soups are a little bland and runny. But if you just got away with lunch for under four bucks, and had the dude behind the counter, with the long hair and smiley-face T-shirt, cheerfully tell you his life story while making your sandwich, you can come away pretty happy—and unusually fresh. –RM

Tien Hong

Dim sum on the weekends—let's make
it a Texan tradition too

food

8.0	6.8
10	10

experience

Chinese $**23**   *Burnet*

Casual restaurant   8301 Burnet Rd.   ***Bar*** Full
Daily 11am-9:45pm. Dim sum   Austin   ***Credit Cards*** Visa, MC, AmEx
Sat.-Sun. 11am-2:30pm.   (512) 458-2263   ***Reservations*** Accepted
Brunch.   www.tienhong.net

There are only a handful of restaurants in town that offer dim sum (that
festive Chinese meal made up of dozens of little dishes usually brought
around on carts), and while none of them is as good as what you'll find
in New York or San Francisco, Tien Hong does a decent job, and a
decent business, in the attempt. The space itself is pretty typical:
Chinese art, fake flowers, red lanterns, and white tablecloths, with the
addition of huge chandeliers hanging from a mirrored ceiling that
noisily reflects the din of families trying to talk over the clatter of carts
and dishes.

The dim sum carts, which operate on weekends from 11am to
2:30pm, whisk around selections from a total of about 60 different
items, ranging from basic egg rolls to the more exotic steamed beef
tripe and sautéed chicken feet. (The feet are tasty, but difficult to eat—
how does one dispose of the bones politely?) Dumplings are the stars
of the show: xiu mai, steamed pork and shrimp dumplings, have a nice
texture; pan-fried chicken dumplings have golden, seared edges and
the delicate crispness of water chestnuts; and steamed barbecued pork
buns are chewy and filled with sweet, rich cubes of pork.

Roast duck, though a bit tough, has a lovely, lush flavor. We also
enjoy the shrimp toast with mayonnaise and the rice soup, though you
may want to pass on the thousand-year egg. For dessert, we like the
toasty, nutty fried sesame seed puff, with its sticky lotus-paste filling.
Another good choice is the sweet rice coconut bun filled with ground
peanuts—it's a lively contrast in textures, but it's only offered during
dim sum on Saturday and Sunday.

Dim sum is good value at Tien Hong, especially if you go with a
group, but it is certainly not the only value. The lobster dinner is
affordable enough not to need an excuse for, and regular menu items
are good as well. –MPN

Tom's Tabooley

Cheery, relaxed, Middle Eastern fare
that has learned the Texas two-step

food

6.8 **5.2**
10   10

experience

Middle Eastern, American $ **8**   *UT Area*

Counter service
Tues.-Thurs. 7am-7pm; Fri.
7am-3pm; Sat. 11am-6pm;
closed Sun.-Mon. *Breakfast. Outdoor dining. Vegetarian-friendly. Wireless Internet.*

2928 Guadalupe St.
Austin
(512) 479-7337

Bar None
Credit Cards Visa and MC
Reservations Not accepted

Tom's Tabooley does indeed have a spirit of lighthearted tomfoolery. An astonishing variety of classic candy is on sale at the counter, chosen with a Wonka-like instinct for which sweets win: extra-sour gummy worms from Spain; crunchy nut chocolates; and those somehow irresistible fake chocolate twigs, usually found sticking out of ice cream scoops.

But the real treats here, of course, are the Middle Eastern specialties, which Tom and Brigid Abdenour have been tweaking and twanging (that is, adding Texas twang to the recipes) to near perfection since they first opened shop with a little cart on the Drag almost 30 years ago. The business has grown considerably since those days; today you'll find Tom's products not only in the Guadalupe restaurant, but also gracing the shelves of many of this city's more enterprising food purveyors.

These consist of the predictable mix of falafel, dolmas, Middle Eastern salads and dips, and sauces. There's certainly better Middle Eastern food out there, but here it's given some unexpected and delightful twists. The dolmas, for example, come not only in the traditional brown rice, lemon, and pine-nut variety (which are tender and flavorful, but a little too allspice-y for our taste), but also in rosemary, dill mint, curry, jalapeño, and habañero flavors. Hummus, too, is jazzed up, and the "Spicy Southwestern" version has become a staple in many Austin households. Then, of course, there's the "tabooley" (tabbouleh) itself, which is lovely, bright, and lemony. Sandwiches such as falafel, wrapped in Phoenicia pita, are excellent— with plenty of perky tzatziki sauce, they're juicy and full of life. You can also order all these products by the pound, making Tom's the perfect source for a large-party picnic.

As you're paying, and contemplating the periodically available Wack-o-Wax cherry-flavored vampire lips by the register, borrow a slogan from Kinky Friedman (whose "Kinky for Governor: How Hard Could it Be" T-shirts hang from the wall): why the hell not? –RM

Tony's Vineyard

Straightforward Italian-American that
doesn't quite manage romance

food
5.6 **6.3**
10   10
experience

Italian $ **37**   *West Campus*

Upmarket restaurant
Daily 11am-midnight. *Brunch.*
Live music. Outdoor dining.

2828 Rio Grande St.
Austin
(512) 476-5600
www.tonysvineyard.com

Bar Beer/wine
Credit Cards Visa, MC, AmEx
Reservations Accepted

Tony has executed a stealthy takeover of the old Piccolo, in this location that has seen the violent death of one restaurant after another. This time, though, the coup was peaceful—Tony's has the same chef, nearly the same menu, the same ambience as Piccolo, and even, for a few months, hung onto the old name, which still clings tenaciously to the restaurant's funky exterior.

This transition, however, has been the smoothest part of the enterprise. While the food isn't bad, we think the place lacks class. It is the kind of restaurant you would go to when its not quite a special occasion, but you want to perk up your evening a little—a dinner-and-a movie spot. In some ways, Tony's fits this bill, but it often messes up the details.

Tony's offers relatively tasty Italian-American food and a nice glass of wine at an affordable price—so far, so good. But when you're sipping your vino at a green plastic table on the patio next to a cherubic fountain probably purchased from the Home Depot garden department, with cheesy fake grapes dangling overhead, or in a cheapo booth inside with the predictable Sinatra on the sound-system, the romance isn't quite there.

Tony's also makes some nagging mistakes in the kitchen. A tasteless bruschetta arrives on dry flatbread, the salads are overdressed, perhaps to protect themselves from the icy temperatures of the refrigerator from which they have only just emerged. Almost everything begs for a hearty salting. The brick-oven pizzas have a pleasant, crisp crust, but their toppings lack luster (the sauce, in particular, is quite bland). We suggest you stick to the heartier Italian-American options, which are actually quite decent. Pastas involving the fennel-flavored Italian sausage are bold and satisfying, and Tony's traditional preparation of baked lasagne is excellent—firm and savory.

On the upside, the slightly cheap feel of this north-campus restaurant clears it of any snobbish pretensions, leaving it friendly both to a student's style and wallet. If you order well, Tony's is not a bad dinner spot, so long as it isn't the evening's main attraction. –RM

Top-Notch Burgers

Sometimes nostalgia goes a long way
down Burnet

food

6.0 | 6.9
10 | 10
experience

Burgers $ **8**   *Burnet*

Counter service   7525 Burnet Rd.   *Bar* None
Mon.-Sat. 11am-8pm;   Austin   *Credit Cards* No credit cards
closed Sun. *Kid-friendly.* (512) 452-2181   *Reservations* Not accepted

It would be hard to argue that Top-Notch Burgers, on Burnet Road, is one of the best places in town for a hamburger. It would be hard to argue that the service is good or that the atmosphere is nice. So why do people still love, and talk about, Top-Notch Burgers so much?

The answer is that we love the past. When Top-Notch Burgers was established in 1971, Austin was a vastly different town. Burnet Road is one of the most interesting neighborhoods in Austin in part because some of it still remains frozen in a different time in the city's history, when motor inns, simple burger joints, and downmarket steakhouses ruled the roost. Today, even amidst ugly recent constructions, nondescript office buildings, modern chains, and auto-mechanic shops, many places remain from the 1970s and earlier—vestiges of Austin's original Miracle Mile.

Even so, it can be hard to pick out the truly authentic on a strip where re-fonting has become legion. These days, some signs have even been retrofitted with nuclear-age futurist fonts—think Jetsons—whose genres anachronistically predate the very establishments that they purport to authenticize. Top-Notch Burgers, unlike retro-Burnet, has not changed with the city *at all*; perhaps that's what led Richard Linklater to use it as a *Dazed and Confused* set. The tasty burgers, grilled over charcoal to well done but not dry or rubbery, certainly haven't changed. Although the slice of American cheese is applied to cheeseburgers after they come off the grill, it still, remarkably, melts. There's a lot to skip, though, including bland, soggy fries and thick, improperly mixed vanilla milkshakes without enough vanilla.

The little room, with its cheesy 1970s paneling, doesn't seem to have changed at all either, nor has the now-kitschy, Sonic-style drive-up option. Pay a visit to Top-Notch burgers only if you're waxing nostalgic. But then, maybe most of us are. –RG

Tree House

Cheesy, contrived décor can be fun—but not so for Italian food

food
1.8 **5.3**
10   10
experience

Italian   **$36**   *St. Edward's Area*

Upmarket restaurant
Mon.-Fri. 11am-2:30pm, 5pm-
10pm; Sat. 5pm-11pm;
Sun. 5pm-10pm. *Live music.*
Outdoor dining.

2201 College Ave.
Austin
(512) 443-4200
www.treehousegrill.com

Bar Beer/wine
Credit Cards Visa, MC, AmEx
Reservations Accepted

South Austin's most ubiquitously advertised Italian-American restaurant makes a good first impression, followed quickly by a bad second one—built around lackluster service and mediocre food.

The space itself is almost magical when you first walk in, with the kind of fantasy décor that burns a lifelong impression into a child's memory. It's a miniature Venetian neighborhood, like the set of a play; the first floor is made of little shops, second-floor balconies are strewn with flowers and plants. Wall murals depict canals and arched bridges, and statues and stone facades make it all seem three-dimensional. With dim lighting, you'd almost think it was real, until the loud, cheesy Italianate music emphasizes the act, and annoyingly nonchalant service dispels the mystery. The timing is off, the staff is occasionally unfamiliar with the kitchen and menu, and none of them really seem to care.

The food at Tree House is as equally unimpressive. An antipasto plate seems pre-made, possibly at an Oscar Mayer plant—the cold cuts are of low quality, quantities are sparse, what looks like feta turns out to be a slab of something like cream cheese, and garnishes of miniature canned corn don't exactly say "class." Deep-fried calamari have often come overcooked, as though the chef went out for a smoking break while they were in the fryer. Salads are boring, and where they manage to find underripe tomatoes at the end of summer is beyond us. Pasta dishes are uniformly overcooked, though sauces are decent, but additions like prosciutto with the texture of poached rubber bands are misguided. Grilled quail on a bed of veggies looks lovely in the low light, but the birds are overdone, and even if they weren't, they would be completely overpowered by the vegetables, which turn out to be pickled. This may not be Rome, but Austinites no longer have to settle for this sorry an excuse for Italian food. –MPN

Tres Amigos

You can get Tex-Mex better and
cheaper elsewhere

food

3.7
10

5.8
10

experience

Mexican

$33

Westlake, Far South, Far NW

Casual restaurant
Mon.-Thurs. 11am-10pm; Fri.-Sat.
11am-11pm; Sun. 11am-9pm.

1801 S. Capital of Texas
Hwy., Austin
(512) 327-1776
www.tresamigos.com

Bar Full
Credit Cards Visa, MC, AmEx
Reservations Accepted

1807 Slaughter Ln.
78748, (512) 292-1001

13435 N. Hwy. 183
78750, (512) 275-0930

The Tres Amigos chain has been around Austin for well over 20 years, and it's just one more Tex-Mex venue serving the same old, same old, but for more. Their front-of-the-menu mission statement claims that they set out to serve high-quality Tex-Mex fare, and signs boast the friendliest staff in town, but Tres Amigos lives up to neither of these promises. It's apparent upon walking in that nothing particularly different or special is going on here—the restaurants' bright, generic interiors could be Tex-Mex Anywhere, as far as we're concerned.

Service is relatively fast, but not overtly friendly, which is actually hard to pull off in neighborly Austin, where Easterners frequently find us so friendly they think we must be faking it. But worst of all, the prices are shockingly high—lunch specials, for instance, run a good two to three bucks higher than at most comparable restaurants—and for no good reason.

Tres Amigos' food isn't bad—it just isn't particularly good. Tortilla soup has lots of chunky vegetables and chicken, but is desperately in need of a squeeze or more of lime. Puffy tacos appear all over the menu in various forms, but are bland, and more like a taco salad bowl, with a sprinkle of meat and a heap of shredded lettuce—they remind us of (shudder) Taco Bell on a good day. These puffy tacos are not the greasy street food we so love in San Antonio. (For some reason, the puffy taco just doesn't seem to travel well, and should remain within the confines of the Alamo City.) Beef enchiladas are heavy on the grease, and their cumin-seasoned chile gravy is too light. Tamales are meaty with good flavor, but the rice and beans tend to be overdone, and at these prices, that's simply intolerable. Seek Tex-Mex elsewhere. Adios, amigos. –MPN

Triumph Café

Well-executed Vietnamese and
American food in a coffeeshop

food

7.2 / 10
8.0 / 10
experience

Vietnamese, Light American $**11**   *Northwest Hills*

Café
Mon.-Thurs. 7am-9pm; Fri. 7am-
10pm; Sat. 8am-10pm; Sun 9am-
3pm. *Breakfast. Kid-friendly. Live
music. Outdoor dining. Wireless Internet.*

3808 Spicewood Springs
Rd., Austin
(512) 343-1875
www.triumphcafe.com

Bar Beer/wine
Credit Cards Visa, MC, AmEx
Reservations Not accepted

The Triumph Café wears many hats—it's a coffeeshop, bakery, Vietnamese restaurant, and gift shop—but it pulls it all off with panache. The space is open and light (a good place to get some work done), and there's a shaded patio out back with a small pond and cypress trees. The patio is absolutely lovely when it's not too hot. Service is friendly and welcoming, the kitchen is pretty quick, and after ordering at the counter you can browse the small gift shop, which is filled mostly with coffee-oriented items and Asian knick-knacks.

In the morning, the pastry case is filled with tempting treats both sweet and savory; bagels and breakfast tacos round out the offerings. At lunch and dinner, Vietnamese food stars here, but there are also many sandwiches to choose from including some vegetarian choices. Sandwiches are served on flat bread with fresh veggies—we like the "Triumph Special," with pastrami, ham, and salami, which is rich and tasty but not too heavy.

Don't miss Vietnamese dishes like the tender shrimp in flavorful yellow curry with lots of onions. We also like the lemongrass chicken over vermicelli, with its solid lemongrass and ginger punch. A chili pork stir-fry is attractively flecked with crimson chili flakes and has bright green beans for crunch, and while it's not so spicy as to be inedible, the dish has a subtle heat that creeps up on you over time. Those who like milder Asian flavors should try the stir-fried noodle combo, with assorted meats and fresh veggies. Soft spring rolls have a fresh texture but are filled mostly with rice noodles, though fried egg rolls are big and surprisingly full of ground meat. With such a diverse menu, this café certainly wins us over as an improved take on the everyday coffeeshop. –MPN

Trudy's

Outstanding queso and well-marketed
Mexican martinis for the college crowd

food

5.6 10 | **7.2** 10

experience

Mexican, American $ **26**   *UT Area, South Lamar, Burnet*

Casual restaurant
Mon.-Fri. 7am-2am; Sat.-Sun.
8am-2am. Kitchen closes Sun.-
Thurs. midnight, Fri.-Sat. 2am.
Breakfast. Brunch. Outdoor dining.

409 W. 30th St.
Austin
(512) 477-5720
www.trudys.com

Bar Full
Credit Cards Visa, MC, AmEx
Reservations Not accepted

141 S. Capital of TX Hwy.   8820 Burnet Rd.
78705, (512) 326-9899   78758, (512) 454-1474

Trudy's Texas Star is a truly venerable institution, famous for its longevity
and for its symbiotic relationship with the University of Texas, which has
lasted since 1977—when the original Texas Star opened right near
campus. How many UT students *haven't* spent at least a night getting
wasted on the Mexican martinis, which includes seemingly bottomless
refills from a silver shaker? The creation of artificial scarcity is a genius
way of creating demand—just ask the Franklin Mint—and Trudy's
"maximum two per customer" rule on the Mexican martinis is a ploy
worthy of a tenured social psychology professor. If we can only order
two (we think to ourselves), then these drinks must contain some DEA
Schedule 2 narcotic. They don't, of course, but they're tasty, avoiding
that dreaded margarita oversweetness.

Trudy's is now a mini-chain; the "South Star," for one, has done a
nice job of recreating the vibe, given its shopping-center location. We
still favor the original, though, which features a beautiful open-air
terrace that becomes a raging bar scene during happy hour (2pm to
6pm) and on weekends. If you're joining the UT crowd during or after a
football game, expect an hour's wait upstairs.

Aside from unusually good salsas, the fare at Trudy's is straight-ahead
Tex-Mex, beginning with a basic, irresistibly creamy chile con queso that
is one of the best-tasting in town, integrating beautifully the peppers
and onions and deftly avoiding skin formation. The "Especial" version,
which sports guacamole and pico de gallo, is another winner. But the
"Hondo Burrito," amongst other Tex-Mex platters, underwhelms. Meats
within, such as smoked chicken, often fall flat—and dry—while chunky
ranchero sauce is a failure, slipping and sliding around and coating its
rolled tortillas only with a thin sheen of juice. Better are the salsa verde
and the murderously creamy Suiza sauce, which takes sour cream and
raises it one. But stick to the queso and the Mexican martinis, and
you'll be even happier. –RG

Truluck's

Upmarket, pompous chain seafood at
unconscionable prices

Seafood, American   **$66**   *Warehouse District, Arboretum*

Upmarket restaurant   400 Colorado St.   *Bar* Full
Mon.-Thurs. 11:30am-2pm,   Austin   *Credit Cards* Visa, MC, AmEx
5:30pm-10pm; Fri. 11:30am-2pm, (512) 482-9000   *Reservations* Accepted
5:30pm-11pm; Sat. 5:30pm-11pm; www.trulucks.com
Sun. 5:30pm-10pm. No lunch at
Arboretum location.   10225 Research Blvd.
                               78759, (512) 794-8300

It would take a stroke of true luck to find anything on the menu that's
worth anywhere near what they're charging for it at this disappointing
downtown chain seafood restaurant. Even if the chain is small enough
to qualify the place for inclusion in *The Fearless Critic,* it feels about as
unique as, say, your average Marriott hotel restaurant. The highly-
touted stone crab claws—they come, we're told (over and over again),
from Truluck's own fishery in Florida—are served cold with mayonnaise.
There's some good flavor and texture there, but it's nothing memorable.
The shocking price, at last check: $27.50 for three large claws, $54.95
for six. Where are we, Monaco?

Then there's a "Seafood Cobb Salad," which comes highly
recommended by the staff. The Cobb, invented at the Brown Derby in
Hollywood, can be a delicious thing, but the ill-inspired Truluck's
variation takes away the classic blue cheese and the bacon (in one case,
at least—bacon was listed on the ingredients, but nowhere to be
found) and replaces it with boring, unseasoned, cold shrimp, small and
flavorless crawfish tails, and shredded crabmeat. Next, the kitchen fails
to chop it up, drowns it in a vinaigrette that's dominated by the
unwanted off-notes of black olives, and then charges you $19.95 for
the plate. Granted, that sum buys you an enormous portion, but that's
not an advantage in this case.

Best amongst mains is hot and crunchy trout; it's much more
palatable than the "simply grilled" pieces of fish, which come bland
and sometimes overcooked. Salmon is overwhelmed with crab, shrimp,
and overrich béarnaise. Then there's the "Florida Stone Crab Platter," a
$35.95 disaster in which the crab is paired with (believe it or not)
broccoli and mashed potatoes. Service is impeccable, but the interior is
modern, overdressed, and extremely dark, full of big booths. The
Arboretum branch is essentially similar—trying to look clubby and
exclusive, when really it's just overpriced. But we wouldn't spend our
money here if they cut all the prices in half. Enough said. –RG

Tuscany

A cafeteria-style wannabe-Italian deli-pizzeria with culinary skill plus attitude

food
7.7 **3.4**
10   10
experience

Italian, Pizza   **$17**   *Far North*

Counter service
Mon.-Thurs. 7am-9pm; Fri.
7am-10pm; Sat. 8am-10pm;
Sun. 10am-8pm. *Breakfast.*

12221 Riata Trace Pkwy.
Austin
(512) 249-1500
www.tuscanymarketandvineyard.com

Bar Beer/wine
Credit Cards Visa, MC, AmEx
Reservations Not accepted

Live music. Outdoor dining. Vegetarian-friendly. Wireless Internet.

This strip-mall Italian "café and wine bar" is one big series of incongruities: An enormous space that boasts modern design and exposed brick, yet is studded by cheap tables with a chain-deli feel. High-end pizza that can only be ordered at a long cafeteria line. An elaborate menu and extensive wine list with different "pour sizes," but a disappointing selection. Delicious pressed sandwiches served amidst confusion and chaos, without the faintest hint of a smile.

Tuscany is pretentious enough to give most items on the menu Italian names, but they're butchered so badly that they'll confuse Italian speakers even more than non-Italian-speakers. Misspelling Italian words like parmigiana, linguine, fettucine, prosciutto, focaccia, and caffè might be common, but amazingly, in addition to those, Tuscany actually manages to misspell even the Italian number one (uno).

This combination of pretentious concept and indifferent execution seems to permeate every aspect of the operation. At one visit to Tuscany, after buying self-serve coffee, we went to fill our cups, only to find all the coffee dispensers empty except hazelnut. When we asked for regular coffee, we were stiffly rebuked—Tuscany did not offer to make another pot of the normal coffee that we'd already paid for, nor did it even offer to refund our money. (Keep in mind that this is a place that calls itself a "café.")

It's frustrating, because this kitchen is actually capable of great things. A Cubano sandwich, with citrus-garlic marinated roast pork, smoked ham, aged Swiss, Dijon mustard, and dill pickles, is pressed exactly as it should be, and the flavors meld together wonderfully. Pizza, too, is excellent. A simple margherita is thin and crispy, with great tomatoes and not a hint of sogginess or over-cheesing. A pizza dubbed "amore del fungo" (love of the mushroom) has Portobello mushrooms, Pennsylvania white mushrooms, oyster mushrooms, and porcini mushrooms along with prosciutto, thyme, roasted garlic, and tomato sauce; the combination is salty and delicious. But the bad attitude and cafeteria feel of this place are such turnoffs that they seriously hinder enjoyment of the food. –RG

219 West

A fun downtown bar that riffs on your
elementary school lunch menu

food
6.9 | 7.0
10 | 10
experience

New American   **$32**   *Warehouse District*

Upmarket restaurant
Mon.-Thurs. 11:30am-2:30pm,
5pm-midnight; Fri.-Sat. 11:30am-
2:30pm, 5pm-2am; Sun. 6pm-2am.
Brunch. Live music. Outdoor dining. Wireless Internet.

219 W. 4th St.
Austin
(512) 474-2194
www.219west.com

Bar Full
Credit Cards Visa, MC, AmEx
Reservations Accepted

219 West is fun on a bun. This swank downtown bar has everything
you could want for a cheeky night out: a lively drinks menu, plenty of
appetizers, and a great sense of humor. Service is attentive and a little
sassy, and a couple of drinks in, you won't really mind the vague yuppie
sameness of the built-in waterfall and deep brown décor.

219's menu presents an appealing mix of old-school middle-American
classics, served with a wink. But the kitchen also clearly has a classier
side, and the two styles of cooking pair up surprisingly amiably. Thus
you'll find corndogs advertised next to beef carpaccio. Chicken-fried
yellowfin tuna, anyone? The dinner menu is divided into sections based
on beverage choice: there is a beer menu, a martini menu, a wine
menu, and so on. Feel free, however, to mix and match. 219's signature
appetizer is the mini-burger—a tiny patty and bun that adapts
chameleon-like to its surroundings; thus the beer menu's mini-burger
has bacon and cheese, while the wine menu's sports fresh mozzarella,
basil, and prosciutto. These are all fairly tasty bites, and definitely good
for a laugh, but our favorite is the plain mini-burger, with bright yellow
mustard and perky pickles. On Tuesdays, these are just 50 cents each,
and all appetizers are half price during happy hour.

There are some dishes to avoid: the chipotle mac and cheese is
inedible gloop, and the quesadillas are bland. But on the fancier side,
the beef carpaccio with plenty of capers is very nice, and the "chicken-
enchilada-stuffed" bell pepper, if a little bit of a mouthful, is sweet and
soft.

And don't forget the cardinal rule of a fun night out: order dessert.
The blueberry bread pudding with Chambord cream is gorgeous, and
the fried Twinkie with warm strawberry sauce a guilty and thoroughly
representative delight. –RM

Uchi

A seductive retreat that takes your
palate for a world-class Japanese joyride

food
9.7 / 10   **9.4** / 10
experience

Japanese $ **69**   *South Lamar*

Upmarket restaurant   801 S. Lamar Blvd.   *Bar* Beer/wine
Sun.-Thurs. 5:30pm-10pm; Fri.- Austin   *Credit Cards* Visa, MC, AmEx
Sat. 5:30pm-11pm.   (512) 916-4808   *Reservations* Not accepted
Date-friendly. Outdoor dining. www.uchiaustin.com

"Uchi" is the Japanese word for house, an apt name for a restaurant
that both bows to the Japanese custom of locating sushi bars in
refurbished homes and follows what is also a local tradition: avoiding
high-priced downtown real estate in favor of homelier settings on the
mixed-use edges of town. But that strategy ends at the door. Enter to
find a warmly colored cocoon that strikes the two notes, played
together, for which this restaurant stands: a cleverly suave, upscale
design and a cleverly suave, upscale Japanese and Japanese-Latin-
inspired fusion cuisine. This formula has been rewarded in spades, with
executive chef Tyson Cole being named as one of *Food & Wine*'s "Best
New Chefs in America."

Without a doubt, much of the food here deserves high praise. The
promises of fusion cuisine can be hard to realize, as the marriages of
ingredients, like marriages between people, have to blend excitement
with orderliness; richness with simplicity; and ambition with modesty.
Mr. Cole carries off this project with remarkable talent. This delicate
balance shines through the sashimi salad, the yellowtail sashimi with
diced chiles, and the sake-steamed mussels in kaffir lime-miso broth.
But Uchi regulars will point to a wide diversity of favorites—a strong
sign that Mr. Cole is on the right trail.

Just as impressive is his menu of sushi and sashimi, with much of the
fish flown in daily from Japan (if a flight is cancelled, you may not be
able to order toro on a particular evening). Full-flavored anago (sea eel),
sensuous uni (sea urchin), impossibly fresh Japanese black bass, buttery
salmon and yellowtail—there's never a weakness and rarely even a blip,
just sheer, all-consuming pleasure.

Nobody's perfect, and not everything about Uchi sings on key.
Appetizers generally outclass most of the mains; acoustic deficiencies,
which the designers haven't worked hard to mediate, inhibit
conversation; waits often exceed reasonable patience; and the prices
they're able to charge should be in a business-school case study of
restaurant success. But we think it's money well spent, and success well
deserved. –JC

Umi Sushi

So-so Japanese fare delivered with a frown

food

5.9 **3.2**
10   10

experience

Japanese $**56**   *Southeast*

Upmarket restaurant
Mon.-Thurs. 11:30am-2:30pm,
5pm-9:30pm; Fri.-Sat. 11:30am-
10:30pm; Sun. 4pm-10pm.

5510 S. IH-35
Austin
(512) 383-8681

Bar Full
Credit Cards Visa, MC, AmEx
Reservations Accepted

Umi is a pricey, modern sushi joint in shopping-center heaven, near the Stassney exit off IH-35 South. Its questionable interior is in the hip-strip (-mall) school of thought. A giant purple oval carves across the ceiling, while recessed lighting shines here and there; it's a bizarre formation that seems to have been chosen from the modern-restaurant-interior catalog by dozens of restaurants around our city. But Umi doesn't stop there. The windows have purple wavy patterns; you might wonder whether you're in American suburbia, circa 1996, or an apocalyptic Hong Kong, circa 2041, as imagined by Ridley Scott.

The mid-21st-century restaurant of our *Blade Runner* dreams, though, would be a lot more affable than this. "No split checks," shout the words thrust before you. You begin to cower. "No substitutions." Brrr. "The lunch menu ends at 2:30 sharp." Are you a wanted criminal? At one visit, after spending considerable time on the phone with Umi trying to find the place, we arrived for lunch at 2:32pm—only to meet a definitive "sorry, no more lunch menu." Did someone dare the new management of Umi to see how quickly they could alienate their once-loyal clientele and drive the business into the ground?

The menu has a fusion aspect, featuring such flights of fancy as miso black cod with carpaccio, but it meets with limited success. Sukiyaki has a sweet broth, but its giant chunks of meat are as grey and tough as dog chews. More people come for sushi, which might be preceded by a salt-happy miso soup with strangely strong-flavored seaweed. The sushi rice is correct, the spicy scallop delicious, the tuna fine, and the salmon soft without off-notes. Red snapper is decent, too, and escolar comes graced with crunchy flakes of roasted garlic. But we've also had fishy yellowtail here. Toro, meanwhile, cost $9 per piece at our last visit ($2 more than world-class Uchi charges). Throw in the bad attitude, and Umi just looks like a big, fat rip-off. –RG

Upper Crust Bakery

A coffeeshop with some of the best
cakes in the city—and sandwiches, too

food

7.1 **7.8**
10   10

experience

Light American, Sweets   **$ 6**   *Burnet*

Café
Mon.-Fri. 6:30am-6:30pm;
Sat. 7am-5pm; Sun. 7am-1pm.
*Breakfast. Kid-friendly. Outdoor
dining. Vegetarian-friendly.*

4508 Burnet Rd.
Austin
(512) 467-0102
www.theuppercrustbakery.com

Bar None
Credit Cards Visa and MC
Reservations Not accepted

The Upper Crust Bakery might just provide one version of the ideal
coffeeshop environment. With comfortable wooden chairs and tables,
lots of local art for sale, and plenty of natural light from the front
windows, the atmosphere is warm and inviting, at once spacious and
intimate.

Upper Crust's wide assortment of pastries and excellent coffees and
teas make it a great place for a mid-morning bite. A moderately priced
daily lunch special of half a sandwich, a cup of soup, and a cookie
(along with Austin's ubiquitous tortilla chips) also draws the midday
crowds. A typical lunch might pair a simple, fresh turkey sandwich on a
light wheat bread with a delicate cheese-and-veggie soup that avoids
the dreaded queso bog, and a delightfully crisp chocolate-chip-pecan
cookie with melting chocolate chips. Other options include a generous,
fluffy slice of ham and cheese quiche; for only a buck extra, you can
add a scoop of chicken salad, with grapes, celery, and pecans in a light
mayonnaise—a real bargain. The Texas croissant is a savory take on a
French staple—a buttery, layered croissant filled with both jack cheese
and pickled jalapeños. It's a little oily, but with all that butter and
cheese, that's to be expected.

Upper Crust also makes some of the best cakes in the city.
"Grandma's Chocolate Cake" is rich and fudgy. The "Gâteau Marisa" is
an elegant white cake layered with sliced strawberries and buttercream.
And the carrot cake is heavenly—the cream cheese frosting is airier
than most with just as rich a flavor, while the cake is dense and moist,
with no raisins or nuts but plenty of shredded carrots.

The counter-to-table service at the Upper Crust Bakery is
knowledgeable and relaxed. The only thing that puts us off is the paper
plates and plastic-ware, which we prefer to reserve for picnics. Such
cheap touches sort of knock the "upper" off the "crust." –MPN

Veggie Heaven

This decent campus vegetarian joint is a little less divine than its name suggests

food
6.7 **6.1**
10 | 10

experience

Light American $ **13**   *West Campus*

Casual restaurant   1914 Guadalupe St.   *Bar* BYO
Mon.-Fri. 11am-9pm;   Austin   *Credit Cards* Visa and MC
Sat.-Sun. noon-9pm.   (512) 457-1013   *Reservations* Accepted
Vegetarian-friendly.

Veggie Heaven is, in a sense, non-denominational. The versatile menu is mainly manned by hearty Chinese options, but it makes a few neighborly, if odd, gestures toward Tex-Mex. Most of the regulars are students; there are several tables for one, which are generally occupied either by laptop fiends or by the numerous members of the Lonely Hearts Club who seem to frequent the place, looking like Dungeons & Dragons might not be too far back in their murky pasts. Gossiping girls, young Chinese families, and the occasional yuppie on a lunch break fill the rest of the tables in the scrappy space.

Unfortunately, while we applaud the well-loved bubble tea and the proprietors' principle that meatless food need not succumb to the sprout and spelt doldrums, the food here does not do the Chinese culinary tradition proud. It is perhaps a bit better than your average campus take-out (we gotta hand it to bad Chinese food joints—they eschew mediocrity and aim for the very bottom), but most of the veggies served here swim in that familiar, gelatinous goo.

There are some nice flavors to be had—we like the spicy yam stir-fry, although the kitchen cheekily substitutes most of the yams with rather hard carrots. And the eggplant in a black-bean tofu dish is sweet and soft, though the black-bean sauce is gray and gloopy. There is a celery-subjugated spring-roll, a bland potato-carrot curry bun (the mutant offspring of a traditional barbecued pork bun and a samosa), and a comical array of nearly identical tofu-veggie dishes (about 40 such dishes are described with, as far as we can tell, the tofu, broccoli, carrot, cabbage, and spicy sauce simply rearranged in different orders; occasionally, they include a noodle).

Most of these are decent enough, and are delivered in a flash by the taciturn staff, but as one diner ruefully remarked, standing up: "that meal lacked meat." –RM

Ventana

The kids are in the kitchen—and they're not just fooling around

food
6.3
10

7.7
10

experience

American

$**42** *Burnet*

Upmarket restaurant
Tues.-Fri. 11am-1:30pm,
5:30pm-9pm; closed Sat.-Mon.
Brunch. Outdoor dining.

11400 Burnet Rd.
Austin
(512) 339-3850

Bar Beer/wine
Credit Cards Visa, MC, AmEx
Reservations Accepted

Ventana, the Texas Culinary Academy's student-run restaurant—where aspiring young chefs take their first tentative steps in a professional kitchen—is lucky to share space with IBM in a North Austin industrial complex, giving it a built-in lunch clientele. The Academy has done its best with the room: floor-to-ceiling windows look out on a massive parking lot, but the space is nicely lit, tables are well dressed, and bright works of art for sale enhance the walls. Puppy-dog student servers are so attentive and enthusiastic it's actually cute, though meal arrival times from the kitchen can make a lunch hour feel like an eternity.

The largely Continental menu features student-created daily specials, and the food has all the hallmarks of our own stints in culinary school: occasional heavy-handedness with seasoning, problematic execution of dishes, and overambitious flavor combinations. Salmon mousse is a French classic, but fresh dill completely overwhelms it. On the other hand, dill-and-sea-salt-topped dinner rolls are dense and chewy with a lovely texture. French onion soup is rich and tasty, but at our last visit, a crouton was added too early and came out soggy.

Amongst mains, "crispy" duck and arugula salad has arrived really cremated, but its dressing has still been light and well balanced, with roasted figs adding an elegant sweetness. A steamed mussel appetizer is served over delicious grilled sourdough, but the last time we tried it, it was Lysol-strength lemony, sprinkled with rubbery ham cubes (interestingly, we've seen virtually this same dish at Zoot). Beef tenderloin has come out unevenly cooked and napped with both a demi-glace and a compound butter, and dry pork chops are lost in a confusion of flavors: lavender butter, caramelized onions, and grilled peach. For dessert, we do recommend the pecan tart—it's nicely made, simple, and sweet. This all said, Ventana is cheap, and with a new batch of student chefs every few weeks, who knows what you'll end up with? –MPN

Veranda

A nice place for a drink, but eat
dinner—or any meal—elsewhere

food

3.0 / 10 **6.2** / 10

experience

American **$31** *North Central*

Casual restaurant
Mon.-Sat. 11am-2am;
Sun. 10am-2am.

2525 W. Anderson Ln.
Austin
(512) 300-2660

Bar Full
Credit Cards Visa, MC, AmEx
Reservations Accepted

The brand-spanking-new Veranda bar and grill in Northcross Mall is trying to fill a niche in its neighborhood by offering late hours, a classy atmosphere, and an array of cuisines in an area that is thick with ethnic restaurants, but boasts few bars. The space is comprised of several small rooms painted in subdued colors and hung with attractive floral paintings, a well-kept outdoor area (which unfortunately overlooks the mall parking lot), and a bar walled in with vermillion and canary-colored glass panes. Service is friendly and helpful, but lacks polish.

Where Veranda falls short is the food, and their encyclopedic menu is the first tip-off. They are just trying to do way too much, which generally means that the entire menu will suffer. And this includes spelling—one of our basic rules is that if you can't even come close to spelling it, you probably shouldn't be making it. Exhibit A: Veranda's baba ganoush—spelled "baba ganuge" on their menu—is the worst we've ever had. It's tinny but otherwise tasteless, and it's disconcertingly lumpy. Another problem child is their burger: the meat has a strange texture, the burger is malformed and too thin to be cooked to temperature, and when topped with congealed shredded cheese, the whole thing takes on the unappealing appearance of a doggy chew toy.

A slightly better bet on this menu is the grilled Hawaiian salad, an overly sweet concoction of grilled chicken, pineapple, pears, and orange over fresh lettuce. It's a bit cloying, but at least everything in it is identifiable. We do enjoy Veranda's spinach queso; lighter in color and texture than its many Velveeta cousins around town, it's blended with spinach leaves and is quite tasty. For dessert, try the key lime pie. Yes, it has the ghostly appearance of paste, but the flavor is bright and tangy. But in this great food town, you have little excuse for ending up here for a meal. –MPN

Vespaio

The best, hippest Italian table in town—
with crowds and noise to prove it

food

9.3 **8.6**
10 10
experience

Italian, Pizza **$62** *South Congress*

Upmarket restaurant
Tues.-Sat. 5:30pm-10:30pm;
Sun. 5:30pm-10pm; closed Mon.
Date-friendly. Vegetarian-friendly.

1610 S. Congress Ave.
Austin
(512) 441-6100

Bar Full
Credit Cards Visa, MC, AmEx
Reservations Not accepted

Vespaio occupies one of the most recognizable spaces on the ever-burgeoning, funky-to-proto-chic South Congress strip. It's been a highly popular addition to the Austin scene since just about the day it opened. And deservedly so. Vespaio's owner, Alan Lazarus, has worked hard for his achievement—a place that serves serious, tasty Italian and Italian-inspired food in a friendly and professional way.

This restaurant, open for dinner only, provides hearty portions of well-made food. The kitchen takes pains over its presentations, which are sometimes so admirable that one draws back to enjoy the sight before tucking in. Reasonable requests as to preparation are carefully honored: tuna asked for almost raw arrives just that way; "al dente" specifications for pasta—difficult to achieve under American working conditions—get fulfilled.

Menu items worth trying include fried calamari—arguably the best in the city—and, when featured, the brilliant crespelle of slow-roasted beef. Seafood cioppino, a dish that is extremely hard to distinguish from the rest, has a marvelously well developed flavor, with long, buttery toasts ideal for sopping. On recent visits, we have been delighted with a special of delicately grilled sardines, something vanishingly rare in Texas. Ravioli have also continued to be uniformly excellent, sometimes integrating unexpected sweetness. The wine list, meanwhile, includes lots of interesting Italian reds, and Vespaio's steward gives valuable advice across the list as a whole.

We must add that Vespaio's reservation policy—as in, mostly forget it—makes time at the long, attractive bar a standard feature of the experience, unless you prefer to linger outdoors or have seen to it to rent the new private room. And the noise level, unless you are willing to eat when the doors first open or are clever enough to request seating in the wine room, is dauntingly high. Try to remain undaunted, as the hordes of this restaurant's fans seem to do. This will go easier if you don't attempt to close a deal or propose marriage here. –JC

Vespaio Enoteca

Vespaio's casual deli offshoot with delicious, humble bowls of pasta

food

9.2 / 10

8.5 / 10

experience

Italian, Pizza

$**32**

South Congress

Casual restaurant
Mon.-Sat. 8am-10pm;
Sun. 10am-3pm. *Date-friendly.*
Outdoor dining. Vegetarian-friendly.

1610 S. Congress Ave.
Austin
(512) 441-6100

Bar Full
Credit Cards Visa, MC, AmEx
Reservations Not accepted

Vespaio Enoteca is an action-packed little place. It has eating areas both outside and in, and a brighter, less stylish ambiance than its revered Italian older sister next door. What the two venues have in common is that neither is much of a place to attempt an intimate conversation, especially indoors, and that at the Enoteca, just as at Vespaio, you can treat reservations as a habit from the past.

While you wait, you can enjoy your time at Vespaio's bar next door, in the company of a wine list as shrewd as it is long; or you can stay in the Enoteca and browse through the delicacies on offer at the deli counter that greets you at the door. Many of the salumi (cured meats), pâtés, and marinated salads on the extensive appetizer menu are available to take out. A remarkable number are made on site and, virtually without exception, these are worth a try. Try, also, the exceptional cabbage, fennel, and sweet pepper slaw—a modest dish that demonstrates the freshness of the restaurant's ingredients. Take note, too, of the fact that the justly-acclaimed Niman Ranch is the source of the Enoteca's hams and some of its other meats. There are also comestibles to purchase that one might well encounter on the shelves of a carriage trade grocer in Florence, including some dried pastas that aren't to be found elsewhere in town. And rest assured that the pastries are well above the Austin average.

We deeply lament the disappearance of our favorite appetizer on the Enoteca's menu, a cone full of delicately deep-fried vegetables such as rapini. But the delightful, minimalist pizzas remain, as do the excellent pasta dishes—some of the most authentic in the city. These include a well-executed Bolognese and a brilliant version of spaghetti carbonara, an Italian staple made from pancetta, eggs, and pasta mixed into a creamy, childishly satisfying concoction. American restaurants are wont to do absurd things to complicate this dish. This cheerful trattoria does not. –JC

Vin Bistro

A charming patio, a competent kitchen, and endless wine ambition

food	
8.3	**8.7**
10	10
	experience

New American $**64**   *Seton Medical Area*

Upmarket restaurant
Mon.-Thurs. 11am-2:30pm, 5pm-10pm; Fri.-Sat. 5pm-11pm; closed Sun. *Date-friendly. Live music. Outdoor dining. Wireless Internet.*

1601 W. 38th St.
Austin
(512) 377-5252
www.vinbistro.com

Bar Full
Credit Cards Visa, MC, AmEx
Reservations Recommended

Alexandre Dumas called wine "the intellectual part of the meal," and it's hard not to be impressed with Vin Bistro's intellectual curiosity. A suggested wine by the glass appears on the menu *above* each dish, not below it, a symbolic gesture that underscores this restaurant's relentless devotion to wine pairings above all else. Some of those wine pairings are truly inspired (for instance, Prosecco, the Italian sparkling aperitif, is paired with fried brie with raspberry coulis). The only two flaws of the ample wine list are an overemphasis on California and the tendency to get carried away with sensory descriptions so esoteric that they are rendered useless (e.g. "elder flower and iris"), but who's to argue with passion?

The place used to be called Zin Bistro (in honor of Zinfandel), but, according to the web site, changed its name to Vin Bistro in order to avoid confusion with Austin's Zen Japanese fast-food chain (never underestimate the power of the Texas accent). The food is ambitious, although we are left with the sense that it could be more than it is. A wild mushroom risotto with black truffle butter and Parmigiano-Reggiano is simple and well executed. Less impressive is grilled salmon with chipotle butter and fire-roasted tomato coulis, an overcooked piece of fish with little evidence of the chipotle. At one visit, a duck breast ordered rare came practically raw and tough to the point of inedibility.

Outdoor seating on the front lawn is a real treat—it feels like you're part of a genteel summer party, and it's in a pleasant neighborhood not overrun with vehicle noise. The indoor room, though, with its prominent television, is considerably less charming and has a certain modern-sports-bar feel. –RG

Vinny's Italian Café

What this Italian-American joint lacks in
quality, it makes up for in quantity

food

3.5 / 10   4.6 / 10
experience

Italian   **$29** *Zilker*

Casual restaurant   1003 Barton Springs Rd.   *Bar* Full
Sun.-Thurs. 11am-10pm; Fri.-Sat.   Austin   *Credit Cards* Visa, MC, AmEx
11am-11pm. *Brunch. Kid-friendly.*   (512) 482-8484   *Reservations* Accepted

Vinny's is a restaurant that seems slightly out of place. An Italian-
American family-dining establishment, it belongs to a genre perhaps
more at home in the vast suburbs of New York City than here in Austin,
where Tex-Mex comfortably fills that role. Vinny's does, in fact, come
from the same folks who brought us the more naturally adapted El
Mercado, but Vinny's does its very best to fit the starch-and-tomato bill.

The result, unfortunately, is something that comes dangerously close
to a parody of an Italian-American family restaurant chain. The inside of
the building—an endless array of tables and booths—looks like a
Friday's or Chili's or the like, with the themes of Italy superimposed
upon it. Plastic vines dangle from every beam; kitschy, modest busts of
Mediterranean women grace the surfaces; gilt cupids flutter over
murals of Roman temples. The color scheme is dutifully red, green, and
white.

Food, too, is true to form. Appetizers are bounteous, deep fried, and
drenched in marinara (like tomato paste) and mozzarella (like glue).
Portions are massive. A smoked chicken lasagne dish arrives with a neat
but indecipherable mush of not-so-fresh spinach, dry meat, tomato,
and cheese. Ravioli remind us of Chef Boyardee; a roasted pepper sauce
has decent flavor, but is floury. One can hardly eat half of a serving.
Puffy, empty white bread accompanies the lot.

Yet everyone means tremendously well. Vinny's is the kind of place
one could happily imagine taking a Little League team for a celebratory
meal. Service is outstandingly friendly, and the waiters bear their heavy
burdens to the tables quickly and with unflinching good cheer. We even
heard one suggest, to some overstuffed patrons, that they order some
dessert to take home for later. Run while you still can. –RM

Vivo Cocina Texicana

Tropical Tex-Mex paradise—if you stick to the basics

food

6.8
10

9.5
10

experience

Mexican   **$28**   *French Place*

Casual restaurant   2015 Manor Rd.   *Bar* Full
Tues.-Thurs. 11am-10pm; Fri.-Sat.   Austin   *Credit Cards* Visa, MC, AmEx
11am-11:30pm; closed Sun.-Mon.   (512) 482-0300   *Reservations* Essential
Date-friendly. Live music. Outdoor   www.vivo-austin.com
dining. Vegetarian-friendly. Wireless Internet.

You hear a lot of chatter about puffy tacos, alfalfa sprouts on the veggie chalupas, brown rice with the enchiladas. You hear a lot about a lot of things coming from Vivo, one of the stars of East Austin's endlessly up-and-coming Manor Road neighborhood. But what's hard to fully comprehend, before you've actually set foot here, is what a beautiful space it is. So surreal is this series of terraced gardens—a waterfall here, birds chirping there, low-hanging trees, speckled shade, and cool mist everywhere—that even on an off-hour on an off-day, you might well have to queue up for a while before staking your claim to one of these tables. And once you do, you won't want to give it up. These are some of the most relaxing seats in Austin.

By that point, you should already have a margarita in your hand. Stick with the large house version, which is a much better deal than the puny top-shelf 'ritas whose in-your-face acidity hides the differences between tequilas anyway. Homemade salsa is a spicy, smoky mix redolent of serrano chiles; a dab of it also peps up the chile con queso, which is a good if slightly unusual version, thicker, saltier, and nacho-cheesier than many. The queso's thickness makes it adhere better to the chip than is the norm, minimizing spillage while maximizing the protein-to-carb ratio per bite.

Less impressive are the puffy tacos, touted though they may be all the way from here to San Antonio. Their tortilla shells are something like the casing that you often see for a taco salad, with a pleasantly crunchy texture; a chicken filling, however, is dry and underseasoned, and the vegetables are poorly integrated. Better is the chile enchilada, which focuses on the more elemental Tex-Mex goodness of melted cheese and onion, with a well-conceived, homemade brown enchilada sauce—a comfortable dish for an even more comfortable place. –RG

The Walburg Mercantile

food 4.9/10 **8.0**/10 *experience*

A German buffet in an 1882 building, with yodeling in the biergarten

German $29   *Walburg*

Casual restaurant
Wed.-Thurs. noon-9pm; Fri.-Sun.
noon-midnight; closed Mon.-Tues.
Kitchen closes Fri.-Sun. 10pm.
Live music. Outdoor dining.

FM 972 and FM 1105
Walburg
(512) 863-8440
www.walburgrestaurant.com

Bar Beer/wine
Credit Cards Visa, MC, AmEx
Reservations Accepted

The history of Williamson County is a history deeply connected with German immigration. In 1882, a man named Hy Doering, of Walburg, Germany, built a mercantile to supply groceries, dry goods, and hardware to the German farmers in Walburg, Texas—a town 33 miles northeast of Austin that, of course, Hy named after his beloved hometown. A century and a quarter later, the building is alive and well, having been taken over by a different set of Germans and turned into a restaurant and dance venue.

It is, perhaps, most successful as a biergarten, with outdoor drinkin', dancin', and partyin' in spring, summer, and fall. Although the outdoor selections are sometimes more limited than those inside the giant space (which still feels like a warehouse), the German draft beer selection is excellent. On tap, at last check, were three versions of Paulaner, two Spatens, and a Warsteiner. For us, it is the Warsteiner that best explains Bavarian beers' assertions of supremacy: clean, balanced, golden, eminently drinkable. Accompany this with ardent two-stepping, yodeling, or accordion music, perhaps courtesy of owner Ron Tippelt's Walburg Boys, and you've got quite a recipe for country entertainment.

A better recipe, perhaps, than the ones used to prepare the food in the hit-or-miss, all-you-can-eat buffet, which most diners choose over à-la-carte menu items. Wiener schnitzel (a fried, breaded veal cutlet) is properly pounded and successful, as are bright kraut and good sausages (how could the sausages not be good in these parts?), but there also are a lot of disappointments mixed into the spread: bland potato salads, mediocre vegetables, tough jaeger schnitzel, leathery roast pork loin, and so on. But guzzle the crisp German beers and two-step the night away, and the side dishes will recede from your memory as quickly as your sorrows into the blazing Texas sunset. –RG

Wanfu

At a certain hour, certain people will
eat anything—and we're amongst them

food **2.3** /10 **1.8** /10 experience

Chinese, Pan-Asian

$21 *Southeast*

Casual restaurant
Sun.-Thurs. 11am-4am,
Fri.-Sat. noon-4am.

2400 E. Oltorf St.
Austin
(512) 462-3535
www.wanfuaustin.com

Bar Beer/wine
Credit Cards Visa, MC, AmEx
Reservations Not accepted

Let's say it's 3am, and you're in South Austin. Maybe you've just
finished a night of dancing at the Broken Spoke, or of having your sorry
butt kicked by old Happy at the shuffleboard table of the legendary
Horseshoe Lounge. Maybe you've been thrown out of Trudy's South for
trying to order a third Mexican martini, or maybe you just got sick of
(or at) that house party in one of those East Oltorf student apartment
complexes. And you're hungry.

That's where Wanfu (not to be confused with Wanfu Too on Barton
Springs) comes into the equation. And that's the *only* time that Wanfu
should come into the equation. This place, with the office-building
ceilings, ratty wall-to-wall carpeting, and cheap recessed lighting, has
all the charm of a run-down Queens diner. (Okay, at least Wanfu's
lighting is dimmer than the diner's would be, better concealing the dirty
rug.) You stumble in, and if it's before 4am, you're seated—maybe not
with a smile, but who's complaining? If you wanted to eat anywhere
else in the neighborhood, you'd have to break in, raid the kitchen, and
risk spending the night in jail.

At Wanfu, the only way you will run into trouble is if you actually try
to make it through the menu. You page through, your eyes blearily
glossing over endless permutations of chicken, shrimp, beef, and brown
sauce. Then, weird things start happening: Vietnamese and Korean
soups make appearances…clay-pot dishes…did you really see Thai
coconut-milk curries, or did you imagine them?

The truth is, it hardly matters what you order. None of it is very good.
The meal might begin with greasy egg rolls or an extraordinarily gummy
hot-and-sour soup with zero depth of flavor. You could do worse than
duck with ginger sauce, which actually brandishes some smokiness—
but be careful to avoid the fatty strips of sinew that work their way into
the mix. Ask for hot sauce, which has more oil than heat but still
improves almost any dish. And as for the after-effects, hey, you
probably weren't going to feel great the next day anyway. –RG

Wanfu Too

All-American Chinese food, with all the
hopes and horrors that entails

food
2.6 **7.9**
10 10
experience

Chinese, Pan-Asian $**21**   *Zilker*

Casual restaurant   1806 Barton Springs Rd.   *Bar* Beer/wine
Daily 10am-2am.   Austin   *Credit Cards* Visa, MC, AmEx
Delivery.   (512) 478-3535   *Reservations* Accepted
                             www.wanfuaustin.com

Wanfu Too would, like its predecessor, have little to recommend it,
were it not for a location on one of the hottest strips in town,
Restaurant Row on Barton Springs Road, in what might be the hottest
restaurant building in town—an absolutely fabulous old diner, with
funky curves and lots of glass bricks. Chinese food in a diner, you ask?
Well, precisely.

A meal at Wanfu Too, in that all-American setting, reminds us of
what is, overall, a quite pleasing fact about Chinese food in this
country: it is, along with McDonald's, perhaps our most democratic—
indeed, American—cuisine. In America almost everyone eats at Mickey
D's: poor, rich, white, black, Yankee and cowboy—a fact that speaks
rather in the super-chain's favor. Chinese food has the same open-
armed appeal. It cuts across class and race, and is enjoyed by the urban
rich and urban poor alike. In a town that tends too much still toward
segregated amusements, Wanfu is a pleasing melting pot, ably serviced
by a diverse staff.

But the cynics who say that democracy breeds mediocrity may be
right when it comes to food. Wanfu's cooking is about as Chinese as its
setting. A short menu boasts all the most familiar options. Soups are
typically gloopy, spring rolls defrosted, dumplings unseasoned. The
orange chicken is stringy and tough, the sauce a heavy syrup. Meat in
the cashew beef is hard to identify, but it is also blissfully hard to find,
hidden in a massive pile of not-so-fresh veggies abundantly led by that
old, indefatigable water chestnut. What is a water chestnut, anyway?
Dare one roast it over an open flame? We suspect that, like the baby
corn—that other take-out standby—it is one of those ingredients that
couldn't possibly exist in nature. Could it? –RM

Waterloo Ice House

An Austin original, with good burgers
and lots of beer but a kid-friendly feel

food

6.0
10
7.8
10
experience

American

$22   *Clarksville, Seton, Westlake*

Pub
Daily 7am-10pm. *Breakfast.*
Brunch. Kid-friendly. Live music.
Outdoor dining. Wireless Internet.

600 N. Lamar Blvd.
Austin
(512) 472-5200
www.waterlooicehouse.com

Bar Full
Credit Cards Visa, MC, AmEx
Reservations Not accepted

1106 W. 38th St.
78705, (512) 451-5245

6203 N. Capital of Texas Hwy.
78731, (512) 418-9700

Since first opening in 1976, Waterloo Ice House has been an Austin
fixture for live music, beer, and down-home Texas cooking. There are
now five Waterloos around town, and they are popular spots for casual
meals and happy hours. If you are dining with the kids, the 2222 and
360 location is for you. Lunchtime is busy, but you'll still be seated fairly
quickly—order your food and head outside to the enclosed playscape,
or if the weather is cool enough, sit outside at the picnic tables under
the oaks. These are the best seats in the house.

The classic cheeseburger is cooked to order and served with all the
fixin's. Opt for crispy, nicely battered onion rings rather than the
scorched fries. The pulled pork sandwich is substantial and pretty with
pickled purple cabbage, but the pork itself is dry and the barbecue
sauce tastes bottled. We prefer the chicken ranch soft tacos, which
sport flavorful grilled chicken, bacon slices, shredded lettuce, diced
tomatoes, and spicy Tabasco ranch dressing. There are several kids'
meals to choose from, but price-wise they are a bit steep.

What really sets Waterloo apart is the service. Servers come outside
to let you know that your food is ready. The manager frequently stops
by tables to make sure guests are happy and to talk to children. A
three-year-old dumps a glass of water all over himself, begins to
scream, and starts stripping right there at the table—and the manager
simply brings out some nice, distracting Blue Bell with the check. There
are certainly places in town with better food and lower prices, but if
you are trying to dine with mercurial children, Waterloo is one of the
best bets in Austin. –MPN

Wheatsville Co-Op Deli

Hippie central, where the hemp meets
the hot sauce

UT Area

Specialty grocery
Daily 9am-9pm. *Breakfast.*
Live music. Outdoor dining.
Vegetarian-friendly.

3101 Guadalupe St.
Austin
(512) 478-1164
www.wheatsville.coop

Bar None
Credit Cards Visa and MC
Reservations Not accepted

Austinites love Wheatsville. The neighborhood grocery sells high-quality
produce and bulk goods at very reasonable prices, and while it
crunches with the best of them, all breeds are welcomed here with the
same glowing, tie-dye-patterned, dreadlocked good cheer, be they
hippie or yuppie, student or slacker. To the Austinite abroad, the sight
of a Corona-inspired "Wheatsville: la cooperativa más fina" T-shirt just
brings you home.

In addition to a well-stocked grocery, Wheatsville has a deli that
dishes out goodies (most with an ethnic influence), some better than
others. Much of the fare is vegan, and almost all of it is vegetarian, so
it's nice to see that the folks here don't shy away from big flavors. Our
favorite snacks here are the Wheatsville samosas, which are spicy and
plentifully filled with potatoes, and come with sweet tamarind chutney.
Avoid things with meat substitutes, but the vegetable fare is perfectly
capable of standing up on its own. The cole slaw is superb—with
poppy seeds, green apple, and apple cider, it's a bright, crunchy
success. There is also a solid daily soup rotation. If you're interested in
the more ethnic side of things, we recommend a large step to the right
of the counter, where you'll find a variety of prepared dishes from the
likes of Tom's Tabooley and Aster's Ethiopian, whose lentil and eggplant
injera wraps are spicy and flavorful (she has a weekly stall at the
Republic Square farmer's market).

And in the end, it's nice to know, as you contemplate the Willie
Nelson for Surgeon General buttons available at the counter, that
you're supporting a local institution. –RM

Whole Foods

A gourmet supermarket empire that
Austin can claim as its own

Clarksville, Arboretum

Specialty grocery
Daily 8am-10pm. *Breakfast.*
Kid-friendly. Live music. Outdoor
dining. Vegetarian-friendly.
Wireless Internet.

525 N. Lamar Blvd.
Austin
(512) 476-1206
www.wholefoodsmarket.com

Bar Beer/wine
Credit Cards Visa, MC, AmEx
Reservations Not accepted

9607 Research Blvd.
78759, (512) 345-5003

Whole Foods is Austin's homegrown health-food market gone
national—the local boy made good. The flagship store downtown is the
Disney World of groceries, and it is gorgeous. The produce, cheese, and
seafood are all beautifully displayed, and the overall experience is quite
simply overwhelming, in part because there is just so much to choose
from. In an America that is all about breadth of choice, it's no wonder,
after a glance around the store and its staggering array of upper-end
food products spanning the globe, that this place has become such a
success story, now gracing such spectacularly ambitious spaces as the
basement of Manhattan's Time Warner Center, one of the most
expensive little swaths of commercial real estate in the history of
mankind.

Sprinkled throughout this store the size of a small village are several
mini-restaurants and buffet stations, which display seafood,
sandwiches, barbecue, pizza, sushi, salads, "living foods," and more.
Foods from around the world (sometimes different parts of the world at
different times of day) can be boxed up or plated, eaten inside or
outside or taken home. In case you get lost in the shuffle, maps to the
store are available at the front information desk; otherwise, just wander
around until something piques your interest, but find it fast before
sensory overload completely incapacitates you.

It is hard to pick out a few dishes to mention from amongst all the
options, but we do love the creamy, rich lobster bisque, with its gentle
Southwestern heat. Satisfying pizza, available by the whole pie or slice,
boasts fresh toppings, a nicely thin crust, and you can get some
interesting vegetarian combinations like artichoke hearts, tomatoes,
Kalamata olives, spinach, and goat cheese. And don't miss the
cannoli—the shells are dense and toasty, the filling is light, and they are
adorned with dark chocolate and pistachio. Not bad for a trip to what
was once just a healthy local supermarket. Austin pride, baby, Austin
pride. –MPN/RG

Wiki Wiki Teriyaki

Semi-fast, semi-good Japanese food
downtown and in the 'burbs

food

5.4
10

5.7
10

experience

Japanese

$ **10**

Congress Avenue Area, Arboretum

Counter service
Mon.-Sat. 11am-8pm;
closed Sun. *Delivery.*
Wireless Internet.

609 Congress Ave.
Austin
(512) 472-9454
www.wikiwikiteriyaki.com

10000 Research Blvd.
78759, (512) 349-9454

Bar None
Credit Cards Visa, MC, AmEx
Reservations Accepted

Austin's latest venture into the widely growing arena of Japanese fast food, Wiki Wiki Teriyaki has opened an ambitious two locations: one downtown, and the other in the Arboretum. The restaurants walk a fine—well, broad, actually—line between formal and fast food. Dining rooms are nicely furnished in blond woods with Asian art, bamboo lanterns, and small garden-like sitting areas decorated with plants, water features, and the occasional smoking dry-ice fountain. But the counters at the back are straight out of a mall food court, with lit signs showing photos of meals, Coke dispensers, and plastic forks and spoons. Service is friendly, but certainly not up to fast food standards of speed. "Wiki wiki" is Hawaiian for fast, and while they might earn a single "wiki" in our book, we'd hardly award them two.

The menu is comprised of basic Japanese foods like katsu, sushi rolls, tempura, and of course, teriyaki. Meals are served in plastic partitioned dishes that resemble black lacquer and are a step up from what you might expect. The char-grilled teriyaki dishes are certainly the best here: chicken comes out moist and tender, with a nice charred flavor, drizzled with a sweet teriyaki sauce that is thick but not too heavy. Sushi rolls are moderately fresh—not up to sushi-bar standards, but much better than what you can buy at the grocery store.

Tempura is much too heavy, though, with a dense batter that seems to soak up grease. We are also disappointed with the tonkatsu—the thin pork cutlets are dried out after being fried, and the sauce has a yucky metallic aftertaste that goes straight to your brain. On the upside, tonkatsu plates are served with a shredded cabbage salad, and dressed with a miso vinaigrette that is crisp and bright. Don't expect much more than basic satisfaction of your sudden Japanese-food craving, and you won't be disappointed here. –MPN

Wink

A high-concept restaurant whose less-is-more ideal doesn't extend to the check

food
9.3
10

8.9
10
experience

New American

$86

House Park Area

Upmarket restaurant
Mon.-Sat. 6pm-11pm.
Date-friendly.

1014 N. Lamar Blvd.
Austin
(512) 482-8868
www.winkrestaurant.com

Bar Full
Credit Cards Visa, MC, AmEx
Reservations Recommended

Rewind to the opening of Wink, a few years ago: the place was filled to over-capacity throughout the evening, and it fairly rippled with well-deserved excitement: Here, in a small, simply-appointed room—tucked improbably behind a sporting goods store and adjacent a dry cleaner—the entire menu displayed delectable choices, as the smiles on all sides made clear. What's more, from the appetizers through the entrees, judicious combinations of flavors dependent on the freshest ingredients came about through just the right amount of tweaking and research—not, as is a fault of many Austin establishments, a piling on of substances in violation of the useful maxim that as regards sophisticated food, less is often more.

Wink still operates at its original location, now with the addition of a trendy wine bar next door. Its menu follows the same, wholesome ideas about new American cuisine with which the establishment began. We continue to marvel over much that comes out of the kitchen—such wonders as veal sweetbreads with flageolets, Alba mushrooms, and baby turnips, all of which lend a revelatory woodsiness to the dish; or a simple and lusciously tender dish of red-wine-braised short ribs.

However, following the owners' acquisition of a second venue, Zoot, the less-is-more maxim is being applied in a more troublesome way. Virtually every dish on offer has shrunk to what have commonly come to be called a "spa"-sized portion, whether it be a single scallop served over a scant bed of puree as an appetizer or the still-delectable pork loin roast. The result is that a diner of average appetite not infrequently has to negotiate with his or her companions over whether to order extra dishes to supplement their meals. Three savory courses per person is standard; four is not unheard of. Since Wink's prices haven't correspondingly dipped, this development has gouged Wink's value proposition. Nonetheless, the restaurant remains one of the city's most successfully ambitious tables. –JC

Y Bar and Grill

Upmarket dining in Oak Hill? Who knew?

food
6.5 **7.2**
10   10
experience

Southwestern   **$45**   *Oak Hill*

Upmarket restaurant
Tues.-Thurs. 11am-10pm; Fri.-Sat.
11am-11pm; Sun. 10am-10pm;
closed Mon. *Brunch. Live music.*
Outdoor dining. Wireless Internet.

7720 W. Hwy. 71
Austin
(512) 394-0220
www.ybargrill.com

Bar Full
Credit Cards Visa, MC, AmEx
Reservations Accepted

Located in unlikely Oak Hill, the Y bar and Grill brings a casually upscale environment to a place far, far south of the river. The restaurant is an interesting combination of adobe materials and Art-Deco-inspired style. The walls are painted in contrasting colors, and diffuse lighting, paired with a vivid crimson ceiling, gives patrons an unfortunate, sunburn-like glow.

There are two bars here—a loungey indoor one, and an acclimatized outdoor one with a stage for frequent live music. The Y Bar and Grill has a particular shtick—several, actually. In their attempt to be everything to everyone, they have something different going on every day of the week. There's "New England Lobster Boil" Tuesday, "Champagne Brunch/Kids-Eat-Free"(ish) Sunday, "A Night of Romance" Saturday…you get the idea.

The food is a little expensive, but the menu has a lot offer in the way of tarted-up Southwestern fare, and the wine list is respectable. The artichoke dip is so cheesy we'd call it queso. Duck quesadillas are loaded with shredded duck and served on grilled corn tortillas that have a nice, toasty flavor. The "Y Bar Shrimp" (available as an app or main) are tasty but rubbery, stuffed with jalapeño and wrapped in bacon, then served with a fiery chile sauce. A corn pudding is creamy, with whole kernels, and tastes faintly of vanilla and coconut; crème brûlée, though it lacks density, has a thick crust of caramelized sugar that gives it the proper bite.

Service is amiable and quick, but although they have a stack of high chairs and a kids' menu, you might want to leave the wee ones at home. Come instead for "Tea Time" (read: happy hour) and enjoy bargain-priced drink and appetizer specials. While the Y Bar and Grill may not be up to downtown standards, it's certainly a step in the right direction. Welcome to the neighborhood. –MPN

Z' Tejas

A margarita-fueled Austin landmark
with sights set on the whole Southwest

Mexican, Southwestern   **$36**   *Clarksville, Arboretum*

Casual restaurant
Downtown branch Mon.-Thurs.
11am-10pm; Fri. 11am-11pm;
Sat. 9am-11pm; Sun. 9am-10pm.
Brunch. Date-friendly. Outdoor dining.

1110 W. 6th St.
Austin
(512) 478-5355
www.ztejas.com

9400A Arboretum Blvd.
78759, (514) 346-3506

Bar Full
Credit Cards Visa, MC, AmEx
Reservations Not accepted

It's hard not to like an Austin original. And it's hard to like a chain that has expanded across the country. So how should we feel about Z' Tejas, the popular Southwestern standby whose glossy menus, vintage-1990s graphic design, and Zorroesque logo, reveal it to be both?

We feel pretty good about it. The popular original branch is on Sixth Street, but the Arboretum locale is a more impressive space, balanced on stilts overlooking the hills, with a soaring interior as well as beautifully situated outdoor tables.

Z' Tejas' flavors are not subtle; they speak loudly and clearly, beginning with the spectacular cornbread that's delivered in a hot pan straight out of the oven, bursting with kernels of corn. Fried shrimp are crusted with cornmeal, crisped properly, and paired with a slaw that has a healthy kick of acidity. Chile con queso is deeply flavored and spiked with sausage, one of the best in the genre. Don't be deceived by the menu's insinuation that the queso is only available as part of a pricey platter with guacamole and pico de gallo: secretly, you can (and should) order it on its own. Fish tacos are crispy and well balanced, but chiles rellenos can vary: at the Arboretum branch, during a green hatch chile festival, we've had one of our favorites in Austin, with a superbly crispy batter, spicy salsa, and cheese with an unexpected burst of flavor. But at another meal downtown, we've had an unbuttered, smoked-chicken version that was less convincing.

Santa Fe chicken enchiladas are good but simpler, with a direct red heat. Creamy wild mushroom enchiladas aren't bad, but fall into that vast Austin middle ground of modified Tex-Mex. Brunch, though, is a successful and popular endeavor, whether you order the obligatory migas or the "breakfast enchiladas" topped with eggs. Margaritas display flawless execution, and it's a good happy-hour drinks-and-apps spot. Throngs of people flock to the place on Friday and Saturday nights, when the waits are often measured in hours, not minutes. At those times, above all, service is iffy—friendly but distracted. Still, it's a reliably fun night out, especially if that night includes queso. –RG

Zax Pints and Plates

Unexpected class from a dolled-up
burger joint

food

6.8 / 10

6.9 / 10

experience

New American $**40**   *Zilker*

Upmarket restaurant
Mon.-Thurs. 11am-10pm; Fri.
11am-10:30pm; Sat. 4pm-
10:30pm; Sun. 11am-2pm.
Brunch. Live music. Outdoor dining. Wireless Internet.

312 Barton Springs Rd.
Austin
(512) 481-0100
www.zaxaustin.com

Bar Full
Credit Cards Visa, MC, AmEx
Reservations Accepted

Zax, hunkered in a concrete island between Barton Springs Road and
Riverside Drive, looks like it might be just another brash bar like the
Aussie Grill beside it—a beer-drinker's haven with a limited, leaden
menu.

Instead, you walk through the doors into an elegant compromise.
Vaulted ceilings and plentiful windows complement a palate of natural
woods and creams. The room is spacious, but judiciously placed
partitions and booths keep it from feeling cavernous. Service, if at times
inattentive, has a friendly flair (it's the kind of place where the waiter
might sit next to you to more closely describe a menu item—a practice
about whose merit customers are deeply split). The result is an
atmosphere of casual sophistication that accounts for the jacked-up
prices on what is, in the end, really a gracefully executed bar menu,
with burgers, salads, pizza, and so on.

Only in some cases are these price hikes merited. Quesadillas, for
example, are fairly bland, despite a lively presentation with ice-cream-
style scoops of sour cream, pico de gallo, and murky guacamole. But
the house salad, with its peppery baby greens, pears, blue cheese, and
crunchy candied pecans, is very nice—it's a typical example of the fare
served here, predictably tarted up but tried and true. Pleasant grilled
shrimp with cilantro-lime cocktail sauce follow in the same line. You
know the drill: the menu abounds in such cheap but successful thrills as
blue cheese, caramelized onions, avocado, and chipotle.

And the burgers here have all the benefits of such pretensions—
they're superb. We particularly like the South Texas burger, which adds
avocado to the usual toppings; it arrives medium-rare as ordered, a
juicy, pleasingly irregular patty. Enjoy it with one of the excellent brews
on offer. Zax's long list includes several local gems such as Real Ale
Fireman's #4 and Independence Bootlegger Brown. Slurp—ahhhh. –RM

Zen Japanese Food Fast

A ubiquitous, efficient, and eminently
mediocre local rice-bowl-and-sushi chain

food
3.8 **5.7**
10 10
experience

Japanese   **$ 9**   *UT Area, S. Congress, N. Central*

Counter service
Mon.-Sat. 11am-11pm;
Sun. 11am-10pm.
Live music. Outdoor dining.
Vegetarian-friendly. Wireless Internet.

3423 Guadalupe St.
Austin
(512) 300-2633
www.eatzen.com

Bar Beer/wine
Credit Cards Visa, MC, AmEx
Reservations Not accepted

1303 S. Congress Ave.
78704, (512) 444-8084

2900 W. Anderson Ln.
78757, (512) 451-4811

Zen (along with the sushi shelves popping up in local supermarkets)
represents the inevitable conclusion to Austin's recent love affair with
Japanese food. It is the other side of the bargain from Uchi—the
counterbalance that keeps the law of averages happy. In many ways, it
keeps us happy too, not because the food is so great—it isn't—but
because it's cheap, it's easy, and it's a guilt-free alternative to the
burger, the slice, or the burrito.

Zen serves sushi, noodles, and rice bowls, but we recommend you
stick with the latter. The sushi is pre-prepared and over-refrigerated.
Skip the tuna sashimi salad, in whose raw fish we have found off-
notes. Rice bowls come closer to the baby-food thing you're there for,
but the dangers of ordering here are fairly predictable. The teriyaki
sauce is a little syrupy, for example, and should be avoided, and in
terms of chicken, we recommend you order the dark meat rather than
light meat, which can be dry and tasteless (it's light meat chicken, after
all). But the vegetables are well steamed and crisp, and the rice, in its
sweet and salty sauces, comforting. We like the oyako bowl, with its
dirty-fried eggs and sweet caramelized onions, and the bohdi bowl, a
virtuous option with celery, sprouts, and nicely browned tofu in a
"spicy" sauce that is actually a fairly mild, sweet, dark teriyaki. Order
these in the regular size, which is a buck or two cheaper and almost as
big as the big.

Zen takes the Buddha thing a little too far (we don't really need to
see pictures of bald, swaddled men meditating on top of oversized tuna
rolls while we eat), but with pleasant, minimalist indoor and outdoor
seating in both its funky South Congress and newer Guadalupe
locations, it's not a bad lunch option if your expectations are modest.
–RM

Zoot

Balance, relaxation, and culinary rigor
at one of Austin's best restaurants

food
9.2 **9.7**
10   10
experience

New American $**64** *Tarrytown*

Upmarket restaurant
Tues.-Sun. 6pm-9:30pm;
closed Mon. *Date-friendly.*
Vegetarian-friendly.

509 Hearn St.
Austin
(512) 477-6535
www.zootrestaurant.com

Bar Beer/wine
Credit Cards Visa, MC, AmEx
Reservations Recommended

It is remarkable when a restaurant can maintain not just impeccable technique, but also a flair for novelty, for a decade and a half. But let us begin with Zoot's enchanting atmosphere. Enter this gracious house, and you will be struck by the sentiment that the customers and the food are taken equally seriously. Tables are neither overdressed nor underdressed; lighting is dim but not too dim; prominent wine racks entertain but do not dominate. The waitstaff describes dishes in loving detail, with an obvious passion for the flavors, for the wines, for the provenance of the ingredients.

And what ingredients! We could write pages about the wonders of the five-course Chef's Tasting Menu ($65 per person), but perhaps even more impressive is the Farmer's Tasting Menu ($45), a meal focusing on seasonal local vegetables that is far and away the best vegetarian dinner in the city. Zoot has a way with soups; on one night, we were impressed by a chilled tomato soup with shaved parmesan. At our last visit, a chilled potato leek soup was like a vichyssoise doused with truffle oil and studded with the crunch of peanuts; the earthy leek and truffle flavors merged in a delightful way. Even better has been a creamy yet balanced spinach and gruyère cannelloni with fennel, brussels sprouts, Texas squash, and sauce mornay.

There are occasional missteps amongst fish mains, but foie gras is treated with reverence, as in a seared version with candied cranberry fennel salad. We have had equally good experiences with quail, veal sweetbreads, and a simple, almost stark plate of roasted chicken with creamy polenta, kale, and tarragon jus, with the moist chicken leg not overcooked one iota, and the flavor of the sauce warm, subtle, and light. It is one of the dishes with which Zoot opened in 1991. That longevity and consistency, for a restaurant at this level, might be the most impressive thing of all. –RG

INDEX